$$SS_{\text{factor B}} = \sum \frac{B^2}{pn} - \frac{G^2}{N} \qquad df_{\text{factor B}} = q - 1$$

$$SS_{A \times B} = SS_{\text{between}} - SS_A - SS_B \qquad df_{A \times B} = (p-1)(q-1)$$

$$SS_{\text{within}} = \sum SS_{\text{inside each treatment}} \qquad df_{\text{within}} = N - pq$$

$$F_A = \frac{MS_A}{MS_{\text{within}}} \qquad F_B = \frac{MS_B}{MS_{\text{within}}} \qquad F_{A \times B} = \frac{MS_{A \times B}}{MS_{\text{within}}}$$

where each $MS = \frac{SS}{df}$

· PEARSON CORRELATION ·

$$r = \frac{SP}{\sqrt{SS_X SS_Y}}$$

where $SP = \sum(X - \bar{X})(Y - \bar{Y}) = \sum XY - \frac{(\sum X)(\sum Y)}{n}$

· REGRESSION ·

$\hat{Y} = bX + a$ where $b = \frac{SP}{SS_X}$ and $a = \bar{Y} - b\bar{X}$

$$\text{Standard error of estimate} = \sqrt{\frac{\sum(Y - \hat{Y})^2}{n-2}} = \sqrt{\frac{(1 - r^2)SS_Y}{n-2}}$$

· CHI-SQUARE STATISTIC ·

$$\chi^2 = \sum \frac{(f_o - f_e)^2}{f_e}$$

· MANN-WHITNEY *U* ·

$$U_A = n_A n_B + \frac{n_A(n_A + 1)}{2} - \sum R_A$$

$$U_B = n_A n_B + \frac{n_B(n_B + 1)}{2} - \sum R_B$$

· SPEARMAN CORRELATION ·

$$r_s = 1 - \frac{6\sum D^2}{n(n^2 - 1)}$$

TO THE STUDENT:

A complete study guide has been prepared by the authors to assist you in mastering concepts presented in this text. The study guide is available from your local bookstore under the title *Study Guide to Accompany Statistics for the Behavioral Sciences second edition.* If you cannot locate it in the bookstore, ask your bookstore manager to order it for you.

STATISTICS FOR THE BEHAVIORAL SCIENCES

A FIRST COURSE FOR STUDENTS OF PSYCHOLOGY AND EDUCATION

SECOND EDITION

STATISTICS FOR THE BEHAVIORAL SCIENCES

A FIRST COURSE FOR STUDENTS OF PSYCHOLOGY AND EDUCATION

SECOND EDITION

FREDERICK J GRAVETTER
STATE UNIVERSITY OF NEW YORK
COLLEGE AT BROCKPORT

LARRY B. WALLNAU
STATE UNIVERSITY OF NEW YORK
COLLEGE AT BROCKPORT

WEST PUBLISHING COMPANY
ST. PAUL · NEW YORK · LOS ANGELES · SAN FRANCISCO

Copyediting Linda Thompson
Problem checking Roxy Peck
Interior design Kathi Townes
Cover design David J. Farr, *IMAGESMYTHE, Inc.*
Art Rolin Graphic Communications
Composition Syntax International
Indexing Lois Oster
Cover art Eugene Boudin, *Races at Deauville* (1866), watercolor on paper.
Courtesy of the Virginia Museum of Fine Arts, Richmond, Virginia.

50 W. Kellogg Boulevard
P.O. Box 64526
St. Paul, MN 55164-1003

Printed in the United States of America
95 94 93 92 91 90 89 8 7 6 5 4 3 2

Library of Congress Cataloging-in-Publication Data

Gravetter, Frederick J.
Statistics for the behavioral sciences: a first course for students of psychology and education/Frederick J. Gravetter, Larry B. Wallnau.—2nd ed.
p. cm.
Includes index.
ISBN 0-314-59996-7
1. Psychometrics. 2. Educational statistics. I. Wallnau, Larry B. II. Title.
BF39.G72 1988
519.5—dc19 87-21281
CIP

For Dyan Marie Alvarez (1952–1985)

My life closed twice before its close-
It yet remains to see
If Immortality unveil
A third event to me

So huge, so hopeless to conceive
As these that twice befell.
Parting is all we know of heaven,
And all we need of hell.

EMILY DICKINSON

Reprinted from *The Complete Poems of Emily Dickinson,* T.H. Johnson (ed.), Little, Brown and Company, 1960.

CONTENTS

CHAPTER 5

z-SCORES: LOCATION OF SCORES AND STANDARDIZED DISTRIBUTIONS 106

CHAPTER 6

PROBABILITY 124

CHAPTER 7

PROBABILITY AND SAMPLES: THE DISTRIBUTION OF SAMPLE MEANS 151

CHAPTER 8

INTRODUCTION TO HYPOTHESIS TESTING 169

CHAPTER 9

DIRECTIONAL TESTS, ESTIMATION, AND POWER 195

CHAPTER 10

INTRODUCTION TO THE t STATISTIC 219

CHAPTER 11

STATISTICAL INFERENCE WITH TWO INDEPENDENT SAMPLES 240

CHAPTER 12

STATISTICAL INFERENCE WITH RELATED SAMPLES 267

CHAPTER 13

INTRODUCTION TO ANALYSIS OF VARIANCE 288

CHAPTER 14

REPEATED-MEASURES ANALYSIS OF VARIANCE (ANOVA) 325

CHAPTER 15

TWO-FACTOR ANALYSIS OF VARIANCE (INDEPENDENT MEASURES) 349

CHAPTER 16

CORRELATION AND REGRESSION 382

CHAPTER 17

THE CHI-SQUARE STATISTIC: TESTS FOR GOODNESS OF FIT AND INDEPENDENCE 415

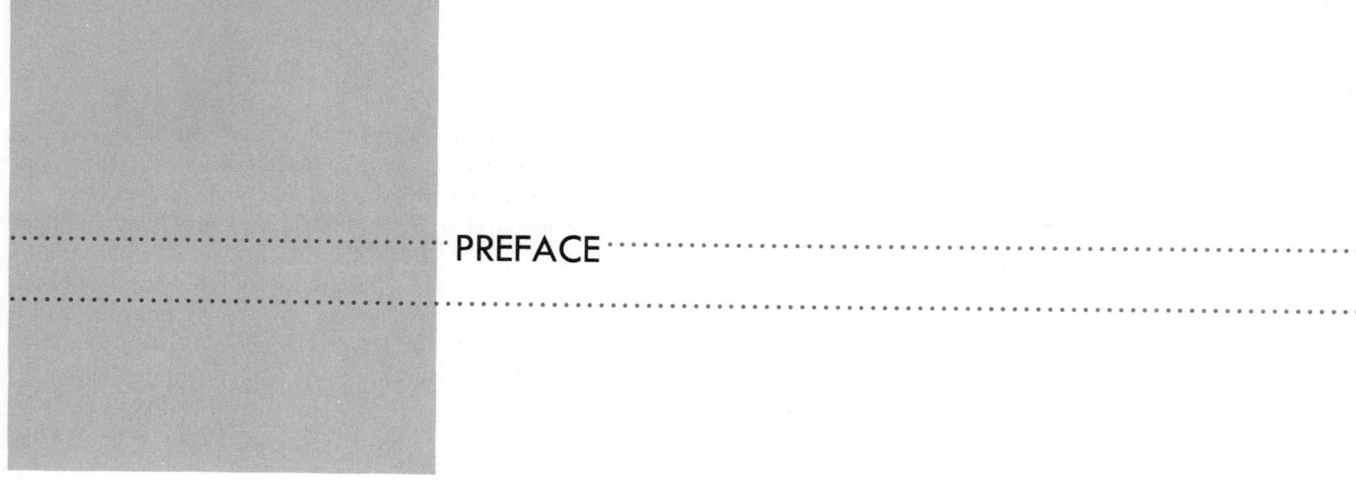

PREFACE

In his autobiography, Mark Twain cites a most memorable comment by Benjamin Disraeli, "There are three kinds of lies: Lies, damned lies, and statistics." The quote reflects a commonly held belief that statistics (or perhaps even statisticians) should not be trusted. Unfortunately, this mistrust is sometimes justified. In this book, we shall see that statistical techniques are tools that are used to organize information and answer questions. Like any other tool, statistics can be misused, which may result in misleading, distorted or incorrect conclusions. It is no small wonder that we are sometimes skeptical when a statistician presents findings. However, if we understand the correct uses of statistical techniques, then we can decide which statistics are more believable. Therefore, the goal of this book is to teach not only the methods of statistics but also how to use these methods appropriately. Finally, a certain amount of mistrust is healthy. That is, we should critically examine information and data before we accept the implications. As you shall see, statistical techniques help us look at things with a critical eye.

For those of you familiar with the first edition, you will notice some things have changed. We have improved sections that were troublesome for our students, included fresh examples and analogies where appropriate, and added more Learning Checks, more computer printouts, more end-of-chapter problems, and new features like the Focus on Problem Solving sections. What has not changed is our approach. We still take the time to explain and discuss each statistical technique and to give the rationale behind the formulas.

As in the first edition of *Statistics for the Behavioral Sciences*, we kept our students in mind in every phase of the writing. They were instrumental in molding this revision, in telling us which elements worked and which did not. We thank them all for their honest feedback and hard work. They have made writing the book and teaching the course both rewarding and fun.

The people at West Publishing have been outstanding. It was easy to delude ourselves that ours was the only book they were publishing because of the time, care, and enthusiasm they put into the project. We give special thanks to Kristi Shuey for her diligent work in marketing and to Jean Cook, who orchestrated the complex production of the book. We know that their tasks were like juggling acts, and yet they gave the project thorough and professional attention. Likewise, we are most appreciative of our editors Nancy Hill-Whilton and Pat Fitzgerald. They were always there to provide focus and momentum. We were fortunate to have outstanding people review all or part of the manuscript. Their remarks and suggestions helped us immeasurably. We thank the following people for their time and assistance:

SURVEY RESPONDENTS

Ronald Holmes
University of Louisville

Horace Keller
Glassboro State College

Robert Yonker
Bowling Green State University

Zita E. Tyer
George Mason University

John D. Frisone
Glassboro State College

Lyle V. Jones
University of North Carolina
Chapel Hill

Carrol S. Perrino
Morgan State University

MANUSCRIPT REVIEWERS

Suzanne Soled
University of Cincinnati

Jack Kirschenbaum
Fuller College

Raymond W. Frankmann
Michigan State University

Michael Lupfer
Memphis State University

Julia Wallace
University of Northern Iowa

Marilyn Boltz
Ohio State University

C. L. Holland
Georgia State University

John M. Davis
Southwest Texas University

James L. Pate
Georgia State University

The authors are grateful to the literary executor of the late Sir Ronald A. Fisher, F.R.S., to Dr. Frank Yates, F.R.S., and to Longman Group Ltd. (London) for permission to adapt Tables III and VI from their book *Statistical Tables for Biological, Agricultural and Medical Research* (6th edition, 1974). The people at SPSS, Inc. and Minitab, Inc. were most cooperative in both checking and providing computer material.

Finally, we are also grateful to the following family and friends for encouraging words, unwavering patience, and eager assistance: Carol, Justin, Naomi, O.J., Patty Smyth, and Henry W. Williams, Jr.

Frederick J Gravetter
Larry B. Wallnau

NOTE ADDED TO PROOF BY LARRY WALLNAU

The following remarks have been surreptitiously added to the page proofs, otherwise Fred Gravetter would have surely protested their inclusion. I arrived at Brockport ten years ago fresh out of graduate school. The undergraduate statistics course was among my first teaching assignments. During my college years, I often looked for excellence in others—others who could ultimately serve as role models for me. My first year at Brockport was no exception. In Fred I found a superb role model—a highly successful teacher who has time for every student, a solid statistician who has time for every colleague, and an exceptional person who has time for every friend.

CHAPTER 1

INTRODUCTION TO STATISTICS

- Preview
- 1.1 Statistics, Science, and Observations
- 1.2 Populations and Samples
- 1.3 The Scientific Method and the Design of Experiments
- 1.4 Scales of Measurement
- 1.5 Discrete and Continuous Variables
- 1.6 Statistical Notation
- Summary
- Focus on Problem Solving
- Problems

PREVIEW

> The procedure is actually quite simple. First you arrange things into different groups depending on their makeup. Of course, one pile may be sufficient, depending on how much there is to do. If you have to go somewhere else due to lack of facilities, that is the next step; otherwise you are pretty well set. It is important not to overdo any particular endeavor. That is, it is better to do too few things at once than too many. In the short run this may not seem important, but complications from doing too many can easily arise. A mistake can be expensive as well. The manipulation of the appropriate mechanisms should be self-explanatory, and we need not dwell on it here. At first the whole procedure will seem complicated. Soon, however, it will become just another facet of life. It is difficult to foresee any end to the necessity for this task in the immediate future, but then one never can tell.*

The preceding paragraph was adapted from a psychology experiment reported by Bransford and Johnson (1972). If you have not read the paragraph yet, go back and read it now.

You probably find the paragraph a little confusing, and most of you probably think it is describing some obscure statistical procedure. Actually, this paragraph describes the everyday task of doing laundry. Now that you know the topic of the paragraph, try reading it again—it should make sense now.

Why did we begin a statistics textbook with a paragraph about washing clothes? Our goal is to demonstrate the importance of context—when not in the proper context, even the simplest material can appear difficult and confusing. In the Bransford and Johnson experiment, people who knew the topic before reading the paragraph were able to recall 73% more than people who did not know that it was about doing laundry. When you have the appropriate background, it is much easier to fit new material into your memory and to recall it later. In this book we begin each chapter with a preview. The purpose of the preview is to provide the background or context for the new material in the chapter. As you read each preview section, you should gain a general overview of the chapter content. Remember, all statistical methods were developed to serve a purpose. If you understand why a new procedure is needed, you will find it much easier to learn the procedure.

The objective for this first chapter is to provide an introduction to the topic of statistics and to give you some background for the rest of the book. We will discuss the role of statistics within the general field of scientific inquiry, and we will introduce some of the vocabulary and notation that are necessary for the statistical methods that follow. In some respects, this chapter serves as a preview section for the rest of the book.

Incidently, we cannot promise that statistics will be as easy as washing clothes. But if you begin each new topic within the proper context, you should eliminate some unnecessary confusion.

1.1 STATISTICS, SCIENCE, AND OBSERVATIONS

DEFINITIONS OF STATISTICS

Why study statistics? is a question countless students ask. One simple answer is that statistics have become a common part of everyday life and therefore deserve some attention. A quick glance at the newspaper yields statistics that deal with crime rates, birth rates, average income, average snowfall, and so on. By a common definition, therefore, statistics consist of facts and figures.

* Copyright by the American Psychological Association. Reprinted by permission of the publisher and author.

· DEFINITION · *Statistics* are facts and figures.

These statistics generally are informative and time saving because they condense large quantities of information into a few simple figures or statements. For example, the average snowfall in Chicago during the month of January is based on many observations made over many years. Few people would be interested in seeing a complete list of day-by-day snowfall amounts for the past 50 years. Even fewer people would be able to make much sense of all those numbers at a quick glance. But nearly everyone can understand and appreciate the meaning of an average.

There is another definition of statistics that applies to many of the topics in this book. When statisticians use the word statistics, they are referring to a set of methods and procedures that help present, characterize, analyze, and interpret observations.

· DEFINITION · *Statistics* consist of a set of methods and rules for organizing and interpreting observations.

These statistical procedures help ensure that the data (or observations) are presented and interpreted in an accurate and informative way. Although facts and figures can be interesting and important, this book will focus on methods and procedures of statistics.

STATISTICS AND SCIENCE

These observations should be public, in the sense that others are able to repeat the observations using the same methods to see if the same findings will be obtained.

It is frequently said that science is *empirical*. That is, scientific investigation is based on making observations. Statistical methods enable researchers to describe and analyze the observations they have made. Thus, statistical methods are tools for science. We might think of science as consisting of methods for making observations and of statistics as consisting of methods for analyzing them.

On one mission of the space shuttle Columbia, so much scientific data were relayed to computers on earth that scientists were hard pressed to convey, in terms the public could grasp, how much information had been gathered. One individual made a few quick computations on a pocket calculator and determined that if all the data from the mission were printed on pages, they would pile up as high as the Washington Monument. Such an enormous amount of scientific observation is unmanageable in this crude form. To interpret the data, many months of work have to be done by many people to statistically analyze them. Statistical methods serve scientific investigation by organizing and interpreting data.

1.2 POPULATIONS AND SAMPLES

WHAT ARE THEY?

A *population* is the entire group of individuals that a researcher wishes to study. By entire group, we literally mean every single individual.

· DEFINITION · A *population* consists of every member of a group that a researcher would like to study.

As you can well imagine, a population can be quite large—for example, the number of women on the planet earth. A researcher might be more specific, limiting the population for study to women who are registered voters in the United States. Perhaps the investigator would like to study the population consisting of women who are heads of state. Populations can obviously vary in size from extremely large to very small, depending on how the investigator defines the population. The population being studied should always be identified by the researcher. In addition, the population need not consist of people—it could be a population of rats, corporations, parts produced in a factory, or anything else an investigator wants to study. In practice, populations are typically very large, such as the population of fourth-grade children in the United States or the population of small businesses.

A *sample* is a subset of a population. It is a part of the population that is selected for study. A sample should always be identified in terms of the population from which it was selected.

· DEFINITION · A *sample* is a portion of the population that is selected for observation.

Just as we saw with populations, samples can vary greatly in size. Imagine that you are about to conduct an opinion poll in a large city. You are going to ask people if they believe the mayor is doing a good job. Since the poll will be conducted by telephone, you define your population as people who live in the city and are listed in the telephone directory. Realizing that it would take more time than you can spend to call everyone in the phone book (the entire population), you call 100 people. Notice that it is often necessary to study a sample because the population is so large that it would be impractical to study every member of the population. If you are more ambitious, you could use a larger sample—for example, 1000 people. Later in this book we will examine the benefits of using large samples.

PARAMETERS AND STATISTICS

When describing data, it is necessary to distinguish whether the data come from a population or a sample. Any characteristic of a population, for example, its average, is called a population *parameter*. On the other hand, a characteristic of a sample is called a *statistic*. The average of the scores for a sample is a statistic. The range of scores for a sample is another type of statistic. As we shall see later, statisticians frequently use different symbols for a parameter and a statistic. By using different symbols, we can readily tell if a characteristic, such as an average, is describing a population or a sample.

· DEFINITIONS · A *parameter* is a measurement that describes a characteristic of a population, such as a population average.

A *statistic* describes a characteristic of a sample.

DESCRIPTIVE AND INFERENTIAL STATISTICAL METHODS

There are two major types of statistical methods. The first type, *descriptive statistics*, is used to simplify and summarize data. Data typically consist of a set of scores called a *distribution*. These scores result from measurements taken during the course of making observations. For example, they may be IQ scores, ages, blood-alcohol levels, or number of correct responses. The original measurements or values in a distribution are called *raw scores*.

· DEFINITIONS · *Descriptive statistical methods* summarize, organize, and simplify data.

A *distribution* is a set of scores.

A *raw score* is an original measurement or value in a distribution.

Descriptive statistics are techniques that take the raw scores from a distribution and summarize them in a form that is more manageable. There are many descriptive procedures, but a common technique is to compute an average. Note that even if the distribution has hundreds of scores, the average of those scores provides a single descriptive value for the entire distribution. Other descriptive techniques, including tables and graphs, will be covered in the next several chapters.

Inferential statistics are techniques that use sample data to make general statements about a population.

· DEFINITION · *Inferential statistics* consist of techniques that allow us to study samples and then make generalizations about the population from which they were selected.

As we saw with the telephone survey, it is usually not practical to make observations of every member of the population of interest. Because the population is much too large to telephone every individual, a sample is selected. By analyzing the results for the sample, we hope to make general statements about the population. In this example, results from the telephone survey (a sample) can be used to draw inferences about the opinions of the general population.

Inferential statistics are a crucial part of conducting experiments. Suppose a researcher would like to test the effectiveness of a new therapy program for depression. It would be too costly and time-consuming to test the program on all depressed individuals. Therefore, the treatment is tested on a sample of depressed patients. Of course, the researcher would like to see these people overcome their misery, but keep in mind that one is not just interested in this sample of individuals. The investigator would like to generalize the findings to the entire population. If the treatment program is effective for the sample of depressed people, it would be great to be able to state with confidence that it will also work for others. It is important to note that inferential statistical methods will allow meaningful generalizations only if the individuals in the sample are representative of the population. One way to ensure that the sample is representative is to use *random selection.* In random sampling, every individual in the population has the same chance of being selected. There will be much more to say about this topic in later chapters.

· DEFINITION · In *random selection,* every individual in the population has the same chance of being selected for the sample.

· LEARNING CHECK ·

1 Science is empirical. This means that science is based on ____________.

2 Science consists of methods for making observations, and statistics are methods for ____________ them.

3 A descriptive characteristic of a population is a ____________. A characteristic of a sample is called a ____________.

4 What are statistics?

5 What is the purpose of descriptive statistics?

6 Inferential statistics attempt to use ____________ to make general statements about ____________.

7 One way to ensure that a sample is representative of a population is to use ____________ selection of the sample.

ANSWERS

1 observation

2 analyzing

3 parameter; statistic

4 By one definition, statistics are facts and figures. In this book, the term statistics refers to a set of methods for analyzing and interpreting data.

5 to simplify and summarize data

6 sample data; a population

7 random

1.3 THE SCIENTIFIC METHOD AND THE DESIGN OF EXPERIMENTS

OBJECTIVITY As noted earlier, science is empirical in that knowledge is acquired by observation. Another important aspect of scientific inquiry is that it should be *objective*. That is, theoretical biases of the researcher should not be allowed to influence the findings. Usually when a study is conducted, the investigator has a hunch about how it will turn out. This hunch, actually a prediction about the outcome of the study, is typically based on a theory that the researcher has. It is important that scientists conduct their studies in a way that will prevent these hunches or biases from influencing the outcome of the research. Experimenter bias can operate very subtly. Rosenthal and Fode (1963) had student volunteers act as experimenters in a learning study. The students were given rats to train in a maze. Half of the students were led to believe that their rats were "maze-bright," while the remainder were told their rats were "maze-dull." In reality they all received the same kind of rat. Nevertheless, the data showed real differences in the rats' performance for the two groups of experimenters. Somehow the students' expectations influenced the outcome of the experiment. Apparently there were differences between the groups in how the students handled the rats, and these differences accounted for the effect. For a detailed look at experimenter bias, you might read the review by Rosenthal (1964).

RELATIONSHIPS BETWEEN VARIABLES Science attempts to discover orderly relationships. Even people of ancient civilizations noted regularity in the world around them—the change of seasons, changes in the moon's phases, changes in the tides—and they were able to make many observations to document these orderly changes. A relationship exists when changes occur interdependently: Whenever X changes, Y also changes in a predictable way. Something that can change or have different values is called a *variable*.

· DEFINITION · A *variable* is something that can change and have different values.

Science involves a search for relationships between variables. For example, there is a relationship between the amount of rainfall and crop growth. Rainfall is one of the variables. It varies from year to year and season to season. Crop growth is the other variable. Some years the corn stalks seem short and stunted; other years they are tall and full. When there is very little rainfall, the crops are short and shriveled. When rain is ample, the crops show vigorous growth. Note that in order to document the relationship, one must make observations—that is, measurements of the amount of rainfall and size of the crops.

The simplest way to look for relationships between variables is to make observations of changes in two variables. This is frequently called an *observational* or *correlational method.*

· DEFINITION · In a *correlational method,* changes are observed in two variables to see if there is a relationship.

Suppose a researcher wants to examine whether or not a relationship exists between length of time in an executive position and assertiveness. A large sample of executives takes a personality test designed to measure assertiveness. Also, the investigator determines how long each person has served in an executive-level job. Suppose the investigator found that there is a relationship between the two variables—that the longer a person had an executive position, the more assertive that person tended to be. Naturally, one might jump to the conclusion that being an executive for a long time makes a person more assertive. The problem with the correlational method is that it provides no information about cause-and-effect relationships. An equally plausible explanation for the relationship is that assertive people choose to stay or survive longer in executive positions than less-assertive individuals. To determine the cause and the effect in a relationship, it is necessary to *manipulate and control* one of the variables being studied. This is accomplished by the experimental method.

THE EXPERIMENTAL METHOD

A distinguishing characteristic of the *experimental method* is that the researcher manipulates and controls one of the variables under study. One then looks for the effect of this manipulation on the other variable.

· DEFINITION · In the *experimental method,* one variable is controlled and manipulated while changes are observed in another variable.

By intentionally altering one variable while at the same time monitoring the other, a cause-and-effect relationship can be established. For example, suppose a psychologist would like to examine the effect of different methods of practice on learning performance. The psychologist solicits volunteers (often called *subjects*) to participate. One group of subjects memorizes a list of words by practicing for 30 minutes. This group is called the massed-practice condition. A second group of people practice for the same total amount of time but in three 10-minute sessions, with a 15-minute rest period between the practice sessions. This group is the distributed-practice condition. Shortly after practice is completed, both groups are tested for how many words were learned. The experiment is diagrammed in Figure 1.1. The experimenter is manipulating the type of practice the people have to use. The amount of learning is measured by the number of words they can jot down after practicing. If method of practice has an effect, these two groups should perform differently on the test. To determine if an effect did occur, the data from the experiment would have to be statistically analyzed.

THE INDEPENDENT AND DEPENDENT VARIABLES

Specific names are used for the two variables that are studied by the experimental method. The variable that is manipulated by the experimenter is called the *independent variable.* It can be identified as the treatment conditions to which subjects are assigned. For the example in Figure 1.1, the method of practice (massed or distributed) is the

· FIGURE 1.1 ·

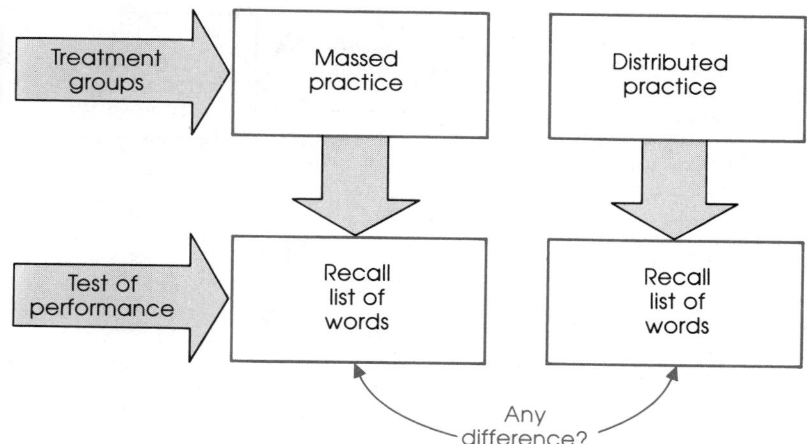

Volunteers are randomly assigned to one of two treatment groups: massed practice or distributed practice. After memorizing a list of words using one of these methods, subjects are tested by having them write down as many words as possible from the list. A difference between the groups in performance is attributed to the treatment—the type of practice.

independent variable. The variable that is observed to assess a possible effect of the manipulation is the *dependent variable.*

· DEFINITIONS · The *independent variable* consists of the treatment conditions to which subjects are exposed. It is the variable that is controlled and manipulated by the researcher.

The *dependent variable* is the one that is observed for changes in order to assess the effect of the treatment.

In psychological research, the dependent variable is typically a measure of some form of behavior. For the practice experiment (Figure 1.1), the dependent variable is the number of words recalled on the learning test. Differences between groups in performance on the dependent variable suggest that the manipulation had an effect. That is, changes in the dependent variable *depend on* the independent variable.

Often we can identify one condition of the independent variable that receives no treatment. It is used for comparison purposes and is called the *control group*. The group that does receive the treatment is the *experimental group*.

· DEFINITIONS · A *control group* is a condition of the independent variable that receives no treatment. It is used for the purpose of making comparisons.

An *experimental group* does receive a treatment.

A trials-to-criterion measure is commonly used in studies of skill acquisition.

Remember, the independent variable consists of treatments, and the dependent variable is the method of assessment.

For example, a researcher performs an experiment to assess the effect of alcohol on motor performance. Volunteers in one group are required to drink three bottles of beer in a 12-minute period. Subjects of the other group drink the same amount of a nonalcoholic beer-type beverage. Thirty minutes later, all people from both groups try to balance a broomstick on the index fingers of their right hands. To make the task more difficult, they must perform the task while seated. Performance is measured by the number of attempts it takes for a subject to balance the stick for 30 seconds. This type of measure is sometimes called a trials-to-criterion task. The structure of the experiment is depicted in Figure 1.2. For this study, the independent variable is the type of beverage consumed (alcoholic or nonalcoholic). The experimental group receives alcohol. In contrast, the control group does not consume alcohol, and it is used for comparison with the experimental group in terms of their performance. The dependent variable is the number of trials required to reach the criterion (30 seconds of

· FIGURE 1.2 ·

Volunteers are randomly assigned to one of two treatment groups: nonalcoholic beverage or alcoholic beverage. Type of beverage is the independent variable. The effects of this manipulation are assessed for motor performance. Specifically, the motor task consists of balancing a stick, and the dependent variable is the number of trials required to reach a criterion (30 seconds of balancing).

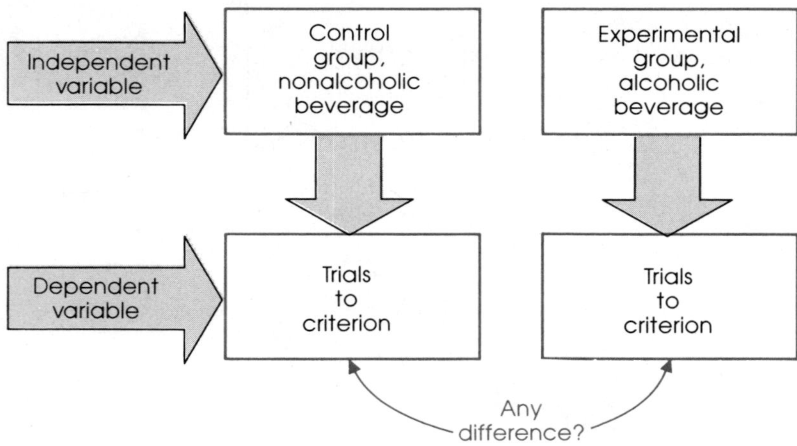

balancing). If alcohol impairs performance for this task, then people in the beer-drinking group should require more attempts at balancing the stick than subjects in the control group. A statistical analysis would have to be performed to determine if an effect occurred.

PROBLEMS THAT CAN ARISE IN EXPERIMENTS

Researchers must use great care in planning and designing an experiment because a seemingly small flaw in a study can make the result uninterpretable. This situation is always unfortunate because time and resources are wasted. There are more ways that an experiment can be flawed than can be enumerated here, but a few examples will alert you to common problems that may occur.

One way an experiment can be flawed is by the presence of *confounding variables.* This problem occurs when a researcher allows the experimental conditions to differ with respect to some characteristic other than the independent variable.

· DEFINITION · A *confounding variable* is an uncontrolled variable that is unintentionally allowed to vary with the independent variable.

For example, an instructor would like to assess the effectiveness of computer laboratory exercises in assisting students to grasp the fundamentals of statistics. There are two treatment conditions. One section of statistics is taught three times a week as a lecture course. A second section of students also meets three times a week, but one of these meetings is devoted to computer exercises in statistics. Professor Smith teaches the lecture, and Professor Jones teaches the second group of students. At the end of the semester, both groups receive the same final exam, and their performances are compared. The experiment is summarized in Figure 1.3.

Let's assume that a statistical analysis determined that the lecture/lab students performed better on the final exam. Can the instructors conclude that the method of instruction had an effect on learning? The answer is emphatically *no.* The independent variable, method of instruction, is not the only way the groups differ in terms of how

· FIGURE 1.3 ·

In this experiment, the effect of instructional method (the independent variable) on test performance (the dependent variable) is examined. However, any difference between groups in performance cannot be attributed to the method of instruction. In this experiment, there is a confounding variable. The instructor teaching the course varies with the independent variable, so that the treatment of the groups differs in more ways than one (instructional method and instructor vary).

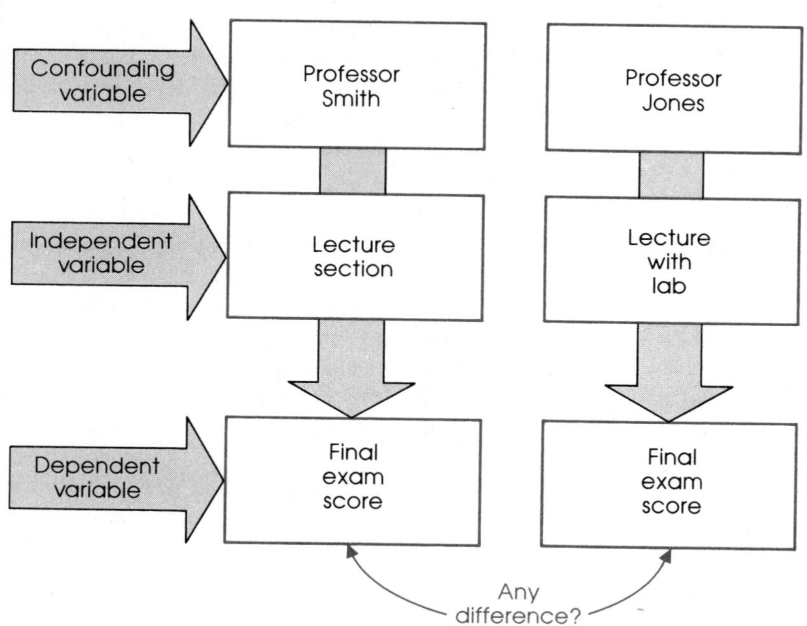

they are treated. The instructor was allowed to vary along with the method of instruction. It is possible that the lecture/lab group performed better because Professor Jones is a better instructor, one who motivates students and can explain concepts in understandable terms. That is, the difference between groups in performance might be due to the different instructors rather than the different treatments. One cannot be sure which interpretation is correct. When a study is confounded, it is impossible to make meaningful conclusions about the results.

Another problem that can occur is that the groups may differ *even before* they receive the treatments. Then the difference in performance between groups at the end of the experiment is incorrectly attributed to the effect of the independent variable. For example, an experiment was done to determine if stress associated with decision making would lead to the development of ulcers (Brady et al., 1958). Four monkeys in the "executive" (decision-making) group were paired with four control monkeys. The monkeys in each pair were restrained in chairs next to each other. The executive had to press a lever often enough to avoid electric shock. If the subject stopped pressing the lever for a short time, *both* monkeys in the pair would get shocked. Thus, the executive and control monkeys received the same number of shocks, but only the executive had to make decisions. After several weeks, it was noted that the executive monkeys had many stomach ulcers, but the controls did not.

This type of pairing of control and experimental subjects is sometimes called a yoked control.

This result would seem to indicate that the stress of responsibility promotes the development of ulcers. However, the outcome of the study may be difficult to interpret because the monkeys were not randomly assigned to treatment groups. The first four monkeys who learned to press the lever to avoid shock were assigned to the executive group, and the remaining animals served as controls. It is possible that the earlier learners were the most sensitive or emotionally reactive of all the animals. On this basis alone, one would expect the early learners to develop more ulcers when shocked. Therefore, the findings of the executive monkey experiment may be due to a bias in group assignments rather than to a treatment (decision-making) effect. The groups may have been different all along.

When we interpret the outcome of an experiment, we assume that the groups were initially the same. If this assumption is violated, then the differences observed following treatment may have nothing to do with the independent variable. Random assignment of subjects to treatments helps avoid this problem, but just to be sure, a researcher may also give the subjects a pretest before the study. That is, one might take measurements of the dependent variable prior to the treatment, as well as after it, to be certain that the groups are initially equivalent. Perspective 1.1 deals with a similar problem in an applied research setting.

THEORIES AND HYPOTHESES

A theory is especially helpful if it generates many testable hypotheses. By testable we mean the hypothesis can be confirmed or disconfirmed by making observations (conducting studies).

Theories are a very important part of psychological research. A psychological theory typically consists of a number of statements about the underlying mechanisms of behavior. Theories are important in that they help organize and unify many observations. They may try to account for very large areas of psychology, such as a general theory of learning. However, they may be more specific, such as a theory of the mechanisms involved in just avoidance learning. A theory is especially useful if it directs and promotes future research and provides specific predictions for the outcomes of that research.

When an investigator designs an experiment, there almost always is a specific hypothesis which is addressed. A *hypothesis* is a hunch about the result that will be obtained from the experiment.

· DEFINITION · A *hypothesis* is a prediction about the outcome of an experiment.

PERSPECTIVE 1.1

OTHER THINGS BEING EQUAL

When assessing the effect of a treatment, we assume that groups differ only with respect to the treatment condition, and that other conditions are the same or equal for the groups in the study. In the following example, Hooke (1983) illustrates the problems of interpretation that arise in research when other things are *not* equal.

> *Ceteris paribus* means "other things being equal," and I drag in this bit of Latin to suggest the antiquity of the phrase. Often we assume that other things are equal without saying so, and then we may forget that the assumption was made. Data pushers like to profit from our habit of making this tacit assumption.
>
> During the 1970s a report was issued describing data for crude cancer mortality rates in two groups of ten American cities, one group that had added fluoride to the drinking water and one that had not. Between 1950 and 1970 the cancer mortality rate rose in both groups of cities, but it rose considerably faster in the fluoridated group. Some data pushers were more than willing to attribute the difference to the fluoride, without pointing out that they were assuming "other things being equal."
>
> The National Cancer Institute asserted that indeed other things were not equal and that the difference between the two groups of cities was explained by differences in the age, race, and sex distributions of the two groups of cities; these three demographic characteristics all have known effects on cancer mortality rates. In Great Britain the Royal College of Physicians asked for comment from the Royal Statistical Society. Two statisticians were chosen to analyze the data, and here is what they found.
>
> The cities that were to be fluoridated already had, before fluoridation, an excess of cancer deaths over the "control," cities that went unfluoridated. Between 1950 and 1970 the demographic differences between the two groups became even greater. Taking into account the known effects of age, race, and sex on cancer death rate, they found that the remaining unaccounted-for part of the cancer mortality rate was actually somewhat smaller in the fluoridated cities than in the others.
>
> Which all goes to show that *ceteris* are not necessarily *paribus,* and that the reason things are often not what they seem is that we may be assuming things about them that are not true.

Excerpt reprinted from R. Hooke, *How to Tell the Liars from the Statisticians,* 1983, pp. 21–22, by courtesy of Marcel Dekker, Inc.

Hypotheses are often derived from the theory that the researcher is developing. An experimenter can state the hypothesis as a prediction—specifically, as a relationship between the independent and dependent variables. Simply stated, a hypothesis is a prediction about the effect of the treatments. Therefore, we can think of an experiment as a test of a hypothesis. A very important part of inferential statistics consists of the statistical analysis of hypothesis tests. Much of the book will focus on this topic.

When an experiment is performed, the researcher is trying to determine if the evidence confirms or refutes a specific hypothesis. Confirming these predictions strengthens the theory, suggesting it is correct and useful for guiding future research. In a sense, an experiment poses a problem of detection. The investigator attempts to detect a treatment effect to support a hypothesis. It is possible to have "false alarms" in an experiment—for the investigator to conclude there is evidence for an effect in the experiment when in reality no such treatment effect exists. The goal of the statistical techniques for testing hypotheses is to detect treatment effects but at the same time reduce the chances of false alarms. As Perspective 1.2 points out, anytime we have a detection situation, there is always a risk of false alarms.

CONSTRUCTS AND OPERATIONAL DEFINITIONS

Theories contain hypothetical concepts which help describe the mechanisms that underlie behavioral phenomena. These concepts are called *constructs,* and they cannot be observed because they are hypothetical. For example, intelligence, personality types, and motives are hypothetical constructs. They are used in theories to organize observations in terms of underlying mechanisms. If constructs are hypothetical and cannot be observed, then how can they possibly be studied? The answer is that we have to *define* the construct so that it can be studied. An *operational definition* defines

PERSPECTIVE 1.2

THE PLAGUE OF FALSE ALARMS

The headline in a Rochester, New York newspaper stated, "City May Charge for False Alarms." The article noted the following:

> The city of Rochester hopes to cut the number of false alarms plaguing its police and fire departments by making negligent alarm owners pay for their mistakes.
>
> Officials estimate that false alarms cost the city about $500,000 a year in such things as police time lost answering the calls. Of the 21,320 alarms automatically called into the city police last year, 96.5 percent were false, according to Police Department statistics. The year before 97 percent of the alarms were false.
>
> A proposed city ordinance will include a $5 annual permit fee for all burglar and fire alarms in the city . . . . At permit renewal time, the owner would pay $50 for each false alarm over three the city responded to during the year.

According to the article, the "$50 charge would provide an incentive for owners to repair faulty burglar alarms and to make sure that they are properly maintained."

Anytime we attempt to detect something, be it a treatment effect or a burglary, there is always the chance that we will make a mistake. A scientist tries to avoid false alarms—that is, concluding there is a treatment effect when there really is no effect. He or she structures and conducts the statistical test in a way that minimizes the likelihood that a false alarm will occur. Faced with a similar and very costly dilemma, the city of Rochester is trying to structure and implement its laws to minimize false alarms in the detection of burglars and fires. As the proposed ordinance suggests, the city officials are willing to risk a maximum of three false alarms per business each year. Like the scientist trying to detect a treatment effect, they are reducing the chances of a certain type of error that can occur in detection situations.

Article excerpts are reprinted courtesy of the *Democrat and Chronicle*, Rochester, New York.

a construct in terms of an observable and measurable response. This definition should include the process and operations involved in making the observations. For example, an operational definition for emotionality might be stated as the amount of increase in heart rate after a person is insulted. An operational definition of intelligence might be the score on the Wechsler Adult Intelligence Scale.

· DEFINITIONS · *Constructs* are hypothetical concepts that are used in theories to organize observations in terms of underlying mechanisms.

An *operational definition* defines a construct in terms of a measurable response.

· LEARNING CHECK ·

1 It is possible for a study to be objective even if the researcher's hypotheses or beliefs are allowed to influence the results. (True or false?)

2 Cause-and-effect relationships cannot be determined by a correlational method. (True or false?)

3 In a memory experiment, subjects memorize a list of words and then must recall as many words as possible after a 6-hour retention interval. One group sleeps during the retention interval, while people in the other group remain awake and go about their daily routine. The number of words recalled is measured for each subject. The experimenter wants to determine if type of activity during the retention interval has an effect on the number of words recalled. For this study, what is the independent variable? What is the dependent variable?

4 A confounding variable will assist the experimenter in making a meaningful interpretation of the data. (True or false?)

5 A hypothesis can be stated as a prediction about the effect of ____________ on ____________.

6 An operational definition defines a construct in terms of ____________.

ANSWERS

1 false

2 true

3 type of activity during the retention interval; the number of words recalled

4 false
5 an independent variable (or treatment); a dependent variable
6 a measurable response

1.4 SCALES OF MEASUREMENT

WHAT IS A MEASUREMENT? It should be obvious by now that data collection requires that we make measurements of our observations. Measurement involves either categorizing events (qualitative measurements) or using numbers to characterize the size of the event (quantitative measurement). There are several types of scales that are associated with measurements. The distinctions among the scales are important because they underscore the limitations of certain types of measurements and because certain statistical procedures are appropriate for data collected on some scales but not on others. If you were interested in people's heights, for example, you could measure a group of individuals by simply classifying them into three categories: tall, medium, and short. However, this simple classification would not tell you much about the actual heights of the individuals, and these measurements would not give you enough information to calculate an average height for the group. Although the simple classification would be adequate for some purposes, you would need more-sophisticated measurements before you could answer more-detailed questions. In this section we examine four different scales of measurement, beginning with the simplest and moving to the most sophisticated.

THE NOMINAL SCALE A *nominal scale* of measurement labels observations so that they fall into different categories.

· DEFINITION · In a *nominal scale* of measurement, observations are labeled and categorized.

The word *nominal* means "having to do with names." Measurements that are made on this scale involve naming things. For example, if we wish to know the sex of a person responding to a questionnaire, it would be measured on a nominal scale consisting of two categories. A product warranty card might have you check the box that best describes your occupation, and it lists "sales," "professional," "skilled trade," "other (please specify)." Occupations are being measured in terms of categories; therefore a nominal scale is being used. A researcher observing the behavior of a group of infant monkeys might categorize responses as playing, grooming, feeding, acting aggressive, or showing submissiveness. Again, this instance typifies a nominal scale of measurement. The nominal scale consists of qualitative distinctions. No attempt is made to measure the size of the event or response. The scales that follow do reflect an attempt to make quantitative distinctions.

THE ORDINAL SCALE In an *ordinal scale* of measurement, observations are ranked in terms of size or magnitude. As the word *ordinal* implies, the investigator simply arranges the observations in rank order.

· DEFINITION · An *ordinal scale* of measurement consists of ranking observations in terms of size or magnitude.

For example, a job supervisor is asked to rank employees in terms of how well they perform their work. The resulting data (Table 1.1) will tell us who the supervisor considers the best worker, the second best, and so on. However, the data provide no information about the amount that the workers differ in job performance. The data may reveal that Jan is viewed as doing better work than Joe but *not how much* better. This is a limitation of measurements on an ordinal scale.

THE INTERVAL SCALE

In an *interval scale* of measurement, intervals between numbers reflect differences in magnitude. That is, it allows you to measure differences in the size or amount of events.

· DEFINITION · In an *interval scale,* the difference (or interval) between numbers on the scale reflects a difference in magnitude. However, ratios of magnitudes are not meaningful.

For example, if on June 1 the temperature is 80°F and on November 1 it is 40°, then we can say that the temperature on June 1 was 40° higher than on November 1. If Jim scored 160 on an IQ test and Sam scored 80, then Jim's is 80 points higher. Note that with an interval scale we can determine which observation is of greater magnitude and by *how much* it is greater.

However, we *cannot* say that it was *twice* as hot on June 1 as on November 1 or that Jim is twice as smart as Sam. These statements require that you form a ratio of the two observations. A ratio will only be meaningful when the scale of measurement has a true zero point. For example, zero on the Fahrenheit scale does not mean there is "no temperature." It certainly can get colder than 0°F. Likewise, there is no meaningful zero point that would indicate that a person has absolutely "no intelligence." These scales start at arbitrary zero points, making ratio comparisons meaningless.

THE RATIO SCALE

A *ratio scale* of measurement has a meaningful zero point, and thus ratios of numbers on this scale do reflect ratios of magnitudes.

· DEFINITION · In a *ratio scale,* ratios of numbers do reflect ratios of magnitudes. Such scale has a meaningful zero point.

Most dependent variables we will encounter can be measured on either an interval or a ratio scale.

For example, two warehouse workers have a contest to see who can lift the heaviest carton. Bill lifts a 200-pound carton and John lifts a 100-pound box. It can be said that Bill is able to lift twice as much as John. Note that a ratio scale of measurement allows one to draw the same conclusions as with ordinal and interval scales, plus it allows one to form ratios to compare the magnitude of measurements. In a psychology laboratory, a researcher might measure people's reaction times to stimuli. For example, it takes Joan 500 milliseconds to respond to a stimulus, and Mary takes only 250 milliseconds. Therefore, Mary responds in half as much time as Joan.

· TABLE 1.1 ·

Rank order of worker's performance according to supervisor

Rank	Worker
1	Sandy
2	Jan
3	Joe
4	Hoyt
5	Ellen
6	Bill

1.5 DISCRETE AND CONTINUOUS VARIABLES

WHAT ARE THEY AND HOW DO THEY DIFFER?

The variables in a study can be characterized by the type of values that can be assigned to them. A *discrete variable* consists of separate, indivisible categories. For this type of variable there are no intermediate values between two adjacent categories. Consider the values displayed when dice are rolled. Between neighboring values—for example, seven dots and eight dots—no other values can ever be observed.

DEFINITION A *discrete variable* consists of separate, indivisible categories. No values can exist between two neighboring categories.

A discrete variable is typically restricted to whole countable numbers—for example, the number of children in a family or the number of students attending class. If you observe class attendance from day to day, you may find 18 students one day and 19 students the next day. However, it is impossible ever to observe a value between 18 and 19. A discrete variable may also consist of observations that differ qualitatively. For example, a psychologist observing patients may classify some as having panic disorders, others as having dissociative disorders, and some as having psychotic disorders. The type of disorder is a discrete variable because there are distinct and finite categories that can be observed. On the other hand, it is possible for a *continuous variable* to take on an infinite number of values. Specifically, between any two observations for a continuous variable, there are an infinite number of other possible values.

DEFINITION For a *continuous variable*, there are an infinite number of possible values that fall between any two observed values. A continuous variable is divisible into an infinite number of fractional parts.

For example, subjects are given problems to solve, and a researcher records the amount of time it takes them to find the solutions. One person may take 31 seconds to solve the problems, whereas another may take 32 seconds. Between these two values it is possible to find any fractional amount—$31\frac{1}{2}$, $31\frac{1}{4}$, $31\frac{1}{10}$—provided the measuring instrument is sufficiently accurate. Time is a continuous variable.

INTERVALS AND CONTINUOUS VARIABLES

A continuous variable can be pictured on a number line that is continuous. That is, there are an infinite number of points on this line. However, when a continuous variable is measured, we typically do not assign our observation to a single point value on the line. In practice we assign the observation to an *interval* on the number line. For example, body weight is a continuous variable because there are an infinite number of possible weights between any two weights. Suppose we measure body weight to the nearest pound. Two people actually weigh 150.3 and 149.6 pounds. Their weights are located on the segment of the number line in Figure 1.4. What weights will we assign to these people? In the first case, 150.3 is rounded down to 150, and for the second person 149.6 is rounded up to 150. Even though their actual weights differ slightly, they are assigned the same value in whole numbers. In fact, any person whose actual weight is somewhere in the interval between 149.5 and 150.5 will be assigned the weight of 150 pounds. Therefore, when we measure weight to the nearest pound, we are actually assigning observations to intervals on the continuum. When body weight is reported, it typically is reported in whole numbers. This practice does not mean that body weight is a discrete variable. Body weight is a continuous variable, but the observations are being assigned to intervals on the

· FIGURE 1.4 ·

When measuring weight to the nearest whole pound, 149.6 and 150.3 are assigned the value of 150 (top). Any value in the interval between 149.5 and 150.5 will be given the value of 150.

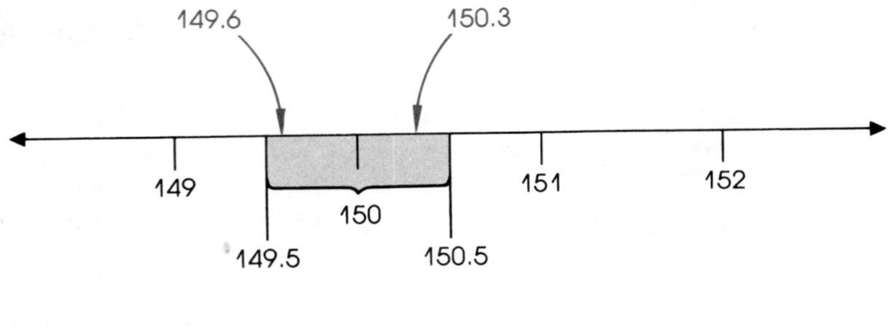

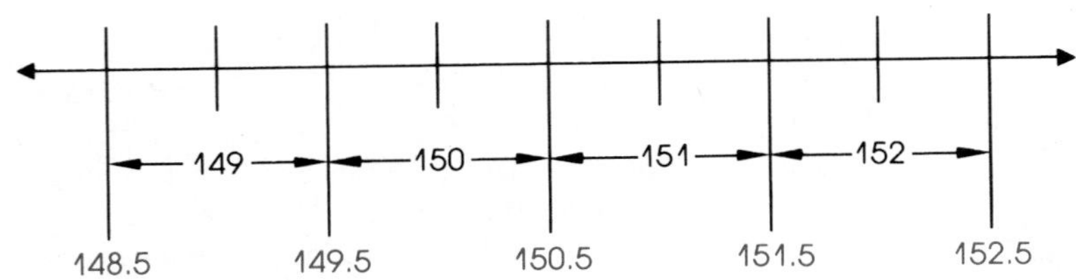

number line rather than points. Sometimes limitations in the precision of a measuring tool (your bathroom scale, for example) necessitates this type of assignment.

A WORD OF CAUTION ABOUT CONTINUOUS VARIABLES

Occasionally the procedure used to measure a continuous variable produces results that make the variable appear to be discrete. For example, a researcher may classify students as slow learners or fast learners depending on how much time they take to solve a set of problems. In this case, the variable is time (which is continuous), but the measurement produces only two distinct categories, slow and fast. Similarly, a researcher may report measurements of time that are rounded to the nearest second. In this case, the data would show a finite number of whole-number categories, with no intermediate values. In both of the situations we have just described, a continuous variable (time) is measured in such a way that the scores appear to be discrete. To determine whether or not a variable is continuous, you must look beyond the actual scores and examine the variable that is being measured. One simple criterion is to ask yourself if it was possible for the researcher to have obtained more-precise measurements. If the answer is yes, chances are that the variable is continuous. For example, time can be measured to the nearest hour, the nearest second, the nearest $\frac{1}{10}$ second, and so on. With a continuous variable there is no limit to the precision of measurement except for the accuracy of the measuring instrument.

· LEARNING CHECK ·

1 An instructor records the order in which students complete their tests—that is, the first to finish, the second to finish, and so on. A(n) __________ scale of measurement is used in this instance.

2 The Scholastic Aptitude Test (SAT) most likely measures aptitude on a(n) __________ scale.

3 In a study on perception of facial expressions, subjects must classify the emotions displayed in photographs of people as either anger, sadness, joy, disgust, fear, or surprise. Emotional expression is measured on a(n) __________ scale.

4 A researcher studies the factors that determine how many children couples decide to have. The variable, number of children, is a __________ (discrete/continuous) variable.

5 An investigator studies how concept-formation ability changes with age. Age is a ____________ (discrete/continuous) variable.

ANSWERS 1 ordinal 2 interval 3 nominal 4 discrete 5 continuous

1.6 STATISTICAL NOTATION

Measurements of behavior will provide data composed of numerical values. These numbers form the basis of the computations that are done for statistical analyses. There is a standardized notation system for statistical procedures, and it is used to identify terms in equations and mathematical operations. Some general mathematical operations, notation, and basic algebra are outlined in the review section of Appendix A. There is also a skills assessment exam (page 467) to help you determine if you need the basic mathematics review. Here we will introduce some statistical notation that is used throughout this book. In subsequent chapters, additional notation will be introduced as it is needed.

SCORES Making observations of a dependent variable in a study will typically yield values or scores for each subject. Raw scores are the original, unchanged set of scores obtained in the study. Scores for a particular variable are represented by the letter X. For example, if performance in your statistics course is measured by tests and you obtain a 35 on the first test, then we could state that $X = 35$. A set of scores can be presented in a column that is headed by X. For example, a list of quiz scores from your class might be presented as follows:

X
37
35
35
30
25
17
16

When observations are made for two variables, there will be two scores for each subject. The data can be presented as two lists labeled X and Y for the two variables. For example, observations for people's height in inches (variable X) and weight in pounds (variable Y) can be presented in the following manner.

X	Y
72	165
68	151
67	160
68	146
70	160
66	133

It is also useful to specify how many scores are in a set. The number of scores in a data set is represented by the letter N. For populations we will use an uppercase N, and for samples we will use a lowercase n. (Throughout the book, notational differences are used to distinguish between samples and populations.) For the height and weight data, $N = 6$ for both variables.

SUMMATION NOTATION

Many of the computations required in statistics will involve adding up a set of scores. Because this procedure is used so frequently, there is a special notation used to refer to the sum of a set of scores. The Greek letter sigma, or $\sum$, is used to stand for summation. The expression $\sum X$ means to add all the scores for variable X. The summation sign $\sum$ can be read as "the sum of." Thus $\sum X$ is read "the sum of the scores." For the following set of quiz scores,

10, 6, 7, 4

$\sum X = 27$ and $N = 4$. There are a number of rules of summation that help identify which scores are added together and which mathematical operation is performed first when several are required. These rules are summarized as follows.

1. When there are two variables X and Y, $\sum X$ indicates the sum of the Xs, and $\sum Y$ refers to the sum of the Ys. For the following data, $\sum X = 16$, and $\sum Y = 34$:

X	Y
3	10
1	4
7	6
3	5
2	9

$$\sum X = 3 + 1 + 7 + 3 + 2 = 16$$
$$\sum Y = 10 + 4 + 6 + 5 + 9 = 34$$

2. When two variables (X and Y) are multiplied together, the product is represented by the symbols XY. Note that the multiplication sign is not written between the symbols ($X \times Y$ can cause confusion). The expression XY is understood to mean "X times Y." The following table shows scores for three individuals. For each person there is a score for variable X, a score for variable Y, and the product of the two scores, XY.

X	Y	XY
2	4	8
3	1	3
4	3	12

The total for the X values, $\sum X = 9$, is obtained by adding the scores in that column, and the sum of the Y values, $\sum Y = 8$, is obtained by adding the Y column. The expression $\sum XY$ means "sum the products of X and Y." The first step is to compute the product for each pair of X and Y scores. These products are displayed in the column headed by XY. In the second step, the products are added together. For this example, the sum of the products is $\sum XY = 23$:

$$\sum XY = 8 + 3 + 12 = 23$$

It is very important to note that $\sum XY$ *does not equal* $\sum X \sum Y$. The latter expression means "the sum of X times the sum of Y." For these data, it is easy to demonstrate that the two expressions are not the same:

$$\sum XY \neq \sum X \sum Y$$

$$23 \neq 9(8)$$

$$23 \neq 72$$

3. When a constant amount C is added to each score, the expression for the resulting scores is $X + C$. In the following example, the constant equals 4. If this value is added to every score, a column headed by $X + 4$ can be made.

X	$X + 4$
1	5
4	8
6	10

When a constant value is added to every score, it is necessary to use parentheses to represent the sum of these new scores, $\sum(X + 4)$. The calculations within the parentheses are always done first. Because the summation symbol is outside the parentheses, finding the sum is performed last. Therefore, to compute $\sum(X + 4)$, the constant 4 is first added to every score, creating the new $X + 4$ column of numbers. Then these new numbers are added together. For this example,

$$\sum(X + 4) = 5 + 8 + 10 = 23$$

A word of caution is necessary. If parentheses are not used, then the meaning of the expression is changed. For example, to compute $\sum X + 4$, you first find the sum of the X values and then add 4 to this total:

$$\sum X + 4 = 11 + 4 = 15$$

Note that $\sum(X + C)$ *does not equal* $\sum X + C$.

Remember, when a number is squared, it is multiplied by itself. A common mistake is to multiply a number by 2 instead of squaring it.

4. The squared value of a score is represented by the symbol X^2. If every score in the group is squared, then a new column of squared values can be listed:

X	X^2
3	9
1	1
4	16
2	4

The expression $\sum X^2$ means the sum of the squared scores. Each score is first squared, and then the sum is found for the squared values (see Perspective 1.3). In this example, adding the X^2 column reveals that

$$\sum X^2 = 9 + 1 + 16 + 4 = 30$$

Be careful! The symbol $(\sum X)^2$ represents a different order of operations, and the resulting value is not the same as that of $\sum X^2$. The operations inside the parentheses are performed first. Therefore, the sum of the X's is determined first. The exponent is outside the parentheses, so the squaring is done last. The expression $(\sum X)^2$ means

PERSPECTIVE 1.3

COMPUTING $\sum X^2$ WITH A CALCULATOR

The sum of squared scores, $\sum X^2$, is a common expression in many statistical calculations. The following steps outline the most-efficient procedure for using a typical, inexpensive hand calculator to find this sum. We assume that your calculator has one memory where you can store and retrieve information. *Caution:* The following instructions work for most calculators but not for every single model. If you encounter trouble, don't panic—check your manual or talk with your instructor.

1. Clear the calculator memory. You may press the memory-clear key (usually MC) or simply turn the calculator off then back on.
2. Enter the first score.
3. Press the multiply key ($\times$); then press the equals ($=$) key. The squared score should appear in the display. (Note you do not need to enter a number twice to square it. Just follow the sequence: number-times-equals.)
4. Put the squared value into the calculator memory. For most calculators, you press the key labeled M+.
5. Enter the next score, square it, and add it to memory (steps 2, 3, and 4). (Note you do not need to clear the display between scores.)
6. Continue this process for the full set of scores. Then retrieve the total ($\sum X^2$) from memory by pressing the memory-recall key (usually labeled MR).

Check this procedure with a simple set of scores such as: 1, 2, 3. You should find $\sum X^2 = 14$.

the *squared total.* In the example, this value is

$$(\sum X)^2 = (10)^2 = 100$$

Therefore, $(\sum X)^2$ is *not the same* expression as $\sum X^2$. It is very important to remember the order of operations for these two expressions. Later we will have to use statistical formulas that contain both of these expressions. It is imperative that you do not confuse them for each other.

· LEARNING CHECK · For the following data, find the values for the listed expressions.

X	Y
3	1
3	2
1	1
2	3
4	5

1 $\sum X$ **2** $\sum X^2$ **3** $(\sum X)^2$ **4** $\sum(Y + 3)$ **5** $(\sum Y)^2$ **6** $\sum X \sum Y$
7 $\sum XY$ **8** N for the X scores

ANSWERS **1** 13 **2** 39 **3** 169 **4** 27 **5** 144 **6** 156 **7** 36 **8** 5

A WORD ABOUT COMPUTERS

Long before computers became commonplace at home, they were routinely used in statistics. The computer can make short work of the statistical analysis of large data sets and can eliminate the tedium that goes along with complex and repetitive computations. As the use of computers became widespread, so did the availability of statistical software packages. The typical software package contains a variety of specialized programs, each one capable of performing a specific type of statistical procedure. The user enters the data to be analyzed and then specifies the program to be used with one or more software commands.

The best known and most popular statistical packages are BMDP, Minitab, SAS, and SPSS^x. Most likely, one or more of these are available at your college. From time to time, we will show you an illustration of a Minitab or SPSS^x analysis applied to an example that has been worked out in a chapter. We will not attempt to train you

The Study Guide accompanying this text contains an introduction to SPSS^x and Minitab.

how to use these software packages. Your instructor can direct you to one of the many guides that are available. Rather, out goal is to familiarize you with reading and finding your way through the printouts of Minitab and SPSS^x analyses and to give you an idea of what these packages are capable of doing.

While we are on the topic of computers and statistics, the authors cannot resist an editorial comment. Many students have approached us with the question: If computers are so good at doing statistical calculations, why not just teach us how to use the computer and forget about teaching us statistics? This question usually is followed with an accurate observation: If I should get a job where I need to use statistics, I probably will just use a computer anyway.

Although there are many ways to answer these comments, we will try to limit ourselves to one or two general ideas. The purpose of this book is to help you gain an understanding of statistics. Notice that we used the word *understanding*. Although computers can do statistics with incredible speed and accuracy, they are not capable of exercising any judgment or interpretation of the material that you feed into them (input) or the results that they produce (output). Too often students (and researchers) rely on computers to perform difficult calculations and have no idea of what the computer is actually doing. In some fields this lack of understanding is acceptable—we are all allowed to use the telephone even if we do not understand how it works. But in scientific research it is critical that you have a complete and accurate understanding of your data. Usually this requires an understanding of the statistical techniques used to summarize and interpret data. So use your computer and enjoy it, but do not rely on it for statistical expertise.

SUMMARY

1 By common usage, the word *statistics* means facts and figures. In this book, the general use of the word is in reference to techniques and procedures for analyzing data.

2 Science is empirical in that it provides methods for making observations. Statistics consist of methods for organizing and interpreting data.

3 A population is composed of every individual from the group one wishes to study. A sample is a subset of the population. Samples are drawn from the population for study because the population in question is usually so large that it is not feasible to study every individual in it.

4 Descriptive statistics simplify and summarize data, so that the data are more manageable. Inferential statistics are techniques that allow one to use sample data to make general statements about a population. Meaningful generalizations are possible only if the sample is representative of the population from which it was drawn. Random sampling helps ensure that it is representative.

5 A correlational method looks for interrelationships between variables but cannot determine the cause-and-effect nature of the relationship. The experimental method is able to establish causes and effects in a relationship.

6 In the experimental method, one variable (the independent variable) is intentionally manipulated and controlled by the experimenter. Then changes are noted in another variable (the dependent variable) as a result of the manipulation. The results of an experiment will be uninterpretable when a confounding variable is present. A confounding variable unintentionally varies along with the independent variable, so that groups differ in terms of how they are treated in more than one way.

7 A hypothesis is a prediction about the effect of an independent variable on a dependent variable. Hypotheses are usually derived from theories. Experiments basically involve the test of a hypothesis.

8 Constructs are hypothetical concepts used in theories to describe the mechanisms of behavior. Because they are hypothetical, they cannot be observed. Constructs are studied by providing operational definitions for them. An operational definition defines a construct in terms of an observable and measurable response or event.

9 A nominal scale labels observations so that they fall into different categories. A nominal scale involves making qualitative distinctions. No attempt is made to measure the magnitude of the event.

10 An ordinal scale involves ranking observations in terms of size or magnitude. Although this scale will tell us which observation is larger, it will not tell us how much larger it is.

11 In an interval scale, intervals between numbers reflect differences in magnitude of observations. It is possible to determine which event is of greater magnitude and how much larger it is.

12 A ratio scale has all of the characteristics of an interval scale, and ratios of measurements on this scale reflect ratios of magnitudes. Unlike the interval scale, a ratio scale has a meaningful zero point.

13 A discrete variable is one that can have only a finite number of values between any two values. It typically consists of whole numbers that vary in countable steps. A continuous variable can have an infinite number of values between any two values. When a continuous variable is measured, we typically assign the observation to an interval on the number line rather than a single point.

14 The letter X is used to represent scores for a variable. If a second variable is used, Y represents its scores. The letter N is used as the symbol for the number of scores in a set. The Greek letter sigma $\sum$ is used to stand for summation. Therefore, the expression $\sum X$ is read "the sum of the scores."

KEY TERMS

statistics
population
sample
population parameter
sample statistic
descriptive statistics
distribution
raw scores
inferential statistics
random selection
variable
correlational method
experimental method
independent variable
dependent variable
control group
experimental group
confounding variable
hypothesis
construct
operational definition
nominal scale
ordinal scale
interval scale
ratio scale
discrete variable
continuous variable

FOCUS ON PROBLEM SOLVING

1. It may help to simplify summation notation if you observe that the summation sign always is followed by a symbol (or symbolic expression)—for example, $\sum X$ or $\sum(X + 3)$. This symbol specifies which values you are to add. If you use the symbol as a column heading and list all the appropriate values in the column, your task is simply to add up the numbers in the column. To find $\sum(X + 3)$ for example, start a column headed with $(X + 3)$ next to the column of X's. List all the $(X + 3)$ values; then find the total for the column.

2. To use summation notation correctly you must be careful of two other factors:

a. When you are determining the "symbol" that follows the summation sign, remember that everything within parentheses is part of the same symbol, for example $\sum(X + 3)$, and a string of multiplied values is considered to be a single symbol, for example, $\sum XY$.

b. Often it is necessary to use several intermediate columns before you can reach the column of values specified by a particular symbol. To compute $\sum(X - 1)^2$, for example, you will need three columns: first, the column of original scores, Xs; second, a column of $(X - 1)$ values; and third, a column of squared $(X - 1)$ values. It is the third column, headed by $(X - 1)^2$, that you should total.

PROBLEMS

***1** Scientific study is empirical and objective. What is meant by this statement?

2 Describe the purposes of descriptive and inferential statistical techniques.

3 What is the shortcoming of the correlational method of study?

*Solutions for problems marked with an asterisk are given in Appendix C.

*4 Describe how the experimental method is conducted. What is the distinction between the two types of variables that are used?

5 What type of problems can occur in the experimental method that may lead to an incorrect interpretation of the findings?

6 A report states that insomniacs given a new sleeping drug fell asleep 20 minutes sooner than insomniacs given a placebo. For this report, what is the independent variable? What is the dependent variable?

A placebo is an inactive or neutral substance (a sugar pill) that is given in place of a drug in psychological or medical research.

7 In a study of memory, the effect of retention interval length is examined. The first group memorizes a list of words. After a 20-minute retention interval, these subjects must write down as many words as they can remember. The second group memorizes a different list and must recall the words after a 1-hour interval. The last group studies a third list of words and is tested for recall 2 hours later. The experimenter measures the number of words recalled for each subject. For this experiment, what is the independent variable? What is the dependent variable? What confounding variable is present and how might it prevent a clear-cut interpretation of any differences that are observed?

*8 A researcher would like to determine whether or not office productivity is influenced by background music.

a Briefly describe how this researcher could gather data using the observational or correlational method.

b Briefly describe how data could be obtained using the experimental method.

c Identify the independent variable and the dependent variable for this experiment.

d Identify some possible confounding variables that could influence the data obtained with the observational method.

9 A researcher would like to examine the effect of the amount of sleep on performance of a vigilance task. One group of subjects is allowed to sleep all night without interruptions. A second group of subjects is awakened six times during the night. In the morning, all the subjects are tested on a vigilance task. They are required to observe a radar screen display and respond anytime a small spot of light briefly flashes somewhere on the screen. The experimenter records the number of errors subjects make. For this experiment, what is the independent variable? What is the dependent variable?

*10 Contrast the nominal scale of measurement to the ordinal scale. What type of scale is used in a list of the order of finish in a horse race? What type of scale is used when describing the sex of the jockeys?

11 Describe the difference between an ordinal scale of measurement and an interval scale.

*12 What is the difference between the interval scale and ratio scale of measurement?

13 What is the distinction between continuous and discrete variables?

14 What is the distinction between a construct and an operational definition?

*15 For the following set of scores, calculate the value for each of the expressions listed:

a $\sum X$
b $\sum X + 5$
c $\sum(X + 5)$
d $\sum(X - 3)$
e $\sum X - 3$
f N

X
5
9
6
7
13

16 For the following set of scores, find the value for the expressions listed:

a $\sum X$
b $\sum Y$
c $\sum X + \sum Y$
d $\sum(X + Y)$
e $\sum XY$
f $\sum X \sum Y$

X	Y
1	3
3	2
2	1
1	5
4	2

*17 For the following set of scores, calculate the value for the expressions:

a $\sum X$
b $\sum X^2$
c $(\sum X)^2$

X
3
5
2
1
4

18 A student was asked to compute $\sum(X + 3)$ for a set of $N = 10$ scores. Rather than add 3 points to each score and find the new sum, the student simply added 30 points (10 times 3) to the old $\sum X$. Explain why this produced the correct answer.

19 Using the following data, calculate each requested value:

a $\sum X$
b $\sum X^2$
c $\sum Y$
d $\sum Y^2$
e $\sum X \sum Y$
f $\sum XY$

X	Y
1	4
7	8
6	11
12	16
8	9
5	13

***20** For the following data, find each requested value:

a $\sum X^2$
b $\sum Y$
c $\sum Y^2$
d $\sum X \sum Y$
e $\sum XY$
f $(\sum X)^2$
g $(\sum Y)^2$

X	Y
2.3	3.1
4.0	11.5
6.7	2.0
4.5	9.4
5.6	7.2
8.0	1.0
3.3	6.7

21 For the following data, calculate the values for the expressions:

a $\sum X$
b $\sum X^2$
c $\sum Y$
d $\sum Y^2$
e $\sum XY$
f $\sum X \sum Y$

X	Y
2	10
6	3
4	2
3	11
9	4

***22** Use summation notation to express each of the following calculations:
a The sum of the squared scores
b The square of the sum of the scores

23 For both samples, calculate the values for the expressions:

Sample 1		Sample 2	
X	Y	X	Y
1	5	1	13
2	7	2	11
3	9	3	9
4	11	4	7
5	13	5	5

a $\sum X$ b $\sum Y$
c $\sum X^2$ d $\sum Y^2$
e $(\sum X)^2$ f $(\sum Y)^2$
g $\sum XY$ h $\sum X \sum Y$
i Explain why the value for $\sum XY$ is different for the two samples, whereas all the other sums are identical.

24 For the following data, find the value for each of the expressions:

a $\sum X$
b $\sum X^2$
c $(\sum X)^2$
d N

X
10.1
9.3
21.5
7.0
8.7
17.4
10.6

25 Use summation notation to represent each of the following calculations:
a Add 3 points to each score and then sum the resulting values.
b Square each score and subtract 1 point. Then sum the resulting values.
c Subtract 2 points from each score and square the result. Add the squared values.
d Add the scores and square the total. Then add 10 points to the squared total.

***26** A researcher has two scores, X and Y, for each individual in a population. Use summation notation to express each of the following calculations with these scores:
a Subtract 1 point from each Y score and then add the resulting values. Then multiply this sum by the sum of the X scores.
b Multiply X times Y for each person and then add the products.
c For each person, subtract 2 points from each X score and then add them. Subtract this sum from the sum of the Y scores.

27 For the following set of scores, find the value of each expression:

a $\sum X$
b $\sum(X - 3)$
c $\sum(X - 3)^2$
d $(\sum X)^2 - \sum X^2$
e $(\sum X + 2)^2 - \sum(X + 2)^2$

X
3
5
10
8
7

***28** For the following set of scores find the value of each expression:

a $\sum X$
b $\sum(X + 2)$
c $\sum X^2$

X
−2
5
−4
0
7
−1

29 For the following set of scores, find the value of each expression:

a $\sum X$
b $\sum Y$
c $\sum XY$
d $\sum X \sum Y$

X	Y
−3	2
4	3
−6	−1
5	−2
−5	4

CHAPTER 2

FREQUENCY DISTRIBUTIONS

TOOLS YOU WILL NEED

The following items are considered essential background material for this chapter. If you doubt your knowledge of any of these items, you should review the appropriate chapter or section before proceeding.

- Proportions (math review, Appendix A)
    - Fractions
    - Decimals
    - Percentages
- Scales of measurement (Chapter 1)
    - Continuous and discrete
    - Nominal, ordinal, interval, and ratio

PREVIEW

Reading a textbook is much different from reading a novel or a newspaper. With a textbook, your goal is to study and to learn the material, not simply to entertain yourself. As a result you must work to identify and understand the important points. You must take time to digest the material, and it helps to stop and question yourself regularly to be sure that you fully comprehend what you are reading. All this may sound like the same old "how to study" lecture that you probably have heard a hundred times by now. But it is true, and it works.

Experiments have demonstrated that reading strategy can significantly affect comprehension and test performance. In 1974, John Boker presented college students with long passages (2500 words) selected from college-level texts (Boker, 1974). One group of students served as a control group and simply read straight through the material from beginning to end. For the experimental group, the passage was divided into 10 sections, each about 250 words, and the students were presented with questions at the end of each section. A week later, both groups were given a 40-question multiple-choice test covering the passage they had read. Hypothetical data similar to those obtained by Boker are shown in Table 2.1.

From looking at the data in Table 2.1, does it appear that one group did better than the other? Because these data are not organized in any systematic way, you probably find it difficult to discern any differences. This is a basic problem confronting any researcher after data are collected. To make sense of the experiment, you must organize the mass of numbers into a simpler form so that it is possible to "see" what happened. One solution is to present the scores in an organized table or a graph. Figure 2.1 shows the same data that are in Table 2.1, but now they are simplified and organized in a graph. Looking at the figure, does it appear that one group did better than the other?

It should be clear that graphing these data makes it easy to see the difference between the two groups. The students who read the passage with interspersed questions performed much better on the test—about 5 points better, which is quite a bit on a 40-question test.

There are two important points to be learned from this discussion. First, you should appreciate the value of simplifying and organizing a set of data. By structuring the data properly, it becomes possible to see at a glance what happened in an experiment. This helps

TABLE 2.1

Hypothetical Data from an Experiment Comparing Two Strategies for Studying College Textbook Material.[a]

Control Group		Experimental Group	
25	32	28	29
27	20	25	31
28	23	31	19
17	21	29	35
24	34	30	28
22	29	24	30
24	25	33	27
21	18	34	26
19	22	29	29
30	24	27	32
26	27	30	36
24	23	22	23
23	25	32	33

[a]The experimental group had questions interspersed through the material as they were reading. The control group read through the material without seeing any questions. One week later both groups were given a 40-item multiple-choice test on the material they had read. The data given are the scores on this test.

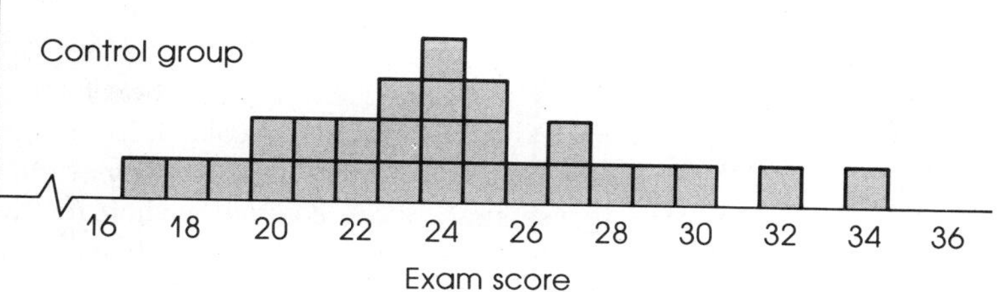

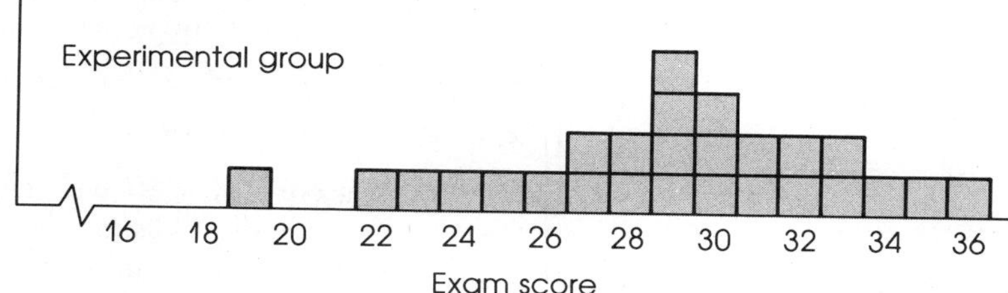

FIGURE 2.1

The two graphs show the same data that were listed in Table 2.1. In these graphs each student is represented by a block that is placed directly above his or her exam score. Notice that the experimental group generally performed better than the control group. For students in the experimental group, the exam scores pile up around $X = 29$. For the control group, the scores pile up around $X = 24$.

researchers to decide exactly how the data should be analyzed and interpreted, and it helps others to understand the significance of the experiment. In this chapter we will examine several statistical techniques for organizing data. The second point concerns the implications of Boker's experiment. The way you study can have a tremendous influence on what you learn. As you read through this book, you will find lots of sample problems in the examples and learning checks that appear in each chapter. Take time to work through these problems, answer the questions, and test yourself. A little extra time and effort can increase your understanding of the material, and it can improve your grade.

2.1 INTRODUCTION

When a researcher finishes the data collection phase of an experiment, the results usually consist of pages of numbers. The immediate problem for the researcher is to organize the scores into some comprehensible form so that any trends in the data can be seen easily and communicated to others. This is the job of descriptive statistics: to simplify the organization and presentation of data. One of the most common procedures for organizing a set of data is to place the scores in a frequency distribution.

DEFINITION A *frequency distribution* is a record of the number of individuals located in each category on the scale of measurement.

A frequency distribution allows the researcher to see "at a glance" the entire set of scores. It shows whether the scores are generally high or low and whether they are concentrated in one area or spread out across the entire scale and generally provides an organized picture of the data. Frequency distributions can be structured either as tables or graphs, but both show the original measurement scale and the frequencies associated with each category. Thus, they present a picture of how the individual scores are distributed on the measurement scale—hence the name *frequency distribution*.

2.2 FREQUENCY DISTRIBUTION TABLES

It is customary to list scores from highest to lowest, but this is an arbitrary arrangement. Many computer programs will list scores from lowest to highest.

The simplest frequency distribution table presents the measurement scale by listing the individual scores in a column from highest to lowest. Beside each score, we indicate the frequency, or number of times the score occurred in the data. It is customary to use an X as the column heading for the scores and an f as the column heading for the frequencies. An example of a frequency distribution table follows.

EXAMPLE 2.1 The following set of $N = 20$ scores was obtained from a 10-point statistics quiz. We will organize these scores by constructing a frequency distribution table. Scores:

8, 9, 8, 7, 10, 9, 6, 4, 9, 8
7, 8, 10, 9, 8, 6, 9, 7, 8, 8

1 The highest score is $X = 10$, and the lowest score is $X = 4$. Therefore, the first column of the table will list scores (X values) from 10 down to 4. Notice that all of the possible values are listed in the table. For example, no one had a score of $X = 5$, but this value is included.

2 The frequency associated with each score is recorded in the second column. For example, two people had scores of $X = 6$, so there is a 2 in the f column beside $X = 6$.

X	f
10	2
9	5
8	7
7	3
6	2
5	0
4	1

Because the table organizes the scores, it is possible to see very quickly the general quiz results. For example, there were only two perfect scores, but most of the class had high grades (8s and 9s). With one exception (the score of $X = 4$) it appears that the class has learned the material fairly well.

You also should notice that the frequencies can be used to find the total number of scores in the distribution. By adding up the frequencies, you will obtain the total number of individuals:

$$\sum f = N$$

PROPORTIONS AND PERCENTAGES

In addition to the two basic columns of a frequency distribution, there are other measures that describe the distribution of scores and can be incorporated into the table. The two most common are proportion and percentage.

Proportion measures the fraction of the total group that is associated with each score. In Example 2.1, there were two individuals with $X = 6$. Thus, 2 out of 20 people had $X = 6$, so the proportion would be $2/20 = 0.10$. In general, the proportion associated with each score is

$$\text{proportion} = p = \frac{f}{N}$$

Because proportions describe the frequency (f) in relation to the total number (N), they often are called *relative frequencies*. Although proportions can be expressed as fractions (for example, 2/20), they more commonly appear as decimals. A column of proportions, headed with a p, can be added to the basic frequency distribution table (see Example 2.2).

In addition to using frequencies (f) and proportions (p), researchers often describe a distribution of scores with percentages. For example, an instructor might describe the results of an exam by saying that 15% of the class earned *A*s, 23% *B*s, and so on. To compute the percentage associated with each score, you first find the proportion (p) and then multiply by 100:

$$\text{percentage} = p(100) = \frac{f}{N}(100)$$

Percentages can be included in a frequency distribution table by adding a column headed with % (see Example 2.2).

EXAMPLE 2.2 The frequency distribution table from Example 2.1 is repeated here. This time we have added columns showing the proportion (p) and the percentage (%) associated with each score.

X	f	$p = f/N$	$\% = p(100)$
10	2	2/20 = 0.10	10%
9	5	5/20 = 0.25	25%
8	7	7/20 = 0.35	35%
7	3	3/20 = 0.15	15%
6	2	2/20 = 0.10	10%
5	0	0/20 = 0	0%
4	1	1/20 = 0.05	5%

GROUPED FREQUENCY DISTRIBUTION TABLES

When a set of data covers a wide range of values, it is unreasonable to list all the individual scores in a frequency distribution table. For example, a set of exam scores ranges from a low of $X = 41$ to a high of $X = 96$. These scores cover a range of over 50 points. The precise range is determined by

In the formula for the range, the $+1$ is included because both extremes (high and low) are counted along with the other scores in determining the range. For example, scores from 1 to 5 cover a range of 5 points.

$$\text{range} = \text{high} - \text{low} + 1$$

For these exam scores the range would be

$$\begin{aligned}\text{range} &= 96 - 41 + 1\\ &= 56\end{aligned}$$

If we were to list all the individual scores, it would take 56 rows to complete the frequency distribution table. This would contradict the goal of a frequency distribution table, which is to simplify the presentation of the data. The solution to this problem is to divide the range of scores into intervals and then list these intervals in the frequency distribution table. For example, we could construct a table showing the number of students who had scores in the 90s, the number with scores in the 80s, etc. The result is called a *grouped frequency distribution table* because we are presenting groups of scores rather than individual values. The groups, or intervals, are called *class intervals*.

There are several rules that help guide you in the construction of a grouped frequency distribution table. These rules should be considered as guidelines rather than as absolute requirements, but they do help produce a simple, well-organized, and easily understood table.

RULE 1 The grouped frequency distribution table should have about 10 class intervals. If a table has many more than 10 intervals, it becomes cumbersome and defeats the purpose of a frequency distribution table. On the other hand, if you have too few intervals, you begin to lose information about the distribution of the scores. At the extreme, with only one interval, the table would not tell you anything about how the scores are distributed. Remember, the purpose for a frequency distribution is to help a researcher see the data. With too few or too many intervals, the table will not provide a clear picture. You should note that 10 intervals is a general guide. If you were constructing a table on a blackboard, for example, you probably would want only 5 or 6 intervals. If the table were to be printed in a scientific report, you may want 12 or 15 intervals. In each case your goal is to present a table that is relatively easy to see and understand.

RULE 2 The width of each interval should be a relatively simple number. For example, 2, 5, 10, or 20 would be good choices for the interval width. Notice that it is easy to count by 5s or 10s. These numbers are easy to understand and make it possible for someone to see quickly how you have divided the range.

RULE 3 The bottom score in each class interval should be a multiple of the width. If you are using a width of 10, for example, the intervals should start with 10, 20, 30, 40, etc. Again, this makes it easier for someone to understand how the table has been constructed.

RULE 4 All intervals should be the same width. They should cover the range of scores completely with no gaps and no overlaps, so that any particular score belongs in exactly one interval.

The application of these rules is demonstrated in Example 2.3.

· EXAMPLE 2.3 · An instructor has obtained the set of $N = 25$ exam scores shown here. To help organize these scores, we will place them in a frequency distribution table. Scores:

82, 75, 88, 93, 53, 84, 87, 58, 72, 94, 69, 84, 61,
91, 64, 87, 84, 70, 76, 89, 75, 80, 73, 78, 60

The first step is to determine the range of scores. For these data, the smallest score is $X = 53$ and the largest score is $X = 94$, so the range is

$$\begin{aligned} \text{range} &= \text{high} - \text{low} + 1 \\ &= 94 - 53 + 1 \\ &= 42 \end{aligned}$$

Because it would require 42 rows to list each individual score in a frequency distribution table, we will have to group the scores into class intervals.

The best method for determining the appropriate interval width is to use Rules 1 and 2 simultaneously. According to Rule 1, we want about 10 intervals; according to Rule 2, we want the width to be a simple number. If we try a width of 2, how many intervals would it take to cover the range of scores? With each interval only 2 points wide, we would need 21 intervals to cover a range of 42 points. This is too many. What about an interval width of 5? What about a width of 10? The following table shows how many intervals would be needed for each possible width:

Width	Number of Intervals Needed to Cover a Range of 42 Points	
2	21	(too many)
5	9	(OK)
10	5	(too few)

Notice that an interval width of 5 will result in about 10 intervals, which is exactly what we want.

The next step is to actually identify the intervals. The lowest score for these data is $X = 53$, so the lowest interval should contain this value. Because the interval should have a multiple of 5 as its bottom score, the interval would be 50 to 54. Notice that this interval contains five values (50, 51, 52, 53, 54), so it does have a width of 5. The next interval would start at 55 and go to 59. The complete frequency distribution table showing all of the class intervals is presented in Table 2.2.

Once the class intervals are listed, you complete the table by adding a column of frequencies or proportions or percentages. The values in the frequency column indicate the number of individuals whose scores are located in that class interval. For this example, there were three students with scores in the 60–64 interval, so the frequency for this class interval is $f = 3$ (see Table 2.2).

CONTINUOUS VARIABLES AND REAL LIMITS

You should recall that a continuous variable has an infinite number of possible values. When measuring individuals on a continuous variable, a researcher must select a unit of measurement and then round off the actual measurements so that the scores correspond to the units selected. For example, if you are measuring time to the nearest second, measurements of 2.34 seconds and 1.98 seconds both would be rounded to scores of $X = 2$ seconds. Thus, a score of $X = 2$ is not a specific point on the scale but rather an interval on the scale. In this example, a score of $X = 2$ seconds actually corresponds to an interval from 1.5 seconds to 2.5 seconds. Any measurement within this interval will be assigned a score of $X = 2$. The boundaries that separate the intervals are called the real limits of the interval.

TABLE 2.2

A Grouped Frequency Distribution Table Showing the Data from Example 2.3[a]

X	f
90–94	3
85–89	4
80–84	5
75–79	4
70–74	3
65–69	1
60–64	3
55–59	1
50–54	1

[a]The original scores range from a high of $X = 94$ to a low of $X = 53$. This range has been divided into nine intervals with each interval exactly five points wide. The frequency column (f) lists the number of individuals with scores in each of the class intervals.

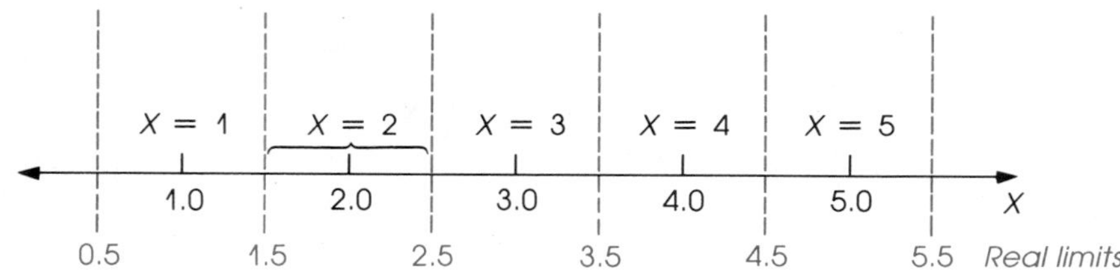

FIGURE 2.2

The relationship between real limits and scores for a continuous variable. Notice that the score $X = 2$ actually corresponds to an interval on the scale bounded by a lower real limit of 1.5 and an upper real limit of 2.5. Any measurement within this interval will be assigned a score of $X = 2$.

DEFINITION For a continuous variable, each score actually corresponds to an interval on the scale. The boundaries that separate these intervals are called *real limits*. The real limit separating two adjacent scores is located exactly halfway between the scores. Each score has two real limits, one at the top of its interval called the *upper real limit* and one at the bottom of its interval called the *lower real limit*. Note that the upper real limit of one interval is also the lower real limit of the next higher interval.

The concept of real limits may be easier to understand if you picture a continuous variable as a line with the scores corresponding to locations on the line (see Figure 2.2).

When data are grouped into class intervals, the concept of real limits applies to the intervals. For example, an interval of 40–49 contains scores from $X = 40$ to $X = 49$. These values are called the *apparent limits* of the interval because it appears that they form the upper and lower boundaries for the class interval. But $X = 40$ is actually an interval from 39.5 to 40.5. Similarly, $X = 49$ is an interval from 48.5 to 49.5. Therefore, the real limits of the interval are 39.5 (the lower real limit) and 49.5 (the upper real limit). Notice that the next higher class interval would be 50–59, which has a lower real limit of 49.5. Thus, the two intervals meet at the real limit 49.5, so there are no gaps in the scale. You also should notice that the width of each class interval becomes easier to understand when you consider the real limits of an interval. For example, the interval 50–54 has real limits of 49.5 and 54.5. The distance between these two real limits (5 points) is the width of the interval.

The concept of real limits will be used later for constructing graphs and for various calculations with continuous scales. For now, however, you should realize that real limits are a necessity whenever measurements are made of a continuous variable.

LEARNING CHECK

1 Place the following scores in a frequency distribution table showing proportion and percentage as well as the frequency for each score. Scores: 2, 3, 1, 2, 5, 4, 5, 5, 1, 4, 2, 2, 5, 5, 4, 2, 3, 1, 5, 4.

2 A set of scores ranges from a high of $X = 142$ to a low of $X = 65$. If these scores are to be placed in a grouped frequency distribution table, then
a What interval width should be used?
b What are the apparent limits of the bottom interval?
c What are the real limits of the bottom interval?

3 Explain why you should avoid having too many rows in a frequency distribution table. What is the problem with having too few rows?

ANSWERS

1

X	f	p	%
5	6	0.30	30%
4	4	0.20	20%
3	2	0.10	10%
2	5	0.25	25%
1	3	0.15	15%

2 **a** The scores cover a range of 78 points. With an interval width of 5 points, you would need 16 intervals to cover the range. With an interval width of 10, you would need 8 intervals. For most purposes, a width of 10 points probably is best.
b With a width of 10, the bottom interval would have apparent limits of 60–69.
c The real limits of the bottom interval would be 59.5 and 69.5.

3 With too many rows the table is not simple and, therefore, fails to meet the goal of descriptive statistics. With too few rows, you lose information about the distribution.

2.3 FREQUENCY DISTRIBUTION GRAPHS

A frequency distribution graph is basically a picture of the information available in a frequency distribution table. We will consider several different types of graphs, but all start with two perpendicular lines called axes. The horizontal line is called the X-axis, or the abscissa. The vertical line is called the Y-axis, or the ordinate. The scores are listed along the X-axis in increasing value from left to right. The frequencies are listed on the Y-axis in increasing value from bottom to top. As a general rule, the point where the two axes intersect should have a value of zero for both the scores and the frequencies. A final general rule is that the graph should be constructed so that its height (Y-axis) is approximately three-quarters of its length (X-axis). Violating these guidelines can result in graphs that give a misleading picture of the data (see Perspective 2.1).

HISTOGRAMS AND BAR GRAPHS

The first type of graph we will consider is called either a histogram or a bar graph. For this type of graph, you simply draw a bar above each score so that the height of the bar corresponds to the frequency of the score. As you will see, the distinction between histograms and bar graphs is determined by the scale of measurement.

When a frequency distribution graph is showing data from an interval or ratio scale, the bars are drawn so that adjacent bars touch each other. The touching bars produce a continuous figure which emphasizes the continuity of the variable. This type of frequency distribution graph is called a histogram. An example of a histogram is presented in Figure 2.3.

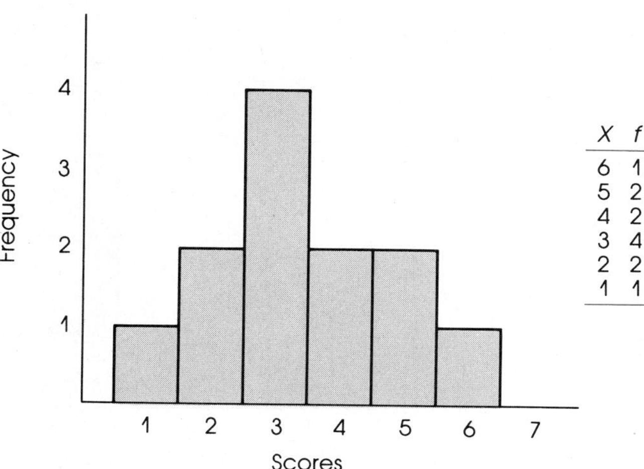

X	f
6	1
5	2
4	2
3	4
2	2
1	1

FIGURE 2.3
An example of a frequency distribution histogram. The same set of data is presented in a frequency distribution table and in a histogram.

· DEFINITION · For a *histogram,* vertical bars are drawn above each score so that

1. The height of the bar corresponds to the frequency.
2. The width of the bar extends to the real limits of the score.

A histogram is used when the data are measured on an interval or ratio scale.

When data have been grouped into class intervals, you can construct a frequency distribution histogram by drawing a bar above each interval so that the width of the bar extends to the real limits of the interval. This process is demonstrated in Figure 2.4.

When you are presenting the frequency distribution for data from a nominal or ordinal scale, the graph is constructed so that there is some space between the bars. In this case the separate bars emphasize that the scale consists of separate, distinct categories. The resulting graph is called a bar graph. An example of a frequency distribution bar graph is given in Figure 2.5.

· DEFINITION · For a *bar graph,* a vertical bar is drawn above each score (or category) so that

1. The height of the bar corresponds to the frequency.
2. There is a space separating each bar from the next.

A bar graph is used when the data are measured on a nominal or ordinal scale.

· FIGURE 2.4 ·

An example of a frequency distribution histogram for grouped data. The same set of data is presented in a grouped frequency distribution table and in a histogram.

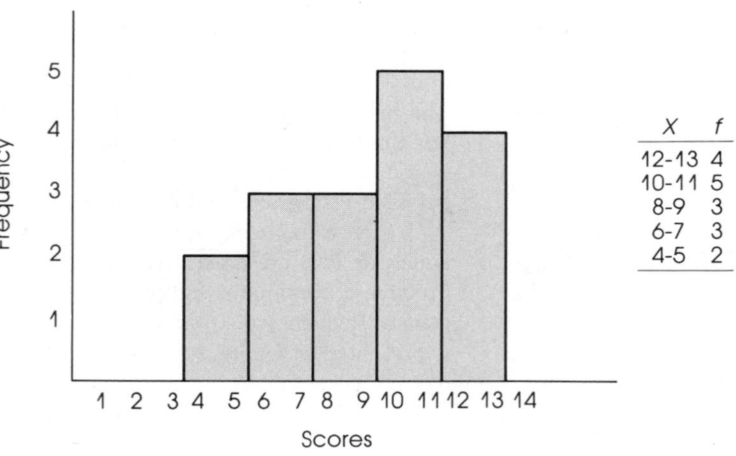

X	f
12-13	4
10-11	5
8-9	3
6-7	3
4-5	2

· FIGURE 2.5 ·

A bar graph showing the distribution of personality types in a sample of college students. Because personality type is a discrete variable measured on a nominal scale, the graph is drawn with space between the bars.

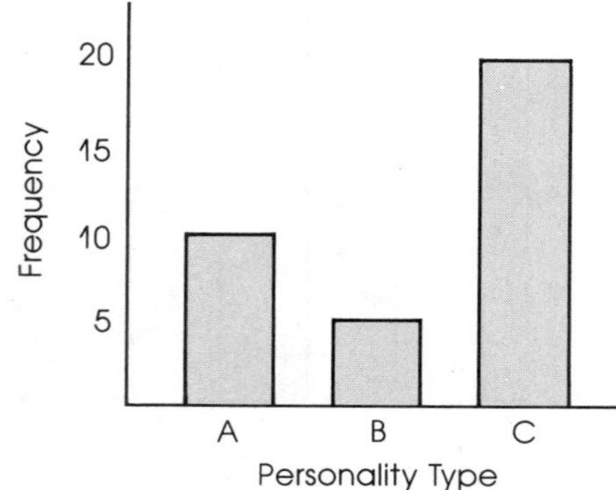

Frequency Distributions on the Computer As we noted in Chapter 1, a computer can be a valuable tool in statistics. For example, imagine having to construct a frequency distribution table and histogram for a distribution of thousands of scores if you are equipped with nothing more than a pencil and paper! Even for simple tasks like making a table and histogram, the work becomes a monumental chore when *N* is so large. Fortunately, software packages for statistical analyses are widely available for many types of computers.

The data shown in the table of Figure 2.3 were used for an SPSS^x analysis. We asked SPSS^x to perform an analysis of the frequencies and to construct a histogram. This is accomplished by using the SPSS^x command FREQUENCIES along with the

TABLE 2.3

An SPSS^x printout for the frequency distribution in Figure 2.3. The analysis provides a frequency distribution table and a histogram.

```
10 JUL 86    SPSS-X RELEASE 2.1+ PRIME

14:46:10     SUNY Brockport Computing Srvcs Prime 9955          Rev 19.4.9
```

SCORE

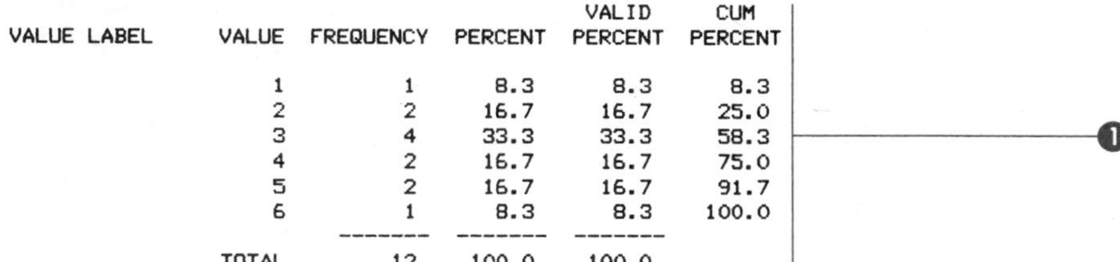

VALUE LABEL	VALUE	FREQUENCY	PERCENT	VALID PERCENT	CUM PERCENT
	1	1	8.3	8.3	8.3
	2	2	16.7	16.7	25.0
	3	4	33.3	33.3	58.3
	4	2	16.7	16.7	75.0
	5	2	16.7	16.7	91.7
	6	1	8.3	8.3	100.0
	TOTAL	12	100.0	100.0	

❶

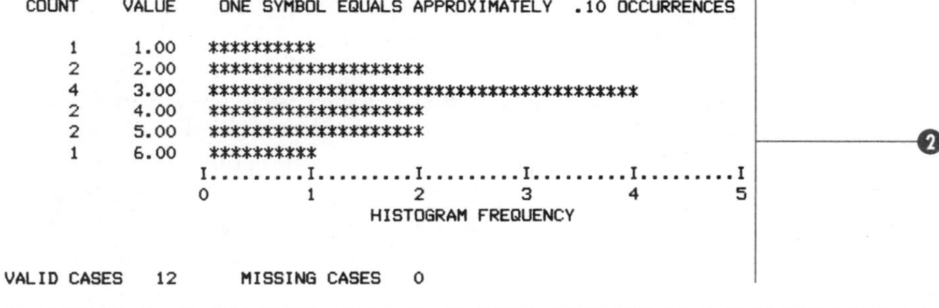

```
COUNT   VALUE    ONE SYMBOL EQUALS APPROXIMATELY  .10 OCCURRENCES

  1     1.00    **********
  2     2.00    ********************
  4     3.00    ****************************************
  2     4.00    ********************
  2     5.00    ********************
  1     6.00    **********
                I.........I.........I.........I.........I.........I
                0         1         2         3         4         5
                               HISTOGRAM FREQUENCY

VALID CASES    12       MISSING CASES    0
```

❷

EXPLANATION OF PRINTOUT:

1 The SPSS^x analysis provides a frequency distribution table. The first column lists the values for the scores in the distribution. Notice that SPSS^x lists the raw score values by beginning with the smallest value at the top of the list. This order is the *opposite* of what we recommend in the text (see page 28). The program also provides columns for frequency, percent and cumulative percent. Cumulative percentages are discussed later in this chapter (page 42). The column labeled "valid percent" is important only when there are missing scores. Because there are not any missing data for this analysis, the "valid percent" column is the same as the "percent" column. In most applications, you should not be concerned with the "valid percent" column.

2 SPSS^x provides a frequency distribution histogram. Notice that the bars are constructed with asterisks and are presented horizontally rather than vertically. The first column (labeled "count") provides the frequencies. The second column lists the values of the scores. As with any histogram, a quick glance at the graph can give you an idea of the shape of the distribution. Compare this histogram to the one in Figure 2.3.

subcommand HISTOGRAM. The result is the frequency distribution table and histogram shown in the printout (Table 2.3). A complete explanation of the printout is provided in the caption of Table 2.3.

FREQUENCY DISTRIBUTION POLYGONS

Instead of a histogram, many researchers prefer to display a frequency distribution using a polygon.

· DEFINITION · In a *frequency distribution polygon,* a single dot is drawn above each score so that

1. The dot is centered above the score.
2. The height of the dot corresponds to the frequency.

A continuous line is then drawn connecting these dots. The graph is completed by drawing a line down to the X-axis (zero frequency) at each end of the range of scores.

As with a histogram, the frequency distribution polygon is intended for use with interval or ratio scales. An example of a polygon is shown in Figure 2.6. A polygon also can be used with data that have been grouped into class intervals. In this case, you position the dots directly above the midpoint of each class interval. The midpoint can be found by averaging the apparent limits of the interval or by averaging the real limits of the interval. For example, a class interval of 40–49 would have a midpoint of 44.5.

$$\text{apparent limits:} \quad \frac{40 + 49}{2} = \frac{89}{2} = 44.5$$

$$\text{real limits:} \quad \frac{39.5 + 49.5}{2} = \frac{89}{2} = 44.5$$

An example of a frequency distribution polygon with grouped data is shown in Figure 2.7.

RELATIVE FREQUENCIES AND SMOOTH CURVES

Often it is impossible to construct a frequency distribution for a population because there are simply too many individuals for a researcher to obtain measurements and frequencies for the entire group. In this case, it is customary to draw a frequency distribution graph showing relative frequencies (proportions) on the vertical axis. For example, a researcher may know that a particular species of animal has three times as many females as males in the population. This fact could be displayed in a bar graph

· FIGURE 2.6 ·

An example of a frequency distribution polygon. The same set of data is presented in a frequency distribution table and in a polygon. Note that these data are shown in a histogram in Figure 2.3.

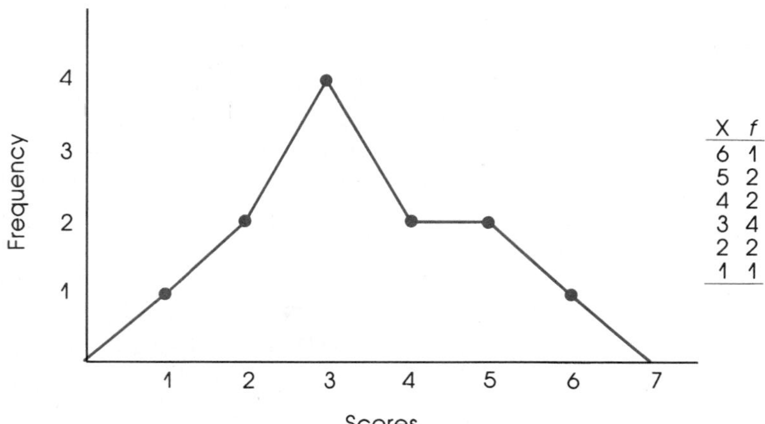

X	f
6	1
5	2
4	2
3	4
2	2
1	1

· FIGURE 2.7 ·

An example of a frequency distribution polygon for grouped data. The same set of data is presented in a grouped frequency distribution table and in a polygon. Note that these data are shown in a histogram in Figure 2.4.

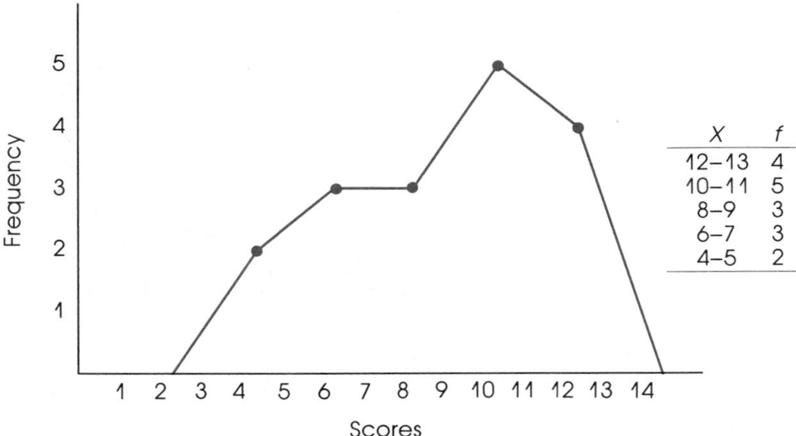

by simply making the bar above "female" three times as tall as the bar above "male." Notice that the actual frequencies are unknown but that the relative frequency of males and females can still be presented in a graph.

It also is possible to use a polygon to show relative frequencies for scores in a population. In this case, it is customary to draw a smooth curve instead of the series of straight lines that normally appears in a polygon. The smooth curve indicates that you are not connecting a series of dots (real frequencies) but rather are showing a distribution that is not limited to one specific set of data. One commonly occurring population distribution is the normal curve. The word *normal* refers to a specific shape that can be precisely defined by an equation. Less precisely, we can describe a normal distribution as being symmetrical, with the greatest frequency in the middle and relatively smaller frequencies as you move toward either extreme. A good example of a normal distribution is the population distribution for IQ scores shown in Figure 2.8. Because normal shaped distributions occur commonly and because this shape is mathematically guaranteed in certain situations, it will receive extensive attention throughout this book.

In the future we will be referring to *distributions of scores*. Whenever the term *distribution* appears, you should conjure up an image of a frequency distribution graph. The graph provides a picture showing exactly where the individual scores are located. To make this concept more concrete, you might find it useful to think of the graph

· FIGURE 2.8 ·

The population distribution of IQ scores: an example of a normal distribution.

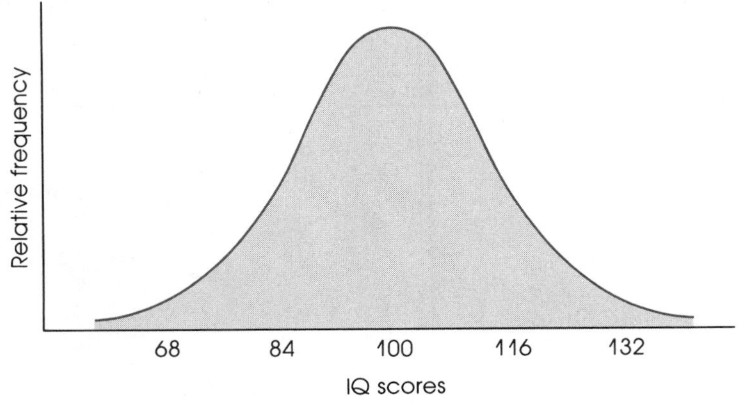

as showing a pile of individuals. In Figure 2.8, for example, the pile is highest at an IQ score of around 100 because most people have "average" IQs. There are only a few individuals piled up at an IQ score of 130; it must be lonely at the top.

2.4 THE SHAPE OF A FREQUENCY DISTRIBUTION

Rather than drawing a complete frequency distribution graph, researchers often simply describe a distribution by listing its characteristics. There are three characteristics that completely describe any distribution: shape, central tendency, and variability. In simple terms, central tendency measures where the center of the distribution is located. Variability tells whether the scores are spread over a wide range or are clustered together. Central tendency and variability will be covered in detail in Chapters 3 and 4. Technically, the shape of a distribution is defined by an equation that prescribes the exact relation between each X and Y value on the graph. However, we will rely on a few less-precise terms that will serve to describe the shape of most distributions.

Nearly all distributions can be classified as being either symmetrical or skewed.

DEFINITIONS

In a *symmetrical distribution* it is possible to draw a vertical line through the middle so that one side of the distribution is an exact mirror image of the other (see Figure 2.9).

In a *skewed distribution* the scores tend to pile up toward one end of the scale and taper off gradually at the other end (see Figure 2.9).

The section where the scores taper off toward one end of a distribution is called the *tail* of the distribution.

A skewed distribution with the tail to the right-hand side is said to be *positively skewed* because the tail points toward the positive (above-zero) end of the X-axis. If the tail points to the left, the distribution is said to be *negatively skewed* (see Figure 2.9).

For a very difficult exam, most scores will tend to be low, with only a few individuals earning high scores. This will produce a positively skewed distribution. Similarly, a very easy exam will tend to produce a negatively skewed distribution, with most of the students earning high scores and only a few with low values.

FIGURE 2.9

Examples of different shapes for distributions.

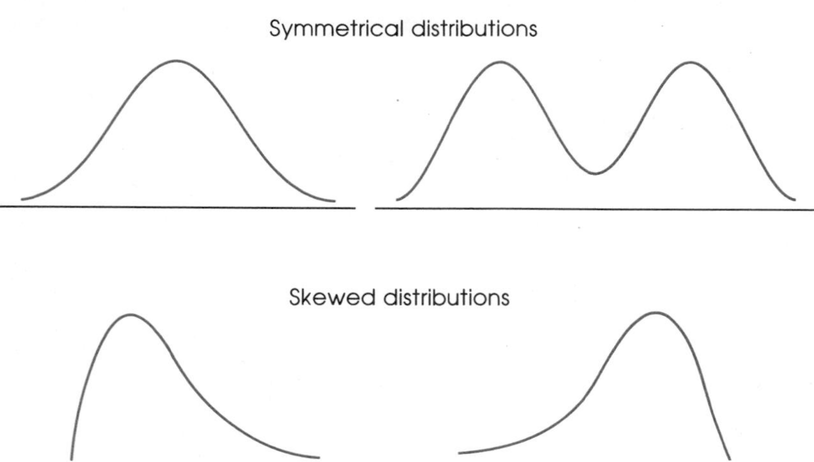

· LEARNING CHECK ·

1 Sketch a frequency distribution histogram and a frequency distribution polygon for the data in the following table:

X	f
5	4
4	6
3	3
2	1
1	1

2 Describe the shape of the distribution in exercise 1.

3 What type of graph would be appropriate to show the number of gold medals, silver medals, and bronze medals won by the United States during the 1984 Olympics?

4 What shape would you expect for the distribution of salaries for all employees of a major industry?

ANSWERS

1 The graphs are shown in Figure 2.10.

2 The distribution is negatively skewed.

3 A bar graph is appropriate for ordinal data.

4 The distribution probably would be positively skewed, with most employees earning an average salary and a relatively small number of top executives with very large salaries.

2.5 OTHER TYPES OF GRAPHS

In addition to displaying frequency distributions, graphs can be used to show relationships between variables. Perhaps the most common use is to show the results of an experiment by graphing the relation between the independent variable and the dependent variable. You should recall that the dependent variable is the score obtained for each subject and that the independent variable distinguishes the different treatment conditions or groups used in the experiment. For example, a researcher testing a new diet drug might compare several different dosages by measuring the amount of food that animals consume at each dose level. Figure 2.11 shows hypothetical data from this experiment. Notice that the four dose levels (the independent variable) are on the X-axis and that food consumption (the dependent variable) is shown on the Y-axis. The points in the graph represent the average food consumption for the group at

· FIGURE 2.10 ·

Answers to Learning Check Exercise 1.

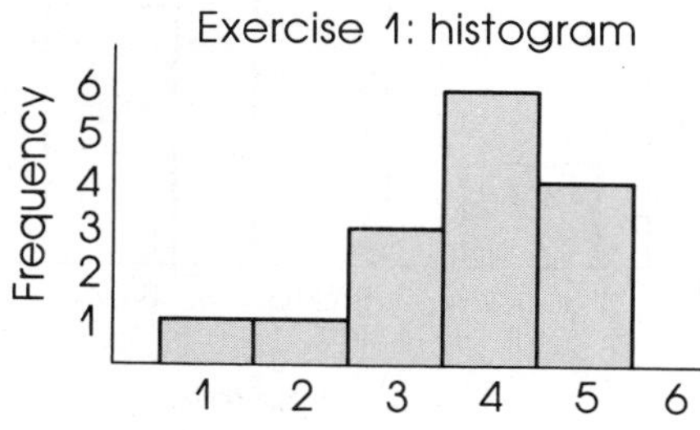

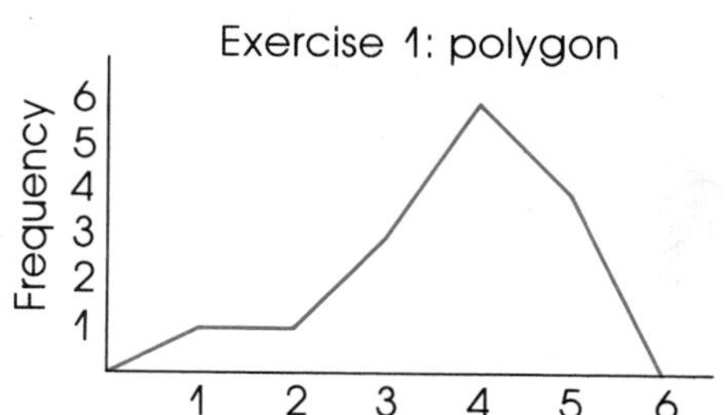

FIGURE 2.11

The relationship between an independent variable (drug dose) and a dependent variable (food consumption). Because drug dose is a continuous variable, a continuous line is used to connect the different dose levels.

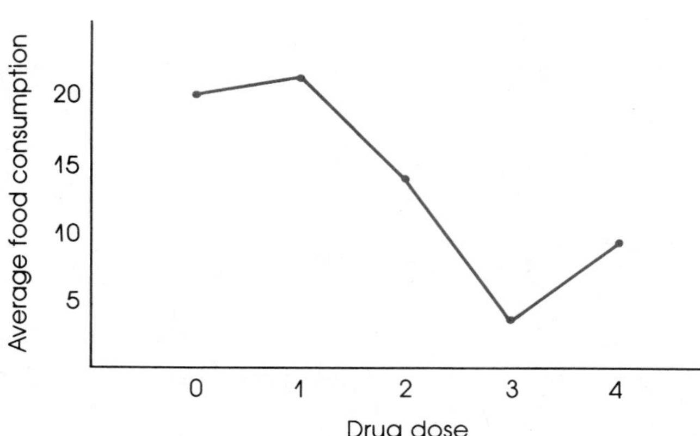

each dose level. In this graph the points are connected with a line because the X-axis variable (drug dose) is continuous (measured on a ratio scale).

Figure 2.12 shows results from another experiment where the independent variable is discrete. In this graph, we have used separate bars for each position on the X-axis to indicate that we are comparing separate categories (measured on a nominal scale).

When constructing graphs of any type, you should recall the basic rules we mentioned earlier:

1. The height of a graph should be approximately three-quarters of its length.
2. Normally, you start numbering both the X-axis and the Y-axis with zero at the point where the two axes intersect.

More importantly, you should remember that the purpose of a graph is to give an accurate representation of the information in a set of data. Perspective 2.1 demonstrates what can happen when these basic principles are ignored.

FIGURE 2.12

The relationship between an independent variable (brand of pain reliever) and a dependent variable (pain tolerance). The graph uses separate bars because the brand of pain reliever is measured on a nominal scale.

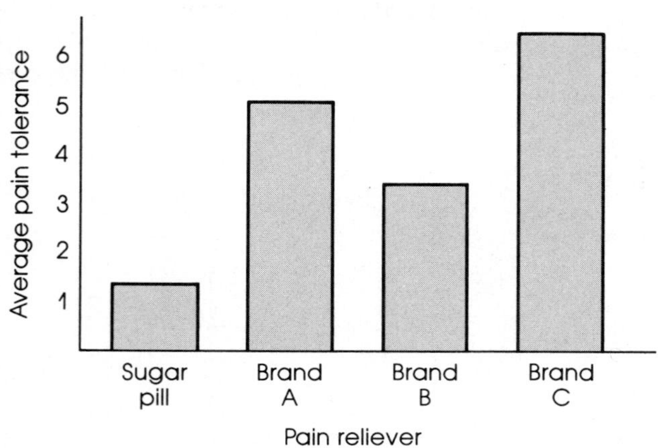

PERSPECTIVE 2.1

THE USE AND MISUSE OF GRAPHS

Although graphs are intended to provide an accurate picture of a set of data, they can be used to exaggerate or misrepresent a set of scores. These misrepresentations generally result from failing to follow the basic rules for graph construction. The following example demonstrates how the same set of data can be presented in two entirely different ways by manipulating the structure of a graph.

For the past several years, the city has kept records of the number of major felonies. The data are summarized as follows:

Year	Number of Major Felonies
1982	218
1983	225
1984	229

These same data are shown in two different graphs in Figure 2.13. In the first graph we have exaggerated the height, and we started numbering the Y-axis at 210 rather than at zero. As a result, the graph seems to indicate a rapid rise in the crime rate over the 3-year period. In the second graph, we have stretched out the X-axis and used zero as the starting point for the Y-axis. The result is a graph that shows no change in the crime rate over the 3-year period.

Which graph is correct? The answer is that neither one is very good. Remember that the purpose of a graph is to provide an accurate display of the data. The first graph in Figure 2.13 exaggerates the differences between years, and the second graph conceals the differences. Some compromise is needed. You also should note that in some cases a graph may not be the best way to display information. For these data, for example, showing the numbers in a table would be better than either graph.

FIGURE 2.13

Two graphs showing the number of major felonies in a city over a 3-year period. Both graphs are showing exactly the same data. However, the first graph gives the appearance that the crime rate is high and rising rapidly. The second graph gives the impression that the crime rate is low and has not changed over the 3-year period.

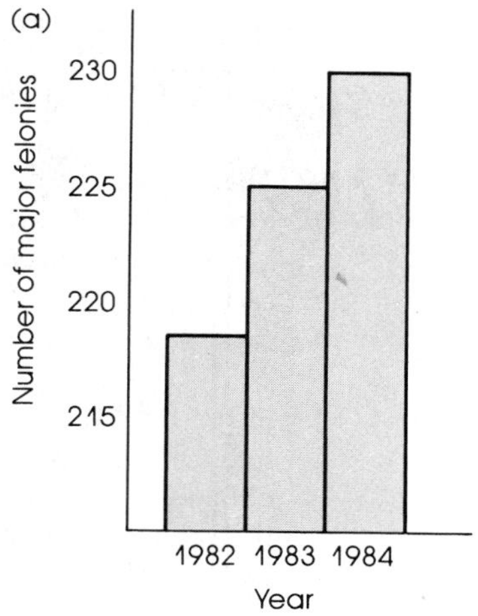

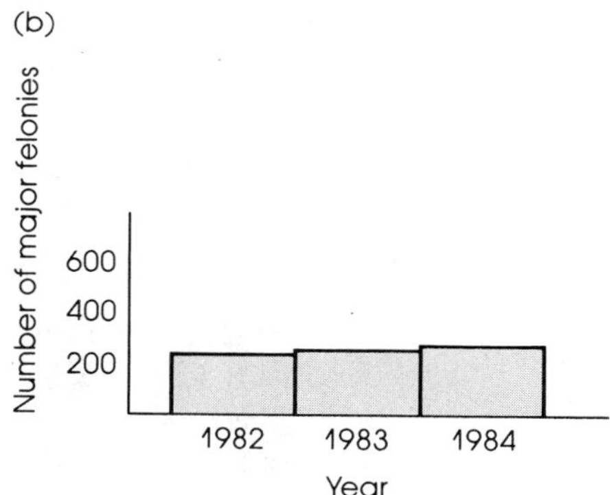

2.6 PERCENTILES AND PERCENTILE RANKS

Although the primary purpose of a frequency distribution is to provide a description of an entire set of scores, it also can be used to describe the position of an individual within the set. Individual scores, or X values, are called raw scores. By themselves, raw scores do not provide much information. For example, if you are told that your score on an exam is $X = 43$, you cannot tell how well you did. To evaluate your score, you need more information such as the average score or the number of people who had scores above and below you. With this additional information you would be able to determine your relative position in the class. Because raw scores do not provide much information, it is desirable to transform them into a more meaningful form. One transformation that we will consider changes raw scores into percentiles.

· DEFINITIONS · The *rank* or *percentile rank* of a particular score is defined as the percentage of individuals in the distribution with scores at or below the particular value.

When a score is identified by its percentile rank, the score is called a *percentile*.

Suppose, for example, that you have a score of $X = 43$ on an exam and that you know that exactly 60% of the class had scores of 43 or lower. Then your score $X = 43$ has a percentile rank of 60%, and your score would be called the 60th percentile. Notice that *percentile rank* refers to a percentage and that *percentile* refers to a score. Also notice that your rank or percentile describes your exact position within the distribution.

CUMULATIVE FREQUENCY AND CUMULATIVE PERCENTAGE

The first step in determining percentiles is to find the number of individuals who are located at or below each point in the distribution. This can be done most easily with a frequency distribution table by simply counting the number who are in or below each category on the scale. The resulting values are called *cumulative frequencies* because they represent the accumulation of individuals as you move up the scale.

· EXAMPLE 2.4 · In the following frequency distribution table we have included a cumulative frequency column headed by *cf*. For each row the cumulative frequency value is obtained by adding up the frequencies in that category or lower. For example, the score $X = 3$ has a cumulative frequency of 14 because exactly 14 individuals had scores in this category or in a lower category.

X	f	cf
5	1	20
4	5	19
3	8	14
2	4	6
1	2	2

The cumulative frequencies show the number of individuals located at or below each score. To find percentiles, we must convert these frequencies into percentages. The resulting values are called *cumulative percentages* because they show the percent of individuals who are accumulated as you move up the scale.

· EXAMPLE 2.5 · This time we have added a cumulative percentage column (c%) to the frequency distribution table from Example 2.4. The values in this column represent the percent of the individuals who are located in each category or lower. For example, 70% of the individuals (14 out of 20) had scores of $X = 3$ or lower. Cumulative percentages can be computed by

$$c\% = \frac{cf}{N}(100\%)$$

X	f	cf	c%
5	1	20	100%
4	5	19	95%
3	8	14	70%
2	4	6	30%
1	2	2	10%

The cumulative percentages in a frequency distribution table give the percent of individuals with scores at or below each X value. However, you must remember that the X values in the table are not points on the scale but rather intervals. A score of $X = 2$, for example, means that the measurement was somewhere between the real limits of 1.5 and 2.5. Thus, when a table shows that a score of $X = 2$ has a cumulative percentage of 30%, you should interpret this as meaning that 30% of the individuals have been accumulated by the time you reach the top of the interval for $X = 2$. Notice that each cumulative percentage value is associated with the upper real limit of its interval. This point is demonstrated in Figure 2.14, which shows the same data that were used in Example 2.5. Figure 2.14 shows that two people, or 10%, had scores of $X = 1$; that is, two people had scores between 0.5 and 1.5. You cannot be sure that both individuals have been accumulated until you reach 1.5, the upper real limit of the interval. Similarly, a cumulative percentage of 30% is reached at 2.5 on the scale, a percentage of 70% is reached at 3.5, and so on.

INTERPOLATION It is possible to determine some percentiles and percentile ranks directly from a frequency distribution table provided that the percentiles are upper real limits and that the ranks are percentages that appear in the table. Using the table in Example 2.5, for example, you should be able to answer the following questions:

1. What is the 95th percentile? (Answer: $X = 4.5$.)
2. What is the percentile rank for $X = 3.5$? (Answer: 70%.)

However, there are many values that do not appear directly in the table, and it is impossible to determine these values precisely. Referring to the table in Example 2.5 again,

1. What is the 50th percentile?
2. What is the percentile rank for $X = 4$?

Because these values are not specifically reported in the table, you cannot answer the questions. However, it is possible to obtain estimates of these intermediate values by using a standard procedure known as interpolation.

Before we apply the process of interpolation to percentiles and percentile ranks, we will use a simple, commonsense example to introduce this method. Suppose you

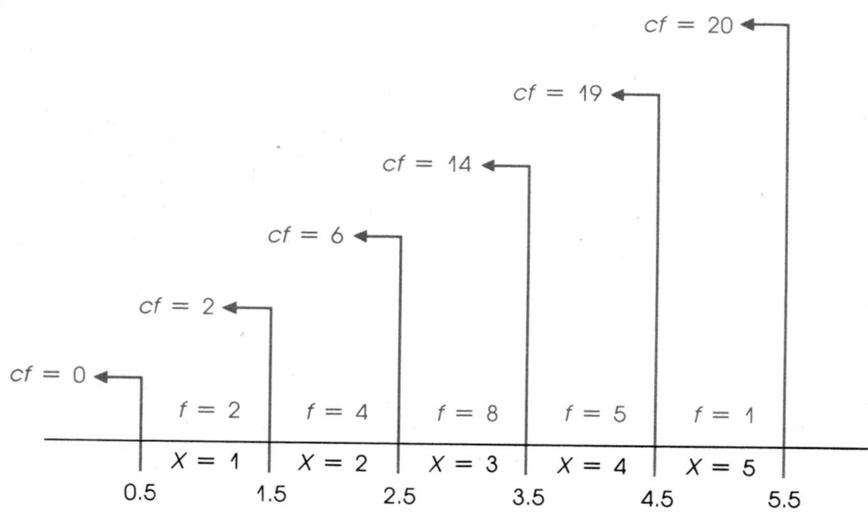

FIGURE 2.14

The relationship between cumulative frequencies (*cf* values) and upper real limits. Notice that two people had scores of $X = 1$. These two individuals are located between the real limits of 0.5 and 1.5. Although their exact locations are not known, you can be certain that both had scores below the upper real limit of 1.5.

hear the weather report at 8 A.M. and again at noon. At 8:00 the temperature was 60°, and at noon it was 68°. What is your estimate of the temperature at 9:00? To make your task a bit easier, we shall sketch a table showing the time and temperature relations:

Time	Temperature
8:00	60
12:00	68

If you estimated the temperature to be 62° at 9:00, you have done interpolation. You probably went through the following logical steps:

1. The total time from 8:00 to 12:00 is 4 hours.
2. During this time, the temperature changed 8°.
3. 9:00 represent 1 hour, or one-fourth of the total time.
4. Assuming that the temperature went up at a constant rate, it should have increased by 2° during the hour because 2° equals one-fourth of the temperature change.

Now try answering the following questions about other times and temperatures:

1. At what time did the temperature reach 64°?
2. What was the temperature at 11:00?

If you got answers of 10:00 and 66°, you have mastered the process of interpolation.

Notice that interpolation provides a method for finding intermediate values, that is, values that are located between two specified numbers. This is exactly the problem we faced with percentiles and percentile ranks. Some values are given in the table, but others are not. Also notice that interpolation only *estimates* the intermediate values. In the time and temperature example we do not know what the temperature was at 10:00. It may have soared to 80° between 8:00 and noon. The basic assumption underlying interpolation is that the change from one end of the interval to the other is a regular, linear change. We assumed, for example, that the temperature went up consistently at 2° per hour throughout the time period. Because interpolation is based on this assumption, the values we calculate are only estimates. The general process of interpolation can be summarized as follows:

1. A single interval is measured on two separate scales (for example, time and temperature). The endpoints of the interval are known for each scale.

2. You are given an intermediate value on one of the scales. The problem is to find the corresponding intermediate value on the other scale.

3. The interpolation process requires four steps:

a. Find the width of the interval on both scales.

b. Locate the position of the intermediate value in the interval. This position corresponds to a fraction of the whole interval:

$$\text{fraction} = \frac{\text{distance from the top of the interval}}{\text{interval width}}$$

c. Use this fraction to determine the distance from the top of the interval on the other scale:

$$\text{distance} = (\text{fraction}) \times (\text{width})$$

d. Use the distance from the top to determine the position on the other scale.

The following examples demonstrate the process of interpolation as it is applied to percentiles and percentile ranks. The key to successfully working these problems is that each cumulative percentage in the table is associated with the upper real limit of its score interval.

You may notice that in each of these problems we use interpolation working from the *top* of the interval. However, this choice is arbitrary, and you should realize that interpolation can be done just as easily working from the bottom of the interval.

· EXAMPLE 2.6 · Using the following distribution of scores, we will find the percentile rank corresponding to $X = 7.0$:

X	f	cf	c%
10	2	25	100%
9	8	23	92%
8	4	15	60%
7	6	11	44%
6	4	5	20%
5	1	1	4%

Note that $X = 7.0$ is located in the interval bounded by real limits of 6.5 and 7.5. The cumulative percentages corresponding to these real limits are 20% and 44%, respectively. These values are shown in the following table:

For interpolation problems, it is always helpful to sketch a table showing the range on both scales.

Scores (X)	Percentages
7.5	44%
7.0	?
6.5	20%

STEP 1 For the scores, the width of the interval is 1 point. For the percentages, the width is 24 points.

STEP 2 Our particular score is located 0.5 point from the top of the interval. This is exactly halfway down in the interval.

STEP 3 Halfway down on the percentage scale would be

$$\tfrac{1}{2}(24 \text{ points}) = 12 \text{ points}$$

STEP 4 For the percentages, the top of the interval is 44%, so 12 points down would be

$$44\% - 12\% = 32\%$$

This is the answer. A score of $X = 7.0$ corresponds to a percentile rank of 32%. ·

This same interpolation procedure can be used with data that have been grouped into class intervals. Once again, you must remember that the cumulative percentage values are associated with the upper real limits of each interval. The following example demonstrates the calculation of percentiles and percentile ranks using data in a grouped frequency distribution.

· EXAMPLE 2 · Using the following distribution of scores, we will use interpolation to find the 50th percentile:

X	f	cf	c%
20–24	2	20	100%
15–19	3	18	90%
10–14	3	15	75%
5–9	10	12	60%
0–4	2	2	10%

A percentage value of 50% is not given in the table; however, it is located between 10% and 60%, which are given. These two percentage values are associated with the upper real limits of 4.5 and 9.5, respectively. These values are shown in the following table:

Scores (X)	Percentages
9.5	60%
?----------------	-50%
4.5	10%

STEP 1 For the scores, the width of the interval is 5 points. For the percentages, the width is 50 points.

STEP 2 The value of 50% is located 10 points from the top of the percentage interval. As a fraction of the whole interval, this is 10 out of 50, or $\frac{1}{5}$ of the total interval.

STEP 3 Using this same fraction for the scores, we obtain a distance of

$$\tfrac{1}{5}(5 \text{ points}) = 1 \text{ point}$$

The location we want is 1 point down from the top of the score interval.

STEP 4 Because the top of the interval is 9.5, the position we want is

$$9.5 - 1 = 8.5$$

This is the answer. The 50th percentile is $X = 8.5$. •

· LEARNING CHECK ·

1 On a statistics exam, would you rather score at the 80th percentile or at the 40th percentile?

2 For the distribution of scores presented in the following table,
   a Find the 60th percentile.
   b Find the percentile rank for $X = 39.5$.

X	f	cf	c%
40–49	4	25	100%
30–39	6	21	84%
20–29	10	15	60%
10–19	3	5	20%
0–9	2	2	8%

3 Use the distribution of scores from exercise 2, and interpolation.
   a Find the 40th percentile.
   b Find the percentile rank for $X = 32$.

ANSWERS

1 The 80th percentile is the higher score.

2 a $X = 29.5$ is the 60th percentile
b $X = 39.5$ has a rank of 84%.

3 a Because 40% is between the values of 20% and 60% in the table, you must use interpolation. The score corresponding to a rank of 40% is $X = 24.5$.
b Because $X = 32$ is between the real limits of 29.5 and 39.5, you must use interpolation. The percentile rank for $X = 32$ is 66%.

2.7 STEM AND LEAF DISPLAYS

The general term display is used because a stem and leaf display combines the elements of a table and a graph.

In 1977 J. W. Tukey presented a technique for organizing data that provides a simple alternative to a frequency distribution table or graph (Tukey, 1977). This technique, called a *stem and leaf display,* requires that each score be separated into two parts: the first digit (or digits) is called the *stem,* and the last digit (or digits) is called the *leaf.* For example, $X = 85$ would be separated into a stem of 8 and a leaf of 5. Similarly, $X = 42$ would have a stem of 4 and a leaf of 2. To construct a stem and leaf display for a set of data, the first step is to list all the stems in a column. For the data in Table 2.4, for example, the lowest scores are in the 30s and the highest scores are in the 90s, so the list of stems would be

Stems
3
4
5
6
7
8
9

The next step is to go through the data, one score at a time, and write the leaf for each score beside its stem. For the data in Table 2.4, the first score is $X = 83$, so you would write 3 (the leaf) beside the 8 in the column of stems. This process is continued for the entire set of scores. The complete stem and leaf display is shown with the original data in Table 2.4.

TABLE 2.4

A set of $N = 24$ scores presented as raw data and organized in a stem and leaf display

Data			Stem and Leaf Display	
83	82	63	3	23
62	93	78	4	26
71	68	33	5	6279
76	52	97	6	283
85	42	46	7	1643846
32	57	59	8	3521
56	73	74	9	37
74	81	76		

COMPARING STEM AND LEAF DISPLAYS WITH FREQUENCY DISTRIBUTIONS

You should notice that the stem and leaf display is very similar to a grouped frequency distribution. Each of the stem values corresponds to a class interval. For example, the stem 3 represents all scores in the 30s, that is, all scores in the interval 30–39. The number of leaves in the display show the frequency associated with each stem. It also should be clear that the stem and leaf display has several advantages over a traditional frequency distribution:

1. The stem and leaf display is very easy to construct. By going through the data only one time, you can construct a complete display.
2. The stem and leaf display allows you to identify every individual score in the data. In the display shown in Table 2.4, for example, you know that there were three scores in the 60s, and you know that the specific values were 62, 68, and 63. A frequency distribution would tell you only the frequency, not the specific values.
3. The stem and leaf display provides both a listing of the scores and a picture of the distribution. If a stem and leaf display is viewed from the side, it is essentially the same as a frequency distribution histogram (see Figure 2.15).
4. Because the stem and leaf display presents the actual value for each score, it is easy to modify a display if you want a more-detailed picture of a distribution. The modification simply requires that each stem be split into two (or more) parts. For example, Table 2.5 shows the same data that were presented in Table 2.4, but now we have split each stem in half. Notice that each stem value is now listed twice in the display. The first half of each stem is associated with the lower leaves (values 0–4), and the second half is associated with the upper leaves (values 5–9). In essence, we have regrouped the distribution using an interval width of 5 points instead of a width of 10 points in the original display.

Although stem and leaf displays are quite useful, you should be warned that they are considered to be a preliminary means for organizing data. Typically, a researcher would use a stem and leaf display to get a first look at experimental data. The final, published report normally would present the distribution of scores in a traditional frequency distribution table or graph.

COMPARING TWO DISTRIBUTIONS WITH STEM AND LEAF DISPLAYS

An additional advantage of stem and leaf displays is that two separate sets of data can be presented in a single display. As before, the stems are listed in a column, and the leaves for one set of data are presented on the right-hand side of this column. The leaf values for the second set of data can be placed on the left-hand side of the stem column. For example, in the preview section of this chapter we presented data from an experiment comparing two different study strategies (see Table 2.1). These same data are reproduced in a stem and leaf display in Table 2.6, with the scores for the experimental group shown on the right-hand side of the stems and the control

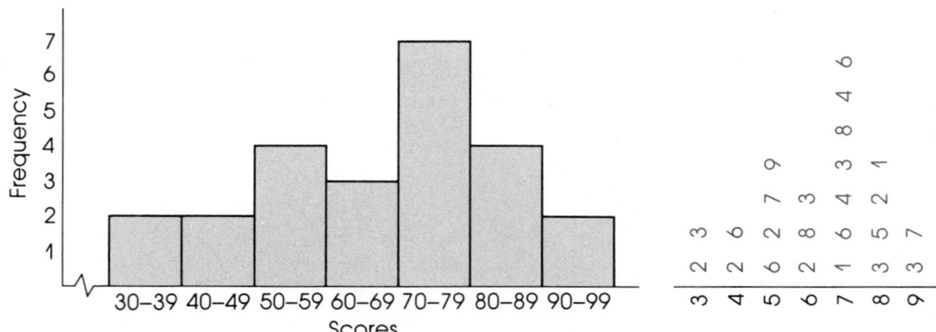

FIGURE 2.15

A grouped frequency distribution histogram and a stem and leaf display showing the distribution of scores from Table 2.4. The stem and leaf display is placed on its side to demonstrate that the display gives the same information that is provided in the histogram.

TABLE 2.5

A stem and leaf display with each stem split into two parts[a]

Stem	Leaf
3	23
3	
4	2
4	6
5	2
5	679
6	23
6	8
7	1434
7	686
8	321
8	5
9	3
9	7

[a]Note that each stem value is listed twice: The first occurrence is associated with the lower leaf values (0–4), and the second occurrence is associated with the upper leaf values (5–9). The data shown in this display are taken from Table 2.4.

group scores on the left. This single display makes it very easy to see that the experimental group generally had higher scores than the control group.

STEM AND LEAF DISPLAYS ON THE COMPUTER

As we noted before, computers are indispensable when we are required to organize or analyze large amounts of data. Even simple tasks, such as constructing a stem and leaf display, become quite tedious when we are dealing with very large data sets. Most software packages for statistics are able to provide summary information of the data in one form or another. The data from Table 2.4 were used to create a stem and leaf display with the Minitab software. The Minitab command STEM-AND-LEAF creates the display. The printout of this program is shown in Table 2.7.

The content of the printout is explained in the table, but a few features are worth noting here. The Minitab analysis provided a stem and leaf display with each stem split into two parts. Minitab does this automatically. The result is a display like the one in Table 2.5.

A unique feature of the Minitab display is the addition of a cumulative frequency column (the first column in the display). Moving down the column from the top,

TABLE 2.6

A stem and leaf display showing two separate sets of data.[a]

Control	Stem	Experimental
	1	
897	1	9
342130341424	2	432
57596875	2	8599798769
420	3	103402102
	3	56

[a]The data are taken from Table 2.1. The scores for the experimental group are shown on the right-hand side of the stems, and the control group scores are on the left-hand side. Note that each stem has been split in half to provide a more detailed picture of the two distributions.

TABLE 2.7

A Minitab printout of a stem and leaf display for the data in Table 2.4.

```
MINITAB RELEASE 5.1 *** COPYRIGHT - MINITAB, INC. 1985
U.S. FEDERAL GOVERNMENT USERS SEE HELP FGU
JUNE 18, 1986 *** S.U.N.Y. BROCKPORT - ACADEMIC COMPUTING SERVICES
STORAGE AVAILABLE 260144

 Type NEWS for information on new features in Minitab Release 5.1

MTB > SET C1                                  (1)
C1
    83    82    63    62  .  .  .

MTB > STEM-AND-LEAF C1

Stem-and-leaf of C1     N = 24                (2)
Leaf Unit = 1.0

    2    3 23
    2    3
    3    4 2
    4    4 6
    5    5 2
    8    5 679
   10    6 23                                 (3)
   11    6 8
   (4)   7 1344
    9    7 668
    6    8 123
    3    8 5
    2    9 3
    1    9 7

MTB > END
MTB > STOP
*** Minitab Release 5.1 *** Minitab, Inc. ***
Storage available 260144  Storage used 30767
```

EXPLANATION OF PRINTOUT:

1 The Minitab program provides a partial list of the raw scores. With very large distributions, this saves a considerable amount of space.

2 The number of scores (N) in the distribution is shown in the output.

3 The stem and leaf display is constructed. The first column shows cumulative frequencies above and below the 50th percentile (see text for explanation). The second column lists the stems, and the last column(s) shows each leaf. Note that the order of some leaves is different than the order in Table 2.5 (for example, for stems of 7). Minitab ignores the order of data entry and automatically places leaves in ascending order for each stem.

cumulative frequencies are entered until you reach the stem that contains the 50th percentile. The frequency for that particular stem is entered in parentheses: (4). That is, the stem and leaves of 7 1344 contain the 50th percentile of the distribution and this stem has 4 scores in it (71, 73, 74, 74). Starting from the bottom of the column and moving up, cumulative frequencies are again entered. These, too, stop when the stem with the 50th percentile is reached. This added feature helps you locate the middle of the distribution at a glance.

LEARNING CHECK

1 Use a stem and leaf display to organize the following set of scores: 86, 114, 94, 107, 96, 100, 98, 118, 107, 132, 106, 127, 124, 108, 112, 119, 125, 115

2 Explain how a stem and leaf display contains more information than a grouped frequency distribution.

ANSWERS 1 The stem and leaf display for these data would be

8	6
9	468
10	70768
11	48295
12	745
13	2

2 A grouped frequency distribution table tells only the number of scores in each interval; it does not identify the exact value for each score. The stem and leaf display gives the individual scores as well as the number in each interval.

SUMMARY

1 The goal of descriptive statistics is to simplify the organization and presentation of data. One descriptive technique is to place data in a frequency distribution table or graph that shows how the scores are distributed across the measurement scale.

2 A frequency distribution table lists scores (from highest down to lowest) in one column and the frequency of occurrence for each score in a second column. The table may include a proportion column showing the relative frequency for each score:

$$\text{proportion} = p = \frac{f}{N}$$

And the table may include a percentage column showing the percentage associated with each score:

$$\text{percentage} = \% = \frac{f}{N}(100)$$

3 When the scores cover a range that is too broad to list each individual value, it is customary to divide the range into sections called class intervals. These intervals are then listed in the frequency distribution table along with the frequency or number of individuals with scores in each interval. The result is called a grouped frequency distribution. The guidelines for constructing a grouped frequency distribution table are as follows:

a There should be about 10 intervals.

b The width of each interval should be a simple number (e.g., 2, 5, or 10).

c The bottom score in each interval should be a multiple of the width.

d All intervals should be the same width, and they should cover the range of scores with no gaps.

4 For a continuous variable, each score corresponds to an interval on the scale. The boundaries that separate intervals are called real limits. The real limits are located exactly halfway between adjacent scores.

5 A frequency distribution graph lists scores on the horizontal axis and frequencies on the vertical axis. The type of graph used to display a distribution depends on the scale of measurement used. For interval or ratio scales, you should use a histogram or a polygon. For a histogram, a bar is drawn above each score so that the height of the bar corresponds to the frequency. Each bar extends to the real limits of the score so that adjacent bars touch. For a polygon, a dot is placed above the midpoint of each score or class interval so that the height of the dot corresponds to the frequency; then lines are drawn to connect the dots. Bar graphs are used with nominal or ordinal scales. Bar graphs are similar to histograms except that gaps are left between adjacent bars.

6 Shape is one of the basic characteristics used to describe a distribution of scores. Most distributions can be classified as either symmetrical or skewed. A skewed distribution that tails off to the right is said to be positively skewed. If it tails off to the left, it is negatively skewed.

7 Cumulative percentage is the percentage of individuals with scores at or below a particular point in the distribution. The cumulative percentage values are associated with the upper real limits of the corresponding score or interval.

8 Percentiles and percentile ranks are used to describe the position of individual scores within a distribution. Percentile rank gives a cumulative percentage associated with a particular score. A score that is identified by its rank is called a percentile.

9 When a desired percentile or percentile rank is located between two known values, it is possible to estimate the desired value using the process of interpolation. Interpolation assumes a regular linear change between the two known values.

10 A stem and leaf display is an alternative procedure for organizing data. Each score is separated into a stem (the first digit or digits) and a leaf (the last digit or digits). The display consists of the stems listed in a column with the leaf for each score written beside its stem. A stem and leaf display combines the characteristics of a table and a graph and produces a concise, well-organized picture of the data.

KEY TERMS

frequency distribution
grouped frequency distribution
range
class interval
upper real limit
lower real limit
apparent limits
histogram
bar graph
polygon
symmetrical distribution
positively skewed distribution
negatively skewed distribution
tail(s) of a distribution
percentile
percentile rank
cumulative frequency (cf)
cumulative percentage ($c\%$)
interpolation
stem and leaf display

FOCUS ON PROBLEM SOLVING

1. The reason for constructing frequency distributions is to transform a disorganized set of raw data into a comprehensible, organized format. Because several different types of frequency distribution tables and graphs are available, one problem is deciding which type should be used. Tables have the advantage of being easier to construct, but graphs generally give a better picture of the data and are easier to understand.

To help you decide exactly which type of frequency distribution is best, consider the following points:

a. What is the range of scores? With a wide range, you will need to group the scores into class intervals.

b. What is the scale of measurement? With an interval or ratio scale you can use a polygon or a histogram. With a nominal or ordinal scale, you must use a bar graph.

2. Percentiles and percentile ranks are intended to identify specific locations within a distribution of scores. When solving percentile problems, especially with interpolation, it is helpful to sketch a frequency distribution graph. Use the graph to make a preliminary estimate of the answer before you begin any calculations. For example, to find the 60th percentile, you would want to draw a vertical line through the graph so that slightly more than half (60%) of the distribution is on the left-hand side of the line. Locating this position in your sketch will give you a rough estimate of what the final answer should be. When doing interpolation problems, there are several points you should keep in mind:

a. Remember that the cumulative percentage values correspond to the upper real limits of each score or interval.

b. You should always identify the interval with which you are working. The easiest way to do this is to sketch a table showing the endpoints on both scales (scores and cumulative percentages). This is illustrated in Example 2.6 on page 45.

c. The word *interpolation* means *between two poles*. Remember, your goal is to find an intermediate value between the two ends of the interval. Check your answer to be sure that it is located between the two endpoints. If not, then check your calculations.

PROBLEMS

*1 A set of scores covers a range of 15 points. Should these scores be presented in a regular table or a grouped table? Explain the advantages and disadvantages of each.

2 A set of $N = 7$ scores ranges from a high of $X = 96$ to a low of $X = 61$. Explain why it would *not* be a good idea to display this set of data in a frequency distribution table.

*3 A researcher collected personality scores from a sample of 100 students and organized the scores in a grouped frequency distribution table. That evening the researcher took the table home in order to use a home computer to do more-detailed calculations. However, the researcher soon found that the table did not provide enough information to do even the simplest arithmetic—for example, it was impossible to find $\sum X$ for the scores. Explain why.

4 What is the difference between a histogram and a bar graph? Under what circumstances is a bar graph appropriate? When is a histogram preferable?

5 Place the following set of scores in a frequency distribution table, and draw a polygon showing the distribution of scores. Scores: 6, 1, 3, 5, 5, 4, 5, 6, 3, 4, 2, 5, 4.

***6** For the set of scores shown in the following frequency distribution table,
a How many scores are in the distribution? ($N = ?$)
b Find $\sum X$ for this set of scores.

X	f
4	6
3	1
2	3
1	2

7 Sketch a histogram and a polygon showing the distribution of scores in the following table:

X	f
10–11	2
8–9	4
6–7	5
4–5	3
2–3	1

***8** For the following set of scores,
a Construct a frequency distribution table to organize the quiz scores.
b Draw a frequency distribution histogram for these data.

3, 5, 4, 6, 2, 3, 4, 1, 4, 3
7, 7, 3, 4, 5, 8, 2, 4, 7, 10

9 Use a frequency distribution table to organize the following set of scores:

206, 350, 590, 473, 450, 483
112, 380, 584, 620, 743, 816
685, 592, 712, 727, 686, 592
542, 490, 684, 491, 520, 380

***10** Place the following 28 scores in a grouped frequency distribution table using
a An interval width of 2
b An interval width of 5

23, 12, 16, 16, 17, 19, 28
20, 14, 21, 18, 24, 29, 24
18, 21, 22, 27, 21, 25, 19
22, 23, 21, 30, 27, 23, 18

11 Five sets of data are described. For each set the range of scores (lowest to highest) is given. Describe how each set should be presented in a grouped frequency distribution. That is, give the interval width that you would suggest and the number of intervals needed.
a 3–24
b 41–93
c 11–18
d 132–207
e 161–786

12 Complete the cumulative frequency column and the cumulative percentage column for the following table:

X	f	cf	c%
5	1		
4	2		
3	4		
2	1		
1	2		

***13** Complete the following frequency distribution table and find each of percentiles and percentile ranks requested:

X	f	cf	c%
10	1		
9	3		
8	5		
7	6		
6	3		
5	2		

a What is the percentile rank for $X = 6.5$?
b What is the percentile rank for $X = 5.5$?
c What is the 80th percentile?
d What score is needed to be in the top 5% of this distribution?

14 Find each value requested for the frequency distribution presented in the following table:

X	f	cf	c%
20–24	10	50	100%
15–19	10	40	80%
10–14	15	30	60%
5–9	10	15	30%
0–5	5	5	10%

a Find the percentile rank for $X = 17$.
b What is the 84th percentile?
c Find the percentile rank for $X = 10$.
d If this were a distribution of quiz scores and the instructor decided to fail the bottom 33% of the class, what score would separate passing from failing?

***15** Using the following frequency distribution, find each of the percentiles and percentile ranks requested:

X	f	cf	c%
6	2	20	100%
5	2	18	90%
4	4	16	80%
3	6	12	60%
2	4	6	30%
1	2	2	10%

a What is the 30th percentile?
b What is the percentile rank for $X = 4.5$?
c What is the 70th percentile?

d What is the percentile rank for $X = 3$?

e What is the minimum score needed to be in the top 25% of this distribution? That is, find the 75th percentile.

16 The following two sets of scores are from two different sections of an introductory statistics class:

Section I						Section II					
70	83	60	68	58	85	93	57	83	70	86	76
73	76	70	67	83	65	85	67	72	82	77	87
77	75	93	89	76	75	69	87	89	91	77	94
92	63	62	79	86	80	97	92	62	85	72	87
74	81	69	78	80	71	65	81	75	90		

a Organize the scores from each section into a grouped frequency distribution polygon using an interval width of 5 for each graph.

b Describe the similarities and differences between the two sections.

17 A psychologist would like to examine the effects of diet on intelligence. Two groups of rats are selected with 12 rats in each group. One group is fed the regular diet of Rat Chow, whereas the second group has special vitamins and minerals added to their food. After 6 months each rat is tested on a discrimination problem. The psychologist records the number of errors each animal makes before it solves the problem. The data from this experiment are as follows:

regular diet scores: 13, 11, 12, 13, 11, 9
12, 10, 12, 14, 10, 12

special diet scores: 9, 8, 7, 8, 9, 10
7, 8, 9, 6, 8, 10

a Identify the independent variable and the dependent variable for this experiment.

b Sketch a frequency distribution polygon for the group of rats with the regular diet. On the same graph (in a different color), sketch the distribution for the rats with the special diet.

c From looking at your graphs, would you say that the special diet had any effect on intelligence? Explain your answer.

***18** The following data are from an experiment with two treatments.

Treatment 1		Treatment 2	
62	45	42	12
52	63	37	28
63	59	21	33
58	68	51	14
38	66	26	15
67	61	47	18
59	60	33	22
68	53	28	39
51	67	56	19
30	48	20	16

a Compare the distributions of both treatments with a single stem and leaf display (see Table 2.6).

b By simply looking at your stem and leaf display, describe how the two distributions differ.

19 For the following scores, construct a frequency distribution table using

a An interval width of 5

b An interval width of 10

64 75 50 67 86 66 62 64 71 47
57 74 63 67 56 65 70 87 48 50
41 66 73 60 63 45 78 68 53 75

20 College officials recently conducted a survey to determine student's attitudes toward extending the library hours. Four different groups of students were surveyed, representing the four major subdivisions of the college. The average score for each group was as follows:

humanities: 7.25
sciences: 5.69
professions: 6.85
fine arts: 5.90

Use a graph to present the results of this survey.

***21** A recent study reports the effect of alcohol on simple reaction time. The relation between reaction time and blood alcohol level is shown in the following table:

Blood Alcohol Level	Reaction Time
0.06	205
0.08	214
0.10	232
0.12	230
0.14	241

Construct a graph showing these data.

22 A researcher examined the effect of amount of relaxation training on insomnia. Four treatment groups were used. Subjects received relaxation training for 2, 4, or 8 sessions. A control group received no training (0 sessions). Following training, the researcher measured how long it took the subjects to fall asleep. The average times for each group are presented in the following table:

Training Sessions	Average Time (in minutes)
0	72
2	58
4	31
8	14

Present these data in a graph.

23 Use a stem and leaf display to organize the following scores:

43, 56, 35, 47, 48, 52, 66, 57, 46
39, 43, 47, 61, 55, 50, 49, 39, 40

24 Place both sets of data from Problem 16 in a single stem and leaf display. (Put the Section I scores on one side of the stems and the Section II scores on the other side.)

***25** Place the following set of scores in a frequency distribution table:

1, 3, 1, 1, 4, 1, 4, 5, 6, 2, 1, 1, 5
1, 3, 2, 1, 6, 2, 4, 5, 2, 3, 2, 3

Compute the proportion and the percentage of individuals with each score. From your frequency distribution table, you should be able to identify the shape of this distribution.

***26** The same set of scores is presented in a regular frequency distribution table and in a grouped frequency distribution table as follows:

X	f	cf	c%
7	2	40	100%
6	4	38	95%
5	4	34	85%
4	11	30	75%
3	9	19	47.5%
2	6	10	25%
1	4	4	10%

X	f	cf	c%
6–7	6	40	100%
4–5	15	34	85%
2–3	15	19	47.5%
0–1	4	4	10%

Notice that when the scores are grouped into class intervals you lose information about the distribution.

a Find the 25th percentile for each frequency distribution table. Note that this value is determined precisely in one table but must be estimated in the other.

b Find the percentile rank for $X = 4$ for each table. Which value would you consider more accurate?

27 The same final exam is given to two different sections of a general psychology course. The scores for each section are as follows:

Section A				Section B			
69	52	74	46	70	86	75	50
37	43	52	58	62	73	72	85
48	59	90	56	95	48	53	79
82	76	35	64	65	47	39	82
81	60	53	39	71	91	88	90
41	45	71	65	83	58	61	77
55				61			

a Construct a grouped frequency distribution histogram using an interval width of 10 points for each of the two sections.

b Describe the differences between the two distributions.

c If Tom had a score of $X = 65$ on the exam, find his percentile rank if he were in section A.

d Find Tom's percentile rank if he were in section B. (Note that percentile rank measures position in a distribution relative to the other scores.)

28 For the past several weeks a bored statistician has kept records of the post position of the winning horse for each race at a local track. The following data represent all races with exactly eight horses:

Post Position of the Winning Horse						
1	3	3	7	4	5	1
3	2	8	5	3	6	1
4	7	1	2	5	8	5
3	4	8	1	8	3	2
6	7	3	4	2	6	5
4	8	2	6	4	7	2

a Construct a frequency distribution graph showing the number of winners for each of the eight post positions.

b Describe the shape of this frequency distribution.

c On the basis of these data, if you were betting on a race where you knew nothing about the horses or the jockeys, which post position would you choose? Explain your answer.

***29** The following data are attitude scores for a sample of 30 students. A high score indicates a positive attitude, and a low score indicates a negative attitude.

Attitude Scores					
9	73	62	52	14	46
31	26	74	61	13	5
79	58	16	62	7	55
77	43	30	18	23	11
42	78	10	66	72	25

a Construct a stem and leaf display to organize these data.

b Using your stem and leaf display, construct a grouped frequency distribution table for these scores.

c Looking at the distribution of scores, which of the following descriptions best fit these data?

1. This group has a generally positive attitude.
2. This group has a generally negative attitude.
3. This group is sharply split with attitudes at both extremes.

CHAPTER 3

CENTRAL TENDENCY

- Preview
- 3.1 Introduction
- 3.2 The Mode
- 3.3 The Median
- 3.4 The Mean
- 3.5 Comparing the Mean, Median, and Mode
- 3.6 Central Tendency and the Shape of the Distribution
- Summary
- Focus on Problem Solving
- Problems

TOOLS YOU WILL NEED

The following items are considered essential background material for this chapter. If you doubt your knowledge of any of these items, you should review the appropriate chapter or section before proceeding.

- Summation notation (Chapter 1)
- Frequency distributions (Chapter 2)
- Cumulative frequency (Chapter 2)
- Interpolation (Chapter 2)

PREVIEW

In a classic study examining the relation between heredity and intelligence, Tryon (1940) used a selective breeding program to develop separate strains of "smart" and "dumb" rats. Starting with a large sample of rats, Tryon tested each animal on a maze-learning problem. Based on their error scores for the maze, the brightest rats and the dullest rats were selected from this sample. The brightest males were mated with the brightest females. Similarly, the dullest rats were interbred. This process of testing and selectively breeding was continued for several generations until Tryon had established a line of maze-bright rats and a separate line of maze-dull rats. The results obtained by Tryon are shown in Figure 3.1.

Notice that after seven generations there is an obvious difference between the two groups. As a rule, the maze-bright animals outperform the maze-dull animals. It is tempting to describe the results of this experiment by saying that the maze-bright rats are better learners than the maze-dull rats. However, you should notice that there is some overlap between the two groups; not all the bright rats are really bright, and not all the dull animals are really dull. In fact, some of the animals bred for brightness are actually poorer learners than some of the animals bred for dullness. What is needed is a simple way of describing the general difference between these two groups while still acknowledging the fact that some individuals may contradict the general trend.

The solution to this problem is to identify the typical or average rat as the representative for each group. Then the experimental results can be described by saying that the typical maze-bright rat is a faster learner than the typical maze-dull rat. On the average, the bright rats really are brighter.

In this chapter we will introduce the statistical techniques used to identify the typical or average score for a distribution. Although there are several reasons for defining the average score, the primary advantage of an average is that it provides a single number that describes an entire distribution and can be used for comparison with other distributions.

As a footnote, you should know that later research with Tryon's rats revealed that the maze-bright rats were not really more intelligent than the maze-dull rats. Although the bright rats had developed specific abilities that are useful in mazes, the dull rats proved to be just as smart when tested on a variety of other tasks.

3.1 INTRODUCTION

The goal in measuring central tendency is to describe a group of individuals (more accurately, their scores) with a single measurement. Ideally, the value we use to describe the group will be the single value that is most representative of all the individuals.

FIGURE 3.1

Distribution of error scores for the original sample of rats (parents, left figure) and for the two separate lines that were selectively bred for either good or poor maze performance (maze-bright and maze-dull, right figure).

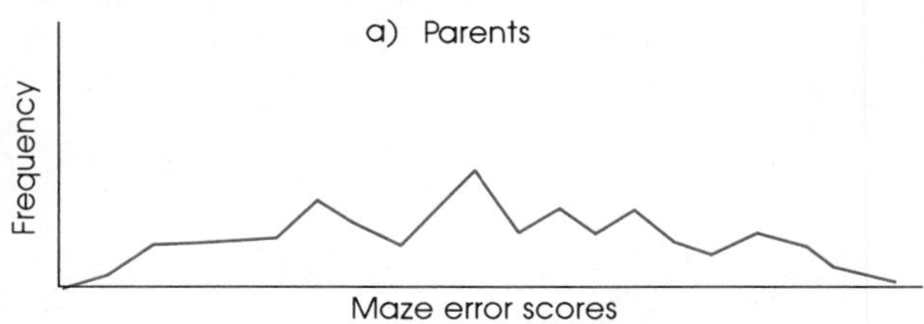

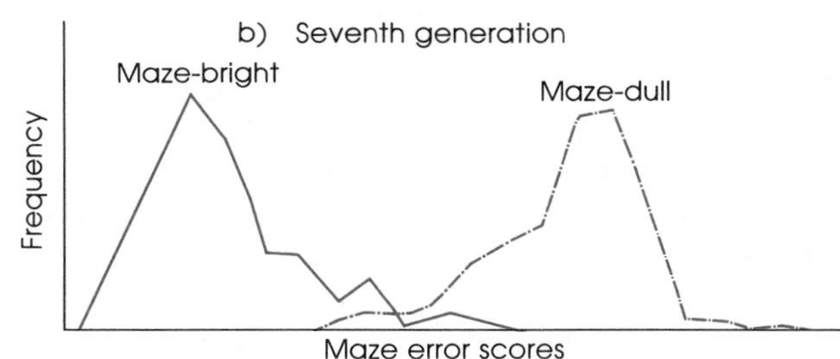

Tryon R. C. (1940). "Genetic differences in maze-learning ability in rats." *The Thirty-ninth Yearbook of the National Society for the Study of Education*, 111–119. Adapted and reprinted with permission of the National Society for the Study of Education.

· DEFINITION · *Central tendency* is a statistical measure that identifies a single score as a representative for an entire distribution.

Usually, we want to choose a value in the middle of the distribution because central scores are often the most representative. In everyday language, the goal of central tendency is to find the "average" or "typical" individual. For example, archeological discoveries indicate that the average height for men in the ancient Roman city of Pompeii was 5 feet 7 inches. Obviously, not all of the men were exactly 5 feet 7 inches, but this average value provides a general description of the population. Measures of central tendency also are useful for making comparisons between groups of individuals or between sets of figures. For example, weather data indicate that during the month of December, Seattle averages only 2 hours of sunshine per day, while Miami averages over 6 hours. The point of these examples is to demonstrate the great advantage of being able to describe a large set of data with a single, representative number. Central tendency characterizes what is typical for a large population and in doing so makes large amounts of data more digestable. Statisticians sometimes use the expression "number crunching" to illustrate this aspect of data description. That is, we take a distribution consisting of many scores and "crunch" them down to a single value that describes them all.

There are three standard ways to measure central tendency: the mode, the median, and the mean. They are computed differently and have different characteristics. To decide which of the three measures is best for any particular distribution, you should keep in mind that the general purpose of central tendency is to find the single most representative score. Each of the three measures we shall present has been developed to work best in a specific situation. We will examine this issue in more detail after we define the three measures.

3.2 THE MODE

In its common usage, the word *mode* means "the customary fashion" or "a popular style." The statistical definition is similar in that the mode is the most common observation among a group of scores.

· DEFINITION · In a frequency distribution, the *mode* is the score or category that has the greatest frequency.

The mode can be used to describe what is typical for any scale of measurement (see Chapter 1). Suppose, for example, you ask a sample of 100 students on campus to name their favorite restaurants in town. Your data might look like the results shown in Table 3.1. These are nominal data because the scale of measurement

· TABLE 3.1 ·

Favorite restaurants named by a sample of $N = 100$ students

Caution: The mode is always a score or category, not a frequency. For this example, the mode is Luigi's, not $f = 42$.

Restaurant	f
College Grill	5
George & Harry's	16
Luigi's	42
Oasis Diner	18
Roxbury Inn	7
Sutter's Mill	12

involves separate, unordered categories (restaurants). For these data, the modal response is Luigi's. This restaurant was named most frequently as a favorite place.

In a frequency distribution graph, the greatest frequency will appear as the tallest part of the figure. To find the mode, you simply identify the score located directly beneath the highest point in the distribution.

It is possible for a distribution to have more than one mode. Figure 3.2 shows the number of fish caught at various times during the day. There are two distinct peaks in this distribution, one at 6 A.M. and one at 6 P.M. Each of these values is a mode in the distribution. Note that the two modes do not have identical frequencies. Twelve fish were caught at 6 A.M., and 11 were caught at 6 P.M. Nonetheless, both of these points are called modes. The taller peak is called the *major mode*, and the shorter one is the *minor mode*. Of course, it also is possible to have a distribution with two (or more) separate peaks that are exactly the same height. A distribution with two modes is said to be *bimodal*. When a distribution has more than two modes, it is called *multimodal*. It also is common for a distribution with several equally high points to be described as having no mode.

· LEARNING CHECK ·

1 Find the mode for the set of scores shown in the following frequency distribution table:

X	f
5	2
4	6
3	4
2	2
1	1

2 In a recent survey comparing picture quality for three brands of color televisions, 63 people preferred brand A, 29 people preferred brand B, and 58 people preferred brand C. What is the mode for this distribution?

3 What is the reason for computing a measure of central tendency?

ANSWERS

1 The mode is $X = 4$.

2 The mode is brand A.

3 The goal of central tendency is to identify a single value to represent an entire distribution.

· FIGURE 3.2 ·

The relationship between time of day and number of fish caught.

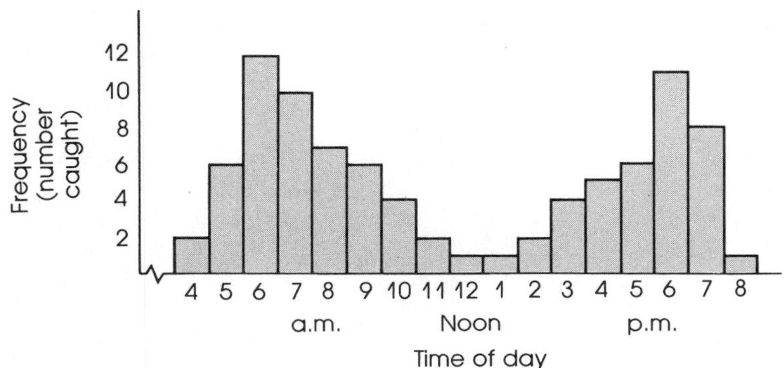

3.3 THE MEDIAN

The median is the score that divides a distribution exactly in half. Exactly one-half of the scores are less than or equal to the median, and exactly one-half are greater than or equal to the median. Because exactly 50% of the scores fall at or below the median, this value is equivalent to the 50th percentile (see Chapter 2).

DEFINITION The *median* is the 50th percentile. Exactly 50% of the individuals in a distribution have scores at or below the median.

By midpoint of the distribution we mean that the area in the graph is divided into two equal parts. We are not locating the midpoint of the range of scores.

The goal of the median is to determine the precise midpoint of a distribution. This commonsense goal is demonstrated in the following three examples. The three examples are intended to cover all of the different types of data you are likely to encounter.

METHOD 1: WHEN *N* IS AN ODD NUMBER

With an odd number of scores, you list the scores in order (lowest to highest), and the median is the middle score in the list. Consider the following set of $N = 5$ scores, which have been listed in order:

3, 5, 8, 10, 11

The middle score is $X = 8$, so the median is equal to 8.0. In a graph, the median divides the space or area of the graph in half (Figure 3.3). The amount of area above the median consists of $2\frac{1}{2}$ "boxes," the same as the area below the median (shaded portion).

METHOD 2: WHEN *N* IS AN EVEN NUMBER

With an even number of scores in the distribution, you list the scores in order (lowest to highest), and then locate the median by finding the point halfway between the middle two scores. Consider the following population:

3, 3, 4, 5, 7, 8

Now we select the middle pair of scores (4 and 5), add them together, and divide by 2:

$$\text{median} = \frac{4 + 5}{2} = \frac{9}{2} = 4.5$$

In terms of a graph, we see again that the median divides the area of the distribution exactly in half (Figure 3.4). There are three scores (or boxes) above the median and three below the median.

FIGURE 3.3

The median divides the area in the graph exactly in half.

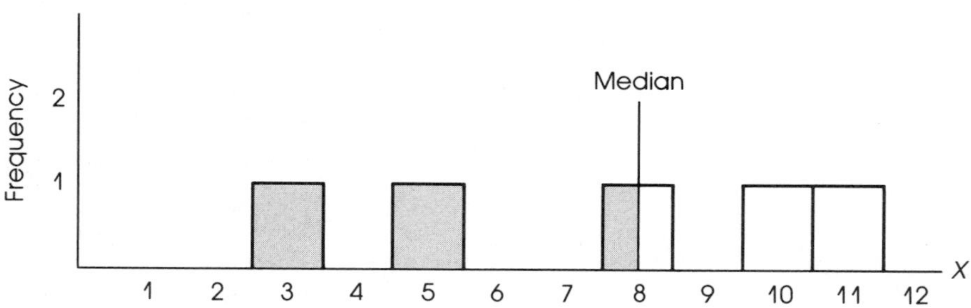

· FIGURE 3.4 ·

The median divides the area of the graph exactly in half.

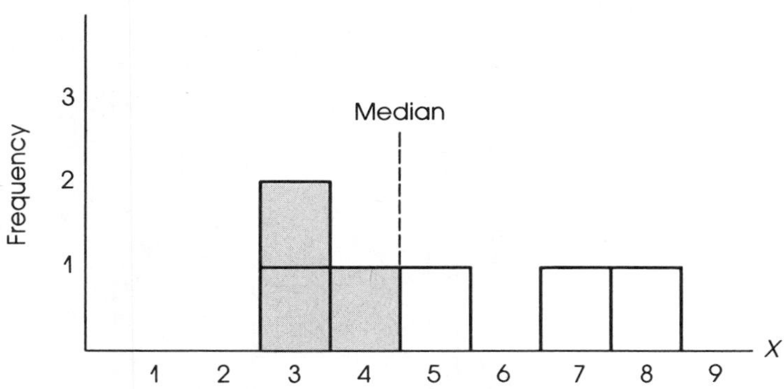

METHOD 3: WHEN THERE ARE SEVERAL SCORES WITH THE SAME VALUE IN THE MIDDLE OF THE DISTRIBUTION

In most cases, one of the two methods already outlined will provide you with a reasonable value for the median. However, when you have more than one individual at the median, these simple procedures may oversimplify the computations. Consider the following set of scores:

1, 2, 2, 3, 4, 4, 4, 4, 4, 5

There are 10 scores (an even number), so you normally would use method 2 and average the middle pair to determine the median. By this method, the median would be 4.

In many ways this is a perfectly legitimate value for the median. However, when you look closely at the distribution of scores (see Figure 3.5), you probably get the clear impression that $X = 4$ is not in the middle. The problem comes from the tendency to interpret the score of 4 as meaning exactly 4.00 instead of meaning an interval from 3.5 to 4.5. The simple method for computing the median has determined that the value we want is located in this interval. To locate the median with greater precision, it is necessary to use the process of interpolation (see Chapter 2, page 43). The following example demonstrates how interpolation is used to find the median.

· EXAMPLE 3.1 · For this example we will use the data shown in Figure 3.5. The data are reproduced in the following frequency distribution table:

X	f	cf	c%
5	1	10	100%
4	5	9	90%
3	1	4	40%
2	2	3	30%
1	1	1	10%

Note that we have included a cumulative frequency column and a cumulative percentage column in this table. Because the median divides the distribution exactly in half, we are looking for the score that corresponds to a cumulative percentage of 50%. However, 50% does not appear in the table. It is located between the *c*% values of 40% and 90%, so we must use interpolation. The cumulative percentage of 40% is reached at a score of $X = 3.5$ (the upper real limit of the 3s). The

· FIGURE 3.5 ·

A distribution with several scores clustered at the median.

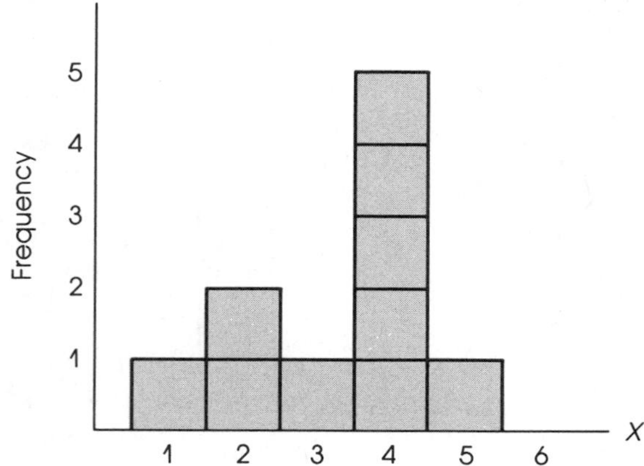

cumulative percentage of 90% is reached at $X = 4.5$. These cumulative percentages and their associated scores are as follows:

Score	Cumulative Percent
4.5	90%
?	50%
3.5	40%

The cumulative percentages cover a range from 90% to 40%. The value we want, $c\% = 50\%$, is located four-fifths of the way down from the top of this interval.

The scores cover a range of one point, so four-fifths of this interval is $\frac{4}{5}(1) = .80$. Starting at the top and moving down .80 gives a score of

$$X = 4.5 - .80 = 3.70$$

The median for this set of scores is 3.70. This is the point that has exactly 50% of the scores at or below it. ·

· LEARNING CHECK ·

1 Find the median for each distribution of scores:
  a 3, 10, 8, 4, 10, 7, 6
  b 13, 8, 10, 11, 12, 10
  c 3, 4, 3, 2, 1, 3, 2, 4
2 A distribution can have more than one median (true or false).
3 If you have a score of 52 on an 80-point exam, then you definitely scored above the median (true or false).

ANSWERS

1 a The median is $X = 7$.
  b The median is $X = 10.5$.
  c The median is $X = 2.83$ (by interpolation).
2 False
3 False. The value of the median would depend on where the scores are located.

3.4 THE MEAN

The mean, commonly known as the arithmetic average, is computed by adding up all the scores in the distribution and dividing by the number of scores. The mean for a population will be identified by the Greek letter mu, μ (pronounced "myoo"), and the mean for a sample will be identified by $\overline{X}$ (read "x-bar").

DEFINITION The *mean* for a distribution is the sum of the scores divided by the number of scores.

The formula for the population mean is

(3.1) $$\mu = \frac{\sum X}{N}$$

First, sum all the scores in the population and then divide by N. For a sample, the computation is done the same way, but the formula uses symbols that signify sample values:

(3.2) $$\text{sample mean} = \overline{X} = \frac{\sum X}{N}$$

In general, we will use Greek letters to identify characteristics of a population and letters of our own alphabet to stand for sample values. If a mean is identified with the symbol $\overline{X}$, you should realize that we are dealing with a sample. Also note that n is used as the symbol for the number of scores in the sample.

EXAMPLE 3.2 For a population of $N = 4$ scores,

3, 7, 4, 6

the mean would be

$$\mu = \frac{\sum X}{N} = \frac{20}{4} = 5$$

An alternative way to think of the mean is to consider it as the amount each individual would get if the total ($\sum X$) were divided equally among all the individuals (N) in the population. This somewhat socialistic viewpoint is particularly useful in problems where you know the mean and must find the total. Consider the following example.

EXAMPLE 3.3 A group of six students decided to earn some extra money one weekend picking vegetables at a local farm. The average earnings for this group was $\mu = \$30$. If they decide to pool all their money together for a party, how much will they have?

You don't know how much money each student earned. But you do know that the mean is \$30. This is the amount that each student would have if the total were divided equally. For each of the six students to have \$30, you must start with $6 \times \$30 = \$180$. The total, $\sum X$, is \$180. To check this answer, use the formula for the mean:

$$\mu = \frac{\sum X}{N} = \frac{\$180}{6} = \$30$$

THE WEIGHTED MEAN

Often it is necessary to combine two sets of scores and then find the overall mean for the combined group. For example, an instructor teaching two sections of introductory psychology obtains an average quiz score of $\overline{X} = 6$ for the 12 students in one section and an average of $\overline{X} = 7$ for the 8 students in the other section. If the two sections are combined, what is the mean for the total group?

The solution to this problem is straightforward if you remember the definition of the mean:

$$\overline{X} = \frac{\sum X}{n}$$

To find the overall mean, we must first find the total number of students (n) for the combined group, and we must find the overall sum of scores for the combined group ($\sum X$). Finding the number of students is easy. If there are $n = 12$ in one group and $n = 8$ in the other, then there must be $n = 20$ $(12 + 8)$ in the combined group. To find the sum of scores for the combined group, we will use this same method: First find the sum for one group, then find the sum for the other, and then add the two sums together.

We know that the first section has $n = 12$ and $\overline{X} = 6$. Using these values in the equation for the mean gives

$$\overline{X} = \frac{\sum X}{n}$$

$$6 = \frac{\sum X}{12}$$

$$12(6) = \sum X$$

$$72 = \sum X$$

The second section has $n = 8$ and $\overline{X} = 7$, so $\sum X$ must be equal to 56. When these two groups are combined, the sum of all 20 scores will be

$$72 + 56 = 128$$

Finally, the mean for the combined group is

$$\overline{X} = \frac{\sum X}{n} = \frac{128}{20} = 6.4$$

Notice that this value is not obtained by simply averaging the two means. (If we had simply averaged $\overline{X} = 6$ and $\overline{X} = 7$, we would obtain a mean of 6.5.) Because the samples are not the same size, one will make a larger contribution to the total group and, therefore, will carry more weight in determining the overall mean. For this reason, the overall mean we have calculated is called the *weighted mean*. In this example, the overall mean of $\overline{X} = 6.4$ is closer to the value of $\overline{X} = 6$ (the larger sample) than it is to $\overline{X} = 7$ (the smaller sample).

COMPUTING THE MEAN FROM A FREQUENCY DISTRIBUTION TABLE

Table 3.2 shows the scores on a quiz for a section of statistics students. Instead of listing all of the individual scores, these data are organized into a frequency distribution table. To compute the mean for this sample, you must use all the information in the table, the f values as well as the X values.

To find the mean for this sample, we will need the sum of the scores ($\sum X$) and the number of scores (n). The number n can be found by summing the frequencies:

$$n = \sum f = 8$$

TABLE 3.2

Statistics quiz scores for a section of $n = 8$ students

Quiz Score (X)	f	fX
10	1	10
9	2	18
8	4	32
7	0	0
6	1	6

It is very common for people to make mistakes when determining ΣX from a frequency distribution table. Often the column labeled X is summed, while the frequency column is ignored. Be sure to use the information in the f column when determining ΣX.

Note that there is one 10, two 9s, four 8s, and one 6 for a total of $n = 8$ scores. To find $\sum X$, you must be careful to add up all eight scores:

$$\sum X = 10 + 9 + 9 + 8 + 8 + 8 + 8 + 6 = 66$$

This sum also can be found by multiplying each score by its frequency and then adding up the results. This is done in the third column (fX) in Table 3.2. Note, for example, that the two 9s contribute 18 to the total.

Once you have found $\sum X$ and n, you compute the mean as usual:

$$\bar{X} = \frac{\sum X}{n} = \frac{\sum fX}{\sum f} = \frac{66}{8} = 8.25$$

LEARNING CHECK

1 Compute the mean for the sample of scores shown in the following frequency distribution table:

X	f
4	2
3	4
2	3
1	1

2 Two samples were obtained from a population. For sample A, $n = 8$ and $\bar{X} = 14$. For sample B, $n = 20$ and $\bar{X} = 6$. If the two samples are combined, will the overall mean be closer to 14 than to 6, closer to 6 than to 14, or halfway between 6 and 14? Explain your answer.

3 A sample of $n = 20$ scores has a mean of $\bar{X} = 5$. What is $\sum X$ for this sample?

ANSWERS

1 $\bar{X} = \frac{27}{10} = 2.7$

2 The mean will be closer to 6. The larger sample will carry more weight in the combined group.

3 $\sum X = 100$

CHARACTERISTICS OF THE MEAN

The mean has many characteristics that will be important in future discussions. In general, these characteristics result from the fact that every score in the distribution contributes to the value of the mean. Specifically, every score must be added into the total in order to compute the mean. Four of the more important characteristics will now be discussed.

1. *Changing a Score or Introducing a New Score.* Changing the value of any score, or adding a new score to the distribution, will change the mean. For example, the quiz scores for a psychology lab section consist of

9, 8, 7, 5, and 1

The mean for this sample is

$$\bar{X} = \frac{\sum X}{n} = \frac{30}{5} = 6.00$$

Suppose that the student who received the score of $X = 1$ returned a few days later and explained that she was ill on the day of the quiz. In fact, she went straight to the infirmary after class and was admitted for two days with the flu. Out of the goodness of the instructor's heart, the student was given a makeup quiz, and she received an 8. By having changed her score from 1 to 8, the distribution now consists of

9, 8, 7, 5, and 8

The new mean is

$$\bar{X} = \frac{\sum X}{n} = \frac{37}{5} = 7.40$$

Changing a single score in this sample has given us a different mean.

2. *Adding or Subtracting a Constant from Each Score.* If a constant value is added to every score in a distribution, the same constant will be added to the mean. Similarly, if you subtract a constant from every score, the same constant will be subtracted from the mean.

Consider the feeding scores for a sample of $n = 6$ rats. See Table 3.3. These scores are the amounts of food (in grams) they ate during a 24-hour testing session. The $\sum X = 26$ for $n = 6$ rats, so $\bar{X} = 4.33$. On the following day, each rat is given an experimental drug that reduces appetite. Suppose that this drug has the effect of reducing the meal size by 2 grams for each rat. Note that the effect of the drug is to subtract a constant (two points) from each rat's feeding score. The new distribution is shown in Table 3.4. Now $\sum X = 14$ and n is still 6, so the mean amount of food consumed is $\bar{X} = 2.33$. Subtracting two points from each score has changed the mean

TABLE 3.3

Amount of food (in grams) consumed during baseline session

Rat's Identification	Amount (X)
A	6
B	3
C	5
D	3
E	4
F	5

$\sum X = 26$
$n = 6$
$\bar{X} = 4.33$

TABLE 3.4

Amount of food (in grams) consumed after drug injections

Rat	Baseline Score Minus Constant	Drug Score (X)
A	6 − 2	4
B	3 − 2	1
C	5 − 2	3
D	3 − 2	1
E	4 − 2	2
F	5 − 2	3

$\sum X = 14$
$n = 6$
$\bar{X} = 2.33$

by the same constant, from $\overline{X} = 4.33$ to $\overline{X} = 2.33$. (It is important to note that experimental effects are practically never so simple as the adding or subtracting of a constant. Nonetheless, the principle of this characteristic of the mean is important and will be addressed in later chapters when we are using statistics to evaluate the effects of experimental manipulations.)

3. *Multiplying or Dividing Each Score by a Constant.* If every score in a distribution is multiplied by (or divided by) a constant value, the mean will be changed in the same way.

Suppose that a sample of $n = 5$ people give estimates of line length in a perception study. Table 3.5 shows the estimates given by the subjects when the stimulus was a 12-inch line. Although the people were asked to estimate length in inches (for their convenience), the metric system of measure usually is used in scientific reports. Therefore, to prepare the data for a report, every person's judgment must be changed to centimeters (cm). There are 2.54 cm in each inch, so each person's estimate must be multiplied by 2.54. As you can see in Table 3.5, multiplying each score by 2.54 causes the mean to be multiplied by exactly the same value. You should note that multiplying by 2.54 did not change any of the lengths. It simply changed the unit of measurement. The average of $\overline{X} = 10$ inches is identical in length to the average of $\overline{X} = 25.4$ cm.

4. *The Mean Is a Balance Point for the Distribution.* In addition to its mathematical definition, the mean can be considered as a balancing point for a distribution of scores. Consider a population consisting of $N = 4$ scores (2, 2, 6, 10). For this population, $\sum X = 20$ and $N = 4$, so $\mu = \frac{20}{4} = 5$.

Imagine that the frequency distribution histogram for this population is drawn so that the X-axis, or number line, is a seesaw, and the scores are boxes of equal weight that are placed on the seesaw (see Figure 3.6). If the seesaw is positioned so that it pivots at the value equal to the mean, it will be balanced and will rest level.

The reason the seesaw is balanced over the mean becomes clear when we measure the distance of each box (score) from the mean:

Score	Distance from the Mean
$X = 2$	3 points below the mean
$X = 2$	3 points below the mean
$X = 6$	1 point above the mean
$X = 10$	5 points above the mean

TABLE 3.5

Length estimates for a 12-inch line

Person	Length Estimate (in.)	Conversion to Centimeters
1	10	25.40
2	9	22.86
3	12	30.48
4	8	20.32
5	11	27.94
	$\sum X = 50$	$\sum X = 127.00$
	$\overline{X} = 10$ in.	$\overline{X} = 25.4$ cm

FIGURE 3.6

The frequency distribution shown as a seesaw balanced at the mean.

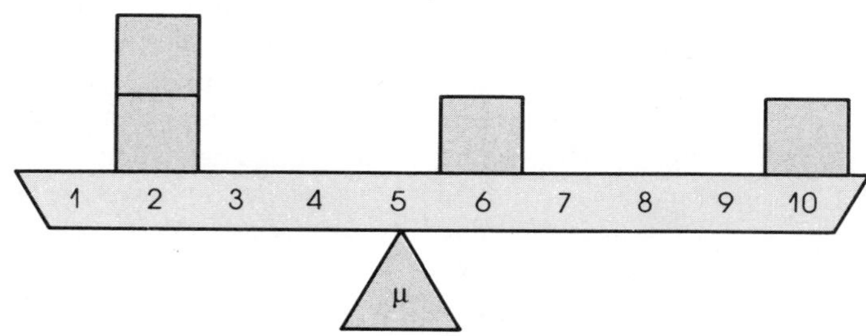

Adapted from *Statistics: An Intuitive Approach*, 4th ed. by G. Weinberg, J. Schumaker, and D. Oltman. Copyright © 1981, 1974, 1969, 1962 by Wadsworth Inc. Reprinted by permission of Brooks/Cole Publishing Co. Monterey, CA 93940.

Notice that the mean balances the distances. That is, the total distance below the mean is the same as the total distance above the mean:

3 points below + 3 points below = 6 points below

1 point above + 5 points above = 6 points above

What happens if we add one more score to the distribution? For instance, another score of $X = 10$ is added so that the distribution now is comprised of 2, 2, 6, 10, and 10. If we place another box at the position of $X = 10$, the seesaw no longer is balanced (see Figure 3.7). Remember, changing a single score, or adding a score, changes the mean. There is a new balance point. Now we have $\sum X = 30$ and $N = 5$, so the new mean is $\mu = \frac{30}{5} = 6$. If we slide the seesaw over so it swings at $\mu = 6$, the seesaw will balance.

LEARNING CHECK

1 **a** Compute the mean for the following sample of scores:

6, 1, 8, 0, 5

b Add four points to each score and then compute the mean.
c Multiply each of the original scores by 5 and then compute the mean.

2 After every score in a distribution is multiplied by 3, the mean is calculated to be $\overline{X} = 60$. What was the mean for the original distribution?

FIGURE 3.7

When a new score ($X = 10$) is added to the distribution, it no longer balances at $X = 5$.

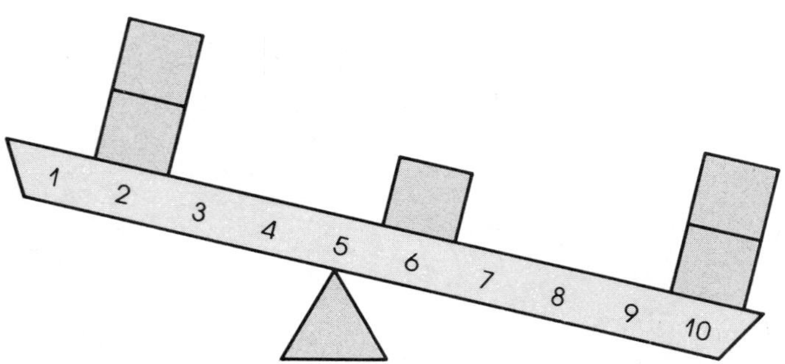

Adapted from *Statistics: An Intuitive Approach*, 4th ed. by G. Weinberg, J. Schumaker, and D. Oltman. Copyright © 1981, 1974, 1969, 1962 by Wadsworth Inc. Reprinted by permission of Brooks/Cole Publishing Co. Monterey, CA 93940.

ANSWERS

1 **a** $\overline{X} = \frac{20}{5} = 4$ **b** $\overline{X} = \frac{40}{5} = 8$ **c** $\overline{X} = \frac{100}{5} = 20$

2 The original mean was $\overline{X} = 20$.

3.5 COMPARING THE MEAN, MEDIAN, AND MODE

How do you decide which measure of central tendency to use? The answer to this question depends on several factors. Before we discuss these factors, however, it should be noted that the mean is most often the preferred measure of central tendency. Because the mean uses every score in the distribution, it usually is a good representative value. Remember, the goal of central tendency is to find the single value that best represents the entire distribution. Besides being a good representative, the mean has the added advantage of being a good measure for purposes of inferential statistics. Specifically, whenever you take a sample from a population, the sample mean will give a good indication of the value of the population mean. For these reasons, and others, the mean generally is considered to be the best of the three measures of central tendency. But there are specific situations where it either is impossible to compute a mean or where the mean is not particularly representative. It is in these situations that the mode and the median are used.

WHEN TO USE THE MODE

The mode has two distinct advantages over the mean. First, it is easy to compute. Second, it can be used with any scale of measurement (nominal, ordinal, interval, ratio; see Chapter 1).

It is a bit misleading to say that the mode is easy to calculate because actually no calculation is required. When the scores are arranged in a frequency distribution, you identify the mode simply by finding the score with the greatest frequency. Because the value of the mode can be determined "at a glance," it is often included as a supplementary measure along with the mean or median as a no-cost extra. The value of the mode (or modes) in this situation is to give an indication of the shape of the distribution as well as a measure of central tendency. For example, if you are told that a set of exam scores has a mean of 72 and a mode of 80, you should have a better picture of the distribution than would be available from the mean alone (see Section 3.6).

The fact that the mode can be used with any scale of measurement makes it a very flexible value. When scores are measured on a nominal scale, it is impossible to calculate either a mean or a median, so the mode is the only way to describe central tendency. Consider the frequency distribution shown in Figure 3.8. These data were

FIGURE 3.8

Major field of study for $n = 9$ students enrolled in an experimental psychology laboratory section.

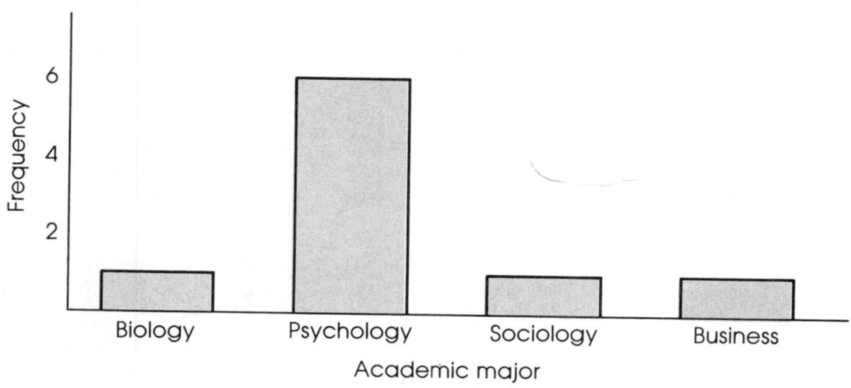

obtained by recording the academic major for each student in a psychology lab section. Notice that "academic major" forms a nominal scale that simply classifies individuals into discrete categories.

You cannot compute a mean for these data because it is impossible to determine $\sum X$. (How much is one biologist plus six psychologists?) Also note that there is no natural ordering for the four categories in this distribution. It is a purely arbitrary decision to place biology on the scale before psychology. Because it is impossible to specify any order for the scores, you cannot determine a median. The mode, on the other hand, provides a very good measure of central tendency. The mode for this sample is psychology. This category describes the typical, or most representative, academic major for the sample.

Because the mode identifies the most typical case, it often produces a more sensible measure of central tendency. The mean, for example, will generate conclusions such as "the average family has 2.4 children and a house with 5.33 rooms." Many people would feel more comfortable saying "the typical, or modal, family has 2 children and a house with 5 rooms" (see Perspective 3.1).

WHEN TO USE THE MEDIAN

There are three specific situations where the median serves as a valuable alternative to the mean. These occur when (1) there are a few extreme scores in the distribution, (2) some scores have undetermined values, and (3) there is an open-ended distribution.

Extreme Scores or Skewed Distributions When a distribution has a few extreme scores, scores that are very different in value from most of the others, then the mean will not be a good representative of the majority of the distribution. The problem comes from the fact that one or two extreme values can have a large influence and cause the mean to be displaced. In this situation, the fact that the mean uses all of the scores equally can be a disadvantage. For example, suppose a sample of $n = 10$ rats is tested in a T-maze for food reward. The animals must choose the correct arm of the T (right or left) to find the food in the goal box. The experimenter records the number of errors each rat makes before it solves the maze. Hypothetical data are presented in Figure 3.9.

The mean for this sample is

$$\bar{X} = \frac{\sum X}{n} = \frac{203}{10} = 20.3$$

Notice that the mean is not very representative of any score in this distribution. Most

FIGURE 3.9

Frequency distribution of errors committed before reaching learning criterion.

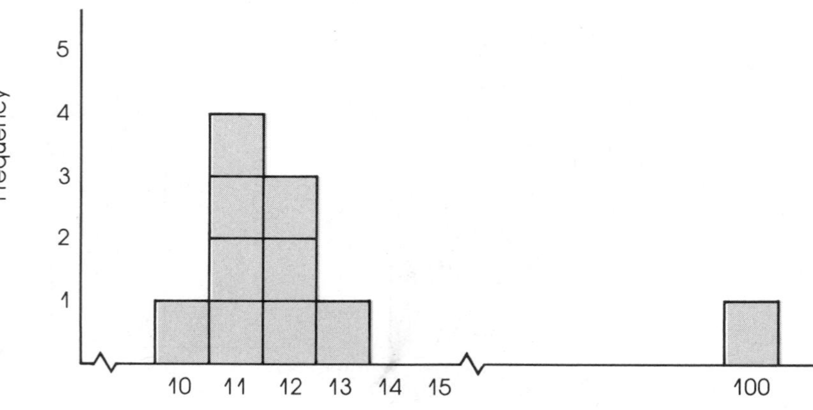

PERSPECTIVE 3.1

WHAT IS THE "AVERAGE"?

The word *average* is used in everyday speech to describe what is typical and commonplace. Statistically, averages are measured by the mean, median, or mode. U.S. Government agencies frequently characterize demographic data, such as average income or average age, with the median. Winners of elections are determined by the mode, the most frequent choice. Scholastic Aptitude Test (SAT) scores for large groups of students usually are described with the mean. The important thing to remember about these measures of central tendency (or the "average") is that they describe and summarize a group of individuals rather than any single person. In fact, the "average person" may not actually exist. Figure 3.10 shows data which were gathered from a sample of $n = 9$ infants. The age

FIGURE 3.10

Frequency distribution showing the age at which each infant in a sample of $n = 9$ uttered his or her first word.

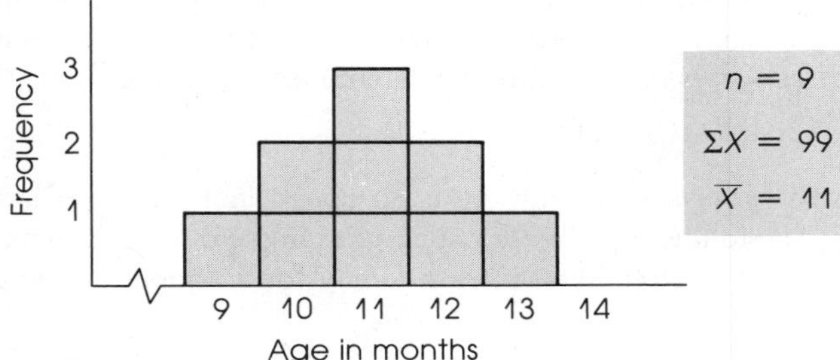

at which each infant said his/her first word was recorded by the parents. Note that the mean for this group is $\overline{X} = 11$ months and that there are three infants who uttered their first intelligible words at this age.

FIGURE 3.11

Frequency distribution showing the age at which each infant in a sample of $n = 6$ uttered his or her first word.

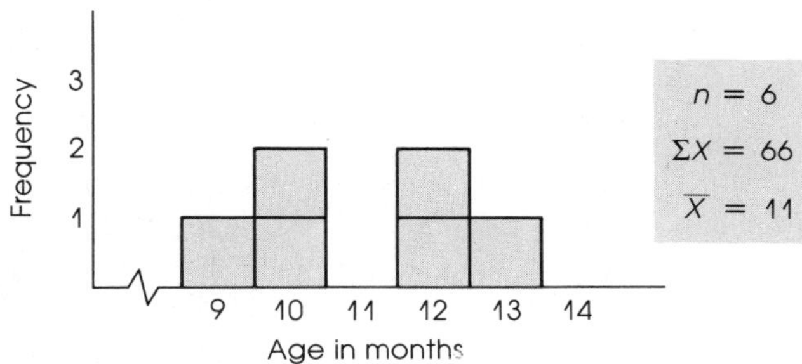

Now look at the results of a different study using a sample of $n = 6$ infants (Figure 3.11). Note that the mean for this group is also $\overline{X} = 11$ months but that the "average infant" does not exist in this sample.

The mean describes the group, not a single individual. It is for this reason that we find humor in statements like "the average American family has 2.4 children," fully knowing that we never will encounter this family.

of the scores are clustered at 10 and 12. The extreme score of $X = 100$ (a slow learner) inflates the value of $\sum X$ and distorts the mean.

The median, on the other hand, is not easily affected by extreme scores. For this sample, $n = 10$, so there should be five scores on either side of the median. The median is 11.50. Notice that this is a very representative value. Also note that the median would be unchanged even if the slow learner made 1000 errors instead of only 100. The median commonly is used when reporting the average value for a skewed distribution. For example, the distribution of personal incomes is very skewed, with a small segment of the population earning incomes that are astronomical. These extreme values distort the mean, so that it is not very representative of the salaries that most of us earn. As in the previous example, the median is the preferred measure of central tendency when extreme scores exist.

Undetermined Values Occasionally, you will encounter a situation where an individual has an unknown or undetermined score. In psychology, this often occurs in learning experiments where you are measuring the number of errors (or amount of time) required for an individual to solve a particular problem. For example, suppose a sample of $n = 6$ people were asked to assemble a wooden puzzle as quickly as possible. The experimenter records how long (in minutes) it takes each individual to arrange all the pieces to complete the puzzle. Table 3.6 presents the outcome of this experiment.

Notice that person 6 never completed the puzzle. After an hour, this person still showed no sign of solving the puzzle, so the experimenter stopped him or her. This

TABLE 3.6

Amount of time to complete puzzle

Person	Time (min.)
1	8
2	11
3	12
4	13
5	17
6	Never finished

person has an undetermined score. (There are two important points to be noted. First, the experimenter should not throw out this individual's score. The whole purpose for using a sample is to gain a picture of the population, and this individual tells us that part of the population cannot solve the puzzle. Second, this person should not be given a score of $X = 60$ minutes. Even though the experimenter stopped the individual after 1 hour, the person did not finish the puzzle. The score that is recorded is the amount of time needed to finish. For this individual, we do not know how long this would be.)

It is impossible to compute the mean for these data because of the undetermined value. We cannot calculate the $\sum X$ part of the formula for the mean. However, it is possible to compute the median. For these data the median is 12.5. Three scores are below the median, and three scores (including the undetermined value) are above the median.

OPEN-ENDED DISTRIBUTIONS

A distribution is said to be *open-ended* when there is no upper limit (or lower limit) for one of the categories. The following table provides an example of an open-ended distribution, showing the number of children in each family for a sample of $n = 20$ households.

Number of Children (X)	f
5 or more	3
4	2
3	2
2	3
1	6
0	4

The top category in this distribution shows that three of the families have "5 or more" children. This is an open-ended category. Notice that it is impossible to compute a mean for these data because you cannot find $\sum X$ (the total number of children for all 20 families). However, you can find the median. For these data, the median is 1.5 (exactly 50% of the families have fewer than 1.5 children).

3.6 CENTRAL TENDENCY AND THE SHAPE OF THE DISTRIBUTION

We have identified three different measures of central tendency, and often a researcher will calculate all three for a single set of data. Because the mean, the median, and the mode are all trying to measure the same thing (central tendency), it is reasonable to expect that these three values should be related. In fact there are some consistent and predictable relationships among the three measures of central tendency. Specifically, there are situations where all three measures will have exactly the same value. On the other hand, there are situations where the three measures are guaranteed to be different. In part, the relationship between the mean, median, and mode is determined by the shape of the distribution. We will consider two general types of distributions.

SYMMETRICAL DISTRIBUTIONS

For a symmetrical distribution, the right-hand side of the graph will be a mirror image of the left-hand side. By definition, the median will be exactly at the center of a symmetrical distribution because exactly half of the area in the graph will be on either side of the center. The mean also will be exactly at the center of a symmetrical distribution, because each individual score in the distribution has a corresponding score on the other side (the mirror image), so that the average of these two values is exactly in the middle. Because all the scores can be paired in this way, the overall average will be exactly at the middle. For any symmetrical distribution, the mean and the median will be the same (Figure 3.12).

If a symmetrical distribution has only one mode, then it must be exactly at the center so that all three measures of central tendency will have the same value (see Figure 3.12). On the other hand, a bimodal distribution that is symmetrical [Figure 3.12(b)] will have the mean and median together in the center with the modes on each side. A rectangular distribution [Figure 3.12(c)] has no mode because all X values occur with the same frequency. Still, the mean and the median will be in the center of the distribution and equivalent in value.

SKEWED DISTRIBUTIONS

Distributions are not always symmetrical. In fact, quite often they are lopsided, or skewed. If an experimenter is measuring reaction times, for example, skewed distributions are very common. Figure 3.13 shows that most subjects can respond very quickly, usually between 250 and 500 milliseconds ($\frac{1}{4}$–$\frac{1}{2}$ second). However, the curve is not symmetrical because there are a few people with relatively long reaction times. Perhaps they were not paying attention to the task, or maybe some subjects were unusually tired that day. This distribution has positive skew; that is, the tail of extreme scores points in the positive direction on the X-axis. Where will the mode, median, and mean be located in skewed distributions?

Figure 3.14 shows a positively skewed distribution. In this distribution, the peak (highest frequency) is on the left-hand side. This is the position of the mode. If you examine Figure 3.14 carefully, it should be clear that the line drawn above the mode does not divide the distribution into two equal parts. In order to have exactly 50% of the distribution on each side, the median must be located to the right of the mode. Finally, the mean will be located to the right of median because it is influenced most by extreme scores and will be displaced farthest to the right by the scores in the tail.

FIGURE 3.12

Measures of central tendency for three symmetrical distributions: normal, bimodal, and rectangular.

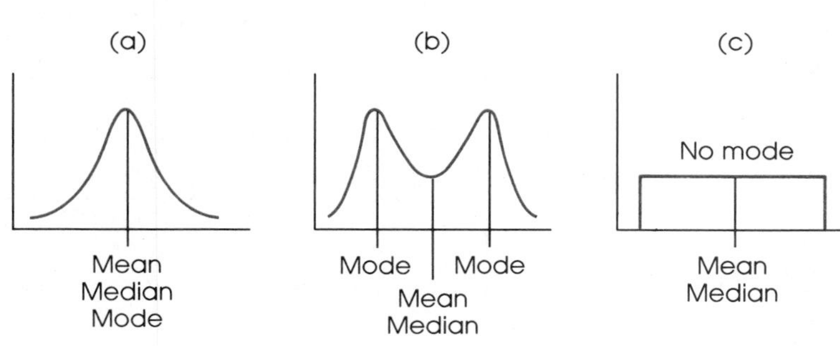

FIGURE 3.13

A positively skewed distribution.

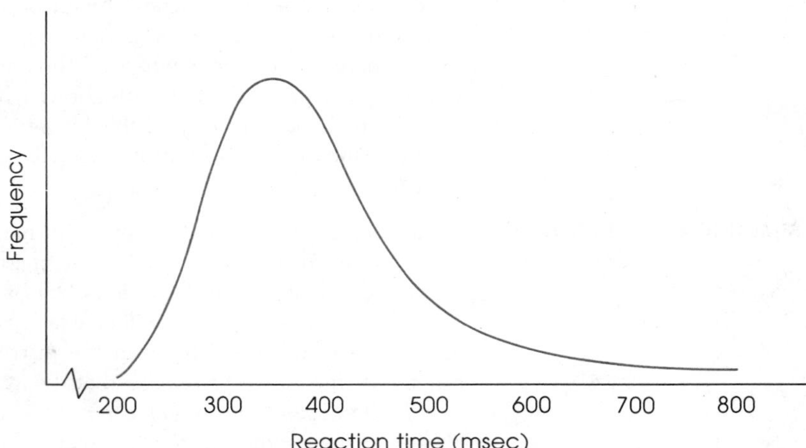

FIGURE 3.14

Measures of central tendency in a positively skewed distribution.

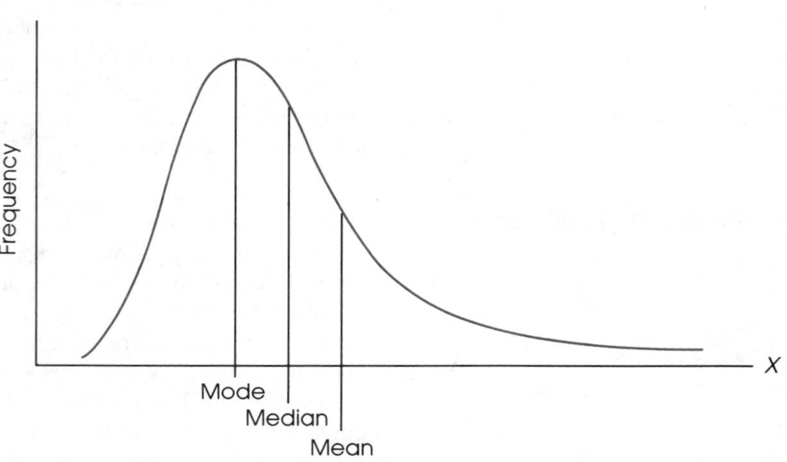

FIGURE 3.15

Measures of central tendency in a negatively skewed distribution.

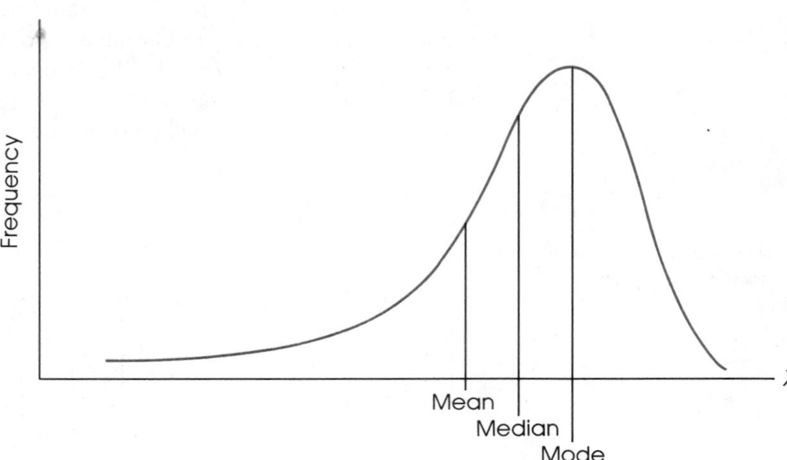

Therefore, in a positively skewed distribution, the mean will have the largest value, followed by the median and then the mode (see Figure 3.14).

Negatively skewed distributions are lopsided in the opposite direction, with the scores piling up on the right-hand side and the tail tapering off to the left. The grades on an easy exam, for example, will tend to form a negatively skewed distribution (see Figure 3.15). For a distribution with negative skew, the mode is on the right-hand side (with the peak), while the mean is displaced on the left by the extreme scores in the tail. As before, the median is located between the mean and the mode. In order from highest value to lowest value, the three measures of central tendency will be the mode, the median, and the mean.

SUMMARY

1 The purpose of central tendency is to determine the single value that best represents the entire distribution of scores. The three standard measures of central tendency are the mode, the median, and the mean.

2 The mean is the arithmetic average. It is computed by adding up all the scores and then dividing by the number of scores. Changing any score in the distribution will cause the mean to be changed. When a constant value is added to (or subtracted from) every score in a distribution, the same constant value is added to (subtracted from) the mean. If every score is multiplied by a constant, the mean will be multiplied by the same constant. In nearly all circumstances, the mean is the best representative value and is the preferred measure of central tendency.

3 The mode is the most frequently occurring score in a distribution. It is easily located by finding the peak in a frequency distribution graph. For data measured on a nominal scale, the mode is the appropriate measure of central tendency. It is possible for a distribution to have more than one mode.

4 The median is the value that divides a distribution exactly in half. The median is the 50th percentile. The median is the preferred measure of central tendency when a distribution has a few extreme scores that displace the value of the mean. The median also is used when there are undetermined (infinite) scores that make it impossible to compute a mean.

5 For symmetrical distributions, the mean will equal the median. If there is only one mode, then it will have the same value too.

6 For skewed distributions, the mode will be located toward the side where the scores pile up, and the mean will be pulled toward the extreme scores in the tail. The median will be located between these two values.

KEY TERMS

central tendency
mode
major mode
minor mode
bimodal distribution
multimodal distribution
median
mean
weighted mean
symmetrical distribution
skewed distribution
positive skew
negative skew

FOCUS ON PROBLEM SOLVING

1. Because there are three different measures of central tendency, your first problem is to decide which one is best for your specific set of data. Usually the mean is the preferred measure, but the median may provide a more representative value if you are working with a skewed distribution. With data measured on a nominal scale, you must use the mode.

2. Although the three measures of central tendency appear to be very simple to calculate, there is always a chance for errors. The most common sources of error are listed next.

a. Many students find it very difficult to compute the mean for data presented in a frequency distribution table. They tend to ignore the frequencies in the table and simply average the score values listed in the X column. You must use the frequencies and the scores! Remember, the number of scores is found by $N = \sum f$, and the sum of all N scores is found by $\sum fX$.

b. The median is the midpoint of the distribution of scores, not the midpoint of the scale of measurement. For a 100-point test, for example, many students incorrectly assume that the median must be $X = 50$. To find the median you must have the *complete set* of individual scores. The median separates the individuals into two equal-sized groups.

c. The most common error with the mode is for students to report the highest frequency in a distribution rather than the score with the highest frequency. Remember, the purpose of central tendency is to find the most representative score. Therefore, for the following data the mode is $X = 3$, not $f = 8$.

X	f
4	3
3	8
2	5
1	2

PROBLEMS

*1 If you change the value of a single score in a distribution, you will sometimes change the median and sometimes leave the median unaffected. Describe the circumstances where the median would change and where the median would not change.

2 Two local archery clubs each sent their three best archers to the annual competition. The individual scores for these six people are as follows:

Rank	Archer	Score
1st place	A	30 points
2nd place	B	15 points
3rd place	C	14 points
4th place	D	13 points
5th place	E	10 points
6th place	F	8 points

Archers A, E, and F are from the Westside Club, and archers B, C, and D are from the Eastside Club.

a Compute the mean score for each club. If the winning team is determined by the highest mean score, which club wins?

b Compute the mean rank (1st, 2nd, and so on) for each club. If the winning team is determined by the highest mean rank, which club wins?

c Explain why the mean score and the mean rank produce different results.

*3 A professor computes grades based on three regular exams and a final. The final exam is weighted twice as much as any of the other tests. If the three regular exams had means of 70, 74, and 76 and the final exam had a mean of 78, what is the overall mean when the test scores are combined? (Assume that the entire class took all four exams.)

4 What is meant when it is said that the median is the *midpoint* of the distribution?

5 What is meant by the following statement: The mean is the balance point of the distribution?

*6 Find the mean, median, and mode for the following set of scores: 2, 4, 3, 4, 1, 5, 4, 2.

7 A sample has a mean of $\overline{X} = 20$. If each X value is multiplied by 6, then what is the value of the new mean?

*8 A set of scores has a total of $\sum X = 400$ and has a mean of $\mu = 50$. How many scores are in this population?

9 For the following set of scores, sketch a frequency distribution histogram and calculate the mean, median and mode.

10, 8, 14, 7, 10, 11, 13, 15, 12, 9, 11, 10

*10 Find the mean, median, and mode for the set of scores in the following frequency distribution table:

X	f
6	1
5	2
4	1
3	1
2	2
1	3

11 **a** Find the mean, median, and mode for the scores in the following frequency distribution table. Note that you must use interpolation to find the median.

b Looking at the values you obtained for the mean, median, and mode, is this distribution positively or negatively skewed?

X	f
8	1
7	1
6	1
5	2
4	2
3	4
2	1

12 A population of $N = 10$ scores has a mean of $\mu = 50$. If one of the scores is changed from $X = 60$ to $X = 80$, what will happen to the mean? Find the value for the new mean.

***13** A sample of $n = 18$ children took a reading test and showed a mean score of $\overline{X} = 24$. A few days later, two children who had previously been absent took the test. Their scores were $X = 36$ and $X = 32$. What will the mean be if their scores are included with the original data?

14 A psychologist has measured how much time is required to solve a problem for each person in a sample of $n = 30$. The average time was $\overline{X} = 330$ seconds. If the psychologist converted all of the scores from seconds to minutes, what value would be obtained for the mean?

***15** A distribution has a mean of 50 and a median of 43. Is it more likely that this distribution is positively skewed or negatively skewed? Explain your answer.

16 Two sets of data follow:

Data set I: 3, 4, 1, 5, 4, 5, 2, 6, 4, 7, 3, 4

Data set II: 3, 1, 4, 3, 2, 1, 7, 1, 2, 5, 1, 6

a Sketch a frequency distribution histogram for each set of scores.

b Without doing any calculations, estimate the mean for each set of scores. You should be able to estimate fairly accurately by simply looking at your graphs.

c Calculate the mean for each set, and compare the results with your estimates.

17 The following data are quiz scores for an introductory psychology class.

18, 21, 16, 21, 20, 17, 15

21, 18, 22, 20, 17, 21, 19

a Compute the mean, median and mode for these data.

b Based on the results of part a, is this distribution positively or negatively skewed?

c Draw a frequency distribution histogram for the data. Note the shape of distribution and compare it to your answer in part b. If parts b and c do not agree, check your computations in part a.

***18** A psychologist would like to determine how many errors are made, on the average, before rats can learn a particular maze. A sample of $n = 10$ rats is obtained, and each rat is tested on the maze. The scores for the first 9 rats are as follows: 6, 2, 4, 5, 3, 7, 6, 2, 1.

a Calculate the mean and the median for these data. On the average, how many errors does each rat make?

b The tenth rat in the sample committed 100 errors before mastering the maze. When this rat is included in the sample, what happens to the mean? What happens to the median? What general conclusion can be drawn from this result?

19 In a problem-solving experiment with $n = 100$ children, 5 of the children failed to complete the problem within 10 minutes and were simply marked as "failed." If the experimenter wanted to find a measure of central tendency to describe the "average" amount of time needed to complete the problem, what measure should be used? Explain your answer.

***20** Four students have part-time jobs in the same store. The mean weekly pay for these students is \$30, and the median weekly pay is \$25.

a If one of the students gets a \$10 raise, what is the new mean?

b If one of the students gets a \$10 raise, what is the new median? (Be careful and explain your answer.)

c If one student gets a \$10 raise and another gets a \$20 raise, what is the new mean?

d If the student with the highest salary gets a \$10 raise, what is the new median?

21 The final exam grades for two sections of the same course are reported as follows:

Section I: $n = 30$, $\overline{X} = 63$

Section II: $n = 70$, $\overline{X} = 78$

If both sections are combined, what is the average grade for the entire set of students?

22 A 20-point quiz is given to each of two sections of an introductory statistics class. The scores for each section are as follows:

Section I: 6, 5, 5, 7, 17, 5, 6, 5

Section II: 9, 8, 10, 7, 8, 9, 1, 0, 9, 9

a Sketch a histogram showing the distribution of scores for section I.

b Sketch a histogram showing the distribution for section II.

c Looking at your graphs, which section would you say had better scores?

d Calculate the mean and the median for each section. Which measure of central tendency best describes the difference between these two distributions?

***23** To evaluate teaching effectiveness, a professor measures each student's attitude toward psychology at the beginning of the course and again at the end. For each person, the change in attitude is computed. A positive score means that the person's opinion of psychology went up; a negative score means that the person's opinion went down. The scores are as follows:

−12,	31,	20,	1,	4,	12,	13,
−6,	7,	−9,	11,	−4,	10,	0,
3,	6,	2,	−18,	−2,	21,	9

a Compute the mean change for this sample of $n = 21$ students.

b Because the professor does not like to work with negative numbers, 20 points are added to each score and then the mean is calculated. How should this mean compare with the value you obtained in part a? Exactly what value should be obtained?

24 A school psychologist has computed the average IQ for a sample of $n = 99$ children and obtained a mean of $\bar{X} = 104$. If one additional student with an IQ of 133 is included in this sample, what will the average IQ be for the entire group of 100 students?

***25** A professor teaches a morning class of $n = 61$ students and an afternoon class of $n = 34$. The same test is given to both classes. The mean for the morning group is $\bar{X} = 44.1$, and the mean for the afternoon group is $\bar{X} = 50.3$. If the two classes are combined, what is the mean for the entire group of students?

26 A social psychologist is interested in the effect of failure on a person's mood. A sample of $n = 9$ students is obtained and each student is given a mood inventory questionnaire. After completing the questionnaire, each student is given a word problem to solve. Although the problem is impossible to solve, the psychologist says that an average student can finish it in about 10 minutes. After working on the problem for 15 minutes, each student is stopped and once again completes the mood questionnaire. The data from this experiment are as follows:

Mood Scores	
Before	After
17	12
25	18
16	19
20	11
30	27
19	14
23	21
26	19
29	18

a Calculate the mean for the initial mood scores and for the scores after failing to solve the problem. What is the difference between these two means?

b Find the change in mood for each individual subject (before versus after). Calculate the mean for these difference scores (remember, some differences may be positive, and some may be negative). You should find that the mean difference is identical to the difference between the means.

27 A psychologist is collecting attitude scores for high school students as part of an experiment. Because the testing room will hold only 15 people, the students are tested in three separate groups. The data for these three groups are as follows:

Group 1: $n = 15$, $\bar{X} = 46.5$

Group 2: $n = 14$, $\bar{X} = 43.2$

Group 3: $n = 11$, $\bar{X} = 50.9$

Find the overall mean for the entire group of high school students.

28 The monthly telephone costs for the Department of Psychology last year are as follows:

Monthly Phone Bills			
Jan.	$121.83	Jul.	$ 83.15
Feb.	$173.21	Aug.	$121.33
Mar.	$165.12	Sep.	$215.50
Apr.	$182.86	Oct.	$201.45
May	$142.67	Nov.	$172.80
Jun.	$104.28	Dec.	$162.25

Find the mean monthly bill.

29 Reaction time data for a sample of $n = 15$ subjects are as follows:

1.0,	.9,	1.2,	1.3,	.9,	.8,	1.0,	
.7,	.9,	1.1,	.7,	1.2,	1.0,	1.1,	.8

Find the mean and the median for these scores. (*Hint:* If you first multiply each score by 10, you will get rid of the decimals.)

***30** The Jones & Jones Corporation is currently involved in negotiations with the employees' labor union. The hourly wages for the 20 employees at Jones & Jones are as follows:

Hourly Wages			
8.50	7.40	7.25	12.00
7.50	8.00	8.55	7.30
7.00	11.00	9.50	7.25
8.20	7.10	10.50	9.00
9.50	7.10	7.25	8.50

The union and the company both have access to these figures. The statewide average hourly wage for this type of industry is $8.25.

a Calculate the mean and the median hourly wage for the Jones & Jones employees.

b If you were a company official arguing that the present salaries are reasonable, which measure of central tendency would you prefer? Using this measure, how does the "average" wage at Jones & Jones compare with the statewide average?

c If you were a union official arguing for a salary increase, which measure of central tendency would you prefer? How does this "average" compare with the statewide average?

31 On a standardized reading achievement test, the nationwide average for seventh grade children is $\mu = 7.00$. A seventh-grade teacher is interested in comparing class reading scores with the national average. The scores for 16 students are as follows:

6.5, 7.2, 7.8, 7.2, 6.8, 7.1, 8.3, 6.9,
8.2, 7.4, 6.2, 6.8, 7.3, 6.2, 8.1, 7.0,

Calculate the mean for this class. On the average, how does this class compare with the national norm?

***32** In the preview section of Chapter 2 we presented test scores for students using two different strategies for studying. One group read straight through the material, and the second group had their reading divided into sections with questions at the end of each section. The data from this experiment are as follows:

Read Straight Through				Interspersed Questions			
25	32	27	20	28	29	25	31
28	23	17	21	31	19	29	35
24	34	22	29	30	28	24	30
24	25	21	18	33	27	34	26
19	22	30	24	29	29	27	32
26	27	24	23	30	36	22	23
23	25			32	33		

Calculate the mean for each group. On the average, how much difference is there between these two study techniques?

CHAPTER 4

VARIABILITY

TOOLS YOU WILL NEED

The following items are considered essential background material for this chapter. If you doubt your knowledge of any of these items, you should review the appropriate chapter or section before proceeding.

- Summation notation (Chapter 1)
- Percentiles (Chapter 2)
- Central tendency (Chapter 3)
    - Mean
    - Median

PREVIEW

It's 10 A.M., and Mary L. is washing her hands for the tenth time today. Before she goes to sleep tonight, she will have washed her hands over 60 times. Is this normal?

To differentiate between normal and abnormal behavior, some psychologists have resorted to using a *statistical model*. For example, we could survey a large sample of individuals and record the number of times each person washes his/her hands during a typical day. Because people are different, the scores should be variable, and the data from this survey should produce a distribution similar to the one shown in Figure 4.1. Notice that most people will have average or moderate scores located in the central part of the distribution. Others, such as Mary L., will deviate from average. According to the statistical model, those who show substantial deviation are abnormal. Note that this model simply defines abnormal as being unusual or different from normal. The model does not imply that abnormal is necessarily negative or undesirable. Mary L. may have a compulsive personality disorder, or she may be a dentist washing her hands between patients.

The statistical model for abnormality requires two statistical concepts: a measure of the average and a measure of deviation from average. In Chapter 3 we examined the standard techniques for defining the average score for a distribution. In this chapter we will examine methods for measuring deviations. The fact that scores deviate from average means that they are variable. Variability is one of the most basic statistical concepts. As an introduction to the concept, this chapter will concentrate on defining and measuring variability. In later chapters we will explore sources of variability and examine how variability affects the interpretation of other statistical measurements.

One additional point should be made before we proceed. You probably have noticed that central tendency and variability are closely related. Whenever one appears, the other usually is close at hand. You should watch for this association throughout the book. The better you understand the relations between central tendency and variability, the better you will understand statistics.

4.1 INTRODUCTION

The term *variability* has much the same meaning in statistics as it has in everyday language; to say that things are variable means that they are not all the same. In statistics our goal is to measure the amount of variability for a particular set of scores, a distribution. In simple terms, if the scores in a distribution are all the same, then there is no variability. If there are small differences between scores, then the variability is small, and if there are big differences between scores, then the variability is large.

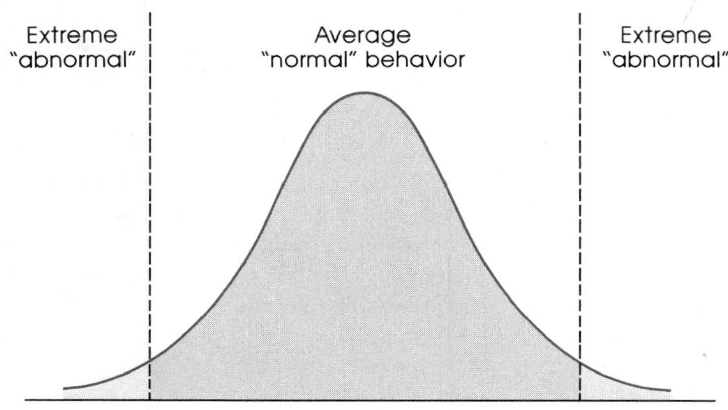

FIGURE 4.1

The statistical model for defining abnormal behavior. The distribution of behavior scores for the entire population is divided into three sections. Those individuals with average scores are defined as normal, and individuals who show extreme deviation from average are defined as abnormal.

· DEFINITION · *Variability* provides a quantitative measure of the degree to which scores in a distribution are spread out or clustered together.

The purpose of measuring variability is to determine how spread out a distribution of scores is. Are the scores all clustered close together, or are they scattered over a wide range of values? A good measure of variability should provide an accurate picture of the spread of the distribution. Variability, along with central tendency and shape, is one of the three basic descriptive indices that are used to describe distributions of scores.

In addition to providing a description of the distribution, a good measure of variability also serves two other valuable purposes. First, variability gives an indication of how accurately the mean describes the distribution. If the variability is small, then the scores are all close together, and each individual score is close to the mean. In this situation, the mean is a good representative of all the scores in the distribution. On the other hand, when variability is large, the scores are all spread out, and they are not necessarily close to the mean. In this case, the mean may be less representative of the whole distribution. To make this point more concrete, consider the two "games of chance" described in Perspective 4.1.

The second valuable purpose served by a good measure of variability is to give an indication of how well an individual score (or group of scores) represents the entire distribution. Although we usually will use the mean as the best representative score for a population, there are occasions where the mean is unknown. In these situations, a sample is selected from the population, and the sample is then used to represent the entire distribution. This is particularly important in the area of inferential statistics where relatively small samples are used to answer general questions about large populations. If the scores in a distribution are all clustered together (small variability), then any individual score will be a reasonably accurate representative of the entire distribution. But if the scores are all spread out, then a single value selected from the distribution often will not be representative of the rest of the group. This point also is illustrated in Perspective 4.1.

In this chapter we will consider three different measures of variability: the range, the interquartile range, and the standard deviation. Of these three, the standard deviation (and the related measure of variance) is by far the most important.

4.2 THE RANGE

· DEFINITION · The *range* is the distance between the largest score and the smallest score in a distribution. Once you have identified the highest and lowest scores, the range is determined by

$$\text{range} = \text{high} - \text{low} + 1$$

Remember, the +1 is included in this formula because both the high score and the low score are counted in determining the range. The range extends from the extreme lower real limit to the extreme upper real limit.

The range is perhaps the most obvious way of describing how spread out the scores are; simply find the distance from the biggest score to the smallest score. The problem with using the range as a measure of variability is that it is completely determined by the two extreme values and ignores the other scores in the distribution. For example, the following two distributions have exactly the same range, 10 points in each case. However, the scores in the first distribution are clustered together at one end of the range, whereas the scores in the second distribution are spread out over the entire range.

PERSPECTIVE 4.1

AN EXAMPLE OF VARIABILITY

To examine the role of variability, we will consider two games of chance.

For the first game you pay $1 to play, and you get back 90 cents every time. That's right, you pay me $1, and I give you back 90 cents. Notice that this game has no variability; exactly the same thing happens every time. On the average, you lose 10 cents each time you play, and, in this case, the average gives a perfect description of the outcome of the game.

For the second game the rules are a little different. It still costs $1 to play, but this time you have a 1-out-of-10 chance of winning $9. The rest of the time you win nothing. For this second game we have added variability; the outcomes are not all the same. Notice, however, that in the long run you still lose 10 cents each time you play. In 10 games, for example, you would expect to win once ($9), but you would have paid $10 to play. You expect to lose $1 during 10 games for an average loss of 10 cents per game.

On the average these two games are identical. But in one case the average perfectly describes every single outcome, and in the other case the average is not at all representative of what actually happens on any single trial. The difference between these two games is the variability.

You also should notice the number of times you would need to watch each game in order to understand it. For the first game, any individual outcome (pay $1 and get back 90 cents) gives a complete description of the game. After only one observation, you know the entire game. For the second game, however, you would need to watch a long time before the nature of the game became clear. In this case it would take a large sample to provide a good description of the game.

Distribution 1: 1, 8, 9, 9, 10, 10

Distribution 2: 1, 2, 4, 6, 8, 10

If, for example, these were scores on a 10-point quiz for two different class sections, there are clear differences between the two sections. Nearly all the students in the first section have mastered the material, but there is a wide range of different abilities for students in the second section. A good measure of variability should show this difference.

Because the range does not consider all the scores in the distribution, it often does not give an accurate description of the variability for the entire distribution. For this reason, the range is considered to be a crude and unreliable measure of variability.

4.3 THE INTERQUARTILE RANGE AND SEMI-INTERQUARTILE RANGE

In Chapter 3 we defined the median as the score that divides a distribution exactly in half. In a similar way, a distribution can be divided into four equal parts using quartiles. By definition, the first quartile ($Q1$) is the score that separates the lower 25% of the distribution from the rest. The second quartile ($Q2$) is the score that has exactly two quarters, or 50%, of the distribution below it. Notice that the second quartile and the median are the same. Finally, the third quartile ($Q3$) is the score that divides the bottom three-fourths of the distribution from the top quarter. The interquartile range is defined as the distance between the first and third quartiles.

DEFINITIONS The *interquartile range* is the distance between the first quartile and the third quartile:

$$\text{interquartile range} = Q3 - Q1$$

When the interquartile range is used to describe variability, it commonly is transformed into the *semi-interquartile range*. As the name implies, the semi-interquartile range is simply

· FIGURE 4.2 ·

Frequency distribution for a population of $N = 16$ scores. The first quartile is $Q1 = 4.5$. The third quartile is $Q3 = 8.0$. The interquartile range is 3.5 points.

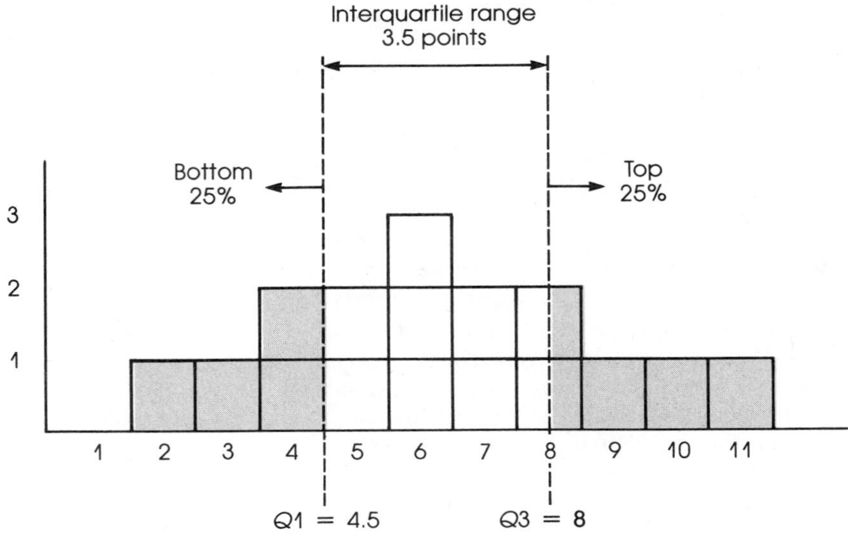

one-half of the interquartile range:

$$\text{semi-interquartile range} = \frac{(Q3 - Q1)}{2}$$

· EXAMPLE 4.1 · Figure 4.2 shows a frequency distribution histogram for a set of 16 scores. For this distribution the first quartile is $Q1 = 4.5$. Exactly 25% of the scores (4 out of 16) are located below $X = 4.5$. Similarly, the third quartile is $Q3 = 8.0$. Note that this value separates the bottom 75% of the distribution (12 out of 16 scores) from the top 25%. For this set of scores the interquartile range is

$$Q3 - Q1 = 8.0 - 4.5 = 3.5$$

The semi-interquartile range is simply one-half of this distance:

$$\text{semi-interquartile range} = \frac{3.5}{2} = 1.75$$

Note: We have used a relatively simple set of data for this example. For most situations, you would need to use interpolation to find $Q1$ and $Q3$ (see page 43)

Because the semi-interquartile range focuses on the middle 50% of a distribution, it is less likely to be influenced by extreme scores and, therefore, gives a better and more-stable measure of variability than the range. Nevertheless, the semi-interquartile range does not take into account the actual distances between individual scores, so it does not give a complete picture of how scattered or clustered the scores are. Like the range, the semi-interquartile range is considered to be a somewhat crude measure of variability.

· LEARNING CHECK ·

1 For the following data, find the range and the semi-interquartile range.

3, 4, 5, 7, 9, 10, 11, 13

2 Consider the distribution of exercise 1, except replace the score of 13 with a score

of 100. What are the new values for the range and the semi-interquartile range? In comparing the answer to the one of the previous problem, what can you conclude about these measures of variability?

ANSWERS

1 Range = high − low + 1 = 13 − 3 + 1 = 11; Semi-interquartile range = $(Q3 - Q1)/2 = (10.5 - 4.5)/2 = 3$.

2 Range = 98, semi-interquartile range = 3. The range is greatly affected by extreme scores in the distribution.

4.4 STANDARD DEVIATION AND VARIANCE FOR A POPULATION

The standard deviation is the most commonly used and the most important measure of variability. Standard deviation uses the mean of the distribution as a reference point and measures variability by considering the distance between each score and the mean. It determines whether the scores are generally near or far from the mean. That is, are the scores clustered together or scattered? In simple terms, the standard deviation approximates the average distance from the mean.

Although the concept of standard deviation is straightforward, the actual equations will appear complex. Therefore, we will begin by looking at the logic that leads to these equations. If you remember that our goal is to measure the average distance from the mean, then this logic and the equations that follow should be easier to remember.

STEP 1 The first step in finding the average distance from the mean is to determine the deviation, or distance from the mean, for each individual score. By definition, the deviation for each score is the difference between the score and the mean.

· DEFINITION · *Deviation* is distance from the mean:

deviation score = $X - \mu$

A deviation score occasionally is identified by a lowercase letter x.

For a distribution of scores with $\mu = 50$, if your score is $X = 53$, then your deviation score is

$$X - \mu = 53 - 50 = 3$$

If your score were $X = 45$, then your deviation score would be

$$X - \mu = 45 - 50 = -5$$

Notice that there are two parts to a deviation score: the sign (+ or −) and the number. The sign tells the direction from the mean, that is, whether the score is located above (+) or below (−) the mean. The number gives the actual distance from the mean. For example, a deviation score of −6 corresponds to score that is below the mean by six points.

STEP 2 *The Mean of the Deviation Scores.* Because our goal is to compute a measure of the average distance from the mean, the obvious next step is to calculate the mean of the deviation scores. To compute this mean, you first add up the deviation scores and then divide by N. This process is demonstrated in the following example.

EXAMPLE 4.2 We start with the following set of $N = 4$ scores. These scores add up to $\sum X = 12$, so the mean is $\mu = \frac{12}{4} = 3$. For each score we have computed the deviation.

X	$X - \mu$
8	+5
1	−2
3	0
0	−3
	$0 = \sum(X - \mu)$

Remember, the mean is the balancing point for the distribution.

Notice that the deviation scores add up to zero. This should not be surprising if you remember that the mean serves as a balance point for the distribution. The distances above the mean are equal to the distances below the mean (see page 67). Logically, the deviation scores must *always* add up to zero.

Because the mean deviation is always zero, it is of no value as a measure of variability. It is zero whether the scores are grouped together or are all scattered out. The mean deviation score provides no information about variability. (You should note, however, that the constant value of zero can be useful in other ways. Whenever you are working with deviation scores, you can check your calculations by making sure that the deviation scores add up to zero.)

STEP 3 The reason that the average of the deviation scores will not work as a measure of variability is that it is always zero. Clearly, this problem results from the positive and negative values canceling each other out. The solution is to get rid of the signs (+ and −). The standard procedure for accomplishing this is to square each deviation score. Before we look at this process, however, we will briefly consider what appears to be a more direct solution; that is, just ignore the signs and use the absolute values of the deviation scores. This procedure will give us what is literally the average distance from the mean or what is called the average deviation.

DEFINITION *Average deviation* is the average of the absolute values of the deviation scores.

To find the absolute value of a number, remove the sign (+ or −) and consider only the magnitude. The absolute value of −3 is 3.

But there is a serious problem with this measure of variability. You should recall that one of the basic principles of statistics is that samples should be representative of the populations they come from. The average deviation violates this principle. The average deviation computed from a sample bears no consistent relationship to the average deviation for its population. Therefore, the sample value will not be representative of the population. For this reason, the average deviation is said to be *unstable under sampling* and is of little value as a measure of variability, especially for inferential statistics.

As noted earlier, the standard procedure of getting rid of the plus and minus signs is to square each deviation score. Using these squared values, you then compute the average squared deviation, which is called variance.

DEFINITION *Population variance* = average squared deviation.

We should note that the process of squaring deviation scores does much more than simply get rid of plus and minus signs. In fact, there is a sophisticated system of mathematical techniques that has been developed for use with squared values. By defining variance in terms of squared deviations, it becomes possible to take advantage of these techniques whenever variance is used as the measure of variability. As a result, variance fits into a mathematical system that can be used to develop other statistical procedures. This makes variance an extremely valuable measure of variability.

STEP 4 Remember that our goal is to compute a measure of the average distance from the mean. Although variance is not exactly what we want, it is a step in the right direction. Variance is the average squared deviation, or the average squared distance from the mean. The final step simply makes a correction for having squared all the distances. Standard deviation is the square root of the variance.

· DEFINITION · *Standard deviation* $= \sqrt{\text{variance}}$.

Technically, standard deviation is the square root of the average squared deviation. But standard deviation is easier to understand if you think of it as describing the average distance from the mean. As the name implies, standard deviation measures the standard, or typical, deviation score.

FORMULAS FOR POPULATION STANDARD DEVIATION AND VARIANCE

The concept of standard deviation (or variance) is the same for a sample as for a population. However, the details of the calculations differ slightly depending on whether you have sample data or a complete population. Therefore, we will consider samples and populations separately, beginning with the formulas for a population.

Variance, you should recall, is defined as the average squared deviation. This average is computed exactly the same way you compute any average: First find the sum; then divide by the number of scores:

$$\text{variance} = \text{average squared deviation} = \frac{\text{sum of squared deviations}}{\text{number of scores}}$$

The value in the numerator of this equation, the sum of the squared deviations, is a basic component of variability, and we will focus on it. To simplify things, it is identified by the notation *SS* (for sum of squared deviations), and it generally is referred to as the *sum of squares.*

· DEFINITION · *SS*, or *sum of squares,* is the sum of the squared deviation scores.

There are two formulas you will need to know in order to compute *SS*. These formulas are algebraically equivalent (they always produce the same answer), but they look different and are used in different situations.

The first of these formulas is called the definitional formula because the terms in the formula literally define the process of adding up the squared deviations:

(4.1) Definitional formula: $SS = \sum(X - \mu)^2$

Note that the formula directs you to square each deviation score $(X - \mu)^2$ and then add them up. The result is the sum of the squared deviations, or *SS*. Following is an example using this formula.

· EXAMPLE 4.3 · We will compute *SS* for the following set of $N = 4$ scores. These scores add up to $\sum X = 8$, so the mean is $\mu = \frac{8}{4} = 2$. For each score, we have computed the deviation and the squared deviation. The squared deviations add up to $SS = 22$.

Caution: The definitional formula requires that you first square the deviations and then add them.

X	$X - \mu$	$(X - \mu)^2$	
1	-1	1	$\sum X = 8$
0	-2	4	$\mu = 2$
6	$+4$	16	
1	-1	1	
		$22 = \sum(X - \mu)^2$	

The second formula for *SS* is called the computational formula (or the machine formula) because it works directly with the scores (*X* values) and, therefore, is generally easier to use for calculations, especially with an electronic calculator:

(4.2) Computational formula; $SS = \sum X^2 - \frac{(\sum X)^2}{N}$

The first part of this formula directs you to square each score and then add them up ($\sum X^2$). The second part requires you to add up the scores ($\sum X$) and then square this total and divide the result by *N* (see Perspective 4.2). The use of this formula is shown in Example 4.4 with the same set of scores we used for the definitional formula.

· EXAMPLE 4.4 · The computational formula is used to calculate *SS* for the same set of $N = 4$ scores we used in Example 4.3. First, compute $\sum X$. Then square each score and compute $\sum X^2$. These two values are used in the formula.

X	X^2	
1	1	$\sum X = 8$
0	0	
6	36	$\sum X^2 = 38$
1	1	

$$
\begin{aligned}
SS &= \sum X^2 - \frac{(\sum X)^2}{N} \\
&= 38 - \frac{(8)^2}{4} \\
&= 38 - \frac{64}{4} \\
&= 38 - 16 \\
&= 22
\end{aligned}
$$

Notice that the two formulas produce exactly the same value for *SS*. Although the formulas look different, they are in fact equivalent. The definitional formula should be very easy to learn if you simply remember that *SS* stands for the sum of the squared deviations. If you use notation to write out "the sum of" ($\sum$) "squared deviations" $(X - \mu)^2$, then you have the definitional formula. Unfortunately, the terms in the computational formula do not translate directly into "sum of squared deviations," so you simply need to memorize this formula.

The definitional formula for *SS* is the most direct way of calculating sum of squares, but it can be awkward to use for most sets of data. In particular, if the mean

PERSPECTIVE 4.2

COMPUTING SS WITH A CALCULATOR

The computational formula for SS is intended to simplify calculations, especially when you are using an electronic calculator. The following steps outline the most efficient procedure for using a typical, inexpensive hand calculator to find SS. (We assume that your calculator has one memory, where you can store and retrieve information.) The computational formula for SS is presented here for easy reference.

$$SS = \sum X^2 - \frac{(\sum X)^2}{N}$$

STEP 1: The first term in the computational formula is $\sum X^2$. The procedure for finding this sum is described in Perspective 1.3 on page 20. Once you have calculated $\sum X^2$, write this sum on a piece of paper so you don't lose it. Leave $\sum X^2$ in the calculator memory and go to the next step.

STEP 2: Now you must find the sum of the scores, $\sum X$. We assume that you can add a set of numbers with your calculator—just be sure to press the equals key (=) after the last score. Write this total on your paper. (*Note:* You may want to clear the calculator display before you begin this process. It is not necessary, but you may feel more comfortable starting with zero.)

STEP 3: Now you are ready to plug the sums into the formula. Your calculator should still have the sum of the scores, $\sum X$, in the display. If not, enter this value.

1. With $\sum X$ in the display, you can compute $(\sum X)^2$ simply by pressing the multiply key ($\times$) and then the equals key (=).
2. Now you must divide the squared sum by N, the number of scores. Assuming that you have counted the number of scores, just press the divide key ($\div$), enter N, and then press the equals key.

Your calculator display now shows $(\sum X)^2/N$. Write this number on your paper.

3. Finally, you subtract the value in your calculator display from $\sum X^2$, which is in the calculator memory. You can do this by simply pressing the memory subtract key (usually M−). The value for SS is now in memory, and you can retrieve it by pressing the memory recall key (MR).

Try the whole procedure with a simple set of scores such as 1, 2, 3. You should obtain $SS = 2$ for these scores.

We asked you to write down values at several steps during the calculation in case you make a mistake at some point. If you have written down the values for $\sum X^2$, $\sum X$, and so on, you should be able to compute SS easily even if the contents of memory were lost.

is not a whole number, then the deviation scores will all be fractions or decimals, and the calculations become difficult. In addition, calculations with decimals or fractions introduce the opportunity for rounding error, which makes the results less accurate. For these reasons, the computational formula is used most of the time. If you have a small group of scores and the mean is a whole number, then the definitional formula is fine; otherwise, use the computational formula.

With the definition and calculation of SS behind you, the equations for variance and standard deviation become relatively simple. Remember, variance is defined as the average squared deviation. The average is the sum divided by N, so the equation for variance is

$$\text{variance} = \frac{SS}{N}$$

Standard deviation is the square root of variance, so the equation for standard deviation is

$$\text{standard deviation} = \sqrt{\frac{SS}{N}}$$

There is one final bit of notation before we work completely through an example computing SS, variance, and standard deviation. Like the mean (μ), variance and standard deviation are parameters of a population and will be identified by Greek letters. To identify the standard deviation, we use the Greek letter sigma (the Greek letter *s*, standing for standard deviation). The capital letter sigma ($\sum$) has been used already, so we now use the lowercase sigma, σ:

(4.3) $$\text{population standard deviation} = \sigma = \sqrt{\frac{SS}{N}}$$

The symbol for population variance should help you remember the relation between standard deviation and variance. If you square the standard deviation, you will get the variance. The symbol for variance is sigma squared, σ^2:

(4.4) $$\text{population variance} = \sigma^2 = \frac{SS}{N}$$

· EXAMPLE 4.5 · The following population of scores will be used to demonstrate the calculation of *SS*, variance, and standard deviation:

1, 9, 5, 8, 7

These five scores add up to $\sum X = 30$, so the mean is $\frac{30}{5} = 6$. Before we do any other calculations, remember that the purpose of variability is to determine how spread out the scores are. Standard deviation accomplishes this by providing a measurement of the standard distance from the mean. The scores we are working with have been placed in a frequency distribution histogram in Figure 4.3 so you can see the variability more easily. Note that the score closest to the mean is $X = 5$ or $X = 7$, both of which are only 1 point away. The score farthest from the mean is $X = 1$, and it is 5 points away. For this distribution, the biggest distance from the mean is five points, and the smallest distance is one point. The average, or standard, distance should be somewhere between 1 and 5. By looking quickly at a distribution in this way, you should be able to make a rough estimate of the standard deviation. In this case, the standard deviation should be between 1 and 5, probably around 3 points. Making a preliminary judgment of standard deviation can help you avoid errors in calculation. If, for example, you worked through the formulas and ended up with a value of $\sigma = 12$, you should realize immediately that you have made an error. (If the biggest deviation is only 5 points, then it is impossible for the standard deviation to be 12.)

Now we will start the calculations. The first step is to find *SS* for this set of scores.

· FIGURE 4.3 ·

A frequency distribution histogram for a population of $N = 5$ scores. The mean for this population is $\mu = 6$. The smallest distance from the mean is one point, and the largest distance is five points. The standard distance (or standard deviation) should be between one and five points.

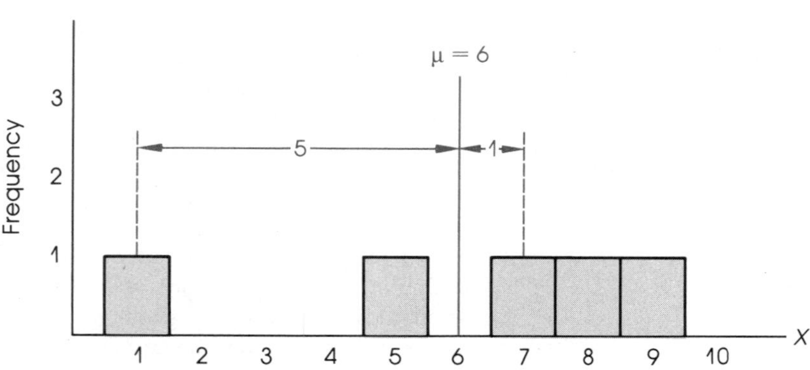

Because the mean is a whole number ($\mu = 6$), we can use the definitional formula for SS:

X	$X - \mu$	$(X - \mu)^2$	
1	-5	25	$\sum X = 30$
9	$+3$	9	$\mu = 6$
5	-1	1	
8	$+2$	4	
7	$+1$	1	
		$40 = \sum(X - \mu)^2 = SS$	

$$\sigma^2 = \frac{SS}{N}$$

$$= \frac{40}{5} = 8$$

$$\sigma = \sqrt{8} = 2.83$$

For this set of scores, the variance is $\sigma^2 = 8$, and the standard deviation is $\sigma = \sqrt{8} = 2.83$. Note that the value for the standard deviation is in excellent agreement with our preliminary estimate of the standard distance from the mean. •

· LEARNING CHECK ·

1 Write brief definitions of variance and standard deviation.

2 Find SS, variance, and standard deviation for the following population of scores: 10, 10, 10, 10, 10. (*Note:* You should be able to answer this question without doing any calculations.)

3 **a** Sketch a frequency distribution histogram for the following population of scores: 1, 3, 3, 9. Using this histogram, make an estimate of the standard deviation (i.e., the standard distance from the mean.)

b Calculate SS, variance, the standard deviation for these scores. How well does your estimate from part a compare with the real standard deviation?

ANSWERS

1 Variance is the average squared distance from the mean. Standard deviation is the square root of variance and provides a measure of the standard distance from the mean.

2 Because there is no variability in the population, SS, variance, and standard deviation are all equal to zero.

3 **a** Your sketch should show a mean of $\mu = 4$. The score closest to the mean is $X = 3$, and the farthest score is $X = 9$. The standard deviation should be somewhere between one point and five points.

b For this population, $SS = 36$; the variance is $\frac{36}{4} = 9$; the standard deviation is $\sqrt{9} = 3$.

GRAPHIC REPRESENTATION OF THE MEAN AND STANDARD DEVIATION

In frequency distribution graphs we will identify the position of the mean by drawing a vertical line and labeling it with μ or $\overline{X}$ (see Figure 4.4). Because the standard deviation measures distance from the mean, it will be represented by a line drawn from the mean outward for a distance equal to the standard deviation (see Figure 4.4). For rough sketches, you can identify the mean with a vertical line in the middle of the distribution. The standard deviation line should extend approximately halfway from the mean to the most extreme score.

FIGURE 4.4

The graphic representation of a population with a mean of $\mu = 40$ and a standard deviation of $\sigma = 4$.

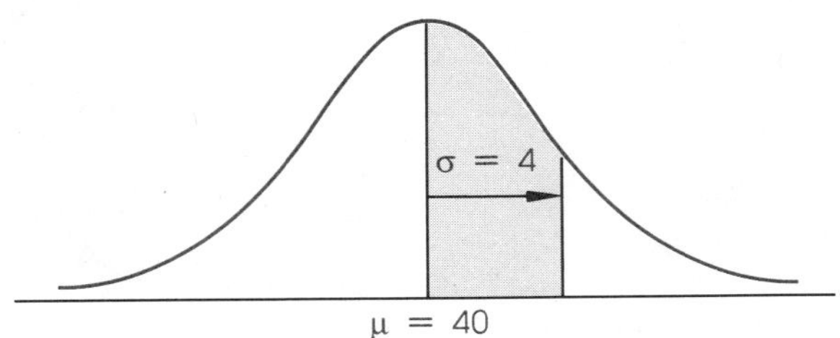

4.5 STANDARD DEVIATION AND VARIANCE FOR SAMPLES

The goal of inferential statistics is to use the limited information from samples to draw general conclusions about populations. The basic assumption of this process is that samples should be representative of the populations from which they come. This assumption poses a special problem for variability because samples consistently tend to be less variable than their populations. An example of this general tendency is shown in Figure 4.5. The fact that a sample tends to be less variable than its population means that sample variability gives a *biased* estimate of population variability. This bias is in the direction of underestimating the population value rather than being right on the mark. To correct for this bias, it is necessary to make an adjustment in the calculation of variability when you are working with sample data. The intent of the adjustment is to make the resulting value for sample variability a more accurate estimate of the population variability.

A sample statistic is said to be *biased* if, on the average, it does not provide an accurate estimate of the corresponding population parameter.

To compute sample variability, we begin by defining the deviation for each score in the sample. As before, deviation measures the distance from the mean, but now we are using the sample mean in place of the population mean:

$$\text{sample deviation score} = X - \overline{X} \tag{4.5}$$

The deviation scores will have a sign and a magnitude. The sign tells the direction from the mean (+ for above, − for below), and the magnitude tells the distance from the mean. The deviation scores always add up to zero.

Variance and standard deviation for sample data have the same basic definitions as they do for populations: Variance measures the average squared distance from the

FIGURE 4.5

The population of adult heights forms a normal distribution. If you select a sample from this population, you are most likely to obtain individuals who are near average in height. As a result, the scores in the sample will be less variable (spread out) than the scores in the population.

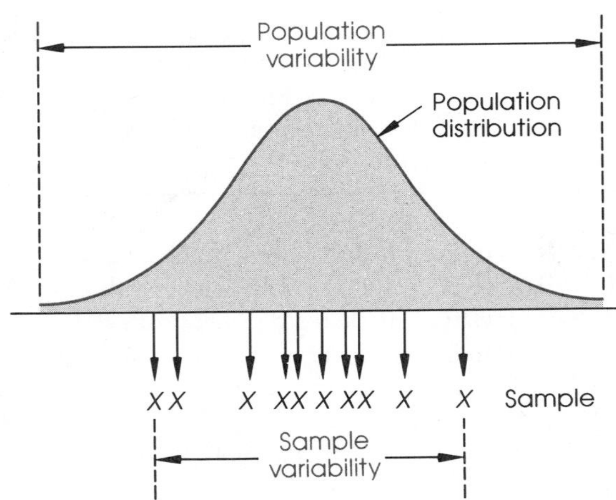

mean, and standard deviation is the square root of variance. To compute the values, we first will need to find *SS*, the sum of squared deviations. The formulas we use to compute sample *SS* are essentially identical to the formulas used for populations:

(4.6) Definitional formula: $SS = \sum(X - \overline{X})^2$

(4.7) Computational formula: $SS = \sum X^2 - \dfrac{(\sum X)^2}{n}$

Note that the only difference between these formulas and the population formulas is a minor change in notation. We have substituted $\overline{X}$ in place of μ and n in place of N. For all practical purposes the population and sample formulas for *SS* are interchangeable. The difference in notation will have no effect on the calculations.

After you compute *SS*, however, it becomes critical to differentiate between samples and populations. To correct for the bias in sample variability, it is necessary to make an adjustment in the formulas for sample variance and standard deviation. With this in mind, sample variance (identified by the symbol s^2) is defined as

(4.8) $$\text{sample variance} = s^2 = \frac{SS}{n - 1}$$

Sample standard deviation (identified by the symbol s) is simply the square root of the variance:

(4.9) $$\text{sample standard deviation} = s = \sqrt{\frac{SS}{n - 1}}$$

Remember, sample variability tends to underestimate population variability unless some correction is made.

Notice that these sample formulas use $n - 1$ instead of n. This is the adjustment that is necessary to correct for the bias in sample variability. The effect of the adjustment is to increase the value you will obtain. Dividing by a smaller number ($n - 1$ instead of n) produces a larger result and makes sample variability an accurate, or unbiased, estimator of population variability. (See Perspective 4.3.)

A complete example showing the calculation of sample variance and standard deviation will now be worked out.

· EXAMPLE 4.6 · We have selected a sample of $n = 7$ scores from a population. The scores are 1, 6, 4, 3, 8, 7, 6. The frequency distribution histogram for this sample is shown in Figure 4.6. Before we begin any calculations, you should be able to look at the sample distribution and make a preliminary estimate of the outcome. Remember that standard deviation measures the standard distance from the mean. For this sample the mean is $\overline{X} = 5$ ($\frac{35}{7} = 5$). The scores closest to the mean are $X = 4$ and $X = 6$, both of which are exactly 1 point away. The score farthest from the mean is $X = 1$, which is 4 points away. With the smallest distance from the

· FIGURE 4.6 ·

The frequency distribution histogram for a sample of $n = 7$ scores. The sample mean is $\overline{X} = 5$. The smallest distance from the mean is one point, and the largest distance from the mean is four points. The standard distance (standard deviation) should be between one and four points.

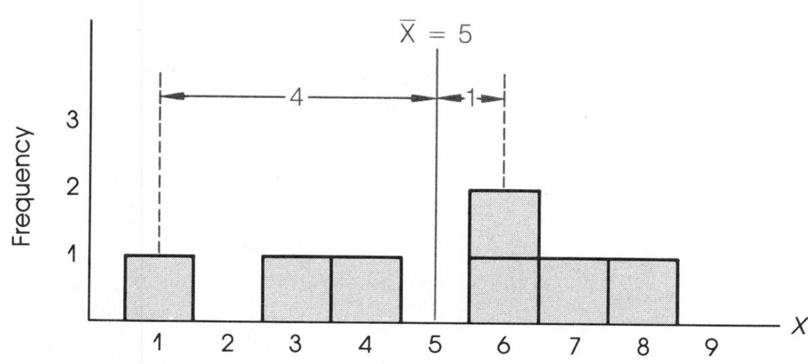

PERSPECTIVE 4.3

USING $n - 1$ TO COMPUTE SAMPLE VARIANCE

The purpose of this example is to demonstrate that using $n - 1$ to compute sample variance produces an unbiased estimate of the population variance. We begin with a very simple population consisting of only four scores: 1, 1, 3, 3. The mean for this population is $\mu = 2$ (halfway between the 1s and the 3s). Note that all the scores in the population are exactly one point away from the mean. Because all the deviations are equal to 1, the standard deviation will be $\sigma = 1$. Therefore, the variance for this population is $\sigma^2 = 1$. (Try computing the variance directly to check this reasoning.)

If you select a sample of $n = 2$ scores from this population, there are only four possible samples that could be obtained. These four samples are listed in Table 4.1.

The next column in the table shows SS for each sample. Note that two of the samples have no variability, so $SS = 0$. For the other two samples, both scores are exactly one point from the mean, so SS (the sum of squared deviations) would be $1 + 1 = 2$.

Next we compute variance for each sample using the $SS/(n - 1)$ formula. And we have computed the variance values that would be obtained using n instead of $n - 1$. These values are shown in the last two columns of the table.

Now look at the four sample variances that were obtained using $n - 1$. These four values add up to 4 $(0 + 2 + 2 + 0)$, so the average is 1. Note that the average of the sample variances is exactly equal to the population variance. This is what is meant when we say that sample variance (using $n - 1$) is an unbiased estimator of population variance. On the average, this sample variance will give a precise estimate of the population variance. Now consider what happens if you were to use n in the formula for sample variance. In this case the four values add up to 2 $(0 + 1 + 1 + 0)$, so the average is $\frac{1}{2}$. Notice that on average this measure of sample variance underestimates the population variance. Using n, instead of $n - 1$, results in a biased measure of sample variance.

TABLE 4.1

All the possible random samples of size $n = 2$ selected from a population consisting of four scores (1, 1, 3, 3)[a]

Sample	First Score	Second Score	Sample SS	Sample Variance Using $n - 1$	Sample Variance Using n
1	1	1	0	0	0
2	1	3	2	2	1
3	3	1	2	2	1
4	3	3	0	0	0

[a]The final two columns show the unbiased variance (using $n - 1$) for each sample and the biased variance (using n).

mean equal to 1 and the largest distance equal to 4, we should obtain a standard distance somewhere around 2.5 (between 1 and 4).

Now let's begin the calculations. First, we will find SS for this sample. Because there are only a few scores and the mean is a whole number, the definitional formula will be easy to use. You should try this formula for practice. Meanwhile, we will work with the computational formula.

X	X^2	
1	1	$\sum X = 35$
6	36	$\sum X^2 = 211$
4	16	
3	9	
8	64	
7	49	
6	36	

Caution: For sample variance, you use $n - 1$ after calculating SS. Do not use $n - 1$ in the formula for SS.

$$SS = \sum X^2 - \frac{(\sum X)^2}{n}$$

$$= 211 - \frac{(35)^2}{7}$$

$$= 211 - \frac{1225}{7}$$

$$= 211 - 175$$

$$= 36$$

SS for this sample is 36. You should obtain exactly the same answer using the definitional formula. Continuing the calculations,

$$\text{sample variance} = s^2 = \frac{SS}{n - 1} = \frac{36}{7 - 1} = 6$$

Finally, the standard deviation is

$$s = \sqrt{s^2} = \sqrt{6} = 2.45$$

Note that the value we obtained is in excellent agreement with our preliminary prediction. •

Remember that the formulas for sample variance and standard deviation were constructed so that the sample variability would provide a good estimate of population variability. For this reason, sample variance is often called *estimated population variance,* and the sample standard deviation is called *estimated population standard deviation.* When you have only a sample to work with, the sample variance and standard deviation provide the best possible estimates of the population variability.

STANDARD DEVIATION ON THE COMPUTER Computer software packages typically provide information about variability for a distribution. Values for standard deviation, for example, are often provided automatically with many of the more-complex statistical analyses. Most packages also have programs that perform basic summary statistics analyses. These provide information about central tendency and variability.

Table 4.2 shows a Minitab printout of descriptive statistics for the data in Example 4.6. This printout was generated by the Minitab command DESCRIBE. As noted before, the computer analysis is especially helpful with very large distributions. It spares you the task of tedious computations and reduces the likelihood of computational errors. An explanation of the printout is given in Table 4.2.

· LEARNING CHECK ·

1 a Sketch a frequency distribution histogram for the following sample of scores: 1, 1, 9, 1. Using your histogram, make an estimate of the standard deviation for this sample.

b Calculate SS, variance, and standard deviation for this sample. How well does your estimate from part a compare with the real standard deviation?

2 If the scores in the previous exercise were a population, what value would you obtain for SS?

3 If the scores in exercise 1 were a population, would you obtain a larger or smaller value for the standard deviation? Explain your answer.

ANSWERS

1 a Your graph should show a sample mean of $\overline{X} = 3$. The score farthest from the mean is $X = 9$, and the closest score is $X = 1$. You should estimate the standard deviation to be between two points and six points.

b For this sample, $SS = 48$; the sample variance is $\frac{48}{3} = 16$; the sample standard deviation is $\sqrt{16} = 4$.

2 $SS = 48$ whether the data are from a sample or a population.

3 Smaller. The formulas for sample data increase the size of variance and standard deviation by dividing by $n - 1$ instead of N. The population formulas will produce smaller values.

TABLE 4.2

A Minitab analysis for descriptive statistics of the data in Example 4.6.

```
MINITAB RELEASE 5.1 *** COPYRIGHT - MINITAB, INC. 1985
U.S. FEDERAL GOVERNMENT USERS SEE HELP FGU
JUNE 17, 1986 *** S.U.N.Y. BROCKPORT - ACADEMIC COMPUTING SERVICES
STORAGE AVAILABLE 260144

 Type NEWS for information on new features in Minitab Release 5.1
```

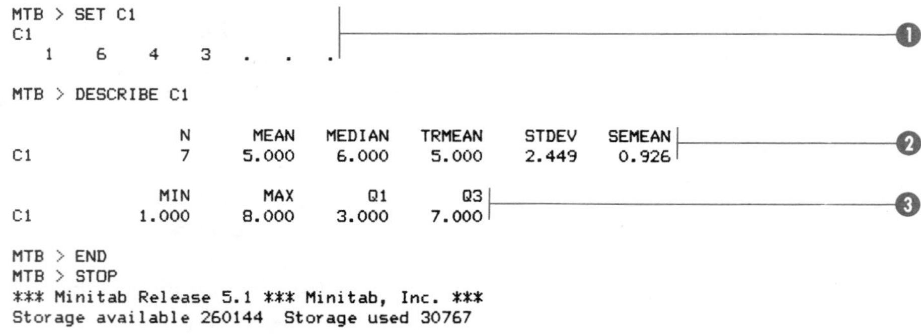

```
MTB > SET C1
C1
   1    6    4    3   .   .   .                                        ❶

MTB > DESCRIBE C1

               N      MEAN    MEDIAN    TRMEAN     STDEV    SEMEAN
C1             7     5.000     6.000     5.000     2.449     0.926     ❷

             MIN       MAX        Q1        Q3
C1         1.000     8.000     3.000     7.000                         ❸

MTB > END
MTB > STOP
*** Minitab Release 5.1 *** Minitab, Inc. ***
Storage available 260144  Storage used 30767
```

EXPLANATION OF PRINTOUT:

1 Minitab provides a partial data list consisting of the first few scores.

2 Relevant to this chapter, Minitab yields values for sample size (N), the mean, the median, and the standard deviation (STDEV).

3 The smallest (MIN) and largest (MAX) values in the distribution are printed. With this information you can easily calculate the range. Also the values for the first ($Q1$) and third ($Q3$) quartiles are determined. These values allow you to compute the interquartile range and the semi-interquartile range.

SAMPLE VARIABILITY AND DEGREES OF FREEDOM

Although the concept of a deviation score and the calculation of *SS* are almost exactly the same for samples and populations, the minor differences in notation are really very important. When you have only a sample to work with, you must use the sample mean as the reference point for measuring deviations. Using $\overline{X}$ in place of μ places a restriction on the amount of variability in the sample. The restriction on variability comes from the fact that you must know the value of $\overline{X}$ before you can begin to compute deviations or *SS*. Notice that if you know the value of $\overline{X}$, then you also must know the value of $\sum X$. For example, if you have a sample of $n = 3$ scores and you know that $\overline{X} = 10$, then you also know that $\sum X$ must be equal to 30 ($\overline{X} = \sum X/n$).

The fact that you must know $\overline{X}$ and $\sum X$ before you can compute variability implies that not all of the scores in the sample are free to vary. Suppose, for example, that you are taking a sample of $n = 3$ scores and you know that $\sum X = 30$ ($\overline{X} = 10$). Once you have identified the first two scores in the sample, the value of the third score is restricted. If the first scores were $X = 0$ and $X = 5$, then the last score would have to be $X = 25$ in order for the total to be $\sum X = 30$. Note that the first scores in this sample could have any values but that the last score is restricted. As a result, the sample is said to have $n - 1$ degrees of freedom; that is, only $n - 1$ of the scores are free to vary.

DEFINITION *Degrees of freedom,* or *df,* for a sample are defined as

$$df = n - 1$$

where n is the number of scores in the sample.

The $n - 1$ degrees of freedom for a sample is the same $n - 1$ that is used in the formulas for sample variance and standard deviation. Remember that variance is defined as the average squared deviation. As always, this average is computed by finding the sum and dividing by the number of scores:

$$\text{average} = \frac{\text{sum}}{\text{number}}$$

To calculate sample variance (average squared deviation), we find the sum of the squared deviations (*SS*) and divide by the number of scores that are free to vary. This number is $n - 1 = df$.

$$s^2 = \frac{\text{sum of squared deviations}}{\text{number of scores free to vary}} = \frac{SS}{df} = \frac{SS}{n-1}$$

Later in this book we will use the concept of degrees of freedom in other situations. For now, you should remember that knowing the sample mean places a restriction on sample variability. Only $n - 1$ of the scores are free to vary; $df = n - 1$.

4.6 PROPERTIES OF THE STANDARD DEVIATION

Because standard deviation requires extensive calculations, there is a tendency for many students to get lost in the arithmetic and forget what standard deviation is and why it is useful. As a measure of variability, standard deviation has the general purpose of describing the extent to which a set of scores is spread out or clustered together. As the name implies, standard deviation measures the standard distance from the mean—are the scores all clustered close to *u*, or are the scores all spread out at great distances from the mean?

Figure 4.7 shows two distributions of quiz scores. Both distributions have $\mu = 20$, but one distribution has small variability, $\sigma = 2$, and the other has larger variability,

FIGURE 4.7

Two hypothetical distributions of test scores for a statistics class. For both distributions, $N = 16$ and $\mu = 20$. In distribution A, where there is little variability, a score of 22 is nearly the top score. In distribution B there is more variability, and the same score occupies a more central position in the distribution.

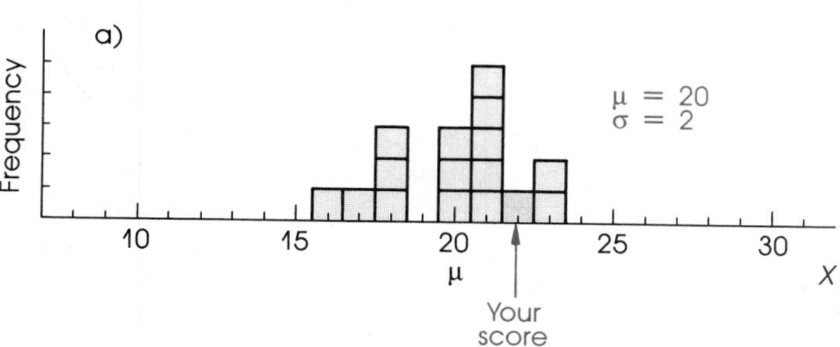

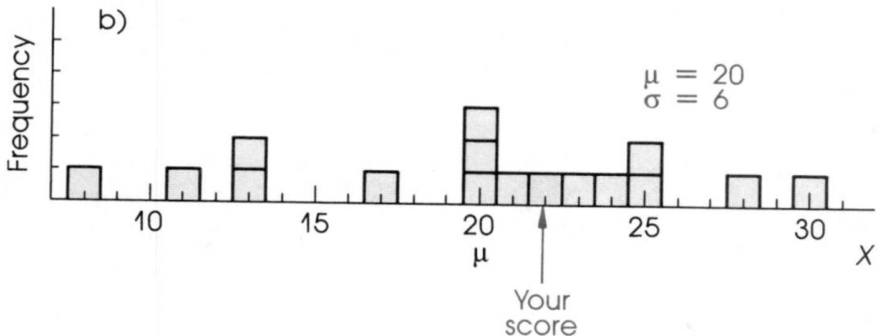

$\sigma = 6$. For one group, the students are all very similar in terms of their quiz performance. For the second group, there are huge differences in performance from one student to the next. You also should recognize that the same score (X value) can have very different meanings in these two distributions. For example, a score of $X = 22$ is one of the highest scores in the low variability group, but it is only average in the high variability distribution.

Standard deviation also helps researchers make predictions about sample data. Referring to the two distributions in Figure 4.7, if you were to select a single score from the low-variability population, you could be very confident of obtaining a value close to $\mu = 20$. On the other hand, you have a much greater chance of obtaining an extreme score if you are picking from the high-variability distribution.

In later chapters you will see that standard deviation plays a valuable role in inferential statistics. You should recall that inferential statistics use sample data to draw inferences about populations. If a sample comes from a population with low variability, you can be reasonably confident that the sample provides a good representation of the general population. But when the standard deviation is large, extreme samples are possible, and any single sample may not accurately reflect the population.

In summary, you should realize that standard deviation is a valuable measure. It will appear repeatedly throughout the remainder of this book.

TRANSFORMATIONS OF SCALE

Occasionally it is convenient to transform a set of scores by adding a constant to each score or by multiplying each score by a constant value. This is done, for example, when you want to "curve" a set of exam scores by adding a fixed amount to each individual's grade or when you want to change the scale of measurement (to convert from minutes to seconds, multiply each X by 60). What happens to the standard deviation when the scores are transformed in this manner?

The easiest way to determine the effect of a transformation is to remember that the standard deviation is a measure of distance. If you select any two scores and see what happens to the distance between them, you also will find out what happens to the standard deviation.

1. *Adding a constant to each score will not change the standard deviation.* If you begin with a distribution that has $\mu = 40$ and $\sigma = 10$, what happens to σ if you add 5 points to every score? Consider any two scores in this distribution: Suppose, for example, that these are exam scores and that you had $X = 41$ and your friend had $X = 43$. The distance between these two scores is $43 - 41 = 2$ points. After adding the constant, 5 points, to each score, your score would be $X = 46$, and your friend would have $X = 48$. The distance between scores is still 2 points. Adding a constant to every score will not affect any of the distances and, therefore, will not change the standard deviation. This fact can be seen clearly if you imagine a frequency distribution graph. If, for example, you add 10 points to each score, then every score in the graph would be moved 10 points to the right. The result is that the entire distribution is shifted to a new position 10 points up the scale. Note that the mean moves along with the scores and is increased by 10 points. However, the variability does not change because each of the deviation scores $(X - \mu)$ does not change.

2. *Multiplying each score by a constant causes the standard deviation to be multiplied by the same constant.* Consider the same distribution of exam scores we looked at earlier. If $\mu = 40$ and $\sigma = 10$, what would happen to σ if each score were multiplied by 2? Again we will look at two scores, $X = 41$ and $X = 43$, with a distance between them equal to 2 points. After all the scores have been multiplied by 2, these scores would become $X = 82$ and $X = 86$. Now the distance between scores is 4 points,

twice the original distance. Multiplying each score causes each distance to be multiplied, and so the standard deviation also is multiplied by the same amount.

The effect of multiplying each score by a constant is demonstrated in the following example.

· EXAMPLE 4.7 · We begin with a sample of $n = 5$ scores. These scores add up to $\sum X = 15$, so the mean is $\overline{X} = 3$. The deviations and squared deviations are computed for each score, and then the squared deviations are added up to find *SS*. Finally, the variance and standard deviation are computed, and we find that $s = 2$ points.

X	$X - \overline{X}$	$(X - \overline{X})^2$
0	−3	9
4	+1	1
5	+2	4
2	−1	1
4	+1	1
		$16 = \sum(X - \overline{X})^2$

$$s^2 = \frac{SS}{n-1} = \frac{16}{4} = 4$$

$$s = \sqrt{s^2} = \sqrt{4} = 2$$

Now each score is multiplied by 3, and we repeat the calculations. Note that the scores now add up to $\sum X = 45$, so the new mean is $\overline{X} = 9$ (three times the original mean).

X	$X - \overline{X}$	$(X - \overline{X})^2$
0	−9	81
12	+3	9
15	+6	36
6	−3	9
12	+3	9
		$144 = \sum(X - \overline{X})^2$

$$s^2 = \frac{SS}{n-1} = \frac{144}{4} = 36$$

$$s = \sqrt{s^2} = \sqrt{36} = 6$$

Notice that multiplying the scores by 3 causes each deviation and the standard deviation also to be multiplied by 3.

Multiplying each score by a constant value is a commonly used method for changing the unit of measurement. If the original scores in this example were measurements in yards, then the mean is $\overline{X} = 3$ yards, and the standard deviation is $s = 2$ yards. Multiplying by 3 would convert the measurements from yards to feet. After multiplying by 3, we find that the mean has been converted to $\overline{X} = 9$ feet, and the standard deviation has been converted to $s = 6$ feet. ·

4.7 COMPARING MEASURES OF VARIABILITY

By far the most commonly used measure of variability is standard deviation (together with the related measure of variance). Nonetheless, there are situations where the range or the semi-interquartile range may be preferred. The advantages and disadvantages of each of these three measures will be discussed.

In simple terms, there are two considerations that determine the value of any statistical measurement:

1. The measure should provide a stable and reliable description of the scores. Specifically, it should not be greatly affected by minor details in the set of data.
2. The measure should have a consistent and predictable relationship with other statistical measurements.

We will examine each of these considerations separately.

FACTORS THAT AFFECT VARIABILITY

1. *Extreme Scores.* Of the three measures of variability, the range is most affected by extreme scores. A single extreme value will have a large influence on the range. In fact, the range is determined exclusively by the two extremes of the distribution. Standard deviation and variance also are influenced by extreme scores. Because these measures are based on squared deviations, a single extreme value can have a disproportionate effect. For example, a score that is 10 points away from the mean will contribute $10^2 = 100$ points to the *SS*. For this reason, standard deviation and variance should be interpreted carefully in distributions with one or two extreme values. Because the semi-interquartile range focuses on the middle of the distribution, it is least affected by extreme values. For this reason, the semi-interquartile range often provides the best measure of variability for distributions that are very skewed or that have a few extreme scores.

2. *Sample Size.* As you increase the number of scores in a sample, you also tend to increase the range because each additional score has the potential to replace the current highest or lowest value in the set. Thus, the range is directly related to sample size. This relationship between sample size and variability is unacceptable. A researcher should not be able to influence variability by manipulating sample size. Standard deviation, variance, and the semi-interquartile range are relatively unaffected by sample size and, therefore, provide better measures.

3. *Stability Under Sampling.* If you take several different samples from the same population, you should expect the samples to be similar. Specifically, if you compute variability for each of the separate samples, you should expect to obtain similar values. Because all of the samples come from the same source, it is reasonable that there should be some "family resemblance." When standard deviation and variance are used to measure variability, the samples will tend to have similar variability. For this reason, standard deviation and variance are said to be stable under sampling. The semi-interquartile range also provides a reasonably stable measure of variability. The range, however, will change unpredictably from sample to sample and is said to be unstable under sampling.

4. *Open-Ended Distributions.* When a distribution does not have any specific boundary for the highest score or the lowest score, it is open-ended. This can occur when you have infinite or undetermined scores. For example, a subject who cannot solve a problem has taken an undetermined or infinite amount of time to reach the solution. In an open-ended distribution, you cannot compute the range, or the standard

deviation, or the variance. In this situation, the only available measure of variability is the semi-interquartile range.

RELATIONSHIP WITH OTHER STATISTICAL MEASURES

As noted earlier, variance and standard deviation are computed from squared deviation scores. Because they are based on squared distances, these measures fit into a coherent system of mathematical relationships that underlies many of the statistical techniques we will examine in this book. Although we generally will not present the underlying mathematics, you will notice that variance and standard deviation appear repeatedly. For this reason, they are valuable measures of variability. Also, you should notice that variance and standard deviation have a direct relation to the mean (they are based on deviations from the mean). Therefore, the mean and standard deviation tend to be reported together. Because the mean is the most common measure of central tendency, the standard deviation will be the most common measure of variability.

Because the median and the semi-interquartile range are both based on percentiles, they share a common foundation and tend to be associated. When the median is used to report central tendency, the semi-interquartile range is commonly used to report variability.

The range has no direct relationship to any other statistical measure. For this reason, it is rarely used in conjunction with other statistical techniques.

SUMMARY

1 The purpose of variability is to determine how spread out the scores are in a distribution. There are four basic measures of variability: the range, the semi-interquartile range, the variance, and the standard deviation.

The range is the distance between the biggest and the smallest scores in the distribution. The semi-interquartile range is one-half the distance between the first quartile (25th percentile) and the third quartile (75th percentile). Variance is defined as the average squared deviation. Standard deviation is the square root of the variance.

Standard deviation and variance are by far the most commonly used measures of variability.

2 The logical steps leading to the formulas for variance and standard deviation are summarized as follows. Remember that the purpose of standard deviation is to provide a measure of the standard distance from the mean.

  a A deviation score is defined as $X - \mu$ and measures the direction and distance from the mean for each score.

  b Because of the plus and minus signs, the sum of the deviation scores and the average of the deviation scores will always be zero.

  c To get rid of the signs, we square each deviation and then compute the average squared deviation, or the variance.

  d Finally, we correct for having squared all the deviations by taking the square root of the variance. The result is the standard deviation, and it gives a measure of the standard distance from the mean.

3 To calculate either variance or standard deviation, you first need to find the sum of the squared deviations, SS. There are two formulas for SS:

Definitional formula: $SS = \sum(X - \mu)^2$

Computational formula: $SS = \sum X^2 - \dfrac{(\sum X)^2}{N}$

4 Variance is the average squared deviation and is obtained by finding the sum of squared deviations and then dividing by the number. For a population, variance is

$$\sigma^2 = \frac{SS}{N}$$

For a sample, only $n - 1$ of the scores are free to vary (degrees of freedom or $df = n - 1$), so sample variance is

$$s^2 = \frac{SS}{n - 1}$$

5 Standard deviation is the square root of the variance. For a population this is

$$\sigma = \sqrt{\frac{SS}{N}}$$

Sample standard deviation is

$$s = \sqrt{\frac{SS}{n - 1}}$$

Using $n - 1$ in the sample formulas makes sample variance and sample standard deviation accurate and unbiased estimates of the corresponding population parameters.

6 Adding a constant value to every score in a distribution will not change the standard deviation. Multiplying every score by a constant, however, will cause the standard deviation to be multiplied by the same constant.

KEY TERMS

variability
range
semi-interquartile range
deviation score
average deviation
variance
standard deviation
sum of squares (*SS*)
degrees of freedom (*df*)

FOCUS ON PROBLEM SOLVING

1. The purpose of variability is to provide a measure of how spread out the scores are in a distribution. Usually this is described by the standard deviation. Because the calculations are relatively complicated, it is wise to make a preliminary estimate of the standard deviation before you begin. Remember, standard deviation provides a measure of the typical, or average, distance from the mean. Therefore, the standard deviation must have a value somewhere between the largest and the smallest deviation scores. As a rule of thumb, the standard deviation should be about one-fourth of the range.

2. Rather than trying to memorize all the formulas for *SS*, variance, and standard deviation, you should focus on the definitions of these values and the logic that relates them to each other:

SS is the sum of squared deviations.
Variance is the average squared deviation.
Standard deviation is the square root of variance.

The only formula you should need to memorize is the computational formula for *SS*.

3. If you heed the warnings in the following list, you may avoid some of the more common mistakes in solving variability problems.

a. Because the calculation of standard deviation requires several steps of calculation, students often get lost in the arithmetic and forget what they are trying to compute. It helps to examine the data before you begin and make a rough estimate of the mean and the standard deviation.

b. The standard deviation formulas for populations and samples are slightly different. Be sure that you know whether the data come from a sample or a population before you begin calculations.

c. A common error is to use $n - 1$ in the computational formula for *SS* when you have scores from a sample. Remember, the *SS* formula always uses n (or N). After you compute *SS* for a sample, you must correct for the sample bias by using $n - 1$ in the formulas for variance and standard deviation.

PROBLEMS

1 Briefly define or explain each of the following:
a *SS* **b** Variance
c Standard deviation

2 For the following population of scores, calculate the mean and then compute the deviation score for each individual. Show that the sum of the deviation scores is zero. Scores: 4, 3, 7, 0, 1, 9.

***3** Compute *SS* for the following set of scores using the definitional formula and then using the computational formula. (You should get the same result from both formulas.) Scores: 1, 3, 2, 7, 1, 0, 3, 2, 1, 0.

***4** Calculate the range, the semi-interquartile range, and the standard deviation for the following sample:

2, 8, 5, 9, 1, 6, 6, 3, 6, 10, 4, 12

5 For the sample data in problem 4, add 2 points to every score in the distribution.
a Find the range, the semi-interquartile range, and the standard deviation the new distribution.

b Compare the results to the previous problem. What happens to the values of these measures of variability when a constant is added to every score?

6 a Using the computational formula, calculate SS for the following population of scores: 0, 1, 9.
b Calculate SS for these scores using the definitional formula. You should notice that the computational formula is much easier to use and that it probably will produce a more accurate answer because it does not require that you constantly round off decimal values.

*7 The quiz scores for a class of $N = 6$ students are as follows: 1, 3, 8, 5, 0, 1.
a Using the definitional formula, compute SS and variance for these scores (assume that the set of scores is a population).
b The instructor would like to "curve" this distribution by adding two points to each score so that the mean becomes $\mu = 5$. Add two points to each score and then recalculate SS and variance.
(You should find that adding a constant does not change any of the deviation scores.)

8 Two samples are as follows:

Sample A: 7, 9, 10, 8, 9, 12

Sample B: 13, 5, 9, 1, 17, 9

a Just by looking at these data, which sample has more variability? Explain your answer.
b Compute the mean and standard deviation for each sample.
c In which sample is the mean more representative (more "typical") of its scores? How does the standard deviation affect the interpretation of the mean?

*9 Two sets of data are presented here. Each set is a population.

Data set A: 3, 5, 7, 3, 5, 6, 4, 7, 4, 6

Data set B: 6, 4, 5, 3, 7

a Sketch a frequency distribution histogram for each population.
b Looking at your graphs, does it appear that one population is more variable than the other?
c Compute SS for each population. You should get different values. Does this mean that one population is more variable than the other?
d Compute variance for each population. The two values should be the same.
e Explain why variance is a better measure of variability than SS.

10 If a population of scores has $\mu = 0$, then $SS = \sum X^2$.
a Make up a set of $N = 4$ scores so that $\mu = 0$.
b Using the definitional formula, compute SS for your scores.
c Explain why $SS = \sum X^2$ whenever $\mu = 0$.

*11 A population has $\mu = 100$ and $\sigma = 20$. If you select a single score from this population, on the average, how close would it be to the population mean? Explain your answer.

12 You can make a rough estimate of the standard deviation for a set of scores by using one-fourth of the range. Explain why this works.

*13 A researcher is measuring student opinions using a standard 7-point scale (1 = "strongly agree" and 7 = "strongly disagree"). For one question, the researcher reports that the student responses averaged $\overline{X} = 5.8$ with a standard deviation of $s = 8.4$. It should be obvious that the researcher has made a mistake. Explain why.

14 The following scores are brain weights in grams for a sample of $n = 5$ fish. Calculate the mean and variance for these data. (*Hint:* Multiply each score by 100 to get rid of the decimal places. Remember to correct for this multiplication before you report your answer.) Scores: .08, .09, .08, .11, .09.

15 Calculate SS, variance, and standard deviation for the following sample of scores. (*Hint:* The calculations will be easier if you first subtract 430 from each score. For example, $431 - 430 = 1$, and $436 - 430 = 6$. (Remember, subtracting a constant will not affect these measures of variability.) Scores: 431, 432, 435, 432, 436, 431, 434.

16 For the following set of scores, calculate SS using the definitional formula and then using the computational formula. (You should get the same answer for each method.) Scores: 2, 6, 3, 7, 6, 1, 3

*17 For the data in the following sample,

1, 4, 3, 6, 2, 7, 18, 3, 7, 2, 4, 3

a Sketch a frequency distribution histogram.
b Compute the mean and standard deviation.
c Find the median and the semi-interquartile range.
d Which measures of central tendency and variability provide a better description of the sample? Explain your answer.

18 A population of scores has $\mu = 50$ and $\sigma = 0$.
a What value would be obtained for SS for this population?
b What value would be obtained for the population variance?
c Describe the scores in the population. (What are the scores)

19 Can SS ever have a value less than zero? Explain your answer.

*20 A set of $n = 20$ quiz scores has a mean of $\overline{X} = 20$. One person is selected from the class to be the "mystery person." If the deviation scores for the other 19 students in the class add up to $+6$, what score did the mystery person have?

21 Two sets of scores are presented here:

Set A: 4, 1, 3, 2

Set B: 9, 6, 8, 9

a Calculate the mean for each set.
b If you had to calculate SS for each set of scores, which formula would you prefer to use for set A? Which formula would you prefer for set B?
(Try both formulas on both sets of data until you are sure which is easier to use. In general, when should you use the definitional formula and when should you use the computational formula for SS?)

22 Find the range, the semi-interquartile range, and the standard deviation for the following population of scores: 1, 3, 5, 4, 2, 8, 4, 5.

***23** Two populations are presented here:

Population A: 53, 58, 52, 55, 57

Population B: 31, 47, 53, 71, 79

a Just looking at these data, which population will have the larger standard deviation? Explain your answer.
b Without precisely calculating the mean, *SS*, and so on, make an estimate of the standard deviation for each population. (First make a rough estimate of the mean. Then judge the average distance from the mean to the rest of the scores.)
c Compute the standard deviation for each population.

24 When a population consists of only two scores, it is very easy to calculate the standard deviation.

a Use the definitional formula to compute *SS*, variance, and standard deviation for the population that consists of $X = 1$ and $X = 5$. You should find that the mean is halfway between these two scores at $\mu = 3$. Each score has the same deviation, two points from the mean. If every score has a deviation of two points, then the standard deviation must be $\sigma = 2$ points.

Use this general rule to find the standard deviation for each of the following populations.
b $X = 20$ and $X = 30$
c $X = 0$ and $X = 1$
d $X = 57$ and $X = 73$

25 Use the following procedure to obtain a sample of $n = 4$ scores: First, close your book. Then, without looking, open to any page and write down the last digit of the left-hand page number. Repeat this procedure until you have four numbers. (*Note:* It is OK if the same digit appears more than once in your sample.)

a Calculate the mean and variance for your sample.
b You probably noticed that the left-hand pages all have even numbers. If you consider only the last digit of these numbers, the whole set of possible values is 0, 2, 4, 6, 8. This is the population for your sample. Calculate the mean and variance for this population.
c How well did your sample statistics (mean and variance) approximate the population parameters? Note that you do not expect the sample values to be identical to the population, but they should be close.

***26** People are most accurate at remembering and describing other individuals when they share some characteristics with the person being described. This fact can be very important in eye-witness testimony. A typical experiment examining this phenomenon is presented here.

Two groups of subjects are used: The first group consists of college students, all 18–20 years old. The second group consists of businesspeople aged 38–40. Each group views a short film of a bank robbery. The criminal in the film is a 40-year-old man wearing a suit and tie. After viewing the film, each subject is asked to describe the bank robber. This description includes an estimate of the robber's age. The data, showing each witness's estimate of age, are as follows:

College students: 35, 30, 55, 40, 40,
50, 45, 28, 33, 50

Businesspeople: 40, 45, 40, 42, 40,
40, 35, 40, 41, 38

a Calculate the mean for each sample. Based on the two means, does it appear that one group is more accurate than the other?
b Calculate the standard deviation for each sample. Based on these values, does it appear that one group is more accurate than the other? Explain your answer.

27 For the following population,

19, 23, 17, 27, 21, 20, 18
22, 19, 18, 25, 21, 29, 24

a Calculate the mean.
b By just looking at the scores, estimate the standard deviation for this population. Remember, standard deviation measures the standard distance from the mean.
c Calculate *SS*, variance, and standard deviation for these scores. Compare the actual standard deviation with your estimate.

28 The following data are from an experiment comparing two treatment conditions:

Treatment A	Treatment B
6	12
0	2
4	8
13	14
1	3
4	12
0	5

a Sketch a histogram showing the distribution of scores for the two treatment conditions. Show both treatments in the same histogram, using different colors to differentiate the two treatment conditions.
b Looking at your graph, does it appear that there is a difference between the two treatments? Are the scores in treatment A noticeably different from the scores in treatment B?
c Calculate the mean and standard deviation for each treatment condition. Is there a mean difference between the treatments?

Note: You should find a 4-point difference between the treatment means. However, the large variability makes the 4-point difference hard to see in the data or in the graph.

*29 The following data represent the daily high temperatures for the month of February and for the month of April:

February			April		
27	24	29	31	38	32
25	19	21	48	32	51
22	31	24	65	46	31
17	23	28	63	73	59
29	32	25	46	29	35
35	28	23	48	64	78
27	21	16	74	52	61
28	25	24	42	48	60
23	32	31	66	73	84
29			81	73	79

a Compute the mean temperature and the standard deviation for each month. Assume each set of data is a sample.

b How well does the mean describe a "typical" day in February? How well does the mean describe a "typical" day in April? In general, how does the standard deviation affect the interpretation of the mean?

30 For the scores in the following sample,

19, 22, 25, 60, 16, 21, 22, 27
26, 22, 20, 15, 17, 21, 23, 29

a Sketch a histogram showing the distribution of scores.

b Calculate the mean and standard deviation for this sample. Calculate the median and the semi-interquartile range for this sample.

d Which measures of central tendency and variability seem to provide the better description of the sample? Why?

*31 A psychologist is interested in the relation between personality types and occupation. A sample of $n = 15$ adult people is obtained to represent the general population. Then a sample of $n = 15$ successful salespeople is obtained. Each individual is given a personality questionnaire measuring introversion/extroversion on a scale from 0 (extreme introvert) to 100 (extreme extrovert). The data for the two samples are as follows:

General Population		Salesmen	
23	49	76	85
61	38	62	77
82	53	71	85
34	58	90	82
79	47	80	74
37	81	84	88
53	86	82	79
41		72	

a Calculate the mean and standard deviation for each sample.

b Based on the sample means, how would you describe the personalities of salespeople relative to personalities in the general population?

c Based on the sample standard deviations, how would you describe the personalities of salespeople relative to personalities in the general population?

CHAPTER 5

z-SCORES: LOCATION OF SCORES AND STANDARDIZED DISTRIBUTIONS

TOOLS YOU WILL NEED

The following items are considered essential background material for this chapter. If you doubt your knowledge of any of these items, you should review the appropriate chapter or section before proceeding.

- The mean (Chapter 3)
- The standard deviation (Chapter 4)
- Basic algebra (math review, Appendix A)

PREVIEW

A friend of mine, John, is 5 feet 10 inches tall and weighs 170 pounds. John plays football. None of this information about John is particularly remarkable, but it does allow us to make some comparisons. First, John is fairly typical in height and weight when compared with American adult males. In relation to professional football players, however, John is tiny. Most of you probably recognized that John does not play in the National Football League. Finally, when I tell you that John is only 10 years old, you should realize that he is a large boy in relation to other children his age.

The point of this example is that information about an individual can be difficult to interpret unless the individual is described in relation to some reference group. John is either average, small, or very large depending on the grou, in which you place him.

It is very common to describe individuals in terms of their relationships to others. Parents want to know the average age at which children begin to walk so that they can judge the developmental progress of their children. (Is my child precocious?) Adults evaluate their salaries by comparison with other people in the same profession. (Am I underpaid?) Students want to know where their exam scores fall in the class distribution. (How did I do on the test?) In each case the goal is to describe a specific individual by his or her relative position within a larger group.

In the preceeding chapters we concentrated on methods for describing entire distributions using the basic parameters of shape, central tendency, and variability. In this chapter we will examine a procedure for describing an individual location within a distribution. The procedure we will introduce is based on the concepts of the mean and the standard deviation. We will use the mean as a reference point to determine whether the individual is above or below average. The standard deviation serves as a yardstick for measuring how much an individual differs from the group average. A good conceptual understanding of the mean and standard deviation will make this chapter much easier.

5.1 *z*-SCORES AND LOCATION IN A DISTRIBUTION

WHAT IS A *z*-SCORE?

Suppose you received a score of $X = 76$ on a statistics exam. How did you do? It should be clear that you need more information to predict your grade. Your score of $X = 76$ could be one of the best scores in the class, or it might be the lowest score the distribution. To find the location of your score, you must have information about the other scores in the distribution. It would be useful, for example, to know the mean for the class. If the mean were $\mu = 70$, you would be in a much better position than if the mean were $\mu = 85$. Obviously, your position relative to the rest of the class depends on the mean. However, the mean by itself is not sufficient to tell you the exact location of your score. Suppose you know that the mean for the statistics exam is $\mu = 70$, and your score is $X = 76$. At this point, you know that your score is above the mean, but you still do not know exactly where it is located. You may have the highest score in the class, or you may be only slightly above average. Figure 5.1 shows two possible distributions of exam scores. Both distributions have $\mu = 70$, but for one distribution $\sigma = 3$ and for the other $\sigma = 12$. Notice that the location of $X = 76$ is very different for these two distributions.

The purpose of the previous example is to demonstrate that a raw score by itself does not provide much information about its position within a distribution. To find the location of a score, you must also know the mean and standard deviation. The goal of *z*-scores is to combine all this information into a single value that specifies a location within a distribution.

· FIGURE 5.1 ·

Two distributions of exam scores. For both distributions, $\mu = 70$, but for one distribution $\sigma = 3$ and for the other, $\sigma = 12$. The position of $X = 76$ is very different for these two distributions.

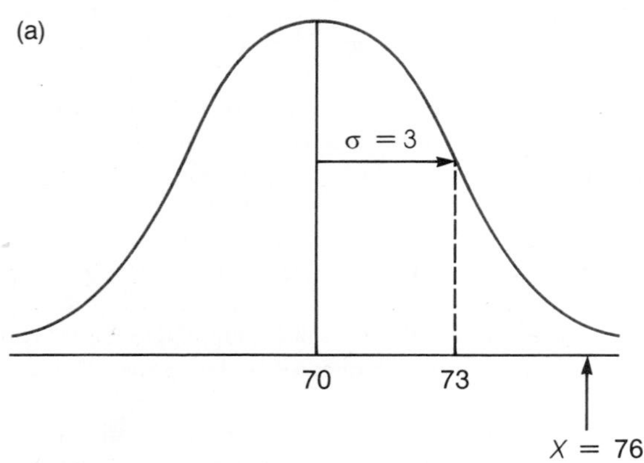

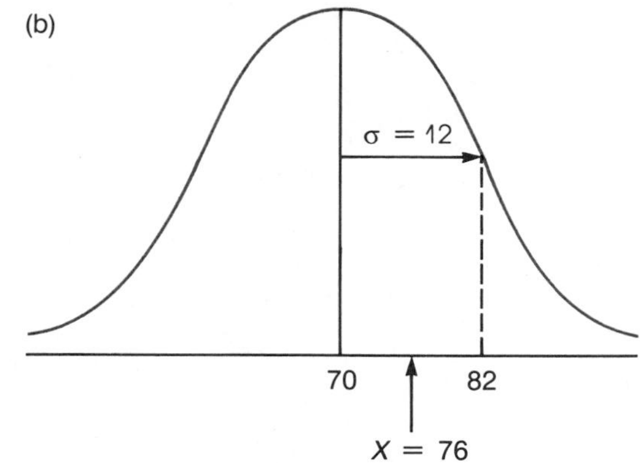

· DEFINITION · A *z-score* specifies the precise location of each X value within a distribution. The sign of the z-score (+ or −) specifies whether the score is above the mean (positive) or below the mean (negative). The numerical value of the z-score specifies the distance from the mean by counting the number of standard deviations between X and μ.

Whenever you are working with z-scores you should imagine or draw a picture similar to Figure 5.2.

Figure 5.2 shows a population distribution with various positions identified by their z-score values. Notice that all z-scores above the mean are positive and all z-scores below the mean are negative. The sign of a z-score tells you immediately whether the score is located above or below the mean. Also, note that a z-score of $z = +1.00$ corresponds to a position above the mean by exactly 1 standard deviation. A z-score of $z = +2.00$ is always located above the mean by exactly 2 standard deviations. The numerical value of the z-score tells you the number of standard deviations from the mean (see Perspective 5.1). Now suppose that the scores from your statistics exam are reported as z-scores and you receive a score of $z = -.50$. How did you do? From this single value you should be able to locate your exact position within the distribution. In this case ($z = -.50$), you are below the mean by one-half of the standard deviation. Find this position in Figure 5.2.

The definition of a z-score indicates that each X value has a corresponding z-score.

· FIGURE 5.2 ·

The relationship between z-score values and locations in a population distribution.

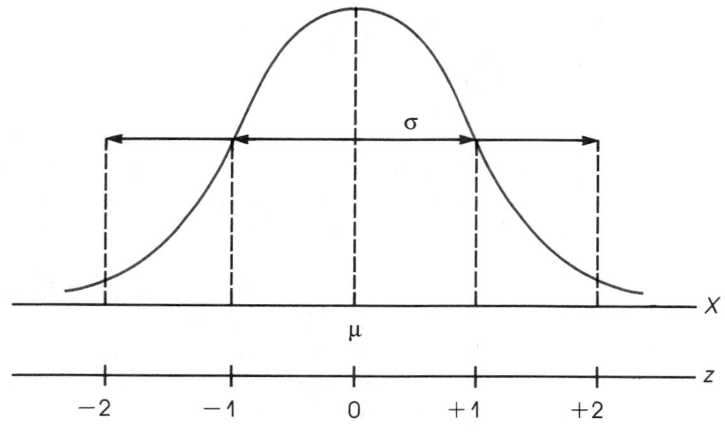

PERSPECTIVE 5.1

RELATIVE POSITION WITHIN A DISTRIBUTION: THE ROLE OF STANDARD DEVIATION

We have now seen that the standard deviation is an essential part of converting any X value to a z-score. It should come as no surprise that the standard deviation affects the value obtained for the z-score. Therefore, in a general sense, the amount of variability in a distribution and the relative position of a particular score are interrelated. This can be demonstrated with a simple example of two distributions.

Suppose that in Caribou, Maine, the average snowfall per year is $\mu = 110$ inches with $\sigma = 30$. In Boston, however, let us assume that the yearly average is only $\mu = 24$ inches with $\sigma = 5$. Last year Caribou enjoyed 125 inches of snow, while Boston was blessed with 39 inches. In which city was the winter much worse than average for its residents?

We are essentially asking a question about the relative position of a raw score in its distribution. In particular, we wish to locate the relative position of last year's accumulation for each city. Thus, in the distribution of annual accumulations for Caribou, where does $X = 125$ fall? Similarly, where does $X = 39$ fall within the distribution for Boston?

If we simply consider deviation scores ($X - \mu$), the snowfall last year was 15 inches above average for both cities. But does this tell the whole story? In this case, it does not. The distributions for each city differ in terms of variability ($\sigma = 30$ for Caribou, $\sigma = 5$ for Boston). Again, the amount of variability affects the relative standing of a score. Therefore, it is misleading to simply look at deviation scores. When determining the position of a score in a distribution, we should measure distance of a score from the mean in terms of standard deviation units (see the definition for a z-score).

If we look at Caribou, we find that $\mu = 100$ and $\sigma = 30$. A winter with $X = 125$ inches of snow is 15 points above the mean, or .5 standard deviations away. For Boston, the distribution has $\mu = 24$ with $\sigma = 5$. Its winter with $X = 39$ inches is also 15 points above the mean, but this is a distance equal to 3 standard deviation units. When we consider the variability in each distribution, we see that it was not an unusual winter for Caribou. Its snowfall was only $\frac{1}{2}$ standard deviation above the mean ($z = +.5$), close to what we would expect for that town. On the other hand, Boston had an extreme winter. Its snowfall was 3 standard deviations above the mean ($z = +3.0$), much more snow than its residents would expect.

The following examples demonstrate the relation between X values and z-scores within a distribution.

EXAMPLE 5.1 A distribution of exam scores has a mean (μ) of 50 and a standard deviation (σ) of 8.

a For this distribution, what is the z-score corresponding to $X = 58$? Because 58 is *above* the mean, the z-score has a positive sign. The score is 8 points greater than the mean. This distance is exactly 1 standard deviation (because $\sigma = 8$), so the z-score is

$$z = +1$$

This z-score indicates that the raw score is one standard deviation above the mean.

b What is the z-score corresponding to $X = 46$? The z-score will be negative because 46 is *below* the mean. The X value is 4 points away from the mean. This distance is exactly one-half of the standard deviation; therefore, the z-score is

$$z = -\tfrac{1}{2}$$

This z-score tells us that the X value is one-half of a standard deviation below the mean.

c For this distribution, what raw score corresponds to a z-score of $+2$? This z-score indicates that the X value is 2 standard deviations above the mean. One standard deviation is 8 points, so two standard deviations would

be 16 points. Therefore, the score we are looking for is 16 points above the mean. The mean for the distribution is 50, so the X value is

$$X = 50 + 16 = 66$$

THE z-SCORE FORMULA

The relation between X values and z-scores can be expressed symbolically in a formula. The formula for transforming raw scores into z-scores is

$$z = \frac{X - \mu}{\sigma} \qquad (5.1)$$

The numerator of the equation, $X - \mu$, is a deviation score (Chapter 4, page 85) and measures the distance in points between X and μ. We divide this difference by σ because we want the z-score to measure distance in terms of standard deviation units. Remember, the purpose of a z-score is to specify an exact location in a distribution. The z-score formula provides a standard procedure for determining a score's location by calculating the direction and distance from the mean.

1. *Direction*. If a raw score is less than the mean, then the z-score will have a negative sign. If X is greater than μ, z will be positive. These points should become obvious when you look at the numerator of the z-score formula, $X - \mu$. If $X = 48$ and $\mu = 51$, then $X - \mu = -3$. When this value is divided by the standard deviation, the result is a z-score that is negative. This indicates that the raw score is below the mean. By similar reasoning, if $X = 56$ and $\mu = 51$, then $X - \mu = +5$. This value in turn will result in a positive z-score. Therefore, the direction (above or below) of a score from the mean is indicated by the sign (+ and −) of the z-score.

Remember, σ is always positive because it is based on squared deviation scores (Chapter 4).

2. *Distance*. The distance of a score from the mean is indicated by the number value of the z-score. The greater the magnitude of this value, the farther X is from μ. A raw score with a z of -3 is farther from the mean than a score with a z of -1. The first score would be 3 standard deviations below the mean, whereas the second is only 1 standard deviation below μ.

EXAMPLE 5.2 A distribution of general psychology test scores has a mean of $\mu = 60$ and a standard deviation of $\sigma = 4$. What is the z-score for a student who received a 66?

Looking at a sketch of the distribution (Figure 5.3), we see that the raw score is above the mean by at least 1 standard deviation but not quite by 2. Judging from the graph, 66 appears to be $1\frac{1}{2}$ standard deviations from the mean. The computation of the z-score with the formula confirms our estimate:

$$z = \frac{X - \mu}{\sigma} = \frac{66 - 60}{4} = \frac{+6}{4} = +1.5$$

EXAMPLE 5.3 The distribution of SAT verbal scores for high school seniors has a mean of $\mu = 500$ and a standard deviation of $\sigma = 100$. Joe took the SAT and scored 430 on the verbal subtest. Locate his score in the distribution by using a z-score.

Joe's score is 70 points below the mean, so the z-score will be negative. Because 70 points is less than 1 standard deviation, the z-score should have a magnitude that is less than 1. Using the formula, his z-score is

$$z = \frac{X - \mu}{\sigma} = \frac{430 - 500}{100} = \frac{-70}{100} = -.70$$

FIGURE 5.3

For the population of general psychology test scores, $\mu = 60$ and $\sigma = 4$. A student whose score is 66 is 1.5σ above the mean or has a z-score of $+1.5$.

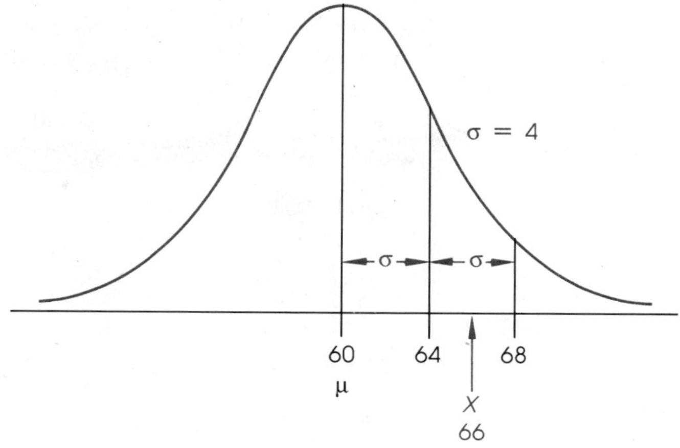

DETERMINING A RAW SCORE FROM A z-SCORE

There may be situations in which you have an individual's z-score and would like to determine the corresponding raw score. When you start with a z-score, you can compute the X value by using a different version of the z-score formula. Before we introduce the new formula, let us look at the logic behind converting a z-score back to a raw score.

EXAMPLE 5.4 A distribution has a mean of $\mu = 40$ and a standard deviation of $\sigma = 6$.

a What raw score corresponds to $z = +1.5$? The z-score indicates that the X value is located 1.5 standard deviations *above* the mean. Because 1 standard deviation is 6 points, 1.5 standard deviations equal 9 points. Therefore, the raw score is 9 points above the mean, or $X = 49$.

b What raw score corresponds to $z = -.5$? The X value for which we are looking is $\frac{1}{2}$ standard deviation *below* (z is negative) the mean. If the standard deviation is 6, then the X value in question must be 3 points below the mean. Thus the raw score is $X = 37$.

In example 5.4 we used the z-score and the standard deviation to determine the deviation for an X value; that is, how much distance lies between the raw score and the mean. The deviation score was then added to or subtracted from the mean (depending on the sign of z) to yield the X value. These steps can be incorporated into a formula so that the X value can be computed directly. This formula is obtained by solving the z-score formula for X:

$$z = \frac{X - \mu}{\sigma}$$

$$z\sigma = X - \mu \qquad \text{(multiply both sides by } \sigma\text{)}$$

$$X - \mu = z\sigma \qquad \text{(transpose the equation)}$$

$$X = \mu + z\sigma \qquad \text{(add } \mu \text{ to both sides)} \tag{5.2}$$

Notice that the third equation in this derivation contains the expression $X - \mu$, the definition for a deviation score (Chapter 4, page 85). Therefore, the deviation score for any raw score can also be found by multiplying the z-score by the standard deviation ($z\sigma$). Essentially, this is the method we used in Example 5.4. If $z\sigma$ provides a deviation score, then we may rewrite equation 5.2 as:

raw score = mean + deviation score

In using formula 5.2, always remember that the sign of the z-score (+ or −) will determine whether the deviation score is added to or subtracted from the mean.

EXAMPLE 5.5 A distribution has a mean of $\mu = 60$ and a standard deviation of $\sigma = 12$.

a What raw score has $z = +.25$?

$$\begin{aligned} X &= \mu + z\sigma \\ &= 60 + .25(12) \\ &= 60 + 3 \\ &= 63 \end{aligned}$$

b What X value corresponds to $z = -1.2$?

$$\begin{aligned} X &= \mu + z\sigma \\ &= 60 + (-1.2)(12) \\ &= 60 - 14.4 \\ &= 45.6 \end{aligned}$$

DETERMINING z-SCORES ON THE COMPUTER

Calculating z-scores for a large sample can be tedious, especially if the standard deviation has a decimal value. The task becomes much simpler when a computer is instructed to perform the repetitive calculations. We used Minitab to compute z-scores for the data from Example 4.5 (Chapter 4, page 90). In that example, the distribution consisted of the following scores: 1, 9, 5, 8, 7. The mean and standard deviation for these data were calculated in Example 4.5 and are $\mu = 6$ and $\sigma = 2.83$, respectively. The printout for the z-score analysis is presented in Table 5.1. The z-score transformation was accomplished by two Minitab commands. The SUBTRACT command found the deviation score for every X value. The DIVIDE command divided each deviation score by the standard deviation.

THE CHARACTERISTICS OF A z-SCORE DISTRIBUTION

It is possible to describe the location of every raw score in the distribution by assigning z-scores to all of them. The result would be a transformation of the distribution of raw scores into a distribution of z-scores. That is, for each and every X value in the distribution of raw scores, there would be a corresponding z-score in the new distribution. This new distribution has specific characteristics—characteristics which make a z-score transformation a very useful tool in statistics. If every X value is transformed into a z-score, then the distribution of z-scores will have the following properties:

1. *Shape*. The shape of the z-score distribution will be the same as the original distribution of raw scores. If the original distribution is negatively skewed, for example, then the z-score distribution will also be negatively skewed. Transforming raw scores into z-scores does not change the shape of the distribution.

2. *The Mean*. When raw scores are transformed into z-scores, the resulting z-score distribution will *always* have a mean of zero. This is the case regardless of the value of μ for the raw score distribution. Suppose a population of scores has $\mu = 75$ and $\sigma = 15$. What is the z-score for the value $X = 75$? Notice that the X value equals the mean of the distribution, so its z-score will also be the z-score for the mean.

$$z = \frac{X - \mu}{\sigma} = \frac{75 - 75}{15} = \frac{0}{15} = 0$$

TABLE 5.1

A z-score transformation of the data in Example 4.3 using Minitab.

```
MINITAB RELEASE 5.1.3 *** COPYRIGHT - MINITAB, INC. 1985
U.S. FEDERAL GOVERNMENT USERS SEE HELP FGU
APRIL 20, 1987 *** S.U.N.Y. BROCKPORT - ACADEMIC COMPUTING SERVICES
STORAGE AVAILABLE 260144

 Type NEWS for information on new features in Minitab Release 5.1
```

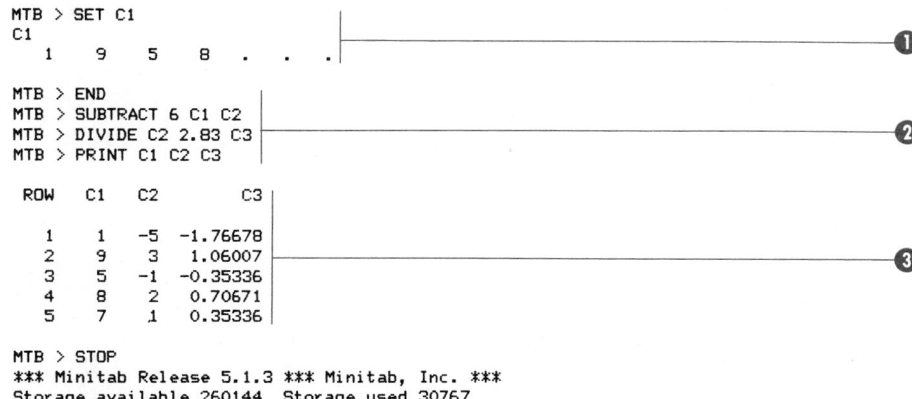

```
MTB > SET C1
C1
   1    9    5    8  .  .  .                    ❶

MTB > END
MTB > SUBTRACT 6 C1 C2
MTB > DIVIDE C2 2.83 C3                          ❷
MTB > PRINT C1 C2 C3

 ROW    C1    C2          C3

   1     1    -5    -1.76678
   2     9     3     1.06007                     ❸
   3     5    -1    -0.35336
   4     8     2     0.70671
   5     7     1     0.35336

MTB > STOP
*** Minitab Release 5.1.3 *** Minitab, Inc. ***
Storage available 260144  Storage used 30767
```

EXPLANATION OF PRINTOUT:

1 Minitab provides a partial list of the data that have been entered for analysis.

2 The SUBTRACT command subtracts 6 (the mean) from each score in column 1 and stores the result in column 2. The DIVIDE command divides the data in column 2 by 2.83 (the standard deviation) and stores the result in column 3. The PRINT command prints all three columns.

3 The first column (labeled C1) displays the raw scores. Column 2 (C2) shows the deviation scores, and the third column (C3) contains z-scores.

The mean of the distribution has a z-score of zero. You will remember that raw scores that fall below the mean have negative z-scores (that is, z-scores *less than zero*) and that X values above the mean have positive z-scores (*greater than zero*). This fact makes the mean a convenient reference point.

3. *The Standard Deviation.* When a distribution of X values is transformed into a distribution of z-scores, the new distribution will have a standard deviation of 1. For example, a distribution of raw scores has $\mu = 100$ and $\sigma = 10$. In this distribution a raw score of 110 will have a z-score of $+1$ (1 standard deviation above the mean). When X is 90, the z will be -1 (or 1 standard deviation below the mean). When X is 120, z is $+2$, and so on. The distribution in Figure 5.4 is labeled in terms of both X values and their corresponding z-scores. Note that 10 points on the X scale is the equivalent of 1 standard deviation. Furthermore, the distance of 1 standard deviation on the X scale corresponds to 1 point on the z-score scale. That is, the X scale has merely been relabeled following a z transformation, so that 1 point on the z scale corresponds to one standard deviation unit on the X scale. This relabeling will give the z-score distribution a standard deviation of 1 point.

DEMONSTRATING THE PROPERTIES OF A z-SCORE TRANSFORMATION

By using a small population of raw scores, it is easy to demonstrate the characteristics of a distribution following a z-score transformation. A population of $N = 6$ scores consists of the following values:

0, 6, 5, 2, 3, 2

FIGURE 5.4

Following a z-score transformation, the X-axis is relabeled in z-score units. The distance that is equivalent to one standard deviation on the X-axis ($\sigma = 10$ points in this example) corresponds to 1 point on the z-score scale.

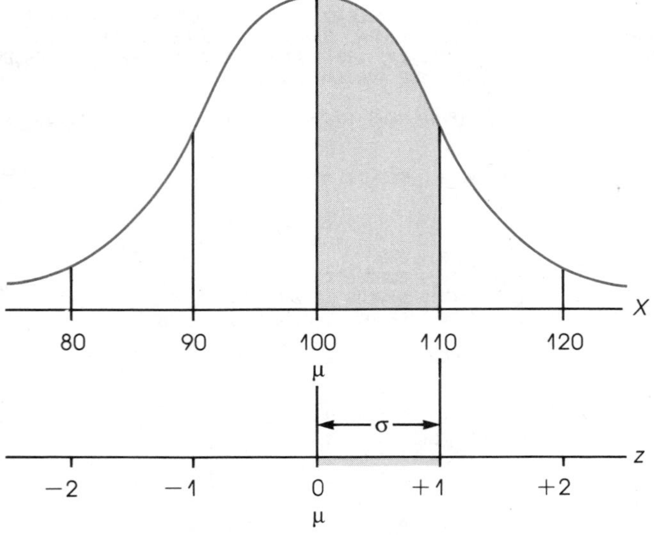

The population mean is

$$\mu = \frac{\sum X}{N} = \frac{18}{6} = 3$$

The population standard deviation is

$$\sigma = \sqrt{\frac{SS}{N}} = \sqrt{\frac{24}{6}} = \sqrt{4} = 2$$

To demonstrate the characteristics of a z-score distribution, we must transform every raw score into a z-score using formula 5.1:

$$z = \frac{X - \mu}{\sigma}$$

Therefore, for $X = 0$,

$$z = \frac{0 - 3}{2} = -1.5$$

For $X = 6$,

$$z = \frac{6 - 3}{2} = +1.5$$

For $X = 5$,

$$z = \frac{5 - 3}{2} = +1.0$$

For $X = 2$,

$$z = \frac{2 - 3}{2} = -.5$$

For $X = 3$,

$$z = \frac{3 - 3}{2} = 0$$

For $X = 2$,

$$z = -.5 \qquad \text{(already computed)}$$

The distribution now consists of $N = 6$ z-scores:

$$-1.5, \ +1.5, \ +1.0, \ -.5, \ 0, \ -.5$$

The distribution of z-scores and the original distribution of raw scores are shown in Figure 5.5. Notice that the shape of the distribution has not been changed by the z-score transformation. All individuals are in the same relative position in the distribution after the transformation to z-scores. For example, the individual with $X = 6$ and $z = +1.5$ has the highest score in both distributions. The X-axis is simply relabeled in z-score units after the transformation.

To find the mean of the z distribution, we add all the z-scores and divide by N:

$$\mu_z = \frac{\sum z}{N} = \frac{-1.5 + 1.5 + 1 + (-.5) + 0 + (-.5)}{6}$$

$$= \frac{-2.5 + 2.5}{6} = \frac{0}{6} = 0$$

The mean of the distribution of z-scores (μ_z) will always equal zero, regardless of the value of the mean for the raw scores.

To determine the standard deviation of the z-scores, we use the standard deviation formula but plug in z-scores in place of X values. Therefore, the sum of squares for a z-score distribution is

$$SS_z = \sum(z - \mu_z)^2$$

FIGURE 5.5

Transforming a distribution of raw scores (top) into z-scores (bottom) will not change the shape of the distribution.

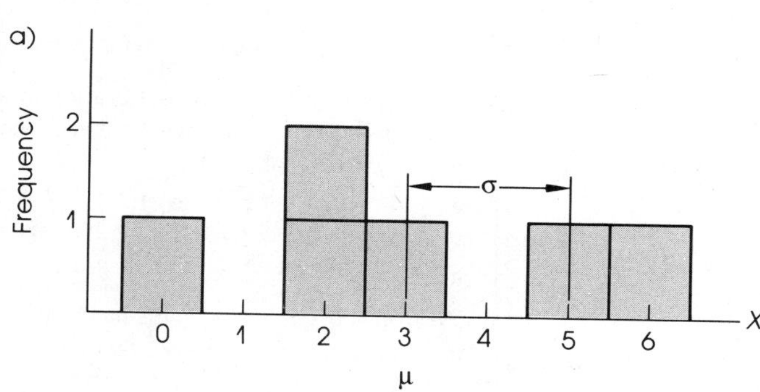

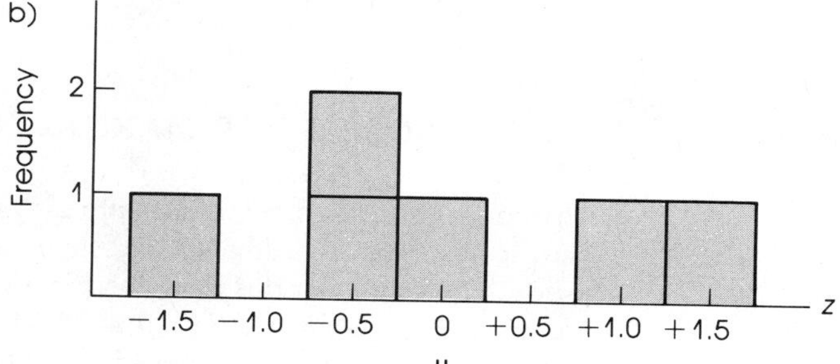

TABLE 5.2

Computation of SS_z for a distribution of z-scores.

Z	$Z - \mu_z$	$(Z - \mu_z)^2$
−1.5	−1.5	2.25
+1.5	+1.5	2.25
+1.0	+1.0	1.00
−.5	−.5	.25
0	0	0
−.5	−.5	.25
		$6.00 = SS_z = \sum(Z - \mu_z)^2$

For a distribution of z-scores, $\mu_z = 0$. Therefore, $z = z - \mu_z$.

Table 5.2 summarizes the steps for the computation of SS_z. For the standard deviation of the z-score distribution (σ_z), we obtain

$$\sigma_z = \sqrt{\frac{SS_z}{N}} = \sqrt{\frac{6}{6}} = \sqrt{1} = 1$$

In summary, transforming raw scores to z-scores will give us a new distribution with the same shape as the original, a mean of zero, and a standard deviation equal to 1 regardless of the parameters of the distribution of raw scores.

LEARNING CHECK

1 What information does a z-score provide?

2 A population of scores has $\mu = 45$ and $\sigma = 5$. Find the z-scores for the following raw scores:

a $X = 47$ **c** $X = 40$ **e** $X = 52$ **g** $X = 45$
b $X = 48$ **d** $X = 44$ **f** $X = 39$ **h** $X = 56$

3 For the same population, determine the raw scores that correspond to the following z-scores:

a $z = +1.3$ **c** $z = -3.0$ **e** $z = +2.8$
b $z = -.4$ **d** $z = -1.5$ **f** $z = 0$

4 What is the advantage of having $\mu = 0$ for a distribution of z-scores?

ANSWERS

1 A z-score identifies a precise location in a distribution. The sign indicates whether the location is above or below the mean, and the magnitude of z indicates the number of standard deviations from the mean.

2 **a** +.4 **c** −1.0 **e** +1.4 **g** 0
b +.6 **d** −.2 **f** −1.2 **h** +2.2

3 **a** 51.5 **b** 43 **c** 30 **d** 37.5 **e** 59 **f** 45

4 With $\mu = 0$ you know immediately that any positive value is above the mean and any negative value is below the mean.

5.2 USING z-SCORES FOR MAKING COMPARISONS

See Perspective 5.2 for other examples of how z-scores are useful in statistics.

The transformation of raw scores into z-scores is very useful when we want to compare scores from two different distributions. For example, Bob received a 60 on a psychology exam. For this class, the mean was 50 and $\sigma = 10$. In biology, Bob's test score was 56, and for this class $\mu = 48$ with $\sigma = 4$. In which course does Bob have a higher standing? First, you should notice that Bob's psychology score is higher than

PERSPECTIVE 5.2

WHY ARE *z*-SCORES IMPORTANT?

We have introduced *z*-scores as a statistical method for describing a specific location within a distribution. As you have seen, *z*-scores can be used to determine the precise location of an individual score, and *z*-scores can be used to compare the relative positions of two or more scores. The ability to describe a location in a distribution is of great value for other statistical purposes. The following is a brief outline of some of the ways that *z*-scores will be used in later chapters.

1. *Probability.* One of the basic goals for statistics is to determine the probability or likelihood of particular events. Often it is possible to use *z*-scores as a starting point for finding probabilities. In many situations, the most likely outcomes are those that are "typical," or average. In other words, observing an individual with a *z*-score near zero (in the middle of the distribution) is much more likely than observing an individual with a *z*-score of +3.00. In Chapter 6, we examine the relation between *z*-scores and probability.

2. *Evaluating Treatment Effects.* Many experiments are done to determine whether or not a particular treatment has any effect on a dependent variable. For example, a researcher testing a new stimulant drug would like to know if the drug affects heart rate. One simple test would be to look at the heart rates of individuals who have taken the drug. If these individuals have heart rates that are still average or typical (i.e., *z*-scores around zero), the researcher could conclude that drug does not seem to influence heart rate. On the other hand, if the individuals had heart rates that were extremely high (i.e., *z*-scores of +3.00 or +4.00), the researcher might conclude that the drug does increase heart rate. In general, *z*-scores provide an easy method for determining whether an individual score is average or extreme. We take a closer look at this inferential procedure in Chapters 8 and 9.

3. *Measuring Relationships.* Some statistical methods are intended to describe and measure the relationship between two variables. For example, a psychologist might be interested in the relation between physical development and mental development for 5-year-old children. Are children who are unusually large also unusually bright? In order to examine the relation, it is first necessary to find the location of each child in the distribution of heights and in the distribution of IQs. Extremely tall children will have large positive *z*-scores, those of average height will have *z*-scores near zero, and small children will have negative *z*-scores. Similarly, each child's IQ can be described as a *z*-score. The researcher can then determine whether there is a consistent relation between the *z*-scores for height and the *z*-scores for IQ. We examine statistical methods for measuring relationships in Chapter 16.

his score in biology ($X = 60$ versus $X = 56$). Also, if you look at deviation scores, Bob is 10 points above the mean in psychology and only 8 points above the mean in biology. Does this mean that he performed better in psychology than in biology? Not necessarily! The problem is that we cannot simply compare his psychology score to his biology score because these scores come from *different distributions.* Any comparisons between these two test scores would be like the proverbial comparison of apples to oranges.

To make a meaningful comparison of Bob's scores, we must standardize the distributions of both classes to make them similar. Remember, a *z*-score transformation will always produce a distribution that has $\mu = 0$ and $\sigma = 1$. Therefore, if every raw score in the psychology and biology classes is transformed into a *z*-score, the resulting distributions for both classes would have $\mu = 0$ and $\sigma = 1$. All we need to do is compare Bob's *z*-score for psychology with his *z*-score for biology to determine which exam score is better. When data transformations are used to make distributions comparable, we are using *standardized distributions.* The *z*-scores in this instance are often called *standard scores.*

DEFINITIONS A *standardized distribution* is composed of transformed scores that result in predetermined values for μ and σ, regardless of their values for the raw score distribution. Standardized distributions are used to make dissimilar distributions comparable.

A *standard score* is a transformed score that provides information of its location in a distribution. A *z*-score is an example of a standard score.

In practice it is not necessary to transform every score in a distribution to make comparisons between two scores. We need to transform only the two scores in question. In Bob's case, we must find the z-scores for his psychology and biology scores. For psychology, Bob's z-score is

Be sure to use the μ and σ values for the distribution to which X belongs.

$$z = \frac{X - \mu}{\sigma} = \frac{60 - 50}{10} = \frac{10}{10} = +1.0$$

For biology, Bob's z-score is

$$z = \frac{56 - 48}{4} = \frac{8}{4} = +2.0$$

Note that Bob's z-score for biology is +2.0, which means that his test score is 2 standard deviations above the class mean. On the other hand, his z-score is +1.0 for psychology, or 1 standard deviation above the mean. In terms of relative class standing, Bob is doing much better in the biology class. Unlike the absolute size of the raw scores, the z-scores describe *relative* positions within a distribution.

· LEARNING CHECK ·

1 Why is it possible to compare scores from different distributions after each distribution is transformed into z-scores?

2 For distribution A, $\mu = 20$ and $\sigma = 7$. Distribution B has $\mu = 23$ and $\sigma = 2$. In which distribution will a raw score of 27 have a higher standing?

ANSWERS

1 Comparisons are possible because both distributions will have the same μ and σ ($\mu = 0$, $\sigma = 1$) following a z-score transformation.

2 For distribution A, a raw score of 27 has a z-score of +1.0. For distribution B, a score of 27 corresponds to a z-score of +2.0. Therefore, a raw score of 27 has a higher relative standing in distribution B.

5.3 OTHER STANDARDIZED DISTRIBUTIONS BASED ON z-SCORES

TRANSFORMING z-SCORES TO A PREDETERMINED μ AND σ

Although z-score distributions have distinct advantages, many people find them cumbersome because they contain negative values and decimals. For these reasons, it is common to standardize a distribution by transforming z-scores to a distribution with a predetermined mean and standard deviation that are whole round numbers. Standardized scores of this type are frequently used in psychological testing. For example, raw scores of the Scholastic Aptitude Test (SAT) are transformed to a standardized distribution that has $\mu = 500$ and $\sigma = 100$. For intelligence tests, raw scores are frequently converted to standard scores that have a mean of 100 and a standard deviation of 15. If the same standardized scale is used for several types of intelligence tests, then the exam scores on different tests can be more readily compared because the distributions will have the same mean and standard deviation. Basically, two steps are involved in standardizing distributions so that they have prespecified μ and σ: (1) All of the raw scores from both distributions are transformed to z-scores, and (2) all z-scores are then converted back into X values so that a particular μ and σ will be achieved.

· EXAMPLE 5.6 · An instructor gives different versions of an exam to two psychology classes. For class 1, the mean is $\mu = 57$ with $\sigma = 14$. Joe and Harry are two of the students in this class, and they have scores of 64 and 43, respectively. For the second class, $\mu = 31$ and $\sigma = 6$. In this class, Mary had a score of 34, and Bill received a 28. These data are summarized in Table 5.3. The instructor would like to make the scores of both classes comparable by transforming all raw scores so that each class distribution will be standardized with $\mu = 50$ and $\sigma = 10$. What will the standardized scores be for Joe, Harry, Mary, and Bill?

STEP 1 Transform all of the raw scores into z-scores. For Joe, $X = 64$, so his z-score is

$$z = \frac{X - \mu}{\sigma} = \frac{64 - 57}{14} = +.5$$

Remember, the values of μ and σ are for the distribution from which X was taken.

For Harry, $X = 43$, and his z-score is

$$z = \frac{X - \mu}{\sigma} = \frac{43 - 57}{14} = -1.0$$

For Mary, $X = 34$, and her z-score is

$$z = \frac{X - \mu}{\sigma} = \frac{34 - 31}{6} = +.5$$

And for Bill, who scored a 28, the z-score is

$$z = \frac{X - \mu}{\sigma} = \frac{28 - 31}{6} = -.5$$

STEP 2 Change the z-scores to the new standardized scores. The instructor wants to have a standardized distribution with $\mu = 50$ and $\sigma = 10$. Joe's z-score is $+.5$. What X value in the new standardized distribution will correspond to $z = +.5$? Joe's z-score indicates that he is $\frac{1}{2}$ standard deviation above the mean. Since the mean of the standardized distribution will be set at 50 and its $\sigma = 10$, Joe is 5 points above 50. That is, he will have a standardized score of 55. Mary's z-score is the same as Joe's, $z = +.5$, so she too will have a score of 55 in the new standardized distribution. Harry is one standard deviation below the mean ($z = -1.0$), so his score will be 10 points below the mean in the standardized distribution, or $X = 40$. Bill is one-half of a standard deviation below the mean ($z = -.5$). His standardized score, therefore, is 5 points below 50, or $X = 45$. These results are summarized in Table 5.3. To complete the construction of the standardized distribution, the instructor must repeat steps 1 and 2 for each raw score in the original distributions for both classes. ·

A FORMULA FOR FINDING THE STANDARDIZED SCORE Earlier in the chapter, we derived a formula [Formula (5.2)] to find the raw score that corresponds to a particular z-score:

$$X = \mu + z\sigma$$

· TABLE 5.3 ·

	Class 1: $\mu = 57, \sigma = 14$		Class 2: $\mu = 31, \sigma = 6$	
	Joe	Harry	Mary	Bill
Raw score	$X = 64$	43	34	28
Step 1: compute z-score	$z = +.5$	-1.0	$+.5$	$-.5$
Step 2: standard score	55	40	55	45

For purposes of computing the new standardized score, we can rewrite the equation:

(5.3) $$\text{standard score} = \mu_{\text{new}} + z\sigma_{\text{new}}$$

The standard score equals the mean of the new standardized distribution plus its z-score times the standard deviation of the new standardized distribution. The z-score in the formula is the one computed for the original raw score (step 1). Notice that $z\sigma$ is the deviation score of the standard score. If the raw score is below the mean, then its z-score and $z\sigma$ will be negative. For scores above the mean, $z\sigma$ is positive.

EXAMPLE 5.7 A psychologist has developed a new intelligence test. For years the test has been given to a large number of people; for this population $\mu = 65$ and $\sigma = 10$. The psychologist would like to make the scores of his subjects comparable to scores on other IQ tests, which have $\mu = 100$ and $\sigma = 15$. If the test is standardized so that it is comparable (has the same μ and σ) to other tests, what would be the standardized scores for the following individuals?

Person	X
1	70
2	75
3	60
4	50
5	80

STEP 1 Compute the z-score for each individual. Remember, the original distribution has $\mu = 65$ and $\sigma = 10$.

STEP 2 Compute the standardized score for each person. Remember that the standardized distribution will have $\mu = 100$ and $\sigma = 15$. Table 5.4 summarizes the computations for these steps and the results.

TABLE 5.4

	Computations	
	Step 1: $z = \frac{X - \mu}{\sigma}$	Step 2: $X = \mu + z\sigma$
Person 1	$z = \frac{70 - 65}{10} = +.5$	$X = 100 + .5(15)$ $= 100 + 7.5 = 107.5$
Person 2	$z = \frac{75 - 65}{10} = +1.0$	$X = 100 + 1(15)$ $= 100 + 15 = 115$
Person 3	$z = \frac{60 - 65}{10} = -.5$	$X = 100 + -.5(15)$ $= 100 - 7.5 = 92.5$
Person 4	$z = \frac{50 - 65}{10} = -1.5$	$X = 100 + -1.5(15)$ $= 100 - 22.5 = 77.5$
Person 5	$z = \frac{80 - 65}{10} = +1.5$	$X = 100 + 1.5(15)$ $= 100 + 22.5 = 122.5$

Summary			
Person	X	z	Standardized Scores
1	70	+.5	107.5
2	75	+1.0	115
3	60	−.5	92.5
4	50	−1.5	77.5
5	80	+1.5	122.5

· LEARNING CHECK ·

1 A population has $\mu = 37$ and $\sigma = 2$. If this distribution is transformed into a new distribution with $\mu = 100$ and $\sigma = 20$, what new values will be obtained for each of the following scores: 35, 36, 37, 38, 39?

2 For the following population, $\mu = 7$ and $\sigma = 4$: 2, 4, 6, 10, 13.
- a Transform this distribution so $\mu = 50$ and $\sigma = 20$.
- b Compute μ and σ for the new distribution. (You should obtain $\mu = 50$ and $\sigma = 20$.)

ANSWERS

1 The five scores 35, 36, 37, 38, and 39 are transformed to 80, 90, 100, 110, and 120, respectively.

2 a The original scores 2, 4, 6, 10, and 13 are transformed to 25, 35, 45, 65, and 80, respectively.
- b The new scores add up to $\sum X = 250$ so the mean is $\frac{250}{5} = 50$. SS for the transformed scores is 2000, the variance is 400, and the new standard deviation is 20.

SUMMARY

1 Each X value can be transformed into a z-score that specifies the exact location of X within the distribution. The sign of the z-score indicates whether the location is above (positive) or below (negative) the mean. The numerical value of the z-score specifies the number of standard deviations between X and μ.

2 The z-score formula is used to transform X values into z-scores:

$$z = \frac{X - \mu}{\sigma}$$

3 To transform z-scores back into X values, solve the z-score equation for X:

$$X = \mu + z\sigma$$

4 When an entire distribution of X values is transformed into z-scores, the result is a distribution of z-scores. The z-score distribution will have the same shape as the distribution of raw scores, and it always will have a mean of 0 and a standard deviation of 1.

5 When comparing raw scores from different distributions, it is necessary to standardize the distributions with a z-score transformation. The distributions will then be comparable because they will have the same parameters ($\mu = 0$, $\sigma = 1$). In practice, it is necessary to transform only those raw scores that are being compared.

6 In certain situations, such as in psychological testing, the z-scores are converted into standardized distributions that have a particular mean and standard deviation.

KEY TERMS

z-score
deviation score
raw score
z-score transformation
standard score
standardized distribution

FOCUS ON PROBLEM SOLVING

1. When you are converting an X value to a z-score (or vice versa), do not rely entirely on the formula. You can avoid careless mistakes if you use the definition of a z-score (sign and numerical value) to make a preliminary estimate of the answer before you begin computations. For example, a z-score of $z = -.85$ identifies a score located *below* the mean by almost one standard deviation. When computing the X value for this z-score, be sure that your answer is smaller than the mean, and check that the distance between X and μ is slightly less than the standard deviation.

A common mistake when computing z-scores is to forget to include the sign of the z-score. The sign is determined by the deviation score $(X - \mu)$ and should be carried through all steps of the computation. If, for example, the correct z-score is $z = -2.0$, then an answer of $z = 2.0$ would be wrong. In the first case, the raw score is 2 standard deviations *below* the mean. But the second (and incorrect) answer indicates that the X value is 2 standard deviations *above* the mean. These are clearly different answers, and only one can be correct. What is the best advice to avoid careless errors? Sketch the distribution, showing the mean and the raw score (or z-score) in question. This way you will have a concrete frame of reference for each problem.

2. When comparing scores from distributions that have different standard deviations, it is important to be sure that you use the correct value for σ in the z-score formula. Use the σ value for the distribution from which the raw score in question was taken.

3. Remember, a z-score specifies a relative position within the context of a specific distribution. A z-score is a relative value, not an absolute value. For example, a z-score of $z = -2.0$ does not necessarily suggest a very low raw score—it simply means that the raw score is among the lowest within that specific group.

PROBLEMS

1 Describe exactly what information is provided by a z-score.

2 Describe the characteristics of a distribution following a z transformation.

***3** At the beginning of the semester the instructor for developmental psychology gave the class an exam to determine how much the students already knew about the topic. The exam results were reported as z-scores, and Tom received a score of $z = +2.40$. Is Tom correct in concluding that he already knows a lot about developmental psychology? Explain your answer.

4 Suppose that two different distributions of raw scores have the same mean, $\mu = 200$. For both distributions, a score of $X = 250$ is 50 points above the mean. In which case would the score probably be a more extreme value, in the first distribution where the amount of variability is small or in the second distribution where there is a large amount of variability? Explain your answer.

***5** For a distribution of raw scores, the mean is $\mu = 45$. The z-score for $X = 55$ is computed and a value of $z = -2.00$ is obtained. Regardless of the value for the standard deviation, why must this z-score be incorrect?

6 For a population of scores with $\mu = 100$ and $\sigma = 16$,

a Find the z-score that corresponds to each of the following X values:

$X = 108$ $\quad X = 104$
$X = 132$ $\quad X = 92$
$X = 100$ $\quad X = 120$
$X = 124$ $\quad X = 84$

b Find the raw scores for each of the following z-scores:

$z = -1.00$ $\quad z = +\frac{1}{2}$
$z = +1.50$ $\quad z = -1.25$
$z = 0$ $\quad z = +.25$
$z = +2.00$ $\quad z = -2.00$

***7** A population has a mean of $\mu = 25$ with $\sigma = 5$.

a Compute the z-scores for the following X values.

27, 31, 29, 17, 15
28, 34, 33, 19, 22

b Compute the X values for the following z-scores.

$-.4$, $+1$, -3, $+2.8$, $+1.4$, $-.4$, -1.4, $+2$

8 A population is composed of the following scores:

13, 7, 12, 15, 5, 10, 11, 11, 10, 6

a Compute μ and σ.
b Find the z-score for each raw score in the population.

***9** For the following population of raw scores,

23	26	23	25	28
22	19	15	21	11
15	15	19	14	18
16	21	21	22	33
24	23	22	10	17
11	24	28	21	23
27	28	22	31	32

a Compute μ and σ.
b Transform the distribution to z-scores.

10 A population of scores has $\mu = 80$ and $\sigma = 20$. Find the z-score corresponding to each of the following X values:

85, 90, 110, 75, 60, 45
130, 82, 68, 80, 95, 30

11 A population has $\mu = 50$ and $\sigma = 6$. Find the raw score for each of the following z-scores:

2.50, 1, -3, -1.33, -1.5, $+\frac{1}{2}$, -2, 0, $-\frac{1}{2}$

***12** For a population with $\mu = 50$, a raw score of 43 corresponds to a z-score of -1.00. What is the standard deviation of this population?

13 For a population with $\sigma = 40$, a score of $X = 320$ corresponds to a z-score of $+2.00$. What is the mean for this population?

***14** The grades from a physics exam were reported in X values and in corresponding z-scores. For this exam, a raw score of 65 corresponds to a z-score of $+2.00$. Also, when $X = 50$, $z = -1.00$. Find the mean and standard deviation for the distribution of exam scores. (*Hint:* Sketch the distribution, and locate the positions for the two scores. How many standard deviations fall between the two X values?)

15 A population has a mean of $\mu = 115$. A raw score of $X = 145$ has a corresponding z-score of $z = +1.5$. What is the standard deviation for the population?

***16** On a statistics quiz you obtain a score of 7. Would you rather be in section A where $\sigma = 2$ or in section B where $\sigma = 1$? Assume that $\mu = 6$ for both sections.

17 Answer the same question in problem 16, but assume that $\mu = 8$ for both sections. Explain your answer.

18 Suppose you have a score of $X = 60$ in a distribution with $\mu = 55$. Explain how the standard deviation could make your score appear to be either "close to" the mean or "far from" the mean.

***19** In psychology, you received an exam score of 37, while the mean for the class is $\mu = 28$ with $\sigma = 6$. In another general psychology section, your friend received a 46. The distribution for this class has $\mu = 35$ and $\sigma = 10$. Who has a higher standing in the class?

20 A distribution of exam scores has a mean of $\mu = 75$ and a standard deviation of 8. On this exam, Mary has a score of $X = 82$, Bill has a z-score of $z = +.75$, and Susan scored at the mean. List these three students in order from highest to lowest score.

21 The mean of a distribution after a z-score transformation is always zero because $\sum z = 0$. Explain why $\sum z$ must always equal zero. (*Hint:* Examine the z-score formula.)

***22** The Wechsler Adult Intelligence Scale is composed of a number of subtests. Each subtest has been standardized so that $\mu = 10$ and $\sigma = 3$. A psychologist is updating some of the subtests. In particular, he has developed a new vocabulary subtest to replace the old one. For the new subtest, the psychologist finds $\mu = 35$ and $\sigma = 6$. Following are the raw scores for some of the subjects who took the new vocabulary subtest:

41, 32, 39, 44, 45, 24, 37, 27

What will their scores be when standardized?

23 A population of $N = 5$ scores consists of

1, 3, 5, 6, 7

a Compute μ and σ for this population.
b Find the z-score for each raw score in the distribution.
c Compute the mean and standard deviation for the set of z-scores (round off all calculations to two decimal places). What is demonstrated about z-score transformations?
d Explain the advantages of the characteristics of z transformations.

***24** For a distribution, $\mu = 20$ and $\sigma = 2$. The raw scores from this distribution are as follows:

16, 17, 18, 18, 18, 20, 20, 20
21, 21, 21, 21, 21, 22, 23, 23

a Transform this distribution so that $\mu = 50$ and $\sigma = 10$.
b Compute the values for μ and σ for the new distribution. They should equal 50 and 10, respectively.

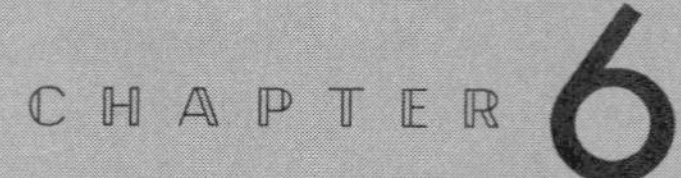

CHAPTER 6

PROBABILITY

TOOLS YOU WILL NEED

The following items are considered essential background material for this chapter. If you doubt your knowledge of any of these items, you should review the appropriate chapter or section before proceeding.

- Proportions (math review, Appendix A)
  - Fractions
  - Decimals
  - Percentages
- Basic algebra (math review, Appendix A)
- Upper and lower real limits (Chapter 2)
- *z*-Scores (Chapter 5)

PREVIEW

As you read through this textbook (or a novel, or a newspaper, etc.), which of the following are you more likely to encounter:

1. A word beginning with the letter K?
2. A word with a K as its third letter?

If you think about this question and answer honestly, you probably will decide that words beginning with a K are more probable.

A similar question was asked of a group of subjects in an experiment reported by Tversky and Kahneman (1973). Their subjects estimated that words beginning with K are twice as likely as words with K in the third position. In truth, the relation is just the opposite: There are more than twice as many words with a K in the third position as there are words beginning with a K. How can people be so wrong? Do they completely misunderstand probability?

When you were deciding which type of K words are more likely, you probably tried to estimate which words are more common in the English language. How many words can you think of that start with the letter K? How many words can you think of that have a K as the third letter? Because you have years of practice alphabetizing words according to their first letter, you find it much easier to search through your memory for words beginning with a K than to search for words with a K in third position. Consequently, you conclude that first-letter K words are more common.

Notice that when you use the strategy of counting words, you are not actually estimating probabilities; rather, you are estimating frequencies or proportions in the population. Most people seem to think of probability in terms of proportion. As you will see later in the chapter, this is a perfectly reasonable concept. Your error in judging the relative probabilities was not due to a misunderstanding of probability; instead, you simply were misled by the availability of the two types of words in your mind. If you had searched through a passage of text (instead of your mind), you probably would have found more third-letter K words, and you would have concluded (correctly) that these words are more probable.

In this chapter we will examine the statistical concept of probability. Although some of the mathematics and definitions may be new to you, there is a good chance that much of the material will be consistent with your present understanding of probability.

6.1 INTRODUCTION

Until this point, we have been concerned primarily with descriptive statistics, that is, finding ways to simplify the description and organization of a set of scores. Now we will begin to lay the foundations for inferential statistics. The goal of inferential statistics is to use the limited information from samples to draw general conclusions about populations. Remember, most experiments start with a general question concerning a population: for example,

Does a new antidepressant drug alter the mood of patients?

Will increased homework assignments improve reading scores for sixth graders?

Will overcrowding increase hostility among monkeys?

In each case the population is much too large to be examined directly. Instead, we must be content to work with a sample and hope that the information from the specific sample will help to answer our general question. The problem for inferential statistics is to define precisely the relationship between the sample and the population. However, when the values in a population are variable (not all the same), it is impossible to specify exactly which scores will be selected for any particular sample. Thus, there is not a perfect, one-to-one relationship between samples and populations. For this reason, relations between samples and populations most often are described in terms of probability. Suppose, for example, you are selecting a sample of 1 marble from a jar that contains 50 black and 50 white marbles. Although you cannot guarantee the exact outcome of your sample, it is possible to talk about the potential outcomes in terms of probabilities. In this case, you have a fifty-fifty chance of getting either color. Now consider another jar (population) that has 90 black and only 10 white marbles. Again, you cannot specify the exact outcome of a sample, but now you know that the sample probably will be a black marble. By knowing the makeup of a population, we can determine the probability of obtaining specific samples. In this way, probability gives us a connection between populations and samples.

You may have noticed that the preceding examples begin with a population and then use probability to describe the samples that could be obtained. This is exactly backward from what we want to do with inferential statistics. Remember, the goal of inferential statistics is to begin with a sample and then answer general questions about the population. We will reach this goal in a two-stage process. In the first stage, we develop probability as a bridge from population to samples. This stage involves identifying the types of samples that probably would be obtained from a specific population. Once this bridge is established, we simply reverse the probability rules to allow us to move from samples to populations (see Figure 6.1). The process of reversing the probability relation can be demonstrated by considering again the two jars of marbles we looked at earlier. (One jar has 50 black and 50 white marbles; the other jar has 90 black and only 10 white marbles.) This time, suppose that you are blindfolded when the sample is selected and that your task is to use the sample to help you to decide which jar was used. If you select a sample of $n = 4$ marbles and all are black, where did the sample come from? It should be clear that it would be relatively unlikely (low probability) to obtain this sample from jar 1; in four draws, you almost certainly would get at least 1 white marble. On the other hand, this sample would have a high probability from jar 2 where nearly all the marbles are black. Your decision, therefore, is that the sample probably came from jar 2. Notice that you now are using the sample to make an inference about the population.

FIGURE 6.1

The role of probability in inferential statistics. The goal of inferential statistics is to use the limited information from samples to draw general conclusions about populations. The relationship between samples and populations usually is defined in terms of probability. Probability allows you to start with a population and predict what kind of sample is likely to be obtained. This forms a bridge between populations and samples. Inferential statistics uses the *probability bridge* as a basis for making conclusions about populations when you have only sample data.

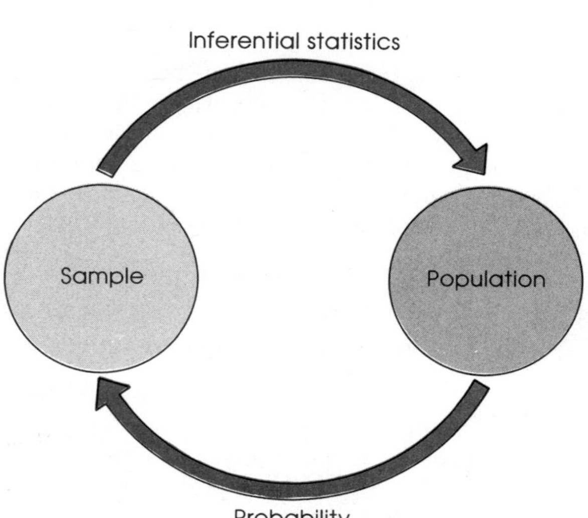

6.2 PROBABILITY DEFINITION

Probability is a huge topic that extends far beyond the limits of introductory statistics, and we will not attempt to examine it all here. Instead, we will concentrate on the few concepts and definitions that are needed for an introduction to inferential statistics. We begin with a relatively simple definition of probability.

DEFINITION In a situation where several different outcomes are possible, we define the *probability* for any particular outcome as a fraction or proportion. If the possible outcomes are identified as *A*, *B*, *C*, *D*, etc., then

$$\text{probability of } A = \frac{\text{number of outcomes classified as } A}{\text{total number of possible outcomes}}$$

For example, when you toss a balanced coin, the outcome will be either heads or tails. Because heads is one of two possible outcomes, the probability of heads is $p = \frac{1}{2}$.

If you are selecting 1 card from a complete deck, there are 52 possible outcomes. The probability of selecting the king of hearts would be $p = \frac{1}{52}$. The probability of selecting an ace would be $p = \frac{4}{52}$ because there are four aces in the deck.

To simplify the discussion of probability, we will use a notation system that eliminates a lot of the words. The probability of a specific outcome will be expressed with a capital *P* (for probability) followed by the specific outcome in parentheses. For example, the probability of selecting a king from a deck of cards would be written as *P*(king). The probability of obtaining heads for a coin toss would be written as *P*(heads).

You should note that probability is defined as a proportion. This definition makes it possible to restate any probability problem as a proportion problem. For example, the probability problem "What is the probability of obtaining a king from a deck of cards?" can be restated as "Out of the whole deck, what proportion are kings?" In each case, the answer is $\frac{4}{52}$ or "four out of fifty-two." This translation from probability to proportion may seem trivial now, but it will be a great aid when the probability problems become more complex. In most situations we are concerned with the probability of obtaining a particular sample from a population. The terminology of *sample* and *population* will not change the basic definition of probability. For example, the whole deck of cards can be considered as a population, and the single card we select is the sample.

The definition we are using identifies probability as a fraction or a proportion. If you work directly from this definition, the probability values you obtain will be expressed as fractions. For example, if you are selecting a card,

$$P(\text{spade}) = \tfrac{13}{52} = \tfrac{1}{4}$$

Or if you are tossing a coin,

$$P(\text{heads}) = \tfrac{1}{2}$$

You should be aware that these fractions can be expressed equally well as either decimals or percentages:

If you are unsure how to convert from fractions to decimals or percentages, you should review the section on proportions in the math review, Appendix A.

$$p = \tfrac{1}{4} = .25 = 25\%$$

$$p = \tfrac{1}{2} = .50 = 50\%$$

By convention, probability values most often are expressed as decimal values. But you should realize that any of these three forms is acceptable.

You also should note that all the possible probability values are contained in a limited range. At one extreme, when an event never occurs, the probability is zero or 0% (see Perspective 6.1). At the other extreme, when an event always occurs, the probability is 1, or 100%. For example, suppose you have a jar containing 10 white marbles. The probability of randomly selecting a black marble would be

$$P(\text{black}) = \frac{0}{10} = 0$$

The probability of selecting a white marble would be

$$P(\text{white}) = \frac{10}{10} = 1$$

RANDOM SAMPLING

For the preceding definition of probability to be accurate, it is necessary that the outcomes be obtained by a process called random sampling.

· DEFINITION · A *random sample* must satisfy two requirements:

1. Each individual in the population has an *equal chance* of being selected.
2. If more than one individual is to be selected for the sample, there must be *constant probability* for each and every selection.

Each of the two requirements for random sampling has some interesting consequences. The first assures that there is no bias in the selection process. For a population with N individuals, each individual must have the same probability, $p = 1/N$, of being selected. This means, for example, that you would not get a random sample of people in your city by selecting names from the yacht club membership list. Similarly, you would not get a random sample of college students by selecting individuals from your psychology classes. You also should note that the first requirement of random sampling prohibits you from applying the definition of probability to situations where the possible outcomes are not equally likely. Consider, for example, the question of whether or not there is life on Mars. There are only two possible alternatives:

1. There is life on Mars.
2. There is no life on Mars.

However, you cannot conclude that the probability of life on Mars is $p = \frac{1}{2}$.

The second requirement also is more interesting than may be apparent at first glance. Consider, for example, the selection of $n = 2$ cards from a complete deck. For the first draw, what is the probability of obtaining the jack of diamonds?

$$P(\text{jack of diamonds}) = \frac{1}{52}$$

Now, for the second draw, what is the probability of obtaining the jack of diamonds? Assuming you still are holding the first card, there are two possibilities:

$$P(\text{jack of diamonds}) = \frac{1}{51} \quad \text{if the first card was not the jack of diamonds}$$

or

$$P(\text{jack of diamonds}) = 0 \quad \text{if the first card was the jack of diamonds}$$

In either case, the probability is different from its value for the first draw. This contradicts the requirement for random sampling which says that the probability must stay constant. To keep the probabilities from changing from one selection to the next, it is necessary to replace each sample before you make the next selection. This is called *sampling with replacement*. The second requirement for random samples (constant

PERSPECTIVE 6.1

ZERO PROBABILITY

An event that never occurs has a probability of zero. However, the opposite of this statement is not always true: A probability of zero does not mean that the event is guaranteed never to occur.

Whenever there is an extremely large number of possible events, the probability of any specific event is assigned the value zero. This is done because the probability value tends toward zero as the number of possible events gets large. Consider, for example, the series

$$\frac{1}{10} \quad \frac{1}{100} \quad \frac{1}{1000} \quad \frac{1}{10{,}000} \quad \frac{1}{100{,}000}$$

Note that the value of the fraction is getting smaller and smaller, headed toward zero. At the far extreme, when the number of possible events is so large that it cannot be specified, the probability of a single, specific event is said to be zero.

$$\frac{1}{\text{infinite number}} = 0$$

Consider, for example, the fish in the ocean. If there were only 10 fish, then the probability of selecting any particular one would be $p = \frac{1}{10}$. Note that if you add up the probabilities for all 10 fish, you get a total of 1.00. Of course, there really are billions of fish in the ocean, and the probability of catching any specific one would be 1 out of billions; for all practical purposes, $p = 0$. However, this does not mean that you are doomed to fail whenever you go fishing. The zero probability simply means that you cannot predict in advance which fish you will catch. Note that each individual fish has a probability of zero, but there are so many fish that when you add up all the zeros you still get a total of 1.00. In probability, a value of zero doesn't mean never. But, practically speaking, it does mean very, very close to never.

probability) demands that you sample with replacement. (*Note:* The definition we are using defines one type of random sampling, often called a *simple random sample* or an *independent random sample.* Other types of random sampling are possible. You also should note that the requirement for replacement becomes relatively unimportant with very large populations. With large populations the probability values stay essentially constant whether or not you use replacement.)

6.3 PROBABILITY RULES

There are two general rules that are used commonly in working with probabilities. They are known as the addition rule and the multiplication rule.

The *addition rule* concerns the probability that either one of two possible events will occur. If A and B are two events, then this rule states that

$$P(A \text{ or } B) = P(A) + P(B) - P(A \text{ and } B \text{ together}) \tag{6.1}$$

EXAMPLE 6.1 If you are tossing a single die (one-half of a pair of dice), what is the probability of rolling either a 2 or a 6? According to the rule,

$$\begin{aligned} P(2 \text{ or } 6) &= P(2) + P(6) - P(2 \text{ and } 6 \text{ together}) \\ &= \tfrac{1}{6} + \tfrac{1}{6} - 0 \\ &= \tfrac{2}{6} = \tfrac{1}{3} \end{aligned}$$

Because it is impossible to get a 2 and a 6 together on one toss, this part of the equation is zero.

To check the rule, we will use the definition of probability. When you toss a die, there are six possible outcomes (1, 2, 3, 4, 5, 6). Two out of these six are either a 2 or a 6. Therefore, according to the definition of probability,

$$P(2 \text{ or } 6) = \tfrac{2}{6} = \tfrac{1}{3}$$

For Example 6.1, the final part of the rule, $P(A \text{ and } B \text{ together})$, did not play any role. When two events cannot occur simultaneously, they are said to be *mutually exclusive:*

The existence of either one excludes the other. In this case, $P(A \text{ and } B \text{ together}) = 0$ and does not contribute to the probability value. The next example shows how this part of Formula 6.1 can be important.

· EXAMPLE 6.2 · If you are selecting a card from a complete deck, what is the probability that you will obtain either a king or a diamond? According to the rule,

$$\begin{aligned} P(\text{king or diamond}) &= P(\text{king}) + P(\text{diamond}) - P(\text{king and diamond together}) \\ &= \tfrac{4}{52} + \tfrac{13}{52} - \tfrac{1}{52} \\ &= \tfrac{16}{52} \end{aligned}$$

This time it is possible to have a king and a diamond together in the same card: the king of diamonds.

Once again, we will use the definition of probability to check the answer. When you select a card from a complete deck, there are 52 possible outcomes. Of the 52 cards, 13 are diamonds (including the king of diamonds), and there are 3 other kings. This gives a total of 16 cards that are either kings or diamonds. Therefore, according to the definition of probability,

$$P(\text{king or diamond}) = \tfrac{16}{52}$$ ·

The *multiplication rule* concerns the probability associated with a sequence of events, or the simultaneous occurrence of two events. If A and B are two possible outcomes, then the probability of A and B occurring in sequence or simultaneously is

$$P(A \text{ and } B) = P(A) \times P(B) \tag{6.2}$$

This rule is valid only if A and B are *independent events*; that is, the probability of A is not affected by the occurrence of B, and the probability of B is not affected by the occurrence of A (see Perspective 6.2). Successive coin tosses, for example, are independent. The probability of heads for any particular toss does not depend on the outcome of previous tosses. (The coin does not remember whether it came up heads or tails on earlier tosses.) On the other hand, if you are selecting cards from a deck, the successive outcomes will be independent only if you sample with replacement. Otherwise, the probabilities will change from one draw to the next depending on which cards you selected on previous draws.

· EXAMPLE 6.3 · If you toss a balanced coin two times, what is the probability that you will get heads both times? According to the rule,

$$\begin{aligned} P(\text{heads then heads}) &= P(\text{heads}) \times P(\text{heads}) \\ &= \tfrac{1}{2} \times \tfrac{1}{2} \\ &= \tfrac{1}{4} \end{aligned}$$

Again, we will check this answer using the definition of probability. When you toss a coin twice, there are four possible outcomes:

Outcome	First Toss	Second Toss
1	Heads	Heads
2	Heads	Tails
3	Tails	Heads
4	Tails	Tails

PERSPECTIVE 6.2

PROBABILITY FALLACIES: THE INDEPENDENCE OF EVENTS

Armed with information on probability, we are likely to make assumptions and inferences about events we observe. Sometimes the assumptions we make are incorrect and lead to misinterpretation. One common source of confusion occurs when we are dealing with the probabilities of independent events. Remember, when events are independent, the probability of one event occurring is not affected by the occurrence of the other. If we fail to recognize this fact, we might make erroneous conclusions and decisions. Two examples of these errors follow.

Probability Fallacy 1: A wary traveler is reassured to learn that the probability of a terrorist bringing a bomb on an airplane is actually quite small (say, for example, 1 out of every 1,000,000 flights). In addition, the traveler knows the multiplication rule for probabilities (Formula 6.2) and calculates that the probability of having two bombs simultaneously on the same flight is 1 out of 1,000,000,000,000 (one in a trillion). Therefore, our wary traveler brings a bomb on the airplane, reasoning that it is essentially impossible that a terrorist would bring a second bomb onto the same plane. His logic of course is faulty, because each person who brings a bomb on board constitutes an independent event. The probability of a terrorist bomb (event A) is not affected by the presence of the traveler's bomb (event B).

Probability Fallacy 2: A gambler has been placing bets for weeks without reward. Every bet made during this period has been a loser. We ask, "With all these losses, why do you continue to place bets?" And the gambler replies confidently, "With all those loses, I'm due for a lucky streak." The fallacy pops up again. The gambler is assuming that each previous bet will affect the probability of future winnings. In reality, each bet placed is an independent event and will not affect the probabilities for future wagers. The gambler obviously never had a course in statistics.

Out of these four possible outcomes, only one has two heads. Therefore, according to the definition of probability,

$$P(\text{heads then heads}) = \tfrac{1}{4}$$

LEARNING CHECK

1 If you are tossing a balanced coin and the first 3 tosses are heads, what is the probability that the 4th toss also will be heads?

2 The animal colony in the psychology department contains 20 male rats and 30 female rats. Of the 20 males, 15 are white and 5 are spotted. Of the 30 females, 15 are white and 15 are spotted. If you randomly select 1 rat from this colony,
a What is the probability of obtaining a female?
b What is the probability of obtaining a white male?
c What is the probability of obtaining a rat that is spotted or female?

ANSWERS

1 Coin tosses are independent events, so the probability of heads will be $p = \frac{1}{2}$, no matter what happened on earlier tosses.

2 **a** $p = \frac{30}{50} = .60$ **b** $p = \frac{15}{50} = .30$ **c** $p = \frac{20}{50} + \frac{30}{50} - \frac{15}{50} = \frac{35}{50} = .70$

6.4 PROBABILITY AND FREQUENCY DISTRIBUTIONS

The situations where we are concerned with probability usually will involve a population of scores that can be displayed in a frequency distribution graph. If you think of the graph as representing the entire population, then different portions of the graph will represent different portions of the population. Because probability and proportion are equivalent, a particular proportion of the graph corresponds to a particular probability in the population. Thus, whenever a population is presented in a frequency distribution graph, it will be possible to represent probabilities as proportions of the graph. The relationship between graphs and probabilities is demonstrated in the following example.

FIGURE 6.2

A frequency distribution histogram for a population that consists of $N = 10$ scores. The shaded part of the figure indicates the portion of the whole population that corresponds to scores greater than $X = 4$. The shaded portion is two-tenths ($p = \frac{2}{10}$) of the whole distribution.

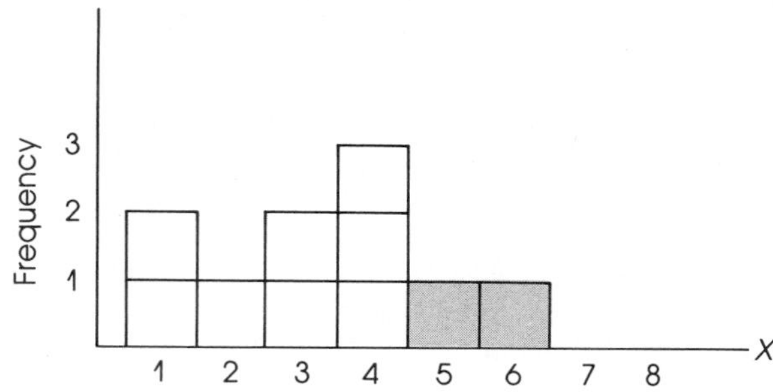

EXAMPLE 6.4 We will use a very simple population that contains only $N = 10$ scores with values 1, 1, 2, 3, 3, 4, 4, 4, 5, 6. This population is shown in the frequency distribution graph in Figure 6.2. If you are taking a random sample of $n = 1$ score from this population, what is the probability of obtaining a score greater than 4? In probability notation,

$$P(X > 4) = ?$$

Using the definition of probability, there are 2 scores that meet this criterion out of the total group of $N = 10$ scores, so the answer would be $p = \frac{2}{10}$. This answer can be obtained directly from the frequency distribution graph if you recall that probability and proportion measure the same thing. Looking at the graph (Figure 6.2), what proportion of the population consists of scores greater than 4? The answer is the shaded part of the distribution, that is, 2 squares out of the total of 10 squares in the distribution. Notice that we now are defining probability as proportion of *area* in the frequency distribution graph. This provides a very con crete and graphic way of representing probability.

Using the same population once again, what is the probability of selecting a score less than 5? In symbols,

$$P(X < 5) = ?$$

Going directly to the distribution in Figure 6.2, we now want to know what part of the graph is not shaded. The unshaded portion consists of 8 out of the 10 blocks ($\frac{8}{10}$ of the area of the graph), so the answer is $p = \frac{8}{10}$.

6.5 PROBABILITY AND THE NORMAL DISTRIBUTION

The normal distribution was first introduced in Chapter 2 as an example of a commonly occurring shape for population distributions. An example of a normal distribution is shown in Figure 6.3. Although the exact shape for the normal distribution is precisely defined by an equation (see Figure 6.3), we can easily describe its general characteristics: It is a symmetrical distribution, with the highest frequency in the middle (mode = mean = median) and the frequencies tapering off gradually as the scores get farther and farther from the mean. In simple terms, in a normal distribution most individuals are around average, and extreme scores are relatively rare. This shape describes many common variables such as adult heights, intelligence scores, personality scores, and so on.

FIGURE 6.3

The normal distribution. The exact shape of the normal distribution is specified by an equation relating each X value (score) with each Y value (frequency). The equation is

$$Y = \frac{1}{\sqrt{2\pi\sigma^2}} e^{-(X-\mu)^2/2\sigma^2}$$

(π and e are mathematical constants.) In simpler terms, the normal distribution is symmetrical with a single mode in the middle. The frequency tapers off as you move farther from the middle in either direction.

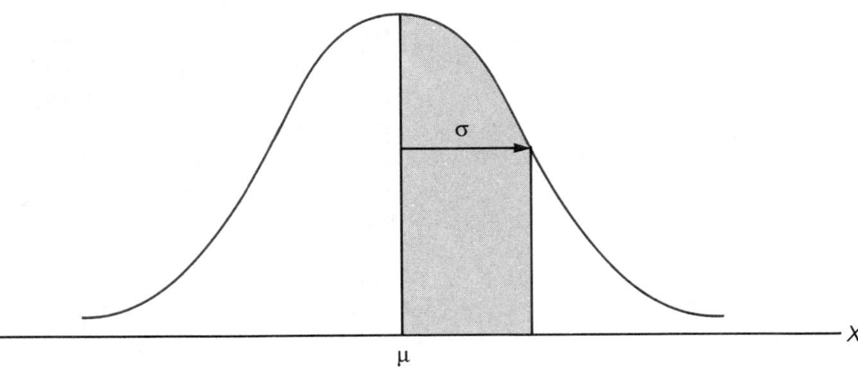

The normal shape also can be defined by the proportions of area contained in each section of the distribution. For instance, all normal shaped distributions will have exactly 34.13% of their total area in the section between the mean and the point that is one standard deviation above the mean (see Figure 6.3). By this definition, a distribution is normal if and only if it has all the right proportions.

Because the normal distribution is a good model for many naturally occurring distributions and because this shape is guaranteed in some circumstances (as you will see in Chapter 7), we will devote considerable attention to this particular distribution.

The process of answering probability questions about a normal distribution is introduced in the following example.

EXAMPLE 6.5 Adult heights form a normal shaped distribution with a mean of 68 inches and a standard deviation of 6 inches. Given this information about the population, our goal is to determine the probability associated with specific samples. For example, what is the probability of randomly selecting an individual who is taller than 6 feet (6 feet = 72 inches)? Restating this question in probability notation, we get

$$P(X > 72) = ?$$

We will follow a step-by-step process to find the answer to this question.

1 First, the probability question is translated to a proportion question: Out of all the possible adult heights, what proportion is greater than 72 inches?

2 You know that "all the possible adult heights" is simply the population distribution. This population is shown in Figure 6.4(a).

FIGURE 6.4

(a) The distribution of adult heights. This is a normal distribution with $\mu = 68$ and $\sigma = 6$. The portion of the distribution corresponding to scores greater than 72 has been shaded. (b) The distribution of adult heights after being transformed into z-scores. The mean is changed to $z = 0$, and the value of $X = 72$ is transformed to $z = +.67$. The portion of the distribution corresponding to z-scores greater than $+.67$ has been shaded.

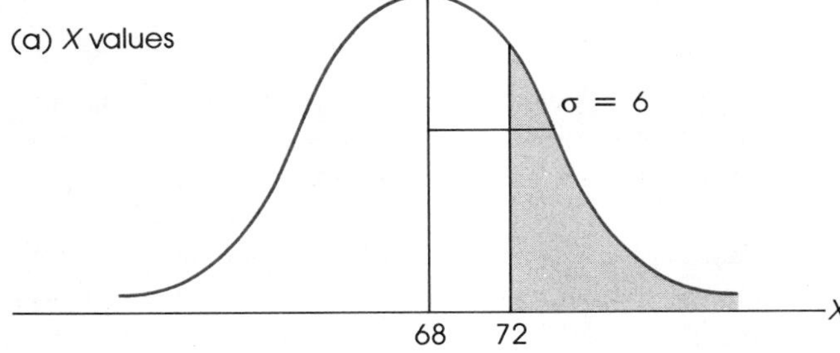

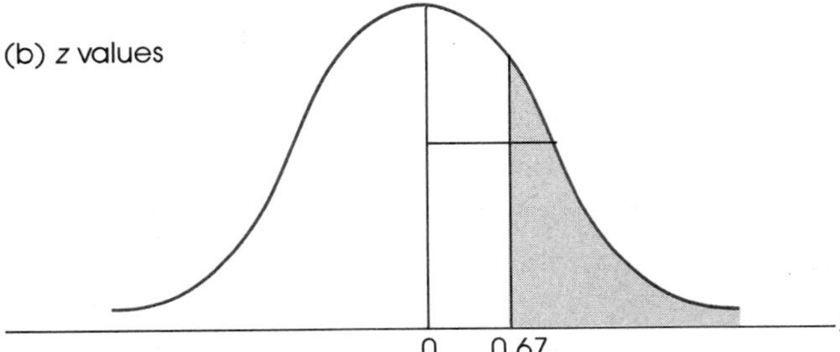

3 We want to find what portion of the distribution (what area) consists of values greater than 72. This part is shaded in the figure.

4 Looking at Figure 6.4(a), it appears that we have shaded in approximately .25 (or 25%) of the distribution. This is the answer we wanted. •

THE UNIT NORMAL TABLE Obviously, the probability answer we obtained for the preceding example was just a rough approximation. To make the answer more precise, we need a way to measure accurately the area in the normal distribution. Conceivably, you could do this by very carefully drawing the distribution on graph paper and then precisely measuring the amount of area in each section. Fortunately, this work already has been done, and the results are available in a table. The table, called the unit normal table, lists areas, or proportions, for all the possible sections of the normal distribution.

To use the unit normal table, you first need to transform the distribution of adult heights into a distribution of z-scores. Remember, changing from X values to z-scores will not change the shape of the distribution (it still will be normal), but it will transform the mean from $\mu = 68$ to $z = 0$ and will transform the standard deviation to 1. This is called *standardizing* the distribution. You should note that standardizing any normal distribution will produce the same result. No matter what mean or standard deviation you begin with, the standardized distribution (of z-scores) will be normal, with $\mu = 0$ and $\sigma = 1$. Because all normal distributions transform to this single standardized normal distribution, it is possible to have a single table that serves for every normal distribution.

Our distribution of adult heights is redrawn and standardized in Figure 6.4(b). Note that we have simply converted X values to z-scores. The value of $X = 72$ corresponds to a z-score of $z = \frac{4}{6}$, or .67. Our problem now is to determine what proportion of the normal distribution corresponds to z-scores greater than +.67. Now the answer can be found in the unit normal table. This table lists the proportion of area corresponding to every possible z-score for the normal distribution.

USING THE UNIT NORMAL TABLE A complete unit normal table is provided in Appendix B on page 484, and a portion of the table is reproduced in Figure 6.5. The table lists z-score values and two proportions associated with each z-score in the normal distribution. The z-scores are listed in column A of the table. Column B lists the proportion of the distribution that is located between the mean and each z-score. Column C lists the proportion of the distribution that lies in the tail beyond each z-score.

To change from a decimal value to a percentage, you multiply by 100 or simply move the decimal point two places to the right.

For a z-score of $z = .25$, for example, the table lists .0987 in column B and .4013 in column C. Of the entire normal distribution, .0987 (9.87%) is located between the mean and a z-score of +.25 (see Figure 6.5). Similarly, the tail of the distribution beyond $z = +.25$ contains .4013 (40.13%) of the distribution (see Figure 6.5). Notice that these two values account for exactly one-half or 50% of the distribution:

$$.0987 + .4013 = .5000$$

The following examples demonstrate several different ways the table can be used to find proportions or probabilities.

• EXAMPLE 6.6a • Occasionally, the answer to a proportion problem can be found directly in the table. For example, what proportion of the normal distribution corresponds to z-scores greater than $z = 1.00$? The portion we want has been shaded in the normal distribution shown in Figure 6.6(a).

In this case, the shaded portion is the tail of the distribution beyond $z = 1.00$. To find this proportion, you simply look up $z = 1.00$ in the table and read the answer directly from column C. The answer is .1587 (or 15.87%). •

· FIGURE 6.5 ·

A portion of the unit normal table. This table lists proportions of the normal distribution corresponding to each z-score value. Column A of the table lists z-scores. Column B lists the proportion of the normal distribution that is located between the mean and the z-score value. Column C lists the proportion of the normal distribution that is located in the tail of the distribution beyond the z-score value.

(A) z	(B) Area Between Mean and z	(C) Area Beyond z
0.00	.0000	.5000
0.01	.0040	.4960
0.02	.0080	.4920
0.03	.0120	.4880
0.20	.0793	.4207
0.21	.0832	.4168
0.22	.0871	.4129
0.23	.0910	.4090
0.24	.0948	.4052
0.25	.0987	.4013
0.26	.1026	.3974
0.27	.1064	.3936
0.28	.1103	.3897
0.29	.1141	.3859
0.30	.1179	.3821
0.31	.1217	.3783
0.32	.1255	.3745
0.33	.1293	.3707
0.34	.1331	.3669

B
Mean z

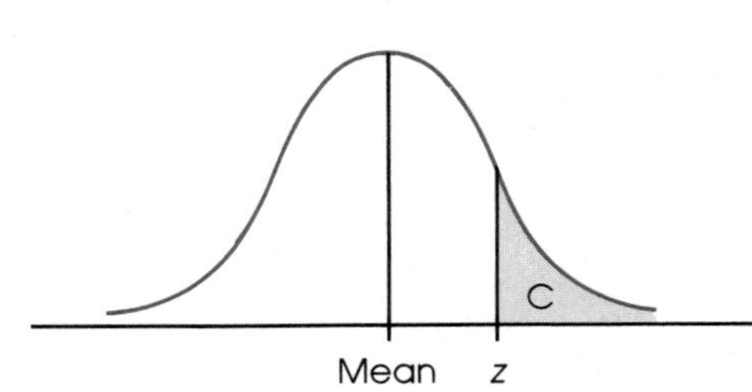

· EXAMPLE 6.6b · Sometimes the table will provide only a part of the required proportion. Suppose, for example, that you want the proportion of the normal distribution corresponding to z-scores less than $z = 1.50$. This portion has been shaded in Figure 6.6(b).

In this example, the shaded area consists of two sections:

1. The section between the mean and the z-score
2. The entire left half of the distribution

To find the area between the mean and the z-score, look up $z = 1.50$ in the table and read the proportion from column B. You should find .4332 in the table. The rest of the shaded area consists of the section to the left of the mean. Because the normal distribution is symmetrical, exactly one-half (.5000, or 50%) is on each

· FIGURE 6.6 ·

Proportions of the normal distribution. (a) The portion consisting of z values greater than $+1.00$. (b) The portion consisting of z values less than $+1.50$. (c) The portion consisting of z values less than $-.50$.

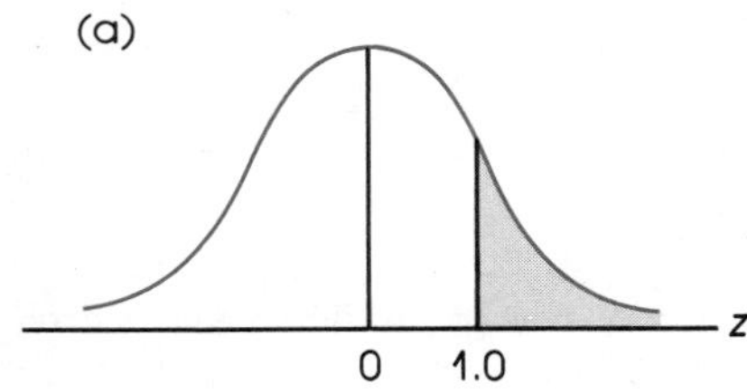

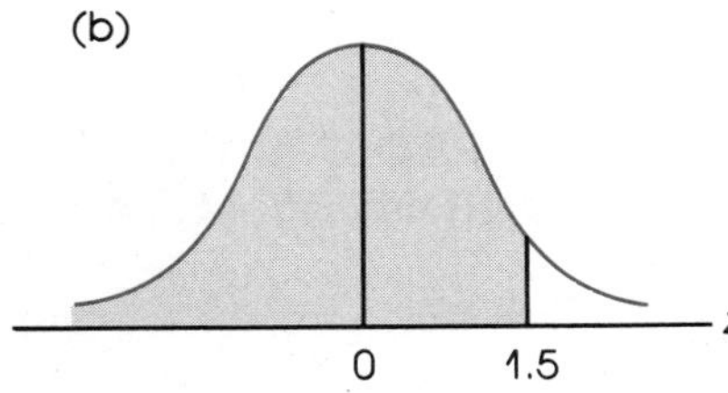

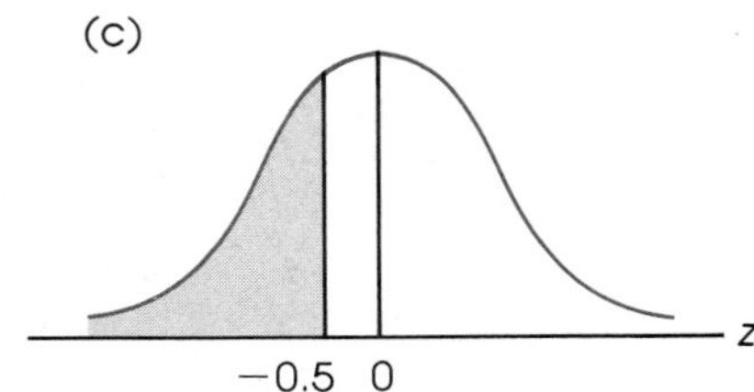

side of $z = 0$. Thus, the shaded area left of the mean is exactly .5000. You add the two sections to obtain the total shaded area:

$$.5000 + .4332 = .9332$$

(*Note:* You could solve this problem by looking up $z = 1.50$ and reading the column C value of .0668 from the table. This proportion corresponds to the unshaded tail of the distribution—precisely the portion of the distribution that you don't want. To find the rest of the distribution, you simply subtract from 1.00: $1.0000 - .0668 = .9332$.) ·

· EXAMPLE 6.6c · Many problems will require that you find proportions for negative z-scores. For example, what proportion of the normal distribution corresponds to z-scores less than $z = -.5$? This portion has been shaded in Figure 6.6(c).

To answer questions with negative z-scores, simply remember that the distribution is symmetrical with a z-score of zero in the middle, positive values to the right, and negative values to the left. The proportion in the left-hand tail beyond $z = -.50$ is exactly the same are the area in the right-hand tail beyond $z = +.50$. To find this proportion, look up $z = .50$ in the table and find the proportion in column C. You should get an answer of .3085. ·

As a general rule when working probability problems with the normal distribution, you should always sketch a distribution, locate the mean with a vertical line, and shade in the portion you are trying to determine. Before you start work, look at your sketch and make an estimate of the answer. (Does the shaded portion look like 20% or like 60% of the total distribution?) If you make a habit of drawing sketches and estimating answers, you will avoid careless errors.

· LEARNING CHECK ·

To help avoid mistakes, always sketch a normal distribution and shade in the portion you want.

1 Find the proportion of a normal distribution that is located in the tail beyond each z-score listed:
a $z = +1.00$ **b** $z = +.80$ **c** $z = -2.00$ **d** $z = -.33$

2 Find the proportion of a normal distribution that is located between the mean and each z-score listed:
a $z = -.50$ **b** $z = -1.50$ **c** $z = +.67$ **d** $z = +2.00$

3 Find the proportion of a normal distribution that is located between the z-score boundaries listed:
a Between $z = -.50$ and $z = +.50$
b Between $z = -1.00$ and $z = +1.00$
c Between $z = -1.96$ and $z = +1.96$

ANSWERS

1 **a** .1587 (15.87%) **b** .2119 (21.19%) **c** .0228 (2.28%) **d** .3707 (37.07%)
2 **a** .1915 (19.15%) **b** .4332 (43.32%) **c** .2486 (24.86%) **d** .4772 (47.72%)
3 **a** .3830 (38.30%) **b** .6826 (68.26%) **c** .9500 (95.00%)

6.6 ANSWERING PROBABILITY QUESTIONS WITH THE UNIT NORMAL TABLE

The unit normal table provides a listing of proportions or probability values corresponding to every possible z-score in a normal distribution. To use this table to answer probability questions, it is necessary that you first transform the X values

PERSPECTIVE 6.3

FINDING PROBABILITIES FROM A NORMAL DISTRIBUTION

Working with probabilities for a normal distribution involves two steps: (1) using a z-score formula and (2) using the unit normal table. However, the order of the steps may vary, depending on the type of probability question you are trying to answer.

In one instance, you may start with a known X value and have to find a probability that is associated with it (as in Example 6.7). First you must convert the X value to a z-score using formula 5.1 (page 110). Then you consult the unit normal table to get the probability associated with the particular area of the graph. *Note:* you cannot go directly from the X value to the unit normal table. You must find the z-score first.

However, suppose you begin with a known probability value and want to find the X value associated with it (as in Example 6.8). In this case you use the unit normal table first, to find the z-score that corresponds with the probability value. Then you convert the z-score into an X value using formula 5.2 (page 111).

Figure 6.7 illustrates the steps you must take when moving from an X value to a probability or from a probability back to an X value. This chart, much like a map, guides you through the essential steps as you "travel" between X values and probabilities.

FIGURE 6.7

This map shows how to find a probability value that corresponds to any specific score, or how to find the score that corresponds to any specific probability value.

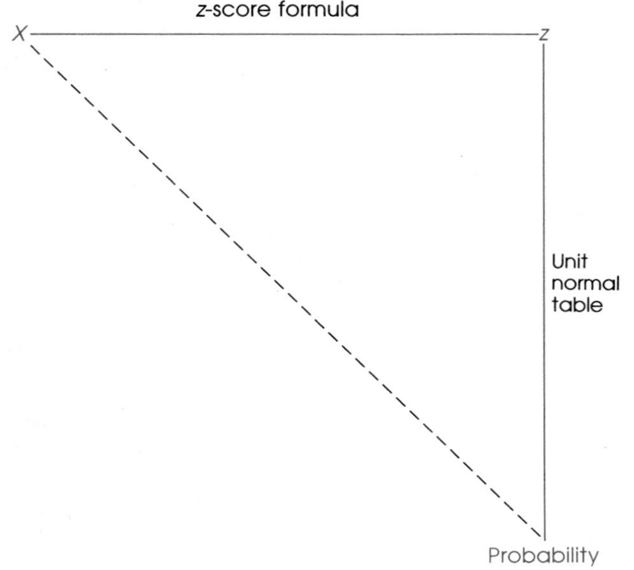

into z-scores (standardize the distribution) and then use the table to look up the probability value. This process is discussed in Perspective 6.3.

EXAMPLE 6.7 We now can use the unit normal table to get a precise answer to the probability problem we started earlier in the chapter (see Example 6.4). The goal is to find the probability of randomly selecting an individual who is taller than 6 feet (72 inches). We know that the distribution of adult heights is normal with $\mu = 68$ and $\sigma = 6$. In symbols, we want

$$P(X > 72) = ?$$

Restated as a proportion question, we want to find the proportion of the whole distribution that corresponds to values greater than 72. The whole distribution is drawn in Figure 6.4, and the part we want has been shaded.

You cannot go directly from a score to the unit normal table. You always must go by way of z-scores.

The first step is to change the X values to z-scores. Specifically, the score of $X = 72$ is changed to

$$z = \frac{X - \mu}{\sigma} = \frac{72 - 68}{6} = \frac{4}{6} = .67$$

Next, you look up this z-score value in the unit normal table. Because we want the proportion of the distribution that is located beyond $z = .67$, the answer will be found in column C. A z-score of .67 corresponds to a proportion of .2514.

The probability of randomly selecting someone taller than 72 inches is .2514, or about 1 out of 4:

$$P(X > 72) = .2514 \qquad (25.14\%)$$

In Example 6.7 we started with an X value and used the table to find the corresponding probability value. Looking at the map in Perspective 6.3, we started at X and moved to P. Like most maps, this one can be used to guide travel in either direction; that is, it is possible to start at P and move to X. To move in this direction means that you start with a specific probability value and then find the corresponding score. The following examples demonstrate this type of problem.

EXAMPLE 6.8 Scores on the Scholastic Appitude Test (SAT) form a normal distribution with $\mu = 500$ and $\sigma = 100$. What is the minimum score necessary to be in the top 15% of the SAT distribution? This problem is shown graphically in Figure 6.8. Notice that this problem is asking you to find the 85th percentile.

In this problem, we begin with a proportion (15% = .15) and we are looking for a score. According to the map in Perspective 6.3, we can move from P (proportion) to X (score) by going via z-scores. The first step is to use the unit normal table to find the z-score that corresponds to a proportion of .15. Because the proportion is located beyond z in the tail of the distribution, we will look in column C for a proportion of .1500. Note that you may not find .1500 exactly, but locate the closest value possible. In this case, the closest value in the table is .1492, and the z-score that corresponds to this proportion is $z = 1.04$.

The next step is to determine whether the z-score is positive or negative. Remember, the table does not specify the sign of the z-score. Looking at the graph in Figure 6.8, you should realize that the score we want is above the mean, so the z-score is positive, $z = +1.04$.

Now you ready for the last stage of the solution, that is, changing the z-score into an X value. Using z-score formula 5.2 (page 111) and the known values of μ, σ, and z, we obtain

$$\begin{aligned} X &= \mu + z\sigma \\ &= 500 + 1.04(100) \\ &= 500 + 104 \\ &= 604 \end{aligned}$$

The conclusion for this example is that you must have an SAT score of at least 604 to be in the top 15% of the distribution.

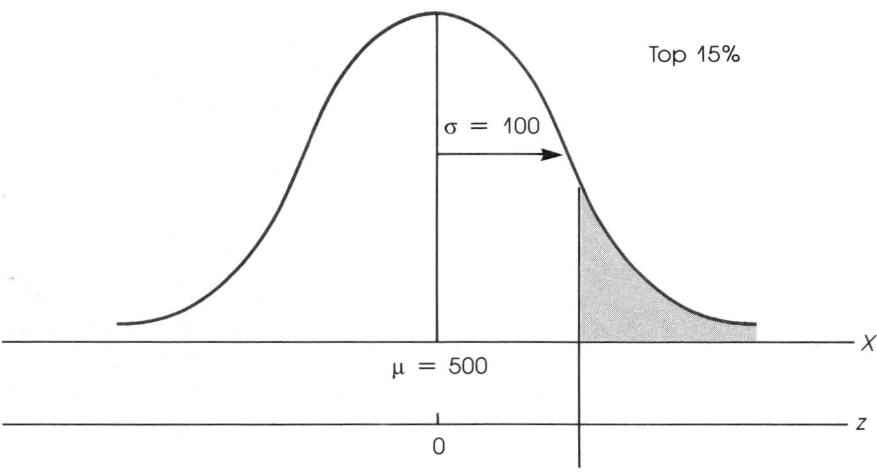

FIGURE 6.8 The distribution of SAT scores. The problem is to locate the score that separates the top 15% from the rest of the distribution. A line is drawn to divide the distribution roughly into 15% and 85% sections.

Because the unit normal table gives only specific portions of the normal distribution, you will encounter some problems where the stated proportion is not directly available in the table. In this case, you must convert the stated proportion into a value that is compatable with the numbers listed in column B or column C of the table. The following example demonstrates this type of problem.

· EXAMPLE 6.9 · A mathematics appitude test is constructed so that the scores for the general population form a normal distribution with $\mu = 100$ and $\sigma = 16$. For this distribution, what score is necessary to place you in the top 60% of the population? In other words, that score separates the top 60% from the rest of the distribution? This problem is shown graphically in Figure 6.9.

Again we are starting with a proportion (60% = .60) and trying to find a score. The first step is to use the unit normal table to find the *z*-score that corresponds to this proportion. But you cannot look up $p = .6000$ in the table. This portion of the distribution (the shaded area in Figure 6.9) does not correspond to the area between the mean and *z* (column B), or the area beyond *z* (column C). Before you can use the table, the proportion stated in the problem must be transformed into one of the listed areas.

Looking again at Figure 6.9, you should see that the 60% that is shaded can be divided into two sections: 50% to the right of the mean and 10% to the left of the mean. You also should note that the 10% on the left is located between the mean and the *z*-score. Similarly, you should see that 40% of the distribution (the unshaded portion) is located in the tail beyond the *z*-score. Thus, you can use either 10% (.1000) in column B or 40% (.4000) in column C to find the *z*-score.

Be careful; the table does not differentiate positive and negative *z*-scores, so you must look at the distribution to determine the sign.

Now we must use the unit normal table to locate a proportion of .1000 in column B (or .4000 in column C). The closest value in column B is $p = .0987$ and the corresponding *z*-score is $z = .25$. For this problem, however, the score we want is below the mean, so the *z*-score is negative, $z = -.25$.

The final step is to transform the *z*-score into an *X* value. The *z*-score of $z = -.25$ indicates that the score we want is located below the mean by one-quarter of a standard deviation. Because a whole standard deviation is 16 points, and the mean is $\mu = 100$, the score we want is $X = 96$.

· FIGURE 6.9 ·

The distribution of mathematics aptitude scores. The problem is to locate the score that separates the top 60% from the rest of the distribution. A line is drawn to divide the distribution roughly into 60% and 40% sections. Because 60% is slightly more than half, the line is placed slightly to the left of the mean.

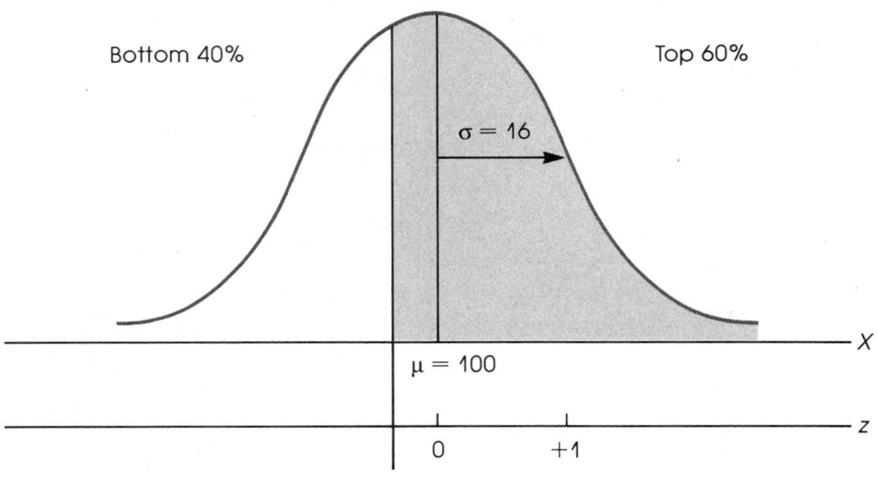

The conclusion for this example is that you must have a mathematics appitude score of at least 96 to be in the top 60% of the population. •

· EXAMPLE 6.10 · This example demonstrates the process of determining a probability associated with a specified range of scores in a normal distribution. Once again, we will use the distribution of SAT scores which is normal with $\mu = 500$ and $\sigma = 100$. For this distribution, what is the probability of randomly selecting an individual with a score between $X = 600$ and $X = 650$? In probability notation, the problem is to find

$$P(600 < X < 650) = ?$$

Figure 6.10 shows the distribution of SAT scores with the relevant portion shaded. Remember, finding the probability is the same as finding the proportion of the distribution located between 600 and 650.

The first step is to transform each of the X values into a z-score:

$$\text{For } X = 600: \quad z = \frac{X - \mu}{\sigma} = \frac{600 - 500}{100} = \frac{100}{100} = 1.00$$

$$\text{For } X = 650: \quad z = \frac{X - \mu}{\sigma} = \frac{650 - 500}{100} = \frac{150}{100} = 1.50$$

The problem now is to find the proportion of the distribution that is located between $z = +1.00$ and $z = +1.50$. There are several different ways this problem can be solved using the information in the unit normal table. One technique is described here.

Using column C of the table, we find that the area beyond $z = 1.00$ is .1587. This includes the portion we want, but is also includes an extra portion in the tail. This extra portion is the area beyond $z = 1.50$, and according to the table (column C), it is .0668 of the total distribution. Subtracting out the extra portion,

· FIGURE 6.10 ·

The distribution of SAT scores. The problem is to find the proportion of this distribution located between the values $X = 600$ and $X = 650$. This portion is shaded in the figure.

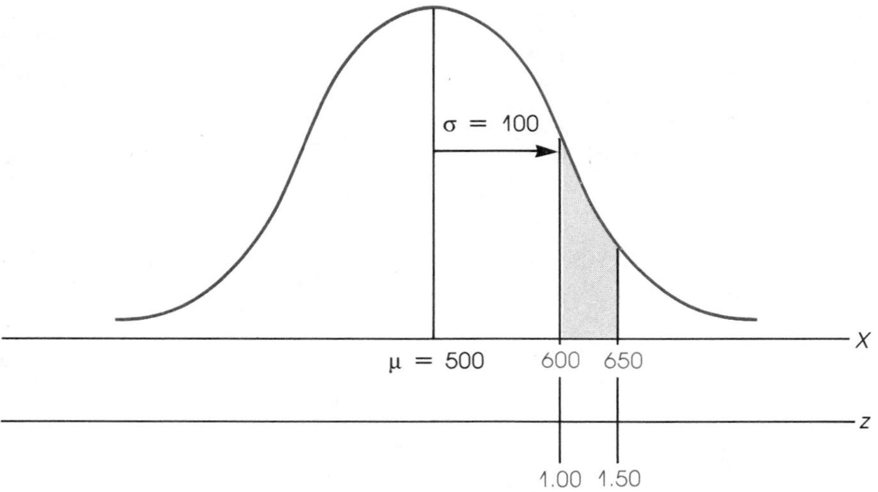

we obtain a final answer of

$$P(600 < X < 650) = .1587 - .0668$$
$$= .0919$$

Thus, the probability of randomly selecting an individual with a SAT score between 600 and 650 is $p = .0919$ (9.19%). •

· LEARNING CHECK ·

1 For a normal distribution with a mean of 80 and a standard deviation of 10, find each probability value requested.
- **a** $P(X > 85) = ?$
- **b** $P(X < 95) = ?$
- **c** $P(X > 70) = ?$
- **d** $P(75 < X < 100) = ?$

2 For a normal distribution with a mean of 100 and a standard deviation of 20, find each value requested.
- **a** What is the 60th percentile?
- **b** What is the minimum score needed to be in the top 5% of this distribution?
- **c** What scores form the boundaries for the middle 60% of this distribution?

3 What is the probability of selecting a score greater than 45 from a positively skewed distribution with $\mu = 40$ and $\sigma = 10$?

ANSWERS

1
- **a** $p = .3085$ (30.85%)
- **b** $p = .9332$ (93.32%)
- **c** $p = .8413$ (84.13%)
- **d** $p = .6687$ (66.87%)

2
- **a** $z = +.25$; $X = 105$
- **b** $z = +1.64$; $X = 132.8$
- **c** $z = \pm.84$; boundaries are 83.2 and 116.8

3 There is no answer. You cannot use the unit normal table to answer this question because the distribution is not normal.

6.7 PROBABILITY AND THE BINOMIAL DISTRIBUTION

When a variable is measured on a scale consisting of exactly two categories, the resulting data are called binomial. The term *binomial* can be loosely translated as "two names," referring to the two categories on the measurement scale.

Binomial data can occur when a variable naturally exists with only two categories. For example, people can be classified as male or female and a coin toss results in either head or tails. It also is common for a researcher to simplify data by collapsing it into two categories. For example, a psychologist may use personality scores to classify people as either high or low in aggression.

In binomial situations, the researcher often knows the probabilities associated with each of the two categories. With a balanced coin, for example, $P(\text{heads}) = P(\text{tails}) = \frac{1}{2}$. The question of interest is the number of times each category occurs in a series of trials or in a sample of individuals. For example:

> What is the probability of obtaining 15 heads in 20 tosses of a balanced coin?
>
> What is the probability of obtaining more than 40 introverts in a sample of 50 college freshmen?

As we shall see, the normal distribution serves as an excellent model for computing probabilities with binomial data.

THE BINOMIAL DISTRIBUTION

To answer probability questions about binomial data, we need to examine the binomial distribution. To define and describe this distribution we first introduce some notation.

1. The two categories are identified as A and B.
2. The probabilities (or proportions) associated with each category are identified as,

$$p = P(A) = \text{the probability of } A$$

$$q = P(B) = \text{the probability of } B$$

Notice that $p + q = 1.00$ because A and B are the only two possible outcomes.

3. The number of individuals or observations in the sample is identified by n.
4. The variable X refers to the number of times category A occurs in the sample. Notice that X can have any value from 0 (none of the sample is in category A) to n (all the sample is in category A).

· DEFINITION · Using the notation presented above, the *binomial distribution* shows the probability associated with each value of X, from $X = 0$ to $X = n$.

A simple example of a binomial distribution is presented next.

· EXAMPLE 6.11 · Figure 6.11 shows the binomial distribution for the number of heads obtained in two tosses of a balanced coin. This distribution shows that it is possible to obtain as many as 2 heads or as few as 0 heads in two tosses. The most likely outcome (highest probability) is to obtain exactly 1 head in two tosses. The construction of this binomial distribution is discussed in detail next.

For this example, the event we are considering is a coin toss. There are two possible outcomes, heads and tails. We assume the coin is balanced so,

$$p = P(\text{heads}) = \tfrac{1}{2}$$

$$q = P(\text{tails}) = \tfrac{1}{2}$$

We are looking at a sample of $n = 2$ tosses and the variable of interest is

$$X = \text{the number of heads}$$

To construct the binomial distribution, we will look at all the possible outcomes from tossing a coin 2 times. The complete set of 4 outcomes is listed below.

1st toss	2nd toss	
Heads	Heads	(both heads)
Heads	Tails	(each sequence has
Tails	Heads	exactly 1 head)
Tails	Tails	(no heads)

Notice that there are 4 possible outcomes when you toss a coin 2 times. Only 1 of the 4 outcomes has 2 heads, so the probability of obtaining 2 heads is $p = \frac{1}{4}$. Similarly, 2 of the 4 outcomes have exactly 1 head, so the probability of one head is $p = \frac{2}{4} = \frac{1}{2}$. Finally, the probability of no heads ($X = 0$) is $p = \frac{1}{4}$. These are the probabilities shown in Figure 6.11.

You should notice that this binomial distribution can be used to answer probability questions. For example, what is the probability of obtaining at least 1

FIGURE 6.11

The binomial distribution showing the probability for the number of heads in two tosses of a balanced coin.

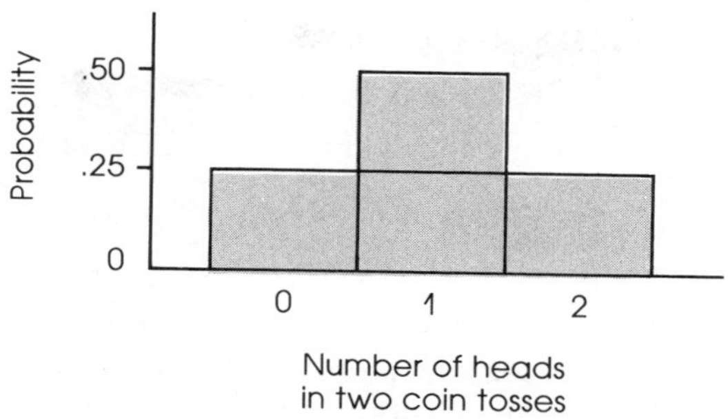

head in 2 tosses? According to the distribution shown in Figure 6.12, the answer would be $\frac{3}{4}$. •

Similar binomial distributions have been constructed for the number of heads in 4 tosses of a balanced coin and for 6 tosses of a coin (Figure 6.12). It should be obvious from the binomial distributions shown in Figures 6.11 and 6.12 that the binomial distribution tends toward a normal shape, especially when the sample size (n) is relatively large.

It should not be surprising that the binomial distribution tends to be normal. With $n = 10$ coin tosses, for example, the most likely outcome would be to obtain around $X = 5$ heads. On the other hand, values far from 5 would be very unlikely—you would not expect to get all 10 heads or all 10 tails (0 heads) in 10 tosses. Notice that we have described a normal-shaped distribution: The probabilities are highest in the middle (around $X = 5$), and they taper off as you move toward either extreme.

THE NORMAL APPROXIMATION TO THE BINOMIAL DISTRIBUTION

We have stated that the binomial distribution tends to approximate a normal distribution, particularly when n is large. To be more specific, the binomial distribution will be a nearly perfect normal distribution when pn and qn are both equal to or greater than 10. Under these circumstances, the binomial distribution will approximate a

FIGURE 6.12

Binomial distributions showing probabilities for the number of heads in 4 tosses of a balanced coin (left) and in 6 tosses of a balanced coin (right).

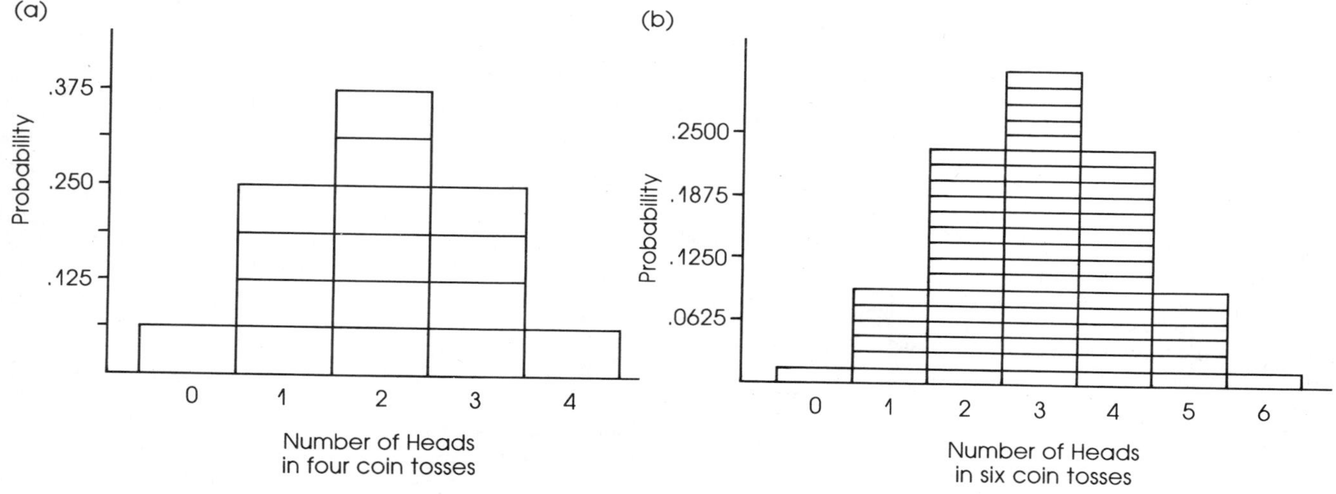

Note: The value of 10 for pn or qn is a general guide, not an absolute cutoff. Values slightly less than 10 still provide a good approximation. However, with smaller values the normal approximation becomes less accurate as a substitute for the binomial distribution.

normal distribution with the following parameters:

a. Mean: $\mu = pn$

b. Standard Deviation: $\sigma = \sqrt{npq}$

Within this normal distribution, each value of X has a corresponding z-score,

$$z = \frac{X - \mu}{\sigma} = \frac{X - pn}{\sqrt{npq}}$$

The fact that the binomial distribution tends to be normal in shape means that we can compute probability values directly from z-scores and the unit normal table.

It is important to remember that the normal distribution is only an approximation of a true binomial distribution. Binomial values, such as the number of heads in a series of coin tosses, are discrete. The normal distribution is continuous. However, the normal approximation provides an extremely accurate model for computing binomial probabilities in many situations. Figure 6.13 shows the difference between the discrete binomial distribution (histogram) and the normal distribution (smooth curve). Although the two distributions are slightly different, the area under the distributions is nearly equivalent. Remember, it is the area under the distribution that is used to find probabilities. To gain maximum accuracy when using the normal approximation, you must remember that each X value in the binomial distribution is actually an interval, not a point on the scale. In Figure 6.13, for example, $X = 6$ is actually an interval bounded by the real limits of 5.5 and 6.5. To find the probability of obtaining a score of $X = 6$, you should find the area of the normal distribution that is contained between the two real limits. If you are using the normal approximation to find the probability of obtaining a score greater than $X = 6$, you should use the area beyond the real limit boundary of 6.5. The following two examples demonstrate how the normal approximation to the binomial distribution is used to compute probability values.

EXAMPLE 6.12 Suppose you are taking a multiple-choice test where each question has four possible answers. If there are 48 questions on the test, what is the probability that you would get exactly 14 questions correct by simply guessing at the answers?

If you are just guessing, then the probability of getting a question correct is $p = \frac{1}{4}$ and the probability of guessing wrong is $q = \frac{3}{4}$. With a sample of $n = 48$ questions, this example meets the criteria for using the normal approximation to the binomial:

$pn = \frac{1}{4}(48) = 12$

$qn = \frac{3}{4}(48) = 36$ (both greater than 10)

Therefore, the distribution showing the number correct out of 48 questions will be

FIGURE 6.13

The relation between the binomial distribution and the normal distribution. The binomial distribution is always a discrete histogram, and the normal distribution is a continuous, smooth curve. Each X value is represented by a bar in the histogram or a section of the normal distribution.

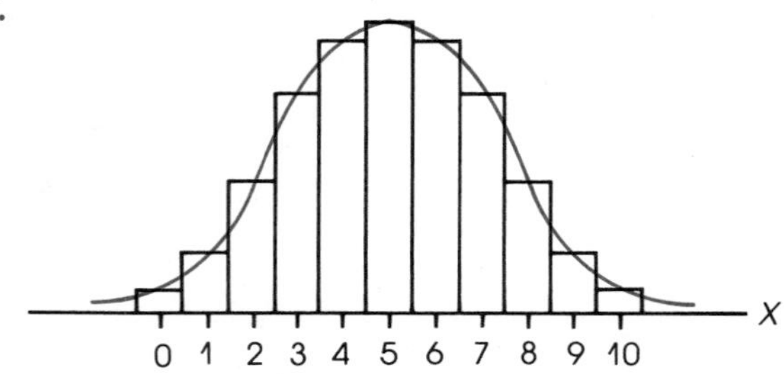

normal with parameters

$$\mu = pn = 12$$

$$\sigma = \sqrt{npq} = \sqrt{9} = 3$$

This distribution is shown in Figure 6.14. We want the proportion of this distribution that corresponds to $X = 14$; that is, the portion bounded by $X = 13.5$ and $X = 14.5$. This portion is shaded in Figure 6.14. To find the shaded portion, we first convert each X value into a z-score. For $X = 13.5$,

$$z = \frac{X - \mu}{\sigma} = \frac{13.5 - 12}{3} = .50$$

For $X = 14.5$,

$$z = \frac{X - \mu}{\sigma} = \frac{14.5 - 12}{3} = .83$$

Looking up these values in the unit normal table, we find

a. The area beyond $z = .50$ is .3085.

b. The area beyond $z = .83$ is .2033.

Therefore, the area between the two z-scores would be

$$.3085 - .2033 = .1052$$

You should remember that this value is an approximation to the exact probability value. However, it is a reasonably accurate approximation. To demonstrate the accuracy of the normal approximation, we have computed the exact probability of getting $X = 14$ questions correct from the binomial distribution. This probability is .1015. Notice that the normal approximation value of .1052 is very close to the exact probability of .1015. As we mentioned earlier, the normal distribution provides an excellent approximation for finding binomial probabilities.

· EXAMPLE 6.13 · Once again suppose that you are taking a multiple-choice test with 4 possible answers for each of 48 questions. If you simply guess the answer for each question, what is the probability that you would get more than 14 correct?

This is the same binomial situation that we considered in the previous example. For each question, the two categories are "correct" and "incorrect," and the probabilities are

$$p = P(\text{correct}) = \tfrac{1}{4}$$

$$q = P(\text{incorrect}) = \tfrac{3}{4}$$

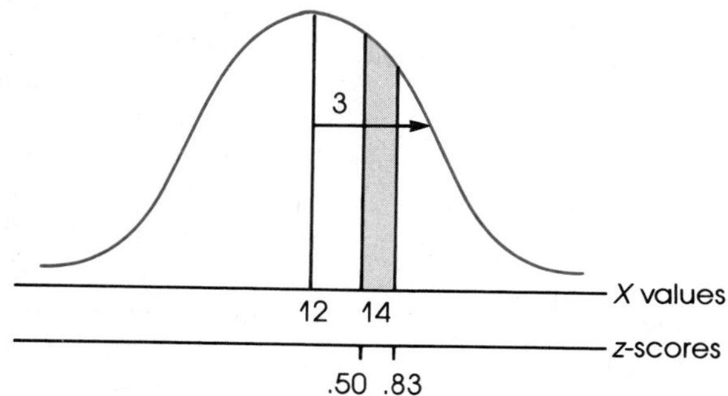

· FIGURE 6.14 ·

The binomial distribution (normal approximation) for the number of answers guessed correctly (X) on a 48-question multiple-choice test. The shaded portion corresponds to the probability of guessing exactly 14 questions. Notice that the score $X = 14$ corresponds to an interval bounded by $X = 13.5$ and $X = 14.5$.

Caution: If the question asked for the probability of 14 or more correct, you would use the area beyond 13.5. Read the question carefully.

The normal approximation for this binomial distribution is shown in Figure 6.14. Because we want the probability of obtaining *more than* 14 correct, we must find the area located in the tail of the distribution beyond $X = 14.5$. (Remember, a score of 14 correct corresponds to the interval from 13.5 to 14.5. We want the area beyond this interval.) The first step is to find the z-score corresponding to the boundary $X = 14.5$.

$$z = \frac{X - \mu}{\sigma} = \frac{14.5 - 12}{3} = .83$$

Now we can look up the probability in the unit normal table. In this case, we want the proportion in the tail of the distribution beyond $z = .83$.

The value from the unit normal table is .2033. This is the answer we want. If you are simply guessing on the exam, the probability of getting more than 14 questions correct is $p = .2033$, or 20.33%. •

· LEARNING CHECK ·

1 Under what circumstances is the normal distribution an accurate approximation to the binomial distribution?

2 A multiple-choice test consists of 48 questions with 4 possible answers for each questions. What is the probability that you would get more than 20 questions correct just by guessing?

3 If you toss a balanced coin 36 times, you would expect, on the average to get 18 heads and 18 tails. What is the probability of obtaining exactly 18 heads in 36 tosses?

ANSWERS

1 When pn and qn are both greater than 10.

2 $p = \frac{1}{4}$, $q = \frac{3}{4}$. $P(X > 20.5) = P(z > 2.83) = .0023$

3 $z = \pm.17$, $p = .1350$

SUMMARY

1 The probability of a particular event A is defined as a fraction or proportion:

$$P(A) = \frac{\text{number of outcomes classified as } A}{\text{total number of possible outcomes}}$$

2 This definition is accurate only for a random sample. There are two requirements that must be satisfied for a random sample:
  a Every individual in the population has an equal chance of being selected.
  b When more than one individual is being selected, the probabilities must stay constant. This means there must be sampling with replacement.

3 All probability problems can be restated as proportion problems. The "probability of selecting a king from a deck of cards" is equivalent to the "proportion of the deck that consists of kings." For frequency distributions, probability questions can be answered by determining proportions of area. The "probability of selecting an individual with an IQ greater than 108" is equivalent to the "proportion of the whole population that consists of IQs above 108."

4 For normal distributions, these probabilities (proportions) can be found in the unit normal table. This table provides a listing of the proportions of a normal distribution that correspond to each z-score value. With this table it is possible to move between X values and probabilities using a two-step procedure:
  a The z-score formula (Chapter 5) allows you to transform X to z or to change z back to X.
  b The unit normal table allows you to look up the probability (proportion) corresponding to each z-score or the z-score corresponding to each probability.

5 The binomial distribution is used whenever the measurement procedure simply classifies individuals into exactly two categories. The two categories are identified as A and B, with probabilities of

$$P(A) = p \quad \text{and} \quad P(B) = q$$

6 The binomial distribution gives the probability for each value of X, where X equals the number of occurrences of category A in a series of n events. For example, X equals the number of heads in $n = 10$ tosses of a coin.

7 When pn and qn are both at least 10, the binomial distribution is closely approximated by a normal distribution with

$$\mu = pn$$

$$\sigma = \sqrt{npq}$$

8 In the normal approximation to the binomial distribution, each value of X has a corresponding z-score:

$$z = \frac{X - \mu}{\sigma} = \frac{X - pn}{\sqrt{npq}}$$

With the z-score and the unit normal table, you can find probability values associated with any value of X. For maximum accuracy, however, you must remember that each X value is actually an interval bounded by real limits. Use the appropriate real limits when computing z-scores and probabilities.

KEY TERMS

probability
random sample
sampling with replacement
the addition rule
the multiplication rule
mutually exclusive events
independent events
unit normal table
binomial distribution
normal approximation (binomial)

FOCUS ON PROBLEM SOLVING

1. We have defined probability as being equivalent to a proportion, which means that you can restate every probability problem as a proportion problem. This definition is particularly useful when you are working with frequency distribution graphs where the population is represented by the whole graph and probabilities (proportions) are represented by portions of the graph. When working problems with the normal distribution, you always should start with a sketch of the distribution. You should shade the portion of the graph that reflects the proportion you are looking for.

2. When using the unit normal table you must remember that the proportions in the table correspond (columns B and C) to specific portions of the distribution. This is important because you will often need to translate the proportions from a problem into specific proportions provided in the table. Also, remember that the table allows you to move back and forth between z-score and proportions. You can look up a given z to find a proportion, or you can look up a given proportion to find the corresponding z-score. However, you cannot go directly from an X value to a probability in the unit normal table. You must first compute the z-score for X. Likewise, you cannot go directly from a probability value to a raw score. First you have to find the z-score associated with the probability (see Perspective 6.3).

3. Remember, the unit normal table shows only positive z-scores in column A. However, since the normal distribution is symmetrical, the probability values in columns B and C also apply to the half of the distribution that is below the mean. To be certain that you have the correct sign for z, it helps to sketch the distribution showing μ and X.

4. A common error for students is to use negative values for proportions on the left-hand side of the normal distribution. Proportions (or probabilities) are always positive: 10% is 10% whether it is in the left or the right tail of the distribution.

5. The proportions in the unit normal table are accurate only for normal distributions. If a distribution is not normal, you cannot use the table.

6. For maximum accuracy when using the normal approximation to the binomial distribution, you must remember that each X value is an interval bounded by real limits. For example, to find the probability of obtaining an X value greater than 10, you should use the real limit 10.5 in the z-score formula. Similarly, to find the probability of obtaining an X value less than 10, you should use the real limit 9.5.

1348

PROBLEMS

1 In a psychology class of 60 students there are 15 males and 45 females. Of the 15 men, only 5 are freshmen. Of the 45 women, 20 are freshmen. If you randomly sample an individual from this class,

a What is the probability of obtaining a female?

b What is the probability of obtaining a freshman?

c What is the probability of obtaining a female or a freshman?

d What is the probability of obtaining a male freshman?

*2 A jar contains 10 black marbles and 20 white marbles. If you are taking a random sample of three marbles from this jar and the first two marbles are both white, what is the probability that the third marble will be black?

3 Find the proportion of the normal distribution that lies in the tail beyond each of the following z-scores:

a $z = .50$ c $z = -1.50$

b $z = 1.75$ d $z = -.25$

*4 Find the proportion of the normal distribution that is located between the following z-score boundaries:

a Between $z = .25$ and $z = .75$

b Between $z = -1.00$ and $z = +1.00$

c Between $z = 0$ and $z = 1.50$

d Between $z = -.75$ and $z = 2.00$

5 Find the z-score that separates a normal distribution into the following two portions:

a Lowest 10% versus highest 90%

b Lowest 25% versus highest 75%

c Lowest 60% versus highest 40%

d Lowest 80% versus highest 20%

*6 For a normal distribution with a mean of $\mu = 80$ and $\sigma = 12$,

a What is the probability of randomly selecting a score greater than 83?

b What is the probability of randomly selecting a score greater than 74?

c What is the probability of randomly selecting a score less than 92?

d What is the probability of randomly selecting a score less than 62?

7 One question on a multiple-choice test asked for the probability of selecting a score greater than $X = 50$ from a normal population with $\mu = 60$ and $\sigma = 20$. The answer choices were:

a .1915 b .3085 c .6915

Sketch a distribution showing this problem, and without looking at the unit normal table, explain why answers a and b cannot be correct.

8 A normal distribution has a mean of 120 and a standard deviation of 20. For this distribution,

a What score separates the top 40% (highest scores) from the rest?

b What score would you need to be in the top 10% of the distribution?

c What range of scores would form the middle 60% of this distribution?

*9 It takes Tom an average of $\mu = 30$ minutes to drive to work. The distribution of driving times is nearly normal with $\sigma = 10$ minutes. If Tom leaves home at 9:05, what is the probability that he will be late for a 9:30 meeting at work?

10 A normal distribution has a mean of 80 and a standard deviation of 10. For this distribution, find each of the following probability values:

a $P(X > 75) = ?$ c $P(X < 100) = ?$

b $P(X < 65) = ?$ d $P(65 < X < 95) = ?$

*11 IQ scores form a normal distribution with $\mu = 100$ and $\sigma = 15$.

a An IQ below 70 is designated as "mentally retarded." What proportion of the population is in this category?

b IQ scores between 90 and 110 are designated "average." What proportion of the population is average?

c IQ scores between 120 and 130 are designated "superior." What proportion of the population is superior?

12 The scores on a psychology exam form a normal distribution with $\mu = 80$ and $\sigma = 8$. On this exam, Tom has a score of $X = 84$. Mary's score is located at the 60th percentile. John's score corresponds to a z-score of $z = .75$. If these three students are listed from highest score to lowest score, what is the correct ordering?

*13 Scores on the college entrance exam are normally distributed with $\mu = 500$ and $\sigma = 100$.

a What is the minimum score needed to be in the top 2% on this exam?

b What is the 70th percentile on this exam?

c John has an exam score of $X = 630$. What is his percentile rank?

d What scores (X values) form the boundaries for the middle 95% of this distribution?

*14 A positively skewed distribution has a mean of 100 and a standard deviation of 12. What is the probability of randomly selecting a score greater than 106 from this distribution? (Be careful; this is a trick problem.)

15 If you are tossing a balanced coin,

a What is the probability of getting two heads in a row?

b What is the probability of getting three heads in a row?

c If you toss the coin four times, which of the following sequences would you predict is more probable:

Sequence 1: heads—heads—heads—heads

Sequence 2: heads—tails—heads—tails

d Calculate the exact probability for each sequence in part c. (You should find that these two sequences are equally probable.)

e If you toss the coin three times, what is the probability that you will obtain at least one tail? (*Hint:* Before you try to calculate this directly, check your answer to part b.)

*16 Three archers A, B, and C each shoot one arrow at a target. The probabilities of hitting the target are

$P(A \text{ hits}) = .5$

$P(B \text{ hits}) = .25$

$P(C \text{ hits}) = .75$

Determine the probability for each of the following outcomes:

a A and B both hit the target.
b A and B both miss the target.
c A or B will hit the target.
d All three will miss the target.
e A or B or C will hit the target.

17 A normal distribution has a mean of 60 and a standard deviation of 10.

a Find the semi-interquartile range for this distribution.
b If the standard deviation were 20, what would be the value for the semi-interquartile range?
c In general, what is the relation between the standard deviation and the semi-interquartile range for a normal distribution?

***18** A mathematics instructor teaches the same algebra course to a section of humanities students and to a section of pre-engineering students. The results of the final exam for each section are summarized as follows. Assume that both distributions are normal.

Humanities	Engineering
$\mu = 63$	$\mu = 72$
$\sigma = 12$	$\sigma = 8$

a Bill is in the humanities section and earned a grade of $X = 74$ on the final. What is his percentile rank in this section? What would his rank be if he were in the pre-engineering section?
b Tom is in the pre-engineering section. His grade on the final exam corresponds to a percentile rank of 40%. What rank would he have if he were in the humanities section?
c Mary scored at the 60th percentile in the humanities section, and Jane scored at the 31st percentile in the pre-engineering section. Who had the better exam score (X value)?

19 All entering freshmen are required to take an English proficiency placement exam (EPPE). Based on these exam scores, the college assigns students to different sections of introductory English. The top 25% of the class goes into the advanced course, the middle 50% goes into the regular English course, and students in the bottom 25% are assigned to a remedial English course. For this year's class the distribution of EPPE scores was approximately normal with $\mu = 68$ and $\sigma = 7.5$. What scores should be used as the cutoff values for assigning students to the three English courses?

***20** The scores on a civil service exam form a normal distribution with $\mu = 100$ and $\sigma = 20$. Only those individuals scoring in the top 20% on this exam are interviewed for jobs.

a What is the minimum score needed to qualify for an interview?
b Because there was an unusually high demand for new employees this year, the civil service board offered job interviews to everyone scoring above $X = 108$. What percentage of the individuals taking the exam were offered interviews?

21 A social psychologist has developed a new test designed to measure social aggressiveness. The scores on this test form a normal distribution with $\mu = 60$ and $\sigma = 9$. Based on these test scores, the psychologist wants to classify the population into five categories of aggressiveness:

I: The meek (the lowest 5%)

II: The mild (the next 20%)

III: The average (the middle 50%)

IV: The aggressive (the next 20%)

V: The dangerous (the top 5%)

What scores should be used to form the boundaries for these categories?

***22** The college admissions office reports that applicants for last year's freshman class had an average SAT score of $\mu = 480$ with $\sigma = 90$. The minimum SAT required for admission last year was $X = 450$. The distribution of SAT scores for this year's applicants has $\mu = 500$ with $\sigma = 80$. This year's cutoff for admission is $X = 470$. Assume that both distributions are normal.

a What proportion of last year's applicants were offered admission?
b What proportion of this year's applicants were offered admission?
c Of the students who were admitted last year, what proportion would have been rejected if the college had been using this year's cutoff?
d Of the students who were rejected this year, what proportion would have been accepted if the college were still using last year's standards?

Caution: For parts c and d of Problem 22 you are asked for a proportion of a proportion.

23 The normal approximation to the binomial distribution is accurate only when both pn and qn are greater than 10. This requirement is violated in both of the following situations. In each case, explain why the normal distribution is not an appropriate substitute for the real binomial distribution. (*Hint:* Calculate the mean and sketch each binomial distribution.)

Situation I: $n = 6$, $p = .5$, and $q = .5$

Situation II: $n = 50$, $p = .9$, and $q = .1$

***24** One common test for extra-sensory perception (ESP) requires subjects to predict the suit of a card that is randomly selected from a complete deck. If a subject has no ESP and is just guessing, find each of the probabilities requested a What is the probability of a correct prediction on each trial?

b What is the probability of correctly predicting more than 18 out of 48 cards?

25 A college dormitory recently sponsored a taste comparison between two major soft drinks. Of the 64 students who participated, 39 selected brand A. If there really is no preference between the two drinks, what is the probability that 39 or more would choose Brand A just by chance?

***26** A trick coin has been weighted so that the probability of heads is .8 and the probability of tails is .2.

a If you toss this coin 100 times, how many heads would you expect on the average?

b What is the probability of obtaining more than 95 heads in 100 tosses?

c What is the probability of obtaining less than 95 heads in 100 tosses?

d What is the probability of obtaining exactly 95 heads in 100 tosses?

27 a What is the probability of getting more than 30 heads in 50 tosses of a balanced coin?

b What is the probability of getting more than 60 heads in 100 tosses of a balanced coin?

c Parts a and b of this question both asked for the probability of getting more than 60% heads in a series of coin tosses ($\frac{30}{50} = \frac{60}{100} = 60\%$). Explain why the two probabilities are different?

***28** A true-false test has 36 questions. If a passing grade on this test is $X = 24$ correct, what is the probability of obtaining a passing grade just by guessing?

CHAPTER 7

PROBABILITY AND SAMPLES: THE DISTRIBUTION OF SAMPLE MEANS

TOOLS YOU WILL NEED

The following items are considered essential background material for this chapter. If you doubt your knowledge of any of these items, you should review the appropriate chapter or section before proceeding.

- Random sampling (Chapter 6)
- Probability and the normal distribution (Chapter 6)
- *z*-Scores (Chapter 5)

PREVIEW

Now that you have some understanding of probability, consider the following problem:

> Imagine an urn filled with balls. Two-thirds of the balls are one color, and the remaining one-third is a second color. One individual selects 5 balls from the urn and finds that 4 are red and 1 is white. Another individual selects 20 balls and finds that 12 are red and 8 are white. Which of these two individuals should feel more confident that the urn contains two-thirds red balls and one-third white balls, rather than the opposite?*

When Tversky and Kahneman (1974) presented this problem to a group of experimental subjects, they found that most people felt that the first sample (4 out of 5) provided much stronger evidence and therefore should give more confidence. At first glance, it may appear that this is the correct decision. After all, the first sample contained $\frac{4}{5} = 80\%$ red balls, and the second sample contained only $\frac{12}{20} = 60\%$ red balls. However, you should also notice that the two samples differ in another important respect: the sample size. One sample contains only $n = 5$, and the other sample contains $n = 20$. The correct answer to the problem is that the larger sample (12 out of 20) gives a much stronger justification for concluding that the balls in the urn are predominately red. It appears that most people tend to focus on the sample proportion and pay very little attention to the sample size.

The importance of sample size may be easier to appreciate if you approach the urn problem from a different perspective. Suppose that you are the individual assigned responsibility for selecting a sample and then deciding which color is in the majority. Before you select your sample, you are offered a choice of selecting either a sample of 5 balls or a sample of 20 balls. Which would you prefer? It should be clear that the larger sample would be better. With a small number, you risk obtaining an unrepresentative sample. By chance, you could end up with 3 white balls and 2 red balls even though the reds outnumber the whites by two to one. The larger sample is much more likely to provide an accurate representation of the population. This is an example of the *law of large numbers*, which states that large samples will be representative of the population from which they are selected. One final example should help demonstrate this law. If you were tossing a coin, you probably would not be greatly surprised to obtain 3 heads in a row. However, if you obtained a series of 20 heads in a row, you almost certainly would suspect a trick coin. The large sample has more authority.

In this chapter we will examine the relation between samples and populations. More specifically, we will consider the relation between sample means and the population mean. As you will see, sample size is one of the primary considerations in determining how well a sample mean represents the population mean. In its more formal statement, the law of large numbers says the following:

> The larger the sample size, the more probable it is that the sample mean will be close to the population mean.

7.1 SAMPLES AND SAMPLING ERROR

The purpose of this chapter is to establish the set of rules that relate samples to populations. These rules primarily will be based on probabilities. For example, what kind of sample will probably be obtained from a particular population or, conversely, what kind of population probably produced a particular sample? Although the general topic of probability has already been discussed (Chapter 6), in this chapter we will be looking

*Adapted from Tversky, A., and Kahneman, D. (1974). Judgments under uncertainty: Heuristics and biases. *Science*, 185, 1124–1131. Copyright 1974 by the AAAS.

at samples that consist of more than a single score, for example, a sample of personality scores for a group of $n = 100$ college freshmen.

In most situations, researchers must depend on the limited data from samples to answer general questions about populations. For example, a researcher might be interested in whether or not a special protein-enriched diet has any effect on intellectual development. To examine this question, the researcher could do the following experiment. First, two random samples of rats are obtained. The rats in one sample are raised on a regular diet, and the animals in the other group are fed the special diet. After 6 months, all of the rats are tested on a learning problem. The researcher now has two sets of data: the performance scores for the regular diet group and the scores for the special diet group. The structure of this experiment is shown in Figure 7.1.

The researcher wants to know whether or not the treatment (the special diet) has any effect on the population; that is, if the entire population of rats was raised on the special diet, would the scores be any different from the scores of rats on the regular diet? The researcher must rely on the two samples to provide accurate information about these two populations. It is reasonable to assume that each sample would give a pretty good picture of its own population. After all, the sample was randomly selected from the population, and therefore it should be a representative group. On the other hand, the rats in each sample are only a small part of the whole population. The data the researcher gets will depend on the individual rats selected for each sample.

The general difficulty in working with samples is that samples generally are not identical to the populations from which they come. More precisely, the statistics calculated for a sample will differ from the corresponding parameters for the population. This difference, or *error*, is referred to as *sampling error*. Furthermore, samples are variable; they are not all the same. If you take two separate samples from the same population, the samples will be different. They will contain different individuals, they will have different scores, and they will have different sample means. How can you tell which sample is giving the best description of the population? Can you even predict how well a sample will describe its population? These are the kinds of questions we will be answering in this chapter.

7.2 THE DISTRIBUTION OF SAMPLE MEANS

As noted, two separate samples probably will be different even if they are taken from the same population. The samples will have different individuals, different scores, different means, etc. In most cases, it is possible to obtain thousands of different samples

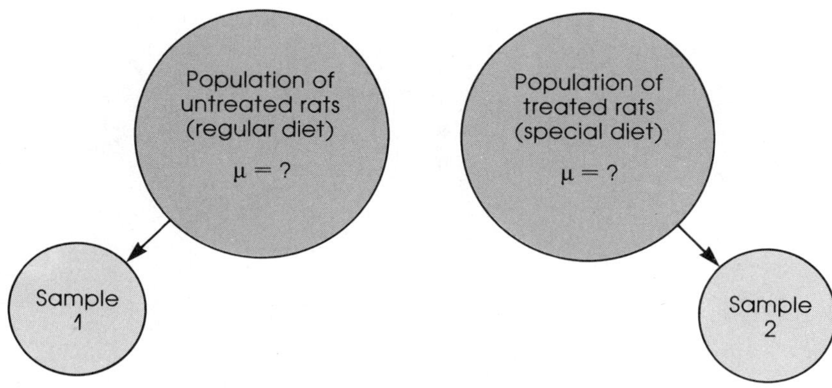

FIGURE 7.1

A diagram of the structure of the experimental design. The purpose of the experiment is to determine whether the special diet has any effect on intelligence. The researcher would like to compare the mean intelligence for rats on the special diet versus rats on the regular diet. Because the populations are too large to work with, the researcher must use samples as the basis for comparing the two populations.

from one population. With all these different samples coming from the same population, it may seem hopeless to try to establish some simple rules for the relations between samples and populations. But fortunately the huge set of possible samples does fall into a relatively simple, orderly, and predictable pattern that makes it possible to accurately predict the characteristics of a sample if you know about the population it is coming from. These general characteristics are specified by the distribution of sample means.

· DEFINITION · *The distribution of sample means* is the collection of sample means for all the possible random samples of a particular size (n) that can be obtained from a population.

You should notice that the distribution of sample means is different from distributions we have considered before. Until now we always have discussed distributions of scores; now the values in the distribution are not scores, they are statistics (sample means). Because statistics are obtained from samples, a distribution of statistics is referred to as a sampling distribution.

· DEFINITION · A *sampling distribution* is a distribution of statistics obtained by selecting all the possible samples of a specific size from a population.

Thus, the distribution of sample means is an example of sampling distribution. In fact, it often is called the sampling distribution of $\overline{X}$.

Before we consider the general rules concerning this distribution, we will look at a simple example that provides an opportunity to examine the distribution in detail.

· EXAMPLE 7.1 · Consider a population that consists of only four scores: 2, 4, 6, 8. This population is pictured in the frequency distribution histogram in Figure 7.2.

We are going to use this population as the basis for constructing the distribution of sample means for $n = 2$. Remember, this distribution is the collection of sample means from all the possible random samples of $n = 2$ from this population. We begin by looking at all the possible samples. Each of the 16 different samples is listed in Table 7.1.

Remember, random sampling requires sampling with replacement.

Next, we compute the mean, $\overline{X}$, for each of the 16 samples (see the last column of Table 7.1). The 16 sample means form the distribution of sample means. These 16 values are organized in a frequency distribution histogram in Figure 7.3.

Notice that the distribution of sample means has some predictable and some very useful characteristics:

1. The sample means tend to pile up around the population mean. For this example, the population mean is $\mu = 5$, and the sample means are clustered around a value of 5. It should not surprise you that the sample means tend to approximate the population mean. After all, samples are supposed to be representative of the population.

· FIGURE 7.2 ·

Frequency distribution histogram for a population of four scores: 2, 4, 6, 8.

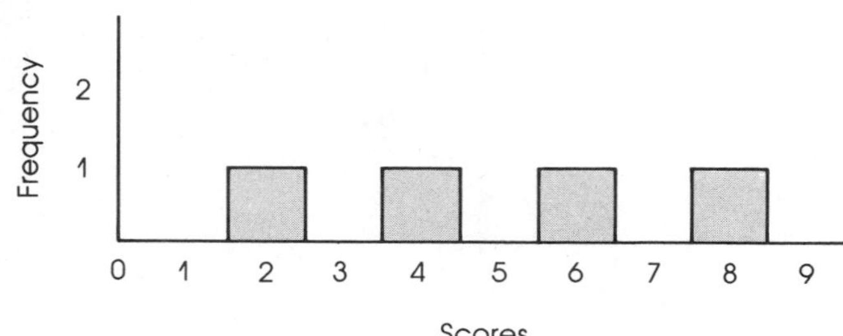

TABLE 7.1

All the possible samples of $n = 2$ scores that can be obtained from the population presented in Figure 7.2[a]

Sample	Scores: First	Scores: Second	Sample Mean, $\overline{X}$
1	2	2	2
2	2	4	3
3	2	6	4
4	2	8	5
5	4	2	3
6	4	4	4
7	4	6	5
8	4	8	6
9	6	2	4
10	6	4	5
11	6	6	6
12	6	8	7
13	8	2	5
14	8	4	6
15	8	6	7
16	8	8	8

[a]Notice that the table lists *random samples*. This requires sampling with replacement, so it is possible to select the same score twice. Also note that samples are listed systematically. The first four samples are all the possible samples that have $X = 2$ as the first score; the next four samples all have $X = 4$ as the first score; etc. This way we are sure to have all the possible samples listed, although the samples probably would not be selected in this order.

2. The distribution of sample means is approximately normal in shape. This is a characteristic that will be discussed in detail later and will be extremely useful because we already know a great deal about probabilities and the normal distribution (Chapter 6).

Remember, our goal in this chapter is to answer probability questions about samples with $n > 1$.

3. Finally, you should notice that we can use the distribution of sample means to answer probability questions about sample means (see Perspective 7.1). For example, if you take a sample of $n = 2$ scores from the original population, what is the probability of obtaining a sample mean greater than 7? In symbols, $P(\overline{X} > 7) = ?$

Because probability is equivalent to proportion, the probability question can be restated as follows: Of all the possible sample means, what proportion have values greater than 7? In this form the question is easily answered by looking at the distribution of sample means. All the possible sample means are pictured (Figure 7.3), and only 1 out of the 16 means has a value greater than 7. The answer, therefore, is 1 out of 16, or $p = \frac{1}{16}$. •

FIGURE 7.3

The distribution of sample means for $n = 2$. This distribution shows the 16 sample means from Table 7.1.

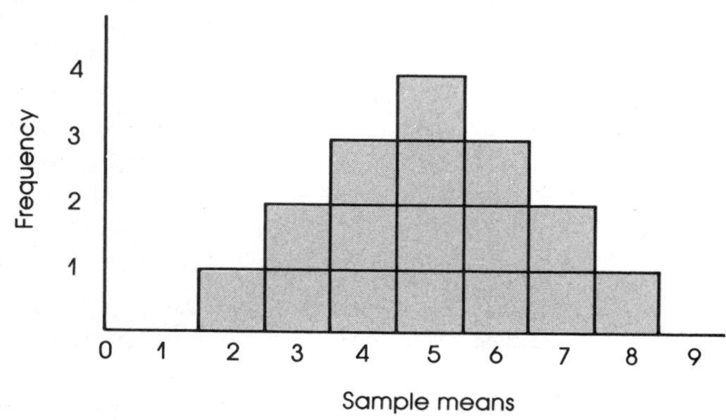

PERSPECTIVE 7.1

PROBABILITY AND THE DISTRIBUTION OF SAMPLE MEANS

I have a bad habit of losing playing cards. This habit is compounded by the fact that I always save the old deck in hope that someday I will find the missing cards. As a result, I have a drawer filled with partial decks of playing cards. Suppose I take one of these almost-complete decks, shuffle the cards carefully, and then randomly select one card. What is the probability that I will draw a king?

You should realize that it is impossible to answer this probability question. To find the probability of selecting a king, you must know how many cards are in the deck and exactly which cards are missing. (It is crucial that you know whether or not any kings are missing.) The point of this simple example is that any probability question requires that you have complete information about the population from which the sample is being selected. In this case, you must know all the possible cards in the deck before you can find the probability for selecting any specific card.

In this chapter we are examining probability and sample means. In order to find the probability for any specific sample mean, you first must know *all the possible sample means.* Therefore, we begin by defining and describing the set of all possible sample means that can be obtained from a particular population. Once we have specified the complete set of all possible sample means (i.e., the distribution of sample means), we will be able to find the probability of selecting any specific sample mean.

THE CENTRAL LIMIT THEOREM

Example 7.1 demonstrates the construction of the distribution of sample means for a relatively simple, specific situation. In most cases, however, it will not be possible to list all the samples and compute all the possible sample means. Therefore, it is necessary to develop the general characteristics of the distribution of sample means that can be applied in any situation. Fortunately, these characteristics are specified in a mathematical proposition known as the *central limit theorem.* This important and useful theorem serves as a cornerstone for much of inferential statistics. Following is the essence of the theorem:

· DEFINITION · *Central Limit Theorem:* For any population with mean μ and standard deviation σ, the distribution of sample means for sample size n will approach a normal distribution with a mean of μ and a standard deviation of $\sigma/\sqrt{n}$ as n approaches infinity.

The value of this theorem comes from two simple facts. First, it describes the distribution of sample means for *any population,* no matter what shape, or mean, or standard deviation. Second, the distribution of sample means "approaches" a normal distribution very rapidly. By the time the sample size reaches $n = 30$, the distribution is almost perfectly normal.

Notice that the central limit theorem describes the distribution of sample means by identifying the three basic characteristics that describe any distribution: shape, central tendency, and variability. Each of these will be examined.

THE SHAPE OF THE DISTRIBUTION OF SAMPLE MEANS

It has been observed that the distribution of sample means tends to be a normal distribution. In fact, this distribution will be almost perfectly normal if either one of the following two conditions is satisfied.

1. The population from which the samples are selected is a normal distribution.
2. The number of scores (n) in each sample is relatively large, around 30 or more.

(As n gets larger, the distribution of sample means will closely approximate a normal distribution. With $n > 30$ the distribution is almost perfectly normal regardless of the shape of the original population.)

The fact that the distribution of sample means tends to be normal should not be surprising. Whenever you take a sample from a population, you expect the sample mean to be near to the population mean. When you take lots of different samples, you expect the sample means to "pile up" around μ, resulting in a normal shaped distribution. This fact is demonstrated in the following example.

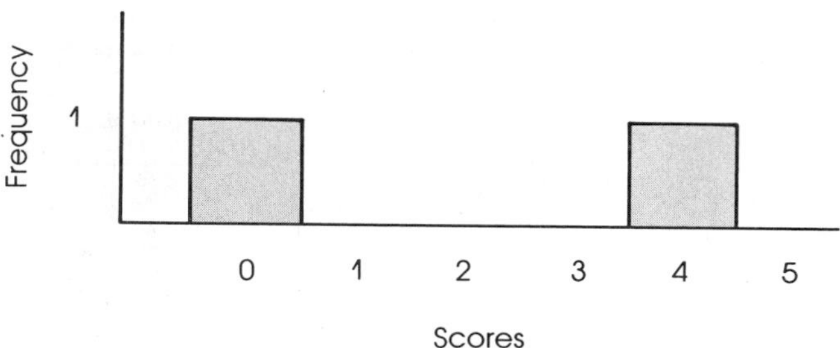

FIGURE 7.4

Original population consisting of only two scores.

EXAMPLE 7.2 Consider a population that consists of only two scores: $X = 0$ and $X = 4$. This population is shown in the frequency distribution graph in Figure 7.4.

Using this population, we first will look at the distribution of sample means based on $n = 2$, that is, the set of all the possible sample means for samples with $n = 2$ in each sample. For this population, there are only four possible random samples, and they are presented in Figure 7.5. The mean for each sample has been computed, and the set of means is presented in the frequency distribution graph. This graph shows the distribution of sample means for $n = 2$. Notice that the distribution has some of the characteristics of the original population (the values at 0 and at 4), plus it has some characteristics of the normal distribution (the sample means are beginning to pile up in the middle of the distribution).

Next, we will look at the distribution of sample means based on $n = 4$. This time there are 16 possible random samples, and they are presented in Figure 7.6. The mean for each of these samples has been computed, and the set of means is presented in the frequency distribution graph. This graph shows the distribution of sample means for $n = 4$. Notice that the distribution of sample means is closer to a normal distribution for $n = 4$ than for $n = 2$. This general trend continues, so that when $n = 30$ or more, the distribution of sample means is essentially a perfect normal distribution.

THE MEAN OF THE DISTRIBUTION OF SAMPLE MEANS: THE EXPECTED VALUE OF $\overline{X}$

You probably have noticed in all the examples so far that the distribution of sample means is centered around the mean of the population from which the samples were obtained. In each case, the average value of all the sample means is exactly equal to the value of the population mean. This fact should be intuitively reasonable; the sam-

FIGURE 7.5

All of the possible samples with $n = 2$ scores and the distribution of sample means for $n = 2$. Samples were selected from the population shown in Figure 7.4.

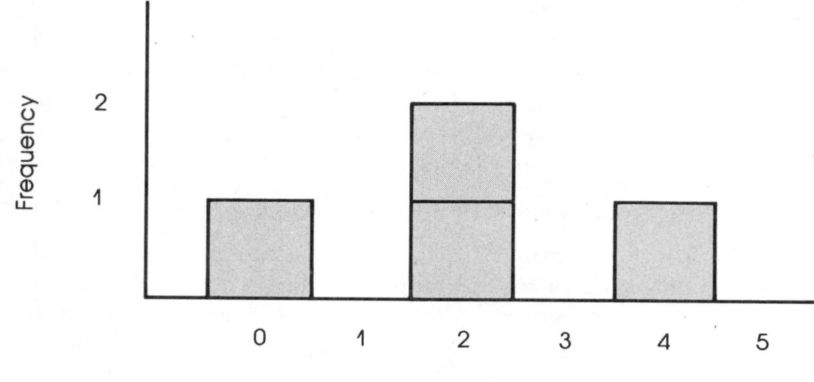

Sample	Scores: First	Scores: Second	Sample mean, $\overline{X}$
1	0	0	0
2	0	4	2
3	4	0	2
4	4	4	4

FIGURE 7.6

All of the possible samples with $n = 4$ scores and the distribution of sample means for $n = 4$. Samples were selected from the population shown in Figure 7.4.

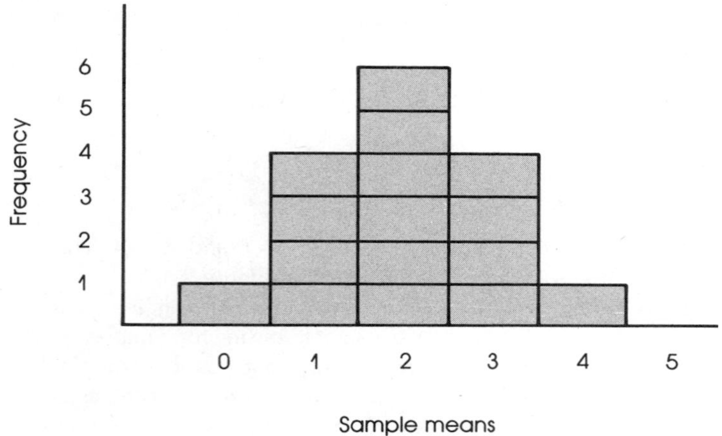

Sample	Scores: First	Second	Third	Fourth	Sample mean, $\overline{X}$
1	0	0	0	0	0
2	0	0	0	4	1
3	0	0	4	0	1
4	0	0	4	4	2
5	0	4	0	0	1
6	0	4	0	4	2
7	0	4	4	0	2
8	0	4	4	4	3
9	4	0	0	0	1
10	4	0	0	4	2
11	4	0	4	0	2
12	4	0	4	4	3
13	4	4	0	0	2
14	4	4	0	4	3
15	4	4	4	0	3
16	4	4	4	4	4

ple means are expected to be close to the population mean, and they do tend to pile up around μ. The formal statement of this phenomenon is that the mean of the distribution of sample means always will be identical to the population mean. This mean value is called the *expected value of* $\overline{X}$.

DEFINITION The mean of the distribution of sample means will be equal to μ (the population mean) and is called the *expected value of* $\overline{X}$.

The expected value of $\overline{X}$ is often identified by the symbol $\mu_{\overline{X}}$, signifying the "mean of the sample means." However, $\mu_{\overline{X}}$ is always equal to μ, so we will continue to use the symbol μ to refer to the mean for the population of scores and the mean for the distribution of sample means.

In commonsense terms, a sample mean is "expected" to be near its population mean. When all of the possible sample means are obtained, the average value will be identical to μ.

THE STANDARD ERROR OF $\overline{X}$

So far we have considered the shape and the central tendency of the distribution of sample means. To completely describe this distribution, we need one more characteristic, variability. The value we will be working with is the standard deviation for the distribution of sample means, and it is called the *standard error of* $\overline{X}$.

DEFINITION The standard deviation of the distribution of sample means is called the *standard error of* $\overline{X}$.

Like any measure of standard deviation, the standard error defines the standard, or typical, distance from the mean. In this case, we are measuring the standard distance between a single sample mean $\overline{X}$ and the population mean μ.

The notation that is used to identify the standard error is $\sigma_{\overline{X}}$. The σ indicates that we are measuring a standard deviation or a standard distance from the mean. The lowercase $\bar{x}$ indicates that we are measuring standard deviation for sample means.

$$\text{standard error} = \sigma_{\overline{X}} = \text{standard distance between } \overline{X} \text{ and } \mu$$

The standard error is an extremely valuable measure because it specifies precisely how well a sample mean estimates its population mean, that is, how much error you should expect, on the average, between $\overline{X}$ and μ. Remember, one basic reason for taking samples is to use the sample data to answer questions about the population. Specifically, we can use the sample mean as an estimate of the population mean. Although we do not expect a sample mean to be exactly the same as the population mean, it should provide a good estimate. The standard error tells how good the estimate will be.

The numerical value of the standard error is determined by two characteristics: (1) the variability of the population from which the sample is selected and (2) the size of the sample. We will examine each of these separately.

1. *Standard Deviation of the Population.* The accuracy with which a sample mean represents its population mean is determined in part by the individual scores in the sample. If the sample contains extreme scores (far from μ), then the sample mean is likely to be very different from μ. On the other hand, if all the individual scores are close to μ, then the sample mean will certainly give an accurate representation of the population mean. Standard deviation measures the standard distance between an individual score (X) and the population mean (μ). When σ is small, each individual score is close to μ, and the average score ($\overline{X}$) is also close to μ. With a large standard deviation, you are likely to obtain extreme scores that can increase the distance between $\overline{X}$ and μ.

Remember the law of large numbers.

2. *The Sample Size.* As a general rule, the larger the sample, the more accurately the sample represents its population. If you were assigned the job of estimating the average IQ for freshmen at your college, you would expect to get a more accurate measure from a group of $n = 100$ than from a sample of $n = 2$. The larger the sample, the smaller the standard error.

Combining these two characteristics results in the following formula for the standard error:

$$\text{standard error} = \sigma_{\overline{X}} = \frac{\sigma}{\sqrt{n}} \tag{7.1}$$

Notice that when the population standard deviation (σ) is small, the standard error will be small. Also, if the sample size (n) is increased, the standard error will get smaller.

The exact derivation of the standard error formula is a bit complex, but we can use a simple example to show that the formula does work.

EXAMPLE 7.3 Earlier we considered a population that consisted of only two scores: $X = 0$ and $X = 4$ (see Figure 7.4). The standard deviation for this population is $\sigma = 2$ (check it for yourself). We also looked at the distribution of sample means based on $n = 2$ (see Figure 7.5). With $n = 2$ there are four possible samples, and each of the four sample means is listed again in Table 7.2. Note that the four sample means are not all the same; they are variable, and we can compute SS and standard deviation for these values.

First, notice that the average value for the four sample means is 2. This is the same as the population mean. Remember, the expected value of $\overline{X}$ is equal to μ.

Second, for each sample we can compute a deviation score. The deviation is

TABLE 7.2

All the possible sample means for samples of $n = 2$ scores taken for a population that consists of two scores: $X = 0$ and $X = 4$.[a]

Sample	Sample Mean, $\overline{X}$	Deviation (Distance from μ)	Squared Deviation
1	0	−2	4
2	2	0	0
3	2	0	0
4	4	+2	4

[a]The four different samples are shown in Figure 7.5.

simply the distance from the mean ($\mu = 2$) and indicates how close the sample mean comes to the population mean (see Table 7.2).

Third, we square each deviation score and compute the sum of squared deviations for the sample means: $SS = 8$.

Next, calculate the variance which is the average squared deviation:

The N in this formula refers to the number of *samples* in the distribution of sample means.

$$\text{variance of sample means} = \frac{SS}{N} = \frac{8}{4} = 2$$

Finally, we calculate the standard deviation for the set of sample means:

$$\text{standard deviation of sample means} = \sqrt{\frac{SS}{N}} = \sqrt{2} = 1.41$$

This is the standard error. It is the standard deviation of the distribution of sample means, and it measures the standard distance between a sample mean and the population mean. Notice that we could have computed this value directly by using the formula for standard error:

$$\text{standard error} = \sigma_{\overline{X}} = \frac{\sigma}{\sqrt{n}} = \frac{2}{\sqrt{2}} = 1.41$$

The formula provides a much more direct way of computing standard error. Again, standard error measures the standard distance between $\overline{X}$ and μ. It tells how much error to expect, on the average, if you are using a sample mean to estimate a population mean. •

• LEARNING CHECK •

1 What is the difference between a distribution of raw scores and a sampling distribution?

2 Under what circumstances is the distribution of sample means guaranteed to be normal?

3 A population of scores is normal with $\mu = 50$ and $\sigma = 12$. Describe the distribution of sample means for samples of size $n = 16$ selected from this population. (Describe shape, central tendency, and variability for the distribution.)

4 A population of scores is normal with $\mu = 100$ and $\sigma = 16$.
   a If you randomly select one score from this population, then, on the average, how close should the score be to the population mean?
   b If you selected a random sample of $n = 4$ scores, how much error would you expect, on the average, between the sample mean and the population mean?
   c If you selected a random sample of $n = 64$ scores, how much error, on the average, should there be between the sample mean and the population mean?

ANSWERS

1 A distribution of raw scores is composed of original measurements, and a sampling distribution is composed of statistics.

2 The distribution of sample means will be normal if the original population is normal or if the sample size is at least 30.

3 The distribution of sample means will be normal because the population is normal. It will have an expected value of $\mu = 50$ and a standard error of $\sigma_{\overline{X}} = 12/\sqrt{16} = 3$.

4 **a** Standard deviation, $\sigma = 16$, measures standard distance from the mean.
   b For a sample of $n = 4$ the standard error would be $16/\sqrt{4} = 8$ points.
   c For a sample of $n = 64$ the standard error would be $16/\sqrt{64} = 2$ points.

MORE ABOUT THE STANDARD ERROR

The concept of standard error is probably the most important new idea is this chapter. The following two examples will demonstrate some important aspects of standard error.

· EXAMPLE 7.4 · Consider a population consisting of $N = 3$ scores: 1, 8, 9. The mean for this population is $\mu = 6$. Using this population, try to find a random sample of $n = 2$ scores with a sample mean ($\overline{X}$) exactly equal to the population mean. (Try selecting a few samples— write down the scores and the sample mean for each of your samples.)

You may have guessed that we constructed this example so that it is impossible to obtain a sample mean that is identical to μ. The point of the example is to emphasize the notion of sampling error. Samples are not identical to their populations, and a sample mean generally will not provide a perfect estimate of the population mean. The purpose of standard error is to provide a quantitative measure of the difference between sample means and the population mean. Standard error is the standard distance between $\overline{X}$ and μ. ·

· EXAMPLE 7.5 · Sample size is a critical factor in determining how well a sample represents its population—the larger the sample, the more accurately the sample represents the population. Suppose you would like to find the average IQ for students at your college. Rather than obtaining IQ scores for the entire population, your job is to get a sample and use the sample mean to estimate μ.

You know that IQ scores form a normal distribution with $\sigma = 15$. For the general population $\mu = 100$, but you want to find μ for your fellow students. Would you rather have a sample of $n = 9$, $n = 25$, or $n = 100$ students? Clearly, the larger your sample, the better you can estimate μ. Standard error tells you exactly how much better.

Figure 7.7 shows distributions of sample means based on $n = 9$, $n = 25$, and $n = 100$. Each distribution shows the collection of all the possible sample means that you could obtain for that particular sample size. Notice that all three sampling distributions are normal because the population of IQ scores is a normal distribution. All three distributions have the same mean, which is the unknown population mean that you are trying to estimate. However, the distributions are very different with respect to variability. With the smallest sample size, $n = 9$, the standard error is

$$\sigma_{\overline{X}} = \frac{\sigma}{\sqrt{n}} = \frac{15}{\sqrt{9}} = \frac{15}{3} = 5$$

With $n = 9$, you expect—on the average—a 5-point error between $\overline{X}$ and μ. Although some samples will give you an $\overline{X}$ very close to μ, it is likely that you will obtain a sample mean that is 5 points or even 10 points different from the population mean that you are trying to estimate.

With larger samples, however, the standard error gets smaller. For $n = 25$, the

· FIGURE 7.7 ·

The distribution of sample means for samples of size $n = 9$ (left), $n = 25$ (center), and $n = 100$ (right). In each case the original population is normal with $\sigma = 15$ and an unknown mean, $\mu = ?$. Notice that the standard error gets smaller as the sample size gets larger.

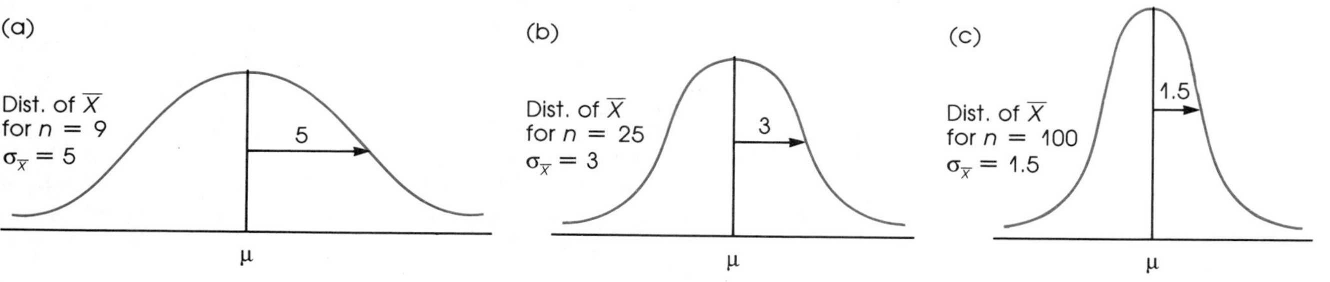

standard error is

$$\sigma_{\bar{X}} = \frac{\sigma}{\sqrt{n}} = \frac{15}{\sqrt{25}} = \frac{15}{5} = 3$$

And with $n = 100$, the standard error is

$$\sigma_{\bar{X}} = \frac{\sigma}{\sqrt{n}} = \frac{15}{\sqrt{100}} = \frac{15}{10} = 1.5$$

A sample of $n = 100$ scores should provide a much better description of the population than you would obtain with a sample of only $n = 9$ scores or a sample of $n = 25$. This fact is clearly seen when you compare the distributions of sample means (Figure 7.7). With $n = 100$, the sample means are clustered very close to the population mean, and there is very little error between $\bar{X}$ and μ. On the average, with $n = 100$, you expect only a 1.5-point difference between $\bar{X}$ and μ. It is almost impossible to obtain a sample of $n = 100$ with a mean that is more than 5 points different from μ.

As sample size increases, the sample becomes a better representative of the population. Standard error defines the relation between the sample size and the accuracy with which $\bar{X}$ represents μ. •

7.3 APPLICATIONS OF THE DISTRIBUTION OF SAMPLE MEANS

The primary use of the distribution of sample means is to find the probability associated with any specific sample. You should recall that probability is equivalent to proportion. Because the distribution of sample means presents the entire set of all possible $\bar{X}$'s, we can use proportions of this distribution to determine probabilities. The following example demonstrates this process.

• EXAMPLE 7.6 • The population of scores on the SAT forms a normal distribution with $\mu = 500$ and $\sigma = 100$. If you take a random sample of $n = 25$ students, what is the probability that the sample mean would be greater than $\bar{X} = 540$?

First, you can restate this probability question as a proportion question: Out of all the possible sample means, what proportion have values greater than 540? You know about "all the possible sample means"; this is simply the distribution of sample means. The problem is to find a specific portion of this distribution. The parameters of this distribution are the following:

Caution: Whenever you have a probability question about a sample mean, you must use the distribution of sample means.

a. The distribution is normal because the population of SAT scores is normal.

b. The distribution has a mean of 500 because the population mean is $\mu = 500$.

c. The distribution has a standard error of $\sigma_{\bar{X}} = 20$:

$$\sigma_{\bar{X}} = \frac{\sigma}{\sqrt{n}} = \frac{100}{\sqrt{25}} = \frac{100}{5} = 20$$

This distribution of sample means is shown in Figure 7.8.

We are interested in sample means greater than 540 (the shaded area in Figure 7.8), so the next step is to use a z-score to locate the exact position of $\bar{X} = 540$ in the distribution. The value 540 is located above the mean by 40 points, which is

FIGURE 7.8

The distribution of sample means for $n = 25$. Samples were selected from a normal population with $\mu = 500$ and $\sigma = 100$.

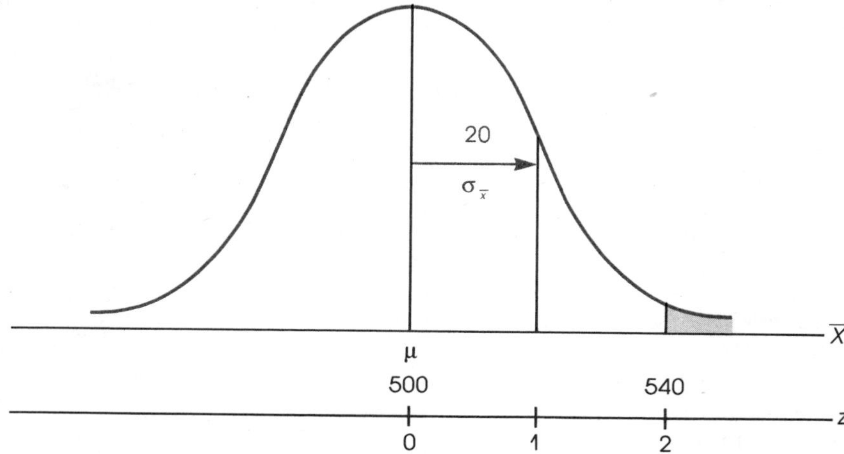

exactly two standard deviations (in this case, exactly two standard errors). Thus, the z-score for $\bar{X} = 540$ is $z = +2.00$.

Because this distribution of sample means is normal, you can use the unit normal table to find the probability associated with $z = +2.00$. The table indicates that .0228 of the distribution is located in the tail of the distribution beyond $z = +2.00$. Our conclusion is that it is very unlikely, $p = .0228$ (2.28%), to obtain a random sample of $n = 25$ students with an average SAT score greater than 540. •

As demonstrated in Example 7.6, it is possible to use a z-score to describe the position of any specific sample within the distribution of sample means. The z-score tells exactly where a specific sample is located in relation to all the other possible samples that could have been obtained. A z-score of $z = +2.00$, for example, indicates that the sample mean is much larger than usually would be expected: It is greater than the expected value of $\bar{X}$ by twice the standard distance. The z-score for each sample mean can be computed by using the standard z-score formula with a few minor changes. First, the value we are locating is a sample mean rather than a score, so the formula uses $\bar{X}$ in place of X. Second, the standard deviation for this distribution is measured by the standard error, so the formula uses $\sigma_{\bar{X}}$ in place of σ (see Perspective 7.2). The resulting formula, giving the z-score value corresponding to any sample mean, is

(7.2) $$z = \frac{\bar{X} - \mu}{\sigma_{\bar{X}}}$$

Every sample mean has a z-score that describes its position in the distribution of sample means. Using z-scores and the unit normal table, it is possible to find the probability associated with any specific sample mean (as in Example 7.6). The following example demonstrates that it also is possible to make quantitative predictions about the kinds of samples that should be obtained from any population.

EXAMPLE 7.7 Suppose you simply wanted to predict the kind of value that would be expected for the mean SAT score for a random sample of $n = 25$ students. For example, what range of values would be expected for the sample mean 80% of the time? The simplest way of answering this question is to look at the distribution of sample means. Remember, this distribution is the collection of all the possible sample means, and it will show which samples are likely to be obtained and which are not.

PERSPECTIVE 7.2

THE DIFFERENCE BETWEEN STANDARD DEVIATION AND STANDARD ERROR

A constant source of confusion for many students is the difference between standard deviation and standard error. You should remember that standard deviation measures the standard distance between a *score* and the population mean. As the name implies, it is the "standard" deviation $(X - \mu)$. Whenever you are working with a distribution of scores, the standard deviation is the appropriate measure of variability. Standard error, on the other hand, measures the standard distance between a *sample mean* and the population mean: the standard $(\bar{X} - \mu)$. Whenever you have a question concerning a sample, the standard error is the appropriate measure of variability.

If you still find the distinction confusing, there is a simple solution. Namely, if you always use standard error, you always will be right. Consider the formula for standard error:

$$\text{standard error} = \sigma_{\bar{X}} = \frac{\sigma}{\sqrt{n}}$$

If you are working with a single score, then $n = 1$, and the standard error becomes

$$\text{standard error} = \sigma_{\bar{X}} = \frac{\sigma}{\sqrt{n}} = \frac{\sigma}{\sqrt{1}} = \sigma = \text{standard deviation}$$

Thus, standard error always measures the standard distance from the population mean, whether you have a sample of $n = 1$ or $n = 100$.

As demonstrated in Example 7.6, the distribution of sample means for $n = 25$ will be normal, will have an expected value of $\mu = 500$, and will have a standard error of $\sigma_{\bar{X}} = 20$. Looking at this distribution, shown again in Figure 7.9, it is clear that the most likely value to expect for a sample mean is around 500. To be more precise, we can identify the range of values that would be expected 80% of the time by locating the middle 80% of the distribution. Because the distribution is normal, we can use the unit normal table. To find the middle 80%, we need exactly 40% (or .40) between the mean and the *z*-score on each side. Looking up a proportion of .40 in the unit normal table (column B) gives a *z*-score of $z = 1.28$. By definition, a *z*-score of 1.28 indicates that the score is 1.28 standard error units from the mean. This distance is $1.28 \times 20 = 25.6$ points. The mean is 500, so 25.6 points either direction would give a range from 474.4 to 525.6. This is the middle 80% of all the possible sample means, so you can expect any particular sample mean to be in this range 80% of the time. •

Remember, when answering probability questions, it always is helpful to sketch a distribution and shade in the portion you are trying to find.

· LEARNING CHECK ·

1 A normal population has $\mu = 80$ and $\sigma = 10$. A sample of $n = 25$ scores has a mean $\bar{X} = 83$. What is the *z*-score corresponding to this sample mean?

2 A random sample of $n = 9$ scores is selected from a normal population with $\mu = 40$ and $\sigma = 6$.
   - **a** What is the probability of obtaining a sample mean greater than 41?
   - **b** What is the probability of obtaining a sample mean less than 46?

3 A skewed distribution has $\mu = 60$ and $\sigma = 8$.
   - **a** What is the probability of obtaining a sample mean greater than $\bar{X} = 62$ for a sample of $n = 4$? (Be careful.)
   - **b** What is the probability of obtaining a sample mean greater than $\bar{X} = 62$ for a sample of $n = 64$?

ANSWERS

1 The standard error is 2. $z = \frac{3}{2} = 1.5$.

2 **a** $\bar{X} = 41$ corresponds to $z = +.50$. The probability is .3085 (30.85%).
   b $\bar{X} = 46$ corresponds to $z = +3.0$. The probability is .9987 (99.87%).

3 **a** Cannot answer because the distribution of sample means is not normal.
   b With $n = 64$ the distribution of sample means will be normal. $\bar{X} = 62$ corresponds to $z = +2.0$. The probability is .0228 (2.28%).

FIGURE 7.9

The middle 80% of the distribution of sample means for $n = 25$. Samples were selected from a normal population with $\mu = 500$ and $\sigma = 100$.

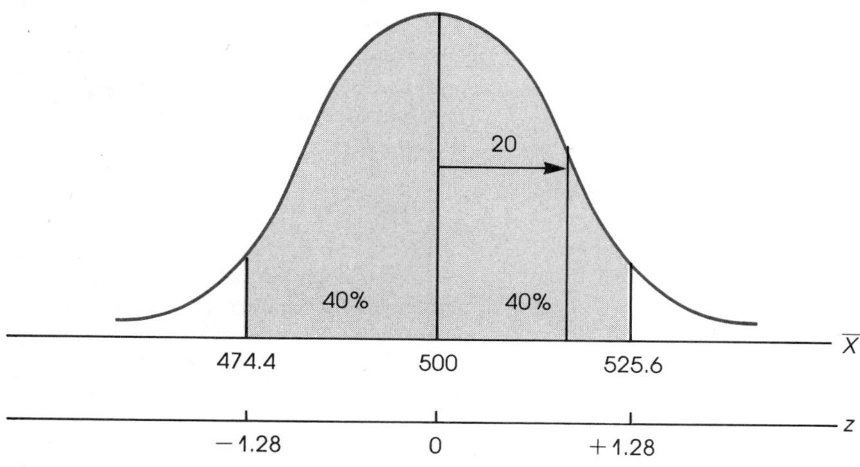

SUMMARY

1 The distribution of sample means is defined as the set of all the possible $\bar{X}$s for a specific sample size (n) that can be obtained from a given population. The parameters of the distribution of sample means are as follows:

a *Shape*. The distribution of sample means will be normal if either one of the following two conditions is satisfied:

(1) The population from which the samples are selected is normal.

(2) The size of the samples is relatively large (around $n = 30$ or more).

b *Central Tendency*. The mean of the distribution of sample means will be identical to the mean of the population from which the samples are selected. The mean of the distribution of sample means is called the expected value of $\bar{X}$.

c *Variability*. The standard deviation of the distribution of sample means is called the standard error of $\bar{X}$ and is defined by the formula

$$\sigma_{\bar{X}} = \frac{\sigma}{\sqrt{n}}$$

Standard error measures the standard distance between a sample mean $\bar{X}$ and the population mean μ.

2 One of the most important concepts in this chapter is the standard error. The standard error is the standard deviation of the distribution of sample means. It measures the standard distance between a sample mean ($\bar{X}$) and the population mean (μ). The standard error tells how much error to expect if you are using a sample mean to estimate a population mean.

3 The location of each $\bar{X}$ in the distribution of sample means can be specified by a z score:

$$z = \frac{\bar{X} - \mu}{\sigma_{\bar{X}}}$$

Because the distribution of sample means tends to be normal, we can use these z-scores and the unit normal table to find probabilities for specific sample means. In particular, we can identify which sample means are likely and which are very unlikely to be obtained from any given population. This ability to find probabilities for samples is the basis for the inferential statistics in the chapters ahead.

KEY TERMS

law of large numbers
sampling error
distribution of sample means
sampling distribution
central limit theorem
expected value of $\bar{X}$
standard error of $\bar{X}$

FOCUS ON PROBLEM SOLVING

1. Whenever you are working probability questions about sample means, you must use the distribution of sample means. Remember, every probability question can be restated as a proportion question. Probabilities for sample means are equivalent to proportions of the distribution of sample means.

2. When computing probabilities for sample means, the most common error is to use standard deviation (σ) instead of standard error ($\sigma_{\bar{X}}$) in the z-score formula.

Standard deviation measures the typical deviation (or "error") for a single score. Standard error measures the typical deviation (or error) for a sample. Remember, the larger the sample, the more accurately the sample represents the population—that is, the larger the sample, the smaller the error.

$$\text{standard error} = \sigma_{\bar{X}} = \frac{\sigma}{\sqrt{n}}$$

3. Although the distribution of sample means is often normal, it is not always a normal distribution. Check the criteria to be certain the distribution is normal before you use the unit normal table to find probabilities. Remember, all probability problems with the normal distribution are easier if you sketch the distribution and shade in the area of interest.

PROBLEMS

1 Briefly define each of the following:
- a The distribution of sample means
- b Expected value of $\bar{X}$
- c Standard error of $\bar{X}$

2 A population consists of exactly three scores: $X = 0$, $X = 2$, and $X = 4$.
- a List all the possible random samples of $n = 2$ scores from this population. (You should obtain 9 different samples—see Example 7.1.)
- b Compute the sample mean for each of the 9 samples, and draw a histogram showing the distribution of sample means.

3 Two samples are randomly selected from a population. One sample has $n = 5$ scores and the second has $n = 30$. Which sample should have a mean ($\bar{X}$) that is closer to μ? Explain your answer.

*4 You have a population with $\mu = 100$ and $\sigma = 30$.
- a If you randomly select a single score from this population, then, on the average, how close would you expect the score to be to the population mean?
- b If you randomly select a sample of $n = 100$ scores, then, on the average, how close would you expect the sample mean to be to the population mean?

5 The distribution of SAT scores is normal with $\mu = 500$ and $\sigma = 100$.
- a If you selected a random sample of $n = 4$ scores from this population, how much error would you expect between the sample mean and the population mean?
- b If you selected a random sample of $n = 25$ scores, how much error would you expect between the sample mean and the population mean?
- c How much error would be expected for a sample of $n = 100$ scores?

*6 A population has $\mu = 200$ and $\sigma = 50$. Find the z-score for each of the following sample means:
- a A sample of $n = 25$ with $\bar{X} = 220$.
- b A sample of $n = 100$ with $\bar{X} = 190$.
- c A sample of $n = 4$ with $\bar{X} = 230$.

7 On an immediate memory test, 10-year-old children can correctly recall an average of $\mu = 7$ digits. The distribution of recall scores is normal with $\sigma = 2$.
- a What is the probability of randomly selecting a child with a recall score less than 6?
- b What is the probability of randomly selecting a sample of $n = 4$ children whose average recall score is less than 6?

*8 Simple reaction times for college students form a normal distribution with $\mu = 200$ milliseconds and $\sigma = 20$.
- a What is the probability of randomly selecting a student whose reaction time is less than 190?
- b What is the probability of randomly selecting a sample of $n = 4$ students with an average reaction time less than 190?
- c What is the probability of randomly selecting a sample of $n = 25$ students with an average reaction time less than 190?

9 If you select a random sample of $n = 36$ scores from a population with $\mu = 80$ and $\sigma = 24$, then
- a What is the probability of obtaining a sample mean greater than 84?
- b What is the probability of obtaining a sample mean less than 72?

*10 A sample is selected from a population with $\sigma = 10$. If the standard error for this sample is $\sigma_{\bar{X}} = 2$, how many scores are in the sample?

11 A researcher obtains a random sample from a population with $\sigma = 12$. The sample mean will be used to estimate the population mean, and the researcher wants to determine how accurately $\bar{X}$ will estimate μ.
- a What is the standard error for a sample of $n = 4$ scores?

b How many scores must be in the sample to have a standard error of 4 points or less?

c How many scores are needed to have a standard error of 2 points or less?

12 If you are taking a random sample from a normal population with $\mu = 100$ and $\sigma = 12$, which of the following outcomes is more likely?

a A sample mean greater than 106 for a sample of $n = 4$ scores

b A sample mean greater than 103 for a sample of $n = 36$ scores

***13** IQ scores form a normal distribution with $\mu = 100$ and $\sigma = 15$.

a What is the probability of randomly selecting a sample of $n = 9$ students so that their average IQ is different by more than one point from the population mean? (What is the probability of obtaining a sample mean greater than 101 or less than 99?)

b What is the probability of randomly selecting a sample of $n = 100$ individuals so that their average IQ is more than one point away from the population mean?

14 Standard error measures the standard distance between a sample mean and the population mean. For a population with $\sigma = 20$,

a How large a sample would be needed to obtain a standard error of less than 10 points?

b How large a sample would be needed to have a standard error smaller than 5 points?

c If you wanted your sample mean to be within 1 point of the population mean (on the average), how large a sample should you use?

***15** The light bulbs used in the U.S. space shuttle have an average life expectancy of $\mu = 100$ hours. The distribution of life expectancies is normal with $\sigma = 10$ hours. For a trip that is expected to last 380 hours, the crew take along four new bulbs (one in place and three spares). Assuming that each bulb is replaced immediately when it burns out, what is the probability that the four bulbs will be sufficient for the entire 380-hour trip? *Note:* For the four bulbs to total 380 hours, they must average 95 hours per bulb.

16 Boxes of sugar are filled by machine with considerable accuracy. The distribution of box weights is normal and has a mean of 32 ounces with a standard deviation of only 2 ounces. A quality control inspector takes a sample of $n = 16$ boxes and finds the sample contains on average $\overline{X} = 31$ ounces of sugar. What is the probability of obtaining a sample with this much shortchanging in its boxes? Should the inspector suspect that the filling machinery needs repair?

17 Scores on a personality questionnaire form a normal distribution with $\mu = 80$ and $\sigma = 12$. If a random sample of $n = 16$ people is selected and the average personality score is computed for this sample, then

a Sketch the distribution of all the possible sample means that could be obtained.

b Of all the possible sample means, what proportion will be greater than 86?

c Of all the possible sample means, what proportion will be within three points of the population mean?

***18** A population is normally distributed with $\mu = 100$ and $\sigma = 20$.

a Find the *z*-score corresponding to each of the following samples:

Sample 1: $n = 4$; $\overline{X} = 110$

Sample 2: $n = 25$; $\overline{X} = 105$

Sample 3: $n = 100$; $\overline{X} = 104$

b Which of the samples in part a is least likely to be obtained by random sampling?

19 A random sample of $n = 36$ scores is obtained from a population with $\sigma = 12$. The sample mean is $\overline{X} = 43$.

a If you had to estimate the mean for the population, what value would you use? Explain the reasoning behind your answer.

b If you use the sample mean to estimate the population mean, then how accurate would you expect this estimate to be?

20 **a** Calculate the mean and standard deviation for the population of digits 0 through 9.

b If you took a random sample of $n = 8$ digits from this population, what is the probability that the digits in your sample would total 50 or more? (*Note:* For 8 digits to total 50, they must average 6.25 each.) Assume the distribution of sample means is normal even though $n = 8$.

c If you took a random sample of 12 digits, what is the probability that they would total 50 or more? Assume the distribution of sample means is normal even though $n = 12$.

***21** The 27 freshmen in Tower Dormatory finished their first semester with a mean grade point average of 2.61. They consider this to be a remarkable achievement because the mean GPA for the entire freshman class was only $\mu = 2.35$. If GPAs are normally distributed with $\sigma = .27$, what is the probability that a random sample of $n = 27$ would have an average GPA of 2.61 or higher? Are the freshmen in Tower Dorm justified in being proud?

22 The local hardware store sells screws in 1-pound bags. Because the screws are not identical, the number of screws per bag varies with $\mu = 115$ and $\sigma = 6$. A carpenter needs a total of 600 screws for a particular project. What is the probability that he will have enough screws if he buys five bags? (Assume the distribution is normal.)

***23** The average age for registered voters in the county is $\mu = 39.7$ years with $\sigma = 11.8$. The distribution of ages is approximately normal. During a recent jury trial in the county courthouse, a statistician noted that the average age for the 12 jurors was $\overline{X} = 51.4$ years.

a How likely is it to obtain a jury this old or older by chance?

b Is it reasonable to conclude that this jury is not a random sample of registered voters?

***24** At the beginning of this chapter we noted that the law of large numbers says that the larger the sample, the more likely that the sample mean will be close to the population mean. This law can be demonstrated using IQ scores which form a normal distribution with $\mu = 100$ and $\sigma = 16$.

a What is the probability of randomly selecting one individual whose IQ is within 5 points of the population mean?

b If you select a sample of five people, how likely is it that their average IQ will be within 5 points of the population mean?

c How likely is it for a sample of 10 people to have an average IQ within 5 points of the population mean?

25 A manufacturer of flashlight batteries claims that its batteries will last an average of $\mu = 34$ hours of continuous use. Of course, there is some variability in life expectancy with $\sigma = 1$ hour. During consumer testing, a sample of 30 batteries lasted an average of only $\overline{X} = 31.5$ hours. How likely is it to obtain a sample that performs this badly if the manufacturer's claim is true?

26 Error scores for laboratory rats on a standardized discrimination problem form a normal distribution with $\mu = 85$ and $\sigma = 15$.

a Sketch the distribution of sample means for samples of size $n = 10$.

b Find the range of values corresponding to the middle 95% of this distribution. Note that 95% of all the possible samples will have a mean in this range.

c What is the range of sample means that would contain 99% of all the possible samples of $n = 10$ rats?

***27** A large grocery store chain in New York has received a shipment of 1000 cases of oranges. The shipper claims that the cases average $\mu = 40$ oranges with a standard deviation of $\sigma = 2$. To check this claim, the store manager randomly selects 4 cases and counts the number of oranges in each case. For these 4 cases, the average number of oranges is $\overline{X} = 38$.

a Assuming that the shipper's claim is true, what is the probability of obtaining a sample mean this small?

b Based on your answer for part a, does the grocery store manager have reason to suspect that he has been cheated? Explain your answer.

CHAPTER 8

INTRODUCTION TO HYPOTHESIS TESTING

TOOLS YOU WILL NEED

The following items are considered essential background material for this chapter. If you doubt your knowledge of any of these items, you should review the appropriate chapter or section before proceeding.

- *z*-Scores (Chapter 5)
- Distribution of sample means (Chapter 7)
    - Expected value
    - Standard error
    - Probability of sample means
- Probability and the binomial distribution (Chapter 6)

PREVIEW

Psychologists have noted that stimulation during infancy can have profound effects on the development of infant rats. It has been demonstrated that stimulation (for example, increased handling) and even stress (mild electric shock) result in eyes opening sooner, more rapid brain maturation, decreases in emotionality, faster growth, and larger body weight (see Levine, 1960). Based on these data, one might theorize that increased stimulation and possibly occasional mild stress early in life can be beneficial. Suppose a researcher who is interested in this developmental theory would like to determine whether or not stimulation during infancy also has an effect on human development. This researcher might propose the following hypothesis:

> For the population of human infants, extra handling early in life will have an effect on growth as measured by body weight.

Notice that the hypothesis makes a specific prediction about the relationship between an independent variable (handling) and a dependent variable (weight). Because the hypothesis identifies specific variables, it can be evaluated in an experiment. Also note that the hypothesis refers to the entire population.

Of course, it would be impossible to test the entire population of human infants in an experiment. It is reasonable, however, to test the effects of handling for a relatively small sample. Thus, a random sample of newborn infants is selected, and the researcher trains the parents to provide increased handling for their children. When each child in the sample reaches 2 years of age, his or her body weight is recorded. The researcher then uses data from the sample to evaluate the hypothesis. For this example, the researcher would determine whether or not the infants receiving extra handling weighed substantially more than normally expected at 2 years of age.

In this example, as in most scientific research, the investigator is using data from a sample to evaluate a hypothesis about a population. You should recall that the general technique of using sample data as the basis for making conclusions about a population is called inferential statistics. The process of testing hypotheses is one of the standard inferential procedures in statistics. In this chapter we introduce the logic, the notation, and the general mechanics of hypothesis testing. We also spend a lot of time discussing errors in hypothesis testing. You should realize that any inferential procedure is subject to errors. Whether you are making judgments about a person after one short meeting or making conclusions about a population based on a single sample, there is a chance that you will reach the wrong decision. One of the general goals in the process of hypothesis testing will be to limit or control the probability of errors.

8.1 THE LOGIC OF HYPOTHESIS TESTING

It is usually impossible or impractical for a researcher to observe every individual in a population. Therefore, researchers usually collect data from a sample. Hypothesis testing is a statistical procedure that allows scientists to use sample data to draw inferences about the population of interest.

DEFINITION *Hypothesis testing* is an inferential procedure that uses sample data to evaluate the credibility of a hypothesis about a population.

As demonstrated in the preview example, a researcher first makes a hypothesis about an unknown population and then obtains a sample from the population to determine whether or not the sample data are consistent with the hypothesis. In this overview of the hypothesis-testing procedure, you can think of the researcher as a police detective gathering evidence. The sample is the evidence that the researcher uses to build a case for or against the hypothesis. Sometimes the evidence is overwhelming, and the researcher can make confident conclusions about the hypothesis. Often the evidence is not very convincing, and the researcher is uncertain about a conclusion. There is always a possibility that the evidence is misleading and the researcher will reach the wrong conclusion.

Because the process of hypothesis testing involves some uncertainty and can lead to errors, the procedure has been formalized to a standard series of operations. In this way, the researcher has a standardized method for evaluating the evidence from an experiment. Other researchers will recognize and understand exactly how the data were evaluated and how conclusions were reached. In addition, the hypothesis-testing procedure is developed so that a researcher can identify and partially control the risk of an error. Throughout this book we will present hypothesis testing as a four-step procedure. The hypothesis testing example from the preview section of this chapter will be used to introduce the four steps. In this example, a psychologist is trying to determine whether increased handling during infancy has an effect on growth as measured by body weight at age 2 years.

STEP 1: STATING THE HYPOTHESES

Suppose our researcher knows from national health statistics that the average weight for 2-year-olds who are not receiving any special treatment is $\mu = 26$ pounds. To determine whether increased handling has any effect, the researcher must compare the weights from the sample data with this national average. To begin this process, the researcher states two opposing hypotheses. Note that both hypotheses are stated in terms of population parameters.

The goal of inferential statistics is to make general statements about the population by using sample data. Therefore, when testing hypotheses, we make our predictions about the population parameters.

The first is the *null hypothesis*, or H_0. This hypothesis states that the treatment has no effect. (The null hypothesis always says that there is no effect, no change, no difference, nothing happened—hence the name *null*.) In this example, the null hypothesis states that additional handling during infancy will have *no effect* on body weight for the population of infants. In symbols, this hypothesis would be

$H_0 : \mu_{\text{infants handled}} = 26$ pounds (Even with extra handling, the mean weight at 2 years is still 26 pounds.)

· DEFINITION · The *null hypothesis* (H_0) predicts that the independent variable (treatment) has no effect on the dependent variable for the population.

The second hypothesis is simply the opposite of the null hypothesis, and it is called the *scientific* or *alternative hypothesis* (H_1). This hypothesis states that the treatment will have an effect on the dependent variable. For this example, it predicts that handling does alter growth for the population. In symbols, it is represented as

$H_1 : \mu_{\text{infants handled}} \neq 26$ (With handling, the mean will be different from 26 pounds.)

Notice that the alternative hypothesis simply states that there will be some type of change. It does not specify whether the effect will be increased or decreased growth. In some circumstances it is appropriate to specify the direction of the effect in H_1. For example, the researcher might hypothesize that increased handling will increase growth ($\mu > 26$ pounds). This type of hypothesis results in a directional hypothesis test, which will be examined in detail in Chapter 9. In this chapter we concentrate on nondirectional tests, where the hypotheses always state that the treatment has some effect (H_1) or has no effect (H_0). A nondirectional hypothesis test is always

FIGURE 8.1

The effect of extra handling during infancy on body weight is assessed. Specifically we ask, What is the mean weight for the population after treatment? This question is answered by sample data. The figure on the left shows the situation if the null hypothesis (H_0) is correct and the treatment has no effect. The figure on the right shows the situation if the alternative hypothesis (H_1) is correct and the treatment has changed the population mean.

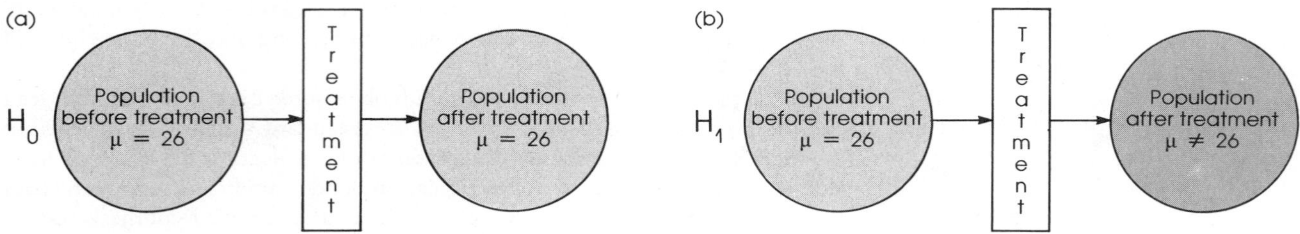

appropriate, even when a researcher has a definite prediction that the treatment will increase (or decrease) scores. For this example, we are examining whether handling in infancy does alter growth in some way (H_1) or has no effect (H_0). You should also note that both hypotheses refer to a population whose mean is unknown—namely, the population of infants who receive extra handling early in life. The two hypotheses are depicted in terms of population distributions in Figure 8.1.

DEFINITION The *alternative hypothesis* (H_1) predicts that the independent variable (treatment) will have an effect on the dependent variable for the population.

STEP 2: SETTING THE CRITERIA FOR A DECISION

Our researcher will eventually use the data from the sample to evaluate the hypotheses. For this example, the null hypothesis states that handling has no effect, so the mean weight for children who receive extra handling is $\mu = 26$ pounds. If this hypothesis is correct, you would expect the children in the experiment to average around 26 pounds. If experiment produces a sample mean near 26 pounds, the researcher will conclude that the data are consistent with the null hypothesis—that is, handling does not appear to affect weight. On the other hand, if the infants in the experiment weigh substantially more (or less) than 26 pounds, the researcher will conclude that the data contradict the hypothesis, so H_0 must be false.

The final decision is based on a comparison of the data versus the null hypothesis. The problem for the researcher is to establish criteria that define precisely how much difference must exist between the data and the null hypothesis to justify a decision that H_0 is false. Suppose the infants in the experiment weighed an average of $\overline{X} = 26.5$ pounds at age 2. Clearly the sample mean is greater than the null hypothesis value of $\mu = 26$. But is it "substantially more"? Does a half-pound difference constitute enough evidence to conclude that the treatment worked?

The procedure for establishing criteria is considered in Section 8.2. For now, you should recognize that criteria are essential for a researcher to make an objective decision about the hypotheses.

STEP 3: COLLECTING SAMPLE DATA

The next step in hypothesis testing is to obtain the sample data. A random sample of infants would be selected and parents would be trained to provide additional daily handling during the first few months of infancy. Then the body weight of the infants would be measured when they reach 2 years of age. Usually the raw data from the sample are summarized in a single statistic, such as the sample mean or a *z*-score. Of course, selecting a sample randomly is important because it helps ensure that the sample is representative of the population. For example, it would help avoid the selection of a group of infants that would be unusually small or large, regardless of the treatment.

PERSPECTIVE 8.1

REJECTING THE NULL HYPOTHESIS VERSUS PROVING THE ALTERNATIVE HYPOTHESIS

It may seem awkward to pay so much attention to the null hypothesis. After all, the purpose of most experiments is to show that a treatment does have an effect, and the null hypothesis states that there is no effect. The reason for focusing on the null hypothesis rather than the alternative hypothesis comes from the limitations of inferential logic. Remember, we want to use the sample data to draw conclusions, or inferences, about a population. Logically, it is much easier to demonstrate that a universal (population) hypothesis is false than to demonstrate that it is true. This principle is shown more clearly in a simple example. Suppose you make the universal statement "all dogs have four legs" and you intend to test this hypothesis by using a sample of one dog. If the dog in your sample does have four legs, have you proved the statement? It should be clear that one four-legged dog does not prove the general statement to be true. On the other hand, suppose the dog in your sample has only three legs. In this case, you have proved the statement to be false. Again, it is much easier to show that something is false than to prove that it is true.

Hypothesis testing uses this logical principle to achieve its goals. It would be difficult to state "the treatment has an effect" as the hypothesis and then try to prove that this is true. Therefore, we state the null hypothesis, "the treatment has no effect," and try to show that it is false. The end result still is to demonstrate that the treatment does have an effect. That is, we find support for the alternative hypothesis by disproving (rejecting) the null hypothesis.

You also should note that the data are collected only after the researcher has stated hypotheses and established criteria for making a decision. This sequence of events helps ensure that a researcher makes an honest, objective evaluation of the data and does not tamper with the decision criteria after the experiment outcome is known.

STEP 4: EVALUATING THE NULL HYPOTHESIS In the final step, the researcher compares the data with the null hypothesis and makes a decision according to the criteria that were established in step 2. There are two possible decisions, and both are stated in terms of the null hypothesis. (See Perspective 8.1.)

One possibility is that the researcher decides to *reject the null hypothesis.* This decision is made whenever the sample data are substantially different from what the null hypothesis predicts. In this case, the data provide strong evidence that the treatment does have an effect.

The second possibility occurs when the data do not provide convincing evidence of a treatment effect. In this case the sample data are consistent with the null hypothesis, and the statistical decision is to *fail to reject the null hypothesis.* The term *fail to reject* is used because the experiment failed to produce evidence that H_0 is wrong.

ERRORS IN HYPOTHESIS TESTING

The problem in hypothesis testing is deciding whether or not the sample data are consistent with the null hypothesis. In the second step of the hypothesis-testing procedure, we identify the kind of data that are expected if the null hypothesis is true. If the outcome of the experiment is consistent with this prediction, then there is no need to be suspicious about the credibility of the null hypothesis. If, on the other hand, the outcome of the experiment is very different from this prediction, then we would reject the null hypothesis because the evidence is overwhelmingly against it. In either case, it is possible that the decision we make about the tenability of H_0 is an incorrect decision. The two possibilities are presented here (and in Perspective 8.2).

Type I Errors It is possible to reject the null hypothesis when in reality the treatment has no effect. The outcome of the experiment could be different from what H_0 predicted just by chance. After all, unusual events do occur. For example, it is possible, although unlikely, to toss a balanced coin five times and have it turn up heads every time. In the experiment we have been considering, it is possible just by chance to

PERSPECTIVE 8.2

A SUMMARY OF STATISTICAL ERRORS

Definitions:

A Type I error is rejecting a true null hypothesis.
A Type II error is failing to reject a false null hypothesis.

Interpretation:

Type I error: The researcher concludes that the treatment does have an effect when, in fact, there is no treatment effect.

Type II error: The researcher concludes that there is no evidence for a treatment effect when, in fact, the treatment does have an effect.

How Does it Happen?:

Type I error: By chance, the sample consists of individuals with extreme scores. As a result, the sample looks different from what we would have expected according to H_0. Note that the treatment has not actually affected the individuals in the sample—they were different from average from the start of the experiment.

Type II error: Although there are several explanations for a type II error, the simplest is that the treatment effect was too small to have a noticeable effect on the sample. As a result, the sample does not appear to have been affected by the treatment. It is also possible that, just by chance, the sample was extreme to start with and in the opposite direction of the treatment effect. The treatment effect, in turn, restores the sample to the average that is expected by H_0. A treatment effect does not appear to have occurred even though it did.

Consequences:

Type I error: Because the sample data appear to demonstrate a treatment effect, the researcher may claim in a published report that the treatment has an effect. This is a false report and can have serious consequences. For one, other researchers may spend precious time and resources trying to replicate the findings to no avail. In addition, the false report creates a false data base upon which other workers develop theories and plan new experiments. In reality, they may be taking a journey down an experimental and theoretical dead end.

Type II error: In this case, the sample data do not provide sufficient evidence to say that the treatment has any effect. The researcher can interpret this finding in two different ways:

First, the researcher can conclude that the treatment probably does have an effect but the experiment was not good enough to find it. Perhaps an improved experiment (larger sample, better measurement, more potent treatment, etc.) would be able to demonstrate the treatment effect. The consequence is that refined experiments may be capable of detecting the effect.

Second, the researcher may believe that the statistical decision is correct. Either the treatment has no effect, or the effect is too small to be important. In this case, the experiment is abandoned. Note that this interpretation can have serious consequences in the event a Type II error has occurred. It means that the researcher is giving up a line of research that could have otherwise provided important findings.

select a sample of exceptional infants who display unusual (much less or much greater than normal) growth patterns even though the handling treatment has no effect. In this situation the data would lead us to reject the null hypothesis even though it is correct. This kind of mistake is called a *Type I error* (see Table 8.1), and in psychology it is very serious mistake. A Type I error results in the investigator making a false report of a treatment effect. In the handling experiment, the researcher would claim that handling during infancy alters growth when in fact no such effect exists.

· DEFINITION · A *Type I error* consists of rejecting the null hypothesis when H_0 is actually true.

Type II Errors It also is possible for the data to be consistent with the null hypothesis even when H_0 is false. Suppose that handling has a small effect on growth so that even with early handling our sample averages slightly above 26 pounds at 2 years of age. However, the difference between the sample and the predicted (H_0) data is too small to reject H_0 confidently. Another possibility is that the sample of infants was exceptionally small at the start. Handling increases their growth but only to the extent that they reach the expected weight of 26 pounds at 2 years. In these cases, we would decide to retain a null hypothesis when in reality it is false, a *Type II error* (Table 8.1). That is, we conclude that the treatment has no effect when in fact it does.

· DEFINITION · In a *Type II error,* the investigator fails to reject a null hypothesis that is really false.

TABLE 8.1

Possible outcomes of a statistical decision

		Actual Situation	
		No Effect, H_0 True	Effect Exists, H_0 False
Experimenter's decision	Reject H_0	Type I error	Decision correct
	Retain H_0	Decision correct	Type II error

Most experiments in psychology are done with the hope of rejecting the null hypothesis. Remember, the null hypothesis states that the treatment has no effect on the dependent variable. However, we face a dilemma in reaching a decision about H_0. On one hand, we would like to establish that there is a treatment effect (reject H_0). But we also would like to avoid a Type I error (rejecting H_0 when it really is true).

A similar dilemma occurs in the "hypothesis testing" that is done in the courtroom. Just as we assume H_0 is true before we collect our data, the jury is instructed to assume that the accused person is innocent of a crime—innocent until proven guilty. A Type I error would occur if the jury decides a person is guilty when in reality that person did not commit the crime (see Table 8.2). A Type I error is serious: An innocent person would be sent to prison. Just as in scientific research, it is desirable to avoid making a Type I error. This may mean that the jury will let a guilty person off the hook, a Type II error (Table 8.2). To deal with the dilemma of testing a person's innocence while avoiding a Type I error, the judge instructs the jury that the accused individual should be found guilty only if the evidence is "beyond a reasonable shadow of a doubt." This guideline will reduce the chance that the jury will commit a Type I error and punish an innocent person.

Likewise, it is important for scientists to minimize the likelihood of making a Type I error in their investigations. It is highly desirable to avoid making a false report that a treatment effect exists. To be sure a Type I error is avoided, the H_0 is rejected only when the sample data are very extreme and unlikely for H_0 to be true. That is, the evidence must be so overwhelming against H_0 that the researcher can reject the null hypothesis with the confidence that the "verdict" is correct "beyond a reasonable shadow of a doubt." How unlikely or overwhelming must the sample data be before the researcher can confidently reject H_0 and conclude there is an effect? The guideline is provided by the level of significance that the investigator uses in testing the hypothesis. We examine this guideline in Section 8.2.

TABLE 8.2

Possible outcomes of a jury's decision

		Actual Situation	
		Did Not Commit Crime	Committed Crime
Jury's Verdict	Guilty	Type I error	Verdict correct
	Innocent	Verdict correct	Type II error

Adapted from *Essence of Statistics*, by G. R. Loftus and E. F. Loftus. Copyright © 1982 by Wadsworth Inc. Reprinted by permission of Brooks/Cole Publishing Company, Monterey, Calif.

· LEARNING CHECK ·

1 What does the null hypothesis predict about a population?
2 Why do we evaluate (decide to reject or not reject) the null hypothesis instead of evaluating the alternative hypothesis?
3 What is a Type I error? A Type II error?
4 Is it possible to commit a Type II error when H_0 is rejected? Explain your answer.
5 Why do we state hypotheses in terms of population parameters?

ANSWERS

1 The null hypothesis predicts that the treatment will have no effect on the dependent variable for the population.
2 It is much easier to disprove a universal (population) statement than to prove one. Therefore, to find support for a treatment effect in the population, we must obtain sample data that suggest we should reject H_0. That is, we support the presence of a treatment effect when we disprove the null hypothesis.
3 A Type I error occurs when the experimenter rejects a null hypothesis that is actually true. An effect is reported when none exists. A Type II error occurs when the decision is "fail to reject H_0" but the null hypothesis is really false. One fails to report an effect that does exist.
4 No. A Type II error results from *failing to reject* a false H_0. Therefore, it cannot result from rejecting the null hypothesis.
5 We make predictions about the population because the goal of inferential statistics is to make general statements about the *population* based on the sample data.

8.2 EVALUATING HYPOTHESES

As previously noted, there is always the possibility for error in making an inference. As a result, we can never be absolutely positive that a hypothesis test has produced the correct decision. Although we cannot know for certain if our decision is right or wrong, we can know the probabilities for being right or wrong. Specifically, the hypothesis testing procedure is structured so that a researcher can specify and control the probability of making a Type I error. By keeping this probability small, a researcher can be confident that the risk of error is very low whenever the null hypothesis is rejected.

ALPHA LEVEL: MINIMIZING THE RISK OF A TYPE I ERROR

To make a decision about a null hypothesis, it is necessary to determine what data are expected if H_0 is true and what data are very unlikely. The *level of significance*, also called the *alpha level*, simply defines the very unlikely data. It marks off the part of the distribution from which it is highly unlikely to obtain sample data if H_0 is true. Obtaining sample data from this part of the distribution would lead us to reject the null hypothesis. To minimize the risk of committing a Type I error, we mark off regions of the distribution that are extreme and improbable. For example, if we use an alpha (α) level of 5%, then the sample data would have to be from the most extreme 5% of the distribution in order to reject H_0. The probability that we would commit a Type I error in that case would equal alpha, or $\alpha = 5\%$.

· DEFINITION · *Alpha* (α) is the risk of committing a Type I error. The selected alpha determines the *level of significance* of a hypothesis test, the level at which we reject H_0 and conclude there is evidence for a treatment effect.

Traditionally, alpha levels are set at 5% (.05), 1% (.01), or .1% (.001). We will examine the role that alpha plays in the hypothesis testing procedures by returning to the example of the effects of increased handling during infancy.

PROCEDURE AND STEPS Recall that the study examines the effect of extra handling during infancy on growth. We will begin with the simplest possible experiment for now, using a sample of only one infant ($n = 1$). The parents are instructed in how to provide additional handling during the first few months of their infant's life, and then the child's weight is measured at 2 years of age. Let us assume that weights are normally distributed with $\mu = 26$ pounds and $\sigma = 4$ for the population of untreated (did not receive additional handling) children. There are four steps to hypothesis testing: (1) state the hypotheses and select an alpha level, (2) use the alpha level to define what kind of sample data would warrant rejection of H_0, (3) analyze the sample data, and (4) make a decision about H_0. We will use these steps to assess the effect of additional handling during infancy on growth.

STEP 1 We must state the hypotheses and select an alpha level. The null hypothesis predicts that no effect will occur. That is, even with additional handling during infancy, the population mean weight for 2-year-olds will still be 26 pounds. In symbols, this hypothesis is stated as follows:

$$H_0 : \mu_{\textbf{handling in infancy}} = 26 \text{ pounds}$$

The alternative hypothesis states that early handling will change the mean weight for the population. In symbols, this hypothesis would state the following:

$$H_1 : \mu_{\textbf{handling}} \neq 26 \text{ pounds}$$

We will select an alpha level of 5%, or in terms of a proportion, $\alpha = .05$. This means that in order to reject the null hypothesis, the sample data must be extremely convincing—the data must be in the most extreme 5% of the distribution. By setting α to this level, we are limiting the probability of a Type I error to only 5%.

STEP 2 We establish criteria that define what kind of sample data would warrant rejection of the null hypothesis. We begin by looking at all the possible data that could be obtained if the null hypothesis were true. If H_0 is true, then the distribution of handled infants would be the same as the original distribution of untreated infants. That is, it would be a normal distribution with $\mu = 26$ and $\sigma = 4$ (Figure 8.2).

If H_0 is true we expect to obtain a score near the population mean, $\mu = 26$. Extreme values in the tails of the distribution would be extremely unlikely.

We have selected the value of $\alpha = .05$ for the level of significance. This proportion is divided evenly between the two tails of the distribution (see Figure 8.2). It is very unlikely that we would sample a score from this area of the distribution if H_0 is true. The area between the tails is the middle 95% of the distribution. This area contains the most likely scores (weights) in the population, and it is very likely that we would obtain a sample score from this region if H_0 is true.

Notice that the boundaries that separate the middle 95% from the extreme 5% (2.5% in each tail) are located at the z-score values of $+1.96$ and -1.96 (from the unit normal table in Appendix B). A z-score of 1.96 indicates that the corresponding score is 1.96 standard deviations away from the mean. For this example, 1.96 standard deviations is equal to 7.84 points. For the population weight distribution, the score that corresponds to $z = +1.96$ is $X = 33.84$, and the score that corresponds to $z = -1.96$ is $X = 18.16$. These values mark off the boundaries between the middle 95% and the extreme tails of the distribution (see Figure 8.2).

Remember, $X = \mu + z\sigma$ (Chapter 5).

· FIGURE 8.2 ·

The distribution of all the possible scores that could be obtained if H_0 is true. The boundaries separate the middle 95% from the most extreme 5% ($\alpha = .05$).

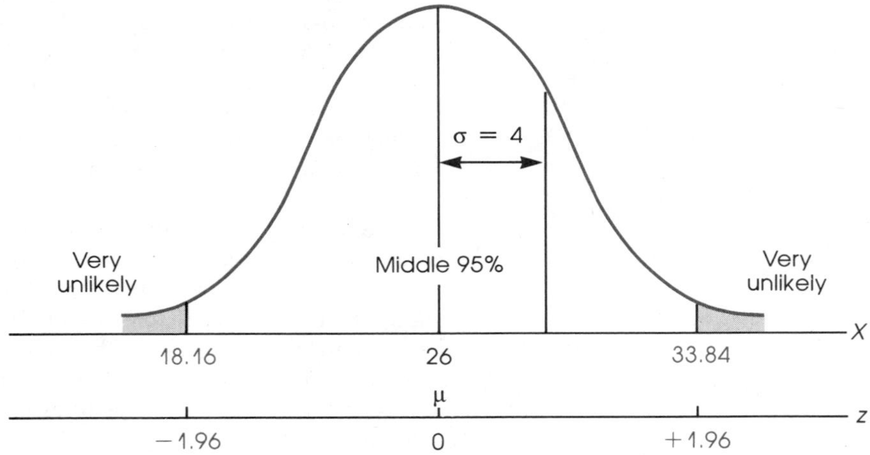

If we randomly select one subject from the population, then we would expect to observe a weight near 26 pounds. Most of the time (95% to be exact) we would expect the score to be in the middle section of the distribution. It is very improbable that we would randomly sample a score that is out in the extreme tails of the distribution if H_0 is true. These extreme tails, the shaded areas in Figure 8.2, are called the *critical region* of the distribution. If H_0 were true, then it would be extremely unlikely to obtain a score in the critical region. Notice that we have defined "extremely unlikely" as meaning "having a probability less than alpha." For this example, the H_0 is rejected only when the sample data are really extreme—when the probability of our sample observation is less than the alpha level ($p < .05$). In other words, H_0 is rejected when the sample data fall in the critical region.

· DEFINITION · The *critical region* is composed of extreme sample values that are very unlikely to be obtained if the null hypothesis is true. The size of the critical region is determined by the alpha level. Sample data that fall in the critical region will warrant the rejection of the null hypothesis.

STEP 3 We now turn our attention to the sample data. In this particular example, the sample size is $n = 1$. Suppose the infant that received extra handling early in life weighed 34 pounds at 2 years of age. What can we conclude about the relationship between handling in infancy and growth?

STEP 4 We must make a decision about the null hypothesis. The result we obtained from the sample, $X = 34$, lies in the critical region (Figure 8.2). The sample is not what we expected if the null hypothesis is true. It is an extremely unlikely outcome ($p < .05$) if H_0 is true. Therefore, we decide to reject the null hypothesis and conclude that extra handling during infancy did have a statistically significant effect on growth. With this statistical decision, we are risking a Type I error. That is, we could be rejecting a true null hypothesis. It is possible that the handling had no effect on growth and that the infant we sampled would have reached 34 pounds anyway. However, this is very unlikely. If H_0 is true, the probability of obtaining any score in the critical region is less than 5%, the alpha level we selected. The maximum probability of committing a Type I error is equal to alpha.

Always state your conclusion in terms of the independent variable and the dependent variable for the particular experiment being examined.

z-SCORES AND HYPOTHESIS TESTING

In the handling example, our decision to reject H_0 was based on the obtained score of $X = 34$, which falls within the critical region. We could have based this decision entirely on z-scores. For this example, the critical region consists of any z value greater than $+1.96$ or less than -1.96 (Figure 8.2). We can simply convert the obtained X value into a z-score to determine its location. That is, we determine whether or not it is in the critical region. For the score obtained,

$$z = \frac{X - \mu}{\sigma} = \frac{34 - 26}{4} = 2.00$$

The obtained z-score is greater than $+1.96$ and thus lies in the critical region. The statistical decision would be the same, H_0 is rejected. Notice that the z-score is being used to test a hypothesis. In this use, the z-score is often called a *test statistic*. We will examine other types of test statistics which are used in hypothesis testing in later chapters.

FAILURES TO REJECT THE NULL HYPOTHESIS

Using the handling example again, let us suppose that we obtained a sample infant that attained a weight of 31 pounds at 2 years. Steps 1 and 2 (stating the hypotheses and locating the critical region) remain the same. For step 3, we can analyze the sample finding by computing a z-score. If $X = 31$, then

$$z = \frac{X - \mu}{\sigma} = \frac{31 - 26}{4} = \frac{5}{4} = 1.25$$

Limitations in the logic of inference make it easier to disprove a hypothesis about the population (Perspective 8.1).

In the final step, the statistical decision is made. The z-score for the obtained sample score is not in the critical region. This is the kind of outcome we would expect if H_0 were true. It is important to note that we have not proved that the null hypothesis is true. The sample provides only limited information about the entire population, and, in this case, we did not obtain sufficient evidence to claim that additional handling early in life does or does not have an effect on growth. For this reason, researchers avoid using the phrase "accepting the null hypothesis," opting instead for "failing to reject the null hypothesis." The latter phrase is more consistent with the logic of hypothesis testing. When the data are not overwhelmingly contrary to H_0, at best all we can say is that the data do not provide sufficient evidence to reject the null hypothesis.

Our decision to "fail to reject" H_0 means that we are risking a Type II error. For this example, a Type II error would mean that the extra handling actually did have some effect and yet we failed to discover it. A Type II error generally is not as serious a mistake as a Type I error. The consequences of a Type II error would be that a real effect is not reported. If a researcher suspects that a Type II error has occurred, there is always the option of repeating the experiment, usually with some refinements or modifications. There are lots of reasons why any particular experiment may fail. When a researcher is personally convinced that a treatment should have an effect, he or she has every right to try to demonstrate it with another experiment (see Perspective 8.3). However, you should realize that it is not reasonable to continue doing the same experiment over and over until it eventually produces the results you want.

Unlike Type I errors where the exact amount of risk is specified by the alpha level (α), there is no simple way to determine the probability of a Type II error. In fact, this probability is not a single value but rather depends on the size of the treatment effect. Although the exact probability of committing a Type II error is not

PERSPECTIVE 8.3

PROBLEMS IN REPLICATION

What does it really mean when we fail to find a treatment effect? What happens when a researcher repeatedly fails to replicate an earlier finding in his or her own laboratory? This problem occurred in the laboratory of Dr. Neal E. Miller, a very prominent psychologist who for years did outstanding research at Yale University and later Rockefeller University. He wanted to see if rats could learn to control their involuntary vital responses by operant conditioning and do so without the aid of voluntary movements. For example, if a rat is given a reward (pleasurable brain stimulation) for slowing down its heart rate, would it learn to control its heart and make it beat slower to get the reward? There was a "catch" to the experiment. The rats had to learn to control heart rate without voluntary movements (like becoming very relaxed) that could slow the heart. So rats were temporarily paralyzed with a drug called curare. Sure enough, even though their muscles were paralyzed, the rats could still learn to control how fast their hearts would beat. Miller and the scientific community in general were excited by the findings and the possible applications for treating psychosomatic disorders. However, after reporting the results of the first few experiments, Miller and his coworkers found that they could no longer get the same effects. He could not replicate the conditioning of involuntary responses by the use of reward. What went wrong? Perhaps the new batch of rats was somehow different from the previous animals. Miller tried a different kind of rat to no avail. Perhaps the paralyzing drug had gone bad and interfered with the conditioning of heart rates. He tried a new sample of curare, but nothing changed. Perhaps the reward was no longer as effective as before, or perhaps changes in the laboratory diet caused general physiological changes in the animals that prevented the effect. The list of possible reasons why the conditioning effect could not be replicated seems endless. As Miller and Dworkin (1974) pointed out,

> The problem is that, whereas there often are millions of ways of doing something wrong, there may be only one or two ways of doing it right. Thus, one positive result can yield vastly more information than many negative ones (p. 315).

Thus, there may be "millions" of ways of doing an experiment incorrectly, each producing no evidence for an effect, each retaining a null hypothesis. Yet we cannot make a general conclusion when we fail to reject H_0. Had we used the right combination of treatment conditions in the experiment, had we done the experiment in the "one or two ways of doing it right," an effect may have emerged. Therefore, retaining the null hypothesis in many experiments will not advance our knowledge as much as finding an effect in a single experiment.

α is for Type I, and β is for Type II.

easily calculated, it is identified by the Greek letter beta, β. We examine β again when statistical power is considered (Chapter 9).

· LEARNING CHECK ·

1 Define alpha.

2 If H_0 is rejected when alpha is .05, will it necessarily be rejected when alpha has been set at .01?

3 What is the critical region? How is it used?

4 Experimenter 1 typically sets alpha to .10, while experimenter 2 always uses an alpha level of .05. In the long run, which experimenter will make more Type I errors?

ANSWERS

1 Alpha is the risk an investigator takes in committing a Type I error. The alpha level determines the level of significance of a statistical test.

2 Not necessarily. The data may be extreme enough to warrant rejecting H_0 at the 5% level of significance but not extreme enough for the same decision at the 1% level.

3 The critical region consists of extreme sample values that are very unlikely to be obtained (probability less than α) if the null hypothesis is true. If sample data fall in the critical region, we reject H_0.

4 Experimenter 1 is taking a greater risk (10%) of committing a Type I error.

8.3 HYPOTHESIS TESTING WITH SAMPLES OF MORE THAN ONE SCORE

Up to this point we have examined the hypothesis-testing procedure with samples consisting of only one subject ($n = 1$). In practice, however, many subjects are selected for the sample. In such a case, our hypothesis no longer hinges on a single X value but on the mean of the sample, $\overline{X}$. The general procedure for hypothesis testing is the same whether you have a sample of $n = 1$ or $n = 100$. In step 1, you state the hypothesis (H_0 and H_1) and specify an alpha level. In step 2, you locate the critical region—that is, you look at all the possible results that could be obtained if H_0 were true and then identify the most extreme, most unlikely outcomes. In step, 3 the sample data are collected and analyzed, and in step 4, a decision is made about the null hypothesis. The size of the sample (n) becomes important in the second and third steps. Instead of looking at all the possible scores that could be obtained (that is, when $n = 1$), we now must look at all the possible sample means that could be obtained. You should recall from the previous chapter that "all the possible sample means" is, by definition, the distribution of sample means. The following example demonstrates how this distribution is used in hypothesis tests with samples of more than $n = 1$.

EXAMPLE 8.1 Once again we will look at the effect of handling early in life on growth. This time, however, a sample of $n = 25$ infants is selected. The parents are instructed in providing additional handling during the first few months. The body weight of all subjects is measured at 2 years of age. As before, body weight for the population of untreated 2-year-olds is normally distributed with $\mu = 26$ and $\sigma = 4$. Suppose that the sample of $n = 25$ children has a mean body weight of $\overline{X} = 30$.

STEPS AND PROCEDURES

STEP 1 The null hypothesis states that the extra handling will have no effect on growth (mean body weight). In symbols, H_0 states that

$$H_0: \mu_{\text{handling}} = 26 \text{ pounds}$$

The alternative hypothesis states that the handling treatment will produce a change in growth. In symbols, it is represented as

$$H_1: \mu_{\text{handling}} \neq 26 \text{ pounds}$$

We select an alpha level of $\alpha = .05$ (5%). This means that we are willing to take a 5% risk of committing a Type I error.

STEP 2 If the null hypothesis is true, it is possible to examine the distribution of all the possible sample means that could be obtained from this experiment. This distribution is the distribution of sample means based on samples of $n = 25$. It will have an expected value of $\mu = 26$ when H_0 is true. Furthermore, this distribution will have a standard error of $\sigma_{\overline{X}} = .8$ according to the following formula:

Remember, a property of the distribution of sample means is that the expected value equals μ.

$$\sigma_{\overline{X}} = \frac{\sigma}{\sqrt{n}} = \frac{4}{\sqrt{25}} = \frac{4}{5} = .8$$

The distribution of sample means is shown in Figure 8.3. It is this distribution for which we locate the critical region. We have set alpha to .05, so the critical region consists of the most extreme 5% of all the possible sample means. Because this distribution is normal, the most extreme 5% consists of values with z-scores greater than $+1.96$ or less than -1.96 (2.5% in each tail, the shaded area in Figure 8.3).

The distribution of sample means is normal when the population is normal.

FIGURE 8.3

The distribution of sample means for $n = 25$ if H_0 is true. This is the set of all the possible experimental outcomes that could be obtained if handling has no effect on weight gain.

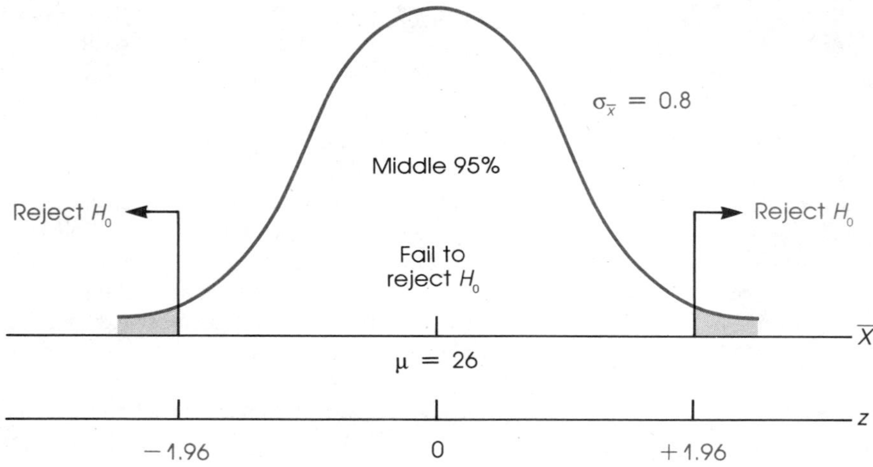

Notice that the middle 95% of the distribution consists of samples with means within 1.96 standard errors of 26 pounds. We would expect to obtain a sample mean in this neighborhood if H_0 were true and handling had no effect. If our data fall in this middle section, we will conclude that the results are consistent with the null hypothesis, and we will retain (fail to reject) H_0. Also note that all of the values in this distribution are possible if H_0 is true. Specifically, it is possible to randomly select a sample whose mean falls in the critical region. However, this is a very unlikely possibility if H_0 is true because of how the critical region was determined. By definition, the critical region consists of the most extreme 5% of all the possible sample means. That is, it is only 5% likely that the sample data will be in the critical region if H_0 were true—which means that there is only a 5% chance of committing a Type I error if H_0 is rejected.

STEP 3 At this stage, the sample data are collected and analyzed. As noted earlier, the obtained sample mean is $\overline{X} = 30$. Where is this sample located within the distribution of sample means shown in Figure 8.3? The most direct way of answering this question is to compute a z-score. The test statistic for these data is

Careful! Be sure to use $\sigma_{\overline{X}}$.

$$z = \frac{\overline{X} - \mu}{\sigma_{\overline{X}}} = \frac{30 - 26}{.8} = \frac{4}{.8} = 5.0$$

Remember, this test statistic finds the location of a sample mean within the distribution of sample means.

STEP 4 It now is possible to make a statistical decision. The result of the study was a sample with a mean weight of $\overline{X} = 30$ pounds. This value corresponds to a z-score of $z = +5.0$. Note that the obtained z-score falls in the critical region on the right-hand side of the distribution (Figure 8.3). This means that the observed sample data are very unlikely to have occurred if H_0 is true. Because the results are overwhelmingly inconsistent with H_0, we reject the null hypothesis. We conclude that additional handling during infancy does have an effect on weight. Of course in making this decision, it is possible that we have made a Type I error—that these extreme data were obtained by chance alone and that handling has no effect. However, this error is not very likely because a level of significance of 5% was used. The probability that we have committed a Type I error, rejecting a true H_0, is $p < .05$. (See Perspective 8.4.) •

PERSPECTIVE 8.4

REPORTING THE RESULTS OF THE STATISTICAL TEST

There is a special jargon and notational system that is used in published reports of hypothesis tests. When you are reading a scientific journal, for example, you will not be told explicitly that the researcher evaluated the data using a *z*-score as a test statistic with an alpha level of .05. Instead, you will see a statement like

"The treatment effect was significant, $z = 3.85$, $p < .05$."

Let us examine this statement part by part.

First, what is meant by the term *significant*? In statistical tests, this word indicates that the result is different from what would be expected by chance. A significant result means that the null hypothesis has been rejected. That is, the data are in the critical region and not what we would have expected to obtain if H_0 were true.

Next, what is the meaning of $z = 3.85$? The *z* indicates that the data were used to compute a *z*-score for a test statistic and that its value was 3.85. Finally, what is meant by $p < .05$? This part of the statement is the conventional way of specifying the alpha level that was used for the hypothesis test. More specifically, we are being told that the result of the experiment would occur by chance with a probability (p) that is less than .05.

In circumstances where the statistical decision is to fail to reject H_0, the report might state that

"There was no evidence for an effect, $z = 1.30$, $p > .10$." In this case, we are saying that the obtained result, $z = 1.30$, is not unusual (not in the critical region) and is relatively likely to occur by chance (the probability is greater than .10).

A z-score Hypothesis Test on the Computer When the size of a sample is large, it is often easier to perform the computations for a hypothesis test on the computer. We used Minitab to do the *z*-score test for Example 8.1. In the example, the sample mean had already been calculated, so you did not need the raw scores. However, for the Minitab analysis, we entered the raw data ($n = 25$ scores) from that experiment which follow:

31	30	26	29	32	28	33	25	28	31	35	27	32
33	29	29	29	28	30	33	29	31	31	33	28	

Using the Minitab command ZTEST, the computer calculates the sample mean, standard error, and the *z*-score. The printout of this analysis with an explanation is shown in Table 8.3.

THE STRUCTURE OF THE z-SCORE FORMULA

It is useful to define the *z*-score formula

$$z = \frac{\overline{X} - \mu}{\sigma_{\overline{X}}}$$

in terms of the important steps and elements of hypothesis testing. The null hypothesis is represented in the formula by μ. The value of μ that we use in the formula is the value predicted by H_0. We test H_0 by collecting sample data, which are represented by the sample mean ($\overline{X}$) in the formula. Thus the numerator of the *z* formula can be rewritten as

$$\overline{X} - \mu = \text{sample data} - \text{population hypothesis}$$

You should recall that the standard error ($\sigma_{\overline{X}}$) measures the standard distance between a sample mean and the population mean. Thus, standard error measures the expected difference (due to chance) between $\overline{X}$ and μ. Now we can restate the entire *z*-score test statistic as

$$z = \frac{\text{sample data} - \text{population hypothesis}}{\text{standard error between } \overline{X} \text{ and } \mu}$$

Notice that the difference between the sample data and the null hypothesis must be

TABLE 8.3

The Minitab printout of a z-score hypothesis test for the data in Example 8.1.

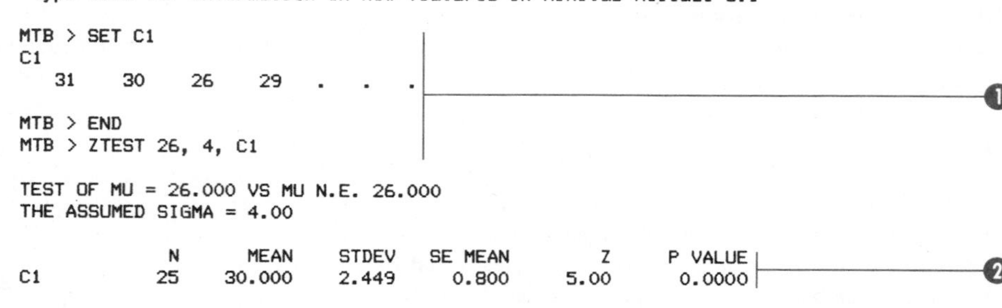

```
MINITAB RELEASE 5.1.3 *** COPYRIGHT - MINITAB, INC. 1985
U.S. FEDERAL GOVERNMENT USERS SEE HELP FGU
MARCH 2, 1987 *** S.U.N.Y. BROCKPORT - ACADEMIC COMPUTING SERVICES
STORAGE AVAILABLE 260144

 Type NEWS for information on new features in Minitab Release 5.1

MTB > SET C1
C1
   31    30    26    29   .  .  .                    (1)

MTB > END
MTB > ZTEST 26, 4, C1

TEST OF MU = 26.000 VS MU N.E. 26.000
THE ASSUMED SIGMA = 4.00

              N      MEAN    STDEV   SE MEAN       Z    P VALUE
C1           25    30.000    2.449     0.800    5.00     0.0000   (2)

MTB > STOP
*** Minitab Release 5.1.3 *** Minitab, Inc. ***
Storage available 260144  Storage used 30767
```

EXPLANATION OF PRINTOUT:

1 Minitab displays a partial list of the raw scores. The ZTEST command selects the analysis and notes that $\mu = 26$ and $\sigma = 4$ and that the data have been entered into column 1 (C1).

2 The results of the analysis show the size (N), the mean (MEAN), and the standard deviation (STDEV) for the sample. The standard error (SE MEAN) and z-score (Z) are also provided. Finally, the printout shows the probability of committing a Type I error (P VALUE) if H_0 is rejected. In this example, that probability is so small that 0.0000 is displayed. Thus, you can reject the null hypothesis with $p < .0001$.

substantially larger than would be expected by chance in order to obtain a z-score that is large enough to fall in the critical region. The structure of this z-score formula will form the basis for some of the test statistics to follow in later chapters.

MORE ABOUT ALPHA—THE LEVEL OF SIGNIFICANCE

As you have seen, the alpha level for a hypothesis test serves two very important functions. First, alpha determines the risk of a Type I error. Second, alpha helps determine the boundaries for the critical region. As you might expect, these two functions interact with each other. When you lower the alpha level—for example, from .05 to .01—you reduce the risk of a Type I error. To gain this extra margin of safety, you must demand more evidence from the data before you are willing to reject H_0. This is accomplished by moving the boundaries for the critical region. With $\alpha = .05$ for example, the z-score boundaries are located at ± 1.96. For $\alpha = .01$, the boundaries move to $z = \pm 2.58$, and with $\alpha = .001$, the boundaries move all the way out to $z = \pm 3.30$ (see Figure 8.4). With $\alpha = .001$, it would take a huge difference between the data and the hypothesis to be significant. In general, as you lower the alpha level, the critical boundaries move farther away from the population mean, and it becomes increasingly more difficult to obtain a sample that is located in the critical region. Thus, sample data that are sufficient to reject H_0 at the .05 level of significance may not provide sufficient evidence to reject H_0 at the .01 level. If you push alpha to an extremely low level, it can become essentially impossible for an experiment ever to demonstrate a significant treatment effect.

Where do you set the critical boundaries so that your experiment has some chance of being successful and (at the same time) minimize your risk of a Type I error? His-

FIGURE 8.4

The location of the critical region boundaries for three different levels of significance: $\alpha = .05$, $\alpha = .01$, and $\alpha = .001$.

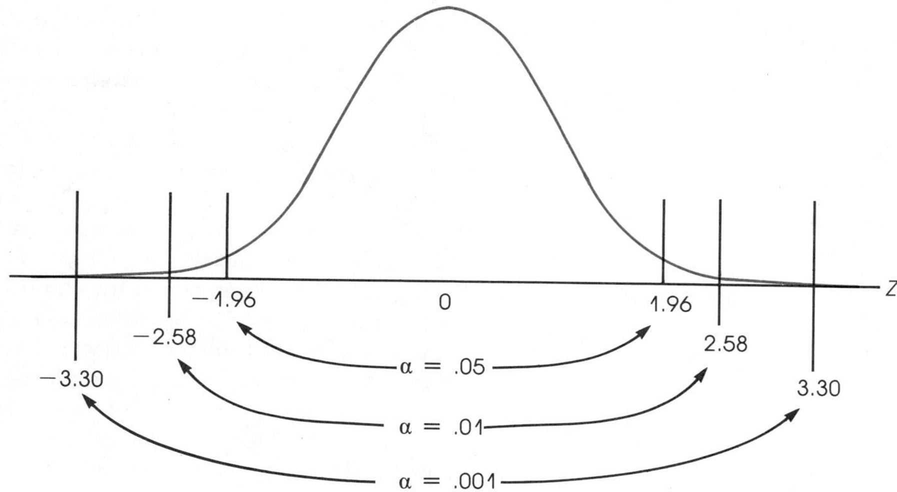

torically, the answer is to use an alpha level of .05. This value was first suggested in 1925 by a well-known statistician named Sir Ronald A. Fisher. Fisher noted that it is convenient to use the .05 level as a limit in judging whether a result is considered to be significant or not, and he suggested that researchers ignore all results that fail to reach this limit. Although Fisher selected $\alpha = .05$ as a personal, arbitrary standard, it has become recognized as the minimum level of significance that is acceptable for publication of research in many journals. In fact, some of the more prestigious journals require an alpha level of .01 for their published results. For most research an alpha level of .05 is appropriate and is generally defined as *statistically significant*. The .01 level of significance is used in situations where you have special reason to fear a Type I error or where you want to make an exceptionally strong demonstration of a treatment effect. The .01 alpha level is generally defined as *highly statistically significant*. (For more information on the origins of the .05 level of significance, see the excellent short article by Cowles and Davis, 1982.)

ASSUMPTIONS FOR HYPOTHESIS TESTS WITH z-SCORES

It will become evident in later chapters that certain conditions must be present for each type of hypothesis test to be an appropriate and accurate procedure. These conditions are assumed to be satisfied when the results of a hypothesis test are interpreted. However, the decisions based on the test statistic (that is, rejecting or not rejecting H_0) may be compromised if these assumptions are not satisfied. In practice, researchers are not overly concerned with the conditions of a statistical test unless they have strong suspicions that the assumptions have been violated. Nevertheless, it is crucial to keep in mind the fundamental conditions that are associated with each type of statistical test to ensure that it is being used appropriately. The assumptions for hypothesis tests with *z*-scores which involve one sample are summarized below.

Random Sampling It is assumed that the subjects used to obtain the sample data were selected randomly. Remember, we wish to generalize our findings from the sample to the population. This task is accomplished when we use sample data to test a hypothesis about the population. Therefore, the sample must be representative of the population from which it has been drawn. Random sampling helps to ensure that it is representative.

The Value of σ is Unchanged by the Treatment The general purpose of hypothesis testing is to determine whether or not a treatment (independent variable) produces a change in the population mean. The null hypothesis, the critical region, and the *z*-score statistic all are concerned with the treated population. In the *z*-score formula we use $\overline{X}$ from the treated sample, a hypothesized value of μ for the treated population and a standard error that indicates how close $\overline{X}$ should be to μ. However, you may have noticed that when we compute the standard error, we use the standard deviation from the untreated population. Thus, the *z*-score appears to be using values from two different populations: $\overline{X}$ and μ for the treated population and σ from the untreated population. To justify this apparent contradiction we must make an assumption. Specifically, we must assume that the value of σ is the same after treatment as it was before treatment.

Actually, this assumption is the consequence of a more general assumption that is part of many statistical procedures. This general assumption states that the effect of the treatment is to add (or subtract) a constant amount to every score in the population. You should recall that adding (or subtracting) a constant will change the mean but will have no effect on the standard deviation. You also should note that this assumption is a theoretical ideal. In actual experiments a treatment generally will not show a perfect and consistent additive effect.

Normal Sampling Distribution To evaluate hypotheses with *z*-scores, we have used the unit normal table to identify the critical region. This table can be used only if the distribution of sample means is normal.

· LEARNING CHECK ·

1 An instructor has been teaching large sections of general psychology for the past 10 semesters. As a group, final exam scores are normally distributed with $\mu = 42$ and $\sigma = 9$. With the current class of $n = 100$ students, the instructor tries a different teaching format. Once a week the class breaks down into smaller groups that meet with the instructor for discussion of recent lecture and reading material. At the end of the semester, the instructor notes that the mean for this section on the final exam was $\overline{X} = 46.5$. Did the teaching format have a significant effect on performance on the final exam? Test with alpha set at .05.

a State the hypotheses.
b Locate the critical region.
c Compute the test statistic.
d Make a decision regarding H_0.
e For this example, identify the independent and dependent variables.

ANSWERS

1 **a** $H_0: \mu_{\text{discussion groups}} = 42$; $H_1: \mu_{\text{discussion groups}} \neq 42$.
b The critical region consists of *z*-score values greater than $+1.96$ or less than -1.96.
c $\sigma_{\overline{X}} = .9$; $z = +5.0$.
d Reject H_0 and conclude that teaching format does affect scores on the final exam. The small-group sessions improve final test performance.
e The independent variable is teaching format. The dependent variable is the score on the final exam.

8.4 HYPOTHESIS TESTS WITH THE BINOMIAL DISTRIBUTION

In Chapter 6 we introduced the binomial distribution and described the process of computing probabilities for binomial events. You should recall that binomial data exist whenever a measurement procedure classifies individuals into exactly two distinct categories. The two categories were identified as *A* and *B*, having probabilities (or proportions) of p and q, respectively. For example, a coin toss results in either heads or tails with probabilities $p = \frac{1}{2}$ and $q = \frac{1}{2}$.

We also noted in Chapter 6 that when pn and qn are both equal to or greater than 10, the binomial distribution approximates a normal distribution. This fact is important because it allowed us to use the unit normal table to answer probability questions about binomial events. It is equally important, because it allows us to use the binomial distribution for inferential statistics. The most commonly used inferential procedure is hypothesis testing, where a researcher uses sample data to evaluate a hypothesis about the values of p and q for a population. This type of hypothesis test is sometimes called a *binomial test.*

· DEFINITION · A *binomial test* uses sample data to evaluate hypotheses about the values of p and q for a population consisting of binomial data.

Consider the following two situations:

1. In a sample of $n = 34$ color-blind students, 30 are male and only 4 are female. Does this sample indicate that color-blindness is significantly more common for males in the general population?

2. In 1980 only 10% of American families had incomes below the poverty level. This year, in a sample of 100 families, 19 were below the poverty level. Does this sample indicate that there has been a significant change in the population proportions?

Notice that both of these examples have binomial data (exactly two categories). Although the data are relatively simple, we are asking the same statistical question about significance that is appropriate for a hypothesis test: Do the sample data provide sufficient evidence to make a conclusion about the population?

Binomial tests using the normal approximation to the binomial distribution will use the z-score formula presented in Chapter 6 (page 144):

For the normal approximation, $\mu = pn$ and $\sigma = \sqrt{npq}$

$$z = \frac{X - pn}{\sqrt{npq}}$$

The same four-step hypothesis-testing procedure presented earlier is used for the binomial test. The four steps are summarized next.

STEP 1 *State the hypotheses.* In the binomial test the null hypothesis specifies the population values for p and q. For example, a null hypothesis might state that a particular coin has $P(\text{heads}) = \frac{1}{2}$ and $P(\text{tails}) = \frac{1}{2}$. Note that the null hypothesis often states that there is "nothing wrong or unusual" about the probabilities. For example, our hypothesis states that the coin is balanced and therefore should come up heads one-half of the time and tails for the other half. Also note that the hypothesis refers to the population (for example, the set of all possible coin tosses). The data will consist of a small sample from this general population.

STEP 2 *Locate the critical region.* For the binomial test using the normal approximation, the critical region is located in the same way as it is for any other z-score test. First, the alpha level is set. Then, the unit normal table is consulted to find the z-scores that form the boundaries of the critical region. Remember, the unit normal table can be used *only* if the condition is satisfied for the normal approximation, that pn and qn are greater than or equal to 10.

STEP 3 *Obtain the data and compute the z-score.* At this point you obtain a sample of n individuals (or events) and count how many times category A occurs in this set. The number of occurrences of A is the X value. The z-score is computed for X using the formula from Chapter 6 (page 144) just given.

STEP 4 *Make a decision about the null hypothesis.* If the *z*-score for the sample *X* value is in the critical region, you should reject H_0. On the other hand, if it is not in the critical region, you should fail to reject H_0.

Example 8.2 demonstrates how the normal approximation can be used to test hypotheses about the probability values *p* and *q* for a population.

· EXAMPLE 8.2 · In 1960 Eleanor Gibson and Richard Walk designed a classic piece of apparatus to test depth perception (Gibson and Walk, 1960). Their device, called a *visual cliff*, consisted of a wide board with a deep drop (the cliff) to one side and a shallow drop on the other side. An infant was placed on the board and then observed to see whether he or she crawled off the shallow side or crawled off the cliff. (*Note:* Infants who moved to the deep side actually crawled onto a sheet of heavy glass, which prevented them from falling. Thus the deep side only appeared to be a cliff—hence the name, visual cliff.)

Gibson and Walk reasoned that if infants are born with the ability to perceive depth, they would recognize the deep side and not crawl off the cliff. On the other hand, if depth perception is a skill that develops over time through learning and experience, then infants should not be able to perceive any difference between the shallow and the deep sides.

Out of 27 infants who moved off the board, only 3 ventured onto the deep side. Is this a chance result, or do the data indicate that infants have a significant preference for the shallow side?

This is a binomial hypothesis testing problem. The two categories are:

A = move off deep side

B = move off shallow side

STEP 1 The null hypothesis would state that for the general population there is no systematic preference between the deep and shallow sides; the direction of movement is determined by chance. In symbols, the hypotheses are

$$H_0: p = P(\text{move to deep side}) = \tfrac{1}{2}$$
$$q = P(\text{move to shallow side}) = \tfrac{1}{2}$$
$$H_1: p \neq \tfrac{1}{2} \text{ and } q \neq \tfrac{1}{2} \text{ (there is a preference)}$$

We will use $\alpha = .05$.

STEP 2 To locate the critical region, we will need to specify the characteristics of the binomial distribution. Because both *pn* and *qn* are greater than 10, we can use the normal approximation of the binomial distribution. This normal distribution is shown in Figure 8.5. Notice that

$$\mu = pn = \tfrac{1}{2}(27) = 13.5$$
$$\sigma = \sqrt{npq} = \sqrt{27(\tfrac{1}{2})(\tfrac{1}{2})} = \sqrt{6.75} = 2.60$$

The critical region consists of the most extreme 5% of this distribution. This portion is bounded by *z*-scores of $z = \pm 1.96$.

STEP 3 For this experiment, the data consist of $X = 3$ out of 27 infants. These data have a corresponding *z*-score of

$$z = \frac{X - pn}{\sqrt{npq}} = \frac{3 - 13.5}{2.60} = \frac{-10.5}{2.60} = -4.04$$

FIGURE 8.5

The normal approximation to the binomial distribution for Example 8.2. The critical region for $\alpha = .05$ is indicated.

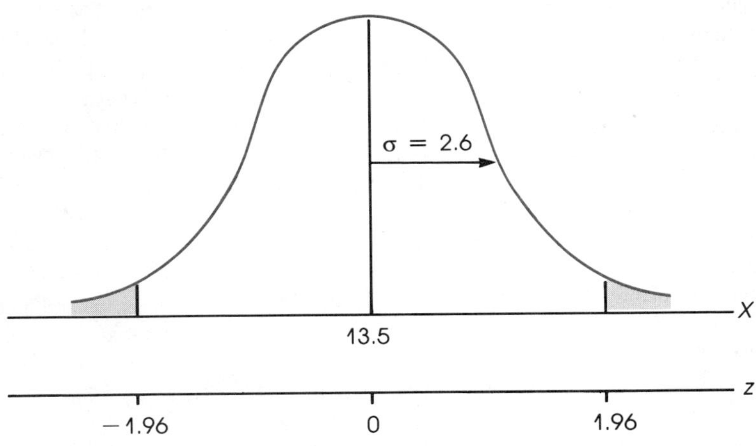

STEP 4 Because the data are in the critical region, our decision is to reject H_0. These data do provide sufficient evidence to conclude that there is a significant preference for the shallow side. Gibson and Walk interpreted these data as convincing evidence that depth perception is innate. •

LEARNING CHECK

1 The makers of Brand X beer claim that people like their beer more than the leading brand. The basis for this claim is an experiment in which 64 beer drinkers compared the two brands in a side-by-side taste test. In this sample, 38 preferred Brand X and 26 preferred the leading brand. Do these data support the claim that there is a significant preference? Test at the .05 level.

ANSWERS

1 $H_0: p = \frac{1}{2} = q$, $X = 38$, $\mu = 32$, $\sigma = 4$, $z = +1.50$, fail to reject H_0. Conclude that there is no evidence for a significant preference.

SUMMARY

1 Hypothesis testing is an inferential procedure for using the limited data from a sample to draw a general conclusion about a population. It begins with hypothesizing values for the mean of an unknown population, generally a population that has received a treatment (Figure 8.1).

2 The null hypothesis (H_0) states that the treatment has not changed the mean. That is, it is the same as the mean for a known and untreated population. At this stage we also select an alpha level, usually $\alpha = .05$ or .01, which sets the risk of committing a Type I error. Alpha determines the level of significance of a statistical test.

3 The second step involves locating the critical region. We examine all the possible experimental outcomes if the null hypothesis is true and then identify the most unlikely values. We define "unlikely according to H_0" as the outcomes with a probability less than alpha. Thus, the selected alpha level determines the critical z-scores that are associated with the critical region. Sample data that produce a z-score that falls within the critical region would imply that H_0 is not tenable.

4 The sample data are collected. Specifically, the sample mean $\overline{X}$ is used to test a hypothesis about μ. To determine how unlikely the obtained sample mean is, we must locate it within the distribution of sample means. This is accomplished by computing a z-score for $\overline{X}$:

$$z = \frac{\overline{X} - \mu}{\sigma_{\overline{X}}}$$

When a z-score is used in the test of a hypothesis, it is called a test statistic.

5 The z-score equation can be expressed as

$$z = \frac{\text{sample mean} - \text{hypothesized population mean}}{\text{standard error between } \overline{X} \text{ and } \mu}$$

That is, the difference between the sample mean and the hypothesized population mean (according to H_0) is compared to (divided by) the amount of error we would expect between $\overline{X}$ and μ.

6 In the fourth step, we compare the obtained data to the set of possible results that were outlined in the second step. That is, if the obtained z-score falls in the critical region, we reject H_0 because it is very unlikely that these data would be obtained if H_0 were true. We would conclude that a treatment effect occurred. If the data are not in the critical region, then there is not sufficient evidence to reject H_0. The statistical decision is "fail to reject H_0." We conclude that we failed to find sufficient evidence for an effect.

7 Whatever decision is reached in a hypothesis test, there is always a risk of making the incorrect decision. There are two types of errors that can be committed.

A Type I error is defined as rejecting a true H_0. This is a serious error because it results in falsely reporting a treatment effect. The risk of a Type I error is determined by the alpha level and, therefore, is under the experimenter's control.

A Type II error is defined as failing to reject a false H_0. In this case, the experiment fails to report an effect that actually occurred. The probability of a Type II error cannot be specified as a single value and depends in part on the size of the treatment effect. It is identified by the symbol β (beta).

8 The binomial test uses sample data to evaluate hypotheses about the values of p and q for a population comprised of binomial data.

9 When pn and qn are greater than or equal to 10, the normal approximation can be used for the binomial test. The test statistic is a z-score,

$$z = \frac{X - pn}{\sqrt{npq}}$$

where X is the frequency of occurrence for category A and $\mu = pn$ with $\sigma = \sqrt{npq}$ for the binomial distribution.

KEY TERMS

hypothesis testing
null hypothesis
alternative hypothesis
Type I error
Type II error
level of significance
alpha level
critical region
test statistic
beta
binomial test

FOCUS ON PROBLEM SOLVING

1. Hypothesis testing involves a set of logical procedures and rules that enable us to make general statements about a population when all we have are sample data. This logic is reflected in the four steps that have been used throughout this chapter. Hypothesis testing problems will become easier to tackle when you learn to follow the steps.

STEP 1 State the hypotheses and set the alpha level.

STEP 2 Locate the critical region.

STEP 3 Compute the z-score for the sample data.

STEP 4 Make a decision about H_0 based on the result of step 3.

A nice benefit of mastering these steps is that all hypothesis tests that will follow use the same basic logic outlined in this chapter.

2. Students often ask, "What alpha level should I use?" Or a student may ask, "Why is an alpha of .05 used?" as opposed to something else. There is no single correct answer to either of these questions. Keep in mind the idea of setting an alpha level in the first place: *to reduce the risk of committing a Type I error.* Therefore, you would not want to set α to something like .20. In that case, you would be taking a 20% risk of committing a Type I error—reporting an effect when one actually does not exist. Most researchers would find this level of risk unacceptable. Instead, researchers generally agree to the convention that $\alpha = .05$ is the greatest risk one should take in making a Type I error. Thus, the .05 level of significance is frequently used and has become the "standard" alpha level. However, some researchers prefer to take even less risk and use alpha levels of .01 and smaller.

3. Take time to consider the implications of your decision about the null hypothesis. The null hypothesis states that there is no effect. Therefore, if your decision is to reject H_0, you should conclude that the sample data provide evidence for a treatment effect. However, it is an entirely different matter if your decision is to fail to reject H_0. Remember, that when you fail to reject the null hypothesis, the results are inconclusive. It is impossible to *prove* that H_0 is correct; therefore, you cannot state with certainty that "there is no effect" when H_0 is not rejected. At best, all you can state is that "there is insufficient evidence for an effect" (see Perspective 8.1 and 8.3).

4. It is very important that you understand the structure of the *z*-score formula (page 183). It will help you understand many of the other hypothesis tests that will be covered later.

5. You can differentiate a binomial hypothesis test from a regular *z*-score test by looking carefully at the data. For a binomial test the data will be frequencies (not scores) for exactly two categories, and the problem will provide information concerning the probability for each category. For a regular *z*-score test, the data will be presented as scores (or summarized as a sample mean), and the problem will specify the population mean and standard deviation.

6. Be careful when stating the values of p and q for the null hypothesis in a binomial test. In some situations, p and q will not be equal to $\frac{1}{2}$ for H_0. Problem 9 in this chapter demonstrates this point.

PROBLEMS

*1 After several years of studying human performance in flight simulators, a psychologist knows that reaction times to an overhead emergency indicator form a normal distribution with $\mu = 200$ milliseconds and $\sigma = 20$. The psychologist would like to determine if placing the indicator in front of the person at eye level has any effect on reaction time. A random sample of $n = 25$ people is selected, they are tested in a simulator with the indicator light at eye level, and their reaction times are recorded.

a Identify the dependent variable and the independent variable.

b State the null hypothesis using a sentence that includes the dependent and independent variables.

c Using symbols, state the hypotheses (H_0 and H_1) that the psychologist is testing.

d Sketch the appropriate distribution and locate the critical region for the .05 level of significance.

e If the psychologist obtained an average reaction time of $\bar{X} = 195$ milliseconds for this sample, then what decision would be made about the null hypothesis?

f If the psychologist had used a sample of $n = 100$ subjects and obtained an average reaction time of $\bar{X} = 195$, then what decision would be made about the effects of the position of the indicator? Explain why this conclusion is different from the one in part e.

2 Suppose that scores on the Scholastic Aptitude Test form a normal distribution with $\mu = 500$ and $\sigma = 100$. A high school counselor has developed a special course designed to boost SAT scores. A random sample of $n = 16$ students is selected to take the course and then the SAT. The sample had an average score of $\bar{X} = 554$. Does the course have an effect on SAT scores?

a What are the dependent and independent variables for this experiment?

b Perform the hypothesis test using the four steps outlined in the chapter. Use $\alpha = .05$.

c If $\alpha = .01$ were used instead, what *z*-score values would be associated with the critical region?

d For part c, what decision should be made regarding H_0? Compare to part b and explain the difference.

3 Explain the structure of the *z*-score formula as it is used for hypothesis testing.

a What does $\bar{X} - \mu$ tell us in a hypothesis-testing situation?

b What does the standard error indicate?

*4 Discuss the errors that can be made in hypothesis testing.

a What is a Type I error? Why might it occur?

b What is a Type II error? How does it happen?

5 Why do we test H_0 to establish an effect instead of H_1?

*6 A developmental psychologist has prepared a training program that, according to a psychological theory, should improve problem-solving ability. For the population of 6-year-olds, the average score on a standardized problem-solving test is known to be $\mu = 80$ with $\sigma = 10$. To test the effectiveness of the training program, a random sample of 6-year-old children is selected. The data for the sample are as follows: 85, 69, 90, 77, 74, 76, 86, 93, 97, 88, 97, 80, 75, 98, 79, 75, 87, 94. Can the experimenter conclude that the program has an effect? Test with alpha set at .05.

a Perform the hypothesis test showing all four steps. When you state the hypotheses, explain what they predict in terms of the independent and dependent variables used in this experiment.

b Would the same decision have been made about H_0 if alpha had been set at .01?

7 A researcher is trying to assess some of the physical changes that occur in addicts during drug withdrawal. For the population, suppose the average body temperature is $\mu = 98.6°F$ with $\sigma = .56$. The following data consist of the body temperatures of a sample of heroin addicts during drug withdrawal: 98.6, 99.0, 99.4, 100.1, 98.7, 99.3, 99.9, 101.0, 99.6, 99.5, 99.4, 100.3. Is there a significant change in body temperature during withdrawal? Test at the .01 level of significance. Show all four steps of the hypothesis test.

***8** Suppose the U.S. Army tested thousands of recruits for their hearing thresholds of high-pitched (10,000-hertz) tones and determined that the average threshold is $\mu = 20$ decibels with $\sigma = 4.4$ and that this distribution is normal. Doctors are interested in the effects of the noise of rifle practice on high-pitched hearing. Following are the hearing thresholds (in decibels) for a 10,000-hertz tone for a sample of individuals that completed the rifle training: 26, 20, 32, 25, 24, 24, 23, 29, 20, 32, 27, 33, 22, 24, 28, 37, 26, 17, 25, 28, 26, 25, 19, 29. Do the trainees need protective ear covers? Test at the .05 level of significance. Provide all four steps of the hypothesis test. In stating the hypotheses, describe what H_0 and H_1 predict in terms of the independent and dependent variables in this study.

***9** An extensive survey 2 years ago indicated that 80% of the population of New York State favored income tax over sales tax as a means of increasing state revenue. In a recent sample of 100 people, 72 preferred income tax, and 28 preferred sales tax. Do these data indicate a significant change in opinion? Test at the .05 level of significance. (*Caution:* Be careful in setting the values of p and q for H_0. They are not equal.)

10 In a recent study examining color preferences in infants, 30 babies were offered a choice between a red rattle and a green rattle. Twenty-five of the 30 selected the red rattle. Do these data provide evidence for a significant color preference? Test at the .01 level of significance.

***11** A college dormitory recently sponsored a taste comparison between two major soft drinks. Of the 64 students who participated, 39 selected brand A, and only 25 selected brand B. Do these data indicate a significant preference? Test at the .05 level of significance.

12 An automobile manufacturer is developing a computer for its cars. Among other things, the computer will "talk" to the driver to warn of open doors, unfastened seat belts, low fuel levels, and so on. The company would like to know whether the computer should have a masculine or a feminine voice. When two voices were tested with a sample of 36 people, 30 preferred the masculine voice and only 6 preferred the feminine voice. Do these data represent a significant preference? Use an alpha of .05.

13 Nationwide, only 4% of the population develops ulcers each year. In a sample of 200 executive vice presidents, 40 had developed ulcers during the previous 12 months. Do these data indicate that vice presidents have an incidence of ulcers different from the general population? Test at the .05 level of significance.

***14** Use $\alpha = .05$ to answer each of the following questions. Use the normal approximation to the binomial distribution.

a For a true-false test with 20 questions, how many would you have to get right to do significantly better than chance?

b How many would you need to get right on a 40-question test?

c How many would you need to get right on a 100-question test?

15 A researcher would like to know if oxygen deprivation at the time of birth has a permanent effect on IQ. It is known that scores on a standard intelligence exam are normally distributed for the population with $\mu = 100$ and $\sigma = 15$. The researcher takes a random sample of individuals for whom complications at birth indicate moderate oxygen deprivation. The sample data are as follows: 92, 100, 106, 78, 96, 94, 98, 91, 83, 81, 86, 89, 87, 91, 89. Is there evidence for an effect?

a Test the hypothesis using the four-step method with alpha set at .05.

b What would the decision be if the .01 level of significance is used instead of the .05 level?

***16** For statistics sections during the past 12 years, an instructor has determined that the final exam scores average $\mu = 61.7$ with $\sigma = 14.6$. These scores are normally distributed. This semester the instructor has acquired two microcomputers and has set them up in a statistics laboratory so that the students in his current class can practice exercises and quiz themselves on the computer. Their final exam scores are as follows: 66, 92, 61, 70, 50, 81, 48, 53, 90, 72, 72, 32, 90, 39, 41, 60, 81, 83, 60, 67, 57, 84, 58, 72, 62, 86, 62, 62, 73, 77, 75. Does it appear that the computerized laboratory has had an effect on their understanding of the course material?

a Test the hypothesis at the .05 level of significance.

b What are the independent and dependent variables for this study?

17 A psychologist develops a new inventory to measure depression. Using a very large standardization group of "normal" individuals, the mean score on this test is $\mu = 55$ with $\sigma = 12$, and the scores are normally distributed. To determine if the test is sensitive in detecting those individuals that are severely depressed, a random sample of patients who are described as depressed by a therapist is selected and given the test. Presumably, the higher the score on the inventory, the more depressed the patient is. The data are as follows: 59, 60, 60, 67, 65, 90, 89, 73, 74, 81, 71, 71, 83, 83, 88, 83, 84, 86, 85, 78, 79. Do patients score significantly different on the test? Test with the .01 level of significance.

***18** On the General Aptitude Test Battery (GATB), scores of engineering graduates are normally distributed with $\mu = 134$ and $\sigma = 15$. The dean of the School of Engineering at a large university is in the process of assessing the engineering program. For part of the assessment, a sample of the current graduates takes the GATB. The data are as follows: 136, 119, 143, 139, 150, 152, 144, 141, 121, 149, 139, 163, 147, 143, 148, 133, 140. Is there a significant difference between the performance of these graduates and those of the standardization group? Test with alpha set at .05.

19 On a vocational/interest inventory that measures interest in several categories, a very large standardization group of adults has an average score on the "literary" scale of $\mu = 22$ with $\sigma = 4$. A researcher would like to determine if scientists differ from the general population in terms of writing interests. A random sample of scientists is selected from the directory of a national scientific society. The scientists are given the inventory, and their test scores on the literary scale are as follows: 21, 20, 23, 28, 30, 24, 23, 19. Do scientists differ from the general population in their writing interests? Test at the .05 level of significance.

***20** Suppose that the average birth weight for the population is $\mu = 2.9$ kilograms with $\sigma = .65$. An investigator would like to see if the birth weights of infants are significantly different for mothers that smoked cigarettes throughout their pregnancy. A random sample of women who smoke is selected, and the birth weight of their infants is recorded. The data (in kilograms) are as follows: 2.3, 2.0, 2.2, 2.8, 3.2, 2.2, 2.5, 2.4, 2.4, 2.1, 2.3, 2.6, 2.0, 2.3. What should the scientist conclude? Use the .01 level of significance.

21 Patients recovering from an appendix operation normally spend an average of $\mu = 6.3$ days in the hospital. The distribution of recovery times is normal with $\sigma = 1.2$ days. The hospital is trying a new recovery program that is designed to shorten the time patients spend in the hospital. The first 10 appendix patients in this new program were released from the hospital in an average of 5.5 days. On the basis of these data, can the hospital conclude that the new program has a significant effect on recovery time. Test at the .05 level of significance.

***22** For the past 2 years the vending machine in the psychology department has charged 40¢ for a soft drink. During this time, company records indicate that an average of $\mu = 185$ cans of soft drinks were sold each week. The distribution of sales is approximately normal with $\sigma = 23$. Recently, the company increased the price to 50¢ a can. The weekly sales for the first 8 weeks after the price increase are as follows: 148, 135, 142, 181, 164, 159, 192, 173. Do these data indicate that there was a significant change in sales after the price increase? Test at the .05 level of significance.

23 IQ scores for the general population form a normal distribution with $\mu = 100$ and $\sigma = 15$. However, there are data that indicate that children's intelligence can be affected if their mothers have German measles during pregnancy. Using hospital records, a researcher obtained a sample of $n = 20$ school children whose mothers all had German measles during their pregnancies. The average IQ for this sample was $\overline{X} = 97.3$. Do these data indicate that German measles have a significant effect on IQ? Test with $\alpha = .05$.

***24** For the past 12 years, an instructor in the Psychology Department has taught a course called "Thinking and Problem Solving." During this time the average enrollment for the course was $\mu = 28.6$ students with $\sigma = 8.2$. The distribution of enrollments is normal. For this semester, the instructor has changed the title of the course to "Higher Mental Processes" and has only 16 students enrolled. Can the instructor conclude that the change in the course title has caused a significant change in enrollment? Test with $\alpha = .05$.

25 In 1965 a nationwide survey revealed that U.S. grade school children spent an average of $\mu = 8.4$ hours per week doing homework. The distribution of homework times was normal with $\sigma = 3.3$. Last year a sample of $n = 200$ students was given the same survey. For this sample, the average number of homework hours was $\overline{X} = 7.1$.

a Do these data indicate a significant change in the amount of homework hours for American grade school children? Test at the .01 level of significance.

b If there had been only $n = 20$ students in the sample, would the data still indicate a significant change? Use the same sample mean, $\overline{X} = 7.1$, and use $\alpha = .01$.

***26** The following sample of $n = 10$ scores was obtained from a normal population with $\sigma = 12$:

78, 90, 54, 77, 71, 99, 85, 74, 93, 84.

a Use these data to test the hypothesis that the population mean is $\mu = 75$. Use $\alpha = .05$ for your test.

b Use these data to test the hypothesis that the population mean is $\mu = 85$. Use $\alpha = .05$ for your test.

c In parts a and b of this problem you should find that $\mu = 75$ and $\mu = 85$ are both acceptable hypotheses. Explain how two different values can both be acceptable.

27 In the general population, 8 out of 10 people can be hypnotized. A researcher suspects that the ability to be hypnotized is partially determined by an individual's personality. A sample of $n = 80$ subjects is obtained. All these subjects are known to be *field independent*, which means that they tend to rely on internal cues rather than external cues for making judgements. The researcher finds that 51 of these 80 subjects can be hypnotized. Do these data indicate that field-independent people are different from the general population in terms of their ability to be hypnotized? Use an alpha of .05.

***28** In a study of human memory, Sachs (1967) demonstrated that people recall the meaning of verbal material but tend to forget the exact word-for-word details. In this study, people read a passage of text. Then the people were shown a test sentence and asked whether or not the identical sentence had appeared in the text. In one condition the test sentence was phrased differently but has the same meaning as a sentence that was in the text. For example, the sentence in the text might be "The boy hit the ball," and the test sentence might be "The ball was hit by the boy." If only 27 out of 45 people correctly notice the change in the sentence, can you conclude that their performance is significantly better than chance? Test at the .05 level of significance.

29 A psychologist examining the psychology of art appreciation selected an abstract painting that had no obvious top or bottom. Hangers were placed on the painting so that it could be hung with any one of the four sides at the top. This painting was shown to a sample of $n = 50$ undergraduates, and each was asked to hang the painting in whatever orientation "looked best." Twenty-five of the subjects in this sample placed the painting so that the correct side was up. Is this significantly better than would be expected by chance? Test with $\alpha = .05$.

CHAPTER 9

DIRECTIONAL TESTS, ESTIMATION, AND POWER

TOOLS YOU WILL NEED

The following items are considered essential background material for this chapter. If you doubt your knowledge of any of these items, you should review the appropriate chapter or section before proceeding.

- Distribution of sample means (Chapter 7)
- Hypothesis tests (Chapter 8)
    - Type I error
    - Type II error
    - Critical region

PREVIEW

It should be obvious that a lot of planning and preparation go into the design of an experiment. Researchers do not blindly collect data and perform hypothesis tests to see whether or not a treatment has any effect. Part of this planning and preparation can be aided by the statistical techniques that will be presented in this chapter.

For example, researchers have access to results of earlier experimental work related to the particular treatment being examined. Almost always there are published research reports that provide some background, and, occasionally, a researcher will conduct some miniexperiments (pilot studies) to gather information about the treatment's effect. This information allows the researcher to predict in advance the magnitude of the treatment effect and the direction (increase or decrease) of the effect. Thus, a researcher is able to plan an experiment with a very detailed and specific hypothesis in mind. For example, a researcher may expect that the treatment will cause scores to increase by an average of approximately 12 points.

With a detailed prediction in mind, it is then possible for a researcher to anticipate the chances of the experiment being successful. It is very discouraging to invest time and money in a major experiment only to find that the final statistical result says "Fail to reject the null hypothesis—there is no evidence for a treatment effect." It would be valuable for a researcher to know in advance that the experiment has a 75% chance of successfully rejecting the null hypothesis. Although there is still some risk, at least you know the odds.

In this chapter we will examine three statistical topics that are relevant to planning experiments and evaluating data. First is the topic of *directional tests,* which allow a researcher to incorporate a directional prediction (increase or decrease) into the hypothesis testing procedure. Second is the technique of *estimation,* which allows a researcher to use sample data to estimate the magnitude of a treatment's effect. Finally, we will examine the topic of *power,* which provides the researcher with an opportunity to compute the probability of success for an experiment.

9.1 INTRODUCTION

The goal of inferential statistics is to use sample data to answer questions about populations. Hypothesis testing is perhaps the most commonly used inferential procedure, but there are others. Also, the format for hypothesis testing that was introduced in Chapter 8 often is modified to produce a slightly different kind of test. In this chapter we will consider some of the alternatives to hypothesis testing and some modifications and expansions of the standard hypothesis testing procedure.

9.2 DIRECTIONAL (ONE-TAILED) HYPOTHESIS TESTS

The hypothesis testing procedure presented in Chapter 8 was the standard, or *two-tailed,* test format. The term *two-tailed* comes from the fact that the critical region is located in both tails of the distribution. This format is by far the most widely accepted procedure for hypothesis testing. Nonetheless, there is an alternative that will be discussed in this chapter.

Usually, a researcher begins an experiment with a specific prediction about the direction of the treatment effect. For example, a special training program is expected to *increase* student performance, or alcohol consumption is expected to *slow* reaction times. In these situations, it is possible to state the statistical hypotheses in a manner that incorporates the directional prediction into the statement of H_0 and H_1. The result is a directional test, or what commonly is called a *one-tailed test.*

· DEFINITION · In a *directional hypothesis test,* or a *one-tailed test,* the statistical hypotheses (H_0 and H_1) specify either an increase or a decrease in the population mean score.

Suppose, for example, a researcher is using a sample of $n = 16$ laboratory rats to examine the effect of a new diet drug. It is known that under regular circumstances these rats eat an average of 10 grams of food each day. The distribution of food consumption is normal with $\sigma = 4$. The expected effect of the drug is to reduce food consumption. The purpose of the experiment is to determine whether or not the drug really works.

THE HYPOTHESES FOR A DIRECTIONAL TEST

Because there is a specific direction expected for the treatment effect, it is possible for the researcher to perform a directional test. The first step (and the most critical step) is to state the statistical hypotheses. Remember that the null hypothesis states that there is no treatment effect and that the alternative hypothesis says that there is an effect. For directional tests, it is easier to begin with the alternative hypothesis. In words, this hypothesis says that with the drug the mean food consumption is *less than* 10 grams per day; that is, the drug does reduce food consumption. In symbols, H_1 would say the following:

$H_1: \mu_{\text{with drug}} < 10$ (mean food consumption is reduced)

The null hypothesis is the opposite of the alternative. In words, the null hypothesis says that even with the diet drug the rats still will eat *at least* 10 grams per day. That is, the drug does not reduce food consumption. In symbols,

$H_0: \mu_{\text{with drug}} \geqslant 10$ (the mean is at least 10 grams per day)

THE CRITICAL REGION FOR DIRECTIONAL TESTS

After stating the hypotheses, the next step is to locate the critical region. The critical region is defined as the most unlikely outcomes (probability less than alpha) if H_0 is true. To find the critical region, you begin by looking at all the possible results that could be obtained if H_0 were true. For our example this is the distribution of sample means for $n = 16$. This distribution is normal (because the population is normal), it has a standard error of $\sigma_{\bar{X}} = 4/\sqrt{16} = \frac{4}{4} = 1$, and it has a mean of $\mu = 10$ if H_0 is true. This distribution is pictured in Figure 9.1.

If the null hypothesis is true and the population mean is 10 or more, you would expect the rats in the sample to average at least 10 grams of food per day. Therefore, a sample mean around 10 or higher would support H_0. The only value that

· FIGURE 9.1 ·

The distribution of sample means for $n = 16$ if H_0 is true. The null hypothesis states that the diet pill has no effect, so the population mean will be $\mu = 10$ or larger.

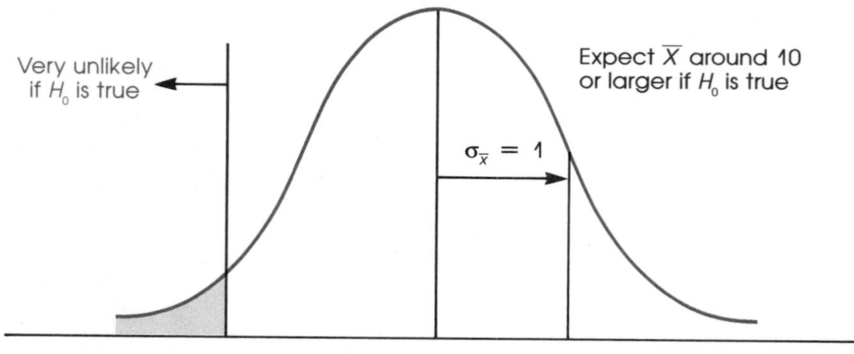

would tend to refute H_0 would be a sample mean substantially less than 10. The result is that the entire critical region is located in one tail of the distribution (see Figure 9.1). This is why the directional test commonly is called *one-tailed*. A complete example of a one-tailed test is presented here.

EXAMPLE 9.1 A psychologist would like to examine the effect of background music on productivity at a local factory. Over the past 2 years it has been determined that the average daily output from this factory is $\mu = 210$ units. The daily output varies with $\sigma = 20$, and the distribution is approximately normal. The psychologist expects that the introduction of background music will improve the work environment and result in increased productivity. To test this hypothesis, a music system is installed, and productivity is measured for a sample period of $n = 25$ days. During this time the average output is $\overline{X} = 217$ units per day. The psychologist wants to use these sample data to test the hypothesis about the music's effect.

Simply because you can do a directional test does not mean that you must use a directional test. A two-tailed test is always acceptable and generally preferred.

STEP 1 *State the hypotheses:* Because the psychologist is predicting an increase in productivity, it is possible to do a directional test. We begin with H_1, the alternative hypothesis, which states that there is a treatment effect. In symbols,

$$H_1: \mu > 210 \qquad \text{(an increase in mean productivity)}$$

The null hypothesis is the opposite of H_1 and states that

$$H_0: \mu \leqslant 210 \qquad \text{(productivity is no greater with the music)}$$

STEP 2 *Locate the critical region:* To find the critical region, we look at all the possible results that could be obtained if H_0 were true and then locate the outcomes that would be extremely unlikely. The set of all possible outcomes is the distribution of sample means for $n = 25$. This distribution will be normal (because the population is normal), it will have a standard error of $\sigma_{\overline{X}} = 20/\sqrt{25} = \frac{20}{5} = 4$, and it will have a mean of $\mu = 210$ if H_0 is true. This distribution is shown in Figure 9.2.

If H_0 is true, we expect the sample to average around 210 units per day or less. It would be very unlikely to obtain a sample mean much greater than 210. Therefore, it is only large values that compose the critical region. With $\alpha = .05$, the most likely 95% of the distribution is separated from the most unlikely 5% by a z-score of $z = +1.65$ (see Figure 9.2).

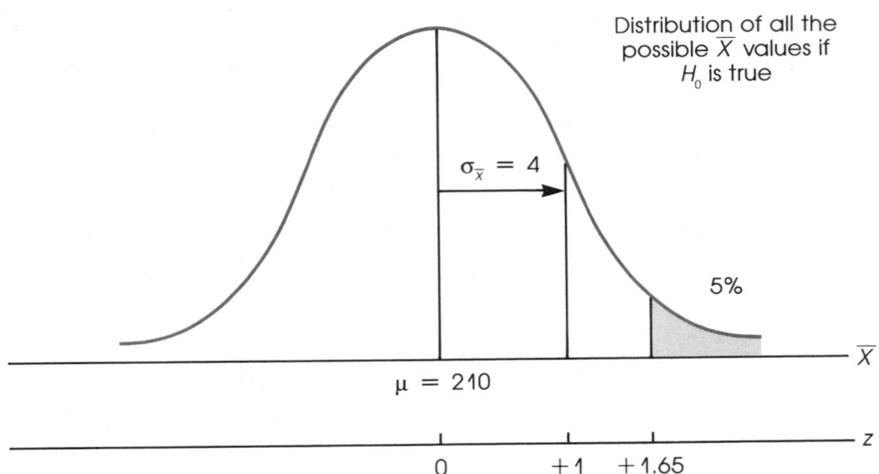

FIGURE 9.2

The distribution of sample means for $n = 25$ if H_0 is true. The null hypothesis says that the music will not increase productivity, so we still expect the mean to be around 210 or smaller.

STEP 3 *Obtain the sample data:* The obtained sample mean is $\bar{X} = 217$. This value corresponds to a z-score of

$$z = \frac{\bar{X} - \mu}{\sigma_{\bar{X}}} = \frac{217 - 210}{4} = \frac{7}{4} = 1.75$$

STEP 4 *Make a statistical decision:* A z-score of $z = +1.75$ indicates that our sample mean is in the critical region. This is a very unlikely outcome if H_0 is true, so the statistical decision is to reject H_0. The conclusion is that the music does increase productivity.

COMPARISON OF ONE-TAILED VERSUS TWO-TAILED TESTS

The general goal of hypothesis testing is to determine whether or not a particular treatment has any effect on a population. The test is performed by selecting a sample, administering the treatment to the sample, and then comparing the result with the original population. If the treated sample is noticeably different from the original population, then we conclude that the treatment has an effect, and we reject H_0. On the other hand, if the treated sample is still similar to the original population, then we conclude that there is no evidence for a treatment effect, and we fail to reject H_0. The critical factor in this decision is the *size of the difference* between treated sample and the original population. A large difference is evidence that the treatment worked; a small difference is not sufficient to say that the treatment has any effect.

The major distinction between one-tailed and two-tailed tests is in the criteria they use for rejecting H_0. A one-tailed test allows you to reject the null hypothesis when the difference between the sample and the population is relatively small, provided the difference is in the specified direction. A two-tailed test, on the other hand, requires a relatively large difference independent of direction. This point is illustrated in the following example.

EXAMPLE 9.2 Consider again the experiment examining background music and factory productivity (see Example 9.1). If we had used a standard two-tailed test, then the hypotheses would have been

$H_0: \mu = 210$ (no change in productivity)

$H_1: \mu \neq 210$ (there is a change)

With $\alpha = .05$, the critical region would consist of any z-score value beyond the $z = \pm 1.96$ boundaries.

If we obtained the same sample data, $\bar{X} = 217$, which corresponds to z-score of $z = +1.75$, our statistical decision would be "fail to reject H_0."

Notice that with the two-tailed test (Example 9.2), the difference between the data ($\bar{X} = 217$) and the hypothesis ($\mu = 210$) is not big enough to conclude that the hypothesis is wrong. In this case, we are saying that the data do not provide sufficient evidence to justify rejecting H_0. However, with the one-tailed test (Example 9.1), the same data led us to reject H_0.

All researchers agree that one-tailed tests are different from two-tailed tests. However, there are several ways to interpret the difference. One group of researchers (the present authors included) contends that one-tailed tests make it too easy to reject H_0 and, therefore, too easy to make a Type I error. According to this position, a two-tailed test requires strong evidence to reject H_0 and thus provides a convincing demonstration that a treatment effect has occurred. A one-tailed test, on the other hand, can result in rejecting the null hypothesis even when the evidence is relatively weak. For this reason, you usually will find two-tailed tests used for research that is published in journal articles for scrutiny by the scientific community. In this type of

Remember, you risk a Type I error every time H_0 is rejected.

research, it is important that the results be convincing, and it is important to avoid a Type I error (publishing a false report). The two-tailed (nondirectional) test satisfies these criteria.

Another group of researchers focuses on the advantages of one-tailed tests. As we have noted, one-tailed tests can lead to rejecting H_0 when the evidence is relatively weak. This statement can be rephrased by saying that one-tailed tests are more sensitive in detecting a treatment effect. If you think of a hypothesis test as a detection device that is used to seek out a treatment effect, then the advantages of a more-sensitive test should be obvious. Although a more-sensitive test will generate more false alarms (Type I errors), it also is more likely to find a significant treatment effect. Thus, one-tailed tests can be very useful in situations where a researcher does not want to overlook any possible significant outcome and where a Type I error is not very damaging. A good example of this situation is in exploratory research. The intent of exploratory research is to investigate a new area or to try an approach that is new and different. Instead of producing publishable results, exploratory research is directed toward generating new research possibilities. In this atmosphere, a researcher is willing to tolerate a few false alarms (Type I errors) in exchange for the increased sensitivity of a one-tailed test.

For the reasons we have outlined, most researchers do not use one-tailed tests except in very limited situations. Even though most experiments are designed with an expectation that the treatment effect will be in a specific direction, the directional prediction is not included in the statement of the statistical hypothesis. Nevertheless, you will probably encounter one-tailed tests and you may find occasion to use them, so you should understand the rationale and the procedure for conducting directional tests.

· LEARNING CHECK ·

1 A researcher predicts that a treatment will lower scores. If this researcher uses a one-tailed test, will the critical region be in the right- or left-hand tail of the distribution?

2 A psychologist is examining the effects of early sensory deprivation on the development of perceptual discrimination. A sample of $n = 9$ newborn kittens is obtained. These kittens are raised in a completely dark environment for 4 weeks, after which they receive normal visual stimulation. At age 6 months, the kittens are tested on a visual discrimination task. The average score for this sample is $\overline{X} = 32$. It is known that under normal circumstances cats score an average of $\mu = 40$ on this task. The distribution of scores is normal with $\sigma = 12$. The researcher is predicting that the early sensory deprivation will reduce the kittens' performance on the discrimination task. Use a one-tailed test with $\alpha = .01$ to test this hypothesis.

ANSWERS

1 The left-hand tail.

2 The hypotheses are $H_0 : \mu \geqslant 40$ and $H_1 : \mu < 40$. The critical region is determined by z-scores less than -2.33. The z-score for these sample data is $z = -2.00$. Fail to reject H_0.

9.3 ················ ESTIMATION

The basic principle underlying all of inferential statistics is that samples are representative of the populations from which they come. The most direct application of this principle is the use of sample values as estimators of the corresponding population values; that is, using statistics to estimate parameters. This process is called estimation.

· DEFINITION · The inferential process of using sample data to estimate population parameters is called *estimation.*

The use of samples to estimate populations is quite common. For example, you often hear news reports such as "Sixty percent of the general public approves of the president's new budget plan." Clearly, the percentage that is reported was obtained from a sample (they don't ask everyone's opinion), and this sample statistic is being used as an estimate of the population parameter.

We already have encountered estimation in earlier sections of this book. For example, the formula for sample standard deviation was developed so that the sample value would give an accurate and unbiased estimate of the population. Now we will examine the process of using the sample mean $\overline{X}$ as an estimator of the population mean μ.

PRECISION AND CONFIDENCE IN ESTIMATION

Before we begin the actual process of estimation, there are a few general points that should be kept in mind. First, a sample will not give a perfect picture of the whole population. A sample is expected to be representative of the population, but there always will be some differences between the sample and the entire population. These differences are referred to as *sampling error.* Second, there are two distinct ways of making estimates. Suppose, for example, you are asked to estimate the weight of this book. You could pick a single value (say, 2 pounds), or you could choose a range of values (say, between 1.5 pounds and 2.5 pounds). The first estimate, using a single number, is called a point estimate. Point estimates have the advantage of being very precise; they specify a particular value. On the other hand, you generally do not have much confidence that a point estimate is correct. You would not bet on it, for example.

· DEFINITION · For a *point estimate,* you use a single number as your estimate of an unknown quantity.

The second type of estimate, using a range of values, is called an interval estimate. Interval estimates do not have the precision of point estimates, but they do give you more confidence. You would feel more comfortable, for example, saying that this book weighs "around 2 pounds." At the extreme, you would be very confident in estimating that this book weighs between .5 and 10 pounds. Notice that there is a trade-off between precision and confidence. As the interval gets wider and wider, your confidence grows. But, at the same time, the precision of the estimate gets worse. We will be using samples to make both point and interval estimates of a population mean. Because the interval estimates are associated with confidence, they usually are called confidence intervals.

· DEFINITIONS · For an *interval estimate,* you use a range of values as your estimate of an unknown quantity.

When an interval estimate is accompanied with a specific level of confidence (or probability), it is called a *confidence interval.*

Estimation is used in situations where you have a population with an unknown mean ($\mu = ?$). Often this is a population that has received some treatment. Suppose you are examining the effect of a special summer reading program for grade school children. Using a standard reading achievement test, you know that the scores for second-graders in the city school district form a normal distribution with $\mu = 80$ and $\sigma = 10$. It is reasonable to assume that a special reading program would increase the students' scores. The question is, How much?

The example we are considering is shown graphically in Figure 9.3. Notice that we have assumed that the effect of the treatment (the special program) is to add a

FIGURE 9.3

A population distribution before the treatment is administered and the same population after treatment. Note that the effect of the treatment is to add a constant amount to each score. The goal of estimation is to determine how large the treatment effect is; i.e., what is the new population mean $\mu = ?$

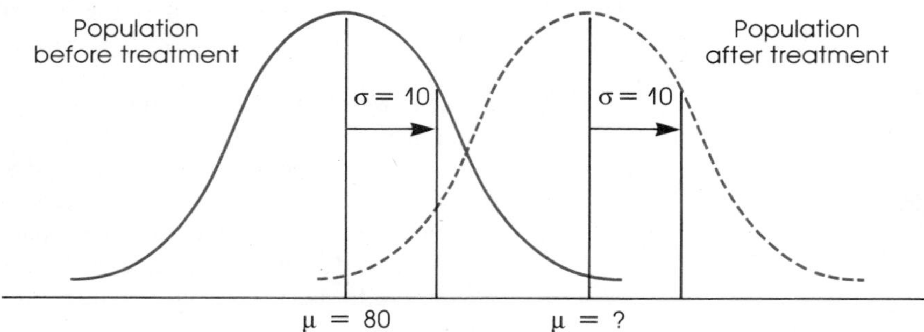

If the treatment simply adds a constant to each score, the standard deviation will not be changed. Although it is common practice to assume that a treatment will add a constant amount, you should realize that in most real-life situations there is a general tendency for variability to increase when the mean increases.

constant amount to each student's reading score. As a result, after the summer reading program the entire distribution would be shifted to a new location with a larger mean. This new mean is what we want to estimate.

Because it would not be reasonable to put all of the students in the special program, we cannot measure this mean directly. However, we can get a sample and use the sample mean to estimate the population value. Suppose, for example, a random sample of $n = 25$ students is selected to participate in the summer program. At the end of the summer, each student takes the reading test and we compute a mean reading score of $\overline{X} = 88$. Note that this sample represents the population after the special program. The goal of estimation is to use this sample mean as the basis for estimating the unknown population mean.

USING A SAMPLE MEAN TO ESTIMATE THE POPULATION MEAN

The procedure for estimating μ is based on the distribution of sample means (see Chapter 7). You should recall that this distribution is the set of all the possible $\overline{X}$ values for a specified sample size (n). The parameters of this distribution are the following:

1. The mean (called expected value) is equal to the population mean.
2. The standard deviation for this distribution (called standard error) is equal to $\sigma/\sqrt{n}$.
3. The distribution of sample means will be normal if either
   a. The population is normal, or
   b. The sample size is at least $n = 30$.

For the example we are considering, the distribution of sample means for $n = 25$ will be normal (because the population is normal), it will have a standard error of $\sigma/\sqrt{n} = 10/\sqrt{25} = \frac{10}{5} = 2$, and it will have a mean that is equal to the unknown population mean ($\mu = ?$). This distribution is shown in Figure 9.4.

Our sample mean, $\overline{X} = 88$, is somewhere in this distribution; that is, we have one value out of all the possible sample means. Unfortunately, we do not know where our sample mean is located in the distribution. Nonetheless, we can specify different locations by using z-scores. The z-score values and their locations have been identified in Figure 9.4.

Our sample mean, $\overline{X} = 88$, has a z-score given by the formula

$$z = \frac{\overline{X} - \mu}{\sigma_{\overline{X}}}$$

Because our goal is to find the population mean (μ), we will solve this z-score equation for μ. The result is

$$\mu = \overline{X} - z\sigma_{\overline{X}} \qquad (9.1)$$

FIGURE 9.4

The distribution of sample means based on $n = 25$. Samples were selected from the unknown population (after treatment) shown in Figure 9.3.

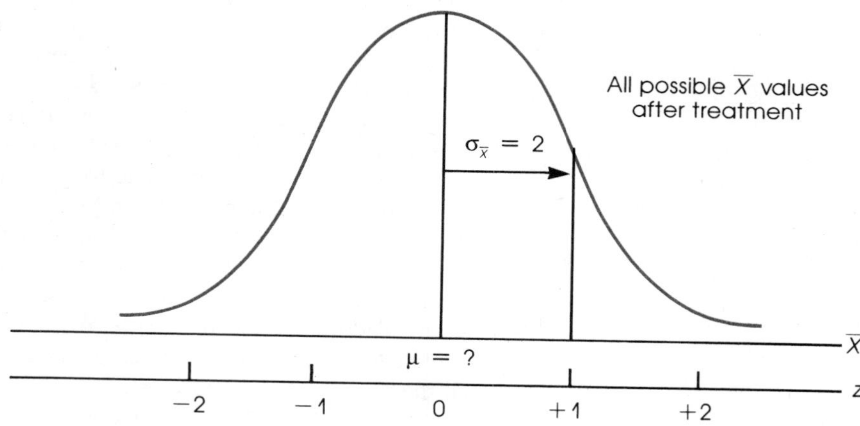

We still do not know the value of μ, but now we have an equation to use. This is the basic equation for estimation. Note that it is simply the z-score formula with some rearrangement of terms.

To use this equation, we begin with the values we know: $\overline{X} = 88$ and $\sigma_{\overline{X}} = 2$. If we also knew the value of z (the location of $\overline{X}$ in the distribution), we would have all the necessary information to compute the value of μ. But we still do not know the z-score value. The solution to this problem is to *estimate* the z-score value for our sample mean. More precisely, we are estimating the location of our sample mean within the distribution of sample mean. The estimated position will determine a z-score value which can be used in the equation to compute μ. It is important to note that the z-score value we will be using is an *estimate*; therefore, the population mean that we compute will also be an estimate.

POINT ESTIMATES For a point estimate, you must select a single value for the z-score. Remember, you are not simply picking a z-score; you are estimating the position of our sample mean ($\overline{X} = 88$) in the distribution of sample means. Looking at Figure 9.4, where would you estimate our sample mean is located?

It should be clear that your best bet is to select the exact middle of the distribution, that is, $z = 0$. It would be unwise to pick an extreme value such as $z = 2$ because there are relatively few samples that far away from the population mean. Most of the sample means pile up around $z = 0$, so this is your best choice. When this z-value is used in the equation, we get

$$\mu = \overline{X} - z\sigma_{\overline{X}}$$

$$\mu = 88 - 0(2)$$

$$= 88$$

This is our point estimate of the population mean. You should notice that this final result is exactly what would be predicted by common sense; we simply have used the sample mean $\overline{X}$ to estimate the population mean μ. Our conclusion is that the special summer program will increase reading scores from an average of $\mu = 80$ to an average of $\mu = 88$. We are estimating that the program will have an eight-point effect on reading scores.

INTERVAL ESTIMATES To make an interval estimate, you select a range of z-score values rather than a single point. Looking again at the distribution of sample means in Figure 9.4, where would you estimate our sample mean is located? Remember, you now can pick a range of values. As before, your best bet is to predict that the sample mean is located somewhere in the center of the distribution. There is a good chance, for example, that our sample mean is located somewhere between $z = +1$ and $z = -1$. You would be almost certain that $\overline{X}$ is between $z = +3$ and $z = -3$. How do you know what range to use? Because several different ranges are possible and each range has its own degree of confidence, the first step is to determine the amount of confidence we want and then use this value to determine the range. Commonly used levels of confidence start at about 60% and go up. For this example, we will use 90%. This means that we want to be 90% confident that our interval estimate of μ is correct.

There are no strict rules for choosing a level of confidence. Researchers must decide how much precision and how much confidence are needed in each specific situation.

To be 90% confident, we simply estimate that our sample mean is somewhere in the middle 90% of the distribution of sample means. This section of the distribution is bounded by z-scores of $z = +1.65$ and $z = -1.65$ (check the table). We are 90% confident that our particular sample mean ($\overline{X} = 88$) is in this range because 90% of all the possible means are there.

The next step is to use this range of z-score values in the estimation equation. We use the two ends of the z-score range to compute the two ends of the interval estimate for μ.

At one extreme, $z = +1.65$, which gives

$$\begin{aligned} \mu &= \overline{X} - z\sigma_{\overline{X}} \\ &= 88 - 1.65(2) \\ &= 88 - 3.30 \\ &= 84.70 \end{aligned}$$

At the other extreme, $z = -1.65$, which gives

$$\begin{aligned} \mu &= \overline{X} - z\sigma_{\overline{X}} \\ &= 88 - (-1.65)(2) \\ &= 88 + 3.30 \\ &= 91.30 \end{aligned}$$

The result is an interval estimate for μ. We are estimating that the population mean after the special summer program is between 84.70 and 91.30. If the mean is as small as 84.70, then the effect of the special program would be to increase reading scores by an average of 4.70 points (from $\mu = 80$ to $\mu = 84.70$). If the mean is as large as 91.30, the program would have increased scores by an average of 11.30 points (from $\mu = 80$ to $\mu = 91.30$). Thus, we conclude that the special summer program will increase reading scores, and we estimate that the magnitude of the increase will be between 4.7 and 11.3 points. We are 90% confident that this estimate is correct because the only thing that was estimated was the z-score range, and we were 90% confident about that. Again, this interval estimate is called a confidence interval. In this case, it is the 90% confidence interval for μ.

Notice that the confidence interval sets up a range of values with the sample mean in the middle. As with point estimates, we are using the sample mean to estimate the population mean, but now we are saying that the value of μ should be *around* $\overline{X}$ rather than exactly equal to $\overline{X}$. Because the confidence interval is built around $\overline{X}$, adding in one direction and subtracting in the other, we will modify the estimation equation in order to simplify the arithmetic:

$$\mu = \overline{X} \pm z\sigma_{\overline{X}} \tag{9.2}$$

To build the confidence interval, start with the sample mean and add $z\sigma_{\overline{X}}$ to get the boundary in one direction; then subtract $z\sigma_{\overline{X}}$ to get the other boundary. Translated into words, the formula says that

population mean = sample mean ± some error

The sample mean is expected to be representative of the population mean with some margin of error. Although it may seem obvious that the sample mean is used as the basis for estimating the population mean, you should not overlook the reason for this result. Sample means, on the average, provide an accurate, unbiased representation of the population mean. You should recognize this fact as one of the characteristics of the distribution of sample means: The mean (expected value) of the distribution of sample means is μ.

INTERPRETING A CONFIDENCE INTERVAL

In the preceding example we constructed a 90% confidence interval that extended from 84.70 to 91.30. The purpose of the interval is to provide an estimate of the unknown population mean. This estimate was obtained by building an interval around the sample mean:

$$\begin{aligned}\mu &= \overline{X} \pm z\sigma_{\overline{X}} \\ &= 88 \pm 1.65(2) \\ &= 88 \pm 3.30\end{aligned}$$

Notice that if we had obtained a different sample mean, for example, $\overline{X} = 90$, we would have obtained a different interval:

$$\begin{aligned}\mu &= \overline{X} \pm z\sigma_{\overline{X}} \\ &= 90 \pm 1.65(2) \\ &= 90 \pm 3.30\end{aligned}$$

Each individual sample mean will generate its own individual confidence interval. However, these confidence intervals will have some common characteristics. First, they all will have exactly the same width, extending from 3.30 points above $\overline{X}$ to 3.30 points below $\overline{X}$. This width is determined by the *z*-score ($z = 1.65$) and the standard error ($\sigma_{\overline{X}} = 2$). You also should note that this width corresponds to the middle 90% of the distribution of sample means. Figure 9.5 shows the distribution of sample means and the confidence intervals associated with several different samples.

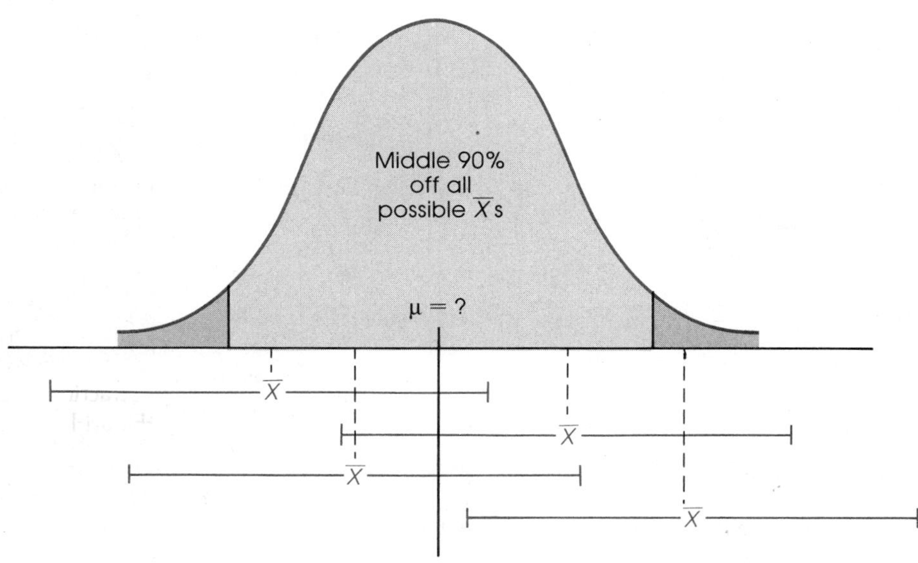

FIGURE 9.5

Confidence intervals for four samples selected from the distribution of sample means. Notice that three of the sample means come from the middle 90% of the distribution and the 90% confidence intervals for these three samples all contain the population mean. However, the one sample mean that is outside the middle 90% produces a confidence interval that does not contain μ.

Notice that as long as the sample mean comes from the middle 90% of this distribution, the population mean ($\mu = ?$) will be included in the interval. Thus, 90% of all the possible sample means will generate a 90% confidence interval that contains μ. Although we do not know exactly where our sample is located in this distribution, we can be 90% confident that it is somewhere in the middle 90%. Thus, we can be 90% confident that the population mean is included in our confidence interval.

FACTORS AFFECTING THE WIDTH OF A CONFIDENCE INTERVAL

There are two characteristics of the confidence interval that should be noted. First, notice what happens to the width of the interval when you change the level of confidence (the percent confidence). To gain more confidence in your estimate, you must increase the width of the interval. Conversely, to have a smaller interval, you must give up confidence. This is the basic trade-off between precision and confidence that was discussed earlier. In the estimation formula, the percent confidence influences the width of the interval by way of the z-score value. For example, if you increase the level of confidence from 90% to 95%, the z-score value increases from 1.65 to 1.96. As confidence gets greater, the z-score gets bigger, and the interval gets wider.

Second, notice what would happen to the interval width if you had a different sample size. This time, the basic rule is as follows: The bigger the sample (n), the smaller the interval. This relation is straightforward if you consider the sample size as a measure of the amount of information. A bigger sample gives you more information about the population and allows you to make a more precise estimate (a narrower interval). The sample size controls the magnitude of the standard error in the estimation formula. As the sample size increases, the standard error decreases, and the interval gets smaller.

COMPARISON OF HYPOTHESIS TESTS AND ESTIMATION

In many ways hypothesis testing and estimation are similar. They both make use of sample means and z-scores to find out about an unknown population. But these two inferential procedures are designed to answer different questions. The example we considered earlier, examining the effect of the special summer reading program, can be used to illustrate the similarities and differences between estimation and hypothesis testing.

For this example, we could have used a hypothesis test to evaluate the effect of the special program. The test would determine whether or not the program has any effect. Notice that this is a yes/no question. The test result would be either

Yes, the treatment has an effect (reject H_0)

or

No, the treatment does not appear to have an effect (fail to reject H_0)

The hypothesis test is done by using the basic z-score formula:

$$z = \frac{\overline{X} - \mu}{\sigma_{\overline{X}}}$$

To calculate the z-score, you use the known values of $\overline{X}$ and $\sigma_{\overline{X}}$ and the hypothesized value of μ (from H_0). The question is whether or not the hypothesized value of μ produces a reasonable z-score.

Estimation, on the other hand, determines *how much* effect the special training has. Our point estimate, for example, is that the population mean after the summer program is $\mu = 88$. This is eight points higher than the original population mean.

The estimation procedure uses the same z-score formula as the hypothesis test, but the terms in the formula are rearranged:

$$\mu = \overline{X} \pm z\sigma_{\overline{X}}$$

As before, you use the known values of $\bar{X}$ and $\sigma_{\bar{X}}$, but now you include the estimated z-score and calculate the value of μ. If you use a reasonable estimate of z, you expect to get a reasonable estimate for μ.

WHEN TO USE ESTIMATION There are three situations where estimation commonly is used.

1. Estimation is used after a hypothesis test where H_0 is rejected. Remember that when H_0 is rejected, the conclusion is that the treatment does have an effect. The next logical question would be, How much effect? This is exactly the question that estimation is designed to answer.

2. Estimation is used when you already know that there is an effect and simply want to find out how much. For example, the city school board probably knows that a special reading program will help students. However, they want to be sure that the effect is big enough to justify the cost. Estimation is used to determine the size of the treatment effect.

3. Estimation is used when you simply want some basic information about an unknown population. Suppose, for example, you want to know about the political attitudes of students at your college. You could use a sample of students as the basis for estimating the population mean.

· LEARNING CHECK ·

1 A cattle rancher is interested in using a newly developed hormone to increase the weight of beef cattle. Before investing in this hormone, the rancher would like to obtain some estimate of its effect. Without the hormone, the cattle weigh an average of $\mu = 1250$ pounds when they are sold at 8 months. The distribution of weights is approximately normal with $\sigma = 80$. A sample of 16 calves is selected to test the hormone. At age 8 months, the average weight for this sample is $\bar{X} = 1340$ pounds.

a Use these data to make a point estimate of the population mean weight if all the cattle were given the hormone.

b Make an interval estimate of the population mean so that you are 95% confident that the true mean is in your interval.

2 If the cattle rancher had used a larger sample, how would the width of the confidence interval change?

3 If the cattle rancher in Problem 1 had used the 80% level of confidence, how would the width of the confidence interval change?

ANSWERS

1 **a** For a point estimate, use the sample mean: $\bar{X} = 1340$ pounds.

b For the 95% confidence interval, $z = +1.96$ and $\sigma_{\bar{X}} = 20$. The interval would be

$$\mu = 1340 \pm 39.20$$

The interval ranges from 1300.80 to 1379.20 pounds.

2 Increasing sample size would result in a smaller interval width.

3 Using a smaller level (%) of confidence would result in a smaller interval width.

9.4 POWER FOR A STATISTICAL TEST

The purpose of a hypothesis test is to determine whether or not a particular treatment has an effect. The null hypothesis states that there is no effect, and the researcher is hoping that the data will provide evidence to reject this hypothesis. In Chapter 8 we saw that the hypothesis testing procedure is structured to minimize the risk of reaching a wrong conclusion. Specifically, the researcher selects an alpha level, generally 5% or 1%, that determines the maximum probability of committing a Type I error (rejecting a true null hypothesis). You also should recall that every hypothesis test has the potential for resulting in a Type II error, failing to reject a false null hypothesis. In everyday terms, a Type II error means that the treatment really does have an effect but that the hypothesis test failed to discover it.

In this section we will reverse our perspective on hypothesis testing; rather than examining the potential for making an error, we will examine the probability of reaching the correct decision. Remember that the researcher's goal is to demonstrate that the experimental treatment actually does have an effect. This is the purpose of conducting the experiment in the first place. When a researcher is correct and the treatment does have an effect, what is the probability that the hypothesis test will correctly identify it? This is a question about the strength or power of the statistical test.

· DEFINITION · The *power* of a statistical test is the probability that the test will correctly reject a false null hypothesis.

It should be clear that the concept of power and the concept of a Type II error are closely related. When a treatment effect exists, the hypothesis test can have one of two conclusions:

1. It can fail to discover the treatment effect (A Type II error), or
2. It can correctly identify the treatment effect (rejecting a false null hypothesis).

We already have defined the probability of a Type II error as β (beta), so the probability of correctly rejecting a false null hypothesis must be $1 - \beta$. If, for example, a hypothesis test has a 20% chance of failing to identify a treatment effect, then it must have an 80% chance of successfully identifying it. Thus, the power of a statistical test is determined by

$$\text{power} = P(\text{reject a false } H_0) = 1 - \beta \tag{9.3}$$

RELATION BETWEEN POWER AND THE TREATMENT EFFECT

Although we now have a definition and an equation for power, we still do not have a value for this probability. The difficulty comes from the fact that power depends on the size of the treatment effect and therefore does not have a single value. When a treatment has a large effect, it is easy to see, and power will be high. On the other hand, when the treatment effect is very small, it can be difficult to discover, and power will be low. Rather than talking about power as a single value, we must examine the different values of power associated with different magnitudes of treatment effect. For example,

What is the power if the treatment produces a 5-point difference?

What is the power if the treatment produces a 10-point difference?

Because the hypothesis test is more likely to detect a 10-point treatment effect, the power will be greater than it would be for a 5-point treatment effect.

One more reminder is necessary before we actually begin the calculation of power. Remember, the null hypothesis is rejected whenever sample data are in the critical region. With this in mind, we can restate the definition of power as follows:

· DEFINITION · *Power* is the probability of obtaining sample data in the critical region when the null hypothesis is false.

Because "data in the critical region" is equivalent to "rejecting the null hypothesis," this definition is equivalent to our original definition of power.

The following example demonstrates the calculation of power for a statistical test.

EXAMPLE 9.3 A researcher is interested in whether cigarette smoke inhaled by pregnant females can affect their offspring. It is known that under normal circumstances newborn rats weigh an average of $\mu = 200$ milligrams with $\sigma = 40$. The distribution of birth weights is approximately normal. A random sample of $n = 25$ pregnant rats is obtained. These animals are placed in closed containers and exposed to cigarette smoke for 4 hours each day. When the pups are born, the researcher plans to randomly select one pup from each litter. The average weight ($\overline{X}$) for this sample of $n = 25$ rats will be used to test the researcher's hypothesis.

The researcher predicts that the cigarette smoke will cause a reduction in birth weight of approximately 20 milligrams. If this is correct, what is the probability that the statistical test will detect this treatment effect and correctly reject H_0? In other words, what is the power of the test if the treatment has a 20-point effect?

Because we want to know the probability of obtaining data in the critical region, the first step is to identify the critical region. This is done by following the usual hypothesis testing procedure.

STEP 1 *State the hypotheses:*

$H_0 : \mu = 200$ (no effect)

$H_1 : \mu \neq 200$ (there is an effect)

We will use $\alpha = .05$.

STEP 2 *Locate the critical region:* If the null hypothesis is true and the smoke has no effect, then we can determine the distribution of all possible sample means for $n = 25$. This distribution of sample means is shown in Figure 9.6. The distribution has an expected value of $\mu = 200$ (if H_0 is true), and it has a standard error of

$$\sigma_{\overline{X}} = \frac{\sigma}{\sqrt{n}} = \frac{40}{5} = 8$$

As usual, the critical region is determined by the most unlikely 5% of all the possible sample means. This region is bounded by z-scores of $+1.96$ and -1.96. To obtain a more general description of the critical region, we will find the $\overline{X}$ value that

FIGURE 9.6

The distribution of sample means assuming that the null hypothesis is true. The critical region (most extreme 5%) is determined by sample means less than 184.32 or greater than 215.68.

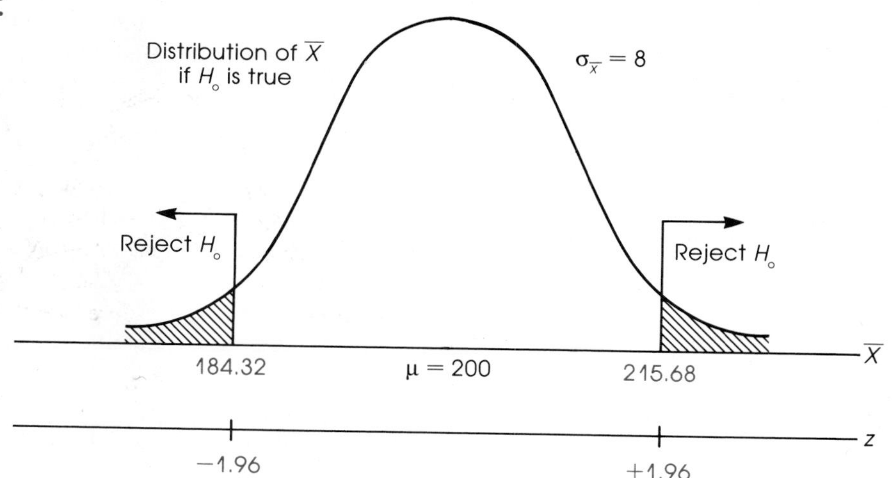

corresponds to each of these z-scores:

At the Lower Boundary	At the Upper Boundary
$z = \dfrac{\overline{X} - \mu}{\sigma_{\overline{X}}}$	$z = \dfrac{\overline{X} - \mu}{\sigma_{\overline{X}}}$
$-1.96 = \dfrac{\overline{X} - 200}{8}$	$+196 = \dfrac{\overline{X} - 200}{8}$
$-15.68 = \overline{X} - 200$	$+15.68 = \overline{X} - 200$
$184.32 = \overline{X}$	$215.68 = \overline{X}$

Thus, any sample mean less than 184.32 or greater than 215.68 will be in the critical region and will result in rejecting the null hypothesis.

Now we are ready to begin the calculation of power. If the treatment has a 20-point effect, then the average birth weight of rats would be reduced from $\mu = 200$ to $\mu = 180$ milligrams. In this case the distribution of sample means should be centered at $\mu = 180$. Figure 9.7 shows this distribution along with the distribution predicted from the null hypothesis. The figure also shows the critical region that we determined earlier using the null hypothesis and $\alpha = .05$.

Remember, the distribution on the left in Figure 9.7 shows all the possible sample means if the treatment has a 20-point effect. Notice that most of this distribution is located in the critical region (shaded portion). Thus, if the treatment does have a 20-point effect, there is a high probability that our sample mean will be in the critical region (less than 184.32). This probability is the power of the statistical test. To find the exact probability, we convert the critical boundary (184.32) into a z-score and then find the probability in the unit normal table.

In this example, we are ignoring the critical region in the other tail of the distribution because the probability of obtaining a sample mean greater than 215.68 would be essentially zero.

If the treatment has reduced the population mean to $\mu = 180$, the z-score corresponding to $\overline{X} = 184.32$ is

$$z = \frac{\overline{X} - \mu}{\sigma_{\overline{X}}} = \frac{184.32 - 180}{8} = \frac{4.32}{8} = +0.54$$

FIGURE 9.7

The distribution of sample means that would be obtained if H_0 were true and the distribution of sample means that would be obtained if the treatment were to reduce the mean by 20 points. Notice that if the treatment does have a 20-point effect, most of the sample means will be in the critical region.

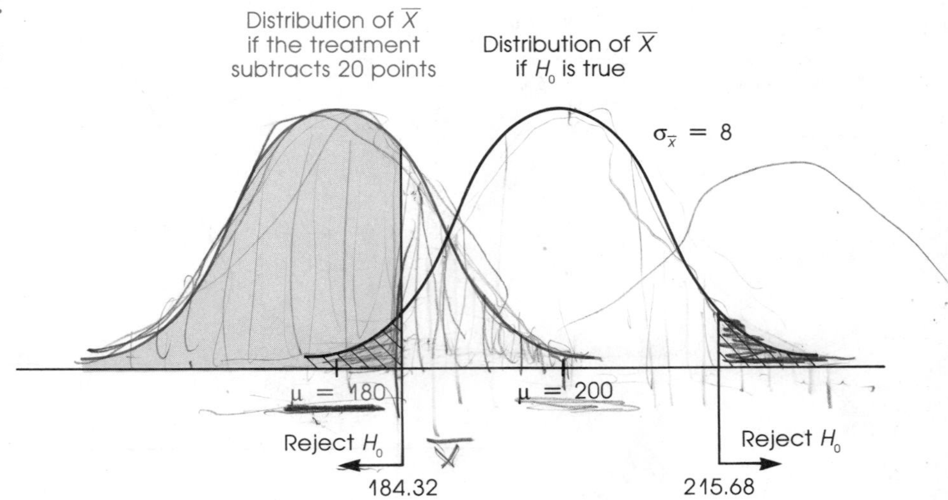

From the unit normal table, the probability of obtaining a z-score smaller than this value is .7054. Thus, the power of the statistical test is .7054 (70.54%).

In summary,

1 The hypothesis test established the critical region as sample means less than 184.32 or greater than 215.68.

2 If the treatment has a 20-point effect, then the distribution of sample means will be centered at $\mu = 180$ with a standard error of 8.

3 The proportion of this distribution that is located in the critical region is .7054.

4 Therefore, if the treatment has a 20-point effect, the probability of obtaining a sample mean in the critical region is .7054. The power of the test is .7054.

POWER AND TYPE II ERRORS In Example 9.3, we found that the power of the hypothesis test was .7054. By assuming that the treatment has a 20-point effect, we calculated a .7054 probability of obtaining sample data in the critical region and correctly rejecting H_0. However, you should note that this means there is an .294 probability that the sample data will not be in the critical region. In this event we would fail to reject the null hypothesis even though the treatment has a 20-point effect. This is a Type II error, failing to reject a false null hypothesis. Just as power $(1 - \beta)$ measures the probability that the experiment will be successful, β measures the probability that the experiment will fail to detect the treatment effect, resulting in a Type II error. These two probabilities always will total 1.00 or 100%.

THE POWER FUNCTION In Example 9.3 we computed power for a single, specific treatment value (a 20-point effect). To provide a complete description of power, you could compute the probability for every possible treatment effect and construct a graph showing the relation between power and the size of the treatment effect. The resulting graph is called a *power function.* An example of a power function graph is shown in Figure 9.8. This graph shows the power function for the cigarette smoke experiment described in Example 9.3. Notice that power increases as the size of the treatment effect increases. The hypothesis test is much more likely to detect a 20-point treatment effect (power = .7054) than it is to detect a 2-point effect (power = .0572). The value

Note that the lowest level of the power function is α. If the treatment effect is zero, then the null hypothesis is true, and the probability of rejecting a true H_0 is α.

FIGURE 9.8

The power function for the hypothesis test described in Example 9.3. Notice that the power increases regularly as the magnitude of the treatment effect increases. The hypothesis test is more likely to detect a large effect than a small treatment effect.

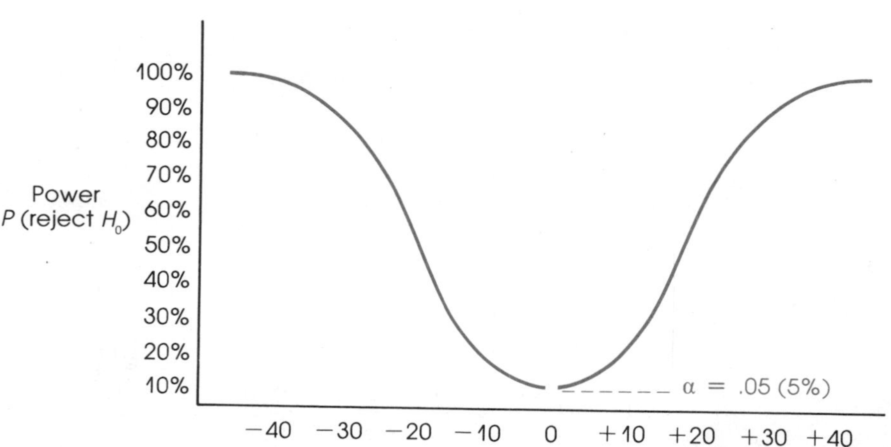

of a power function is that it allows a researcher to predict the success of an experiment. If, for example, the researcher expected the cigarette smoke to have a 10-point effect, the power curve in Figure 9.8 would specify that the experiment has only an .2396 (23.96%) probability of detecting a treatment effect of this magnitude.

FACTORS AFFECTING POWER

There are three factors under the direct control of a researcher that have an effect on the power of a statistical test. Each of these factors will be discussed briefly.

The Alpha Level Reducing the alpha level will reduce the power of a statistical test. For example, reducing α from .05 to .01 moves the critical region boundaries from $z = \pm 1.96$ out to $z = \pm 2.58$. The result is that the smaller alpha level makes it harder to reject the null hypothesis. Thus, a smaller α means that you are less likely to reject a true H_0 (Type I error), but also you are less likely to reject a false null hypothesis (power).

One-Tailed Versus Two-Tailed Tests You should recall that one-tailed tests make it easier to reject the null hypothesis. With $\alpha = .05$, for example, the critical boundary for a one-tailed test is located at $z = 1.65$. For a two-tailed test, the boundary would be at $z = \pm 1.96$. Because one-tailed tests increase the probability of rejecting H_0, they also increase the power of the test.

Sample size In general, the larger the sample, the better it will represent the population. If there is a real treatment effect in the population, you are more likely to find it with a large sample than with a small sample. Thus, the power of a test can be increased by increasing the size of the sample. This fact can be demonstrated using the same experimental situation described in Example 9.3. In this example, the null hypothesis states that $\mu = 200$, and we are computing the power of the test if the treatment has a 20-point effect. Figure 9.9 shows the distribution for the null hypothesis ($\mu = 200$) and the distribution that would be obtained if the treatment had a 20-point effect ($\mu = 180$). We also assume that the original population of scores has a standard deviation of $\sigma = 40$.

In the left-hand portion of Figure 9.9, we show the power of the test for a sample of $n = 25$. With $n = 25$, the standard error is

$$\sigma_{\bar{X}} = \frac{\sigma}{\sqrt{n}} = \frac{40}{\sqrt{25}} = \frac{40}{5} = 8$$

· FIGURE 9.9 ·

The relation between power and sample size. The left figure shows power of $p = .7054$ (shaded area) when H_0 is tested with a sample of $n = 25$. The right figure shows power of $p = .9988$ when H_0 is tested with a sample of $n = 100$. The same null hypothesis, $\mu = 200$, and the same treatment effect, 20 points, are used in both figures.

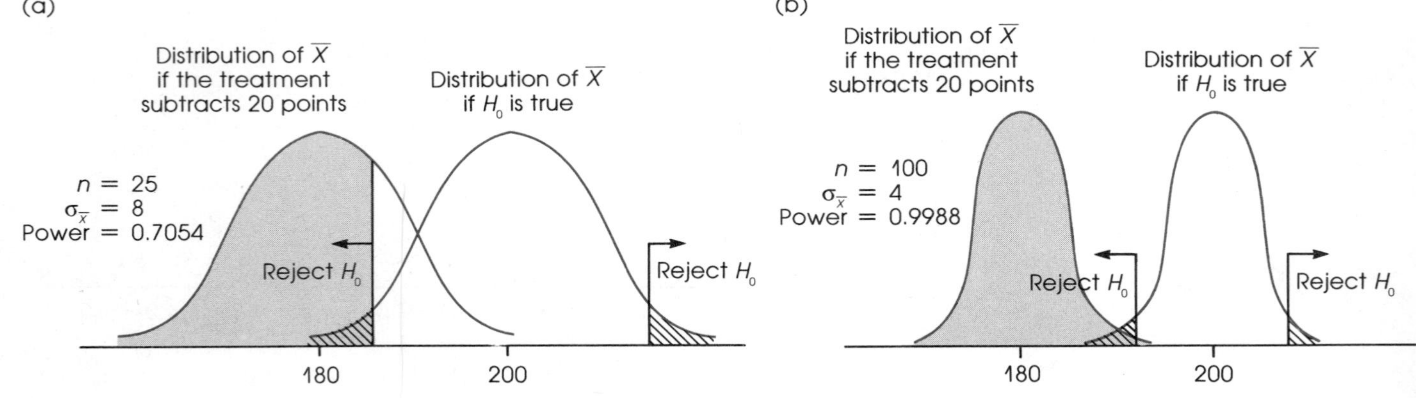

The right-hand portion of the figure shows the calculation of power for $n = 100$. With $n = 100$, the standard error is

$$\sigma_{\bar{X}} = \frac{\sigma}{\sqrt{n}} = \frac{40}{\sqrt{100}} = \frac{40}{10} = 4$$

Note that the larger the sample, the greater the power of the test.

USING POWER TO DETERMINE SAMPLE SIZE

In Figure 9.9, we showed that increasing the sample size will increase the power of a hypothesis test. The increased power results from the fact that the larger sample has a smaller standard error. If you compare the left- and right-hand parts of Figure 9.9, this effect should be clear. In both figures there is a 20-point difference between the two distribution means (180 versus 200). However, in the left figure the standard error is 8 and the 20-point difference amounts to only $2\frac{1}{2}$ standard errors. In the right-hand portion of Figure 9.9, the standard error is 4, so the 20-point difference corresponds to 5 standard errors. In general, a larger sample will have a smaller standard error, which makes the separation between the two distributions more apparent and thereby increases power.

· EXAMPLE 9.4 · A researcher is planning an experiment to demonstrate that increased salt intake will produce a corresponding increase in fluid consumption. It is known that under regular circumstances laboratory rats drink an average of $\mu = 80$ milliliters of water each day. The distribution of water consumption scores is normal with $\sigma = 10$. Based on previous data, the researcher predicts that increased salt will produce an 8-milliliter increase in fluid consumption. The researcher is planning to obtain a sample of rats, add extra salt to their food, and then measure water consumption. How large a sample is needed for this experiment to have an 80% chance of success? That is, what n is necessary to ensure that the hypothesis test will have power of .80 or larger? Assume that the researcher is planning a standard two-tailed test with $\alpha = .05$.

The first step is to sketch the two distributions and locate the critical region. If the null hypothesis is true, the distribution of sample means will be centered at $\mu = 80$. Within this distribution the critical region consists of z-score values greater than $+1.96$ or less than -1.96. On the other hand, if the treatment (more salt) increases the mean by 8 points, the distribution of sample means will be centered at $\mu = 88$. These two distributions are shown in Figure 9.10.

The second step is to specify the desired level of power. For this example, the researcher wants power equal to 80% or more. To achieve this level of power, at least 80% of the alternative distribution must be in the critical region (see the shaded portion in Figure 9.10). Therefore, in the alternative distribution the boundary for the critical region must have z-score of $z = -.84$ (check the unit normal table).

Looking at Figure 9.10, you will see that the distance between the two population means can be described in two different ways:

1 The distance is equal to 8 points ($\mu = 80$ versus $\mu = 88$).

2 The distance is equal to 2.80 standard errors. This description comes from the fact that the critical boundary is 1.96 standard errors above $\mu = 80$ (the z-score is $+1.96$) and this same boundary is .84 standard errors below $\mu = 88$ (z-score is $-.84$). Thus, the total distance between the means is $1.96\sigma_{\bar{X}} + .84\sigma_{\bar{X}} = 2.80\sigma_{\bar{X}}$.

· FIGURE 9.10 ·

The distribution of sample means that would be obtained if H_0 were true (left) and the distribution that would be obtained if the treatment adds 8 points to each score (right). To have power = .80 it is necessary that 80% of the alternative distribution be located in the critical region.

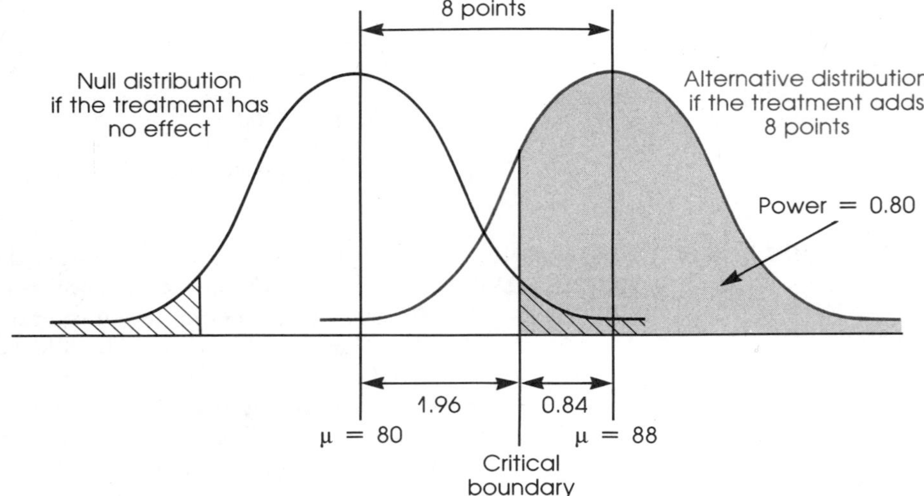

Because these two distances are identical, we can incorporate them into an equation.

$$2.80\sigma_{\bar{X}} = 8 \text{ points}$$

Solving this equation, we obtain $\sigma_{\bar{X}} = 2.86$. Finally, we use the formula for the standard error and solve for the value of n.

$$\sigma_{\bar{X}} = \frac{\sigma}{\sqrt{n}}$$

$$2.86 = \frac{10}{\sqrt{n}}$$

$$\sqrt{n} = \frac{10}{2.86}$$

$$n = 12.22$$

Thus, the researcher must use a sample of $n = 12.22$ or larger (actually $n = 13$ or larger) to ensure that the power of the hypothesis test is at least .80. ·

· LEARNING CHECK ·

1 For a particular hypothesis test, power equals .50 for a 5-point treatment effect. Will the power be greater or lower for a 10-point treatment effect?

2 As the power of a test increases, what happens to the probability of a Type II error?

3 A researcher knows that a population of learning scores is approximately normal with $\mu = 50$ and $\sigma = 8$. This researcher plans to use a sample of $n = 16$ to evaluate a particular treatment that is expected to affect learning. Assuming the researcher uses a two-tailed test with $\alpha = .05$,

   a What is the power of the statistical test if the treatment adds six points to each person's learning score?

   b What is the power of the test if the treatment adds only two points to each person's score? (Be careful; both tails of the critical region will contribute to the power in this case.)

ANSWERS

1 The hypothesis test is more likely to detect a 10-point effect, so power will be greater.

2 As power increases, the probability of a Type II error decreases.

3 a With a standard error of 2, the critical region consists of sample means greater than 53.92 or less than 46.08. If the treatment adds 6 points, the distribution of sample means will have $\mu = 56$. In this distribution, the critical boundary of 53.92 has a z-score of $z = -1.04$. The power (area in the critical region) is .8508 (85.08%).

b The critical region consists of sample means greater than 53.92 or less than 46.08. If the treatment adds two points, the distribution of sample means will have $\mu = 52$. In this distribution, the critical boundary of 53.92 has a z-score of $z = +.96$, and the boundary of 46.08 has a z-score of $z = -2.96$. The power (total area in the critical region) is .1700 (i.e., .1685 + .0015).

SUMMARY

1 When a researcher predicts that a treatment effect will be in a particular direction (increase or decrease), it is possible to do a directional or one-tailed test. The first step in this procedure is to state the alternative hypothesis (H_1). This hypothesis states that the treatment works and, for directional tests, specifies the direction of the predicted treatment effect. The null hypothesis is the opposite of H_1. To locate the critical region, you must identify the kind of experimental outcome that refutes the null hypothesis and demonstrates that the treatment works. These outcomes will be located entirely in one tail of the distribution. The entire critical region (5% or 1%, depending on α) will be in one tail.

2 Directional tests should be used with caution because they may allow the rejection of H_0 when the experimental evidence is relatively weak. Even though a researcher may have a specific directional prediction for an experiment, it is generally safer and never inappropriate to use a nondirectional (two-tailed) test.

3 Estimation is a procedure that uses sample data to obtain an estimate of a population mean. The estimate can be either a point estimate (single value) or an interval estimate (range of values). Point estimates have the advantage of precision, but they do not give much confidence. Interval estimates provide confidence, but you lose precision as the interval grows wider.

4 The formula for estimation is

$$\mu = \overline{X} \pm z\sigma_{\overline{X}}$$

This is the basic z-score formula with the terms rearranged. To use the formula, you first plug in the value of $\overline{X}$ from your sample and the value of $\sigma_{\overline{X}}$ (from the sample size n and the known value of σ). Next, you estimate the value of z. Note that you are using the z value to estimate the location of your particular sample mean within the distribution of sample means. For point estimates, use $z = 0$. For interval estimates, select a level of confidence (percent confidence); then use this percentage to determine the range of z-score values (for example, 80% confidence gives $+1.28$ to -1.28). Finally, plug in the estimate of z and calculate the estimate of μ.

5 The width of a confidence interval is an indication of its precision: A narrow interval is more precise than a wide interval. The interval width is influenced by sample size and the level of confidence.

a As sample size (n) gets larger, the interval width gets smaller (greater precision).

b As the percent confidence increases, the interval width gets greater (less precision).

6 Estimation and hypothesis testing are similar processes: Both use sample data to answer questions about populations. However, these two procedures are designed to answer different questions. Hypothesis testing will tell you whether or not a treatment effect exists (yes or no). Estimation will tell you how much treatment effect there is.

7 The power of a statistical test is defined as the probability that the test will correctly reject the null hypothesis. Power is identified as

$$\text{power} = 1 - \beta$$

where β is the probability of a Type II error.

8 To compute the power for a statistical test, you must first identify a specific alternative to the null hypothesis. That is, you must specify the magnitude of the treatment effect. Next, you locate the critical region as if you were doing a regular hypothesis test. Finally, you construct the distribution of all possible sample outcomes using the specified treatment effect. The power of the test is the portion of this distribution that is located in the critical region.

9 The power of a test is affected by several factors that can be controlled by the experimenter:

a Increasing the alpha level will increase power.

b A one-tailed test will have greater power then a two-tailed test.

c A large sample will result in more power than a small sample.

KEY TERMS

estimation
point estimate
interval estimate
confidence interval
directional hypothesis test
one-tailed test
two-tailed test
power

FOCUS ON PROBLEM SOLVING

1. Although hypothesis tests and estimation are similar in some respects, you should remember that they are separate statistical techniques. A hypothesis test is used to determine whether or not there is evidence for a treatment effect. Estimation is used to determine how much effect a treatment has.

2. When students perform a hypothesis test and estimation with the same set of data, a common error is to take the z-score from the hypothesis test and use it in the estimation formula. For estimation the z-score value is determined entirely by the level of confidence, and you always find the z-score value in the unit normal table.

3. When you are doing a directional hypothesis test, read the problem carefully and watch for key words (such as increase or decrease, raise or lower, and more or less) that tell you which direction the researcher is predicting. The predicted direction will determine the alternative hypothesis (H_1) and the critical region. For example, if a treatment is expected to *increase* scores, H_1 would contain a *greater than* symbol and the critical region would be in the tail associated with high scores.

4. When calculating power you use two separate distributions—one determined by the null hypothesis and one determined by a specific alternative hypothesis. Always begin with the distribution from the null hypothesis and locate the critical region as if you were doing a routine hypothesis test. After the critical region is specified, you shift attention to the alternative distribution. Power is the proportion of the alternative distribution located in the critical region.

PROBLEMS

***1** An extensive survey in 1970 revealed that preschool children spend an average of $\mu = 6.3$ hours per day watching television. The distribution of TV times is normal with $\sigma = 2$. Last year a sample of $n = 100$ preschool children gave a mean of $\bar{X} = 5.8$ hours of television per day.
  a Use these sample data to make a point estimate of the population mean for last year.
  b Based on your point estimate, how much change has occurred in children's television habits since 1970?
  c Make an interval estimate of last year's population mean so that you are 80% confident that the true mean is in your interval.

2 What happens to power as the alternative hypothesis gets closer to the null hypothesis?

***3** A researcher has constructed a 90% confidence interval of 87 ± 10, based on a sample of $n = 25$ scores. Note that this interval is 20 points wide (from 77 to 97). How large a sample would be needed to produce a 90% interval that is only 10 points wide?

***4** Performance scores on a motor skills task form a normal distribution with $\mu = 20$ and $\sigma = 4$. A psychologist is using this task to determine the extent to which increased self-awareness affects performance. The prediction for this experiment is that increased self-awareness will reduce a subject's concentration and result in lower performance scores. A sample of $n = 16$ subjects is obtained, and each subject is tested on the motor skills task while seated in front of a large mirror. The purpose of the mirror is to make the subjects more self-aware. The average score for this sample is $\bar{X} = 15.5$. Use a one-tailed test with $\alpha = .05$ to test the psychologist's prediction.

5 Use the data from Problem 4 to estimate how much performance is reduced by the presence of the mirror.
  a Make a point estimate of the population mean performance score with the mirror present.
  b Make an interval estimate of the population mean so that you are 95% confident that the true mean is in your interval.

***6** Based on a sample of $n = 20$, a 90% confidence interval is found to have boundaries of 36.7 and 43.4. A common misinterpretation of confidence intervals would lead you to predict that if we took another sample of $n = 20$ scores from the same population, there is a 90% probability that the sample mean would be in this interval. Explain why this conclusion is incorrect, and give the correct interpretation of the confidence interval.

7 Researchers have developed a filament that should add to the life expectancy of light bulbs. The standard 60-watt bulb burns for an average of $\mu = 750$ hours with $\sigma = 20$. A sample of $n = 100$ bulbs is prepared using the new filament. The average life for this sample is $\overline{X} = 820$ hours.
a Use these sample data to make a point estimate of the mean life expectancy for the new filament.
b Make an interval estimate so that you are 80% confident that the true mean is in your interval.
c Make an interval estimate so that you are 99% confident that the true mean is in your interval.

***8** Scores on the Scholastic Aptitude Test (SAT) form a normal distribution with $\mu = 500$ and $\sigma = 100$. A school counselor has proposed a special training program for high school juniors that is intended to improve performance on the SAT. The counselor expects the program to improve scores by an average of 40 points. This year a sample of $n = 25$ students will participate in the program in order to evaluate its effectiveness.
a If the counselor uses a one-tailed hypothesis test with $\alpha = .05$, what is the probability that the sample data will lead to rejecting H_0? Assume that the program does produce a 40-point increase in the mean score.
b What would the power of the test be if the counselor used a standard two-tailed hypothesis test?

9 Suppose that the sample of $n = 25$ students described in Problem 8 achieved an average SAT score of $\overline{X} = 535$ after completing the training program.
a Use a one-tailed test with $\alpha = .05$ to determine whether or not these data provide sufficient evidence to conclude that the program is successful.
b What decision would be made if the counselor used a two-tailed test with these data?

***10** After years of working in the area of animal learning, a psychologist has observed that laboratory rats that have participated in several experiments tend to perform much better on a new task than rats with no previous experience. To determine the magnitude of this effect, the psychologist selects a random sample of $n = 9$ experienced rats and tests each rat on a standardized maze. On the maze, the error scores for naive rats form a normal distribution with $\mu = 55$ and $\sigma = 18$. Although none of the rats in the sample has seen this particular maze before, they solve the maze with an average of $\overline{X} = 46$ errors. Using a one-tailed test with $\alpha = .05$, can the psychologist conclude that previous experience results in a significant decrease in errors?

11 For smokers at a large company, the average worker smokes $\mu = 24$ cigarettes daily with $\sigma = 8$. Assume the distribution of cigarette smokers is normal. A sample of $n = 4$ workers is placed in a program to help them break the habit. After just one week of treatment, the average cigarette consumption among workers in the sample is $\overline{X} = 14$. Is this a significant reduction?
a Use a one-tailed test with $\alpha = .01$.
b Would you make the same decision about H_0 if you used a two-tailed test with $\alpha = .01$?

12 For the data in problem 11, estimate how much the treatment reduces smoking behavior.
a Make a point estimate for the population mean of cigarette consumption following the treatment.
b Make an interval estimate for μ at the 95% confidence level.

***13** A researcher did a one-tailed hypothesis test using an alpha level of .01. For this test, H_0 was rejected. A colleague analyzed the same data but used a two-tailed test with $\alpha = .05$. In this test H_0 was *not* rejeccted. Can both analyses be correct? Explain your answer.

14 The manufacturers of a gasoline additive would like to include some statistical data in their advertisements. Specifically, they would like to claim that their product significantly increases gas mileage, and they would like to make a statement concerning the magnitude of this increase. Based on published EPA figures, they know that the average mileage for a particular model car is $\mu = 24$ miles per gallon with $\sigma = 4$. They obtain a sample of $n = 16$ of these cars and measure the mileage obtained with their gasoline additive. The average for this sample is $\overline{X} = 26.5$ miles per gallon.
a In using a one-tailed test with $\alpha = .05$, does the additive produce a significant increase in mileage?
b Use these data to make a point estimate of the average mileage with the additive. Based on this estimate, how much effect does the additive have?

***15** A psychological theory predicts that individuals who grow up as an only child will have above-average IQs. A sample of $n = 64$ people from single-child families is obtained. The average IQ for this sample is $\overline{X} = 104.9$. In the general population, IQs form a normal distribution with $\mu = 100$ and $\sigma = 15$.
a Use a one-tailed test with $\alpha = .01$ to evaluate the theory.
b Use these sample data to construct a 90% confidence interval for the mean IQ of the population of single children.

16 A psychologist is interested in the long-term effects of a divorce on the children in a family. A sample is obtained of $n = 10$ children whose parents were divorced at least 5 years ago. Each child is given a personality questionnaire measuring depression. In the general population, the scores on this questionnaire form a normal distribution with $\mu = 80$ and $\sigma = 12$. The scores for this sample are as follows: 83, 81, 75, 92, 84, 107, 63, 112, 92, 88. The psychologist is predicting that children from divorced families will be more depressed than children in the general population. Use a one-tailed test with $\alpha = .05$ to test this hypothesis.

17 Use the data from Problem 16 to estimate the population mean depression score for children from divorced families.
a Make a point estimate of the population mean.
b Make an interval estimate so that you are 95% confident that the true mean is in your interval.

***18** A psychologist is examining the effect of chronic alcoholism on memory. In this experiment, a standardized memory test will be used. Scores on this test for the general population form a normal distribution with $\mu = 50$ and $\sigma = 5$. The psychologist expects alcoholics to average at least five points below the general population. The proposed experiment will use a sample of $n = 20$ alcoholics.
a Compute the power for a two-tailed hypothesis test with $\alpha = .05$. Assume that alcoholism does lower memory scores by an average of five points.
b Compute the power for a one-tailed hypothesis test with $\alpha = .05$. Again, assume alcoholism lowers memory scores by an average of five points.
c What is the probability that the two-tailed test will result in a Type II error?
d What is the probability that the one-tailed test will result in a Type II error?

19 A poultry farm supplies chickens to a fast-food restaurant chain. The chickens are sold by weight and average $\mu = 65$ ounces. The distribution of weights is normal with $\sigma = 4.9$ ounces. The farmer is interested in changing to a new brand of chicken food. However, the new food is more expensive and will not be economically feasible unless it results in an average weight increase of at least 3 ounces per chicken. A sample of $n = 30$ chicks is selected to be tested on the new food. At maturity, the weights for these chickens are as follows: 74, 72, 65, 79, 75, 73, 68, 75, 78, 69, 72, 75, 79, 81, 73, 63, 69, 73, 77, 73, 64, 73, 63, 78, 72, 71, 62, 72, 71, 74.
a Construct an 80% confidence interval for the population mean weight for chickens raised on the new feed.
b Based on your confidence interval, should the farmer switch to the new food? Explain your answer.

***20** A state inspector is checking the machinery at a canning factory. The canning machine is supposed to put an average of $\mu = 16$ ounces in each can. There is some variability, so the distribution of actual weights is normal with $\sigma = .15$ ounce. The inspector selects a random sample of 15 cans and carefully weighs the contents of each. The weights from this sample are are follows: 15.8, 16.1, 15.9, 15.8, 16.0, 15.9, 15.7, 16.2, 15.8, 15.7, 15.9, 16.1, 16.0, 15.9, 15.9. Use a one-tailed test with $\alpha = .05$ to determine whether the machine is averaging below 16 ounces per can.

***21** Suppose that the canning machine described in Problem 20 is really averaging only 15.9 ounces per can. If the inspector uses a one-tailed test with a sample of 20 cans, what is the probability that this error will be detected? Assume that α is set at .05.

22 A psychologist is investigating the degree to which personality disorders are familial. The psychologist selects a sample of 40 adolescents who have at least one parent with a history of personality disorder. Each individual in the sample is given a personality inventory questionnaire. For the general population, scores on this questionnaire are known to have a mean of $\mu = 100$ with $\sigma = 20$. The average score for the sample is $\bar{X} = 93.7$. Use a one-tailed statistical test with $\alpha = .05$ to determine whether a family history of personality disorder results in personality scores significantly lower than the general population.

***23** In a nationwide survey, women were asked to use a 20-point scale to rate the personal importance of their jobs as well as other aspects of their lives (such as family, money, children, etc.). In this survey, the average rating for jobs was $\mu = 7.5$ with $\sigma = 2$. A psychologist suspects that women who were "tomboys" as children will have attitudes that are different from average. For a sample of $n = 28$ of these women, the average rating for job importance was $\bar{X} = 9.2$. Do these data indicate that former tomboys rate their jobs higher than the rating given by the national survey? Use a one-tailed test with $\alpha = .05$.

24 Calculating the power of a statistical test can help a researcher plan the number of subjects needed for an experiment. For example, a researcher is testing a drug that is expected to lower blood pressure by five points. It is known that under regular conditions the distribution of blood pressure scores is normal with $\mu = 120$ and $\sigma = 10$. Assuming that the drug works as expected, how large a sample should the researcher use to obtain power of at least 75%. The researcher plans a standard two-tailed test with $\alpha = .05$. (*Hint:* See Example 9.4.)

***25** In 1970 a nationwide survey measured the attitudes of college students concerning appropriate behavior for women. Each student was given a checklist of adjectives describing traditionally masculine behaviors (aggressive, assertive, competitive, etc.). The students had to rate on a scale from 1 to 100 how appropriate the behavior was for women. In 1970 the average rating was $\mu = 52$ with $\sigma = 13.5$. Last year the same survey was given to a sample of $n = 35$ students. The average rating for this sample was $\bar{X} = 59$.
a On the basis of these data, has there been a significant increase in the appropriateness of these behaviors for women? Use a one-tailed test with $\alpha = .05$.
b Use the sample data to estimate the magnitude of the change in attitude. Make a point estimate and a 90% confidence interval estimate.

26 Explain why power for a statistical test can never be less than the alpha level for the test. (*Hint:* Sketch a null distribution and then add several different alternative distributions to your sketch. What happens to power as the alternative gets closer to the null?)

CHAPTER 10

INTRODUCTION TO THE *t* STATISTIC

TOOLS YOU WILL NEED

The following items are considered essential background material for this chapter. If you doubt your knowledge of any of these items, you should review the appropriate chapter or section before proceeding.

- Sample standard deviation (Chapter 4)
- Degrees of freedom (Chapter 4)
- Hypothesis testing (Chapter 8)
- Estimation (Chapter 9)

PREVIEW

Numerous accounts suggest that for many animals, including humans, a direct stare from another animal is aversive (e.g., Cook, 1977). Try it out for yourself. Make direct eye contact with a stranger in a cafeteria. Chances are the person will display avoidance by averting his or her gaze or turning away from you. Some insects, such as moths, have even developed eye-spot patterns on the wings or body to ward off predators (mostly birds) who may have a natural fear of eyes (Blest, 1957). Suppose a comparative psychologist is interested in determining whether or not the birds that feed on these insects show an avoidance of eye-spot patterns.

Using methods similar to those of Scaife (1976), the researcher performed the following experiment. A sample of $n = 16$ moth-eating birds is selected. The animals are tested in an apparatus that consists of a two-chambered box. The birds are free to roam from one side of the box to the other through a doorway in the partition that separates the two chambers. In one chamber, there are two eye-spot patterns painted on the wall. The other side of the box has plain walls. One at a time, the researcher tests each bird by placing it in the doorway between the chambers. Each subject is left in the apparatus for 60 minutes, and the amount of time spent in the plain chamber is recorded.

What kind of data should the experimenter expect if the null hypothesis is true? If the animals show no aversion to the eye spots, they should spend, on average, half of the time in the plain side. Therefore, the null hypothesis would predict that

$$H_0: \mu_{\text{plain side}} = 30 \text{ minutes}$$

Suppose the researcher collected data for the sample and found that the average amount of time spent on the plain side was $\overline{X} = 35$ minutes. The researcher now has two of the needed pieces of information to compute a z-score test statistic—the sample data ($\overline{X}$) and the hypothesized mean (according to H_0). All that is needed is the population standard deviation, so that the standard error can be computed. Note that the investigator does not have this information about the population. All that is known is that the population of animals should, on average, spend half of the 60-minute period in the plain chamber if the eye spots have no effect on behavior. Without complete information about the population, how can the comparative psychologist test the hypothesis with a z-score? The answer is simple—z cannot be used for the test statistic because the standard error cannot be computed. However, it is possible to estimate the standard error using the sample data and to compute a test statistic that is similar in structure to the z-score. This new test statistic is called the t statistic.

10.1 INTRODUCTION

In the preceding two chapters we presented the statistical procedures that permit researchers to use a sample mean to draw inferences about a population. These statistical procedures were based on a few basic notions which we summarize as follows:

Remember, the expected value of the distribution of sample means is μ, the population mean.

1. A sample mean $\overline{X}$ is expected more or less to approximate its population mean μ. This permits us to use the sample mean to test a hypothesis about the population mean or to estimate its value.

2. The standard error provides a measure of how well a sample mean approximates the population mean.

$$\sigma_{\overline{X}} = \frac{\sigma}{\sqrt{n}}$$

3. To quantify our inferences about the population, we convert each sample mean to a z-score using the formula

$$z = \frac{\overline{X} - \mu}{\sigma_{\overline{X}}}$$

When the z-scores form a normal distribution, we are able to use the unit normal table (Appendix B) to find the probabilities that are needed to relate the sample to the population, be it for the test of a hypothesis or for the estimation of μ.

The shortcoming of using the z-score as an inferential statistic is that the z-score formula requires more information than is usually available. Specifically, z-scores require that we know the value of the population standard deviation, which is needed to compute the standard error. Most often the standard deviation of the population is not known, and the standard error of sample means cannot be computed. Without the standard error, we have no way of quantifying the expected amount of distance (or error) between $\overline{X}$ and μ. We have no way of making precise, quantitative inferences about the population based on z-scores.

THE *t* STATISTIC—A SUBSTITUTE FOR *z* Fortunately, there is a relatively simple solution to the problem of not knowing the population standard deviation. When the value of σ is not known, we use the sample standard deviation in its place. In Chapter 4 (page 92), the sample standard deviation was developed specifically to be an unbiased estimate of the population standard deviation. You should recall that the formula for the sample standard deviation is

$$s = \sqrt{\frac{SS}{n-1}}$$

Using this sample statistic, we can now estimate the standard error. The estimated standard error $s_{\overline{X}}$ is obtained by the formula

$$s_{\overline{X}} = \frac{s}{\sqrt{n}} \tag{10.1}$$

Notice that we have substituted the sample standard deviation (s) in place of the unknown population standard deviation (σ). Also notice that the symbol for the estimated standard error is $s_{\overline{X}}$ instead of $\sigma_{\overline{X}}$, indicating that the value is computed from sample data rather than from the population parameter.

· DEFINITION · *The estimated standard error* ($s_{\overline{X}}$) is used as an estimate of $\sigma_{\overline{X}}$ when the value of σ is unknown. It is computed from the sample standard deviation and provides an estimate of the standard distance between a sample mean $\overline{X}$ and the population mean μ.

Now we can substitute the estimated standard error in the denominator of the z-score formula. This new test statistic is called a *t statistic*:

$$t = \frac{\overline{X} - \mu}{s_{\overline{X}}} \tag{10.2}$$

The only difference between the *t* formula and the z-score formula is that the z-score formula uses the actual population standard deviation (σ) and the *t* statistic uses the sample standard deviation as an estimate when σ is unknown:

$$z = \frac{\overline{X} - \mu}{\sigma_{\overline{X}}} = \frac{\overline{X} - \mu}{\sigma/\sqrt{n}} \qquad t = \frac{\overline{X} - \mu}{s_{\overline{X}}} = \frac{\overline{X} - \mu}{s/\sqrt{n}}$$

Structurally, these two formulas have the same form:

$$z \text{ or } t = \frac{\text{sample mean} - \text{population mean}}{\text{(estimated) standard error}}$$

Both z, and t formulas are used for hypothesis testing and for estimation of μ. There is only one rule to remember:

> When you know the value of σ, use a z-score. If σ is unknown, use the t statistic.

· DEFINITION · The t *statistic* is used to test hypotheses about μ and to estimate the value of μ when the value for σ is not known. The formula for the t statistic is similar in structure to the z-score, except that the t statistic uses estimated standard error.

DEGREES OF FREEDOM AND THE *t* STATISTIC

In this chapter we have introduced the t statistic as a substitute for a z-score. The basic difference between these two is that the t statistic uses sample standard deviation (s), and the z-score uses the population standard deviation (σ). To determine how well a t statistic approximates a z-score, we must determine how well the sample standard deviation approximates the population standard deviation.

In Chapter 4 we introduced the concept of degrees of freedom. Reviewing briefly, you must know the sample mean before you can compute sample standard deviation. This places a restriction on sample variability such that only $n - 1$ scores in a sample are free to vary (page 96). The value $n - 1$ is called the *degrees of freedom* (or *df*) for the sample standard deviation.

$$\text{degrees of freedom} = df = n - 1 \tag{10.3}$$

· DEFINITION · *Degrees of freedom* describe the number of scores in a sample that are free to vary. Because the sample mean places a restriction on the value of one score in the sample, there are $n - 1$ degrees of freedom for the sample (see Chapter 4).

The greater the value of df for a sample, the better s represents σ, and the better the t statistic approximates the z-score. This should make sense because the larger the sample (n), the better the sample represents its population. Thus, the degrees of freedom associated with s also describe how well t represents z.

THE *t* DISTRIBUTIONS

Every sample from a population can be used to compute a z-score or a t statistic. If you select all the possible samples of a particular size (n), then the entire set of resulting z-scores will form a z-score distribution. In the same way, the set of all possible t statistics will form a t distribution. As we saw in Chapter 7, the distribution of z-scores computed from sample means tends to be a normal distribution. For this reason, we consulted the unit normal table to find the critical region or to determine a confidence interval when using z-scores to make inferences about a population. The t distribution, on the other hand, is generally not normal. However, the t distribution will approximate a normal distribution in the same way that a t statistic approximates a z-score. How well a t distribution approximates a normal distribution is determined by degrees of freedom. In general, the greater the sample size (n), the larger the degrees of freedom ($n - 1$), and the better the t distribution approximates the normal distribution (see Figure 10.1).

THE SHAPE OF THE *t* DISTRIBUTION

The exact shape of a t distribution changes with degrees of freedom. In fact, statisticians speak of a "family" of t distributions. That is, there is a different sampling distribution of t (a distribution of all possible sample t values) for each possible number of degrees

PERSPECTIVE 10.1

THE CRITICAL VALUES IN A NORMAL z DISTRIBUTION AND A t DISTRIBUTION: THE INFLUENCE OF DEGREES OF FREEDOM

As previously noted, a t distribution approximates a normal z distribution. How well it approximates a normal distribution depends on the value of df. This can be seen by simply comparing critical values for z with critical values of t at various degrees of freedom. For example, if we test a hypothesis with a z-score using a two-tailed test and $\alpha = .05$, the critical z-scores will be $+1.96$ and -1.96. However, suppose the population standard deviation were not known and we conducted this hypothesis test with a t statistic. For a sample of $n = 4$, the t statistic would have $df = 3$. For three degrees of freedom, the critical values of t would be $+3.182$ and -3.182 (with alpha still set at .05). When df is small, the t distribution is flatter and more spread out. Consequently, the tails have a greater area for the t distribution compared to a normal distribution (see Figure 10.1). The extreme 5% of the distribution will be farther from the mean and have a larger critical value in the t distribution. If, however, we use a sample of $n = 31$, then $df = 30$, and the critical t values will be $+2.042$ and -2.042. These values are very close to the critical z-score values (± 1.96). If the sample is made even larger, say $n = 121$, the critical values get even closer to the z values. For 120 degrees of freedom, the critical values of t are $+1.980$ and -1.980 when $\alpha = .05$. Thus, the difference between a t distribution and a normal z-distribution becomes negligible when a sample of more than 30 individuals is used. (Note: Determining critical values for t is discussed on page 224.)

of freedom. As df gets very large, the t distribution gets closer in shape to a normal z-score distribution (see Perspective 10.1). A quick glance at Figure 10.1 reveals that distributions of t are bell-shaped and symmetrical and have a mean of zero. However, the t distribution has more variability than a normal z distribution, especially when df values are small (Figure 10.1). The t distribution tends to be flatter and more spread out, whereas the normal z distribution has more of a central peak.

Why is the t distribution flatter and more variable than a normal z distribution? For a particular population, the top of the z-score formula, $\overline{X} - \mu$, can take on different values because $\overline{X}$ will vary from one sample to another. However, the value of the bottom of the z-score formula, $\sigma_{\overline{X}}$, is constant. The standard error will not vary from sample to sample because it is derived from the population standard deviation. The implication is that samples which have the same value for $\overline{X}$ should also have the same z-score.

On the other hand, the standard error in the t formula is not a constant because it is estimated. That is, $s_{\overline{X}}$ is based on the sample standard deviation, which will vary

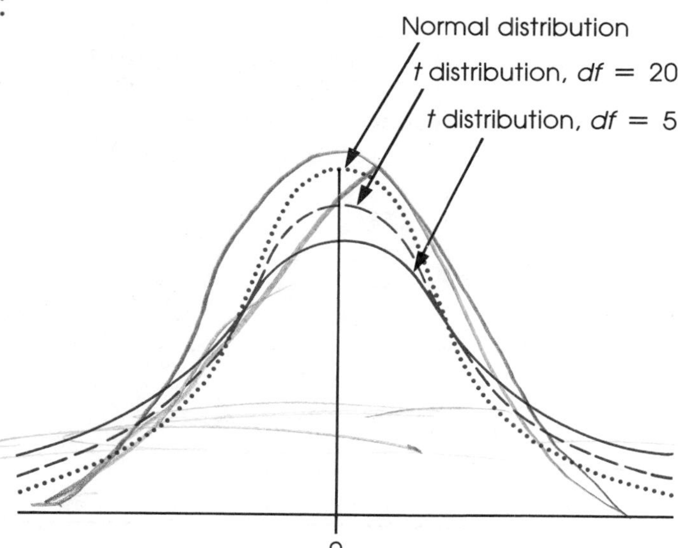

FIGURE 10.1

Distributions of the t statistic for different values of degrees of freedom are compared to a normal z-score distribution. Like the normal distribution, t distributions are bell-shaped and symmetrical and have a mean of zero. However, t distributions have more variability, indicated by the flatter and more spread-out shape. The larger the value of df, the more closely the t distribution approximates a normal distribution.

TABLE 10.1

A portion of the t distribution table

	Proportion in One Tail					
	.25	.10	.05	.025	.01	.005
	Proportion in Two Tails					
df	.50	.20	.10	.05	.02	.01
1	1.000	3.078	6.314	12.706	31.821	63.657
2	0.816	1.886	2.920	4.303	6.965	9.925
3	0.765	1.638	2.353	3.182	4.541	5.841
4	0.741	1.533	2.132	2.776	3.747	4.604
5	0.727	1.476	2.015	2.571	3.365	4.032
6	0.718	1.440	1.943	2.447	3.143	3.707

The numbers in the table are the values of t that separate the tail from the main body of the distribution. Proportions for one or two tails are listed at the top of the table and df values for t are listed in the first column.

in value from sample to sample. The result is that samples can have the same value for $\overline{X}$ yet different values of t because the estimated error will vary from one sample to another. Therefore, a t distribution will have more variability than the normal z distribution. It will look flatter and more spread out. When the value of df increases, the variability in the t distribution decreases, and it more closely resembles the normal distribution, because with greater df, $s_{\overline{X}}$ will more closely estimate $\sigma_{\overline{X}}$, and when df is very large, they are nearly the same.

DETERMINING PROPORTIONS AND PROBABILITIES FOR t DISTRIBUTIONS

Just as we used the unit normal table to locate proportions associated with z-scores, we will use a t distribution table to find proportions for t statistics. The complete t distribution table is presented in Appendix B, page 484, and a portion of this table is reproduced in Table 10.1. The two rows at the top of the table show proportions of the t distribution contained in either one or two tails, depending on which row is used. The first column of the table lists degrees of freedom for the t statistic. Finally, the numbers in the body of the table are the t values that mark the boundary between the tails and the rest of the t distribution.

For example, with $df = 3$, exactly 5% of the t distribution is located in the tail beyond $t = 2.353$ (see Figure 10.2). To find this value, you locate $df = 3$ in the first column and locate .05 (5%) in the one-tail proportion row. When you line up these two values in the table, you should find $t = 2.353$. Similarly, 5% of the t distribution is located in the tail beyond $t = -2.353$ (see Figure 10.2). Finally, you should notice that a total of 10% is contained in the two tails beyond $t = \pm 2.353$ (check the proportion value in the "two-tails" row at the top of the table).

FIGURE 10.2

The t distribution with $df = 3$. Note that 5% of the distribution is located in the tail beyond $t = 2.353$. Also, 5% is in the tail beyond $t = -2.353$. Thus, a total proportion of 10% (.10) is in the two tails beyond $t = \pm 2.353$.

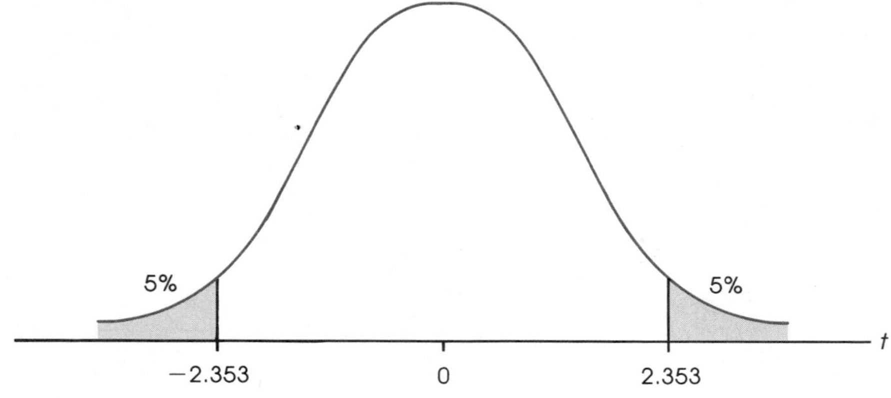

· LEARNING CHECK ·

1 A hypothesis test with a z-score can be performed only when the population standard deviation is known. (true/false)

2 To compute estimated standard error, $s_{\bar{X}}$, you must know the value for the population standard deviation. (true/false)

3 As the value for *df* gets smaller, the *t* distribution resembles a normal distribution more and more. (true/false)

4 As the value for *df* gets larger, *s* provides a better estimate of σ. (true/false)

5 For $df = 10$, what *t* value(s) are associated with:

a The top 1% of the *t* distribution?

b The bottom 5% of the *t* distribution?

c The most-extreme 1% of the distribution?

ANSWERS

1 True. (With large samples, z-scores and *t* statistics are very similar. For this reason, some statisticians allow the use of a z-score instead of *t* when the sample size is at least $n = 30$. However, there is always some difference between *z* and *t*, so we recommend that you use a z-score only when the population standard deviation is known.)

2 false 3 false 4 true

5 a $+2.764$ b -1.812 c $+3.169$ and -3.169

10.2 HYPOTHESIS TESTS WITH THE *t* STATISTIC

The *t* statistic formula is used in exactly the same way that the z-score formula is used to test a hypothesis about a population mean. Once again, the *t* formula and its structure are

$$t = \frac{\bar{X} - \mu}{s_{\bar{X}}} = \frac{\text{sample mean} - \text{population mean}}{\text{estimated standard error}}$$

In the hypothesis-testing situation, we have a population with an unknown mean, often a population that has received some treatment (Figure 10.3). The goal is to use a sample from the treated population as the basis for determining whether or not the treatment has any effect. As always, the null hypothesis states that the treatment has no effect. Specifically, H_0 predicts that the population mean is unchanged. The hypothesized value for the population mean is put into the *t* formula along with the sample mean (from the obtained data) and the estimated standard error (also computed from the sample data). When the resulting *t* statistic is near zero, we can conclude that the sample mean is not significantly different from the hypothesized value and the

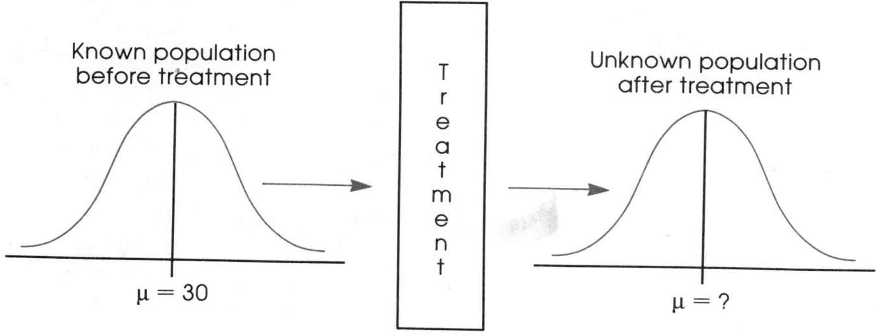

· FIGURE 10.3 ·
The basic experimental situation for using the *t* statistic or the z-score is presented. It is assumed that the parameter μ is known for the population before treatment. The purpose of the experiment is to determine whether or not the treatment (exposure to eye-spot patterns) has an effect on time spent on the plain side of the test box. We ask, Is the population mean after treatment the same as or different from the mean before treatment? A sample is selected from the treated population to help answer this question.

decision is "fail to reject H_0." In other words, there is no support for a treatment effect. If there is a substantial difference between the sample mean and the hypothesized μ, we will obtain a large value for t (large positive or large negative value). In this case, we would conclude that the data are not consistent with the null hypothesis and our decision would be to "reject H_0." The evidence suggests the existence of a treatment effect. The basis steps of the hypothesis-testing procedures will now be reviewed.

STEPS AND PROCEDURES For hypothesis tests with a t statistic, we use the same steps that were used with z-scores (Chapter 8). The major difference is that we are now required to estimate standard error because σ is unknown. Consequently, we compute a t statistic rather than a z-score and consult the t distribution table rather than the unit normal table to find the critical region.

STEP 1 The hypotheses are stated and the alpha level is set. The experimenter states the null hypothesis, that is, what should happen if no treatment effect exists. On the other hand, the alternative hypothesis predicts the outcome if an effect does occur. These hypotheses are always stated in terms of the population parameter, μ.

STEP 2 Locate the critical region. The exact shape of the t distribution, and therefore the critical t values, vary with degrees of freedom. Thus, to find a critical region in a t distribution, it is necessary to determine the value for df. Then the critical region can be located by consulting the t distribution table (Appendix B, page 484).

STEP 3 The sample data are collected and the test statistic is computed. When σ is unknown, the test statistic is a t statistic (Formula 10.2).

STEP 4 The null hypothesis is evaluated. If the t statistic we obtained in step 3 falls within the critical region (exceeds the value of a critical t), then H_0 is rejected. It can be concluded that a treatment effect exists. However, if the obtained t value does not lie in the critical region, then we fail to reject H_0, and we conclude that we failed to observe evidence for an effect in our study (see Perspective 10.2).

HYPOTHESIS-TESTING EXAMPLE Let us return to the research problem posed in the beginning of the chapter to demonstrate the procedures of hypothesis testing. Recall that direct eye contact is avoided by many animals. Some animals, such as moths, have even developed large eye-spot patterns, presumably to ward off predators that avoid a direct gaze. The experiment will assess the effect of exposure to eye-spot patterns on the behavior of moth-eating birds.

· EXAMPLE 10.1 · To test the effectiveness of eye-spot patterns in deterring predation, a sample of $n = 16$ insectivorous birds is selected. The animals are tested in a box that has two separate chambers. The birds are free to roam from one chamber to another through a doorway in a partition. On the wall of one chamber, two large eye-spot patterns have been painted. The other chamber has plain walls. The birds are tested one at a time by placing them in the doorway in the center of the apparatus. Each animal is left in the box for 60 minutes, and the amount of time spent in the plain chamber is recorded. Suppose that the sample of $n = 16$ birds spent an average of $\overline{X} = 35$ minutes in the plain side, with $SS = 1215$. Can we conclude that eye-spot patterns have an effect on behavior? Note that while it is possible to predict a value for μ, we have no information about the population standard deviation.

STEP 1 State the hypotheses and select an alpha level. If the null hypothesis were true, then the eye-spot patterns would have no effect on behavior. The animals should show no preference for either side of the box. That is, they should spend half of the 60-minute test period in the plain chamber. In symbols the null hypothesis would

PERSPECTIVE 10.2

A RECIPE FOR MAKING *t* STATISTICS

The *t* statistic formula, like any formula, can be thought of as a recipe. If you follow the instructions and use all the right ingredients, the formula will always produce a *t* statistic. In hypothesis testing situations, however, you do not have all the necessary ingredients. Specifically, you do not know the value for the population mean (μ), which is one component (or ingredient) in the formula.

This situation is similar to trying to follow a cake recipe where one of the ingredients is not clearly listed. For example, a cake recipe may call for flour but not specify exactly how much flour is needed. In this situation, you could proceed with the recipe and just add whatever amount of flour you think is appropriate. Your "hypothesis" about the amount of flour would be confirmed or rejected depending on the outcome of the cake. If the cake was good you could reasonably assume that your hypothesis was correct. But if the cake was horrid, you would conclude that your hypothesis was wrong.

In a hypothesis test with the *t* statistic, you do not know the value for μ. Therefore, you take a hypothesized value from H_0, plug it into the *t* formula, and see how it works. If your hypothesized value produces a reasonable outcome (a *t* statistic near zero), you conclude that the hypothesis was acceptable. But if the formula produces an extreme *t* statistic (in the critical region), you conclude that the hypothesis was wrong.

state that

$$H_0 : \mu_{\text{plain side}} = 30 \text{ minutes}$$

The alternative hypothesis would state that the eye patterns have an effect on behavior. There are two possibilities: (1) The animals may avoid staying in the chamber with the eye spots as we suspect, or (2) maybe for some reason the animals may show a preference for the patterns painted on the wall. A non-directional hypothesis (for a two-tailed test) would be represented in symbols as follows:

Directional hypotheses could be used and would specify whether the average time on the plain side is more or less than 30 minutes.

$$H_1 : \mu_{\text{plain side}} \neq 30 \text{ minutes}$$

We will set the level of significance at $\alpha = .05$ for two tails.

STEP 2 Locate the critical region. The test statistic is a *t* statistic because the population standard deviation is not known. The exact shape of the *t* distribution and therefore the proportions under the *t* distribution depend on the number of degrees of freedom associated with the sample. To find the critical region, *df* must be computed:

$$df = n - 1 = 16 - 1 = 15$$

For a two-tailed test at the .05 level of significance and with 15 degrees of freedom, the critical region consists of *t* values greater than $+2.131$ or less than -2.131. Figure 10.4 depicts the critical region in this *t* distribution.

FIGURE 10.4

The critical region in the *t* distribution for $\alpha = .05$ and $df = 15$.

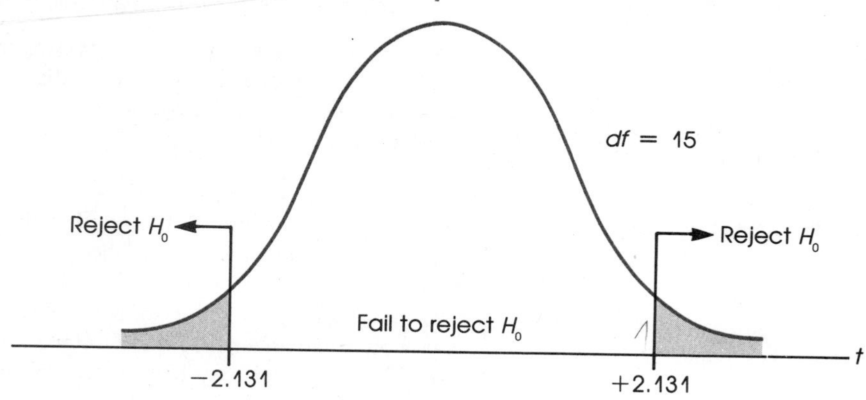

STEP 3 Calculate the test statistic. To obtain the value for the *t* statistic, we first must compute s and then $s_{\bar{X}}$. The sample standard deviation is

$$s = \sqrt{\frac{SS}{n-1}} = \sqrt{\frac{1215}{15}} = \sqrt{81} = 9$$

The estimated standard error is

$$s_{\bar{X}} = \frac{s}{\sqrt{n}} = \frac{9}{\sqrt{16}} = 2.25$$

Finally, we can compute the *t* statistic for these sample data:

$$t = \frac{\bar{X} - \mu}{s_{\bar{X}}} = \frac{35 - 30}{2.25} = \frac{5}{2.25} = 2.22$$

STEP 4 Make a decision regarding H_0. The obtained *t* statistic of 2.22 falls into the critical region on the right-hand side of the *t* distribution (Figure 10.4). Our statistical decision is to reject H_0 and conclude that the presence of eye-spot patterns does influence behavior. As can be seen from the sample mean, there is a tendency for animals to avoid the eyes and spend more time on the plain side of the box. For this example, alpha was set at .05. Therefore, the probability that a Type I error has been committed is $p < .05$. It is common practice in scientific literature to report the results of the *t* test in the following manner:

> The data suggest that the birds spent significantly more time in the chamber without eye-spot patterns; $t(15) = +2.22$, $p < .05$, two-tailed.

Note that the degrees of freedom are reported in parentheses right after the symbol *t*. The value for the obtained *t* statistic follows (2.22) and next is the probability of committing a Type I error (less than 5%). Finally, the type of test (one- versus two-tailed) is noted. •

DIRECTIONAL HYPOTHESES AND ONE-TAILED TESTS

As we noted in Chapter 9, the nondirectional (two-tailed) test is commonly used for research that is intended for publication in a scientific journal. On the other hand, a directional (one-tailed) test may be used in some research situations, such as exploratory investigations or pilot studies. Although one-tailed tests are used occasionally, you should remember that the two-tailed test is preferred by most researchers. Even though a researcher may have a specific directional prediction for an experiment, it is generally safer and always appropriate to use a nondirectional (two-tailed) test. The following example demonstrates a directional hypothesis test with a t statistic, using the same experimental situation that was presented in Example 10.1.

EXAMPLE 10.2 The research question is whether eye-spot patterns will affect the behavior of birds placed in a special testing box. The researcher is expecting the birds to avoid the eye-spot patterns. Therefore, the researcher predicts that the birds will spend most of the hour on the plain side of the box.

STEP 1 State the hypotheses and select an alpha level. With most directional tests it is easier to begin by stating the alternative hypothesis. Remember, H_1 states that the treatment does have an effect. For this example, the eye patterns should cause the birds to spend most of their time on the plain side. In symbols,

$$H_1: \mu_{\text{plain side}} > 30 \text{ minutes}$$

The null hypothesis states that the treatment will not have the predicted effect. In this case, H_0 says that the eye patterns will not cause the birds to spend more time on the plain side. In symbols,

$$H_0: \mu_{\text{plain side}} \leqslant 30 \text{ minutes} \qquad \text{(not greater than 30 minutes)}$$

We will set the level of significance at $\alpha = .05$.

STEP 2 Locate the critical region. In this example, the researcher is predicting that the sample mean ($\overline{X}$) will be greater than 30. The null hypothesis states that the population mean is $\mu = 30$ (or less). If you examine the structure of the t statistic formula, it should be clear that a positive t statistic would support the researcher's prediction and refute the null hypothesis.

$$t = \frac{\overline{X} - \mu}{s_{\overline{X}}}$$

The problem is to determine how large a positive value is necessary to reject H_0. To find the critical value you must look in the t distribution table using the one-tail proportions. With a sample of $n = 16$, the t statistic will have $df = 15$; using $\alpha = .05$, you should find a critical t value of 1.753. Figure 10.5 depicts the critical region in the t distribution.

STEP 3 Calculate the test statistic. The computation of the t statistic is the same for either a one-tailed or a two-tailed test. Earlier (in Example 10.1), we found that the data for this experiment produce a test statistic of $t = 2.22$.

FIGURE 10.5

The critical region in the t distribution for $\alpha = .05$, $df = 15$, one-tailed test.

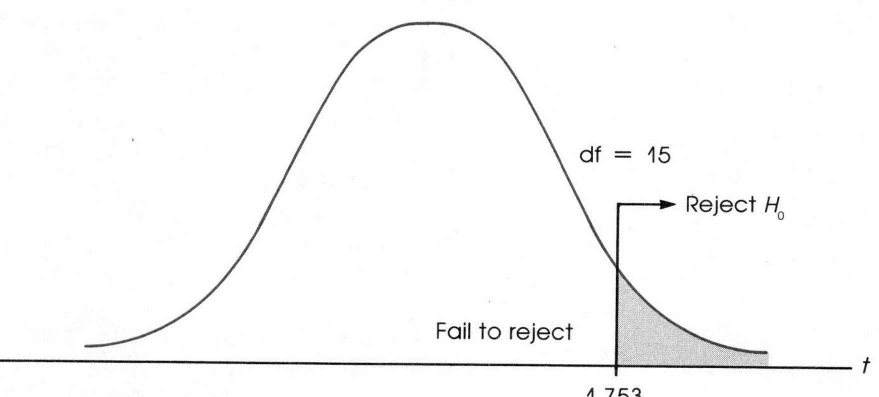

STEP 4 Make a decision. The test statistic is in the critical region so we reject H_0. In terms of the experimental variables, we have decided that the birds spent significantly more time on the plain side of the box than on the side with eye-spot patterns. •

ASSUMPTIONS OF THE *t* TEST

As noted earlier (Chapter 8), for each statistical test it is assumed that a certain set of conditions exists. Severe violations of one or more of these assumptions may compromise the validity of the statistical test. Of course, for a *t* test it is assumed that the sample has been randomly selected. This condition helps to ensure that the sample is representative of the population so that valid generalizations can be made from sample to population. Another important assumption for the *t* test is that the population distribution of scores is normal. If this condition is not met, the *t* distribution table cannot be used to locate the critical region. It is difficult to determine the exact *t* distribution that will be appropriate for the test when the population is not normally distributed.

Some statisticians have suggested that the *t* test is "robust." By robust, they mean the *t* test will still be a valid statistical test even when there are departures from the assumption of normality. However, the *t* statistic is more likely to be robust to violations of normality when large samples (for example, $n > 30$) are used. It should be noted that the assumption of normality is a condition that applies to all types of *t* tests that follow in later chapters.

THE VERSATILITY OF THE *t* TEST

The obvious advantage of hypothesis testing with the *t* statistic (as compared to *z*-scores) is that you do not need to know the value of the population standard deviation. This means that we still can do a hypothesis test even though we have little or no information about the population. One result of this extra versatility is that it is possible to do *t* tests in circumstances where hypothesis tests with *z*-scores would not even allow for the statement of a null hypothesis.

Both the *t* statistic and *z*-score tests have been introduced as a means of determining whether or not a treatment has any effect on the dependent variable. Recall that the null hypothesis states that the treatment has no effect. That is, the population mean after treatment has the same value that it had before treatment. Notice that this experimental situation requires that we know the value of the population mean before the treatment. This requirement is often unrealistic and limits the usefulness of *z*-score tests. Although the *t* statistic often is used in this before-and-after type of experiment (Figure 10.3), the *t* test also permits hypothesis testing in situations where we do not have a "known" population to serve as a before-treatment standard. Specifically, the *t* test can be used in situations where the value for the null hypothesis can come from a theory, a prediction, or just wishful thinking. Some examples follow. Notice in each example that the hypothesis is not dependent on knowing the actual population mean before treatment and that the rest of the *t* statistic can be computed entirely from the obtained sample data.

1. A researcher would like to examine the accuracy of people's judgment of time when they are distracted. Individuals are placed in a waiting room where many distracting events occur for a period of 12 minutes. The researcher then asks each person to judge how much time has passed. The null hypothesis would state that distraction has no effect and that time judgments are accurate. That is,

$$H_0 : \mu = 12 \text{ minutes}$$

2. A local fund-raising organization has set a goal of receiving $25 per contributor. After 1 week, a sample of contributions is selected to see if they deviate significantly from the goal. The null hypothesis would state that the contributions do not deviate

from the goal of the organization. In symbols, it is

$H_0: \mu = \$25.00$

3. A soft-drink company has developed a new, improved formula for its product and would like to determine how consumers respond to the new formula. A sample is obtained, and each individual is asked to taste the original soft drink and the new formula. After tasting, the subjects are required to state whether the new formula is better or worse than the original formula using a 7-point scale. A rating of 4 indicates no preference between the old and new formulas. Ratings above 4 indicate that the new formula is better (5 = slightly better, 6 = better, and 7 = much better). Similarly, ratings below 4 indicate that the new formula tastes worse than the old formula. The null hypothesis states that there is no perceived difference between the two formulas. In symbols, the new formula would receive an average rating of

$H_0: \mu = 4$

· LEARNING CHECK ·

1 A professor of philosophy hypothesizes that an introductory course in logic will help college students with their other studies. To test this hypothesis, a random sample of $n = 25$ freshmen is selected. These students are required to complete a logic course during their freshman year. At the time of graduation, the final grade point average is computed for each of these students. The mean GPA for this sample is $\overline{X} = 2.83$ with $SS = 6$. Can the professor conclude that the grades for the sample were significantly different from the rest of the graduating class, which had an average GPA of $\mu = 2.58$? Test with a two-tailed test at $\alpha = .05$.

a State the hypotheses.
b Determine the value for df and locate the critical region.
c Compute the test statistic.
d Make a decision regarding H_0.

ANSWERS

1 a $H_0: \mu_{\text{with logic course}} = 2.58$ (even with the logic course, the population mean GPA will still be 2.58)

$H_1: \mu_{\text{with logic course}} \neq 2.58$ (for the population, the logic course has an effect on GPA)

b $df = 24$; the critical region begins at t values of $+2.064$ and -2.064.
c $s = .5$; $s_{\overline{X}} = .1$; $t = +2.5$.
d Reject H_0.

10.3 ESTIMATION OF THE POPULATION MEAN

The t statistic not only can be used for hypothesis testing but also for estimating the value of a population mean. Hypothesis testing addresses the question of whether or not a treatment effect exists. Estimation asks, "How much?" Therefore, estimation is not only useful to estimate the value of μ, but may also be used to determine the approximate size of a treatment effect (estimate the value of μ *after* treatment). Applications of the estimation procedure are discussed in Chapter 9.

The estimation procedure is used when we want to determine the average value for a population of scores (the average income for women lawyers, the average IQ scores for U.S. college students, etc.) but we do not have access to the entire population to find μ. Thus, a sample is selected from the population, and the goal is to use the sample mean as the basis for estimating the population mean. In Chapter 9, we used *z*-scores to assist in this estimation. However, in instances where σ is unknown, we cannot perform estimation with *z*-scores because $\sigma_{\overline{X}}$ cannot be computed. Just as we saw with hypothesis testing, when σ is unknown, we must use the *t* statistic. Because the purpose of estimation is to find the approximate value for the population mean μ, we begin by solving the *t* statistic equation for μ. The algebra in this process is as follows:

$$t = \frac{\overline{X} - \mu}{s_{\overline{X}}}$$

$$ts_{\overline{X}} = \overline{X} - \mu \qquad \text{(multiply both sides of the equation by } s_{\overline{X}}\text{)}$$

$$\mu + ts_{\overline{X}} = \overline{X} \qquad \text{(add } \mu \text{ to both sides of the equation)}$$

$$\mu = \overline{X} - ts_{\overline{X}} \qquad \text{(subtract } ts_{\overline{X}} \text{ from both sides of the equation)}$$

Because *t* can have a positive or negative value in interval estimates, we can simplify the arithmetic of the formula:

$$\mu = \overline{X} \pm ts_{\overline{X}} \tag{10.4}$$

This is the basic formula for estimation using the *t* statistic. You should notice that this formula is very similar to the *z*-score formula used for estimation in Chapter 9 (page 204). Also note that either formula (using *t* or *z*) can be expressed conceptually in words as

population mean = sample mean ± some error

In the case of estimation when σ is unknown, we are using a *t* value and the *estimated* standard error rather than $\sigma_{\overline{X}}$.

PROCEDURES OF ESTIMATION USING A *t* STATISTIC

To obtain an estimate of μ using formula 10.4, we first find the value for the sample mean (from the sample data) and calculate the estimated standard error (also computed from the sample data). Next, we must obtain a value for *t*. Remember that you cannot calculate *t* because you do not know the population mean μ. However, you know that every sample has a corresponding *t* value, and this *t* value is located somewhere within the *t* distribution. Therefore, the next step is to estimate where your particular sample is located in the *t* distribution. For a point estimate you use the most likely value in the distribution, namely, $t = 0$. For an interval estimate you use a range of *t* values determined by the level of confidence you have selected (for example 95% or 99%). Because the *t* value in the formula is an estimate, the result we obtain is an estimate for the value of μ. The process of estimation using both a point estimate and an interval estimate is nearly identical to previous accounts (Chapter 9) and is demonstrated in the following example.

· EXAMPLE 10.3 ·

In this example we are simply trying to estimate the value of μ. Because no particular treatment is involved here, we are not trying to determine the size of a treatment effect.

A marketing researcher for a major U.S. jeans manufacturer would like to estimate the mean age for the population of people who buy its products. This information will be valuable in making decisions about how to spend advertising dollars. For example, should the company place more advertisements in *Seventeen* magazine or in *Cosmopolitan*? These represent publications that are directed at different age groups. It would be too costly and time consuming to record the age of every person in the population of their consumers, so a random sample is taken to estimate the value of μ. A sample of $n = 30$ people is drawn from the consumers who purchase the jeans from several major clothing outlets. The mean age of this sample is $\overline{X} = 30.5$ years, with $SS = 709$. The marketing researcher wishes to make a point estimate and to determine the 95% confidence interval for μ.

Notice that nothing is known about the population parameters. Estimation of the value for μ will be based solely on the sample data. Because σ is unknown, a t statistic will be used for the estimation. The confidence level has been selected (95%), and the sample data have been collected. Now we can turn our attention to the computational steps of estimation.

Compute s and $s_{\bar{X}}$ The population standard deviation is not known; therefore, to estimate μ, it is necessary to use the estimated standard error. To obtain $s_{\bar{X}}$, we must first compute the sample standard deviation. Using the information provided, we obtain

$$
\begin{aligned}
s &= \sqrt{\frac{SS}{n-1}} \\
&= \sqrt{\frac{709}{29}} \\
&= \sqrt{24.45} \\
&= 4.94
\end{aligned}
$$

For estimated standard error we obtain

$$
\begin{aligned}
s_{\bar{X}} &= \frac{s}{\sqrt{n}} \\
&= \frac{4.94}{\sqrt{30}} \\
&= \frac{4.94}{5.48} \\
&= .90
\end{aligned}
$$

Compute the Point Estimate The value for t that is used depends on the type of estimate being made. A single t value is used for a point estimate and an interval of values is used for the confidence interval. Just as we observed with the z-score distribution, t values are symmetrically distributed with a mean of zero. Therefore, we will use $t = 0$, the center of the distribution, as the best choice for the point estimate. Using the sample data, the estimation formula yields a point estimate of

$$
\begin{aligned}
\mu &= \bar{X} \pm ts_{\bar{X}} \\
&= 30.5 + 0(.90) \\
&= 30.5 + 0 \\
&= 30.5
\end{aligned}
$$

As noted before (Chapter 9), the sample mean is the most appropriate point estimate of the population mean.

Construct an Interval Estimate For an interval estimate of μ we construct an interval around the sample mean in which the value for μ probably falls. We now use a range of t values to define this interval. For example, there is a good chance that the sample has a t value somewhere between $t = +2$ and $t = -2$ and even a much better chance it is between $t = +4$ and $t = -4$. The level of confidence (percent confidence) will determine the t values that mark off the boundaries of this interval. However, unlike the normal z distribution, there is a family of t distributions in which the exact shape of the distribution depends on the value of degrees of freedom. Therefore, the value of df that is associated with

We do not know the actual t value associated with the $\bar{X}$ we obtained. For that information, we would need the value for μ—which we are trying to estimate. So we use values of t, just as we did with z, to define an interval around $\bar{X}$ that probably contains the value of μ.

FIGURE 10.6

The 95% confidence interval for $df = 29$ will have boundaries that range from $t = -2.045$ to $+2.045$. Because the t distribution table presents proportions in both tails of the distribution, for the 95% confidence interval you find the t values under $p = .05$ (proportions of t-scores in two tails) for $df = 29$.

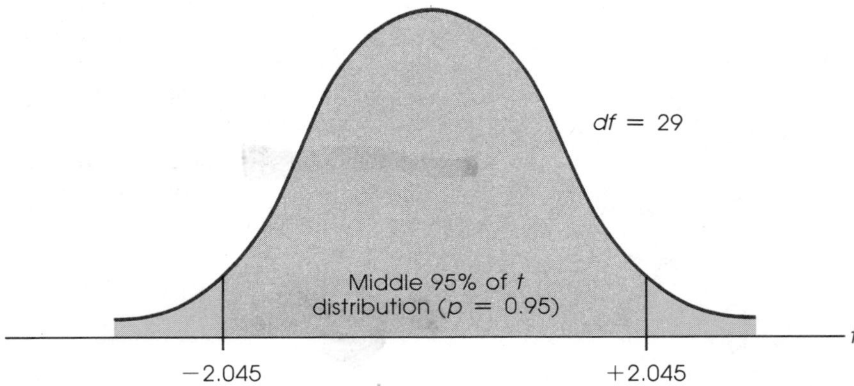

the sample is another determining factor of the t values to be used in the interval estimate. For this example,

$$df = n - 1 = 30 - 1 = 29$$

The marketing researcher selected the 95% confidence interval. Figure 10.6 depicts the t distribution for $df = 29$. To obtain the t values associated with the 95% confidence interval, we must consult the t distribution table. We look under the heading of proportions in *two tails*. If the middle 95% of the distribution is of interest to us, then both tails outside of the interval together will contain 5% of the t values. Therefore, to find the t values associated with the 95% confidence interval, we look for the entry under $p = .05$, two tails, for $df = 29$. The values of t used for the boundaries of this confidence interval are -2.045 and $+2.045$ (Figure 10.6). Using these values in the formula for μ, we obtain, for one end of the confidence interval,

$$\begin{aligned}\mu &= \overline{X} - ts_{\overline{X}}\\ &= 30.5 - 2.045(.90)\\ &= 30.5 - 1.84\\ &= 28.66\end{aligned}$$

For the other end of the interval

$$\begin{aligned}\mu &= \overline{X} + ts_{\overline{X}}\\ &= 30.5 + 2.045(.90)\\ &= 30.5 + 1.84\\ &= 32.34\end{aligned}$$

Therefore, the marketing researcher can be 95% confident that the population mean age for consumers of his product is between 28.66 and 32.34 years. The confidence level (%) determines the range of t values used in constructing the interval. As long as the obtained sample really does have a t value that falls within the estimated range of t values, the population mean will be included in the confidence interval. •

This point is demonstrated in Figure 9.5 for estimation with z-scores.

FACTORS AFFECTING THE WIDTH OF THE CONFIDENCE INTERVAL

As noted in Chapter 9, increasing the confidence level for an interval estimate will result in a larger interval width. In Example 10.3, suppose the marketing researcher had wanted to construct the 99% confidence interval instead of 95%. For the 99% confidence interval, 1% (or $p = .01$) of the distribution would fall in the two tails outside of the interval. For example 10.3, $df = 29$, and therefore the t values for the 99%

confidence interval are +2.756 and −2.756. Note that the t values are more extreme than those for the 95% confidence interval (±2.045). These larger t values will result in a wider interval (try to compute the 99% confidence interval for Example 10.3). As the confidence level gets greater, the values of t that define the boundaries of the interval get bigger. As a result, the interval is wider.

When a larger sample (n) is used, the interval tends to be smaller. All other factors being held constant, increasing n will reduce the size of the estimated standard error used in the estimation formula. Less error will result in a narrower interval width. There is another aspect of sample size to consider. As the sample size gets larger, the value of degrees of freedom ($n - 1$) gets larger. Remember that the exact shape of the t distribution depends on degrees of freedom. As df gets larger, the t values associated with the boundaries of the interval get smaller. For a 95% confidence ($p = .05$ in two tails) interval with $df = 11$, the t values are +2.201 and −2.201. However, for $df = 20$ the t values for the interval are +2.086 and −2.086. As df increases, the range of t values decreases, and the width of the confidence interval gets smaller.

· LEARNING CHECK ·

1 In the previous Learning Check (page 231), the effect of a course in logic on grade point average was examined. The statistical decision was to reject H_0, indicating there was evidence for an effect. Using the sample data in that problem, estimate how much of an effect the professor can expect. Specifically, make a point estimate and an interval estimate for the mean GPA of the population of students that take the course. Use a confidence level of 99%. Sample data: $\bar{X} = 2.83$, $SS = 6$, and $n = 25$.

2 Suppose the sample data consisted of $\bar{X} = 2.83$, $SS = 6$, and $n = 16$. Make a point estimate and construct the 99% confidence interval.

ANSWERS

1 Point estimate: $\mu = 2.83$. 99% confidence interval: μ is between 3.11 and 2.55.

2 Point estimate: $\mu = 2.83$. 99% confidence interval: $s = .63$; $s_{\bar{X}} = .16$; μ is between 3.30 and 2.36.

SUMMARY

1 When σ is unknown, the standard error cannot be computed, and a hypothesis test based on a z-score is impossible.

2 In order to test a hypothesis about μ when σ is unknown, σ must first be estimated using the sample standard deviation s:

$$s = \sqrt{\frac{SS}{n - 1}}$$

Next, the standard error is estimated by substituting s for σ in the standard error formula. The estimated standard error ($s_{\bar{X}}$) is calculated in the following manner:

$$s_{\bar{X}} = \frac{s}{\sqrt{n}}$$

Finally, a t statistic is computed using the estimated standard error. The t statistic serves as a substitute for a z-score, which cannot be computed because σ is unknown.

$$t = \frac{\bar{X} - \mu}{s_{\bar{X}}}$$

3 The structure of the t formula is similar to that of the z-score in that

$$z \text{ or } t = \frac{\text{sample mean} - \text{population mean}}{\text{(estimated) standard error}}$$

4 The t distribution is an approximation of the normal z distribution. To evaluate a t statistic that is obtained for a sample mean, the critical region must be located in a t distribution. There is a family of t distributions, with the exact shape of a particular distribution of t values depending on degrees of freedom ($n - 1$). Therefore, the critical t values will depend on the value for df associated with the t test. As df increases, the shape of the t distribution approaches a normal distribution.

5 Estimation of the value of the population mean can be performed when σ is unknown by solving the t formula for μ:

$$\mu = \bar{X} \pm t s_{\bar{X}}$$

6 For a point estimate, $t = 0$ is the best value to use in the estimation formula. The result is that the sample mean $\bar{X}$ is the best point estimate for μ.

7 For confidence intervals, a range of t values is used in the estimate. The t values that form the boundaries of the interval are determined by the selected level (percent) of confidence and the number of degrees of freedom asssociated with the sample.

8 Increasing the level of confidence results in an increase in the width of the confidence interval. Increasing sample size (n) or the df associated with the sample decreases the interval width.

KEY TERMS

t statistic

estimated standard error

degrees of freedom

t distribution

FOCUS ON PROBLEM SOLVING

1. The first problem we confront in analyzing data is determining the appropriate statistical test. Remember, you can use a z-score for the test statistic only when the value for σ is known. If the value for σ is not provided, then you must use the t statistic.

2. For a t test, students sometimes use the unit normal table to locate the critical region. This, of course, is a mistake. The critical region for a t test is obtained by consulting the t distribution table. Notice that to use this table you first must compute the value for degrees of freedom (df).

3. For the t test, the sample standard deviation is used to find the value for estimated standard error. Remember, when computing the sample standard deviation use $n - 1$ in the denominator (see Chapter 4). When computing estimated standard error, use $\sqrt{n}$ in the denominator.

4. When constructing a confidence interval after a hypothesis test, students are sometimes tempted to use the t value obtained in the hypothesis test for the interval estimate formula. This is not correct. The t values for the interval estimate are determined by the level (%) of confidence that has been selected.

PROBLEMS

*1 For the following studies, state which statistical procedure should be used: estimation or hypothesis testing.

a At a large university, the GPA for all students enrolled in the past four years is $\mu = 2.45$. A professor would like to determine if students who take a course overload have GPAs that differ significantly from the general student population. The professor collects data (GPAs) from a sample of students taking more than 15 credit hours per semester.

b A marketing researcher is interested in knowing the average income for the population of people who subscribe to *Newsweek* magazine. To answer this question, a sample of subscribers is selected. They are contacted by telephone and asked to report how much they earn per year.

c On a particular reaction time task, it is known that people can respond to a stimulus in $\mu = 300$ milliseconds. A researcher would like to determine the effect of a drug on reaction time. A sample of subjects receives the drug and reaction times are recorded for each person.

2 When a t statistic is used, why is it necessary to estimate the standard error?

*3 Why is the t statistic more versatile for inferential statistics then the z-score?

4 What assumptions (or set of conditions) must be satisfied for a t test to be valid?

5 Why is a t distribution generally more variable than a normal distribution?

*6 What is the relationship between the value for degrees of freedom and the shape of the t distribution? What happens to the critical value of t for a particular alpha level when df increases in value?

7 What factors affect the width of the confidence interval? How is the width affected by each of these factors?

*8 A distribution is known to be normal with $\mu = 50$ and $\sigma = 12$. A researcher would like to evaluate the effect of a particular treatment on this population. A sample of $n = 4$ individuals is selected, and the treatment is administered. After treatment, this sample yielded an average score of $\overline{X} = 64$ with $SS = 300$.

a Because σ is known, you can use a z-score hypothesis test. Also you could ignore the fact that σ is known and just use the sample data to compute a t statistic. Which of these two tests do you think is more likely to produce a correct decision? Explain your answer.

b Do the z-score test with $\alpha = .05$.

c Do the t statistic test with $\alpha = .05$.

(Note that the same data can lead to different conclusions depending on which test you use.)

9 For a standard set of discrimination problems that have been used for years in primate research, it is known that monkeys require an average of $\mu = 20$ trials before they can successfully reach the criterion (five consecutive correct solutions). A psychologist hypothesizes that the animals can learn the task vicariously—that is, simply by watching other animals perform the task. To test this hypothesis, the researcher selects a random sample of $n = 4$ monkeys. These animals are placed in neighboring enclosures from which they can watch another animal learn the task. After a week of viewing other animals, the four monkeys in the sample are tested on the problem. These animals require an average of $\overline{X} = 15$ trials to solve the problem, with $SS = 300$. On the basis of these data, can the psychologist conclude that there is evidence that the animals perform significantly better after viewing others. Use a one-tailed test at the .01 level of significance

a State the hypotheses using symbols. Explain what they predict for this experiment.

b Sketch the distribution and locate the critical region.

c Calculate the test statistic.

d Make a decision regarding H_0 and state your conclusion.

*10 A group of students recently complained that all of the statistics classes are offered early in the morning. They claim that they "think better" later in the day and therefore would do better in the course had it been offered in the afternoon. To test this claim, the instructor scheduled the course this past semester for 3 p.m. The afternoon class was given the same final exam that has been used in previous semesters. The instructor knows that for previous students the scores are normally distributed with a mean of 70. The afternoon class with 16 students had an average score on the final of $\overline{X} = 76$ with $SS = 960$. Do the students perform significantly better in the afternoon section?

a Test with alpha set at .05 and with a one-tailed test.

b Identify the independent and dependent variables.

11 A psychologist has developed a new personality questionnaire for measuring self-esteem and would like to estimate the population parameters for the test scores. The questionnaire is administered to a sample of $n = 25$ subjects. This sample has an average score of $\overline{X} = 43$ with $SS = 2400$.

a Provide an unbiased estimate for the population standard deviation.

b Make a point estimate for the population mean.

c Make an interval estimate of μ so that you are 90% confident that the value for μ is in your interval.

*12 A toy manufacturer asks a developmental psychologist to test children's responses to a new product. Specifically, the manufacturer wants to know how long, on average, the toy captures children's attention. The psychologist tests a sample of $n = 9$ children and measures how long they play with the toy before they get bored. This sample had a mean of $\overline{X} = 31$ minutes with $SS = 648$.

a Make a point estimate for μ.

b Make an interval estimate for μ using a confidence level of 95%.

13 A recent national survey reports that the general population gives the president an average rating of $\mu = 62$ on a scale of 1 to 100. A researcher suspects that college students are likely to be more critical of the president than people in the general population. To test these suspicions, a random sample of college students is selected and asked to rate the president. The data for this sample are as follows: 44, 52, 24, 45, 39, 57, 20, 38, 78, 74, 61, 56, 49, 66, 53, 49, 47, 88, 38, 51, 65, 47, 35, 59, 23, 41, 50, 19.

a On the basis of this sample, can the researcher conclude that college students rate the president differently? Test at the .01 level of significance, two tails.

b Use these data to estimate the average rating for the population of college students. In addition to a point estimate, determine the 95% confidence interval for μ.

*14 A fund raiser for a charitable organization has set a goal of averaging $20 per donation. To see if the goal is being met, a random sample of recent donations is selected. The data from this sample are as follows: 20, 5, 10, 15, 25, 5, 8, 10, 30, 10, 15, 24, 50, 10, 7, 15, 10, 5, 5, 15.

a Do the contributions differ significantly from the goal of the fund raiser? Test at the .05 level of significance.

b Would you reach the same conclusion had the .01 level of significance been used?

15 A random sample of $n = 11$ scores is selected from a population with unknown parameters. The scores in the sample are as follows: 12, 5, 9, 9, 10, 14, 7, 10, 14, 13, 8.

a Provide an unbiased estimate of the population standard deviation.

b Use the sample data to make a point estimate for μ and to construct the 95% confidence interval for μ.

*16 A researcher would like to examine the effect of labor unions on the average pay of workers. The investigator obtains information from the National Carpenters Union, which states that the average pay for union carpenters is $\mu = \$7.80$ per hour. The researcher then obtains a random sample of eight carpenters who do not belong to a union and records the pay for each. The data from this sample are as follows: 6.25, 7.50, 6.75, 6.90, 7.10, 7.15, 8.00, 6.15.

a Does the average pay of nonunion carpenters differ significantly from union members? Test at the .01 level of significance.

b Make a point estimate and an interval estimate at the 95% confidence level for the population average pay of nonunion carpenters.

17 After many studies of memory, a psychologist has determined that when a standard list of 40 words is presented at a rate of 2 words per second, college students can recall an average of $\mu = 17.5$ words from the list. The psychologist would like to determine if the rate of presentation affects memory. A random sample of $n = 15$ students is selected, and each is given the standard list of words at a rate of only 1 word per second. At the end of the presentation of the list, each student is tested for recall. The number of words recalled is as follows: 14, 21, 23, 19, 17, 20, 24, 16, 27, 17, 20, 21, 18, 20, 19.

a Is there evidence for an effect of presentation rate? Test at the .05 level of significance and with two tails.

b Would you arrive at the same conclusion had the .01 level of significance been used?

c Find the 99% confidence interval for μ with the 1-word-per-second presentation rate.

***18** A researcher knows that the average weight of American men between the ages of 30 and 50 is $\mu = 166$ pounds. The researcher would like to determine if men who have heart attacks between those ages are heavier than the average male. For a random sample of heart patients, body weights are recorded. The data are as follows: 153, 176, 201, 188, 157, 182, 208, 186, 163, 187, 230, 196, 167, 193, 171, 198, 191, 193, 233, 197, 196.

a Are these patients significantly heavier than expected? Use a one-tailed test at the .01 level of significance.

b Make an interval estimate of the population mean weight for this class of patient using the 99% level of confidence.

19 A psychologist assesses the effect of distraction on time perception. Subjects are asked to judge the length of time between signals given by the experimenter. The actual interval of time is 10 minutes. During this period, the subjects are distracted by noises, conversation between the experimenter and his assistant, and questions from the assistant. The experimenter expects that the subjects' judgments will average around 10 minutes if the distraction has no effect. The data are as follows:

11	9.5	14	8
8	14	15	15
12	7.5	15	18
15	12	11	10
20	10	9	14

Is there a significant effect? Test at the .05 level of significance. What conclusion can be made?

***20** A researcher would like to determine whether humidity can have an effect on eating behavior. It is known that under regular circumstances laboratory rats eat an average of $\mu =$ 10 grams of food each day. The researcher selects a random sample of $n = 15$ rats and places them in a controlled atmosphere room where the relative humidity is maintained at 90%. The daily food consumption for each of these rats is as follows:

Food Consumption				
9.1	8.3	7.6	10.2	8.4
6.9	9.3	10.7	11.2	9.8
8.5	12.1	8.4	7.7	9.2

On the basis of these data, can the researcher conclude that humidity affects eating behavior? Test with $\alpha = .05$?

21 A manufacturer of office furniture is designing a new computer table. Although it is known that the standard height for typing tables is 26 inches, the manufacturer is concerned that the best height for a computer might be different. A sample of $n = 18$ computer operators is obtained, and each is asked to position the height of an adjustable table at its most comfortable level. The heights for this sample are as follows:

Heights (Inches)		
27.50	26.25	25.75
29.50	26.50	29.00
27.25	26.00	28.25
26.25	28.00	26.25
26.75	27.00	27.50
28.00	26.25	25.75

a On the basis of this sample, should the company conclude that the best height for a computer table is different from 26 inches? Test with $\alpha = .05$.

b Use these data to estimate the average "best height" for the general population. Make a point estimate and a 90% confidence interval estimate.

***22** Recently the college newspaper conducted a survey to assess student attitudes toward spending student government money to help support college athletic teams. Student responses were recorded on a scale from 0 (totally opposed) to 10 (completely in favor). A value of 5 on this scale represented a neutral point. The results from $n = 327$ students gave an average opinion score of $\overline{X} = 6.3$ with $SS = 1343$. Do these data indicate that the general student opinion is significantly different from neutral. Test with $\alpha = .01$.

23 A vocabulary skills test designed for 6-year-old children has been standardized to produce a mean score of $\mu = 50$. A researcher would like to use this test in an experiment with 5-year-old children. Before beginning the experiment, however, the researcher would like some indication of how well 5-year-olds can perform on this test. Therefore, a sample of

$n = 21$ 5-year-old children is given the test. The data for this sample are as follows:

Vocabulary Test Scores						
42	56	49	37	43	46	47
48	57	39	40	51	49	50
36	45	52	47	49	40	53

a Use the data to make a point estimate of the population mean for 5-year-old children.

b Make an interval estimate of the mean so that you are 95% confident that the true mean is in your interval.

c On the basis of your confidence interval, can the researcher be 95% confident that the population mean for 5-year-olds is lower than the mean for 6-year-olds?

***24** For several years the members of the faculty in the Department of Psychology have been teaching small sections of the introductory statistics course because they believe that students learn better in small classes. For these small classes, the average score on the standardized final exam is $\mu = 73.5$. This year, for the first time, the department offered one large section. For the 81 students in this large class, the scores on the final exam averaged $\overline{X} = 71.2$ with $SS = 9647$. The psychologist would like to use these data to determine whether there is any difference between students' performance in large versus small classes. Perform the appropriate test with $\alpha = .05$.

25 A curious student would like to know the average number of books owned by college professors. A random sample of 12 professors is selected, and the student counts the number of books owned by each professor. The data obtained by the student are as follows:

346, 134, 208, 640, 276, 318
211, 453, 152, 281, 109, 334

a Use these sample data to make a point estimate of the population mean.

b Use the data to make an interval estimate of the population mean so that you are 95% confident that the mean is in your interval.

c Based on these data, the 80% confidence interval for the population mean extends from 229.87 to 347.13. Does this mean that 80% of all college professors own between 229.87 and 347.13 books? Explain your answer.

CHAPTER 11

STATISTICAL INFERENCE WITH TWO INDEPENDENT SAMPLES

TOOLS YOU WILL NEED

The following items are considered essential background material for this chapter. If you doubt your knowledge of any of these items, you should review the appropriate chapter or section before proceeding.

- Sample variance (Chapter 4)
- The *t* statistic (Chapter 10)
    - Distribution of *t* values
    - *df* for the *t* statistic
    - Estimated standard error

PREVIEW

In a classic study in the area of problem solving, Katona (1940) compared the effectiveness of two methods of instruction. One group of subjects was shown the exact, step-by-step procedure for solving a problem, and then these subjects were required to memorize the solution. This method was called *learning by memorization* (later called the *expository* method). Subjects in a second group were encouraged to study the problem and find the solution on their own. Although these subjects were given helpful hints and clues, the exact solution was never explained. This method was called *learning by understanding* (later called the *discovery* method).

Katona's experiment included the problem shown in Figure 11.1. This figure shows a pattern of five squares made of matchsticks. The problem is to change the pattern into exactly four squares by moving only three matches. (All matches must be used, none can be removed, and all the squares must be the same size.) Two groups of subjects learned the solution to this problem. One group learned by understanding, and the other group learned by memorization. After 3 weeks both groups returned to be tested again. The two groups did equally well on the matchstick problem they had learned earlier. But when they were given two new problems (similar to the matchstick problem), the *understanding* group performed much better than the *memorization* group.

The outcome of Katona's experiment probably is no surprise. However, you should realize that the experimental design is different from any we have considered before. This experiment involved *two separate samples*. Previously we have examined statistical techniques for evaluating the data from only one sample. In this chapter we will present the statistical procedures that allow a researcher to use two samples to evaluate the difference between two experimental treatment conditions.

Incidentally, if you still haven't discovered the solution to the matchstick problem, keep trying. According to Katona's results, it would be very poor teaching strategy for us to give you the answer.

11.1 INTRODUCTION

Until this point, all the inferential statistics we have considered have involved using one sample as the basis for drawing conclusions about one population. Although these *single-sample* techniques are used occasionally in real research, most of the interesting experiments require two (or more) sets of data in order to compare two (or more) populations. For example, a social psychologist may want to compare men and women in terms of their attitudes toward abortion, or an educational psychologist may want to compare two methods for teaching mathematics. In both of these examples, the basic question concerns a mean difference between two populations or between two

FIGURE 11.1

A pattern of five squares made of matchsticks. The problem is to change the pattern into exactly four squares by moving only three matchsticks.

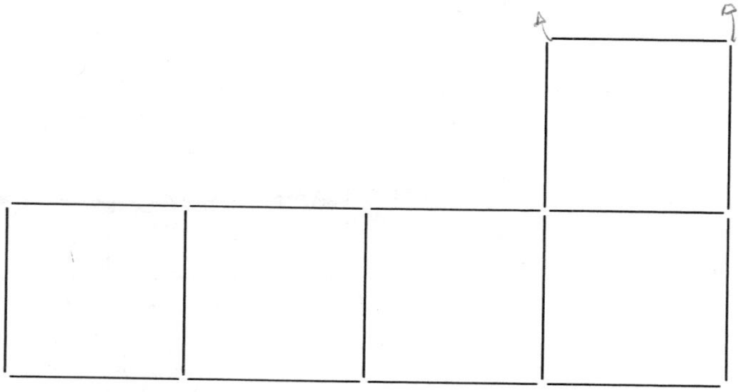

Katona, G. (1940) *Organizing and Memorizing*. New York: Columbia University Press. Reprinted by permission.

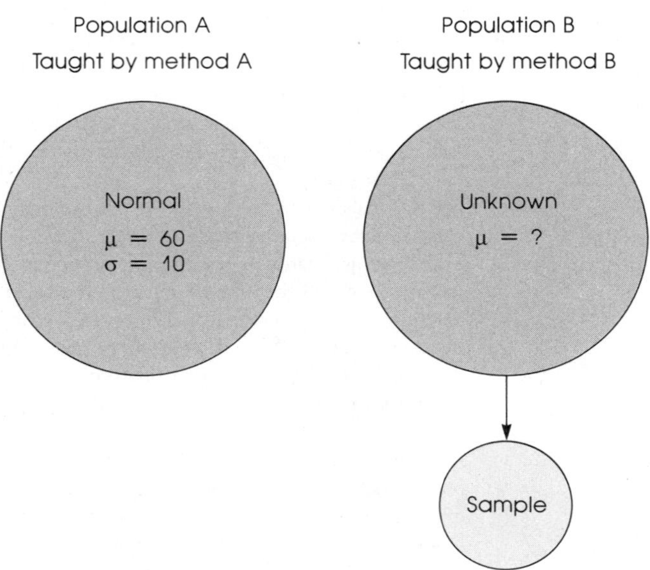

· FIGURE 11.2 ·

Do the achievement scores for children taught by method A differ from the scores for children taught by method B? In statistical terms, is the mean for population A different from the mean for population B? If you already know that the mean for population A is $\mu = 60$, then the only question is whether or not the mean for population B also is equal to 60. This is a question about one population, so you would need only one sample.

treatments. Is the average attitude for men any different from the average attitude for women? Do children who are taught math by method A score higher than children who are taught by method B?

To answer these questions with the single-sample techniques, it is necessary that we know in advance the population parameters for one of the two distributions. For example, we might know that students taught by method A have math-achievement scores that form a normal distribution with $\mu = 60$ and $\sigma = 10$. When one of the two populations is known, the problem simplifies to a question about only one unknown population. To find out about one population, you need only one sample. (See Figure 11.2.)

In most situations, it is not reasonable to expect a researcher to have prior knowledge about either of the two populations being compared. In this case, the researcher has a question about two unknown populations. To find out about two separate populations, it will be necessary to take two separate samples. (See Figure 11.3.)

The remainder of this chapter will present the statistical techniques that permit a researcher to examine the data obtained from two separate samples. More specifically, our goal is to use the data from two samples as the basis for evaluating the mean difference between two populations.

· DEFINITION · An experiment that uses a separate sample for each treatment condition (or each population) is called an *independent-measures* experimental design.

The term *independent measures* comes from the fact that the experimental data consist of two *independent* sets of measurements, that is, two separate samples. On occasion, you will see an independent measures experiment referred to as a *between-subjects* or a *between-groups* design. This terminology reflects the fact that an independent-measures design evaluates differences between treatments by looking at differences between the groups of subjects.

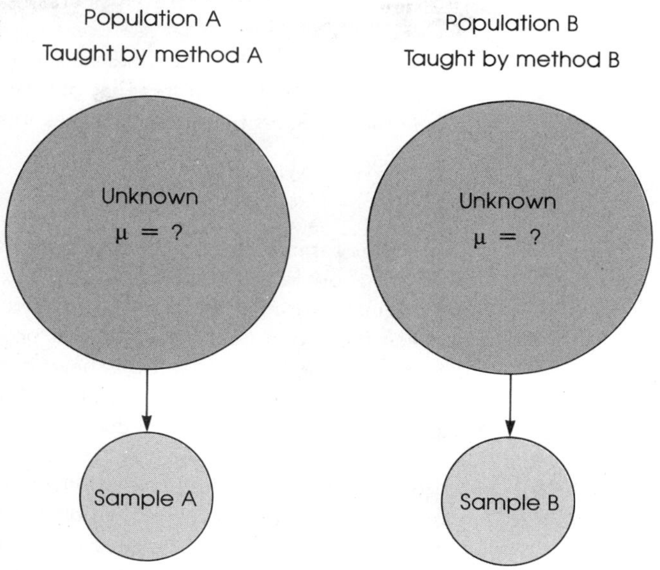

FIGURE 11.3

Do the achievement scores for children taught by method A differ from the scores for children taught by method B? In statistical terms, are the two population means the same or different? Because neither of the two population means is known, it will be necessary to take two samples, one from each population. The first sample will provide information about the mean for the first population, and the second sample will provide information about the second population mean.

11.2 THE *t* STATISTIC FOR AN INDEPENDENT-MEASURES EXPERIMENT

Because an independent-measures experiment involves two separate samples, we will need some special notation to help specify which data go with which sample. This notation involves the use of subscripts, which are small numbers written beside each sample statistic. For example, the number of scores in the first sample would be identified by n_1; for the second sample, the number of scores would be n_2. The sample means would be identified by $\overline{X}_1$ and $\overline{X}_2$. The sums of squares would be SS_1 and SS_2.

Recall that our goal is to evaluate the mean difference between two populations (or between two treatment conditions). In symbols, the mean difference between the two populations can be written as $\mu_1 - \mu_2$. For hypothesis tests we will hypothesize a value for this mean difference. Generally, the null hypothesis says there is no difference between the two population means: $\mu_1 - \mu_2 = 0$. For estimation, we will use the two samples to estimate the size of this mean difference.

The basis for either hypothesis tests or estimation will be a *t* statistic. The formula for this *t* statistic will have the same general structure as the single-sample *t* formula that was introduced in Chapter 10:

$$t = \frac{\overline{X} - \mu}{s_{\overline{X}}} = \frac{\text{sample data} - \text{population parameter}}{\text{estimated standard error}}$$

However, the details of the formula must be modified to accommodate the independent measures experimental design. Now the population parameter of interest is the difference between the two population means $(\mu_1 - \mu_2)$. The corresponding sample data would be the difference between the two sample means $(\overline{X}_1 - \overline{X}_2)$. The standard error in the denominator of the formula measures the standard distance between the sample data $(\overline{X}_1 - \overline{X}_2)$ and the population parameter $(\mu_1 - \mu_2)$. As always, standard error tells how well a sample value is expected to approximate the corresponding population value. In this case, the standard error tells how well the sample mean difference should approximate the population mean difference. The symbol for this standard error is $s_{\bar{X}_1 - \bar{X}_2}$. The s indicates an estimated standard distance and the lowercase $\bar{X}_1 - \bar{X}_2$ simply indicates that our sample value is the difference between two sample means. Substituting these values into the general t formula gives

$$t = \frac{(\bar{X}_1 - \bar{X}_2) - (\mu_1 - \mu_2)}{s_{\bar{X}_1 - \bar{X}_2}}$$

This is the t formula that will be used with data from an independent measures experiment. You should note that this is still a t statistic; it has the same basic structure as the original t formula that was introduced in Chapter 10. However, to distinguish between these two t formulas, we will occasionally refer to the original formula as the *single-sample t statistic* and this new formula as the *independent measures t statistic.* To complete the independent measures t formula, we must define more precisely the calculations needed for the standard error $s_{\bar{X}_1 - \bar{X}_2}$.

THE STANDARD ERROR FOR A SAMPLE MEAN DIFFERENCE

In general, the purpose of standard error is to provide a measure of how accurately a sample statistic approximates the population parameter. In the independent measures t formula, the sample statistic consists of two sample means, and the population parameter consists of two population means. We expect the sample data $(\bar{X}_1 - \bar{X}_2)$ to be close to the population parameter $(\mu_1 - \mu_2)$, but there will be some error. Our goal is to determine how much error. To develop the formula for this standard error, we will consider two points:

1. First, we know that each of the two sample means provides an estimate of its own population mean:

$\bar{X}_1$ approximates μ_1 with some error.

$\bar{X}_2$ approximates μ_2 with some error.

The amount of error from each sample is defined by the standard error of $\bar{X}$,

See Equation (10.1).

$$s_{\bar{X}} = \frac{s}{\sqrt{n}}$$

which measures how accurately a sample mean approximates the population mean.

2. We want to know the total amount of error involved in using two sample means to approximate two population means. To do this, we will find the error from each sample separately and then add the two errors together.

As noted in point 1, the standard error between $\bar{X}$ and μ is specified by

$$s_{\bar{X}} = \frac{s}{\sqrt{n}}$$

Before we continue, we will change the appearance of this standard error formula. To accomplish this change, we first will square the standard error:

$$s_{\bar{X}}^2 = \frac{s^2}{n}$$

Then we take the square root of this squared value:

$$s_{\bar{X}} = \sqrt{\frac{s^2}{n}}$$

PERSPECTIVE 11.1

THE VARIABILITY OF DIFFERENCE SCORES

It may seem odd that the independent measures t statistic *adds* together the two sample errors when it *subtracts* to find the difference between the two sample means. The logic behind this apparently unusual procedure is demonstrated here.

We begin with two populations, I and II (see Figure 11.4). The scores in population I range from a high of 70 to a low of 50. The scores in population II range from 30 to 20. We will use the range as a measure of how spread out (variable) each population is:

FIGURE 11.4

Two population distributions. The scores in population I vary from 50 to 70 (a 20-point spread), and the scores in population II range from 20 to 30 (a 10-point spread). If you select one score from each of these two populations, the closest two values would be $X_1 = 50$ and $X_2 = 30$. The two values that are farthest apart would be $X_1 = 70$ and $X_2 = 20$.

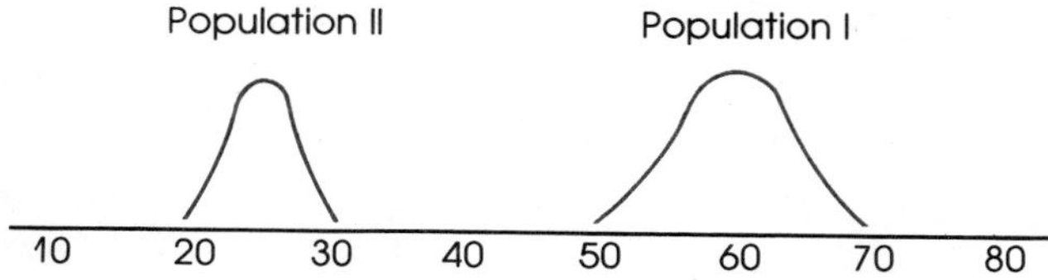

For population I, the scores cover a range of 20 points.

For population II, the scores cover a range of 10 points.

If we randomly select a score from population I and a score from population II and compute the difference between these two scores ($X_1 - X_2$), what range of values is possible for these differences? To answer this question, we need to find the biggest possible difference and the smallest possible difference. Look at Figure 11.4; the biggest difference occurs when $X_1 = 70$ and $X_2 = 20$. This is a difference of $X_1 - X_2 = 50$ points. The smallest difference occurs when $X_1 = 50$ and $X_2 = 30$. This is a difference of $X_1 - X_2 = 20$ points. Notice that the differences go from a high of 50 to a low of 20. This is a range of 30 points:

range for population I (X_1 scores) $= 20$ points
range for population II (X_2 scores) $= 10$ points
range for the differences ($X_1 - X_2$) $= 30$ points

The variability for the difference scores is found by *adding* together the variabilities for the two populations.

In the independent measures t statistic we are computing the variability (standard error) for a sample mean difference. To compute this value, we add together the variability for each of the two sample means.

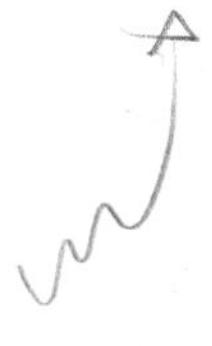

Note that by squaring and then taking the square root, we are right back where we started from. The value of the standard error is the same, but the appearance of the formula has changed. The reason for constructing this new appearance is that it helps to introduce the standard error for the independent-measures t statistic. Because we now have two sample means approximating two population means, we now have two sources of error. The formula for this independent-measures standard error is

$$s_{\bar{X}_1 - \bar{X}_2} = \sqrt{\frac{s^2}{n_1} + \frac{s^2}{n_2}}$$

Note that this standard error simply adds together the error from the first sample mean and the error from the second sample mean. (See Perspective 11.1.)

Before we continue, let's pause to compare the formula for the single-sample t statistic with the formula for the new independent measures t statistic. For the single-sample case,

$$t = \frac{\bar{X} - \mu}{s_{\bar{X}}} = \frac{\bar{X} - \mu}{s/\sqrt{n}} = \frac{\bar{X} - \mu}{\sqrt{s^2/n}}$$

For the independent measures case,

$$t = \frac{(\bar{X}_1 - \bar{X}_2) - (\mu_1 - \mu_2)}{\sqrt{\frac{s^2}{n_1} + \frac{s^2}{n_2}}}$$

The relationship between the two formulas should be obvious. The single-sample formula has one sample mean, one population mean, and one standard error. The independent measures formula simply doubles everything; there are two sample means, two population means, and two sources of error.

POOLED VARIANCE One more detail must be addressed in order to complete the *t* formula. You should recall that the original *t* statistic was developed to be used in situations where the population variability is unknown. The general strategy of the *t* statistic is to use the sample data to compute an estimate of the variability in the population. With an independent measures experiment, we have two samples which are combined to obtain a single estimate of population variance. The result is called the *pooled variance* because it is obtained by averaging or "pooling" the two sample variances. To compute this pooled variance, we will find the average of the two sample variances, but we will allow the bigger sample to carry more weight in determining the average. This process is demonstrated in the following example.

· EXAMPLE 11.1 · Suppose we have two samples from the same population. The first sample has $n = 4$ scores and $SS = 36$. For the second sample, $n = 8$ and $SS = 56$. From these data, we can compute a variance for each sample.

For sample 1,

$$s^2 = \frac{SS}{n - 1} = \frac{36}{3} = 12$$

For sample 2,

$$s^2 = \frac{SS}{n - 1} = \frac{56}{7} = 8$$

Because these two samples are from the same population, each of the sample variances provides an estimate of the same population variance. Therefore, it is reasonable somehow to average these two estimates together in order to get a better estimate. Before we average the two variances, however, you should notice that one of the samples is much bigger than the other. Because bigger samples tend to give better estimates of the population, we would expect the sample variance based on $n = 8$ to be a better value than the variance based on $n = 4$. When we pool the two variances, we will let the "better" value carry more weight.

To compute the pooled variance, we will weight each of the sample variances by its degrees of freedom ($df = n - 1$). The degrees of freedom indicate how well the sample variance approximates the population variance (the bigger the sample, the bigger the *df*, and the better the estimate). To find the pooled variance, or the weighted mean for two sample variances, you follow two steps:

1. Multiply each s^2 by its *df* and then add the results together (this weights each variance).
2. Divide this total by the sum of the two *df* values.

The equation for this process is

$$\text{pooled variance} = s_p^2 = \frac{df_1 s_1^2 + df_2 s_2^2}{df_1 + df_2}$$

For this example, the calculation can be described in words as follows: You take 3 of the first variance ($df = 3$) and 7 of the second variance ($df = 7$). This gives you a total of 10 variances ($df_1 + df_2 = 10$). To find the average, you must divide by

10. For this example,

$$\text{pooled variance} = \frac{3(12) + 7(8)}{3 + 7} = \frac{36 + 56}{10} = 9.2$$

Notice that the value we obtained is not halfway between the two sample variances. Rather it is closer to $s^2 = 8$ (the big sample) than it is to $s^2 = 12$ (the small sample), because the larger sample carried more weight in computing the average.

You may have noticed that the calculation of the pooled variance in Example 11.1 can be simplified greatly. In the numerator of the formula, each sample variance is multiplied by its *df*. When you do this, you always obtain *SS*:

$$df(s^2) = df\frac{SS}{df} = SS$$

Therefore, we can use *SS* in place of $df(s^2)$ in the formula. The simplified result is

$$\text{pooled variance} = s_p^2 = \frac{SS_1 + SS_2}{df_1 + df_2}$$

THE FINAL FORMULA AND DEGREES OF FREEDOM

The complete equation for the independent measures t statistic is as follows:

(11.1)
$$t = \frac{(\bar{X}_1 - \bar{X}_2) - (\mu_1 - \mu_2)}{s_{\bar{X}_1 - \bar{X}_2}} = \frac{(\bar{X}_1 - \bar{X}_2) - (\mu_1 - \mu_2)}{\sqrt{\frac{s_p^2}{n_1} + \frac{s_p^2}{n_2}}}$$

with the pooled variance s_p^2 defined as

(11.2)
$$s_p^2 = \frac{SS_1 + SS_2}{df_1 + df_2}$$

The degrees of freedom for this t statistic are determined by the *df* values for the two separate samples:

(11.3)
$$\begin{aligned} df &= df \text{ for first sample} + df \text{ for second sample} \\ &= df_1 + df_2 \end{aligned}$$

Remember, we pooled the two sample variances to compute the t statistic. Now we combine the two *df* values to obtain the overall *df* for the t statistic.

Occasionally, you will see degrees of freedom written in terms of the number of scores in each sample:

(11.4)
$$\begin{aligned} df &= (n_1 - 1) + (n_2 - 1) \\ &= n_1 + n_2 - 2 \end{aligned}$$

This t formula will be used for hypothesis testing and for estimation. In each case, we will use the sample data $(\bar{X}_1 - \bar{X}_2)$ as the basis for drawing inferences about the population parameter $(\mu_1 - \mu_2)$.

· LEARNING CHECK ·

1 Describe the general experimental situation in which an independent-measures statistic would be used.

2 Identify the two sources of error that are reflected in the standard error for the independent-measures t statistic.

3 Sample 1 of an experiment has dozens of subjects, and $s_1^2 = 32$. On the other hand, sample 2 has fewer than 10 subjects, and its variance is $s_2^2 = 57$. When these variances are pooled, which sample variance will s_p^2 more closely resemble?

ANSWERS

1 Independent-measures statistics are used whenever an experiment uses separate samples to represent the different treatment conditions or populations being compared.

2 The two sources of error come from the differences between the mean of both samples and their respective population means. That is, $\overline{X}_1$ approximates μ_1 with some error and $\overline{X}_2$ approximates μ_2 with some error.

3 The value for s_p^2 will be closer to $s_1^2 = 32$ because the size of sample 1 is larger.

11.3 HYPOTHESIS TESTS WITH THE INDEPENDENT-MEASURES *t* STATISTIC

The independent-measures t statistic can be used to test a hypothesis about the mean difference between two populations (or between two treatments). As always, the null hypothesis states that there is no difference:

$$H_0: \mu_1 - \mu_2 = 0$$

The alternative hypothesis says that there is a mean difference:

$$H_1: \mu_1 - \mu_2 \neq 0$$

The hypothesis test procedure will determine whether or not the data provide evidence for a mean difference between the two populations. At the conclusion of the hypothesis test, we will decide either to

a. Reject H_0: We conclude that the data indicate a significant difference between the two populations, or to

b. Fail to reject H_0: The data do not provide sufficient evidence to conclude that a difference exists.

For hypothesis tests, we will use the t formula as follows:

$$t = \frac{\text{sample data} - \text{hypothesized population parameter}}{\text{estimated standard error}}$$

Notice that we simply take the value from the null hypothesis ($\mu_1 - \mu_2 = 0$) and use it in the formula along with the data from the experiment. When the sample data are close to the hypothesis, we should get a t statistic near zero, and our decision will be to fail to reject H_0 (see Figure 11.5). On the other hand, when the data are very different from the hypothesis, we should obtain a large value for t (large positive or large negative), and we will reject H_0.

A complete example of a hypothesis test with two independent samples follows. Notice that the hypothesis testing procedure follows the same four steps that we have used before:

STEP 1 State the hypotheses H_0 and H_1 and select an alpha level. For the independent measures t test, the hypotheses concern the difference between two population means.

STEP 2 Locate the critical region. The critical region is defined as sample data that would be extremely unlikely ($p < \alpha$) if the null hypothesis were true. In this case, we will be locating extremely unlikely t values.

STEP 3 Get the data and compute the test statistic. Here we compute the t value for our data using the value from H_0 in the formula.

STEP 4 Make a decision. If the t statistic we compute is in the critical region, we reject H_0. Otherwise we conclude that the data do not provide sufficient evidence that the two populations are different.

EXAMPLE 11.2 In recent years psychologists have demonstrated repeatedly that using mental images can greatly improve memory. A hypothetical experiment, designed to examine this phenomenon, is presented here.

The psychologist first prepares a list of 40 pairs of nouns (for example, dog/bicycle, grass/door, lamp/piano). Next, two groups of subjects are obtained (two separate samples). Subjects in the first group are given the list for 5 minutes and instructed to memorize the 40 noun pairs. Subjects in the second group receive the same list of words, but in addition to the regular instructions these people are told to form a mental image for each pair of nouns (imagine a dog riding a bicycle, for example). Notice that the two samples are identical except that the second group is using mental images to help learn the list.

Remember, an independent-measures design means that there are separate samples for each treatment condition.

Later each group is given a memory test, and the psychologist records the number of words correctly recalled for each individual. The data from this experiment are as follows. On the basis of these data, can the psychologist conclude that mental images affected memory?

DATA (Number of Words Recalled)

Group 1 (No Images)		Group 2 (Images)	
24	13	18	31
23	17	19	29
16	20	23	26
17	15	29	21
19	26	30	24
$n = 10$		$n = 10$	
$\bar{X} = 19$		$\bar{X} = 25$	
$SS = 160$		$SS = 200$	

STEP 1 State the hypothesis and select α.

Directional hypotheses could be used and would specify whether imagery should increase or decrease recall scores.

$H_0: \mu_1 - \mu_2 = 0$ (no difference; imagery has no effect)

$H_1: \mu_1 - \mu_2 \neq 0$ (imagery produces a difference)

We will set $\alpha = .05$.

STEP 2 This is an independent-measures design. The t statistic for these data will have degrees of freedom determined by

$$\begin{aligned} df &= df_1 + df_2 \\ &= (n_1 - 1) + (n_2 - 1) \\ &= 9 + 9 \\ &= 18 \end{aligned}$$

The t distribution for $df = 18$ is presented in Figure 11.5. For $\alpha = .05$, the critical region consists of the extreme 5% of the distribution and has boundaries of $t = +2.101$ and $t = -2.101$.

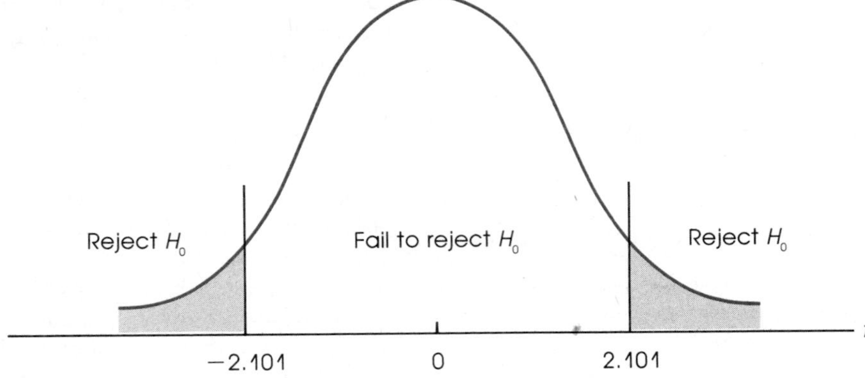

FIGURE 11.5

The t distribution with $df = 18$. The critical region for $\alpha = .05$ is shown.

STEP 3 Obtain the data and compute the test statistic. The data are as given, so all that remains is to compute the t statistic. Because the independent measures t formula is relatively complex, the calculations can be simplified by dividing the process into three parts.

Caution: The pooled variance combines the two samples to obtain a single estimate of variance. In the formula the two samples are combined in a single fraction.

First, find the pooled variance for the two samples:

$$s_p^2 = \frac{SS_1 + SS_2}{df_1 + df_2} = \frac{160 + 200}{9 + 9} = \frac{360}{18} = 20$$

Second, use the pooled variance to compute the standard error:

Caution: The standard error adds the errors from two separate samples. In the formula these two errors are added as two separate fractions.

$$s_{\bar{X}_1 - \bar{X}_2} = \sqrt{\frac{s_p^2}{n_1} + \frac{s_p^2}{n_2}} = \sqrt{\frac{20}{10} + \frac{20}{10}} = \sqrt{4} = 2$$

Third, compute the t statistic:

$$t = \frac{(\bar{X}_1 - \bar{X}_2) - (\mu_1 - \mu_2)}{s_{\bar{X}_1 - \bar{X}_2}} = \frac{(19 - 25) - 0}{2} = \frac{-6}{2} = -3.00$$

STEP 4 Make a decision. The obtained value ($t = -3.00$) is in the critical region. This result is very unlikely if H_0 is true. Therefore, we reject H_0 and conclude that using mental images produced a significant difference in memory performance. More specifically, the group using images recalled significantly more words than the group with no images.

In the scientific literature it is common to report the results of a hypothesis test in a concise, standardized format. For the test described in Example 11.2, the report would state the following: $t(18) = -3.00$; $p < .05$. This statement indicates that the t statistic has $df = 18$, the value obtained from these sample data is $t = -3.00$; and this value is in the critical region with $\alpha = .05$.

The independent-measures *t* test on the computer The independent-measures t test is a commonly used statistical analysis. For this reason, most statistical software packages have a program to run this type of analysis. The advantages of these programs become obvious when you have many subjects in each sample or when the measurements for the dependent variable produce large numbers or decimal values. We used Minitab to perform the t test for the data of Example 11.2. This is accomplished with the Minitab command TWOSAMPLE and the subcommand POOLED. The printout of this analysis, along with an explanation, is provided in Table 11.1.

TABLE 11.1

An independent-measures t test for the data in Example 11.2 performed by Minitab.

```
MINITAB RELEASE 5.1.3 *** COPYRIGHT - MINITAB, INC. 1985
U.S. FEDERAL GOVERNMENT USERS SEE HELP FGU
AUG. 28, 1987 *** S.U.N.Y. BROCKPORT - ACADEMIC COMPUTING SERVICES
STORAGE AVAILABLE 260144

 Type NEWS for information on new features in Minitab Release 5.1


MTB > READ C1 C2
     10 ROWS READ

 ROW    C1     C2

   1    24     18
   2    23     19         ——————————— 1
   3    16     23
   4    17     29
   .     .     .

MTB > TWOSAMPLE C1 C2;
SUBC>      POOLED.

TWOSAMPLE T FOR C1 VS C2                                 ——————————— 2
      N        MEAN        STDEV      SE MEAN
C1   10       19.00         4.22          1.3
C2   10       25.00         4.71          1.5

95 PCT CI FOR MU C1 - MU C2: (-10.2, -1.8)
TTEST MU C1 = MU C2 (VS NE): T =-3.00 P=0.0077 DF=18.0   ——— 3

MTB > END
MTB > STOP
*** Minitab Release 5.1.3 *** Minitab, Inc. ***
Storage available 260144  Storage used 30767
```

EXPLANATION OF PRINTOUT:

1 The data from sample 1 and sample 2 are read into columns 1 and 2 (C1 and C2), respectively. Minitab prints only a portion of these data.

2 The command TWOSAMPLE and the subcommand POOLED initiate the independent-measures t test. Descriptive statistics are provided for samples 1 and 2 (C1 and C2). This summary includes the sample size, mean, standard deviation (STDEV), and the standard error (SE MEAN) for both groups.

3 Inferential statistics are provided. These include a confidence interval estimate and the t test. For the t test, the obtained t value is given along with the df value. Note that a probability value is also printed ($p = .0077$) after the t value. This is the probability of committing a Type I error for the obtained t. As you can see, this value for this example is considerably less than the .05 level of significance that was used.

DIRECTIONAL HYPOTHESES AND ONE-TAILED TESTS

When planning an independent-measures experiment, a researcher usually has some expectation or specific prediction for the outcome. For the memory experiment described in Example 11.2, the psychologist clearly expects the group using images to have higher memory scores than the group without images. This kind of directional prediction can be incorporated into the statement of the hypotheses, resulting in a directional, or one-tailed, test. You should recall from Chapter 9 that one-tailed tests are used only in limited situations, where a researcher wants to increase the chances of finding a significant difference. In general, a nondirectional (two-tailed) test is preferred, even in research situations where there is a definite directional prediction. The following example demonstrates the procedure for stating hypotheses and locating the critical region for a one-tailed test using the independent-measures t statistic.

EXAMPLE 11.3 We will use the same experimental situation that was described in Example 11.2. The researcher is using an independent-measures design to examine the effect of mental images on memory. The prediction is that the imagery group will have higher memory scores.

STEP 1 State the hypotheses and select α. As always, the null hypothesis says that there is no effect, and H_1 says that there is a difference between the treatments. With a one-tailed test, it usually is easier to begin with the statement of H_1.

For this example, we will identify the no-imagery condition as treatment 1 and the imagery condition as treatment 2. Because images are expected to produce higher scores, the alternative hypothesis would be

$$H_1: \mu_1 - \mu_2 < 0 \qquad \text{(imagery produces higher scores)}$$

The null hypothesis states that the treatment does not work. For this example,

$$H_0: \mu_1 - \mu_2 \geqslant 0 \qquad \text{(imagery scores are not higher)}$$

We will set $\alpha = .05$.

STEP 2 Locate the critical region. The researcher predicts that the imagery group (sample 2) will have higher scores. If this is correct, then $\bar{X}_2$ will be greater than $\bar{X}_1$, and the data will produce a negative t statistic.

$$t = \frac{(\bar{X}_1 - \bar{X}_2) - (\mu_1 - \mu_2)}{s_{\bar{X}-\bar{X}}}$$

The table lists critical values without signs. You must determine whether the sign is positive or negative.

Thus, a negative value for t will tend to support the researcher's prediction and refute H_0. The question is, How large a negative t value is needed to reject H_0? With $n = 10$ scores in each sample, the data will produce an independent-measures t statistic with $df = 18$. To find the critical value, look in the t distribution table with $df = 18$ and $\alpha = .05$ for a one-tailed test. You will find a critical t value of 1.734. Figure 11.6 shows the one-tailed critical region in the t distribution. The data from this example produce a test statistic of $t = -3.00$ (see Example 11.2). This value is in the critical region, so we reject H_0 and conclude that recall is significantly better in the imagery condition than in the no-imagery condition.

THE t STATISTIC AS A RATIO

You should note that the magnitude of the t statistic is determined not only by the mean difference between the two samples but also by the sample variability. The bigger the difference between the sample means (the numerator of the t formula), the bigger the t value. This relation is reasonable because a big difference between the samples is a clear indication of a difference between the two populations. However, the sample variability (in the denominator of the t formula) is just as important. If the variability is large, t will tend to be small. The role of variability becomes clearer

FIGURE 11.6

The critical region in the t distribution for $\alpha = .05$, $df = 18$, one-tailed test.

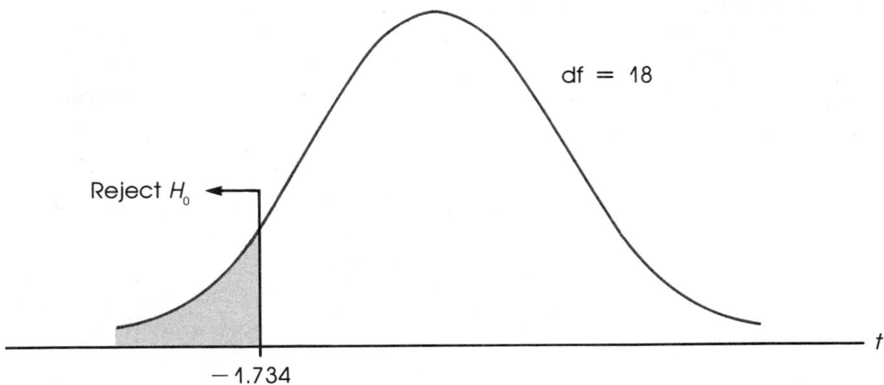

if you consider a simplified version of the t formula:

$$t = \frac{\text{sample mean difference}}{\text{variability}}$$

Notice that we have left out the population mean difference because the null hypothesis says that this is zero. Also, we have used the general term *variability* in place of standard error. In this simplified form, t becomes a ratio involving only the sample mean difference and the sample variability. It should be clear that large variability will make the t value smaller (or small variability will make t larger). The importance of sample variability is demonstrated in the following example.

EXAMPLE 11.4 The following two hypothetical experiments demonstrate the influence of variability in the computation and interpretation of an independent-measures t statistic. Each of these experiments compares attitude scores for men versus women. Both experiments use a sample of $n = 7$ individuals from each of the populations, and both experiments obtain the same sample mean values ($\overline{X} = 8$ for the men and $\overline{X} = 12$ for the women). The only difference between the two experiments is in the amount of sample variability.

The data from experiment I are pictured in Figure 11.7. In this experiment the scores in each sample are clustered around the mean, so the sample variability is relatively small. The hypothesis test using these data gives a t statistic of $t = 9.16$.

FIGURE 11.7

Data from experiment I comparing attitude scores for men versus women. The independent measures t test for these data gives a t statistic of $t = 9.16$. This value is in the critical region, so we reject H_0 and conclude that the two samples come from different populations.

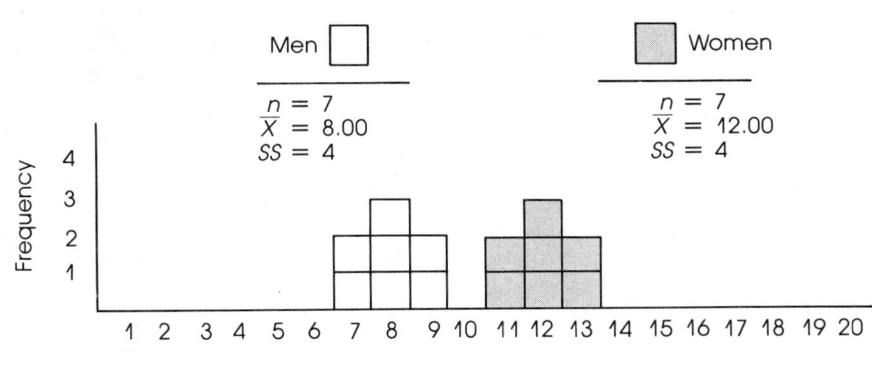

· FIGURE 11.8 ·

Data from experiment II comparing attitude scores for men versus women. The independent measures t test for these data gives a t statistic of $t = 1.18$. This value is not in the critical region, so we fail to reject H_0 and conclude that there is not sufficient evidence to say that the two samples come from different populations.

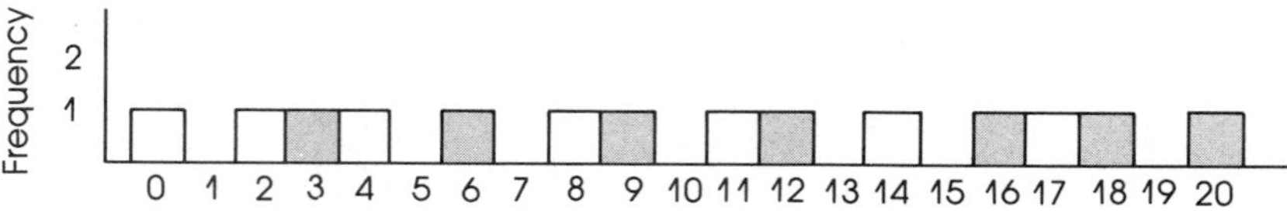

With $df = 12$, this value is in the critical region, so we would reject H_0 and conclude that the population mean for men is different from the population mean for women.

If you look at the data in Figure 11.7, the statistical decision should be easy to understand. The two samples look like they come from different populations. By visually examining a graph of the data, you often can predict the outcome of a statistical test.

Now consider the data from experiment II, which are shown in Figure 11.8. Do these two samples look like they came from two separate populations? It should be clear that it is no longer easy to see a difference between the two samples. The scores completely overlap, and it appears likely that all 14 scores could have come from the same population.

The impression that the two samples do not look different is supported by the hypothesis test. The data from experiment II give a t statistic of $t = 1.18$. This value is not in the critical region, so we fail to reject H_0. In this case, we conclude that there is not enough evidence to say that the samples come from two different populations.

There are two general points to be made from this example. First, variability plays an important role in the independent measures hypothesis test. In both experiments there was a 4-point difference between the two sample means. In experiment I this difference was easy to see, and it was statistically significant. In experiment II this 4-point difference gets lost in all the variability.

The second point is that the t statistic you obtain from a hypothesis test should be intuitively reasonable. In the first experiment, it looks like there are two separate populations, and the t statistic supports this appearance. In the second experiment, there does not appear to be any difference, and the t statistic says that there is no difference. The t value should not be a mysterious number; it simply is a precise, mathematical way of determining whether or not it "looks like" there is a difference between two samples. •

· LEARNING CHECK ·

1 A development psychologist would like to examine the difference in mathematical skills for 10-year-old boys versus 10-year-old girls. A sample of 10 boys and 10 girls is obtained, and each child is given a standardized mathematical abilities test. The data from this experiment are as follows:

Boys	Girls
$\bar{X} = 37$	$\bar{X} = 31$
$SS = 150$	$SS = 210$

Do these data indicate a significant difference in mathematical skills for boys versus girls? Test at the .05 level of significance.

2 A psychologist is interested in the effect of aging on memory. A sample of 10 college graduates is obtained. Five of these people are between 30 and 35 years old. The other 5 are between 60 and 65 years old. Each person is given a list of 40 words to memorize. A week later each person is asked to recall as many of the words as possible. The data from this experiment are as follows:

30-Year-Olds	60-Year-Olds
$\overline{X} = 21$	$\overline{X} = 16$
$SS = 130$	$SS = 190$

Do these data provide evidence for a significant change in recall ability with age? Test at the .05 level of significance.

ANSWERS

1 Pooled variance = 20; standard error = 2; $t = 3.00$. With $df = 18$, this value is in the critical region, so the decision is to reject H_0: There is a significant difference.

2 Pooled variance = 40; standard error = 4; $t = 1.25$. With $df = 8$, this value is not in the critical region, so the decision is to fail to reject H_0. These data do not provide evidence for a significant difference.

11.4 ESTIMATION

The independent-measures t statistic can be used for estimation as well as for hypothesis testing. In either case, the t statistic provides a means for using sample data to draw inferences about the difference between two population means. For the hypothesis test, the goal is to answer a yes-no question: Is there any mean difference between the two populations? For estimation, the goal is to determine *how much* difference.

Recall that the basic structure of the independent-measures t formula is the same as we observed for the initial z-score or single-sample t:

$$t = \frac{\text{sample data} - \text{population parameter}}{\text{estimated standard error}}$$

Because we are interested in finding the population parameter, we will rewrite this equation as follows:

$$\text{population parameter} = \text{sample data} \pm t(\text{estimated standard error})$$

This is the basic formula for estimation. With an independent-measures experimental design, we must solve formula 11.1 for $\mu_1 - \mu_2$. The formula we obtain for estimation is

$$\mu_1 - \mu_2 = (\overline{X}_1 - \overline{X}_2) \pm t s_{\overline{X}_1 - \overline{X}_2} \qquad (11.5)$$

In words, we are using the sample mean difference, plus or minus some error, to estimate the population mean difference. To use this equation to estimate $\mu_1 - \mu_2$ requires two steps:

1. Use the sample data to compute the sample mean difference $(\overline{X}_1 - \overline{X}_2)$ and the standard error $(s_{\overline{X}_1 - \overline{X}_2})$.

2. The sample mean difference, $\bar{X}_1 - \bar{X}_2$, is used for the estimate of $\mu_1 - \mu_2$. Because $\mu_1 - \mu_2$ is unknown, we cannot compute a t statistic. Instead, we must estimate the t value that is associated with $\bar{X}_1 - \bar{X}_2$. This is accomplished by selecting a t value that is appropriate for the type of estimate we are using. That is, we can either make a point estimate, in which case $t = 0$, or we select a level of confidence and use a range of t values for the estimate. With 90% confidence, for example, you would estimate that the t statistic for $\bar{X}_1 - \bar{X}_2$ is located somewhere in the middle 90% of the t distribution.

Remember, we are not simply choosing a t value but are estimating the location of our sample data within the t distribution.

At this point you have all the values on the right-hand side of the equation (formula 11.5), and you can compute the value for $\mu_1 - \mu_2$. If you have used a single number to estimate the location of t, you will get a single, point estimate for $\mu_1 - \mu_2$. If you have used a range of values for t, you will compute a confidence interval for $\mu_1 - \mu_2$. A complete example of this estimation procedure follows.

· EXAMPLE 11.5 · Recent studies have allowed psychologists to establish definite links between specific foods and specific brain functions. For example, lecithin (found in soybeans, eggs, liver) has been shown to increase the concentration of certain brain chemicals that help regulate memory and motor coordination. This experiment is designed to demonstrate the importance of this particular food substance.

The experiment involves two separate samples of newborn rats (an independent measures experiment). The 10 rats in the first sample are given a normal diet containing standard amounts of lecithin. The 5 rats in the other sample are fed a special diet, which contains almost no lecithin. After 6 months, each of the rats is tested on a specially designed learning problem that requires both memory and motor coordination. The purpose of the experiment is to demonstrate the deficit in performance that results from lecithin deprivation. The score for each animal is the number of errors before the learning problem was solved. The data from this experiment are as follows:

Regular Diet	No-Lecithin Diet
$n = 10$	$n = 5$
$\bar{X} = 25$	$\bar{X} = 33$
$SS = 250$	$SS = 140$

Because we fully expect that there will be a significant difference between these two treatments, we will not do the hypothesis test (although you should be able to do it). We want to use these data to obtain an estimate of the size of the difference between the two population means; that is, how much does lecithin affect learning performance? The basic equation for estimation with an independent measures experiment is

$$\mu_1 - \mu_2 = (\bar{X}_1 - \bar{X}_2) \pm t s_{\bar{X}_1 - \bar{X}_2}$$

The first step is to obtain the known values from the sample data. The sample mean difference is easy; one group averaged $\bar{X} = 25$, and the other averaged $\bar{X} = 33$, so there is an 8-point difference. Notice that it is not important whether you call this a +8 or a −8 difference. In either case the size of the difference is 8 points, and the regular diet group scored lower. Because it is easier to do arithmetic with positive numbers, we will use

$$\bar{X}_1 - \bar{X}_2 = 8$$

To find the standard error, you first must pool the two variances:

$$s_p^2 = \frac{SS_1 + SS_2}{df_1 + df_2} = \frac{250 + 140}{9 + 4}$$
$$= \frac{390}{13}$$
$$= 30$$

Next, the pooled variance is used to compute the standard error:

$$s_{\bar{X}_1 - \bar{X}_2} = \sqrt{\frac{s_p^2}{n_1} + \frac{s_p^2}{n_2}} = \sqrt{\frac{30}{10} + \frac{30}{5}} = \sqrt{3 + 6} = \sqrt{9} = 3$$

You should recall that this standard error combines the error from the first sample and the error from the second sample. Because the first sample is much larger, $n = 10$, it should have less error. This difference shows up in the formula. The larger sample contributes an error of three points, and the smaller sample contributes six points, which combine for a total error of nine points under the square root.

Sample 1 has $df = 9$, and sample 2 has $df = 4$. The t statistic has $df = 9 + 4 = 13$.

The final value needed on the right-hand side of the equation is t. The data from this experiment would produce a t statistic with $df = 13$. With 13 degrees of freedom, we can sketch the distribution of all the possible t values. This distribution is shown in Figure 11.9. The t statistic for our data is somewhere in this distribution. The problem is to estimate where. For a point estimate, the best bet is to use $t = 0$. This is the most likely value, located exactly in the middle of the distribution. To gain more confidence in the estimate, you can select a range of t values. For 80% confidence, for example, you would estimate that the t statistic is somewhere in the middle 80% of the distribution. Checking the table, you find that the middle 80% is bounded by values of $t = +1.350$ and $t = -1.350$.

Using these t values and the sample values computed earlier, we now can estimate the magnitude of the performance deficit caused by lecithin deprivation.

For a point estimate, use the single-value (point) estimate of $t = 0$:

$$\mu_1 - \mu_2 = (\bar{X}_1 - \bar{X}_2) \pm t s_{\bar{X}_1 - \bar{X}_2}$$
$$= 8 \pm 0(3)$$
$$= 8$$

FIGURE 11.9

The distribution of t values with $df = 13$. Note that t values pile up around zero and that 80% of the values are between $+1.350$ and -1.350.

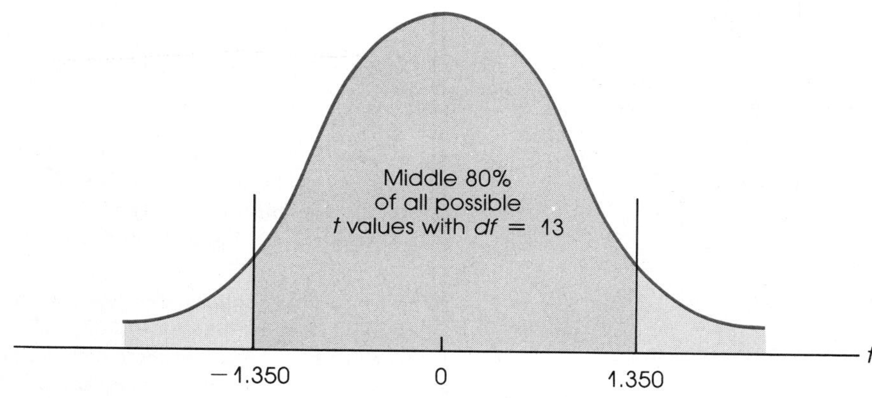

Notice that the result simply uses the sample mean difference to estimate the population mean difference. The conclusion is that lecithin deprivation produces an average of 8 more errors on the learning task. (Based on the fact that the normal animals averaged around 25 errors, an 8-point increase would mean a performance deficit of approximately 30%.)

For an interval estimate, or confidence interval, use the range of t values. With 80% confidence, at one extreme,

$$\begin{aligned}\mu_1 - \mu_2 &= (\bar{X}_1 - \bar{X}_2) + ts_{\bar{X}_1 - \bar{X}_2} \\ &= 8 + 1.350(3) \\ &= 8 + 4.05 \\ &= 12.05\end{aligned}$$

and at the other extreme,

$$\begin{aligned}\mu_1 - \mu_2 &= (\bar{X}_1 - \bar{X}_2) - ts_{\bar{X}_1 - \bar{X}_2} \\ &= 8 - 1.350(3) \\ &= 8 - 4.05 \\ &= 3.95\end{aligned}$$

This time we are concluding that the effect of lecithin deprivation is to increase errors with an average increase somewhere between 3.95 and 12.05 errors. We are 80% confident of this estimate because the only thing estimated was the location of the t statistic, and we use the middle 80% of all the possible t values.

Note that the result of the point estimate is to say that lecithin deprivation will increase errors by exactly 8. To gain confidence, you must lose precision and say that errors will increase by around 8 (for 80% confidence, we say that the average increase will be 8 ± 4.05). •

· LEARNING CHECK ·

1 In families with several children, the first-born children tend to be more reserved and serious, whereas the last-born children tend to be more outgoing and happy-go-lucky. A psychologist is using a standardized personality inventory to measure the magnitude of this difference. A sample of eight first-born and eight last-born children is obtained. Each child is given the personality test. The results of this test are as follows:

First-Born	Last-Born
$\bar{X} = 11.4$	$\bar{X} = 13.9$
$SS = 26$	$SS = 30$

a Use these sample data to make a point estimate of the population mean difference in personality for first-born versus last-born children.

b Make an interval estimate of the population mean difference so that you are 80% confident that the true mean difference is in your interval.

ANSWERS

1 **a** For a point estimate, use the sample mean difference: $\bar{X}_1 - \bar{X}_2 = 2.5$ points.

b With $df = 14$, the middle 80% of all possible t statistics is bounded by $t = +1.345$ and $t = -1.345$. For these data the pooled variance is 4, and the standard error is 1. The 80% confidence interval is 1.155 to 3.845.

11.5 ASSUMPTIONS UNDERLYING THE t FORMULA

In addition to random sampling, there are two assumptions that should be satisfied before you use the independent-measures t formula for either hypothesis testing or estimation:

1. The distribution of the sample mean differences should be normal.
2. The two populations from which the samples are selected must have the same variances.

The first assumption should be very familiar by now. In both the z-score formula and the single-sample t formula, it was necessary that the sample data come from a normal distribution. For an independent measures experiment, the sample data consist of a mean difference ($\bar{X}_1 - \bar{X}_2$), and, once again, these data should form a normal distribution. To satisfy this assumption, it is necessary that the distribution of sample means for both samples ($\bar{X}_1$ and $\bar{X}_2$) be normal. You should recall from Chapter 7 that these sampling distributions do tend to be normal. Specifically, these distributions will be normal and the assumption will be satisfied if either

a. The two populations are normal or
b. Both samples are relatively large (n around 30 or more).

In general, this assumption is satisfied easily and is not a cause for concern in most research. When there is reason to suspect that the populations are far from normal in shape, you should compensate by ensuring that samples are relatively large.

The second assumption is referred to as *homogeneity of variance* and states that the two populations being compared must have the same variance. You may recall a similar assumption for both the z-score and the single-sample t. For those tests, we assumed that the effect of the treatment was to add (or subtract) a constant amount to each individual score. As a result, the population standard deviation after treatment was the same as it had been before treatment. We now are making essentially the same assumption but phrasing it in terms of variances.

Remember, adding (or subtracting) a constant to each score does not change the standard deviation.

You should recall that the pooled variance in the t statistic formula is obtained by averaging together the two sample variances. It makes sense to average these two values only if they both are estimating the same population variance, i.e., if the homogeneity of variance assumption is satisfied. If the two sample variances represent different population variances, then the average would be meaningless. (*Note:* There is no meaning to the value obtained by averaging two unrelated numbers. For example, what is the significance of the number obtained by averaging your shoe size and the last two digits of your social security number?)

The homogeneity of variance assumption is quite important because violating this assumption can negate any meaningful interpretation of the data from an independent measures experiment. Specifically, when you compute the t statistic in a hypothesis test, all the numbers in the formula come from the data except for the population mean difference which you get from H_0. Thus, you are sure of all the numbers in the formula except for one. If you obtain an extreme result for the t statistic (a value in the critical region), you conclude that the hypothesized value was wrong. But consider what happens when you violate the homogeneity of variance assumption. In this case, you have two questionable values in the formula (the hypothesized population value and the meaningless average of the two variances). Now if you obtain an extreme t statistic, you do not know which of these two values is responsible. Specifically, you cannot reject the hypothesis because it may have been

PERSPECTIVE 11.2

HARTLEY'S *F*-MAX TEST FOR HOMOGENEITY OF VARIANCE

Although there are many different statistical methods for determining whether or not the homogeneity of variance assumption has been satisfied, Hartley's *F*-max test is one of the simplest to compute and to understand. An additional advantage is that this test can be used to check homogeneity of variance with two or more independent samples. In later chapters we will examine statistical methods involving several samples, and Hartley's test will be useful again.

The *F*-max test is based on the principle that a sample variance provides an unbiased estimate of the population variance. Therefore, if the population variances are the same, the sample variances should be very similar. The procedure for using the *F*-max test is as follows:

1. Compute the sample variance, $s^2 = SS/df$, for each of the separate samples.
2. Select the largest and the smallest of these sample variances and compute

$$F\text{-max} = \frac{s^2(\text{largest})}{s^2(\text{smallest})}$$

A relatively large value for *F*-max indicates a large difference between the sample variances. In this case, the data suggest that the population variances are different and that the homogeneity assumption has been violated. On the other hand, a small value of *F*-max (near 1.00) indicates that the sample variances are similar and that the homogeneity assumption is reasonable.

3. The *F*-max value computed for the sample data is compared with the critical value found in Table B3 (Appendix B, page 484). If the sample value is larger than the table value, then you conclude that the variances are different and that the homogeneity assumption is not valid.

To locate the critical value in the table, you need to know

a. k = number of separate samples. (For the independent measures t test, $k = 2$.)

b. $df = n - 1$ for each sample variance. The Hartley test assumes that all samples are the same size.

c. The α level. The table provides critical values for $\alpha = .05$ and $\alpha = .01$. Generally, a test for homogeneity would use the larger alpha level.

Example: Two independent samples each have $n = 10$. The sample variances are 12.34 and 9.15. For these data,

$$F\text{-max} = \frac{s^2(\text{largest})}{s^2(\text{smallest})} = \frac{12.34}{9.15} = 1.35$$

With $\alpha = .05$, $k = 2$, and $df = n - 1 = 9$, the critical value from the table is 4.03. Because the obtained *F*-max is smaller than this critical value, you conclude that the data do not provide evidence that the homogeneity of variance assumption has been violated.

the pooled variance that produced the extreme t statistic. Without satisfying the homogeneity of variance requirement, you cannot accurately interpret a t statistic, and the hypothesis test becomes meaningless.

How do you know whether or not the homogeneity of variance requirement is satisfied? There are statistical tests that can be used to determine if the two population variances are the same or different (see Perspective 11.2), but there is a simple rule of thumb that works most of the time. If the two population variances are the same, then the two sample variances should be very similar. You can just look at the two sample variances to see whether or not they are close. If one of the sample variances is more than four times larger than the other, you probably have violated the homogeneity of variance requirement. Otherwise the two population variances are close enough to proceed with the hypothesis test.

SUMMARY

1 The independent measures t statistic is used to draw inferences about the mean difference between two populations or between two treatment conditions. The term *independent* is used because this t statistic requires data from two separate (or independent) samples.

2 The formula for the independent measures t statistic has the same structure as the original z-score or the single-sample t:

$$t = \frac{\text{sample data} - \text{population parameter}}{\text{estimated standard error}}$$

For the independent measures statistic, the data consist of the difference between the two sample means ($\bar{X}_1 - \bar{X}_2$). The population parameter of interest is the difference between the two population means ($\mu_1 - \mu_2$). The standard error is computed by combining the errors for the two sample means. The resulting formula is

$$t = \frac{(\bar{X}_1 - \bar{X}_2) - (\mu_1 - \mu_2)}{s_{\bar{X}_1 - \bar{X}_2}} = \frac{(\bar{X}_1 - \bar{X}_2) - (\mu_1 - \mu_2)}{\sqrt{\frac{s_p^2}{n_1} + \frac{s_p^2}{n_2}}}$$

The pooled variance in the formula, s_p^2, is the weighted mean of the two sample variances:

$$s_p^2 = \frac{SS_1 + SS_2}{df_1 + df_2}$$

This t statistic has degrees of freedom determined by the sum of the df values for the two samples:

$$df = df_1 + df_2 = (n_1 - 1) + (n_2 - 1)$$

3 For hypothesis testing, the formula has the following structure:

$$t = \frac{\text{sample data} - \text{hypothesized population parameter}}{\text{estimated standard error}}$$

The null hypothesis normally states that there is no difference between the two population means:

$$H_0: \mu_1 = \mu_2 \quad \text{or} \quad \mu_1 - \mu_2 = 0$$

4 For estimation, the formula is solved for the value of $\mu_1 - \mu_2$:

$$\mu_1 - \mu_2 = (\bar{X}_1 - \bar{X}_2) \pm t s_{\bar{X}_1 - \bar{X}_2}$$

To use this formula, you first decide on a degree of precision and a level of confidence desired for the estimate. If your primary concern is precision, use $t = 0$ to make a point estimate of the mean difference. Otherwise you select a level of confidence (percent confidence) that determines a range of t values to be used in the formula.

5 Appropriate use and interpretation of the t statistic requires that the data satisfy the homogeneity of variance assumption. This assumption stipulates that the two populations have equal variances. An informal test of this assumption can be made by simply comparing the two sample variances: If the two sample variances are approximately equal, the t test is justified. Hartley's F-max test provides a statistical technique for determining whether or not the data satisfy the homogeneity assumption.

KEY TERMS

independent-measures experimental design

between-subjects experimental design

pooled variance

homogeneity of variance

FOCUS ON PROBLEM SOLVING

1. As you learn more about different statistical methods, one basic problem will be deciding which method is appropriate for a particular set of data. Fortunately, it is easy to identify situations where the independent-measures t statistic is used. First, the data will always consist of two separate samples (two n's, two $\bar{X}$'s, two SS's, and so on). Second, this t statistic always is used to answer questions about a mean difference: On the average, is one group different (better, faster, smarter) than the other group. If you examine the data and identify the type of question that a researcher is asking, you should be able to decide whether or not an independent-measures t is appropriate.

2. When computing an independent-measures t statistic from sample data, we suggest that you routinely divide the formula into separate stages rather than trying to do all the calculations at once. First, find the pooled variance. Second, compute the standard error. Third, compute the t statistic.

3. One of the most common errors for students involves confusing the formulas for pooled variance and standard error. When computing pooled variance, you are "pooling" the

two samples together into a single variance. This variance is computed as a *single fraction*, with two SS values in the numerator and two *df* values in the denominator. When computing the standard error, you are adding the error from the first sample and the error from the second sample. These two separate errors add as *two separate fractions* under the square root symbol.

4. When you do a hypothesis test and estimation with the same data, remember that the t value in the estimation formula is determined by the percent confidence you select. Do not use the t value obtained from the hypothesis test.

PROBLEMS

*1 For each situation described, decide whether the appropriate statistic is a single-sample t or an independent-measures t. Also, indicate whether the research question calls for estimation or a hypothesis test.

a A researcher would like to know the average weight for 6-week-old rats.

b A researcher would like to know whether there is any difference in mathematical aptitude for 6-year-old boys versus 6-year-old girls.

c A researcher would like to compare subjects in a behavior-modification program versus subjects in a control group to determine how much effect behavior modification has on the eating habits of obese people.

2 For the independent-measures t statistic, what is the goal of estimation? What is the goal of hypothesis testing?

*3 What is measured by the estimated standard error that is used for the independent-measures t statistic?

*4 Describe the "homogeneity of variance" assumption, and explain why it is important for the independent measures hypothesis test.

5 A psychologist would like to compare the amount of information that people get from television versus newspapers. A random sample of 20 people is obtained. Ten of these people agree to get all of their news information from TV (no newspapers) for 4 weeks. The other 10 people agree to get all of their news information from newspapers. At the end of 4 weeks all 20 people are given a test on current events. The average score for the TV group was $\overline{X} = 41$ with $SS = 200$. The average for the newspaper group was $\overline{X} = 49$ with $SS = 160$. On the basis of these data, can the psychologist conclude that there is a significant difference between TV news and newspapers? Test at the .05 level of significance.

6 A local politician would like to compare the political attitudes for the older people and the younger people in his district. He develops a questionnaire which measures political attitude on a scale from 0 (very conservative) to 100 (very liberal) and administers this questionnaire to a sample of 10 young voters and a sample of 10 elderly voters. The data from these two samples are as follows:

Old	Young
$\overline{X} = 39$	$\overline{X} = 52$
$SS = 4200$	$SS = 4800$

On the basis of these data, should the politician conclude that there is a significant difference between political attitudes for younger voters and older voters? Test with $\alpha = .05$.

*7 A psychologist is studying the relation between weight and hormone levels. A random sample of rats is selected, and the sample is divided into two groups of five rats each. The rats in one group are given daily injections of a "growth" hormone, and the rats in the second group are injected with a harmless salt solution. During a 2-week test period, the psychologist records the amount of weight gained by each rat. The data are as follows:

Hormone	Control
$\overline{X} = 22$	$\overline{X} = 8$
$SS = 140$	$SS = 180$

a Use these data to determine whether the hormone injections have any significant effect on weight gain. Test at the .05 level.

b Use the data to estimate how much extra weight gain the hormone produces. Make a point estimate and an interval estimate so that you are 80% confident that the true mean difference is in your interval.

*8 For the study described in Problem 7, the researcher probably anticipates that the animals getting the growth hormone will show larger weight gains. If a one-tailed test had been used instead, how would you express H_0 and H_1 using symbols? (Assume that the "hormone" group is designated as group 1 and the control group is group 2.)

*9 The following data are from two separate independent-measures experiments. Without doing any calculations, which experiment is more likely to demonstrate a significant difference between treatments A and B? Explain your answer. *Note:* You do not need to compute the t statistics; just look carefully at the data.

Experiment I		Experiment II	
Treatment A	Treatment B	Treatment A	Treatment B
$n = 10$	$n = 10$	$n = 10$	$n = 10$
$\bar{X} = 42$	$\bar{X} = 52$	$\bar{X} = 61$	$\bar{X} = 71$
$SS = 180$	$SS = 120$	$SS = 986$	$SS = 1042$

10 The two given sets of data were computer-generated from populations with predetermined parameters. Sample A was generated from a normal population with $\mu = 30$ and $\sigma = 5$. Sample B comes from a normal population with $\mu = 35$ and $\sigma = 5$.

Sample A: 28, 36, 26, 31, 27

Sample B: 38, 42, 30, 35, 29

a Use a hypothesis test to determine whether or not these two samples provide sufficient evidence to differentiate the two populations. Use $\alpha = .05$.

b What do you think would happen if we used larger samples (say $n = 100$)? First, what would happen to the two sample means? Second, what would happen to the pooled variance? Third, what would happen to the standard error for the t statistic? Finally, what outcome would you expect for the hypothesis test?

***11** A researcher selects two random samples from a population with $\mu = 60$. Sample 1 is given treatment A, and sample 2 is given treatment B. The resulting data for these two samples are as follows:

Sample 1	Sample 2
$n = 9$	$n = 9$
$\bar{X} = 58$	$\bar{X} = 62$
$SS = 72$	$SS = 72$

a Do the data from sample 1 indicate that treatment A has a significant effect? Use a single-sample t statistic with $\alpha = .05$.

b Do the data from sample 2 indicate that treatment B has significant effect? Use a single-sample t statistic with $\alpha = .05$.

c Use an independent-measure t statistic to determine whether there is a significant difference between treatment A and treatment B. Test at the .05 level of significance.

d The results from parts a and b should indicate that neither treatment has a significant effect. However, the results from the independent-measures test should show a significant difference between the two treatments. Are these results contradictory? Explain your answer.

12 In an experiment designed to examine the effect that personality can have on practical decisions, a psychologist selects a random sample of $n = 5$ people who are classified as "impulsive" and a sample of $n = 10$ people who are classified as "reflective." Each person is given a brief description of a crime and then is asked for his or her judgment of a reasonable prison sentence for the criminal. The impulsive people gave an average sentence of 14 years with $SS = 130$, and the reflective people gave an average sentence of 12.5 years with $SS = 260$. On the basis of these samples, can the psychologist conclude that there is a significant difference in the harshness of judgment for impulsive versus reflective people? Test with $\alpha = .01$.

***13** A researcher has done a series of experiments to determine whether there is any significant different between two treatments. The data from three of these experiments are as follows:

Experiment I		Experiment II		Experiment III	
A	B	A	B	A	B
$n = 5$	$n = 5$	$n = 5$	$n = 5$	$n = 5$	$n = 5$
$\bar{X} = 40$	$\bar{X} = 35$	$\bar{X} = 40$	$\bar{X} = 35$	$\bar{X} = 40$	$\bar{X} = 38$
$SS = 36$	$SS = 44$	$SS = 120$	$SS = 200$	$SS = 36$	$SS = 44$

a Use the data from each experiment to determine whether there is any significant difference between treatment A and treatment B. Test at the .05 level of significance.

b How do you explain the fact that the results of experiments I and II lead to different conclusions? Notice that the sample means are identical for these two experiments.

c How do you explain that experiments I and III lead to different conclusions? Note that the sample SS values are identical for these two experiments.

14 A local hospital is planning a fund-raising campaign to raise money for the expansion of their pediatrics ward. Part of the campaign will involve visits to local industries to present their case to employees and to solicit contributions. One factory is selected as a test site to compare two different campaign strategies. Within this factory the employees are randomly divided into two groups. The individuals in one group are presented the "hard facts" (number of people served, costs, and the like) about the hospital. The individuals in the second group receive an "emotional appeal" that describes in detail the personal histories of two children recently treated at the hospital. The average contribution for the 20 employees in the hard-facts group was \$21.50 with $SS = 970$. The average for the 20 employees in the emotional group was \$29.80 with $SS = 550$.

a On the basis of these sample data, should the hospital conclude that one strategy is significantly better than the other? Test at the .05 level of significance.

b Use Hartley's F-max test to determine whether these data satisfy the homogeneity of variance assumption.

***15** A psychologist would like to know how much difference there is between the problem-solving ability of 8-year-old children versus 10-year-old children. A random sample of 10 children is selected from each age group. The children are given a problem-solving test, and the results are summarized as follows:

8-Year-Olds	10-Year-Olds
$n = 10$	$n = 10$
$\overline{X} = 36$	$\overline{X} = 43$
$SS = 110$	$SS = 250$

a Use the sample data to make a point estimate of the mean difference between 8-year-olds' and 10-year-olds' problem-solving ability.
b Make an interval estimate of the mean difference so that you are 90% confident that the real difference is in your interval.

16 Do the data in Problem 15 satisfy the homogeneity of variance assumption? Use Hartley's *F*-max test with $\alpha = .05$.

***17** A psychologist would like to examine the effects of fatigue on mental alertness. An attention test is prepared which requires subjects to sit in front of a blank TV screen and press a response button each time a dot appears on the screen. A total of 110 dots are presented during a 90-minute period, and the psychologist records the number of errors for each subject. Two groups of subjects are selected. The first group ($n = 5$) is tested after they have been kept awake for 24 hours. The second group ($n = 10$) is tested in the morning after a full night's sleep. The data for these two samples are as follows:

Awake 24 Hours	Rested
$\overline{X} = 35$	$\overline{X} = 24$
$SS = 120$	$SS = 270$

On the basis of these data, can the psychologist conclude that fatigue significantly increases errors on an attention task? Use a one-tailed test with $\alpha = .05$.

18 A school psychologist would like to examine cheating behavior for 10-year-old children. A standardized achievement test is used. One sample of $n = 8$ children is given the test under unsupervised conditions where cheating is possible. A second sample of 8 children receives the same test under very strict supervision. The test scores for these children are summarized as follows:

Unsupervised	Supervised
$\overline{X} = 78$	$\overline{X} = 65$
$SS = 3000$	$SS = 2600$

Can the psychologist conclude that the unsupervised (cheating?) group did significantly better than the strictly supervised group? Test at the .05 level of significance.

19 A psychologist would like to measure the effects of air pollution on life expectancy. Two samples of newborn rats are selected. The first sample of 10 rats is housed in cages where the atmosphere is equivalent to the air in a severely polluted city. The second sample with $n = 20$ is placed in cages with clean air. The average life span for the first group is $\overline{X} = 478$ days with $SS = 5020$ and for the second group $\overline{X} = 511$ with $SS = 10{,}100$.
a Does pollution cause a difference in life expectancy? Test with $\alpha = .01$.
b Make a point estimate of the mean difference in life span for polluted versus clean air.
c Make an interval estimate of the mean difference so that you are 95% confident that the true difference is in your interval.

***20** A psychologist studying human memory would like to examine the process of forgetting. One group of subjects is required to memorize a list of words in the evening just before going to bed. Their recall is tested 10 hours later in the morning. Subjects in the second group memorize the same list of words in the morning, and then their memories are tested 10 hours later after being awake all day. The psychologist hypothesizes that there will be less forgetting during sleep than during a busy day. The recall scores for two samples of college students are as follows:

Asleep Scores				Awake Scores			
15	13	14	14	15	13	14	12
16	15	16	15	14	13	11	12
16	15	17	14	13	13	12	14

a Sketch a frequency distribution polygon for the "asleep" group. On the same graph (in a different color) sketch the distribution for the "awake" group. Just by looking at these two distributions, would you predict a significant difference between the two treatment conditions?
b Use the independent measures *t* statistic to determine whether there is a significant difference between the treatments. Conduct the test with $\alpha = .05$.

21 The experiment described in Problem 20 was repeated using samples of 6-year-old children. The data for this experiment are as follows:

Asleep Scores				Awake Scores			
15	13	8	10	6	8	5	8
7	10	6	9	4	7	12	9
14	11	5	12	3	10	13	11

a Again, sketch a frequency distribution polygon for each group on the same graph. Does there appear to be a significant difference between the two treatments?
b Use the independent measures *t* statistic to test for significance with $\alpha = .05$.
c Note that the data from Problem 20 and the data here show the same mean difference. Explain why the statistical analysis produces different conclusions for these two problems.

***22** An instructor would like to evaluate the effectiveness of a new programmed learning course in statistics. The class is randomly divided in half. One group gets the regular lecture series and textbook, while the other group takes the programmed course. At the end of the semester all students take the same final exam. The scores are as follows:

Regular Course Grades			Programmed Course Grades		
82	73	93	92	82	97
61	89	99	81	80	62
73	91	84	72	74	68
71	68	81	84	81	71
75	72	69	63	65	73

Use these data to determine whether there is any significant difference between the programmed course and the regular course. Test at the .05 level.

23 Although the instructor from Problem 22 found no significant difference in grades for the two different statistics courses, it is possible that the students preferred one teaching method over the other. At the end of the course, each student was given a course-evaluation questionnaire that included a question about how much he or she enjoyed the course. The responses range from 1 (not at all) to 5 (very much). The data for the two sections of students are as follows:

Regular Course				Programmed Course			
4	4	3	4	3	4	2	3
4	2	4	5	4	4	2	2
3	4	5	5	4	3	2	2
4	5	5		3	2	5	

Do these data indicate a significant preference between the two teaching methods? Test with $\alpha = .05$.

24 A researcher is interested in testing the opinions of college students concerning the value of their college education. She suspects that seniors will place more value on their education than will sophomores. A sample of 20 seniors and 20 sophomores is selected, and each subject is given an opinion questionnaire. The data for each sample are as follows:

Sophomores				Seniors			
18	21	24	21	25	19	23	22
20	19	23	26	23	21	21	18
19	24	19	28	27	18	28	21
22	17	27	18	26	25	22	16
25	22	14	17	21	29	18	20

Using a one-tailed test with $\alpha = .05$, do these data indicate that seniors have significantly higher value scores?

***25** A principal for a city high school would like to determine parents' attitudes toward a proposed sex education program. A sample of 15 families is selected, and each set of parents is requested to fill out an opinion questionnaire. Part of this questionnaire requires the parent's names and occupations. Looking over the data, the principal noticed that the opinions seemed to be a lot more favorable than had been expected. The principal suspected that the parents might have felt "forced" into stating a favorable opinion because they were required to identify themselves. They might have responded more honestly if the questionnaire had been anonymous. Therefore, a second sample of 15 families was selected, and they were requested to complete the same questionnaire without reporting their names or occupations. The data from both questionnaires are as follows:

First Questionnaire					Second Questionnaire				
60	56	54	58	63	51	50	53	48	42
61	52	49	57	58	52	57	47	49	50
65	59	42	51	67	51	43	48	53	41

Use these data to test the principal's hypothesis. Set $\alpha = .05$.

26 In a test of cognitive dissonance theory, Festinger and Carlsmith (1959) had college students participate in a really boring experiment. Later these students were asked to recruit other subjects for the same experiment by pretending that it was an interesting experience. Some of these students were paid \$20 to recruit others, and some were paid only \$1. Afterward, each student was asked to report how he or she really felt about the experiment. Hypothetical data representing these reports are as follows:

Students Paid \$1				Students Paid \$20			
3	3	4	6	1	2	5	2
5	5	5	7	3	5	4	5
8	5	4	8	2	3	4	4
2	6	4	4	1	2	3	3
6	7	5	5	5	1	1	3

Cognitive dissonance theory predicts that those paid only \$1 would come to believe that the experiment really was interesting. It must have been, or they wouldn't have worked so hard for only \$1. The students paid \$20 were working for money, not for the experiment, so they should have no reason to change their opinions. Do the preceding data support this prediction? Test for a significant difference between the two groups with $\alpha = .01$.

***27 a** Sketch a frequency distribution polygon showing the following samples. Use a different color for each set of scores.

Sample 1			Sample 2		
14	18	12	15	21	16
11	18	15	22	14	12
15	17	16	19	20	18
15	18	14	20	21	17
16	14	15	22	19	20
16	17	13	20	19	18

b By just looking at your polygon, does it appear that these two samples came from different populations or from the same population?

c Calculate the independent-measures t statistic for these data. Does the t statistic indicate that the samples came from different populations? Set $\alpha = .05$.

28 The following data came from an independent-measures experiment comparing two different treatment conditions. The score for each subject is the amount of time (measured in minutes) required to complete a set of math problems.

Treatment 1 (Sample 1)		Treatment 2 (Sample 2)	
2.5	3.2	1.8	2.1
3.4	2.9	2.0	1.6
2.4	2.6	1.9	2.3
2.5	3.0	2.2	2.5
2.7	3.1	1.8	2.1

a Use an independent-measures t statistic to determine whether or not there is a significant difference between the two treatments. Use $\alpha = .05$.

b The experimenter would like to convert each subject's score from minutes to seconds. To do this, each value must be multiplied by 60. After each value is multiplied, what will happen to the sample means? What will happen to the sample standard deviations? What do you expect will happen to the t statistic for these data?

c Multiply each of the original scores by 60 (i.e., change them from minutes to seconds). Now compute the independent measures t statistic for the new scores? How does this t statistic compare with the t statistic for the original data?

CHAPTER 12

STATISTICAL INFERENCE WITH RELATED SAMPLES

TOOLS YOU WILL NEED

The following items are considered essential background material for this chapter. If you doubt your knowledge of any of these items, you should review the appropriate chapter or section before proceeding.

- Introduction to the *t* statistic (Chapter 10)
    - Estimated standard error
    - Degrees of freedom
    - *t* distribution
    - Hypothesis tests with the *t* statistic
    - Estimation using the *t* statistic
- Independent-measures design (Chapter 11)

PREVIEW

Have you ever wondered what is going to happen to your mental faculties as you grow older? Many people, especially young people, are convinced that they face an inevitable decline in intellectual skills as they age. In fact many scientific studies show that average IQ scores peak around 20 years of age, decline gradually until about age 50, and then drop sharply (Horn, 1978).

On the other hand, there is a separate group of scientific studies that show little, if any, decline in IQ between ages 20 and 50. After age 50, these studies show some drop in performance on speed-related tasks and spatial reasoning, but other intelligence skills such as general knowledge and vocabulary appear to hold constant, even up to age 85 (Horn, 1978).

How can two sets of data be so completely different? One answer lies in a closer examination of how the data were collected. The data that show IQ declining with age are generally obtained from *cross-sectional* studies that compare separate samples representing each age group. In statistical terminology, these are *independent-measures* studies. Suppose that you went out today and obtained a sample of 20-year-old, a sample of 50-year-old, and a sample of 80-year-old individuals. Besides differing in age, your three samples are probably very different in terms of educational background, work experience, and living environment. Any of these other factors could affect IQ scores and could be the source of the IQ differences between age groups. Using statistical terminology again, these other factors are known as *confounding variables*, and they make it impossible to conclude that age alone is responsible for the IQ differences.

The second group of studies, showing stable IQ, use a different experimental methodology. Rather than comparing different samples, these studies monitor IQ scores for the same set of people over a long period of time. This type of research is often called a *longitudinal* study. In statistical terms it is referred to as a *repeated-measures* experiment because the researcher is repeatedly measuring the same individuals. The advantages of the repeated-measures experiment should be obvious. In these studies, for example, the researcher can be certain that the 20-year-olds and the 50-year-olds grew up in the same environment and have the same educational background—after all, they are the same people. Equally obvious is the fact that this kind of research can take 20 or 30 years to complete—a tremendous disadvantage.

In this chapter we will examine the statistical methods used to evaluate data from repeated-measures experiments. In addition, we will take a closer look at the differences between independent-measures and repeated-measures experiments and discuss the advantages and disadvantages of each.

12.1 INTRODUCTION TO REPEATED MEASURES

Previously we discussed inferential techniques using two separate samples to examine the mean difference between two populations. Usually, our goal was to evaluate the difference between two treatment conditions. For example, if a researcher would like to assess the effect of a new drug on depression, he or she might use two treatment conditions: a drug treatment and a no-drug treatment. With an independent-measures design (Chapter 11), one sample of patients receives the drug, and the other sample receives an ineffective placebo. Depression can be measured by the subjects' scores on a depression inventory. Differences in the severity of depression between these two samples may then be used to test the effectiveness of the new drug. This independent-measures design can be recognized by the assignment of separate, or "independent," samples of subjects for each treatment condition.

It should be obvious that there is a different experimental technique that could be used to evaluate the drug. Specifically, you could use a single sample of subjects and measure their depression scores before they receive the drug and then repeat the measurements after they have received the drug. This experimental design is called *repeated measures* because you are repeating measurements on a single sample of subjects.

· DEFINITION · A *repeated-measures* study is one in which a single sample of individuals is tested more than once on the dependent variable. The same subjects are used for every treatment condition.

The main advantage of a repeated-measures experiment is that it uses exactly the same subjects in all treatment conditions. Thus, there is no risk that the subjects in one treatment are substantially different from the subjects in another. With an independent-measures design, on the other hand, there is always a risk that the results are biased by the fact that one sample was much different (smarter, faster, more extroverted, and so on) than the other.

Occasionally, researchers will try to approximate the advantages of a repeated-measures experiment by using a technique known as *matched subjects*. For example, suppose a researcher is testing the effectiveness of a special reading program. One sample of fourth graders takes the reading course, and a second sample serves as the control group. The researcher plans to compare these two groups in terms of reading comprehension. However, the researcher is concerned that there might be differences in intelligence between the two samples, which could confound the results. Therefore, the researcher matches the subjects in terms of IQ. That is, if a person assigned to the control group has an IQ of 120, the researcher assigns another individual with the same IQ to the treatment group (see Table 12.1). The result is called a *matched-subjects* experiment.

· DEFINITION · In a *matched-subjects* experiment, each individual in one sample is matched with a subject in the other sample. The matching is done so that the two individuals are equivalent (or nearly equivalent) with respect to a specific variable that the researcher would like to control.

In a repeated-measures, or a matched-subjects, design all the subjects in one treatment are directly related, one-to-one, with the subjects in another treatment. For this reason, these two experimental designs are often called *related-samples* experiments (or correlated-samples experiments). In this chapter we will focus our discussion on repeated-measures experiments because they are overwhelmingly the more common example of related-groups designs. However, you should realize that the statistical techniques used for repeated-measures experiments can be applied directly to data from a matched-subjects experiment.

A matched-subjects experiment occasionally is called a *matched-samples design*. But the subjects in the samples must be matched one-to-one before you can use the statistical techniques in this chapter.

Now we will examine the statistical techniques that allow a researcher to use the sample data from a repeated-measures experiment to draw inferences about the general population.

· TABLE 12.1 ·

Group assignment of subjects matched for IQ

Control		Reading Program	
Subject	IQ	Subject	IQ
A	120	E	120
B	105	F	105
C	110	G	110
D	95	H	95

TABLE 12.2

Scores on a depression inventory before and after

Person	Before Treatment, X_1	After Treatment, X_2	D
A	72	64	−8
B	68	60	−8
C	60	50	−10
D	71	66	−5
E	55	56	+1
			$\sum D = -30$

$$\bar{D} = \frac{\sum D}{n} = \frac{-30}{5} = -6$$

DIFFERENCE SCORES Table 12.2 presents hypothetical data for a drug evaluation study. The first score for each person (X_1) is the score obtained on the depression inventory before the drug treatment. The second score (X_2) was obtained after the drug treatment. Because we are interested in how much change occurs as a result of the treatment, each person's scores are summarized as a single difference score. This is accomplished by subtracting the first score (before treatment) from the second score (after treatment) for each person:

$$\text{difference score} = D = X_2 - X_1 \tag{12.1}$$

In a matched-subjects design, *D* is the difference between scores for two matched subjects.

The difference scores, or *D* values, are shown in the last column of the table. Note that the sign of each *D* score tells you the direction of change. For example, person A showed a decrease in depression, as indicated by the negative difference score.

The researcher's goal is to use this sample of difference scores to answer questions about the general population. Notice that we are interested in a population of *difference scores.* More specifically, we are interested in the mean for this population of difference scores. We will identify this population mean difference with the symbol μ_D (using the subscript letter *D* to indicate that we are dealing with *D* values rather than *X* scores). Because populations usually are too large to test in an experiment, investigators must rely on the data from samples. Do these data indicate that the drug has a significant effect (more than chance)? How big is the effect? Our problem is to use the limited data from a sample to draw inferences about the population. This problem is diagrammed in Figure 12.1.

Notice that the problem we are facing here is essentially identical to the situation we encountered in Chapter 10. We have a single sample of scores that must be used to draw inferences about a single population. In Chapter 10 we introduced a *t* statistic that allowed us to use the sample mean as a basis for testing hypotheses about the population mean and for estimating the population mean. This *t* statistic formula will be used again here to develop the repeated measures *t* test.

THE *t* STATISTIC FOR REPEATED MEASURES To refresh your memory, the single-sample *t* statistic (Chapter 10) is defined by the formula

$$t = \frac{\bar{X} - \mu}{s_{\bar{X}}}$$

The sample mean $\bar{X}$ comes from the data. The standard error $s_{\bar{X}}$ (also computed from the sample data) gives a measure of the error between the sample mean and the population mean μ.

FIGURE 12.1

Because populations are usually too large to test in a study, the researcher selects a random sample from the population. The sample data are used to make inferences (hypothesis tests or estimation) about the population mean μ_D. The data of interest in the repeated-measures study are difference scores (D scores) for each subject.

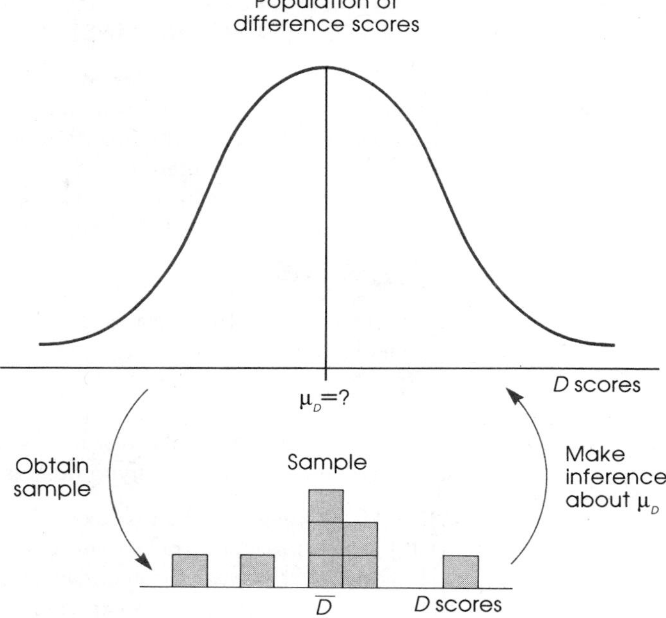

For the repeated measures experiment, the sample data are difference scores and are identified by the letter *D* rather than *X*. Therefore, we will substitute *D*'s in the formula in place of *X*'s to emphasize that we are dealing with difference scores instead of *X* values. Also, the population mean that is of interest to us is the population mean difference (the mean amount of change for the entire population), and we identify this parameter with the symbol μ_D. With these simple changes, the *t* formula for the repeated-measures design becomes

(12.2) $$t = \frac{\bar{D} - \mu_D}{s_{\bar{D}}}$$

The standard error in this formula, $s_{\bar{D}}$, is computed exactly as it was in the original single-sample *t* statistic. First, we compute the standard deviation for the sample (this time a sample of *D* scores):

$$s = \sqrt{\frac{SS}{n-1}}$$

Then we divide this value by the square root of the sample size:

(12.3) $$s_{\bar{D}} = \frac{s}{\sqrt{n}}$$

Notice that the sample data we are using consist of the *D* scores and that there is only one *D* value for each subject. Because there are only *n* difference scores in the sample, our *t* statistic will have degrees of freedom equal to

(12.4) $$df = n - 1$$

Note that this formula is identical to the *df* equation used for the single-sample *t* statistic (Chapter 10). However, *n* refers to the number of *D* scores, not the number of *X* values.

12.2 HYPOTHESIS TESTS WITH THE REPEATED MEASURES *t* TEST

THE HYPOTHESES In a repeated-measures experiment we are interested in whether or not any change occurs between scores in the first treatment and scores in the second treatment. In statistical terms, we are interested in the population mean difference μ_D. Is the population mean difference equal to zero (no change), or has a change occurred? As always, the null hypothesis states that there is no treatment effect. In symbols, this is

$$H_0: \mu_D = 0$$

The alternative hypothesis states that there is a difference between the treatments. In symbols, this is

$$H_1: \mu_D \neq 0$$

The two examples that follow will illustrate the repeated-measures experiment in situations where (1) the null hypothesis is true and (2) the null hypothesis is false.

When H_0 Is True In the first example, a researcher is examining whether or not the IQ scores for ninth graders are affected by a course in speed reading. For the sake of argument, we will assume that the course actually has no effect on IQ; that is, the null hypothesis is true. This experiment would require measuring each individual's IQ before and after taking the speed-reading course. Even though the course has no effect, you generally will find some difference between the first score and the second score for individual subjects. For some cases there will be a slight increase in IQ; in others a decrease will occur. These differences are due to chance and represent the influence of uncontrolled variables. Some subjects, for example, might have a sleepless night between the first and second test and show a temporary decrease in IQ score caused by fatigue. Others may be more rested and more alert for the second test and, therefore, show an increase in IQ. Because these and similar changes are random and unsystematic, they will average zero for the entire population. (See Figure 12.2.) You also should note that even though the population mean difference is zero, the sample mean probably will not be exactly equal to zero. Remember, samples are not

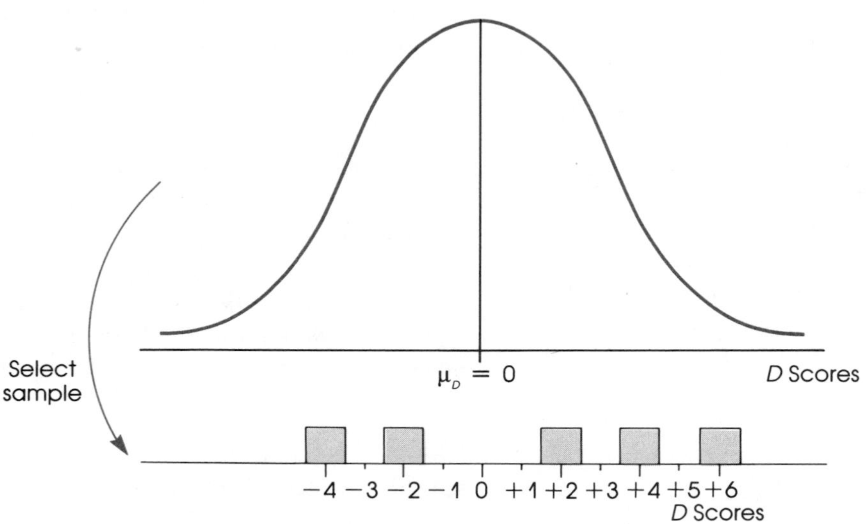

FIGURE 12.2

For the population of difference scores, $\mu_D = 0$ when the null hypothesis is true (no treatment effect). Notice that the mean for the sample of difference scores is not exactly zero (the value of the population mean). However, the sample mean, $\bar{D} = +1.20$, is close to zero.

expected to be exactly the same as the populations they come from. The sample mean should be close to the population mean but probably will not be identical.

When H_0 Is False For our second example, we will assume that H_0 actually is false and that the speed-reading course does work. Suppose it has the effect of adding 10 points to each individual's IQ score. Now we expect an average increase in IQ of approximately 10 points. Notice that the difference score for any particular subject probably will not be exactly equal to 10. In addition to the systematic change caused by the course, we still have the random changes caused by uncontrolled variables. For example, one subject who failed to have breakfast before the second IQ test might be fatigued and hungry and show an increase of only 8 points: a 10-point increase caused by the course and a 2-point decrease resulting from no breakfast. Again, this random variability should average to zero so that the mean change in IQ for the population will be 10 points. (See Figure 12.3.) As in the first example, you should realize that a sample selected from this population probably will not have a mean difference of exactly 10 points. However, the sample mean is expected to be close to the population mean.

PROCEDURES AND STEPS

As we saw in previous tests, the level of significance defines what values are sufficiently "far away" to reject H_0.

As a statistician, your job is to determine whether the sample data support or refute the null hypothesis. In simple terms, we must decide whether sample mean difference is close to zero (indicating no change) or far from zero (indicating there is a change). The t statistic helps us determine if the sample data are "close to" or "far from" zero.

The repeated-measures t test procedure follows the same outline we have used in other situations. The basic steps for hypothesis testing are reviewed here.

STEP 1 The hypotheses are stated, and an alpha level is selected. For the repeated-measures experiment, the null hypothesis is stated symbolically as

Directional hypotheses can be used as well and would predict whether μ_D is greater or smaller than zero. A one-tailed test is used in those instances (Chapter 9).

$$H_0 : \mu_D = 0$$

The alternative hypothesis is

$$H_1 : \mu_D \neq 0$$

FIGURE 12.3

For this example, the null hypothesis is false. The treatment effect for the population is reflected by its mean, $\mu_D = +10$. Notice that the mean for the sample of difference scores, $\overline{D} = 11.2$, is not identical to the mean of the population.

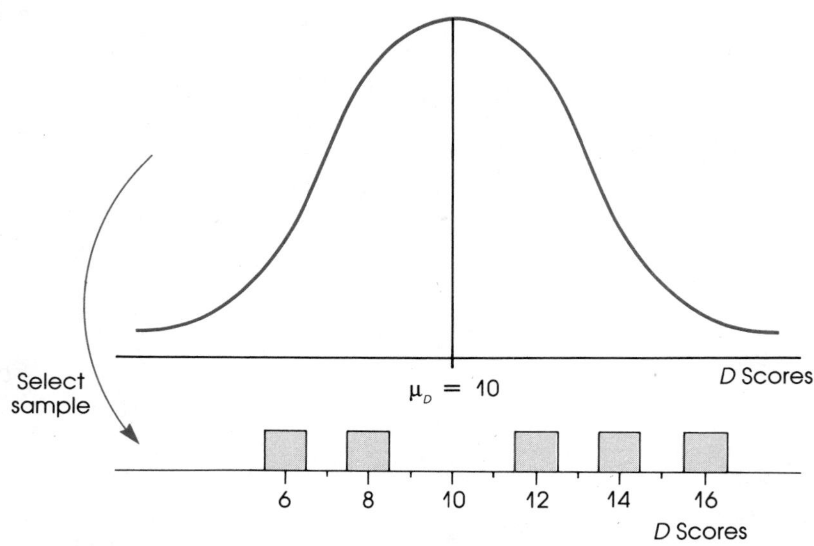

STEP 2 The critical region is located. As before, the critical region is defined as values that would be very unlikely (probability less than alpha) if H_0 is true. Because the repeated-measures test uses a t statistic with $df = n - 1$, we simply compute df and look up the critical values in the t distribution table.

STEP 3 Compute the test statistic, in this case, the t statistic for repeated measures. We first must find the sample mean $\bar{D}$ and SS for the set of difference scores. From SS we compute the estimated standard error $s_{\bar{D}}$. These values are then put into the t formula along with the hypothesized value of μ_D from H_0.

STEP 4 If the obtained value falls in the critical region, we reject H_0 and conclude that there is a significant treatment effect. Remember, it is very unlikely for the t value to be in the critical region if H_0 is true. On the other hand, if the obtained t is not in the critical region, then we fail to reject H_0 and conclude that the sample data do not provide sufficient evidence for a treatment effect.

The complete hypothesis testing procedure is demonstrated in Example 12.1.

EXAMPLE 12.1 A researcher in behavioral medicine believes that stress often makes asthma symptoms worse for people who suffer from this respiratory disorder. Because of the suspected role of stress, the investigator decides to examine the effect of relaxation training on the severity of asthma symptoms. A sample of five patients is selected for the study. During the week before treatment, the investigator records the severity of their symptoms by measuring how many doses of medication are needed for asthma attacks. Then the patients receive relaxation training. For the week following training, the researcher once again records the number of doses required by each patient. Table 12.3 shows the data and summarizes the findings. Do these data indicate that relaxation training alters the severity of symptoms?

STEP 1 State hypotheses and select alpha:

$H_0: \mu_D = 0$ (no change in symptoms)

$H_1: \mu_D \neq 0$ (there is a change)

The level of significance is set at $\alpha = .05$ for a two-tailed test.

STEP 2 Locate the critical region. For this example, $n = 5$, so the t statistic will have $df = n - 1 = 4$. From the t distribution table, you should find that the critical values are $+2.776$ and -2.776. These values are shown in Figure 12.4.

TABLE 12.3

The number of doses of medication needed for asthma attacks before and after relaxation training

Patient	Week Before Training	Week After Training	D	D^2
A	9	4	−5	25
B	4	1	−3	9
C	5	5	0	0
D	4	0	−4	16
E	5	1	−4	16
			$\sum D = -16$	$\sum D^2 = 66$

$$\bar{D} = \frac{\sum D}{n} = \frac{-16}{5} = -3.2$$

$$SS = \sum D^2 - \frac{(\sum D)^2}{n} = 66 - \frac{(-16)^2}{5}$$

$$= 66 - 51.2 = 14.8$$

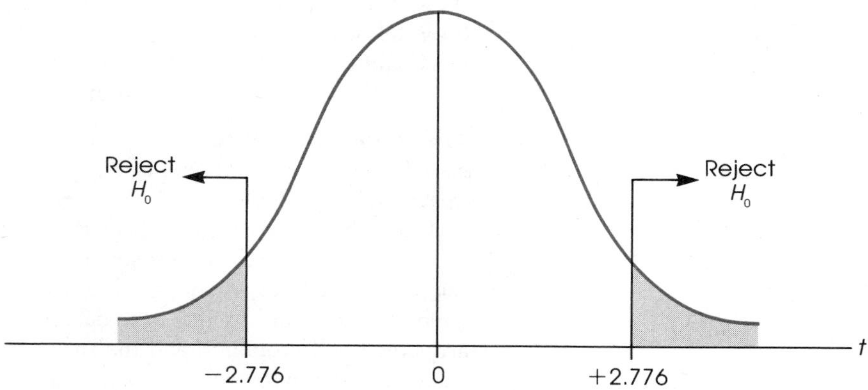

FIGURE 12.4

The critical regions with $\alpha = .05$ and $df = 4$ begin at $+2.776$ and -2.776 in the t distribution. Obtained values of t that are more extreme than these values will lie in a critical region. In that case, the null hypothesis would be rejected.

STEP 3 Calculate the repeated-measures t statistic. The mean for this example is $\bar{D} = -3.2$. To compute the SS for the D scores, we will use the computational formula:

$$SS = \sum X^2 - \frac{(\sum X)^2}{n}$$

Because we are using difference scores (D values) in place of X scores, this formula can be rewritten as

$$SS = \sum D^2 - \frac{(\sum D)^2}{n}$$

Remember, the computations for SS and s are based on the D scores for the subjects in the sample.

For our data, the SS is

$$\begin{aligned} SS &= 66 - \frac{(-16)^2}{5} \\ &= 66 - 51.2 \\ &= 14.8 \end{aligned}$$

Next, use the SS value to compute the sample standard deviation:

$$s = \sqrt{\frac{SS}{n-1}} = \sqrt{\frac{14.8}{4}} = \sqrt{3.7} = 1.92$$

Finally, the estimated standard error is computed:

$$s_{\bar{D}} = \frac{s}{\sqrt{n}} = \frac{1.92}{\sqrt{5}} = \frac{1.92}{2.24} = .86$$

Now these values are used to calculate the value of t:

$$t = \frac{\bar{D} - \mu_D}{s_{\bar{D}}} = \frac{-3.2 - 0}{.86} = -3.72$$

STEP 4 The t value we obtained falls in the critical region (see Figure 12.4). The investigator rejects the null hypothesis and concludes that relaxation training does affect the amount of medication needed to control the asthma symptoms. For this example, a journal report might summarize the conclusion as follows:

> Relaxation training resulted in a significant reduction in the dose of medication needed to control asthma symptoms, $t(4) = -3.72$, $p < .05$, two tails.

As is customary, the number of degrees of freedom is contained in parentheses after the t, followed by the obtained value. The probability of a Type I error (the alpha level) and the type of test (one or two tails) also are reported.

The repeated-measures t test on the computer A repeated-measures t test can easily be done with any one of a number of software packages. The scores for both treatments are entered, and a set of commands instructs the computer to perform the analysis. The advantage, of course, is that the computer program eliminates the need for you to calculate difference scores, SS, s, $s_{\bar{D}}$, and t. This is especially helpful when samples are large or when the scores have decimal places. We used SPSS[x] to perform a repeated-measures t test for the data in Example 12.1. The SPSS[x] command T-TEST activates t test programs, and the subcommand PAIRS initiates a repeated-measures analysis. The printout of the analysis and its explanation are shown in Table 12.4.

DIRECTIONAL HYPOTHESES AND ONE-TAILED TESTS

In most repeated-measures experiments, the researcher has a specific prediction concerning the direction of the treatment effect. For example, in the study described in Example 12.1, the researcher expects relaxation training to reduce the severity of asthma symptoms and, therefore, to reduce the amount of medication needed for asthma attacks. This kind of directional prediction can be incorporated into the statement of hypotheses, resulting in a directional, or one-tailed, hypothesis test. You should recall from earlier chapters that directional tests should be used with caution. The standard two-tailed test usually is preferred and is always appropriate, even in situations where the researcher has a specific directional prediction. The following

TABLE 12.4

The printout of the repeated measures t test for Example 12.1 using SPSS[x]

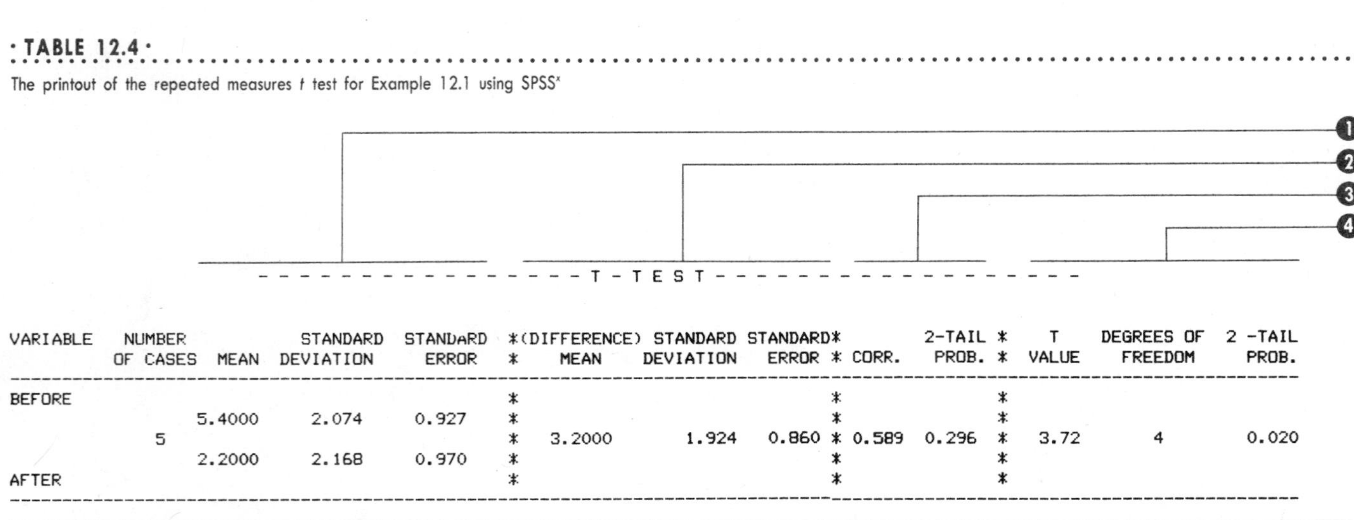

VARIABLE	NUMBER OF CASES	MEAN	STANDARD DEVIATION	STANDARD ERROR	(DIFFERENCE) MEAN	STANDARD DEVIATION	STANDARD ERROR	CORR.	2-TAIL PROB.	T VALUE	DEGREES OF FREEDOM	2 -TAIL PROB.
BEFORE		5.4000	2.074	0.927								
	5				3.2000	1.924	0.860	0.589	0.296	3.72	4	0.020
AFTER		2.2000	2.168	0.970								

EXPLANATION OF PRINTOUT:

1 The first section of the printout provides descriptive statistics for both measurements before and after training. These include the sample size (NUMBER OF CASES), the means for both measurements, the standard deviations, and the standard errors.

2 The next section summarizes the analysis of the *difference scores*, showing the values for $\bar{D}$, standard deviation, and standard error.

3 The third section provides a correlation coefficient (CORR). This measures the strength of the relationship between the first and second measurements. Correlation is covered in Chapter 16.

4 Finally, the value for the repeated-measures t statistic and its df are displayed. The two-tailed probability shown with the t value is the probability of committing a Type I error if the null hypothesis is rejected. In this case, p is considerably less than the .05 level of significance. Therefore, H_0 is rejected.

· FIGURE 12.5 ·

The one-tailed critical region for $\alpha = .05$ in the t distribution with $df = 4$.

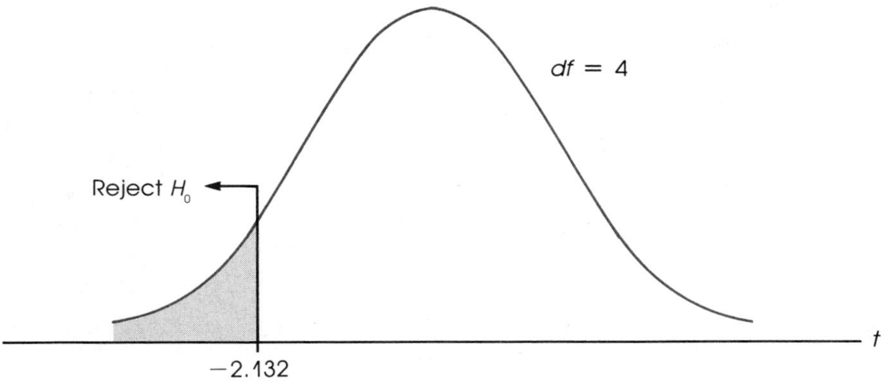

example demonstrates how the hypotheses and critical region are determined in a directional test.

· EXAMPLE 12.2 · We will reexamine the experiment presented in Example 12.1. The researcher is using a repeated-measures experiment to investigate the effect of relaxation training on the severity of asthma symptoms. The researcher predicts that people will need less medication after training than before, which will produce negative difference scores.

$$D = X_2 - X_1 = \text{after} - \text{before}$$

STEP 1 State the hypotheses and select α. With most one-tailed tests, it is easiest to incorporate the researcher's prediction directly into H_1. In this example, the researcher predicts a negative difference, so

$H_1: \mu_D < 0$ (medication is reduced after training)

The null hypothesis states that the treatment does not have the predicted effect. In this example,

$H_0: \mu_D \geq 0$ (medication is not reduced after training)

STEP 2 Locate the critical region. The researcher is predicting negative difference scores if the treatment works. Hence, a negative t statistic would tend to support the experimental prediction and refute H_0. With a sample of $n = 5$ subjects, the t statistic will have $df = 4$. Looking in the t distribution table for $df = 4$ and $\alpha = .05$ for a one-tailed test, we find a critical value of 2.132. Thus, a t statistic that is more extreme than -2.132 would be sufficient to reject H_0. The t distribution with the one-tailed critical region is shown in Figure 12.5. For this example, the data produce a t statistic of $t = -3.72$ (see Example 12.1). Therefore, we reject H_0 and conclude that the relaxation training did significantly reduce the amount of medication needed for asthma attacks. ·

· LEARNING CHECK ·

1 A researcher would like to examine the effect of hypnosis on cigarette smoking. A sample of smokers ($n = 4$) is selected for the study. The number of cigarettes smoked on the day prior to treatment is recorded. The subjects are then hypnotized and given the posthypnotic suggestion that each time they light a cigarette they will experience a horrible taste and feel nauseous. The data are as follows.

The number of cigarettes smoked before and after hypnosis

Subject	Before Treatment	After Treatment
1	19	13
2	35	37
3	20	14
4	31	25

a Find the difference scores (D values) for this sample.
b The difference scores have $\bar{D} = -4$ and $SS = 48$. Do these data indicate that hypnosis has a significant effect on cigarette smoking? Test with $\alpha = .05$.

ANSWER

1 a The difference scores are -6, 2, -6, -6.
b For these data $s = 4$, $s_{\bar{D}} = 2$, and $t = -2.00$. With $\alpha = .05$, we fail to reject H_0; these data do not provide sufficient evidence to conclude that hypnosis has a significant effect on cigarette smoking.

12.3 A CLOSER LOOK AT THE REPEATED-MEASURES *t* TEST

ASSUMPTIONS OF THE REPEATED-MEASURES *t* TEST

As in the previous statistical tests, it is required that the sample of individuals is randomly selected from the population. This requirement helps ensure that the sample is representative of the population from which it was selected. There is also an assumption of normality for the repeated-measures t test. Specifically, the population distribution of difference scores (D) should be normal. Ordinarily, researchers do not worry about this assumption unless there is ample reason to suspect a violation of this requirement of the test. In the case of severe departure from normality, the validity of the t test may be compromised. However, as noted before, the t statistic is robust to violations of normality when large samples ($n > 30$) are used.

USES OF REPEATED-MEASURES STUDIES

The repeated-measures experiment differs from an independent-measures study in a fundamental way. In the latter type of study, a separate sample is used for each treatment. In the repeated-measures design, only one sample of subjects is used, and measurements are repeated for the same sample in each treatment. There are many situations where it is possible to examine the effect of a treatment by using either type of study. However, there are situations where one type of experimental design is more desirable or appropriate than the other. For example, if a researcher would like to study a particular type of subject (a rare species, people with an unusual illness, etc.) that is not commonly found, a repeated-measures study will be more economical in the sense that fewer subjects are needed. Rather than selecting several samples for the study (one sample per treatment), a single sample can be used for the entire experiment.

There are situations where only an independent-measures design can be used. When one wants to compare two different populations (for example, the attitudes of Republicans and Democrats), it is necessary to use two independent samples.

Another factor in determining the type of experimental design is the specific question being asked by the experimenter. Some questions are better studied with a repeated-measures design, especially those concerning changes in response across time. For example, a psychologist may wish to study the effect of practice on how well a person performs a task. To show that practice is improving a person's performance, the experimenter would typically measure the person's responses very early in the experiment (when there is little or no practice) and repeat the measurement later when the person has had a certain amount of practice. Most studies of skill acquisition examine practice effects by using a repeated-measures design. Another situation where a repeated-measures study is useful is in developmental psychology. By repeating observations of the same individuals at various points in time, an investigator can watch behavior unfold and obtain a better understanding of developmental processes (for example, see the Preview).

There are situations where a repeated-measures design cannot or should not be used. Specifically, when you are comparing two different populations (men versus women, first-born versus last-born children, and the like), you must use an independent-measure design with separate samples from each population.

Finally, it should be noted that there are certain statistical advantages to repeated-measures designs, particularly when you are studying a population with large differences from one individual to the next. One of the sources of variability that contributes to the standard error is due to these individual differences—that is, subjects all respond differently because they enter the experiment with different abilities, experiences, and the like. Large individual differences would produce larger standard errors, which might mask a mean difference. A repeated-measures design reduces the amount of this error variability in the analysis by using the same subjects for every treatment. The result is that the size of the standard error is reduced, and the t test will be more likely to detect the presence of a treatment effect. That is, the repeated-measures t test is more powerful than an independent-measures test when individual differences are large. The statistical advantages of a repeated-measures design will be more evident in Chapter 14, when we examine the components of variability in an experiment.

CARRY-OVER EFFECTS IN REPEATED-MEASURES EXPERIMENTS

Sometimes the outcome of a repeated-measures study is contaminated by the presence of a carry-over effect. This will occur when a subject's response in the second treatment is altered by lingering aftereffects of the first treatment. As a result, the outcome of the study may be uninterpretable. A common type of carry-over effect is fatigue. For example, suppose an experimenter studies the effects of distraction on task performance with a repeated-measures design. Two treatment conditions are used: a no-distraction treatment and a distraction treatment. A sample of four subjects work on math problems requiring multiplication of large numbers. For the first 30 minutes, the subjects work on the problems in the no-distraction condition in a quiet room. Then the subjects are moved to the distraction condition. Now they must work on a similar set of math problems in the presence of loud background noise. The experimenter records the number of errors made by each subject. Table 12.5 summarizes the results.

Notice that the subjects in the experiment made an average of eight more errors in the distraction condition, $\bar{D} = +8$. A repeated-measures t test would confirm that the mean difference between treatments is statistically significant, $t(3) = 8.79$, $p < .05$ for two tails. The experimenter might conclude that distraction has an effect on task performance. However, there may be another explanation of the effect. It is possible that the mean difference was observed because of a carry-over effect rather than a

TABLE 12.5

The number of errors made under conditions of no distraction and distraction

Person	No Distraction	Distraction	D
A	6	15	+9
B	5	15	+10
C	11	17	+6
D	6	13	+7
			$\bar{D} = +8$

TABLE 12.6

The number of errors made under conditions of no distraction and distraction with a rest period between the treatments

Person	No Distraction	Rest	Distraction	D
A	6	Rest	7	+1
B	5	Rest	4	−1
C	11	Rest	11	0
D	6	Rest	5	−1
				$\bar{D} = -.25$

treatment effect. Perhaps the subjects became fatigued during the no-distraction condition. After all, they had to work on a boring, tedious task for 30 minutes. By the time the subjects are switched to the distraction condition, they might be bored, tired, and poorly motivated to do any more multiplication problems. Therefore, the increase in errors may have nothing to do with the introduction of distraction. It may have simply been due to the buildup of boredom and fatigue during the first condition. This buildup would in turn affect performance in (that is, "carry over" to) the second condition. If the significant mean difference were due solely to a carry-over effect of fatigue, then providing the subjects with a rest period between the two treatment conditions would lead to a different outcome. As shown in Table 12.6, the introduction of a rest period would eliminate the influence of fatigue on the second treatment. With the carry-over effect prevented, the data show no systematic effect, and the mean difference between treatments is negligible. On the other hand, if the effect were not due to fatigue, the significant mean difference would still be found when a rest period is introduced.

Another way a researcher can reduce the contribution of a carry-over effect is to balance the order of presentation of treatments. That is, the treatments can be presented in one order for some subjects and in the reverse order for others. This procedure may eliminate a systematic contribution of a carry-over effect to any one treatment condition.

LEARNING CHECK

1 What assumptions must be satisfied for the repeated-measures t tests to be valid?

2 Describe some situations for which a repeated-measures design is well suited?

3 How is a matched-subjects design similar to a repeated-measures design? How do they differ?

4 What is a carry-over effect?

ANSWERS

1 The sample must be randomly selected from the population. The population distribution of D scores is assumed to be normal.

2 The repeated-measures design is suited to situations where a particular type of subject is not readily available for study. This design is helpful because it uses fewer subjects (only one sample is needed). Certain questions are addressed more adequately by a repeated-measures design—for example, anytime one would like to study changes across time in the same individuals. Also, when individual differences are large, a repeated-measures design is helpful because it reduces the amount of this type of error in the statistical analysis.

3 They are similar in that the role of individual differences in the experiment is reduced. They differ in that there are two samples in a matched-subjects design and only one in a repeated-measures study.

4 A carry-over effect occurs in a repeated-measures study when lingering aftereffects of the first treatment alter performance on the second—for example, fatigue.

12.4 ESTIMATION WITH THE REPEATED-MEASURES t STATISTIC

INTRODUCTION The hypothesis-testing procedure addresses the question of whether or not any mean difference exists. Occasionally, a researcher is interested in approximating *how much* difference can be expected for the population. This is a question for estimation. The repeated-measures t statistic allows researchers to use sample data to estimate the value of μ_D, that is, to estimate the magnitude of the mean difference for the general population. Once again, the repeated-measures t formula is

$$t = \frac{\bar{D} - \mu_D}{s_{\bar{D}}}$$

Because we want to estimate the value of the population mean difference, this formula is solved for μ_D:

$$\mu_D = \bar{D} \pm t s_{\bar{D}} \quad (12.5)$$

In words, this formula may be stated as

population mean difference = sample mean difference $\pm$ some error

That is, to estimate the mean difference for the population, we use the sample mean difference plus or minus some error.

PROCEDURE FOR ESTIMATION OF μ_D The process of estimation with the repeated-measures t statistic follows exactly the same steps that were used for estimation with the single-sample t statistic (see Chapter 10, page 232). First you calculate the sample mean ($\bar{D}$) and the estimated standard error ($s_{\bar{D}}$) using the sample of difference scores. Next, you determine the appropriate values for t ($t = 0$ for a point estimate or a range of values from the t distribution for an interval estimate). Finally, these values are used in the estimation formula (12.5) to compute an estimate of μ_D. The following example demonstrates this process.

Remember, we are not simply choosing a t value but are estimating the location of our sample data within the t distribution.

EXAMPLE 12.3 A school psychologist has determined that a remedial reading course increases scores on a reading comprehension test. The psychologist now would like to estimate how much improvement might be expected for the whole population of students in his city. A random sample of $n = 16$ children is obtained. These children are first tested for level of reading comprehension and then enrolled in the course. At the completion of the remedial reading course, the students are tested again, and the difference between the second score and the first score is recorded for each child. For this sample, the average difference was $\bar{D} = +21$, and the SS for the difference scores was $SS = 1215$. The psychologist would like to use these data to make a point estimate and a 90% confidence interval estimate of μ_D.

STEP 1 The formula for estimation requires that we know the values of $\bar{D}$, $s_{\bar{D}}$, and t. We know that $\bar{D} = +21$ points for this sample, so all that remains is to compute $s_{\bar{D}}$ and look up the value of t in the t distribution table.

To find the standard error, we first must compute the sample standard deviation:

$$s = \sqrt{\frac{SS}{n-1}} = \sqrt{\frac{1215}{15}} = \sqrt{81} = 9$$

Now the estimated standard error is

$$s_{\bar{D}} = \frac{s}{\sqrt{n}} = \frac{9}{\sqrt{16}} = \frac{9}{4} = 2.25$$

FIGURE 12.6

The t values for the 90% confidence interval are obtained by consulting the t table for $df = 15$, $p = .10$.

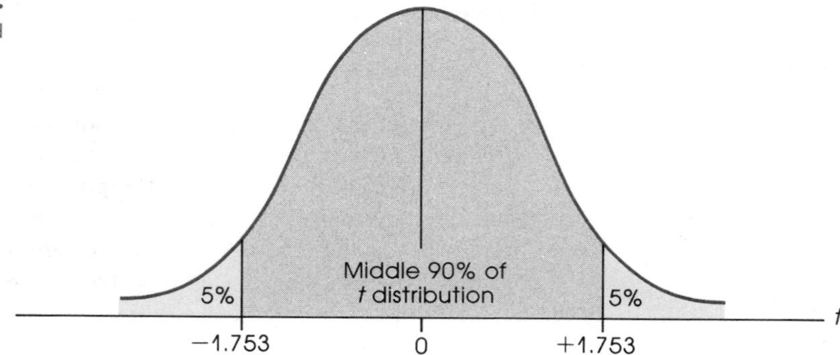

To complete the estimate of μ_D, we must identify the value of t. We will consider the point estimate (step 2) and the interval estimate (step 3) separately.

STEP 2 *Point Estimation of* μ_D. To obtain a point estimate, a single value of t is selected to approximate the location of $\bar{D}$. Remember that the t distribution is symmetrical and bell-shaped with a mean of zero (see Figure 12.6). Because $t = 0$ is the most frequently occurring value in the distribution, this is the t value that is used for the point estimate. Using this value in the estimation formula gives

$$\mu_D = \bar{D} \pm ts_{\bar{D}}$$
$$= 21 \pm 0(2.25)$$
$$= 21$$

As noted several times before, the sample mean, $\bar{D} = 21$, provides the best point estimate of μ_D.

STEP 3 *Interval Estimation of* μ_D. The psychologist also wanted to make an interval estimate in order to be 90% confident that the interval contains the value of μ_D. To get the interval, it is necessary to determine what t values form the boundaries of the middle 90% of the t distribution. To use the t distribution table, we first must determine the proportion associated with the tails of this distribution. With 90% in the middle, the remaining area in both tails must be 10%, or $p = .10$. Also note that our sample has $n = 16$ scores, so the t statistic will have $df = n - 1 = 15$. Using $df = 15$ and $p = .10$ for two tails, you should find the values $+1.753$ and -1.753 in the t table. These values form the boundaries for the middle 90% of the t distribution. (See Figure 12.6.) We are confident that the t value for our sample is in this range because 90% of all the possible t values are there. Using these values in the estimation formula, we obtain the following: On one end of the interval,

$$\mu_D = \bar{D} - ts_{\bar{D}}$$
$$= 21 - 1.753(2.25)$$
$$= 21 - 3.94$$
$$= 17.06$$

and on the other end of the interval,

Remember, in estimation we use values of t and the estimated standard error to define an interval around the sample mean that probably contains μ.

$$\mu_D = 21 + 1.753(2.25)$$
$$= 21 + 3.94$$
$$= 24.94$$

Therefore, the school psychologist can be 90% confident that the average amount of improvement in reading comprehension for the population (μ_D) will be somewhere between 17.04 and 24.94 points.

· LEARNING CHECK ·

1 A government researcher believes that driving and automotive tips will result in energy-saving habits. A sample of nine subjects is given a brochure containing energy-saving tips and is asked to follow this advice. Before and after using the tips, the subjects maintain gasoline consumption records for their automobiles. For this sample, the average improvement in gasoline mileage (in miles per gallon) was $\bar{D} = 6.50$ with $SS = 72$. A repeated measures t test indicated that the mean change was statistically significant. However, before the government prints millions of copies of the brochure, the researcher is requested to estimate how much mean change can be expected for the population of drivers. The investigator decides to report the 95% confidence interval. What will this interval be?

ANSWER

1 For this sample $s = 3$ and $s_{\bar{D}} = 1$. For the 95% confidence interval with $df = 8$, $t = \pm 2.306$; the 95% confidence interval for μ_D is from 4.194 to 8.806.

SUMMARY

1 In a repeated-measures experiment, a single sample of subjects is randomly selected, and measurements are repeated on this sample for each treatment condition. This type of experiment may take the form of a before-and-after study.

2 The data analysis for a repeated-measures t test is done on the basis of the difference between the first and second measurement for each subject. These difference scores (D scores) are obtained by

$$D = X_2 - X_1$$

3 The formula for the repeated-measures t statistic is

$$t = \frac{\bar{D} - \mu_D}{s_{\bar{D}}}$$

where the sample mean is

$$\bar{D} = \frac{\sum D}{n}$$

the estimated standard error is

$$s_{\bar{D}} = \frac{s}{\sqrt{n}}$$

and the value of degrees of freedom is obtained by

$$df = n - 1$$

4 A repeated-measures design may be more useful than an independent-measures study when one wants to observe changes in behavior in the same subjects, as in learning or developmental studies. The repeated-measures design has the advantage of reducing error variability due to individual differences. A potential problem with repeated-measures studies is the presence of carry-over effects that can cloud the interpretation of the findings.

5 Estimation of the amount of mean change for the population is accomplished by solving the t statistic formula for μ_D:

$$\mu_D = \bar{D} \pm ts_{\bar{D}}$$

For a point estimate, a t value of zero is used. A range of t values is used to construct an interval around $\bar{D}$. As in previous estimation problems, the t values that mark the interval boundaries are determined by the confidence level that is selected and by degrees of freedom.

KEY TERMS

repeated-measures design
repeated-measures t statistic
difference scores
estimated standard error for $\bar{D}$
individual differences
matched-subjects design
carry-over effects

FOCUS ON PROBLEM SOLVING

1. Once data have been collected, we must then select the appropriate statistical analysis. How can you tell if the data call for a repeated-measures t test? Look at the experiment carefully. Is there only one sample of subjects? Are the same subjects tested a second time? If

your answers are yes to both of these questions, then a repeated-measures t test should be done. There is only one situation in which the repeated-measures t can be used for data from two samples, and that is for *matched-subjects* experiments (page 269).

2. The repeated-measures t test is based on difference scores. In finding difference scores, be sure you are consistent with your method. That is, you may use either $X_2 - X_1$ or $X_1 - X_2$ to find D scores, but you must use the same method for all subjects.

3. For interval estimates of μ_D, remember that the t values for the formula are determined by the percent confidence you select. Do not use the t value obtained from a hypothesis test.

PROBLEMS

*1 For the following studies, indicate whether or not a repeated-measures t test is the appropriate analysis. Explain your answers.

- **a** A researcher examines the effect of relaxation training on test anxiety. One sample of subjects receives relaxation training for 3 weeks. A second sample serves as a control group and does not receive the treatment. The researcher then measures anxiety levels for both groups in a test-taking situation.
- **b** Another researcher does a similar study. Baseline levels of test anxiety are recorded for a sample of subjects. Then all subjects receive relaxation training for 3 weeks and their anxiety levels are measured again.
- **c** In a test-anxiety study, two samples are used. Subjects are assigned to groups so that they are matched for self-esteem and for grade-point average. One sample receives relaxation training for 3 weeks and the second serves as a no-treatment control group. Test anxiety is measured for both groups at the end of 3 weeks.

2 For the following studies, state whether estimation or hypothesis testing is required. Also, is an independent- or a repeated-measures t statistic appropriate?

- **a** An educator wants to determine how much mean difference can be expected for the population in SAT scores following an intensive review course. Two samples are selected. The first group takes the review course and the second receives no treatment. SAT scores are subsequently measured for both groups.
- **b** A psychiatrist would like to test the effectiveness of a new antipsychotic medication. A sample of patients is first assessed for the severity of psychotic symptoms. Then the patients are placed on drug therapy for 2 weeks. The severity of their symptoms is assessed again at the end of the treatment.

*3 A psychologist would like to evaluate the effectiveness of a special course intended to help students prepare for the SAT exam. A sample of 8 students is selected to participate in the course, and a second sample of 8 students is selected as a control group (no special course). All 16 students take the SAT in November; then the eight students in the experimental group participate in the special course. When the course is over, all 16 students take the SAT again. The psychologist records the difference between the first and second test score for each student. The data are as follows:

Experimental Group (special course)	Control Group (no special course)
+40	+10
+10	−20
+20	+30
+40	+20
+70	−10
−10	+40
+60	+10
+20	+20

- **a** Do the data from the experimental group indicate that the special course had a significant effect on SAT scores? Test at the .05 level.
- **b** Using the data from both groups, did the students in the special course show significantly more improvement on the SAT than students who did not take the course? Test at the .05 level. (*Caution:* You are now comparing two separate samples; this is not a repeated-measures test.)
- **c** Write a brief statement describing the outcome of both tests and explaining why this result might have been obtained.

4 What is a carry-over effect? Give an example of one.

*5 What is the advantage of a matched-subjects design over an independent-measures design?

*6 A psychologist would like to know if there are any changes in personality during imprisonment. She selects a random sample of $n = 25$ people who have been sentenced to at least 5 years of prison. The psychologist interviews each of these people during their first week in prison and administers a personality test which measures introversion/extroversion on a scale from 0 to 50 (low scores indicate introversion). After 1 year, the investigator returns for a second interview with the prisoners and again administers the personality test. For each person, she calculates the difference between their initial score and the score after 1 year of confinement.

The average for this sample of difference scores is $\bar{D} = -5$ with $SS = 2400$.

a Test the hypothesis that imprisonment changes personality variables. Set alpha at .05.

b Would the same decision be made had alpha been set at .01?

c Estimate how much change in personality is caused by 1 year of confinement for the population of prisoners. Make a point estimate and an interval estimate at the 80% level of confidence.

7 A researcher arguing for stricter laws for drunk driving argues that even one can of beer can produce a significant effect on reaction time. In an attempt to prove his claim, he selects a random sample of $n = 4$ people and measures their baseline reaction times. This is accomplished by having the subjects view a stimulus display and press a button as fast as they can when a light flashes on. The subjects then consume a 12-ounce can of beer. After 30 minutes, they are tested again on the task. The researcher computed the difference scores and determined that for this sample $\bar{D} = 32$ milliseconds. That is, on average it took the group of subjects 32 milliseconds longer to respond. Also, the sample had $SS = 1200$. Do the data support the investigator's claim? Test at the .05 level of significance.

8 For the data in Problem 7, estimate the amount of mean change in reaction time for the population as a result of drinking a single can of beer. Make an interval estimate at the 90% level of confidence.

***9** For the experiment described in Problem 7, the researcher probably expects reaction times to increase following beer consumption. If a one-tailed test were performed, how would H_0 and H_1 be expressed in symbols? (Assume that difference scores are computed by $D = X_2 - X_1$.)

10 A college professor performed a study to assess the effectiveness of computerized exercises in teaching mathematics. She decides to use a *matched-subjects design*. One group of subjects is assigned to be regular lecture section of introductory mathematics. A second group must attend a computer laboratory in addition to the lecture. These students work on computerized exercises for additional practice and instruction. Both samples are matched in terms of general mathematics ability, as measured by mathematical SAT scores. At the end of the semester, both groups are given the same final exam. For $n = 16$ matched pairs of subjects, the professor found a mean improvement of $\bar{D} = 9.3$ points for the computer group. The SS for the D values was 2160. Does the computerized instruction lead to a significant improvement? Test at the .01 level of significance.

11 For the study in Problem 10, estimate the amount of mean change for the population (μ_D) using the 95% level of confidence.

***12** A psychologist for NASA examines the effect of cabin temperature on reaction time. A random sample of $n = 10$ astronauts and pilots is selected. Each person's reaction time is measured in a simulator, where the cabin temperature is maintained at 70°F, and again the next day at 95°F. The subjects are run through a launch simulation. Their reaction time (in milliseconds) is measured when an emergency indicator flashes and they must quickly press the appropriate switch. The data from this experiment are as follows:

Experiment 1

70°	95°	D
180	190	10
176	201	25
204	220	16
216	240	24
194	217	23
183	206	23
207	228	21
229	255	26
231	245	14
210	228	18

a Using the results from this experiment, can the psychologist conclude that temperature has a significant effect on reaction time? Test at the .05 level of significance.

b To verify the results of the first experiment, the psychologist repeats the experiment with another sample of $n = 10$. The data for the replication are as follows:

Experiment 2

70°	95°	D
178	252	74
194	244	50
217	200	−17
186	231	45
242	218	−24
212	214	2
221	201	−20
194	236	42
187	247	60
219	207	−12

Again, test for a significant difference at the .05 level of significance.

c Both experiments showed reaction times that were on average 20 milliseconds longer with the hotter cabin temperature. Why are the results of one experiment significant and of the other not significant? (*Hint:* Compare the two experiments in terms of the consistency of the effect for all subjects. How does the consistency (or inconsistency) of the effect affect the analysis?)

***13** A high school counselor has developed a course designed to help students with the mathematics portion of the SAT. A random sample of students is selected for the study. These students take the SAT at the end of their junior year. During the summer, they take the SAT review course. When they begin their senior year, they all take the SAT again. The data for the sample are as follows:

SAT scores (mathematics)

Before	After
402	468
486	590
543	625
516	553
475	454
403	447
522	543
480	416
619	652
493	495
485	496
551	585
573	610
437	491
472	544
409	492

Did the students perform significantly better on the SAT after taking the special course? Use a one-tailed test with alpha at .05.

14 For the data in Problem 13, estimate how much improvement (μ_D) can be expected for the population. Use the 95% level of confidence for the interval estimate.

***15** A psychologist tests a new drug for its pain-killing effects. Pain threshold is measured for a sample of subjects by determining the intensity (in milliamperes) of electric shock that causes discomfort. After the initial baseline is established, subjects receive the drug, and their thresholds are once again measured. The data are as follows:

Pain thresholds (milliamperes)

Before	After
2.1	3.2
2.3	2.9
3.0	4.6
2.7	2.7
1.9	3.1
2.1	2.9
2.9	2.9
2.7	3.4
3.2	5.3
2.5	2.5
3.1	4.9

Is there an effect of the drug treatment? Test with an alpha of .05.

***16** Estimate the mean amount of change (μ_D) in threshold for the population for the study in Problem 15. Use a confidence level of 90% for the interval estimate.

***17** A researcher examines the effects of sensitization on cigarette smoking in habitual smokers. A random sample of $n = 12$ smokers is selected. The number of cigarettes smoked per day is first determined for these people. The subjects are then sensitized to the effects of smoking by having them view a film that graphically shows the harm caused by cigarette smoke. A week later, the subjects are asked to count the number of cigarettes they smoke that day. The data are as follows:

Number of cigarettes smoked

Before	One Week Later
19	15
22	7
32	31
17	10
37	28
20	12
23	23
24	17
28	19
21	24
15	11
18	16

Did sensitization cause a reduction in smoking? Use the .05 level of significance.

18 Estimate the average amount of reduction (μ_D) that sensitization will produce for the population using the data in Problem 17. Use a confidence level of 90% for the interval estimate.

***19** A researcher tests the effectiveness of a drug called Ritalin on hyperkinetic children. The researcher uses a sample of $n = 12$ hyperkinetic children ranging in age from 8 to 9 years of age. The children are told several brief stories. After each story, the experimenter asks the children questions about the story. The total number of questions answered correctly for all the stories is recorded as the child's score. Because hyperkinetic children have attentional deficits, they should not perform well on this task when they are not treated. The researcher tests all of the children under two conditions: following administration of a sugar pill (placebo condition) and after receiving Ritalin. For the following data, determine if the drug treatment has an effect on performance. Use an alpha level of .01.

Subject	Placebo	Ritalin
A	10	15
B	8	15
C	11	13
D	6	17
E	7	8
F	9	17
G	6	18
H	8	3
I	5	14
J	10	20
K	7	18
L	2	19

20 For the data in Problem 19, estimate the mean amount of change in performance (μ_D) for the population due to Ritalin treatment. Use the 95% level of confidence for the interval estimate.

***21** A statistics instructor was unable to decide between two potential textbooks. To help with this decision, a random sample of 12 students was obtained, and each student was to rate both books using a scale from 1 (very bad) to 10 (excellent). The data from these 12 students are as follows:

Student	Book 1	Book 2
1	3	5
2	6	7
3	8	7
4	7	8
5	5	6
6	3	5
7	8	6
8	6	3
9	2	5
10	5	6
11	7	5
12	4	7

Do these data indicate that students perceive a significant difference between the books? Test at the .05 level of significance.

22 Although psychologists do not completely understand the phenomenon of dreaming, it does appear that people need to dream. One experiment demonstrating this fact shows that people who are deprived of dreaming one night will tend to have extra dreams the following night, as if they were trying to make up for the lost dreams. In a typical version of this experiment, the psychologist first records the number of dreams (by monitoring rapid eye movements (REMs)) during a normal night's sleep. The next night, each subject is prevented from dreaming by being awakened as soon as he or she begins a dream. During the third night, the psychologist once again records the number of dreams. Hypothetical data from this experiment are as follows:

Subject	First Night	Night After Deprivation
1	4	7
2	5	5
3	4	8
4	6	7
5	4	10
6	5	7
7	4	7
8	4	6

Do these data indicate a significant increase in dreams after one night of dream deprivation? Test at the .05 level of significance.

***23** A pharmaceutical company would like to test the effectiveness of a new antidepressant drug. A sample of 15 depressed patients is obtained, and each patient is given a mood inventory questionnaire before and after receiving the drug treatment. The data for this experiment are as follows:

Patient	Before	After
1	18	23
2	21	20
3	16	17
4	19	20
5	14	13
6	23	22
7	16	18
8	14	18
9	21	21
10	18	16
11	17	19
12	14	20
13	16	15
14	14	15
15	20	21

On the basis of these data, can the company conclude that the drug has a significant effect on mood? Test with $\alpha = .01$.

24 A consumer protection agency is testing the effectiveness of a new gasoline additive that claims to improve gas mileage. A sample of 10 cars is obtained, and each car is driven over a standard 100-mile course with and without the additive. The researchers carefully record the miles per gallon for each test drive. The results of this test are as follows:

Car	With Additive	Without Additive
1	23.0	21.6
2	20.2	19.8
3	17.4	17.5
4	19.6	20.7
5	22.8	23.1
6	20.4	19.8
7	26.8	26.4
8	23.7	24.0
9	17.2	15.9
10	18.5	18.3

Does the new gasoline additive have a significant effect on gas mileage? Test at the .05 level of significance.

CHAPTER 13

INTRODUCTION TO ANALYSIS OF VARIANCE

TOOLS YOU WILL NEED

The following items are considered essential background material for this chapter. If you doubt your knowledge of any of these items, you should review the appropriate chapter or section before proceeding.

- Variability (Chapter 4)
    - Sum of squares
    - Sample of variance
    - Degrees of freedom
- Introduction to hypothesis testing (Chapter 8)
    - The logic of hypothesis testing
- Independent-measures *t* statistic (Chapter 11)

PREVIEW

"But I read the chapter four times! How could I possibly have failed the exam?"

Most of you probably have had the experience of reading a textbook and suddenly realizing that you have no idea of what was said on the past few pages. Although you have been reading the words, your mind has wandered off, and the meaning of the words never reaches memory. In an influential paper on human memory, Craik and Lockhart (1972) proposed a *levels of processing* theory of memory that can account for this phenomenon. In general terms, this theory says that all perceptual and mental processing leaves behind a memory trace. However, the quality of the memory trace depends on the level or the depth of the processing. If you superficially skim the words in a book, your memory also will be superficial. On the other hand, when you think about the meaning of the words and try to understand what you are reading, the result will be a good, substantial memory that should serve you well on exams. In general, deeper processing results in better memory.

Rogers, Kuiper, and Kirker (1977) conducted an experiment demonstrating the effect of levels of processing. Subjects in this experiment were shown lists of words and asked to answer questions about each word. The questions were designed to require different levels of processing, from superficial to deep. In one experimental condition, subjects were simply asked to judge the physical characteristics of each printed word ("Is it printed in capital letters or small letters?") A second condition asked about the sound of each word ("Does it rhyme with 'boat'?"). In a third condition, subjects were required to process the meaning of each word ("Does it have the same meaning as 'attractive'?"). The final condition required subjects to understand each word and relate its meaning to themselves. ("Does this word describe you?"). After going through the complete list, all subjects were given a surprise memory test. As you can see in Figure 13.1, deeper processing resulted in better memory. Remember, none of these subjects was trying to memorize the words; they were simply reading through the list answering questions. However, the more they processed and understood the words, the better they recalled the words on the test.

In terms of human memory the Rogers et al. experiment is notable because it demonstrates the importance of "self" in memory. You are most likely to remember material that is directly related to you. In terms of statistics, however, this study is notable because it compares four different treatment conditions in a single experiment. Although it may seem like a small step to go from two treatments (as in the t tests in Chapters 11 and 12) to four treatments, there is a tremendous gain in experimental sophistication. Suppose, for example, that Rogers et al. had decided to examine only two levels of processing: one based on physical characteristics and one based on sound. In this simplified experiment, they would have made only *one* comparison: physical versus sound. In the real experiment, however, they

FIGURE 13.1

Mean recall as a function of the level of processing. Rogers, T. B., Kuiper, N. A., & Kirker, W. S. (1977). Self-reference and the encoding of personal information. *Journal of Personality and Social Psychology*, 35, 677–688. Copyright (1977) by the American Psychological Association. Adapted by permission of the author.

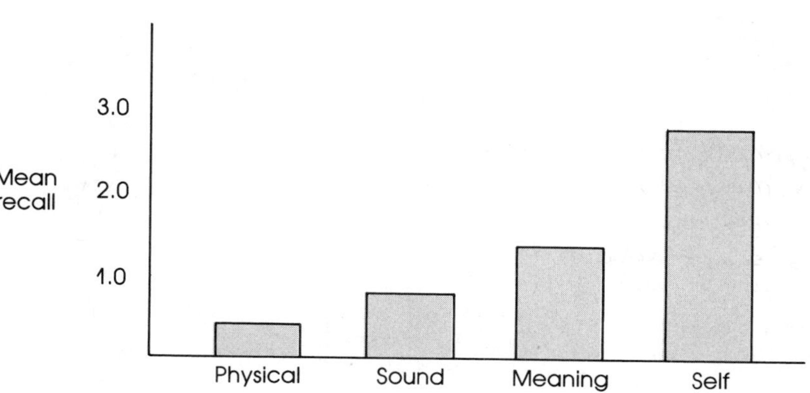

used four conditions and were able to make *six* different comparisons:

Physical versus sound
Physical versus meaning
Physical versus self
Sound versus meaning
Sound versus self
Meaning versus self

To gain this experimental sophistication, there is some cost. Specifically, you no longer can use the familiar t tests we encountered in Chapters 11 and 12. Instead, you now must learn a new statistical technique which is designed for experiments consisting of two or more sets of data. This new, general-purpose procedure is called analysis of variance.

13.1 INTRODUCTION

Analysis of variance (ANOVA) is a hypothesis-testing procedure used to determine if mean differences exist for two or more treatments (or populations). As with all inferential procedures, ANOVA uses sample data as the basis for drawing conclusions about populations. A diagram of a situation where analysis of variance would be used is shown in Figure 13.2.

Remember, we would expect samples to differ because of sampling error (Chapter 7).

For an independent-measures experiment, a separable sample is taken for each of the treatment conditions. Because it is very unlikely that any two samples will be identical, even if they come from the same population, we have assumed that the samples in Figure 13.2 have different scores and different means. The purpose of ANOVA is to decide whether the differences between the samples are simply due to chance (sampling error) or whether there are systematic treatment effects that have caused the scores in one group to be different from the scores in another. More pre-

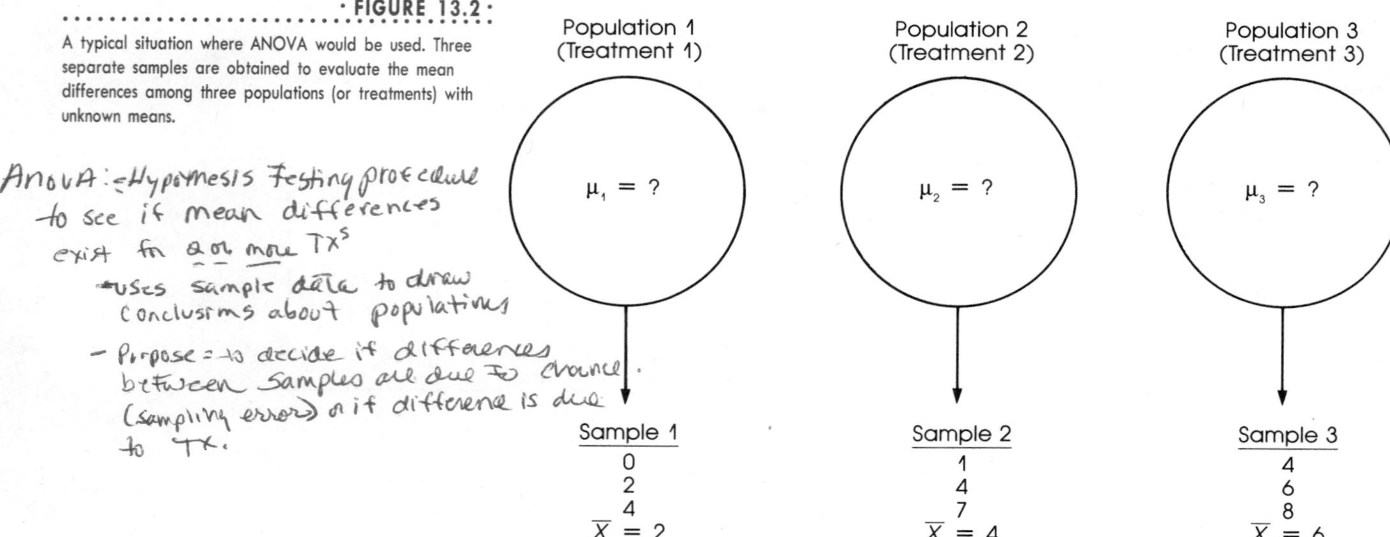

FIGURE 13.2
A typical situation where ANOVA would be used. Three separate samples are obtained to evaluate the mean differences among three populations (or treatments) with unknown means.

cisely, the alternatives can be stated as follows:

1. The populations for all treatments are really the same (u's for each population are identical); the mean difference between the samples occurred due to chance; that is, sampling error.
2. The populations for the treatments are different (they have different u's); the mean difference between the samples is due to the effect of the treatment.

STATISTICAL HYPOTHESES FOR ANOVA These alternatives (a treatment effect versus a mean difference due to chance) can be seen more clearly when stating the hypotheses for ANOVA. For example, suppose a psychologist examined learning performance under three temperature conditions: 50°, 70°, and 90°. Three samples of subjects are selected, one sample for each treatment condition. The purpose of the study is to determine whether room temperature affects learning performance. In statistical terms, we want to decide between two hypotheses: the null hypothesis (H_0), which says temperature has no effect, and the alternative hypothesis (H_1), which states that temperature does affect learning. In symbols, the null hypothesis states

$$H_0 : \mu_1 = \mu_2 = \mu_3$$

That is, there are no differences among the means of the populations that receive the three treatments. The population means are all the same. Once again, notice that hypotheses are always stated in terms of population parameters, even though we use sample data to test them.

For the alternative hypothesis we may state that

H_1 : At least one mean is different from the others

Notice that we have not given any specific alternative hypothesis. This is because there are many different alternatives possible, and it would be tedious to list them all. One alternative, for example, would be that the first two populations are identical but that the third is different. Another alternative states that the last two means are the same but that the first is different. Other alternatives might be

$H_1 : \mu_1 \neq \mu_2 \neq \mu_3$ all three means are different

$H_1 : \mu_1 = \mu_3$ μ_2 is different

It should be pointed out that a researcher typically entertains only one (or at most a few) of these alternative hypotheses. Usually a theory or the outcomes of previous studies will dictate a specific prediction concerning the treatment effect. For example, previous research has demonstrated that most tasks are performed best with a room temperature around 70°. With this in mind, our researcher probably would predict that performance would be better in the intermediate temperature treatment (70°) and worse at the extreme temperatures (50° and 90°). In symbols, this alternative would be

$$H_1 : \mu_2 > \mu_1 \quad \text{and} \quad \mu_2 > \mu_3$$

For the sake of simplicity, we will state a general alternative hypothesis rather than try to list all the possible specific alternatives.

It may appear that analysis of variance and t tests are simply two different ways of doing exactly the same job: testing for mean differences. In some respects this is true—both tests use sample data to test hypotheses about population means. However, ANOVA has a tremendous advantage over t tests. Specifically, t tests are limited to situations where there are only two treatments to compare. The major advantage of ANOVA is that it can be used to compare two or more treatments. Thus, ANOVA provides researchers with much greater flexibility in designing experiments and interpreting results.

13.2 THE LOGIC OF ANALYSIS OF VARIANCE

The formulas and calculations required in ANOVA are somewhat complicated, but the logic that underlies the whole procedure is fairly straightforward. Therefore, this section will attempt to give a general picture of analysis of variance before we start looking at the details. We will introduce the logic of ANOVA with the help of the hypothetical data in Table 13.1. These data represent the results of an independent measures experiment comparing learning performance under three temperature conditions.

One obvious characteristic of the data in Table 13.1 is that the scores are not all the same. In everyday language, the scores are different: in statistical terms, the scores are variable. Our goal is to measure the amount of variability (the size of the differences) and to explain where it comes from.

The first step is to determine the total variability for the entire set of data. To compute the total variability, we will combine all the scores from all the separate samples to obtain one general measure of variability for the complete experiment. Once we have measured the total variability, we can begin to break it apart into separate components. The word *analysis* means dividing into smaller parts. Because we are going to analyze variability, the process is called *analysis of variance*. This analysis process divides the total variability into two basic components:

1. *Between-Treatments Variability*. Looking at the data in Table 13.1, we clearly see that much of the variability in the scores is due to general differences between treatment conditions. For example, the scores in the 70° condition tend to be much higher ($\bar{X} = 4$) than the scores in the 50° condition ($\bar{X} = 1$). We will calculate the variability between treatments to provide a measure of the overall differences between treatment conditions—that is, the differences among sample means.

2. *Within-Treatments Variability*. In addition to the general differences between treatment conditions, there is variability within each sample. Looking again at Table 13.1, the scores in the 70° condition are not all the same; they are variable. The within-treatments variability will provide a measure of the variability inside each treatment condition.

TABLE 13.1

Hypothetical data from an experiment examining learning performance under three temperature conditions[a]

Treatment 1 50° (Sample 1)	Treatment 2 70° (Sample 2)	Treatment 3 90° (Sample 3)
0	4	1
1	3	2
3	6	2
1	3	0
0	4	0
$\bar{X} = 1$	$\bar{X} = 4$	$\bar{X} = 1$

[a]Note that there are three separate samples, with $n = 5$ in each sample. The dependent variable is the number of problems solved correctly.

Analyzing the total variability into these two components is the heart of analysis of variance. We will now examine each of the components in more detail.

BETWEEN-TREATMENTS VARIABILITY

Whenever you compare two samples representing two treatment conditions, there are three possible explanations for the differences (variability) between sample means:

1. *Treatment Effect.* It is possible that the different treatments have caused the samples to be different. In Table 13.1, the scores in sample 1 were obtained in a 50° room, and the scores in sample 2 were obtained in a 70° room. It is possible that the difference between these two samples is due in part to the different temperatures.

2. *Individual Differences.* Subjects enter an experiment with different backgrounds, abilities, and attitudes; that is, they are unique individuals. Whenever you compare separate samples (different groups of individuals), it is possible that the differences between samples are simply the result of individual differences.

In this chapter we are examining *independent-measures* designs (separate samples). In Chapter 14 we will look at ANOVA for repeated-measures experiments.

3. *Experimental Error.* Whenever you make a measurement, there is a chance of error. The error could be caused by poor equipment, lack of attention, or unpredictable changes in the event you are measuring. This kind of uncontrolled and unexplained difference is called *experimental error,* and it can cause two samples to be different.

Thus, when we compute the variability between treatments, we are measuring differences that could be due to any of these three factors or any combination of the three.

WITHIN-TREATMENTS VARIABILITY

There are only two possible explanations for variability within a treatment condition:

1. *Individual Differences.* The scores are obtained from different individuals, which could explain why the scores are variable.
2. *Experimental Error.* There always is a chance that the differences are caused by experimental error.

Notice that the variability inside a treatment condition cannot be attributed to any treatment effect because all subjects within a treatment condition are treated exactly the same. Thus, the differences within a treatment are not systematic or predictable but rather are due to chance. The analysis, or partitioning, of variability is diagrammed in Figure 13.3.

THE *F*-RATIO: THE TEST STATISTIC FOR ANOVA

Once we have analyzed the total variability into two basic components (between treatments and within treatments), we simply compare them. The comparison is made

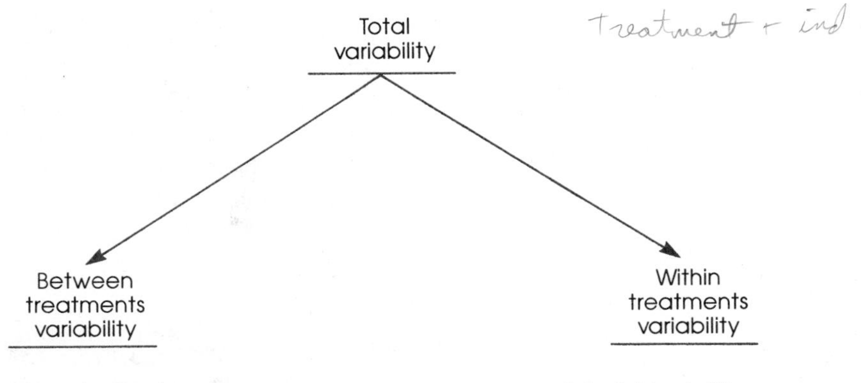

FIGURE 13.3

The independent measures analysis of variance partitions, or analyzes, the total variability into two components: variability between treatments and variability within treatments.

PERSPECTIVE 13.1

COMPARISON OF ANOVA AND *t* TESTS: A FIRST LOOK

It may help you to understand ANOVA if we compare the structure of the *F*-ratio with the structure of the *t* statistics that were used for hypothesis testing in previous chapters. With both ANOVA and the *t* tests, our goal is to use sample means (the data) to evaluate hypotheses about the population means. With the *t* tests (independent or repeated measures), we used a very direct method to measure the difference between the samples. Because these tests compare only two treatments, we simply computed the sample mean difference using either $(\bar{X}_1 - \bar{X}_2)$ or $\bar{D}$. This sample mean difference was used in the numerator of the *t* statistic and provided a measure of the actual difference between samples. With ANOVA, however, we somehow must measure the differences among several sample means. In other words, we must determine whether several sample means are all clustered together (small mean differences) or are all spread out (large mean differences). Fortunately, we already have learned a procedure for measuring the degree to which a set of values is clustered together or spread out—we simply compute variability. Thus, the numerator of the *F*-ratio contains a measure of the variability between treatments rather than mean differences.

For the *t* tests we computed a standard error, either $s_{\bar{X}-\bar{X}}$ or $s_{\bar{D}}$, for the denominator of the *t* statistic. You should recall that standard error provides a measure of the standard distance between a sample and its population. Thus, the structure of the *t* statistic compares the actual difference between the samples (numerator) with the standard difference that would be expected by chance (denominator).

$$t = \frac{\text{mean difference}}{\text{standard error}} = \frac{\text{difference between samples}}{\text{difference expected by chance}}$$

In a similar way, the denominator of the *F*-ratio provides a measure of uncontrolled, unsystematic differences—that is, differences due to chance. The structure of the *F*-ratio (like the structure of the *t* statistic) compares the actual differences between samples versus the differences due to chance.

$$F = \frac{\text{variability between treatments}}{\text{variability within treatments}} = \frac{\text{differences between samples}}{\text{differences expected by chance}}$$

For either the *t* statistic or the *F*-ratio, a large value indicates that the difference between the samples is more than would be expected by chance. When the value of *t* or *F* is sufficiently large, we reject the null hypothesis and conclude that there is a significant difference between treatments.

Later in this chapter (Section 13.7) we continue to explore the relation between ANOVA and *t* tests.

by computing a statistic called an *F*-ratio (see Perspective 13.1). For the independent-measures ANOVA, the *F*-ratio has the following structure:

$$F = \frac{\text{variability between treatments}}{\text{variability within treatments}} \tag{13.1}$$

When we express each component of variability in terms of its sources (see Figure 13.3), the structure of the *F*-ratio is

$$F = \frac{\text{treatment effect} + \text{individual differences} + \text{experimental error}}{\text{individual differences} + \text{experimental error}} \tag{13.2}$$

You should note that the between treatments variability and the within treatments variability differ in only one respect: the variability (mean differences) caused by the treatment effect. This single difference between the numerator and denominator of the *F*-ratio is crucial in determining if a treatment effect has occurred. Remember, the whole purpose for doing the experiment and the analysis is to find out whether or not the treatment has any effect. Let's consider the two possibilities:

1. H_0 is true, and there is no treatment effect. In this case, the numerator and denominator of the *F*-ratio are measuring the same variance:

$$F = \frac{0 + \text{individual differences} + \text{experimental error}}{\text{individual differences} + \text{experimental error}}$$

When H_0 is true and the treatment effect is zero, the *F*-ratio is expected to equal 1.

2. If H_0 is false, then a treatment effect does exist, and the *F*-ratio becomes

$$F = \frac{\text{treatment effect} + \text{individual differences} + \text{experimental error}}{\text{individual differences} + \text{experimental error}}$$

The numerator of the ratio should be larger than the denominator, and the *F*-ratio is expected to be larger than 1.00. Ordinarily, the presence of a large treatment effect is reflected in a large value for the *F*-ratio.

In more general terms, the denominator of the *F*-ratio measures only uncontrolled and unexplained (often called *unsystematic*) variability. For this reason, the denominator of the *F*-ratio is called the *error term*. The numerator of the *F*-ratio always includes the same unsystematic variability as in the error term, but it also includes any systematic differences caused by the treatment effect. The goal of ANOVA is to find out whether or not a treatment effect exists.

· DEFINITION · For ANOVA, the denominator of the *F*-ratio is called the *error term*. The error term provides a measure of the variance due to chance. When the treatment effect is zero (H_0 is true), the error term measures the same sources of variance as the numerator of the *F*-ratio, so the value of the *F*-ratio is expected to be nearly equal to 1.00. (Technically, the average value for *F*-ratios is slightly larger than 1.00 when H_0 is true.)

· LEARNING CHECK ·

1 ANOVA is a statistical procedure that compares two or more treatment conditions for differences in variance. (True or False)

2 In ANOVA what value is expected on the average for the *F*-ratio when the null hypothesis is true?

3 What happens to the value of the *F*-ratio if differences between treatments are increased? What happens to the *F*-ratio if variability inside the treatments is increased?

4 In ANOVA, the total variability is partitioned into two parts. What are these two variability components called, and how are they used in the *F*-ratio?

ANSWERS

1 False. Although ANOVA uses variability in the computations, the purpose of the test is to evaluate differences in *means* between treatments.

2 When H_0 is true, the expected value for the *F*-ratio is 1.00 because the top and bottom of the ratio are both measuring the same variance.

3 As differences between treatments increase, the *F*-ratio will increase. As variability within treatments increases, the *F*-ratio will decrease.

4 The two components are between-treatments variability and within-treatments variability. Between treatments is the numerator of the *F*-ratio and within treatments is the denominator.

13.3 ANOVA VOCABULARY, NOTATION, AND FORMULAS

Before we introduce the notation, let's look at some special terminology that is used for ANOVA. The first term we will need from the ANOVA vocabulary is the word *factor*. This term is used in place of the words *independent variable*. Therefore, for the experiment shown in Table 13.1, the factor is temperature.

· DEFINITION · In analysis of variance, a *factor* is an independent variable.

Because this experiment has only one independent variable, it is called a *single-factor experiment*. In Chapter 15, we will examine *two-factor experiments*; that is, experiments with two independent variables.

The second term you need to know is *levels*. The levels in an experiment consist of the different values used in the factor. For example, in the learning experiment

TABLE 13.2

Hypothetical data from an experiment examining learning performance under three temperature conditions[a]

Temperature Conditions			
1	2	3	
50°	70°	90°	
0	4	1	
1	3	2	$\sum X^2 = 106$
3	6	2	$G = 30$
1	3	0	$N = 15$
0	4	0	$k = 3$
$T_1 = 5$	$T_2 = 20$	$T_3 = 5$	
$SS_1 = 6$	$SS_2 = 6$	$SS_3 = 4$	
$n_1 = 5$	$n_2 = 5$	$n_3 = 5$	
$\bar{X}_1 = 1$	$\bar{X}_2 = 4$	$\bar{X}_3 = 1$	

[a]Summary values and notation for an analysis of variance also are presented.

(Table 13.1) we are using three values of temperature. Therefore, the temperature factor has three levels.

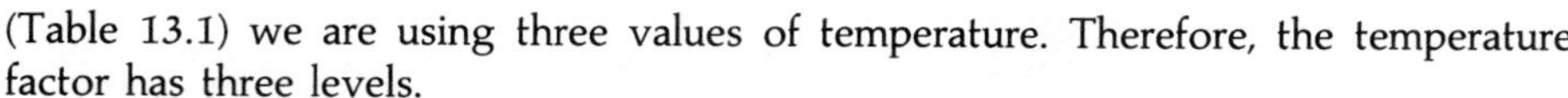

DEFINITION The individual treatment conditions that make up a factor are called *levels* of the factor.

Because ANOVA most often is used to examine data from more than two treatment conditions (and more than two samples), we will need a notation system to help keep track of all the individual scores and totals. To help introduce this notational system, we will use the hypothetical data from Table 13.1 again. The data are reproduced in Table 13.2 along with some of the notation and statistics that will be described.

1. The letter k is used to identify the number of treatment conditions, that is, the number of levels of the factor. For an independent measures experiment, k also specifies the number of separate samples. For the data in Table 13.2, there are three treatments, so $k = 3$.

2. The number of scores in each treatment is identified by a lowercase letter n. For the example in Table 13.2, $n = 5$ for all the treatments. If the samples are of different sizes, you can identify a specific sample by using a subscript. For example, n_2 is the number of scores in treatment 2.

3. The total number of scores in the entire experiment is specified by a capital letter N. When all the samples are the same size (n is constant), $N = kn$. For the data in Table 13.2, there are $n = 5$ scores in each of the $k = 3$ treatments, so $N = 3(5) = 15$.

Because ANOVA formulas require $\sum X$ for each treatment and $\sum X$ for the entire set of scores, we have introduced new notation (T and G) to help identify which $\sum X$ is being used. Remember, T stands for *treatment total* and G stands for *grand total*.

4. The total ($\sum X$) for each treatment condition is identified by the capital letter T. The total for a specific treatment can be identified by adding a numerical subscript to the T. For example, the total for the second treatment in Table 13.2 is $T_2 = 20$.

5. The sum of all the scores in the experiment (the grand total) is identified by G. You can compute G by adding up all N scores or by adding up the treatment totals: $G = \sum T$.

6. Although there is no new notation involved, we also have computed SS and $\bar{X}$ for each sample, and we have calculated $\sum X^2$ for the entire set of $N = 15$ scores in the experiment. These values are given in Table 13.2 and will be important in the formulas and calculations for ANOVA.

ANOVA FORMULAS

The F-ratio used in analysis of variance is composed of two variances, both computed from sample data: variance between treatments in the numerator and variance within treatments in the denominator. You should recall that variance for a sample has been defined as

$$\text{sample variance} = s^2 = \frac{SS}{df}$$

To compute the final *F*-ratio, we will need an *SS* and a *df* for each of the two variances. Thus the process of analyzing variability will occur in two parts. First, we will compute *SS* for the total experiment and analyze it into two components (between treatments and within treatments). Second, we will conduct a similar analysis for degrees of freedom.

ANALYSIS OF SUM OF SQUARES (SS) The ANOVA requires that we first compute a total variability and then partition this value into two components: between treatments and within treatments. This analysis is outlined in Figure 13.3. We will examine each of the three components separately.

1. *Total Sum of Squares,* SS_{total}. As the name implies, SS_{total} is simply the sum of squares for the entire set of *N* scores. We calculate this value by using the computational formula for *SS*:

$$SS = \sum X^2 - \frac{(\sum X)^2}{N}$$

To make this formula consistent with the ANOVA notation, we substitute the letter *G* in place of $\sum X$ and obtain

(13.3) $$SS_{\text{total}} = \sum X^2 - \frac{G^2}{N}$$

Applying this formula to the set of data in Table 13.2, we obtain

$$SS_{\text{total}} = 106 - \frac{30^2}{15}$$
$$= 106 - 60$$
$$= 46$$

2. *Within-Treatments Sum of Squares,* SS_{within}. Now we are looking at the variability inside each of the treatment conditions. We already have computed the *SS* within each of the four treatment conditions: $SS_1 = 6$, $SS_2 = 6$, and $SS_3 = 4$. To find the overall within treatment sum of squares, we simply add these values together:

(13.4) $$SS_{\text{within}} = \sum SS_{\text{inside each treatment}}$$

For the data in Table 13.2, this formula gives

$$SS_{\text{within}} = 6 + 6 + 4$$
$$= 16$$

3. *Between-Treatments Sum of Squares,* SS_{between}. Before we introduce the equation for SS_{between}, consider what we have found so far. The total variability for the data in Table 13.2 is $SS_{\text{total}} = 46$. We intend to partition this total into two parts (see Figure 13.3). One part, SS_{within}, has been found to be equal to 16. This means that SS_{between} must be equal to 30 in order for the two parts (16 and 30) to add up to the total (46). The equation for the between treatments sum of squares should produce a value of $SS_{\text{between}} = 30$. You should recall that the variability between treatments is measuring the differences between treatment means. Conceptually, the most direct way of measuring the amount of variability among the treatment means is simply to compute the sum of squares for the set of means.

To do this, we begin by computing the overall mean for the entire set of N scores in the experiment. This overall mean will be identified by the symbol $\bar{G}$, indicating the grand mean. For the data in Table 13.2, the grand total is $G = 30$ for a set of $N = 15$ scores, so the grand mean is $\bar{G} = \frac{30}{15} = 2$. Next, we measure the extent to which each individual sample mean deviates from the grand mean:

$$\text{deviation} = (\bar{X} - \bar{G})$$

Then we square these deviations and sum the results to obtain the sum of squared deviations (SS) for the set of sample means.

$$SS_{\text{means}} = \sum(\bar{X} - \bar{G})^2$$

Because each individual treatment mean represents a sample of n scores, each of the squared deviations is multiplied by n to obtain a complete measure of the between-treatments sum of squares:

$$SS_{\text{between}} = \sum n(\bar{X} - \bar{G})^2 \qquad (13.5)$$

Applying this formula to the data in Table 13.2, we obtain

$$\begin{aligned} SS_{\text{between}} &= 5(1-2)^2 + 5(4-2)^2 + 5(1-2)^2 \\ &= 5 + 20 + 5 \\ &= 30 \end{aligned}$$

At this point of the analysis, the work may be checked to see if total SS equals between-treatments SS plus within-treatments SS.

Notice that the result, $SS_{\text{between}} = 30$, is exactly what we predicted. The two parts from the analysis (between and within) add up to the total:

$$\begin{aligned} SS_{\text{total}} &= SS_{\text{within}} + SS_{\text{between}} \\ 46 &= 16 + 30 \end{aligned}$$

Although formula 13.5 is conceptually the most direct way of computing the amount of variability among the treatment means, this formula can be awkward to use, especially when the means are not whole numbers. For this reason, we generally will use an algebraically equivalent formula that uses the treatment totals (T values) instead of the means:

$$SS_{\text{between}} = \sum \frac{T^2}{n} - \frac{G^2}{N} \qquad (13.6)$$

For the derivation of this formula, see Perspective 13.2.

Using this new formula with the data in Table 13.2, we obtain

$$\begin{aligned} SS_{\text{between}} &= \frac{5^2}{5} + \frac{20^2}{5} + \frac{5^2}{5} - \frac{30^2}{15} \\ &= 5 + 80 + 5 - 60 \\ &= 90 - 60 \\ &= 30 \end{aligned}$$

Notice that this result is identical to the value we obtained using formula 13.5.

The formula for each SS and the relationships among these three values are shown in Figure 13.4.

THE ANALYSIS OF DEGREES OF FREEDOM (*df*)

The analysis of degrees of freedom (df) follows the same pattern as the analysis of SS. First, we will find df for the total set of N scores, and then we will partition this value into two components: degrees of freedom between treatments and degrees of

PERSPECTIVE 13.2

ALTERNATIVE FORMULAS FOR ANOVA

Part I: Formulas for SS_{between}. We have presented two different formulas for SS_{between}. To show that these formulas are equivalent, we begin with formula 13.5 and derive formula 13.6:

$$SS_{\text{between}}$$
$$= \sum n(\bar{X} - \bar{G})^2$$
$$= \sum n(\bar{X} - \bar{G})(\bar{X} - \bar{G})$$
$$= \sum n(\bar{X}^2 - 2\bar{G}\bar{X} + \bar{G}^2)$$
$$= \sum n\bar{X}^2 - 2\bar{G}\sum n\bar{X} + \bar{G}^2\sum n$$
$$= \sum n\left(\frac{T}{n}\right)^2 - 2\left(\frac{G}{N}\right)\sum n\left(\frac{T}{n}\right) + \left(\frac{G}{N}\right)^2\sum n \quad \left(\text{substituting } \frac{T}{n} = \bar{X} \text{ and } \frac{G}{N} = \bar{G}\right)$$
$$= \sum\frac{T^2}{n} - 2\left(\frac{G}{N}\right)\sum T + \frac{G^2}{N^2}\sum n$$
$$= \sum\frac{T^2}{n} - 2\left(\frac{G}{N}\right)G + \left(\frac{G^2}{N^2}\right)N \quad \left(\text{substituting } G = \sum T \text{ and } N = \sum n\right)$$
$$= \sum\frac{T^2}{n} - 2\frac{G^2}{N} + \frac{G^2}{N}$$
$$= \sum\frac{T^2}{n} - \frac{G^2}{N} \quad \left(\text{combining terms with } \frac{G^2}{N}\right)$$

Part II: Formulas for SS_{within}. You also should know that there is an alternative formula for finding SS_{within}. This formula is developed briefly in the following three steps:

1. First, recall that the two components add up to the total:

$$SS_{\text{within}} + SS_{\text{between}} = SS_{\text{total}}$$

2. By simple algebra we obtain the relation

$$SS_{\text{within}} = SS_{\text{total}} - SS_{\text{between}}$$

3. Finally, substituting the equations for SS_{total} and SS_{between}, we obtain

$$SS_{\text{within}} = \sum X^2 - \frac{G^2}{N} - \left(\sum\frac{T^2}{n} - \frac{G^2}{N}\right)$$
$$= \sum X^2 - \frac{G^2}{N} - \sum\frac{T^2}{n} + \frac{G^2}{N}$$
$$= \sum X^2 - \sum\frac{T^2}{n}$$

Note: This alternative formula for SS_{within} can help simplify the calculations for ANOVA. To find all three SS values, you must compute only three numbers: $\sum X^2$, $\sum T^2/n$, and G^2/N. These three values are sufficient to satisfy the three SS formulas.

freedom within treatments. In computing degrees of freedom, there are two important considerations to keep in mind:

1. Each df value is associated with a specific SS value.
2. Normally, the value of df is obtained by counting the number of items that were used to calculate SS and then subtracting 1. For example, if you compute SS for a set of n scores, then $df = n - 1$.

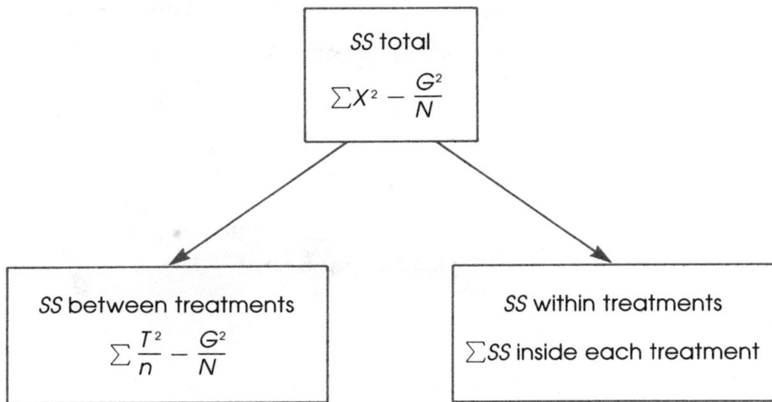

FIGURE 13.4

Partitioning the sum of squares (SS) for the independent-measures analysis of variance.

With this in mind, we will examine the degrees of freedom for each part of the analysis:

1. *Total Degrees of Freedom, df_{total}.* To find the df associated with SS_{total}, you must first recall that this SS value measures variability for the entire set of N scores. Therefore, the df value will be

(13.7) $$df_{\text{total}} = N - 1$$

For the data in Table 13.2, the total number of scores is $N = 15$, so the total degrees of freedom would be

$$df_{\text{total}} = 15 - 1$$
$$= 14$$

2. *Within-Treatments Degrees of Freedom, df_{within}.* To find the df associated with SS_{within}, we must look at how this SS value is computed. Remember, we first find SS inside each of the treatments and then add these values together. Each of the treatment SS values measures variability for the n scores in the treatment, so each SS will have $df = n - 1$. When all these individual treatment values are added together, we obtain

(13.8) $$df_{\text{within}} = \sum(n - 1)$$

For the experiment we have been considering, each treatment has $n = 5$ scores. This means there are $n - 1 = 4$ degrees of freedom inside each treatment. Because there are three different treatment conditions, this gives a total of 12 for the within-treatments degrees of freedom. Notice that this formula for df simply adds up the number of scores in each treatment (the n values) and subtracts 1 for each treatment. If these two stages are done separately, you obtain

(13.9) $$df_{\text{within}} = N - k$$

(Adding up all the n values gives N. If you subtract 1 for each treatment, then altogether you have subtracted k because there are k treatments.) For the data in Table 13.2, $N = 15$ and $k = 3$, so

$$df_{\text{within}} = 15 - 3$$
$$= 12$$

3. *Between-Treatments Degrees of Freedom, df_{between}.* The df associated with SS_{between} can be found by considering the SS formula. This SS formula measures the variability among the treatment means or totals. To find df_{between}, simply count the number of T values (or means) and subtract 1. Because the number of treatments is specified by the letter k, the formula for df is

(13.10) $$df_{\text{between}} = k - 1$$

For the data in Table 13.2, there are three different treatment conditions (three T values), so the between treatments degrees of freedom are

$$df_{\text{between}} = 3 - 1$$
$$= 2$$

Notice that the two parts we obtained from this analysis of degrees of freedom add up to equal the total degrees of freedom:

$$df_{\text{total}} = df_{\text{within}} + df_{\text{between}}$$
$$14 = 12 + 2$$

The complete analysis of degrees of freedom is shown in Figure 13.5.

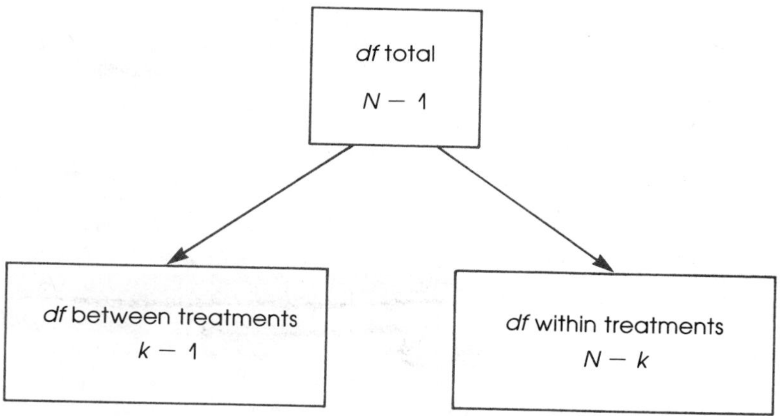

FIGURE 13.5
Partitioning degrees of freedom (*df*) for the independent measures analysis of variance.

CALCULATION OF VARIANCES (*MS*) AND THE *F*-RATIO The final step in the analysis of variance procedure is to compute the variance between treatments and the variance within treatments in order to calculate the *F*-ratio. You should recall (from Chapter 4) that variance is defined as the average squared deviation. For a sample, you compute this average by the following formula:

$$\text{variance} = \frac{SS}{n-1} = \frac{SS}{df}$$

In ANOVA it is customary to use the term *mean square, or simply MS,* in place of the term *variance.* Note that variance is the *mean squared* deviation, so this terminology is quite sensible. For the final *F*-ratio you will need an *MS* between treatments and an *MS* within treatments. In each case,

$$MS = \frac{SS}{df} \tag{13.11}$$

For the data we have been considering,

$$MS_{\text{between}} = \frac{SS_{\text{between}}}{df_{\text{between}}} = \frac{30}{2} = 15$$

and

$$MS_{\text{within}} = \frac{SS_{\text{within}}}{df_{\text{within}}} = \frac{16}{12} = 1.33$$

We now have a measure of the variance (or differences) between the treatments and a measure of the variance within the treatments. The *F*-ratio simply compares these two variances:

$$F = \frac{MS_{\text{between}}}{MS_{\text{within}}} \tag{13.12}$$

For the experiment we have been examining, the data give an *F*-ratio of

$$F = \frac{15}{1.33} = 11.28$$

The obtained value of $F = 11.28$ indicates that the numerator of the *F*-ratio is substantially bigger than the denominator. If you recall the conceptual structure of the *F*-ratio as presented in formulas 13.1 and 13.2, the *F* value we obtained indicates that the differences between treatments are substantially greater than would be expected by chance, providing evidence that a treatment effect really exists. Stated in terms of the experimental variables, it appears that temperature does have an effect on learning performance. However, to properly evaluate the F-ratio, we must examine the F distribution.

13.4 THE DISTRIBUTION OF F-RATIOS

In analysis of variance, the F-ratio is constructed so that the numerator and denominator of the ratio are measuring exactly the same variance when the null hypothesis is true (see formula 13.2). In this situation we expect the value of F to be around 1.00. The problem now is to define precisely what we mean by "around 1.00." What values are considered to be close to 1.00, and what values are far away? To answer this question, we need to look at all the possible F values, that is, the distribution of F-ratios.

Before we examine this distribution in detail, you should note two obvious characteristics:

1. Because F-ratios are computed from two variances (the numerator and denominator of the ratio), F values always will be positive numbers. Remember, variance is always positive.
2. When H_0 is true, the numerator and denominator of the F-ratio are measuring the same variance. In this case, the two sample variances should be about the same size, so the ratio should be near 1. In other words, the distribution of F-ratios should pile up around 1.00.

With these two factors in mind we can sketch the distribution of F-ratios. The distribution is cut off at zero (all positive values), piles up around 1.00, and then tapers off to the right (see Figure 13.6). The exact shape of the F distribution depends on the degrees of freedom for the two variances in the F-ratio. You should recall that the precision of a sample variance depends on the number of scores or the degrees of freedom. In general, the variance for a large sample (large *df*) provides a more

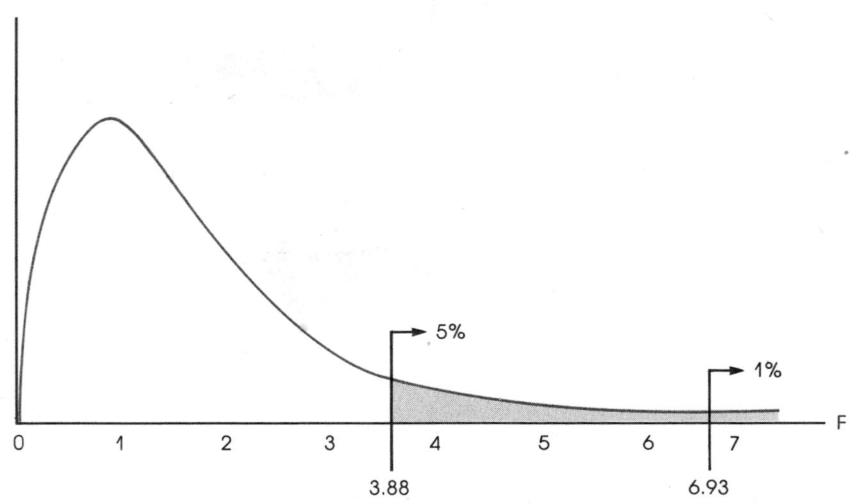

FIGURE 13.6 The distribution of F-ratios with $df = 2, 12$. Of all the values in the distribution, only 5% are larger than $F = 3.88$, and only 1% are larger than $F = 6.93$.

accurate estimate of the population variance. Because the precision of the *MS* values depends on *df*, the shape of the *F* distribution also will depend on the *df* values for the numerator and denominator of the *F*-ratio. With very large *df* values, nearly all the *F*-ratios will be clustered very near to 1.00. With smaller *df* values, the *F* distribution is more spread out.

For analysis of variance we expect *F* near 1.00 if H_0 is true, and we expect a large value for *F* if H_0 is not true. In the *F* distribution, we need to separate those values that are reasonably near 1.00 from the values that are significantly greater than 1.00. These critical values are presented in an *F* distribution table in Appendix B, page 484. To use the table, you must know the *df* values for the *F*-ratio (numerator and denominator), and you must know the alpha level for the hypothesis test. It is customary for an *F* table to have the *df* values for the numerator of the *F*-ratio printed across the top of the table. The *df* values for the denominator of *F* are printed in a column on the left-hand side. A portion of the *F* distribution table is shown in Table 13.3. For the temperature experiment we have been considering, the numerator of the *F*-ratio (between treatments) has $df = 2$ and the denominator of the *F*-ratio (within treatments) has $df = 12$. This *F*-ratio is said to have "degrees of freedom equal to 2 and 12." The degrees of freedom would be written as $df = 2, 12$. To use the table, you would first find $df = 2$ across the top of the table and $df = 12$ in the first column. When you line up these two values, they point to a pair of numbers in the middle of the table. These numbers give the critical cutoffs for $\alpha = .05$ and $\alpha = .01$. With $df = 2, 12$, for example, the numbers in the table are 3.88 and 6.93. These values indicate that the most unlikely 5% of the distribution ($\alpha = .05$) begins at a value of 3.88. The most extreme 1% of the distribution begins at a value of 6.93 (see Figure 13.6).

In the temperature experiment we obtained an *F*-ratio of 11.28. According to the critical cutoffs in Figure 13.6, this value is extremely unlikely (it is in the most extreme 1%). Therefore, we would reject H_0 with α set at either .05 or .01 and conclude that temperature does have a significant effect on learning performance.

TABLE 13.3

A portion of the *F* distribution table. Entries in roman type are critical values for the .05 level of significance and bold type values are for the .01 level of significance.

Degrees of Freedom Denominator	Degrees of Freedom: Numerator					
	1	2	3	4	5	6
10	4.96	4.10	3.71	3.48	3.33	3.22
	10.04	**7.56**	**6.55**	**5.99**	**5.64**	**5.39**
11	4.84	3.98	3.59	3.36	3.20	3.09
	9.65	**7.20**	**6.22**	**5.67**	**5.32**	**5.07**
12	4.75	3.88	3.49	3.26	3.11	3.00
	9.33	**6.93**	**5.95**	**5.41**	**5.06**	**4.82**
13	4.67	3.80	3.41	3.18	3.02	2.92
	9.07	**6.70**	**5.74**	**5.20**	**4.86**	**4.62**
14	4.60	3.74	3.34	3.11	2.96	2.85
	8.86	**6.51**	**5.56**	**5.03**	**4.69**	**4.46**
15	4.54	3.68	3.29	3.06	2.90	2.79
	8.68	**6.36**	**5.42**	**4.89**	**4.56**	**4.32**
16	4.49	3.63	3.24	3.01	2.85	2.74
	8.53	**6.23**	**5.29**	**4.77**	**4.44**	**4.20**
17	4.45	3.59	3.20	2.96	2.81	2.70
	8.40	**6.11**	**5.18**	**4.67**	**4.34**	**4.10**
18	4.41	3.55	3.16	2.93	2.77	2.66
	8.28	**6.01**	**5.09**	**4.58**	**4.25**	**4.01**

· LEARNING CHECK ·

1 Calculate SS_{total}, $SS_{between}$, and SS_{within} for the following set of data:

Treatment 1	Treatment 2	Treatment 3	
$n = 10$	$n = 10$	$n = 10$	$N = 30$
$T = 10$	$T = 20$	$T = 30$	$G = 60$
$SS = 27$	$SS = 16$	$SS = 23$	$\sum X^2 = 206$

2 A researcher uses an ANOVA to compare three treatment conditions with a sample of $n = 8$ in each treatment. For this analysis, find df_{total}, $df_{between}$, and df_{within}.

3 With $\alpha = .05$, what value forms the boundary for the critical region in the distribution of *F*-ratios with $df = 2, 24$?

ANSWERS

1 $SS_{total} = 86$; $SS_{between} = 20$; $SS_{within} = 66$

2 $df_{total} = 23$, $df_{between} = 2$, and $df_{within} = 21$

3 The critical value is 3.40.

13.5 EXAMPLES OF HYPOTHESIS TESTING WITH ANOVA

Although we have seen all the individual components of ANOVA, the following example demonstrates the complete ANOVA process using the standard four-step procedure for hypothesis testing.

· EXAMPLE 13.1 · The data depicted in Table 13.4 were obtained from an independent measures experiment designed to measure the effectiveness of three pain relievers (A, B, and C). A fourth group that received a placebo (sugar pill) also was tested.

The purpose of the analysis is to determine whether these sample data provide evidence of any significant differences among the four drugs. The dependent variable is the amount of time (in seconds) that subjects can withstand a painfully hot stimulus.

STEP 1 The first step is to state the hypotheses and select an alpha level:

$$H_0: \mu_1 = \mu_2 = \mu_3 = \mu_4 \qquad \text{(no treatment effect)}$$

H_1: At least one of the treatment means is different

We will use $\alpha = .05$.

STEP 2 To locate the critical region for the *F*-ratio, we first must determine degrees of freedom for $MS_{between}$ and MS_{within} (the numerator and denominator of *F*). For

· TABLE 13.4 ·

The effect of drug treatment on the amount of time (in seconds) stimulus is endured

Placebo	Drug A	Drug B	Drug C	
0	1	3	7	$N = 12$
0	2	4	4	$G = 36$
3	3	5	4	$\sum X^2 = 154$
$T = 3$	$T = 6$	$T = 12$	$T = 15$	
$SS = 6$	$SS = 2$	$SS = 2$	$SS = 6$	

these data, the total degrees of freedom would be

$$df_{\text{total}} = N - 1 = 12 - 1 = 11$$

Analyzing this total into two components, we obtain

Note that the two df components (between and within) add up to equal df_{total}.

$$df_{\text{between}} = k - 1 = 4 - 1 = 3$$

$$df_{\text{within}} = N - k = 12 - 4 = 8$$

The F-ratio for these data will have $df = 3, 8$. The distribution of all the possible F-ratios with $df = 3, 8$ is presented in Figure 13.7. Almost always (95% of the time) we should obtain an F-ratio less than 4.07 if H_0 is true.

STEP 3 We already have the data for this experiment, so it now is time for the calculations.

Analysis of SS: First we will compute the total SS and then the two components as indicated in Figure 13.4:

$$SS_{\text{total}} = \sum X^2 - \frac{G^2}{N} = 154 - \frac{36^2}{12} = 154 - 108 = 46$$

$$SS_{\text{within}} = \sum SS_{\text{inside each treatment}} = 6 + 2 + 2 + 6 = 16$$

FIGURE 13.7

The distribution of F-ratios with $df = 3, 8$. The critical value for $\alpha = .05$ is $F = 4.07$.

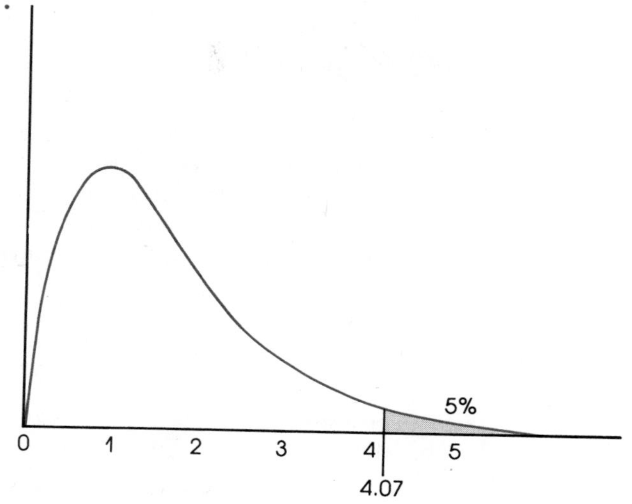

$$SS_{\text{between}} = \sum \frac{T^2}{n} - \frac{G^2}{N}$$

$$= \frac{3^2}{3} + \frac{6^2}{3} + \frac{12^2}{3} + \frac{15^2}{3} - \frac{36^2}{12}$$

$$= 3 + 12 + 48 + 75 - 108$$

$$= 30$$

Note that the two variability components (between and within) add up to equal SS_{total}.

Calculation of Mean Squares. Now we must compute the variance or MS for each of the two components:

$$MS_{\text{between}} = \frac{SS_{\text{between}}}{df_{\text{between}}} = \frac{30}{3} = 10$$

$$MS_{\text{within}} = \frac{SS_{\text{within}}}{df_{\text{within}}} = \frac{16}{8} = 2$$

Calculation of F. Finally, we compute the F-ratio:

$$F = \frac{MS_{\text{between}}}{MS_{\text{within}}} = \frac{10}{2} = 5.00$$

STEP 4 *Statistical Decision.* The F value we obtained, $F = 5.00$, is in the critical region (see Figure 13.7). It is very unlikely ($p < .05$) that we will obtain a value this large if H_0 is true. Therefore, we reject H_0 and conclude that there is a significant treatment effect.

Example 13.1 demonstrated the complete, step-by-step application of the ANOVA procedure. There are three additional points that can be made using this example.

First, you should look carefully at the statistical decision. We have rejected H_0 and concluded that not all the treatments are the same. But we have not determined which ones are different. Is drug A different from the placebo? Is drug A different from drug B? Unfortunately, these questions remain unanswered. We do know that at least one difference exists (we rejected H_0), but additional analysis is necessary to find out exactly where this difference is. This problem is addressed in Section 13.6.

Second, it is common in experimental reports to present the obtained F-ratio, the degrees of freedom, and the alpha level in one concise phrase. For the data in Example 13.1, this phrase would be

$F(3, 8) = 5.00, \quad p < .05$

This phrase indicates that our F-ratio has $df = 3, 8$, we obtained a value of $F = 5.00$ from the data, and the F value was in the critical region with alpha equal to .05.

Third, all of the parts of the analysis (the SS, df, F, etc.) can be presented together in one table called an *analysis of variance summary table.* Although these tables are no longer commonly used in published research reports, they do provide a concise means for presenting the results of an analysis. The summary table for the analysis in Example 13.1 is as follows:

Source	SS	df	MS	
Between treatments	30	3	10	$F = 5.00$
Within treatments	16	8	2	
Total	46	11		

· LEARNING CHECK ·

1 The following data summarize the results of an experiment using three separate samples to compare three treatment conditions:

Treatment 1	Treatment 2	Treatment 3	
$n = 5$	$n = 5$	$n = 5$	
$T = 5$	$T = 10$	$T = 30$	$\sum X^2 = 325$
$SS = 45$	$SS = 25$	$SS = 50$	

Do these data provide evidence of any significant mean differences among the treatments? Test with $\alpha = .05$.

2 A researcher reports an F-ratio with $df = 2, 30$ for an independent measures analysis of variance. How many treatment conditions were compared in the experiment? How many subjects participated in the experiment?

ANSWERS

1 The following summary table presents the results of the analysis:

Source	SS	df	MS	
Between	70	2	35	$F = 3.5$
Within	120	12	10	
Total	190	14		

The critical value for F is 3.88. The obtained value for F is not in the critical region and we fail to reject H_0.

2 There were 3 treatment conditions ($df_{\text{between}} = k - 1 = 2$). A total of $N = 33$ individuals participated ($df_{\text{within}} = 30 = N - k$).

13.6 POST HOC TESTS

In analysis of variance, the null hypothesis states that there is no treatment effect:

$$H_0: \mu_1 = \mu_2 = \mu_3 \cdots$$

When you reject the null hypothesis, you conclude that the means are not all the same. Although this appears to be a simple conclusion, in most cases it actually creates more questions than it answers. When there are only two treatments in an experiment, H_0 will state that $\mu_1 = \mu_2$. If you reject this hypothesis, the conclusion is quite straightforward; i.e., the two means are not equal ($\mu_1 \neq \mu_2$). However, when you have more than two treatments, the situation immediately becomes more complex. With $k = 3$, for example, rejecting H_0 indicates that not all the means are the same. Now you must decide which ones are different. Is μ_1 different from μ_2? Is μ_2 different from μ_3? Is μ_1 different from μ_3? Are all three different? The purpose of post hoc tests is to answer these questions.

As the name implies, post hoc tests are done after an analysis of variance. More specifically, these tests are done after ANOVA when

1. You reject H_0 and
2. There are three or more treatments ($k \geq 3$).

Rejecting H_0 indicates that at least one difference exists among the treatments. With $k = 3$ or more, the problem is to find where the differences are.

In general, a post hoc test enables you to go back through the data and compare the individual treatments two at a time. In statistical terms, this is called making *pairwise comparisons*. For example, with $k = 3$, we would compare μ_1 versus μ_2, then μ_2

versus μ_3, and then μ_1 versus μ_3. In each case, we are looking for a significant mean difference.

You might wonder why we do not perform *t* tests for all possible pairs of groups. This approach may cause a problem in avoiding Type I errors. Remember, each time you do a hypothesis test, you select an alpha level. For this reason, researchers often make a distinction between the *testwise* alpha level and the *experimentwise* alpha level. The testwise alpha level is simply the alpha level you select for each individual hypothesis test. The experimentwise alpha level is the total probability of a Type I error that is accumulated from all the separate tests in the experiment. It is the experimentwise alpha level that is most important when doing multiple comparisons between all possible pairs of groups. The more comparisons you make, the greater the experimentwise alpha level and the greater the risk of a Type I error. The problem with simply doing *t* tests for all possible pairs of treatment groups is that the experimentwise alpha level may be quite large.

Fortunately, many post hoc tests have been developed that attempt to control the experimentwise alpha level. These tests can be classified into two broad categories: *a priori*, or planned, comparisons and *a posteriori*, or unplanned, comparisons.

· DEFINITION · *A priori tests* are intended to compare specific treatment conditions that are identified before the experiment begins. These tests generally make little attempt to control the alpha level. They should be used cautiously and only when you have a small number of preplanned comparisons. Planned comparisons can be made even when the overall *F*-ratio is not significant.

Technically, an *a priori* test cannot also be a *post hoc* test. However, these tests are done after an ANOVA, so we will discuss them along with other post tests.

Having a specific hypothesis (that is, making a prediction about the outcome of a portion of the experiment) justifies planned comparisons that will test this hypothesis.

The rationale for these tests is that the researcher has a specific small experiment (comparing two treatments) contained within a larger experiment. Because the investigator has specific hypotheses for just this portion of the experiment, it is reasonable to test its results separately.

· DEFINITION · *A posteriori tests* are used for treatment comparisons that were not necessarily planned at the beginning of the experiment. These tests attempt to control the overall alpha level by making adjustments for the number of different samples (potential comparisons) in the experiment. To justify a posteriori tests, the *F*-ratio from the overall ANOVA must be significant.

TUKEY'S HONESTLY SIGNIFICANT DIFFERENCE (HSD) TEST

The first post hoc test we will consider is Tukey's HSD test. We have selected Tukey's HSD test because it is a good representative of a posteriori tests, and it is a commonly used test in psychological research. Tukey's test allows you to compute a single value that determines the minimum difference between treatment means that is necessary for significance. This value, called the *honestly significant difference*, or HSD, is then used to compare any two treatment conditions. If the mean difference exceeds Tukey's HSD, you conclude that there is a significant difference between the treatments. Otherwise you cannot conclude that the treatments are significantly different. The formula for Tukey's HSD is

$$\text{HSD} = q\sqrt{\frac{MS_{\text{within}}}{n}} \tag{13.12}$$

The q value used in Tukey's *HSD* test is called a Studentized range statistic.

where the value of q is found in Table B5 (Appendix B, page 484), MS_{within} is the within-treatments variance from the ANOVA, and n is the number of scores in each treatment. Tukey's test requires that the sample size n be the same for all treatments. To locate the appropriate value of q, you must know the number of treatments in the overall experiment (k) and the degrees of freedom for MS_{within} (the error term in the F-ratio) and select an alpha level (generally the same α used for the ANOVA).

TABLE 13.7

Pain threshold data for four different pain relievers

1, Placebo	2, Drug A	3, Drug B	4, Drug C
$n = 3$	$n = 3$	$n = 3$	$n = 3$
$T = 3$	$T = 6$	$T = 12$	$T = 15$
$\overline{X} = 1$	$\overline{X} = 2$	$\overline{X} = 4$	$\overline{X} = 5$

EXAMPLE 13.4 To outline the procedure for conducting post hoc tests with Tukey's HSD, we will use the data from the pain-reliever study in Example 13.1. The data are reproduced in summary form in Table 13.7. The within-treatments variance for these data is $MS_{\text{within}} = 2.00$ with $df = 8$.

With $\alpha = .05$ and $k = 4$, the value of q for these data is $q = 4.53$. Tukey's HSD is

$$\text{HSD} = q\sqrt{\frac{MS_{\text{within}}}{n}}$$

$$= 4.53\sqrt{\frac{2.00}{3}}$$

$$= 3.70$$

Therefore, the mean difference between any two samples must be at least 3.70 to be significant. Using this value, we can make the following conclusions:

1 Drug A is not significantly different from the placebo ($\overline{X} = 2$ versus $\overline{X} = 1$).

2 Drug B is not significantly different from the placebo ($\overline{X} = 4$ versus $\overline{X} = 1$).

3 Drug C is significantly different from the placebo ($\overline{X} = 5$ versus $\overline{X} = 1$).

Thus, drug C is the only one that produced significantly more pain relief than the placebo.

You also may notice that Tukey's HSD test can lead to the conclusion that there are no significant differences among the drugs (check the mean differences). This may seem to contradict the finding that drug C is the only one different from the placebo. However, you should recall that saying "no significant difference" is not equivalent to saying "no difference." There may be differences among the three drugs; however, these differences are not large enough to satisfy the criterion of statistical significance. For these data, the only mean difference large enough to be statistically significant is between drug C ($\overline{X} = 5$) and the placebo ($\overline{X} = 1$).

THE SCHEFFÉ TEST A second commonly used a posteriori test is the Scheffé test. Because it uses an extremely cautious method for reducing the risk of a Type I error, the Scheffé test has the distinction of being one of the safest of all possible post hoc tests.

The Scheffé test uses an *F*-ratio to test for a significant difference between any two treatment conditions. The numerator of the *F*-ratio is an *MS* between treatments that is calculated using only the two treatments you want to compare. The denominator is the same *MS* within treatments that was used for the overall ANOVA. The "safety factor" for the Scheffé test comes from the following two considerations:

1. Although you are only comparing two treatments, the Scheffé test uses the value of k from the original experiment to compute df between treatments. Thus, df for the numerator of the *F*-ratio is $k - 1$.

2. The critical value for the Scheffé *F*-ratio is the same as was used to evaluate the *F*-ratio from the overall ANOVA. Thus, Scheffé requires that every post test satisfy the same criteria used for the complete analysis of variance.

The following example uses the data from Table 13.7 to demonstrate the Scheffé post test procedure.

EXAMPLE 13.5 Rather than test all the possible comparisons of the four treatment conditions shown in Table 13.7, we will begin with the largest mean difference and then test progressively smaller differences until we find one that is not significant. For these data, the largest difference is between the placebo ($T = 3$) and drug C ($T = 15$). The first step is to compute SS_{between} for these two treatments.

The grand total, G, for these two treatments is found by adding the two treatment totals ($G = 3 + 15$), and N is found by adding the number of scores in the two treatments ($N = 3 + 3$).

$$SS_{\text{between}} = \sum \frac{T^2}{n} - \frac{G^2}{N}$$
$$= \frac{3^2}{3} + \frac{15^2}{3} - \frac{18^2}{6}$$
$$= 24$$

Although we are comparing only two treatments, these two were selected from an experiment consisting of $k = 4$ treatments. The Scheffé test uses the overall experiment ($k = 4$) to determine the degrees of freedom between treatments. Therefore, $df_{\text{between}} = k - 1 = 3$, and the MS between treatments is

$$MS_{\text{between}} = \frac{SS_{\text{between}}}{df_{\text{between}}} = \frac{24}{3} = 8$$

Scheffé also uses the within-treatments variance from the complete experiment, $MS_{\text{within}} = 2.00$ with $df = 8$, so the Scheffé F-ratio is

$$F = \frac{MS_{\text{between}}}{MS_{\text{within}}} = \frac{8}{2} = 4.00$$

With $df = 3, 8$ and $\alpha = .05$, the critical value for F is 4.07 (see Table B.4). Therefore, our F-ratio is not in the critical region, and our decision is that these data fail to provide sufficient evidence to conclude that there is a significant difference between the placebo and drug C. Because we started with the largest mean difference and found that it is not significant, we also can conclude that none of the other pairwise comparisons would be significant with the Scheffé test.

This example provides an excellent demonstration of the cautious nature of the Scheffé test. You should recall that the decision from the overall ANOVA was to reject H_0 and conclude that there are significant differences among the four treatment conditions (see Example 13.1). However, none of the mean differences was large enough to satisfy the Scheffé test criteria for significance. By Scheffé's standards, these data do not provide sufficient evidence to conclude that there are any differences among the four treatments.

13.7 THE RELATION BETWEEN ANOVA AND *t* TESTS

When you have data from an independent-measures experiment with only two treatment conditions, you can use either a t test (Chapter 11) or independent-measures ANOVA. In practical terms, it makes no difference which you choose. These two statistical techniques always will result in the same statistical decision. In fact, the two methods use many of the same calculations and are very closely related in several other respects. The basic relation between t statistics and F-ratios can be stated in an equation:

$$F = t^2$$

The details of this relationship are presented in Example 13.6, but we will discuss some of the more general aspects of the relation before looking at the example.

1. The general relation between the t and F formulas was discussed on page 294, when we introduced the conceptual structure of the F-ratio in Perspective 13.1. Remember, both formulas evaluate the actual difference between samples (numerator) relative to the difference that would be expected by chance (denominator). The numerator and denominator of the t formula both measure distance. The distance between the two sample means is in the numerator, and the standard error, or standard distance, is in the denominator. For the F-ratio, both the numerator and denominator measure variance, or mean squared distance. The fact that the t statistic is based on distances and the F-ratio is based on *squared* distances leads to the basic relation $F = t^2$.

2. It should be obvious that you will be testing the same hypotheses whether you choose a t test or ANOVA. With only two treatments, the hypotheses for either test are

$$H_0: \mu_1 = \mu_2$$
$$H_1: \mu_1 \neq \mu_2$$

3. The degrees of freedom for the t statistic and the df for the denominator of the F-ratio (df_{within}) are identical. For example, if you have two samples, each with six scores, the independent-measures t statistic will have $df = 10$, and the F-ratio will have $df = 1, 10$. In each case, you are adding the df from the first sample $(n - 1)$ and the df from the second sample.

4. The distribution of t and the distribution of F-ratios match perfectly if you take into consideration the relation $F = t^2$. Consider the t distribution with $df = 18$ and the corresponding F distribution with $df = 1, 18$ that are presented in Figure 13.8.

FIGURE 13.8

The distribution of t-scores with $df = 18$ and the corresponding distribution of F-ratios with $df = 1, 18$. Notice that the critical values for $\alpha = .05$ are $t = \pm 2.101$ and that $F = 2.101^2 = 4.41$.

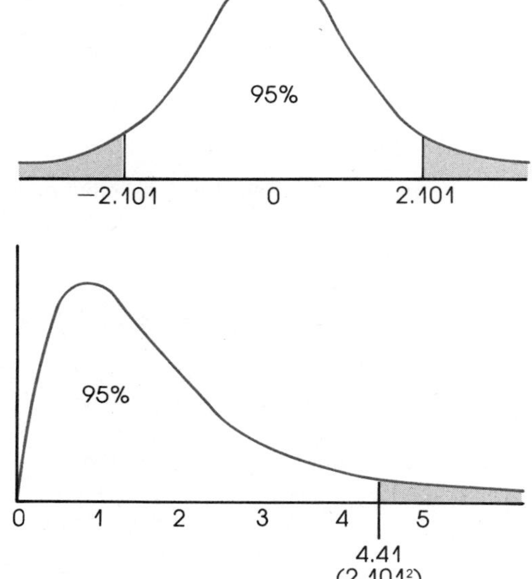

Notice the following relationships:

a. If each of the t values is squared, then all of the negative values will become positive. As a result, the whole left-hand side of the t distribution (below zero) will be flipped over to the positive side. This creates a nonsymmetrical, positively skewed distribution, that is, the F distribution.

b. For $\alpha = .05$, the critical region for t is determined by values greater than $+2.101$ or less than -2.101. When these boundaries are squared, you get

$$\pm 2.101^2 = 4.41$$

Notice that 4.41 is the critical value for $\alpha = .05$ in the F distribution. Any value that is in the critical region for t will end up in the critical region for F-ratios after it is squared.

The details of the relation between the t statistic and the F-ratio are examined in the following example.

EXAMPLE 13.6 We will use the following data to examine the relation between ANOVA and the t test when there are only two treatments being compared.

Hormone	Control
$n = 10$	$n = 10$
$SS = 40$	$SS = 50$
$\bar{X} = 3$	$\bar{X} = 7$

The data represent the results of an experiment designed to examine whether hormone levels in a pregnant rat can affect the intelligence of the offspring. A psychologist selects two groups of pregnant rats. The animals in one group receive regular injections of the hormone, and the rats in the second group serve as a control (no hormone injections). When the pups are 2 months old, one is randomly selected from each litter and tested on a problem-solving task. The dependent variable is the number errors.

STEP 1 The hypotheses are the same for the t test and the analysis of variance:

$$H_0: \mu_1 = \mu_2 \quad \text{(no difference)}$$

$$H_1: \mu_1 \neq \mu_2 \quad \text{(there is an effect)}$$

We will use $\alpha = .05$.

STEP 2 For these data, the t statistic will have $df = 18$, and the F-ratio will have $df = 1, 18$. With $\alpha = .05$, the critical values for t are ± 2.101. For the F-ratio, the critical value is 4.41. Notice that $4.41 = 2.101^2$. The t statistic and the F-ratio distributions are shown in Figure 13.8.

STEP 3 To compute the t statistic for these data, we first need the pooled variance:

$$s_p^2 = \frac{SS_1 + SS_2}{df_1 + df_2} = \frac{40 + 50}{9 + 9} = \frac{90}{18} = 5$$

Then the standard error is computed:

$$s_{\bar{X}-\bar{X}} = \sqrt{\frac{s_p^2}{n_1} + \frac{s_p^2}{n_2}} = \sqrt{\frac{5}{10} + \frac{5}{10}} = \sqrt{1} = 1$$

Finally, t is

$$t = \frac{(\bar{X}_1 - \bar{X}_2) - (\mu_1 - \mu_2)}{s_{\bar{X}-\bar{X}}} = \frac{4 - 0}{1} = 4$$

To compute the F-ratio for these data, we will need MS_{between} and MS_{within}. (Note that we do not have the individual scores, so we cannot compute the total sum of squares directly. However, this value is not essential in order to find the F-ratio.)

For MS_{within} we need values for SS and df:

$$SS_{\text{within}} = \sum SS_{\text{inside each treatment}}$$
$$= 40 + 50$$
$$= 90$$

$$df_{\text{within}} = N - k$$
$$= 20 - 2 = 18$$

These two values give

(Note that MS_{within} is the same value we computed earlier as the pooled variance for the t statistic.)

$$MS_{\text{within}} = \frac{SS_{\text{within}}}{df_{\text{within}}} = \frac{90}{18} = 5$$

To compute SS_{between} we need the treatment totals (Ts) and the grand total (G). Although these values are not given explicitly in the data, they are easy to find. In the hormone group, for example, we have $n = 10$ scores with an average of $\bar{X} = 3$. If the 10 scores average 3, the total must be $T = 10(3) = 30$. Similarly, the total for the control group would be $T = 70$. With these two values you can compute the grand total, $G = 30 + 70 = 100$.

$$SS_{\text{between}} = \sum \frac{T^2}{n} - \frac{G^2}{N} = \frac{30^2}{10} + \frac{70^2}{10} - \frac{100^2}{20}$$
$$= 90 + 490 - 500$$
$$= 80$$

$$df_{\text{between}} = k - 1$$
$$= 2 - 1 = 1$$

With the SS and the df values we can compute

$$MS_{\text{between}} = \frac{SS_{\text{between}}}{df_{\text{between}}}$$
$$= \frac{80}{1} = 80$$

Notice that the value for F and the value for t are related by the formula $F = t^2$.

Finally, the F-ratio for this analysis is

$$F = \frac{MS_{\text{between}}}{MS_{\text{within}}} = \frac{80}{5} = 16$$

STEP 4 The t test and the analysis of variance both reach the same decision. In each case, the data fall in the critical region, and we reject H_0. These data provide evidence that hormone levels in the mother affect the intelligence of the offspring. •

13.8 ASSUMPTIONS FOR ANALYSIS OF VARIANCE

For analysis of variance, as well as other inferential techniques, there is the requirement that the samples be randomly selected from the population. There are two basic assumptions that must be satisfied for the independent-measures ANOVA to be valid. The first assumption is that the population distribution for each treatment condition is normal. For the other assumption to be met, the population variances for all treatments should be equal (homogeneity of variance). These conditions are the same as those required for the independent measures t test (Chapter 11).

Ordinarily, researchers are not overly concerned with the assumption of normality, especially when large samples are used, unless there are strong reasons to suspect the assumption has not been satisfied. The assumption of homogeneity of variance is an important one. If a researcher suspects it has been violated, it can be tested by Hartley's F-max test for homogeneity of variance (Chapter 11, page 260).

LEARNING CHECK

1 If a Scheffé post hoc test is significant, then the same test would certainly be significant using Tukey's HSD test. (True or False)

2 An ANOVA produces an F-ratio with $df = 1, 34$. Could the data have been analyzed with a t test? What would be the degrees of freedom for the t statistic?

3 With $k = 2$ treatments, are post hoc tests necessary when the null hypothesis is rejected? Explain why or why not.

ANSWERS

1 True. Scheffé is the more-cautious test.

2 If the F-ratio has $df = 1, 34$, then the experiment compared only two treatments, and you could use a t statistic to evaluate the data. The t statistic would have $df = 34$.

3 No. Post hoc tests are used to determine which treatments are different. With only two treatment conditions, there is no uncertainty as to which two treatments are different.

SUMMARY

1 Analysis of variance is a statistical technique that is used to test for mean differences among two or more treatment conditions or among two or more populations. The null hypothesis for this test states that there are no differences among the population means. The alternative hypothesis states that at least one mean is different from the others. Although analysis of variance can be used with either an independent- or a repeated-measures experiment, this chapter examined only independent measures designs, that is, experiments with a separate sample for each treatment condition.

2 The test statistic for analysis of variance is a ratio of two variances called an F-ratio. The F-ratio is structured so that the numerator and denominator measure the same variance when the null hypothesis is true. In this way, the existence of a significant treatment effect is apparent if the data produce an "unbalanced" F-ratio. The variances in the F-ratio are called mean squares or MS values. Each MS is computed by

$$MS = \frac{SS}{df}$$

3 For the independent-measures analysis of variance the F-ratio is

$$F = \frac{MS_{\text{between}}}{MS_{\text{within}}}$$

The MS_{between} measures differences among the treatments by computing the variability of the treatment means or totals.

These differences are assumed to be produced by three factors:
a Treatment effects (if they exist)
b Individual differences
c Experimental error
The MS_{within} measures variability inside each of the treatment conditions. This variability is assumed to be produced by two factors:
a Individual differences
b Experimental error
With these factors in mind, the *F*-ratio has the following structure

$$F = \frac{\text{treatment effect} + \text{individual diff's.} + \text{experimental error}}{\text{individual diff's.} + \text{experimental error}}$$

When there is no treatment effect (H_0 is true), the numerator and denominator of the *F*-ratio are measuring the same variance, and the obtained ratio should be near 1.00. If there is a significant treatment effect, the numerator of the ratio should be larger than the denominator, and the obtained *F* value should be much greater than 1.00.

4 The formulas for computing each *SS*, *df*, and *MS* value are presented in Figure 13.9, which also shows the general structure for the analysis of variance.

5 The *F*-ratio has two values for degrees of freedom, one associated with the *MS* in the numerator and one associated with the *MS* in the denominator. These *df* values are used to find the critical value for the *F*-ratio in the *F* distribution table.

6 When the decision from an analysis of variance is to reject the null hypothesis and when the experiment contained more than two treatment conditions, it is necessary to continue the analysis with post hoc tests such as Scheffé or Tukey's HSD tests. The purpose of these tests is to determine exactly which treatments are significantly different and which are not.

FIGURE 13.9

The complete structure and formulas for the independent measures analysis of variance.

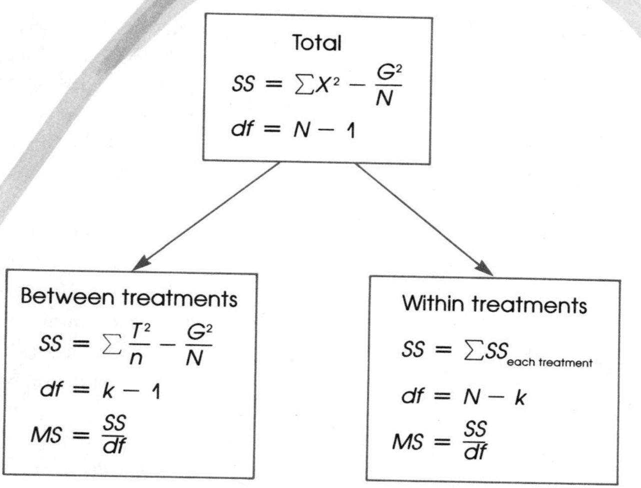

KEY TERMS

analysis of variance (ANOVA)
factor
levels
between-treatments variability
within-treatments variability
treatment effect
individual differences
experimental error
F-ratio
error term
mean squares
distribution of *F*-ratios
ANOVA summary table
post hoc tests
a priori tests
a posteriori tests
Tukey's HSD test
Scheffé's test

FOCUS ON PROBLEM SOLVING

1. The words and labels used to describe the different components of variance can help you remember the ANOVA formulas. For example, *total* refers to the total experiment. Therefore, the SS_{total} and df_{total} values are based on the whole set of *N* scores. The word *within* refers to the variability inside (within) the treatment groups. Thus, the value for SS_{within} is based on an *SS* value from each group, computed from the scores *within* each group. Finally, *between* refers to the variability (or differences) between treatments. The SS_{between} component measures

the differences between treatments (T_1 versus T_2, and so on), and $df_{between}$ is simply the number of T values (k) minus one.

2. When you are computing SS and df values, always calculate all three components (total, between, and within) separately, then check your work by making sure that the *between-treatments* and *within-treatments* components add up to the *total.*

3. Because ANOVA requires a fairly lengthy series of calculations, it helps to organize your work. We suggest that you compute all of the SS values first, followed by the df values, then the two MS values, and finally the F-ratio. If you use the same system all the time (practice it!), you will be less likely to get lost in the middle of a problem.

4. The previous two focus points are facilitated by using an ANOVA summary table (for example, see p. 306). The first column has the heading *source*. Listed below the heading are the three sources of variability (between, within, and total). The second and third columns have the heading SS and df. These can be filled in as you perform the appropriate computations. The last column is headed MS for the mean square values.

5. Remember that an F-ratio has two separate values for df: A value for the numerator and one for the denominator. Properly reported, the $df_{between}$ value is stated first. You will need both df values when consulting the F distribution table for the critical F value. You should recognize immediately that an error has been made if you see an F-ratio reported with a single value for df.

6. When you encounter an F-ratio and its df values reported in the literature, you should be able to reconstruct much of the original experiment. For example, if you see "$F(2, 36) = 4.80$," you should realize that the experiment compared $k = 3$ treatment groups (because $df_{between} = k - 1 = 2$), with a total of $N = 39$ subjects participating in the experiment (because $df_{within} = N - k = 36$).

7. Keep in mind that a large value for F indicates evidence for a treatment effect. A combination of factors will yield a large F value. One such factor is a large value for $MS_{between}$ in the numerator of the ratio. This will occur when there are large differences between groups, as would be expected when a treatment effect occurs. Another factor that contributes to a large F value would be a small value for MS_{within} on the bottom of the F ratio. This will occur when there is a little error variability, reflected in low variability within groups.

PROBLEMS

***1** Why is the expected value for an F-ratio equal to 1.00 when there is no treatment effect?

2 Describe the similarities between an F-ratio and a t statistic.

***3** A social psychologist would like to examine the relationship between personal appearance and authority. A special questionnaire is prepared, which requires very careful attention to instructions in order to fill it in correctly. Three random samples of college students are obtained. For the first group the psychologist dresses very casually (blue jeans and T-shirt) when the questionnaire is administered. For the second sample, the psychologist wears a suit, and for the third sample the psychologist wears a very "scientific" laboratory coat. The psychologist records the number of errors made by each individual while completing the questionnaire. These data are as follows:

Blue Jeans	Suit	Lab Coat	
5	3	1	
2	3	0	$G = 30$
2	0	1	$\sum X^2 = 86$
4	2	2	
2	2	1	
$T = 15$	$T = 10$	$T = 5$	
$SS = 8$	$SS = 6$	$SS = 2$	

Should the psychologist conclude that appearance had an influence on the amount of attention people paid to the instructions? Test at the .05 level of significance.

4 A psychologist would like to examine how the rate of presentation affects people's ability to memorize a list of words.

A list of 20 words is prepared. For one group of subjects the list is presented at the rate of one word every $\frac{1}{2}$ second. The next group gets one word every second. The third group has one word every 2 seconds, and the fourth group has one word every 3 seconds. After the list is presented, the psychologist asks each person to recall the entire list. The dependent variable is the number of errors in recall. The data from this experiment are as follows:

$\frac{1}{2}$ Second	1 Second	2 Seconds	3 Seconds	
4	0	3	0	
6	2	1	2	$G = 32$
2	2	2	1	$\sum X^2 = 104$
4	0	2	1	
$T = 16$	$T = 4$	$T = 8$	$T = 4$	
$SS = 8$	$SS = 4$	$SS = 2$	$SS = 2$	

a Can the psychologist conclude that the rate of presentation has a significant effect on memory? Test on the .05 level.
b Use Tukey's HSD test to determine which rates of presentation are statistically different and which are not.

***5** The following data represent scores from three different treatment conditions.

Treatment 1	Treatment 2	Treatment 3	
1	3	2	
1	3	2	$N = 12$
1	3	2	$\sum X^2 = 56$
1	3	2	$G = 24$
$T = 4$	$T = 12$	$T = 8$	

a Just looking at the data, describe the relative amount of variability between treatments versus within treatments.
b Calculate SS_{total}, $SS_{between}$, and SS_{within}. You should find that all of the variability for these data comes from differences between treatments.

6 A psychologist would like to show that background noise can interfere with a student's concentration and therefore cause poorer performance on complex mental tasks. A sample of 12 students is obtained, and the psychologist randomly assigns these students to three separate groups. Each group is given a standard problem-solving task. One group works on this task under quiet conditions, one group works with soft background music, and the third group works with a loud radio tuned to a popular rock station. For each student the psychologist measures the number of errors on the task. The results from this experiment are summarized as follows:

Quiet	Soft Music	Loud Music	
$n = 4$	$n = 4$	$n = 4$	
$T = 4$	$T = 6$	$T = 14$	$\sum X^2 = 71$
$SS = 2$	$SS = 4$	$SS = 3$	

Can the psychologist conclude that the background noise had an effect on performance? Test at the .05 level of significance.

***7** A psychologist using an independent-measures experimental design to compare different teaching methods reports an F-ratio of $F = 3.87$ with $df = 3, 28$.
a How many teaching methods (treatments) were being compared?
b How many subjects participated in the total experiment?
c Were there significant differences among the teaching methods?

8 The following data represent the results of an independent-measures experiment comparing two treatment conditions.

Treatment 1	Treatment 2
1	5
2	4
2	3
4	2
1	6

a Use an analysis of variance with $\alpha = .05$ to test for a significant difference between the two treatment means.
b Use an independent-measures t statistic to test for a significant difference. (Remember, you should find the basic relation, $F = t^2$.)

9 An experiment compares two treatment conditions with separate samples of $n = 5$ in each treatment.
a If the treatment means are $\bar{X}_1 = 2$ and $\bar{X}_2 = 4$, compute $SS_{between}$ for this experiment.
b Suppose there were $n = 10$ subjects in each treatment and you obtained the same treatment means ($\bar{X}_1 = 2$ and $\bar{X}_2 = 4$). Again, compute $SS_{between}$.
c Explain how increasing the sample size affects $SS_{between}$ and the F-ratio.

***10** Use an analysis of variance with $\alpha = .05$ to determine whether the following data provide evidence of any significant differences among the three treatments:

Treatment 1	Treatment 2	Treatment 3	
$n = 4$	$n = 5$	$n = 6$	$N = 15$
$T = 2$	$T = 10$	$T = 18$	$G = 30$
$SS = 13$	$SS = 21$	$SS = 26$	$\sum X^2 = 135$

***11** A psychologist administers an art appreciation questionnaire to a group of five science students and a group of five English majors. The average score for the science students was $\bar{X} = 6$ with $SS = 200$, and the average score for the English majors was $\bar{X} = 8$ with $SS = 120$.
a Use an analysis of variance to determine whether or not these two populations differ significantly in art appreciation. Use $\alpha = .05$.

b Use a t test to compare the two groups. You should find that $F = t^2$.

***12** A pharmaceutical company has developed a drug that is expected to reduce hunger. To test the drug, three samples of rats are selected with $n = 10$ in each sample. The first sample receives the drug every day. The second sample is given the drug once a week, and the third sample receives no drug at all. The dependent variable is the amount of food eaten by each rat over a 1-month period. These data are analyzed by an analysis of variance, and the results are reported in the following summary table. Fill in all missing values in the table. (*Hint:* Start with the *df* column.)

Source	SS	df	MS	
Between treatments	24	____	____	$F =$ ____
Within treatments	____	____	2	
Total	____	____		

13 The following summary table presents the results of an ANOVA from an experiment comparing four treatment conditions with a sample of $n = 10$ in each treatment. Complete all missing values in the table.

Source	SS	df	MS	
Between treatments	____	____	____	$F = 8.00$
Within treatments	72	____	____	
Total	____	____		

***14** A developmental psychologist is examining problem-solving ability for grade school children. Random samples of 5-year-old, 6-year-old, and 7-year-old children are obtained with $n = 3$ in each sample. Each child is given a standardized problem-solving task, and the psychologist records the number of errors. These data are as follows:

5-Year-Olds	6-Year-Olds	7-Year-Olds	
5	6	0	$G = 30$
4	4	1	$\sum X^2 = 138$
6	2	2	
$T = 15$	$T = 12$	$T = 3$	
$SS = 2$	$SS = 8$	$SS = 2$	

a Use these data to test whether there are any significant differences among the three age groups. Use $\alpha = .05$.

b Use Tukey's HSD test to determine which groups are different.

15 A researcher would like to know whether infants can be affected by alcohol consumed by a mother during pregnancy. A sample of 24 pregnant rats is obtained. The researcher randomly divides these rats into four groups with $n = 6$ in each group. All groups receive the same diet of rat chow but during the last 2 weeks of pregnancy one group has $\frac{1}{4}$ ounce of vodka mixed with their food. The second group receives $\frac{1}{2}$ ounce, the third group receives 1 ounce, and the final group has no alcohol. One of the offspring of each rat is randomly selected to be weighed at birth. The data were examined using an ANOVA, and the results are summarized in the following table. Fill in all missing values.

Source	SS	df	MS	
Between treatments	____	____	10	$F =$ ____
Within treatments	40	____	____	
Total	____	____		

***16** A psychologist would like to demonstrate that the combination of two drugs can often produce much different effects than either of the drugs taken separately. Four random samples are selected with $n = 5$ in each sample. One group is given a sugar pill (no drug), one group is given drug A, another group is given drug B, and the final group is given drugs A and B together. Each person is then given a logic test measuring basic reasoning ability. The data are summarized as follows:

Sugar Pill	Drug A	Drug B	Drugs A and B	
$T = 0$	$T = 5$	$T = 5$	$T = 20$	$\sum X^2 = 122$
$SS = 7$	$SS = 8$	$SS = 7$	$SS = 10$	

a Can the psychologist conclude that there are any significant differences among the treatments? Test at the .05 level.

b Use the Scheffé test to determine which treatments are different.

17 Several studies indicate that handedness (left-handed/right-handed) is related to differences in brain function. Because different parts of the brain are specialized for specific behaviors, this means that left- and right-handed people should show different skills or talents. To test this hypothesis, a psychologist tested pitch discrimination (a component of musical ability) for three groups of subjects: left-handed, right-handed, and ambidextrous. The data from this study are as follows:

Right-Handed	Left-Handed	Ambidextrous	
6	1	2	
4	0	0	
3	1	0	$G = 30$
4	1	2	$\sum X^2 = 102$
3	2	1	
$T = 20$	$T = 5$	$T = 5$	
$SS = 6$	$SS = 2$	$SS = 4$	

Each score represents the number of errors during a series of pitch discrimination trials.

a Do these data indicate any differences among the three groups? Test with $\alpha = .05$.

b Use the *F*-max test to determine whether these data satisfy the homogeneity of variance assumption.

*18 The following data are from a study for which the ANOVA revealed a significant treatment effect.

Treatment 1	Treatment 2	Treatment 3
$n = 4$	$n = 4$	$n = 4$
$T = 24$	$T = 40$	$T = 100$
$SS = 10$	$SS = 14$	$SS = 12$

a Compute the treatment means and determine which ones differ using Tukey's HSD test. Use the .05 level of significance.

b Use Scheffe's test to determine which pairs of treatments differ significantly (at the .05 level). Compare the results to part a. Which post hoc test is more conservative?

19 In a paired-associate learning task, subjects are required to learn pairs of words. The first word in each pair is called the stimulus word, and the second is the response word. On each trial, the experimenter presents the stimulus word and asks the subject to recall the correct response. If the subject fails, the correct response word is given, and the experimenter continues through the list. The dependent variable is the number of times the experimenter must go through the entire list before the subject can recall all response words perfectly. This task often is used to demonstrate the effectiveness of mental imagery as an aid to memory. In a typical experiment, subjects in one group are instructed to form a mental image combining the two words in each pair. A second group is instructed to form a sentence that uses both of the words. A third group receives no special instructions. The data from this experiment are as follows:

No instructions			Images			Sentences		
6	7	5	3	6	5	5	8	6
5	8	10	5	3	4	4	5	8
8	9	10	4	5	3	5	10	9

a Compute the mean for each treatment. Draw a bar graph of these means. (See Chapter 2 for assistance.)

b Do the data indicate significant differences among the instruction groups? Test with alpha set at .05.

c Use the Scheffé test to determine which groups are different.

d In a few sentences, explain what happened in this study.

20 A researcher would like to evaluate systematically the effects of food deprivation on learning. Five groups of rats are selected with each group receiving a different level of deprivation before testing. The scores for these rats are as follows:

Hours of Deprivation				
6	12	18	24	30
9	10	18	14	7
7	8	16	12	9
10	17	23	17	13
12	14	24	20	16
13	18	21	19	15

a Can the researcher conclude that the level of deprivation has an effect on learning performance? Test at the .05 level of significance.

b Sketch a graph showing the mean learning score for each treatment condition. Describe the relation between hours of deprivation and learning.

c Use Tukey's HSD test to determine which treatment conditions are different.

21 A school administrator would like to know whether students tend to select college majors that are consistent with their skills. A sample of $n = 12$ psychology majors and a sample of $n = 12$ English majors are selected. Each of these students completed a verbal abilities test when he or she first entered college. The scores for these two samples are as follows:

Psychology			English		
18	14	21	19	23	16
17	20	19	22	19	21
15	18	13	20	18	15
16	21	14	19	16	23

a Use an analysis of variance to determine whether these data indicate any significant difference in verbal ability for English versus psychology majors. Test with $\alpha = .05$.

b Use a t test to determine whether there is any mean difference between the two populations. Again, test at the .05 level of significance. (*Note:* You should find $F = t^2$.)

*22 Betz and Thomas (1979) have reported a distinct connection between personality and health. They identified three personality types who differ in their susceptibility to serious, stress-related illness (heart attack, high blood pressure, etc.). The three personality types are Alphas, who are cautious and steady; Betas, who are carefree and outgoing; and Gammas, who tend toward extremes of behavior such as being overly cautious or very careless. Sample data representing general health scores for each of these three groups are as follows. A low score indicates poor health.

Alphas		Betas		Gammas	
43	44	41	52	36	29
41	56	40	57	38	36
49	42	36	48	45	42
52	53	51	55	25	40
41	21	52	39	41	36

a Compute the mean for each personality type. Do these data indicate a significant difference among the three types? Test with $\alpha = .05$.

b Use the Scheffé test to determine which groups are different. Explain what happened in this study.

23 Do weather conditions affect people's moods? To examine this question, a researcher selected three samples of college students and administered a mood inventory questionnaire to each student. One group was tested on a dreary, overcast, and drizzly day. The second group was tested during a violent thunderstorm, and the third group was tested on a bright sunny day. The data are as follows:

Dreary		Stormy		Bright	
6	9	8	12	13	10
10	12	10	6	6	13
5	7	8	9	10	8
12	8	14	10	9	12
7	10	7	7	15	11

Do these data indicate that weather has an effect on mood? Test at the .05 level of significance.

***24** A psychologist is interested in the extent to which physical attractiveness can influence judgment of other personal characteristics such as intelligence or ability. The psychologist selected three groups of subjects who were to play the role of a company personnel manager. Each subject was given a stack of job applications which included a photograph of the applicant. One of these applications was previously selected as the test stimulus. For one group of subjects, this application contained a photograph of a very attractive woman. For the second group, the photograph was of an average-looking woman. For the third group, a photo of a very unattractive woman was attached to the application. The subjects were instructed to rate the quality of each job applicant (0 = "very poor" to 10 = "excellent"). The psychologist recorded the rating of the test stimulus for each subject. These data are as follows:

Attractive			Average			Unattractive		
5	4	4	6	5	3	4	3	1
3	5	6	6	6	7	3	1	2
4	3	8	5	4	6	2	4	3
3	5	4	8	7	8	2	1	2

a Compute the means of the groups and draw a graph showing the results.
b Use an ANOVA with $\alpha = .05$ to determine whether there are any significant differences among these three groups.
c Use Tukey's HSD test to determine which groups are different.
d Based on the results of the post hoc test, describe the relation between physical attractiveness and the job ratings.

25 Does coffee help people become sober more quickly after drinking too much? The ensuing data represent results from an experiment designed to answer this question. A sample of volunteers is randomly divided into four groups. One of these groups serves as a control and receives no alcohol. Subjects in each of the other three groups drink a fixed amount of alcohol in a 1-hour period. During the next $\frac{1}{2}$ hour, subjects in the second group drink two cups of decaffeinated coffee, subjects in another group drink two cups of regular coffee, and subjects in the final group drink two cups of water. Finally, all subjects are given a reaction-time test to determine mental alertness. The data from this experiment are as follows:

Control	Decaffeinated Coffee	Regular Coffee	Water
184	221	189	196
197	218	219	201
189	226	206	215
197	230	214	198
179	205	221	229
171	216	192	228
201	195	215	209

a Compute the mean for each treatment group.
b Are there any differences among these four groups? Use ANOVA with an alpha level of .01.
c Use Tukey's HSD test to determine which groups are different.
d Describe the findings of this experiment based on the analyses you have just completed.

***26** A researcher evaluating the effects of a drug designed an experiment using three different drug doses (small, medium, and large). A separate sample of subjects was tested for each drug dose, and the researcher obtained the following scores:

Small	Medium	Large
14	16	24
19	20	18
13	15	20
17	18	18
18	19	22
21	23	24

a Use an analysis of variance to determine whether there are any significant differences among these three drug doses. Set $\alpha = .05$.
b Suppose the researcher had collected data only for the small-dose and the large-dose conditions. If an analysis of variance is used only on the data from these two conditions, is there evidence for a significant difference between the two drug doses? Test with $\alpha = .05$.
c You should find that there is a significant difference between the small dose and the large dose in part b but no significant difference in part a. How would you explain this apparent contradiction? (*Hint:* Analysis of variance evaluates mean differences. Compute all the mean differences among treatments when all three drug doses are included in the experiment. Now compute the mean difference between treatments when only two drug doses are used.)

CHAPTER 14

REPEATED-MEASURES ANALYSIS OF VARIANCE (ANOVA)

TOOLS YOU WILL NEED

The following items are considered essential background material for this chapter. If you doubt your knowledge of any of these items, you should review the appropriate chapter or section before proceeding.

- Introduction to analysis of variance (Chapter 13)
- The logic of analysis of variance
- ANOVA notation and formulas
- Distribution of *F*-ratios
- Repeated-measures design (Chapter 12)

PREVIEW

In the early 1970s, it was discovered that the brain manufactures and releases morphine-like substances called endorphins (see Snyder, 1977). Among many possible functions, these substances are thought to act as natural pain killers. For example, acupuncture may relieve pain because the acupuncture needles stimulate a release of endorphins in the brain. It also is thought that endorphins are responsible for reducing pain for long-distance runners and may produce the "runner's high."

Gintzler (1980) studied changes in pain threshold during pregnancy and examined how these changes are related to endorphin activity. Gintzler tested pregnant rats in several sessions spaced at regular intervals throughout their pregnancies (a rat's pregnancy lasts only 3 weeks). In a test session, a rat received a series of foot shocks that increased in intensity. The intensity of shock that elicited a jump response was recorded as the index of pain threshold. In general, the rats showed less sensitivity to shock (increased thresholds) as the pregnancy progressed. The change in threshold from one session to another was gradual, up until just a day or two before birth of the pups. At that point there was an abrupt increase in pain threshold. Gintzler also found evidence that the change in pain sensitivity was due to enhanced activity of endorphins. Perhaps a natural pain-killing mechanism prepares these animals for the stress of giving birth.

You should recognize Gintzler's experiment as an example of a repeated-measures design: each rat was observed repeatedly at several different times during the course of pregnancy. You also should recognize that it would be inappropriate to use the repeated-measures t statistic to evaluate the data because each subject is measured in *more than* 2 conditions. As noted in Chapter 13, whenever the number of levels of a treatment is greater than 2, analysis of variance (ANOVA) should be performed rather than multiple t tests. Because each t test has a risk of Type I error, doing several t tests would result in an unacceptably large experimentwise alpha level, making the probability of a Type I error for the entire set of tests undesirably high. The ANOVA, on the other hand, provides a single test statistic (the F-ratio) for the experiment.

In this chapter we will examine how the repeated-measures design is analyzed with ANOVA. As you will see, many of the notational symbols and computations are the same as those used for the independent-measures ANOVA. In fact, your best preparation for this chapter is a good understanding of the basic ANOVA procedure presented in Chapter 13.

14.1 INTRODUCTION

In the previous chapter we introduced the statistical technique of analysis of variance, and we examined how this hypothesis-testing procedure is used for independent-measures experimental designs. In this chapter we will examine how data from a repeated-measures experiment are evaluated using ANOVA. You should recall that an independent-measures design uses a separate sample for each treatment condition. A repeated-measures experiment, on the other hand, uses a single sample, so that the same individuals are measured in each of the treatment conditions. In both experimental designs, ANOVA is used to determine whether or not the sample data provide evidence of mean differences between two or more treatment conditions. As always, the null hypothesis states that there are no mean differences among the treatments: In symbols,

$$H_0: \mu_1 = \mu_2 = \mu_3 = \cdots$$

The alternative hypothesis states that the treatments are not all the same. As before, we will not list all the possible alternative hypotheses but rather will simply state

$$H_1: \text{At least one treatment mean is different from the others}$$

When repeated-measures designs were first introduced in Chapter 12, we noted that this type of experiment is particularly useful when a researcher wants to examine how behavior changes over time or across different treatment conditions in the same individuals. As a result, repeated-measures designs are used commonly to examine development (over time), to chart the course of learning (at different levels of practice), or simply to examine performance under different conditions. We also noted in Chapter 12 that a repeated-measures experiment has the advantage of being more powerful than an independent-measures design because it eliminates individual differences. Because the same individuals are tested in each treatment condition, differences between treatments cannot be attributed to differences between groups of subjects.

As we shall see, many of the notational symbols and computations for repeated-measures ANOVA are identical to those used for the independent-measures design. However, the fact that the repeated-measures analysis eliminates individual differences will produce a fundamental change in the structure of the final F-ratio. To introduce this change, we will begin with the general logic of the repeated-measures ANOVA and then look at the details of notation and formulas.

14.2 THE LOGIC OF REPEATED-MEASURES ANOVA

ANOVA evaluates mean differences between two or more treatments by comparing the actual differences versus the amount of difference that would be expected by chance. This comparison is made in an F-ratio, which is a ratio of two variances.

$$F = \frac{\text{variance between treatments}}{\text{variance due to chance}} \tag{14.1}$$

We will examine in more detail the two variance components that comprise the numerator and denominator of the F-ratio.

VARIANCE BETWEEN TREATMENTS The variance between treatments provides a measure of the actual mean differences between treatment conditions in an experiment. What might cause the scores in one treatment to be different from scores in another treatment? For a repeated-measures design, there are only two answers to this question.

1. *Treatment Effect*. It is possible that the different treatment conditions actually do produce different effects and therefore cause the individuals' scores to be higher (or lower) in one condition than in another. Remember, the purpose of the experiment is to determine whether or not a treatment effect exists.
2. *Experimental Error*. Any time behavior is measured, error may be introduced. The error may be inherent in the accuracy of the measurement tools, or it might be attributed to uncontrolled conditions in the laboratory, such as noises or changes in room temperature. This kind of uncontrolled and unsystematic error may cause the individuals' scores in one condition to be different from their scores in another condition.

Notice that we have not listed "individual differences" as a possible explanation for variance between treatments. Remember, a repeated-measures design uses the same individuals in every treatment condition, so any differences between treatments cannot be attributed to individual differences.

VARIANCE DUE TO CHANCE: THE ERROR TERM The error term (denominator of the F-ratio) is intended to provide a measure of the amount of variance expected by chance. In addition, the error term is intended to produce a balanced F-ratio when the null hypothesis is true and there is no treatment

FIGURE 14.1

The partitioning of variability for a repeated-measures experiment.

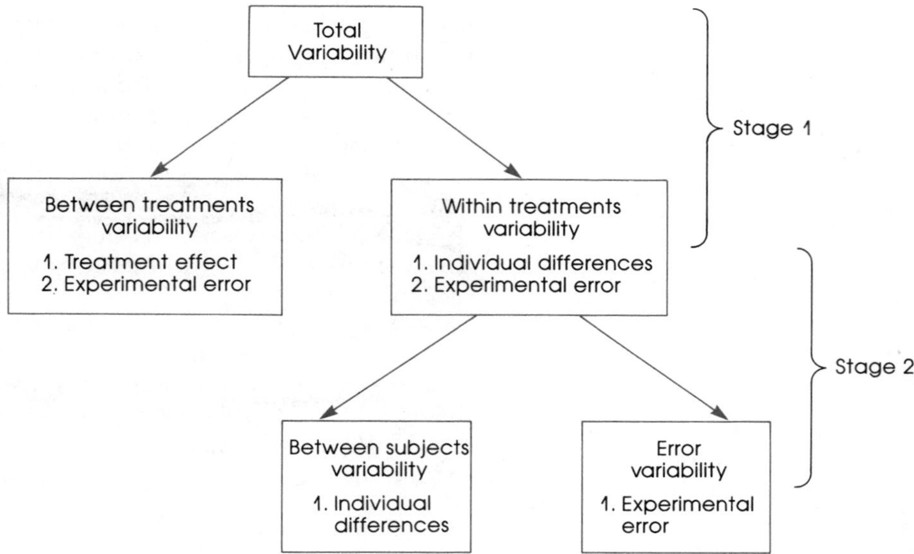

effect. For the repeated-measures ANOVA, this means that the denominator of the *F*-ratio should provide a measure of variance due to experimental error, so the final *F*-ratio has the following structure:

$$F = \frac{\text{treatment effect} + \text{experimental error}}{\text{experimental error}} \tag{14.2}$$

Notice that when the treatment effect is zero, the top and bottom of the *F*-ratio are measuring the same variance, and the expected value of *F* is 1.00.

To obtain a measure of variance due to experimental error, we begin with the variance within treatments. You should recall that the differences (or variance) inside each treatment condition come from two sources:

1. *Individual Differences.* Within each treatment, the scores come from different individuals.
2. *Experimental Error.* This uncontrolled and unsystematic error always could be the source of differences between scores.

Because we want to obtain a measure of variance that is due *only* to experimental error, we will separate the variance within treatments into two components: the variance from individual differences and the variance from experimental error.

Figure 14.1 summarizes the complete analysis of variance for a repeated-measures design. Note that the analysis consists of a two-stage process. In the first stage, the total variance is partitioned into two components: (1) variance between treatments, and (2) variance within treatments. This stage is identical to the analysis we conducted for an independent-measures design (see Chapter 13). The second stage of the analysis is necessary to separate individual differences and experimental error. This is accomplished by computing the variance between subjects and subtracting it from the variance within treatments. The residual, error variance, provides a measure of experimental error and is used as the error term in the *F*-ratio.

The term *residual* is often used in place of *error*.

LEARNING CHECK

1 What sources contribute to between-treatments variability for the repeated-measures design?

2 What sources of variability contribute to within-treatments variability?

3 (a) Describe the structure of the *F*-ratio for a repeated-measures ANOVA. (b) Compare it to the *F*-ratio structure for the independent-measures ANOVA (Chapter 13). How do they differ?

4 In the second stage of analysis, within-treatments variability is partitioned into ________ variability and ________ variability.

ANSWERS

1 Treatment effect, experimental error.

2 Individual differences, experimental error.

3 a $F = \dfrac{\text{treatment effect} + \text{experimental error}}{\text{experimental error}}$

b For the independent-measures ANOVA, individual differences contribute variability to both between-treatments variability and the error term of the *F*-ratio.

4 Between-subjects variability, error variability.

14.3 NOTATION AND FORMULAS FOR REPEATED-MEASURES ANOVA

We will use the data in Table 14.1 to help introduce the notation and formulas for the repeated-measures ANOVA. The data represent manual dexterity scores for a sample of $n = 4$ people measured over a series of three practice sessions. The goal of the experiment is to examine changes in manual dexterity performance (dependent variable) as a function of practice (independent variable). Most of the notation for a repeated-measures study is identical to the notation used in an independent-measures experiment. The following list reviews the notation system.

1. The letter k identifies the number of treatment conditions. For Table 14.1, $k = 3$.
2. The number of scores in each treatment is identified by the lowercase letter n. For a repeated-measures study, n is the same for all treatments because the same sample is used in all treatments. In Table 14.1, $n = 4$.
3. The total number of scores in the entire experiment is identified by an uppercase N. For these data, $N = 12$.
4. The sum of all the scores in the experiment is G. The value of G corresponds to $\sum X$ for all N scores and specifies the grand total for the experiment. For Table 14.1, $G = 36$.

Remember, we are using T and G to help differentiate $\sum X$ for treatments and $\sum X$ for the entire set of scores.

TABLE 14.1

Manual dexterity scores as a function of amount of practice (Test session)

	Test Session			
Person	Session 1	Session 2	Session 3	P
A	3	3	6	12
B	2	2	2	6
C	1	1	4	6
D	2	4	6	12
	$T_1 = 8$ $SS_1 = 2$	$T_2 = 10$ $SS_2 = 5$	$T_3 = 18$ $SS_3 = 11$	

$G = 36 \quad \Sigma X^2 = 140 \quad k = 3 \quad n = 4 \quad N = 12$

5. The sum of the scores in each treatment condition is identified by the letter T, for treatment total.
6. We also identify the sum of squares for each treatment (SS) and the sum of the squared scores ($\sum X^2$) for the entire experiment.

The repeated-measures design includes one new notational symbol. The total of the scores for each individual is identified by the letter P, for "person total." In Table 14.1, person A has scores of 3, 3, and 6, so the total for this person is $P = 12$. The P values are used to help measure individual differences in the analysis.

FORMULAS FOR REPEATED-MEASURES ANOVA

The F-ratio for ANOVA requires two measures of sample variance: between-treatments variance and error variance. As always, sample variance is computed by

$$\text{sample variance} = s^2 = \frac{SS}{df}$$

To compute each of the variances in the F-ratio we will need an SS value and a df value. These values are obtained by conducting a complete analysis of the sum of squares following the outline shown in Figure 14.1 and a separate analysis of degrees of freedom. These two analyses are described in detail in the following sections.

ANALYSIS OF THE SUM OF SQUARES (SS)

We will continue to use the data in Table 14.1 to demonstrate the ANOVA formulas. The complete analysis of SS is shown in Figure 14.2. You may find it helpful to refer to this figure as we introduce the SS formulas.

The first step in the analysis of SS is to compute SS_{total}, which measures the total variability for the entire set of N scores.

$$SS_{\text{total}} = \sum X^2 - \frac{G^2}{N} \tag{14.3}$$

Using this formula for the data in Table 14.1, we obtain

$$SS_{\text{total}} = 140 - \frac{(36)^2}{12}$$
$$= 140 - 108 = 32$$

FIGURE 14.2

The partitioning of sum of squares (SS) for a repeated-measures analysis of variance.

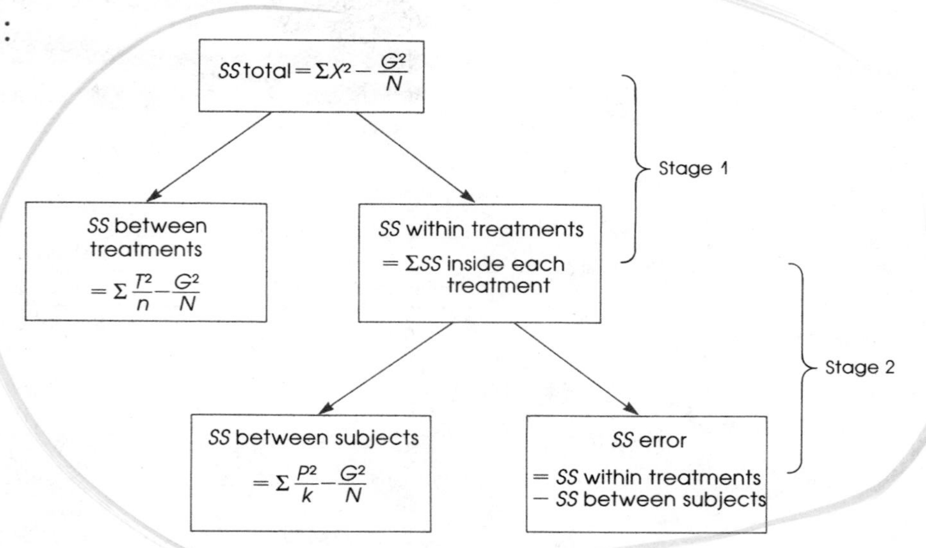

The next step is to partition SS_{total} into two components: between treatments and within treatments (see Figure 14.2). The $SS_{\text{between treatments}}$ measures the mean differences among the treatment conditions and is computed using the treatment totals (T's). The formula for this SS value is

(14.4) $$SS_{\text{between treatments}} = \sum \frac{T^2}{n} - \frac{G^2}{N}$$

For the data in Table 14.1, we obtain

$$\begin{aligned} SS_{\text{between treatments}} &= \frac{8^2}{4} + \frac{10^2}{4} + \frac{18^2}{4} - \frac{36^2}{12} \\ &= 16 + 25 + 81 - 108 \\ &= 14 \end{aligned}$$

The $SS_{\text{within treatments}}$ measures the variability inside the treatment conditions. To compute this value, we simply add the SS values from each of the separate treatment conditions.

(14.5) $$SS_{\text{within treatments}} = \sum SS_{\text{inside each treatment}}$$

For the experiment in Table 14.1, we obtain

$$\begin{aligned} SS_{\text{within treatments}} &= 2 + 5 + 11 \\ &= 18 \end{aligned}$$

To check your calculations, you should always compute all three SS values and verify that the two components add up to the total.

This completes the first stage of the analysis (see Figure 14.2). You should notice that the formulas and computations up to this point are identical to those of the independent-measures ANOVA. You also should note that the two SS components (between and within) add up to the total SS.

The second stage of the analysis involves partitioning the SS_{within} into two components: $SS_{\text{between subjects}}$ and SS_{error} (see Figure 14.2). As you will see, we actually compute only $SS_{\text{between subjects}}$ and then subtract this value from SS_{within}. The residual is SS_{error}.

Because the same individuals are used in every treatment in a repeated-measures experiment, it is possible to measure the variability due to individual differences. If you examine the data in Table 14.1, you will notice that some individuals tend to have higher scores than others. These individual differences are reflected in the P values, or person totals. To evaluate the individual differences, we compute an $SS_{\text{between subjects}}$ that measures the variability among the person totals, the P values. The formula for $SS_{\text{between subjects}}$ is

(14.6) $$SS_{\text{between subjects}} = \sum \frac{P^2}{k} - \frac{G^2}{N}$$

Notice that the formula for $SS_{\text{between subjects}}$ is similar in structure to the formula for $SS_{\text{between treatments}}$. The person totals ($P$ values) are used instead of treatment totals (T values). Each P value is divided by the number of scores that were added together to obtain P, or by k. Remember, each person was measured repeatedly, once for each treatment. There are k treatment conditions, and thus k scores are used to get a

PERSPECTIVE 14.1

DERIVATION OF FORMULA FOR SS_{error}

It is possible to derive a formula for SS_{error} based on the information and formulas that have been reviewed for the repeated-measures ANOVA. First, we saw that (Figure 14.2)

$$SS_{total} = SS_{between\ treatments} + SS_{within\ treatments}$$

and that

$$SS_{within\ treatments} = SS_{between\ subjects} + SS_{error}$$

By substituting for $SS_{within\ treatments}$, the equation for SS_{total} becomes

$$SS_{total} = SS_{between\ treatments} + SS_{between\ subjects} + SS_{error}$$

If we now solve the equation for SS_{error}, we obtain

$$SS_{error} = SS_{total} - SS_{between\ treatments} - SS_{between\ subjects}$$

The actual computational formulas for SS_{total}, $SS_{between\ treatments}$, and $SS_{between\ subjects}$ may be placed in the equation for SS_{error}. These substitutions yield

$$SS_{error} = \left(\sum X^2 - \frac{G^2}{N}\right) - \left(\sum\frac{T^2}{n} - \frac{G^2}{N}\right) - \left(\sum\frac{P^2}{k} - \frac{G^2}{N}\right)$$

$$= \sum X^2 - \frac{G^2}{N} - \sum\frac{T^2}{n} + \frac{G^2}{N} - \sum\frac{P^2}{k} + \frac{G^2}{N}$$

$$= \sum X^2 - \sum\frac{T^2}{n} - \sum\frac{P^2}{k} + \frac{G^2}{N}$$

For the data in Table 14.1, this formula yields

$$SS_{error} = 140 - 122 - 120 + 108$$

$$= 248 - 242$$

$$= 6$$

This formula may seem more difficult to use than

$$SS_{error} = SS_{within\ treatments} - SS_{between\ subjects}$$

However, many researchers prefer to use it because it eliminates the need to compute SS_{within} and $SS_{between\ subjects}$.

---

person total. For the example, $SS_{between\ subjects}$ is

$$SS_{between\ subjects} = \sum\frac{P^2}{k} - \frac{G^2}{N}$$

$$= \frac{12^2}{3} + \frac{6^2}{3} + \frac{6^2}{3} + \frac{12^2}{3} - \frac{36^2}{12}$$

$$= 48 + 12 + 12 + 48 - 108$$

$$= 120 - 108$$

$$= 12$$

The final step in the analysis is to obtain SS_{error} by subtracting $SS_{between\ subjects}$ from SS_{within} (see Figure 14.2).

$$SS_{error} = SS_{within\ treatments} - SS_{between\ subjects} \quad (14.7)$$

Substituting the values we have already obtained for SS_{within} and $SS_{between\ subjects}$ into the formula, we obtain

$$SS_{error} = 18 - 12$$

$$= 6$$

Subtracting the variability due to individual differences from $SS_{within\ treatments}$ is the easiest way to compute SS_{error}. There is, however, a more-complicated formula that can be used to compute this value directly (see Perspective 14.1).

ANALYSIS OF DEGREES OF FREEDOM (*df*)

Each of the *SS* values in analysis of variance has a corresponding degrees of freedom. In general terms, *SS* measures the variability for a set of "things," such as scores, treatment totals, people, and so on, and the *df* value for each *SS* is determined by the number of items minus one. For a set of n scores, for example, $df = n - 1$. The *df* formulas for the first stage of the repeated-measures analysis are identical to those in the independent-measures ANOVA. Figure 14.3 presents the complete analysis of degrees of freedom. You may want to refer to this figure as you read the following section on *df* formulas.

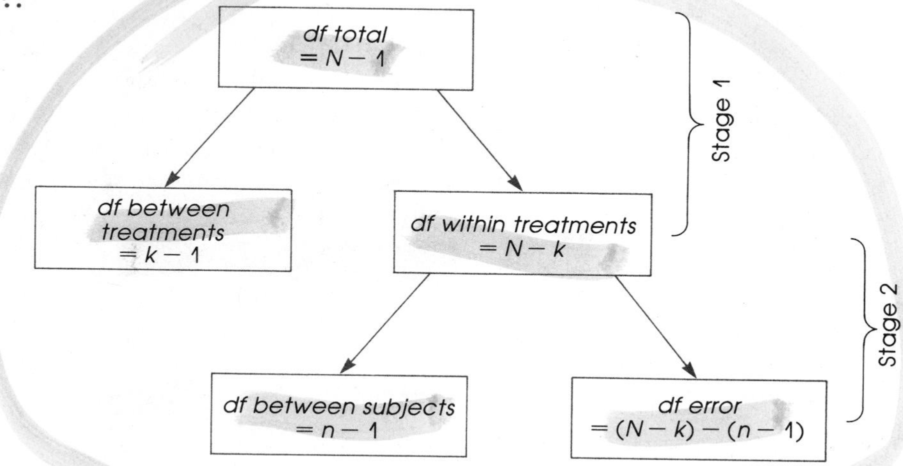

FIGURE 14.3
The partitioning of degrees of freedom for a repeated-measures experiment.

Remember, the total *SS* measures the variability for the entire set of *N* scores. The total *df* is computed by

(14.8) $$df_{\text{total}} = N - 1$$

For the data in Table 14.1,

$$df_{\text{total}} = 12 - 1$$
$$= 11$$

The between-treatments *SS* is based on the *k* treatment totals (*T*'s), and the corresponding *df* is

(14.9) $$df_{\text{between treatments}} = k - 1$$

For the data in Table 14.1

$$df_{\text{between treatments}} = 3 - 1$$
$$= 2$$

The within-treatments *SS* was obtained by summing the *SS* values for each of the treatment conditions. Each of these *SS* values has $df = n - 1$, and $df_{\text{within treatments}}$ is obtained by summing these *df* values.

(14.10) $$df_{\text{within}} = \sum(n - 1) = N - k$$

For the data in Table 14.1

$$df_{\text{within}} = 12 - 3$$
$$= 9$$

This completes the first stage of the analysis of degrees of freedom (see Figure 14.3). As always, you should check that the two components (between and within) add up to the total.

In the second stage of the analysis, the variability within treatments is partitioned into two components: between subjects and error. The between-subjects *SS* measures the variability among the person totals, the *P* values. Because the number of *P* values is *n*, the between-subjects *df* is given by

(14.11) $$df_{\text{between subjects}} = n - 1$$

Using the data from Table 14.1,

$$df_{\text{between subjects}} = 4 - 1$$
$$= 3$$

The final step in the analysis is to find df for the error variance. Remember, the variability due to error is not computed directly but rather is defined as the residual that is left when you subtract between subject variability (individual differences) from the within-treatments variability. We obtain df_{error} in exactly the same manner.

(14.12) $$df_{\text{error}} = df_{\text{within}} - df_{\text{between subjects}}$$
$$= (N - k) - (n - 1)$$

For the data in Table 14.1,

$$df_{\text{error}} = 9 - 3$$
$$= 6$$

CALCULATION OF THE VARIANCES (*MS*) AND THE *F*-RATIO

The F-ratio is a ratio of two variances. These variances, called mean squares (MS), are obtained by dividing a sum of squares by degrees of freedom. The MS in the numerator of the F-ratio, in part, is influenced by the amount of treatment effect that is present. This is the between-treatments MS, and it is calculated by dividing the between-treatments SS by between-treatments df:

(14.13) $$MS_{\text{between treatments}} = \frac{SS_{\text{between treatments}}}{df_{\text{between treatments}}}$$

The error term of the F-ratio consists of MS_{error} for a repeated-measures ANOVA. This MS is computed by dividing the error SS by the error df:

(14.14) $$MS_{\text{error}} = \frac{SS_{\text{error}}}{df_{\text{error}}}$$

The F-ratio therefore consists of

(14.15) $$F = \frac{MS_{\text{between treatments}}}{MS_{\text{error}}}$$

Once again, notice that the repeated-measures F-ratio uses MS_{error} as an error term in place of MS_{within}. The new error term is used because it maintains the expected F-ratio of 1.00 if the null hypothesis is true. This is confirmed when the structure of the repeated-measures F-ratio is examined:

$$F = \frac{\text{treatment effect} + \text{experimental error}}{\text{experimental error}}$$

When H_0 is true, the treatment effect will be zero, and the expected value of the F-ratio is 1.00. Alternatively, when H_0 is false, the presence of a treatment effect in the numerator of the F-ratio should give us a large value that falls in the critical region.

For the data in Table 14.1, we obtain the following MS values:

$$MS_{\text{between treatments}} = \frac{SS_{\text{between treatments}}}{df_{\text{between treatments}}}$$
$$= \frac{14}{2}$$
$$= 7$$

$$MS_{\text{error}} = \frac{SS_{\text{error}}}{df_{\text{error}}} = \frac{6}{6} = 1$$

The F-ratio for the example is obtained by dividing the between-treatments MS by the error MS:

$$F = \frac{MS_{\text{between treatments}}}{MS_{\text{error}}} = \frac{7}{1} = 7$$

The degrees of freedom for the F ratio are determined by the two variances that form the numerator and denominator. For the repeated-measures ANOVA, the numerator and denominator are between treatments and error, respectively. The df values for the F-ratio are reported as

$$df = df_{\text{between treatments}}, df_{\text{error}}$$

Caution! A very common mistake is to use the value of within-treatments df instead of error df. Remember, the error term for a repeated-measures ANOVA is not the same as that of an independent-measures ANOVA.

Therefore, the df values associated with the repeated-measures F-ratio in our example are

$$df = 2, 6$$

The obtained F-ratio is evaluated by the same general procedure used for the independent measures ANOVA. The experimenter must consult the F distribution table (page 489) to find the critical value of F. The df values printed across the top of the table are values for the df associated with the numerator of the F-ratio (between-treatments df). The column on the left-hand side of the table contains df values associated with the denominator of the F-ratio. For a repeated-measures ANOVA, this value is the error df.

· LEARNING CHECK ·

1 $SS_{\text{within treatments}} - SS_{\text{between subjects}} =$ __________.

2 What two df components are associated with the repeated-measures F-ratio? How are they computed?

3 For the following set of data, compute all of the SS components for a repeated-measures ANOVA:

Subject	Treatment 1	2	3	4	
A	2	2	2	2	$G = 32$
B	4	0	0	4	$\sum X^2 = 96$
C	2	0	2	0	
D	4	2	2	4	

4 Which two MS components are used to form the F-ratio of the repeated-measures ANOVA? How are they computed?

ANSWERS

1 SS_{error}

2 Between-treatments df and error df; $df_{\text{between treatments}} = k - 1$; $df_{\text{error}} = (N - k) - (n - 1)$.

3 $SS_{\text{total}} = 32$, $SS_{\text{between treatments}} = 10$, $SS_{\text{within treatments}} = 22$, $SS_{\text{between subjects}} = 8$, $SS_{\text{error}} = 14$.

4 Between-treatments *MS* and error *MS*;

$$MS_{\text{between treatments}} = \frac{SS_{\text{between treatments}}}{df_{\text{between treatments}}}$$

$$MS_{\text{error}} = \frac{SS_{\text{error}}}{df_{\text{error}}}$$

14.4 TESTING HYPOTHESES WITH THE REPEATED-MEASURES ANOVA

Let us consider a complete example of hypothesis testing with a repeated-measures study. This task will be accomplished in the four steps that should be familiar by now: (1) State hypotheses and set the alpha level, (2) compute *df* and locate the critical region, (3) compute the test statistic, and (4) evaluate the hypotheses.

EXAMPLE 14.1 A school psychologist would like to test the effectiveness of a behavior-modification technique in controlling classroom outbursts of unruly children. A teacher is instructed to use the response-cost technique. Every time a child disrupts the class, he or she is told that the behavior has cost him or her 10 minutes of free time. That is, the free-time period is shortened for each unruly act. For a sample of $n = 4$ children, the number of outbursts is measured for a day before the treatment is initiated and again 1 week, 1 month, and 6 months after the response-cost technique began. Note that the measurements taken after the response-cost technique is administered serve as a long-term follow-up on the effectiveness of the treatment. This underscores the usefulness of the repeated-measures design in evaluating the effectiveness of clinical treatments. The data are summarized in Table 14.2.

STEP 1 *State the hypotheses and select an alpha level.* According to the null hypothesis, the response-cost technique will be ineffective in producing a change in the number of classroom disruptions. In symbols the null hypothesis states that

$$H_0: \mu_{\text{before}} = \mu_{\text{1 week}} = \mu_{\text{1 month}} = \mu_{\text{6 months}}$$

The alternative hypothesis may take on many forms. Somewhere among the four

TABLE 14.2

The effect of response-cost treatment on the number of outbursts in class after different periods of time

Subject	Before Treatment	One Week After	One Month After	Six Months After	*P*
A	8	2	1	1	12
B	4	1	1	0	6
C	6	2	0	2	10
D	8	3	4	1	16
	$T_1 = 26$ $SS_1 = 11$	$T_2 = 8$ $SS_2 = 2$	$T_3 = 6$ $SS_3 = 9$	$T_4 = 4$ $SS_4 = 2$	

$n = 4$ $k = 4$ $N = 16$ $G = 44$ $\Sigma X^2 = 222$

levels of the treatment there will be a difference. Because there are a number of possibilities, the alternative hypothesis states that

H_1: At least one mean is different from the others

For the level of significance, the experimenter selects $\alpha = .05$. In other words, the researcher is willing to take only a 5% chance of committing a Type I error.

STEP 2 *Find df and locate the critical region.* For a repeated-measures study, the degrees of freedom associated with the *F*-ratio are between-treatments *df* and error *df*. In this example

We have computed only those *df* values that are needed to evaluate the *F*-ratio. However, it is useful to compute all *df* components of ANOVA in order to check the computations (see Figure 14.3).

$$df_{\text{between treatments}} = k - 1 = 4 - 1 = 3$$

$$df_{\text{error}} = (N - k) - (n - 1) = (16 - 4) - (4 - 1) = 12 - 3 = 9$$

Therefore, for this *F*-ratio $df = 3, 9$. Consulting the *F* distribution table for $\alpha = .05$, we observe that the critical region begins with $F = 3.86$. Figure 14.4 illustrates the distribution. An obtained *F*-ratio that exceeds this critical value justifies rejecting H_0.

STEP 3 *Compute the test statistic.* To compute the *F*-ratio, we must first calculate the values for *SS*, *df*, and *MS*. This analysis begins by finding the value for total *SS*:

$$SS_{\text{total}} = \sum X^2 - \frac{G^2}{N} = 222 - \frac{44^2}{16} = 222 - 121 = 101$$

FIGURE 14.4

The critical region in the *F* distribution for $\alpha = .05$ and $df = 3, 9$.

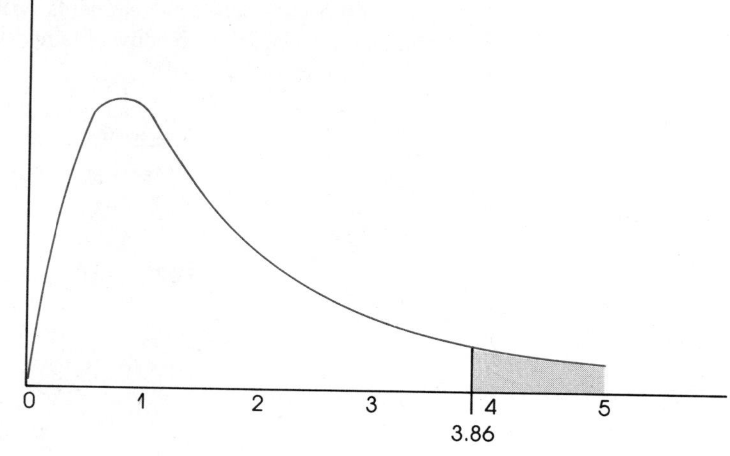

Total variability is partitioned into between-treatments *SS* and within-treatments *SS*. For between-treatments variability, we get

$$\begin{aligned} SS_{\text{between treatments}} &= \sum \frac{T^2}{n} - \frac{G^2}{N} \\ &= \frac{26^2}{4} + \frac{8^2}{4} + \frac{6^2}{4} + \frac{4^2}{4} - \frac{44^2}{16} \\ &= 169 + 16 + 9 + 4 - 121 \\ &= 77 \end{aligned}$$

The first stage of the partitioning of variability is completed by computing within-treatments *SS*:

At this point of the analysis, the work may be checked to see if total *SS* equals between-treatments *SS* plus within-treatments *SS*.

$$\begin{aligned} SS_{\text{within treatments}} &= \sum SS_{\text{inside each treatment}} \\ &= 11 + 2 + 9 + 2 \\ &= 24 \end{aligned}$$

In the second stage of the analysis, within-treatments *SS* is partitioned into between-subjects *SS* and error *SS*. This analysis is accomplished by first calculating between-subjects *SS* and then subtracting it from within-treatments *SS*. The residual will be error *SS*:

$$\begin{aligned} SS_{\text{between subjects}} &= \sum \frac{P^2}{k} - \frac{G^2}{N} \\ &= \frac{12^2}{4} + \frac{6^2}{4} + \frac{10^2}{4} + \frac{16^2}{4} - \frac{44^2}{16} \\ &= 36 + 9 + 25 + 64 - 121 \\ &= 13 \end{aligned}$$

$$\begin{aligned} SS_{\text{error}} &= SS_{\text{within treatments}} - SS_{\text{between subjects}} \\ &= 24 - 13 \\ &= 11 \end{aligned}$$

Finally, we can compute the *MS* values and then the *F*-ratio. The repeated-measures *F*-ratio uses between-treatments *MS* in the numerator and error *MS* in the denominator. These are readily obtained by dividing *SS* by the appropriate number of degrees of freedom:

$$\begin{aligned} MS_{\text{between treatments}} &= \frac{SS_{\text{between treatments}}}{df_{\text{between treatments}}} \\ &= \frac{77}{3} \\ &= 25.67 \end{aligned}$$

$$\begin{aligned} MS_{\text{error}} &= \frac{SS_{\text{error}}}{df_{\text{error}}} \\ &= \frac{11}{9} \\ &= 1.22 \end{aligned}$$

$$F = \frac{MS_{\text{between treatments}}}{MS_{\text{error}}} = \frac{25.67}{1.22} = 21.04$$

STEP 4 *Evaluate the hypotheses.* The obtained F-ratio is 21.04. This value falls in the critical region that begins at 3.86. The statistical decision is to reject the null hypothesis. The school psychologist may conclude that the response-cost technique had an effect on the number of disruptions. A report might state:

> There was a significant effect of response-cost training on the number of outbursts exhibited by the children, $F(3, 9) = 21.04$, $p < .05$.

The complete results of the analysis are summarized in Table 14.3.

TABLE 14.3

Analysis of variance summary

Source	SS	df	MS	F
Between treatments	77	3	25.67	21.04
Within treatments	24	12		
Between subjects	13	3		
Error	11	9	1.22	
Total	101	15		

POST HOC TESTS WITH REPEATED MEASURES

Recall that ANOVA provides an overall test of significance for the treatment. When the null hypothesis is rejected, it only indicates that there is a difference between at least two of the treatment means. If $k = 2$, it is obvious where the difference lies in the experiment. However, when k is greater than 2, the situation becomes more complex. To determine exactly where significant differences exist, the researcher must follow the ANOVA with post hoc tests. In Chapter 13 we used Tukey's HSD and the Scheffé test to make these multiple comparisons among treatment means. As a posteriori tests, these two procedures attempt to control the overall alpha level by making adjustments for the number of potential comparisons.

For a repeated-measures ANOVA, Tukey's HSD and the Scheffé test can be used in the exact same manner as was done for the independent-measures ANOVA, *provided* that you substitute MS_{error} in place of MS_{within} in the formulas and use df_{error} in place of df_{within} when locating the critical value in a statistical table. It should be noted that statisticians are not in complete agreement about the appropriate error term in post hoc tests for repeated-measures designs (for an excellent discussion, see Keppel, 1973).

14.5 ADVANTAGES OF THE REPEATED-MEASURES DESIGN

When we first encountered the repeated-measures design (Chapter 12), it was noted that this type of experiment has certain advantages and disadvantages. On the bright side, a repeated-measures study may be desirable if the supply of subjects is limited. A repeated-measures experiment is economical in that the experimenter can get by using fewer subjects. However, the disadvantages may be very great. These take the form of carry-over effects, such as fatigue, that can make the interpretation of the data very difficult.

Now that we have examined the repeated-measures ANOVA, we can introduce another advantage, namely, the elimination of the role of variability due to individual differences. Consider the structure of the F-ratio for both the independent- and repeated-measures designs. For the independent measures design the F-ratio takes the following form:

$$F = \frac{\text{treatment effect} + \text{individual differences} + \text{experimental error}}{\text{individual differences} + \text{experimental error}}$$

The structure of the repeated-measures F-ratio reveals that the influence of individual differences has been eliminated altogether:

$$F = \frac{\text{treatment effect} + \text{experimental error}}{\text{experimental error}}$$

The removal of individual differences from the analysis becomes an advantage in situations where very large individual differences exist among the subjects being studied. When individual differences are extraordinarily large, the presence of a treatment effect may be masked if an independent-measures study is performed. In this case, a repeated-measures design would be more sensitive in detecting a treatment effect, because individual differences do not influence the value of the F-ratio.

This point will become evident in the following example. Suppose an experiment is performed in two ways, with an independent-measures design and a repeated-measures experiment. Also, let's suppose that we know how much variability is accounted for by the different sources of variance. For example,

$$\begin{aligned}\text{treatment effect} &= 10 \text{ units of variance}\\ \text{individual differences} &= 1000 \text{ units of variance}\\ \text{experimental error} &= 1 \text{ unit of variance}\end{aligned}$$

Notice that a very large amount of the variability in the experiment is due to individual differences. By comparing the F-ratios of both types of experiments, we will be able to see a fundamental difference between the two types of experimental designs. For the independent-measures experiment, we obtain

$$\begin{aligned}F &= \frac{\text{treatment effect} + \text{individual differences} + \text{experimental error}}{\text{individual differences} + \text{experimental error}}\\ &= \frac{10 + 1000 + 1}{1000 + 1}\\ &= \frac{1011}{1001}\\ &= 1.01\end{aligned}$$

However, the repeated-measures F-ratio provides a different outcome:

$$\begin{aligned}F &= \frac{\text{treatment effect} + \text{experimental error}}{\text{experimental error}}\\ &= \frac{10 + 1}{1}\\ &= \frac{11}{1}\\ &= 11\end{aligned}$$

PERSPECTIVE 14.2

DATA THAT PRODUCE A LARGE MS_{error}

To get some idea of a situation that results in a large MS_{error}, it is useful to examine hypothetical data in the form of a graph. Suppose an experimenter examines the effect of amount of reward on maze performance in rats. A sample of $n = 4$ rats that have learned to solve a maze is subsequently tested in all four reward conditions: 2, 4, 6, and 8 grams of food reward. The experimenter measures the speed with which they solve the maze after experiencing the new amount of reward. The broken line in Figure 14.5 represents a graph of the means of each treatment. The speed of maze running seems to increase with amount of reward.

Figure 14.5 also shows a set of hypothetical data for each individual (solid lines) that would produce the treatment means (broken line). Notice that there are individual differences in these data. The subject totals (P values) differ, indicating that some subjects generally run faster than others. Also note that the individual differences are consistent from one treatment to the next. For example, in all four treatment conditions subject 1 is fastest, and subject 2 is slowest. This means that much of the variability within treatments is due to consistent, predictable individual differences. When the individual differences are subtracted out of the analysis, the result will be a very small value for MS_{error}. Remember that a small value for MS_{error} will tend to produce a large value for the F-ratio, indicating a significant difference between treatments. The consistency in these data can be described in another way that may help you to understand the F-ratio. For the data in Figure 14.5 the effect of the treatment is consistent for all subjects: Every rat shows an increase in speed when the amount of reward is increased. Because the treatment effect is very consistent, you should expect to find a significant difference between treatments.

Figure 14.6 depicts another possibility for individual subjects. Although these data will produce the same treatment means as the previous example (Figure 14.5), the treatment effect is no longer consistent across subjects. Now when the amount of reward is increased, some subjects run faster, and some run slower. Because the treatment effect is not consistent, you should not expect to find significant differences between treatments. Also note that the data in Figure 14.6 do not show consistent individual differences from one treatment to another. For example, subject 2 is the slowest rat in the first treatment but is the fastest in the second treatment. Because there are no consistent individual differences, most of the variability within treatments is due to experimental error. As a result, MS_{error} will be large and will tend to produce a relatively small F-ratio.

· FIGURE 14.5 ·

The effect of amount of reward on running speed. Treatment means are depicted by the broken line. Individual scores for each subject at each level of reward are shown by solid lines.

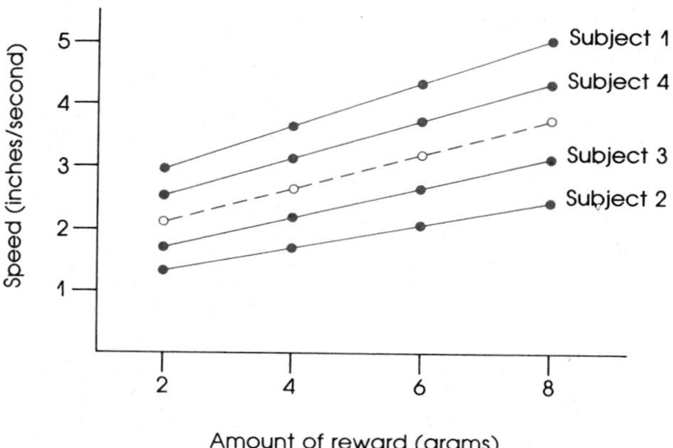

· FIGURE 14.6 ·

The effect of amount of reward on running speed. The treatment means are depicted by the broken line. Individual scores for each subject at each level of reward are shown by solid lines.

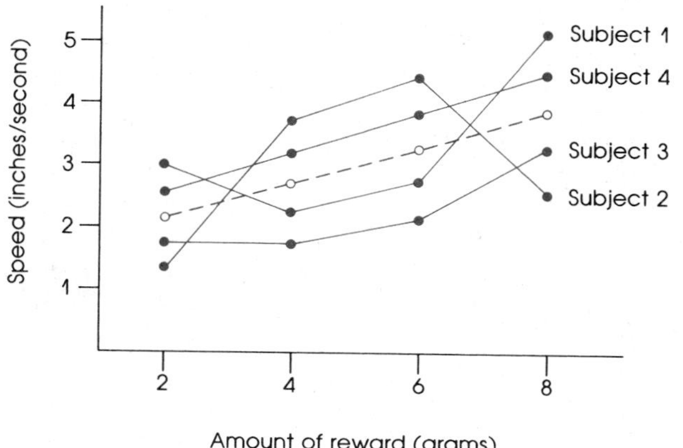

All things (sources of variability) being equal, the repeated-measures F-ratio is larger. In this example, the F-ratio is much larger for the repeated-measures study because the individual differences, which are extremely large, have been removed (see Perspective 14.2). In the independent ANOVA, the presence of a treatment effect is obscured by the influence of individual differences. This problem is remedied by the repeated-measures design in which variability due to individual differences has been partitioned out of the analysis. When the amount of individual differences is great, a repeated-measures experiment may provide a more sensitive test for a treatment effect. In statistical terms, a repeated-measures test has more *power* than an independent-measures test; that is, it is more likely to reject a false H_0.

14.6 ASSUMPTIONS OF THE REPEATED-MEASURES ANOVA

In Chapter 11, we introduced the *F*-max test for the assumption of homogeneity of variance.

Of course, random sampling is a requirement for the repeated measures ANOVA. Also, it is assumed that the population distribution for each treatment is normal. As we noted in Chapter 13, homogeneity of variance is required for analysis of variance. That is, the variances of the population distributions for each treatment should be equivalent. These assumptions are essentially the same as those for the independent-measures ANOVA.

For the repeated-measures ANOVA, there is an additional assumption, called homogeneity of covariance. Basically, it refers to the requirement that the relative standing of each subject is maintained in each treatment condition. This assumption will be violated if the effect of the treatment is not consistent for all of the subjects or if carry-over effects exist for some but not other subjects. This issue is a very complex one and beyond the scope of this book. However, methods do exist for dealing with violations of this assumption (for a discussion, see Keppel, 1973).

· LEARNING CHECK ·

1 It has been suggested that pupil size increases during emotional arousal. A researcher, therefore, would like to see if the increase in pupil size is a function of the type of arousal (pleasant versus aversive). A random sample of five subjects is selected for the study. Each subject views *all* three stimuli: neutral, pleasant, and aversive photographs. The neutral photograph portrays a plain brick building. The pleasant photograph consists of a young man and woman sharing a large ice cream cone. Finally, the aversive stimulus is a graphic photograph of an automobile accident. Upon viewing each stimulus, the pupil size is measured (in millimeters) with sophisticated equipment. The data are as follows. Perform an ANOVA and make a conclusion about the findings.

	Stimulus		
Subject	Neutral	Pleasant	Aversive
A	4	8	3
B	3	6	3
C	2	5	2
D	3	3	6
E	3	8	1

ANSWER

1

Source	SS	df	MS	F
Between treatments	30	2	15	4.29
Within treatments	34	12		
Between subjects	6	4		
Error	28	8	3.5	
Total	64	14		

$F(2, 8) = 4.29$. For an alpha level of .05, the obtained *F*-ratio fails to reach statistical significance. The null hypothesis cannot be rejected. There is not sufficient evidence for an effect of stimulus type on pupil size.

SUMMARY

1 ANOVA for a repeated-measures design initially partitions total variability into between-treatments *SS* and within-treatments *SS*.

2 Between-treatments *SS* is influenced by the treatment effect and experimental error. Individual differences do not play a role in this source of variability because the same sample of subjects serves in all treatments.

3 Within-treatments *SS* is affected by individual differences and experimental error.

4 The structure of the repeated-measures *F* is

$$F = \frac{\text{treatment effect} + \text{experimental error}}{\text{experimental error}}$$

5 To obtain the error term for the *F*-ratio, within-treatments *SS* is partitioned into between-subjects *SS* and error *SS*.

6 Degrees of freedom are partitioned in a similar fashion. That is, there is a *df* value for each *SS* value in the analysis.

7 The estimated variances, or *MS* values, are computed by dividing each *SS* used in the *F*-ratio by the appropriate *df* value. For the repeated-measures ANOVA,

$$MS_{\text{between treatments}} = \frac{SS_{\text{between treatments}}}{df_{\text{between treatments}}}$$

$$MS_{\text{error}} = \frac{SS_{\text{error}}}{df_{\text{error}}}$$

8 The *F*-ratio for the repeated-measures ANOVA is computed by

$$F = \frac{MS_{\text{between treatments}}}{MS_{\text{error}}}$$

9 When the obtained *F*-ratio is significant (that is, H_0 is rejected), it indicates that a significant difference lies between at least two of the treatment conditions. To determine exactly where the difference lies, unplanned, post hoc comparisons may be made. Unplanned tests, such as Tukey's HSD, use MS_{error} rather than $MS_{\text{within treatments}}$ and df_{error} instead of $df_{\text{within treatments}}$.

10 A repeated-measures ANOVA eliminates the influence of individual differences from the analysis. If individual differences are extremely large, a treatment effect might be masked in an independent-measures experiment. In this case, a repeated-measures design might be a more sensitive test for a treatment effect.

KEY TERMS

between-treatments variability
within-treatments variability
between-subjects variability
error variability
treatment effect
individual differences
experimental error
mean squares
F-ratio

FOCUS ON PROBLEM SOLVING

1. Before you begin a repeated-measures ANOVA, complete all the preliminary calculations needed for the ANOVA formulas. This requires that you find the total for each treatment (*T*'s), the total for each person (*P*'s), the grand total (*G*), the *SS* for each treatment condition, and $\sum X^2$ for the entire set of *N* scores. As a partial check on these calculations, be sure that the *T* values add up to *G* and that the *P* values have a sum of *G*.

2. To help remember the structure of the repeated-measures ANOVA, keep in mind that a repeated-measures experiment eliminates the contribution of individual differences. There are no individual differences contributing to the numerator of the *F*-ratio ($MS_{\text{between treatments}}$) because the same individuals are used for all treatments. Therefore, you must also eliminate individual differences in the denominator. This is accomplished by partitioning within-treatments variability into two components: between-subjects variability and error variability. It is the *MS* value for error variability that is used in the denominator of the *F*-ratio.

3. As with any ANOVA, it helps to organize your work so you do not get lost. Compute the *SS* values first, followed by the *df* values. You can then calculate the *MS* values and the *F*-ratio. Filling in the columns on an ANOVA summary table (for example, page 339) as

you do the computations will help guide your way through the problem.

4. Be careful when using *df* values to find the critical *F* value. Remember, df_{error} (*not* df_{within}) is used for the denominator.

PROBLEMS

1 What advantages does a repeated-measures design have over an independent-measures design?

2 How does the error term differ for repeated- versus independent-measures ANOVA?

***3** It has been demonstrated that when subjects must memorize a list of words serially (in the order of presentation) words at the beginning and end of the list are remembered better than words in the middle. This observation has been called the *serial-position effect*. The following data represent the number of errors made in recall of the first eight, second eight, and last eight words in the list:

	Serial Position		
Person	First	Middle	Last
A	1	5	0
B	3	7	2
C	5	6	1
D	3	2	1

a Compute the mean number of errors for each position and draw a graph of the data.

b Is there evidence for a significant effect of serial position? Test at the .05 level of significance. Based on the ANOVA, explain the results of the study.

***4** A researcher reports an *F*-ratio with $df = 3, 36$ for a repeated-measures ANOVA.

a How many treatment conditions were evaluated in this experiment?

b How many subjects participated in this experiment?

5 A researcher conducts a repeated-measures experiment using a sample of $n = 12$ subjects to evaluate the differences among three treatment conditions. If the results are examined with an ANOVA, what would be the *df* values for the *F*-ratio?

6 The following data were obtained to compare three experimental treatments:

Treatments		
1	2	3
2	4	6
5	5	5
1	2	3
0	1	2

a If these data were obtained from an *independent-measures design*, then could you conclude that there is a significant difference among the treatment conditions? Test with alpha set at .05.

b If these data were obtained from a *repeated-measures design*, so that each row of scores represents data from a single subject, then could you conclude that there is a significant difference among the treatments? Test at the .05 level of significance.

c Explain the difference in the results of part a and part b.

***7** To determine the long-term effectiveness of relaxation training on anxiety, a researcher uses a repeated-measures study. A random sample of $n = 10$ subjects is first tested for the severity of anxiety with a standardized test. In addition to this pretest, subjects are tested again 1 week, 1 month, 6 months, and 1 year after treatment. The investigator used ANOVA to evaluate these data, and portions of the results are presented in the following summary table. Fill in the missing values. (*Hint:* Start with the *df* values.)

Source	SS	df	MS	
Between treatments	____	____	____	$F = 5$
Within treatments	500	____		
Between subjects	____	____		
Error	____	____	10	
Total	____	____		

8 A company researcher examines the sales performance of $n = 5$ new employees at the real estate firm. To see if there is a significant trend toward improvement, the number of homes sold is recorded each month for the first 3 months of employment. The data are as follows:

Person	Month 1	Month 2	Month 3
A	1	3	4
B	4	6	8
C	3	3	5
D	2	4	7
E	0	4	6

a Compute the mean number of sales that were made in each month.

b Is there a significant change in sales performance with more experience? Test at the .05 level of significance.

The researcher examines the role of experience on sales performance at another branch office. Again, a sample of $n = 5$

new employees is studied, and the number of sales is noted for each of the first 3 months of employment:

Person	Month 1	Month 2	Month 3
A	4	0	10
B	0	10	0
C	0	6	4
D	6	0	14
E	0	4	2

c Compute the mean number of sales that were made in each month. Compare these values to those obtained in part a.

d Is there a significant change in sales across months? Set the alpha level to .05.

e Compare the results of the ANOVA for the first branch office (part b) to those of the second branch (part d). Even though the means are the same at each branch (part a versus part c), why are the results of the ANOVA so different?

9 A teacher studies the effectiveness of a reading skills course on comprehension. A sample of $n = 20$ students is studied. The instructor assesses their comprehension with a standardized reading test. The test is administered at the beginning of the course, at midterm, and at the end of the course. The instructor uses analysis of variance to determine whether or not a significant change has occurred in the students' reading performance. The following summary table presents a portion of the ANOVA results. Provide the missing values in the table. (Start with *df* values.)

Source	SS	df	MS	
Between treatments	____	____	18	$F = 9.0$
Within treatments	170	____		
Between subjects	____	____		
Error	____	____	____	
Total	____	____		

***10** A psychologist studies the effect of practice on maze learning in rats. Rats are tested in the maze in one daily session for 4 days. The psychologist records the number of errors made in the trials on each daily session. The data are as follows:

	Session			
Rat	1	2	3	4
1	3	1	0	0
2	3	2	2	1
3	6	3	1	2

Is there evidence for a practice effect? Use the .05 level of significance.

***11** A researcher studies the interference of old habits on new tasks in the following manner: He presents three types of stimuli, one at a time, on a slide projector. In the first type, the subject views the name of a color, such as "green," printed in the same color ink as the name. For the second type of stimulus the name of a color, such as "red," is printed in ink that is *different* in color from the name. The third type of stimulus is a random string of consonants printed in ink of one of several possible colors (such as blue ink). The task for the subject is to name the color of the ink as soon as possible. The reaction time (the latency of response to the stimulus presentation) is recorded for each type of stimulus. Because reading words is such a strong habit, subjects should have difficulty in quickly naming the color of ink for the second type of stimulus. This method of studying interference effects is known as a Stroop task. A random sample of $n = 6$ subjects is selected for this study. The data are as follows:

	Type of Stimulus		
Subject	1 Same Color (ms)	2 Different Color (ms)	3 Consonants (ms)
1	180	220	190
2	198	233	201
3	174	218	187
4	185	221	193
5	207	240	209
6	191	215	189

a Compute the mean for each stimulus type.

b Perform an ANOVA to determine if there is an effect of stimulus type on reaction time. Test at the .01 level of significance.

c In a few sentences, interpret the findings in light of the ANOVA. What happened in the experiment?

12 When a stimulus is presented continuously and it does not vary in intensity, the individual will eventually perceive the stimulus as less intense or not perceive it at all. This phenomenon is known as sensory adaptation. Years ago Zigler (1932) studied adaptation for skin (cutaneous) sensation by placing a small weight on part of the body and measuring how much time lapsed until subjects reported they felt nothing at all. Suppose a researcher does a similar study, comparing adaptation for four regions of the body for a sample of $n = 7$ subjects. A 500-milligram weight is gently placed on the region, and the latency (in seconds) for a report that it is no longer felt is recorded for each subject. The data are as follows:

	Area of Stimulation			
Subject	Back of Hand	Lower Back	Middle of Palm	Chin Below Lower Lip
1	6.5	4.6	10.2	12.1
2	5.8	3.5	9.7	11.8
3	6.0	4.2	9.9	11.5
4	6.7	4.7	8.1	10.7
5	5.2	3.6	7.9	9.9
6	4.3	3.5	9.0	11.3
7	7.4	4.8	10.8	12.6

Is there a significant effect of area of stimulation on the latency of adaptation? Set the alpha level to .01.

***13** A psychologist has $n = 7$ subjects fitted with glasses containing prisms that make everything look upside down. The psychologist has the subjects wear these glasses for 5 days to see if they eventually learn to compensate for the inversion of their visual field. On each of the 5 days, the subjects must assemble a wooden puzzle, and the experimenter measures the amount of time to completion (in seconds). The data are as follows:

	Day				
Subject	1	2	3	4	5
1	112	107	83	87	69
2	135	130	110	74	46
3	89	33	27	36	29
4	37	60	62	32	19
5	73	66	54	43	37
6	56	58	51	59	60
7	95	89	125	70	31

Is there an effect of practice? Test at the .05 level of significance.

14 A psychologist is asked by a dog food manufacturer to determine if animals will show a preference among three new food mixes recently developed. The psychologist takes a sample of $n = 6$ dogs. They are deprived of food overnight and presented simultaneously with three bowls of the mixes on the next morning. After 10 minutes, the bowls are removed, and the amount of food (in ounces) consumed is determined for each type of mix. The data are as follows:

	Mix		
Subject	1	2	3
1	3	2	1
2	0	5	1
3	2	7	3
4	1	6	5
5	1	2	3
6	3	0	3

Is there evidence for a significant preference? Test at the .05 level of significance.

***15** A repeated-measures experiment comparing only two treatments can be evaluated with either a t statistic or an ANOVA. As we found with the independent-measures design, the t test and the ANOVA will produce equivalent conclusions, and the two test statistics are related by the equation $F = t^2$.

The following data are from a repeated-measures study.

Subject	Treatment 1	Treatment 2	Difference
1	2	4	+2
2	1	3	+2
3	0	10	+10
4	1	3	+2

a Use a repeated-measures t statistic with $\alpha = .05$ to determine whether or not the data provide evidence of a significant difference between the two treatments.
b Use a repeated-measures ANOVA with $\alpha = .05$ to evaluate the data. (You should find $F = t^2$.)

Caution: ANOVA calculations are done with the X values, but for t you use the difference scores.

16 A psychologist performs an experiment to demonstrate a generalization gradient in instrumental conditioning. Pigeons are trained to peck a key for food reward whenever a 1000-hertz tone is presented. The animals are trained until they satisfactorily learn that the discriminative stimulus (the tone) signals the availability of reward and until their response rates are high and stable. The experimenter then tests the pigeons for stimulus generalization by presenting tones of 200, 600, 1000, 1400, and 1800 hertz to all of the animals. The number of responses are recorded in each of these generalization tests. In a generalization gradient, the more difference between the test stimulus and the original stimulus, the less the animal will respond. The data from the experiment are as follows:

Number of responses in a test session

	Test Tone (Hz)				
Pigeon	200	600	1000	1400	1800
1	63	129	356	240	94
2	95	110	123	120	90
3	45	190	251	154	33
4	80	181	180	75	30
5	68	135	277	124	65
6	32	79	286	174	81

a Compute the mean number of responses for each test tone. Draw a graph of these means.
b Perform an ANOVA on the results. Is there an effect of the frequency (hertz) of the test tone? Set alpha at .01.
c Based on the "picture" of the results in part a and the analysis in part b, explain what occurred in this experiment.

17 A scientist tests two drugs for their effects on insomnia. A sample of $n = 8$ insomniacs is pretested with a placebo before bedtime, and the latency to onset of sleep is measured to serve as a baseline. A week later, the subjects receive the first drug before bedtime, and the time that lapses between drug administration and sleep onset is measured again. Finally, a week later the second drug is tested in the same fashion. The latency to sleep onset (in minutes) is presented for each subject on every test. The data are as follows:

Subject	Pretest	Drug 1	Drug 2
E.B.	136	24	33
K.F.	92	107	21
T.Z.	117	98	111
J.R.	65	51	49
R.E.	129	29	37
A.G.	172	112	70
P.S.	89	122	145
D.W.	84	22	16

Is there a significant effect on latency? Test at the .05 level of significance.

***18** A sample of 14-week-old infants is studied in a perception experiment. The infants are presented with three line drawings successively for 5 minutes each. The designs vary in their complexity. The researcher records how much time (in seconds) is spent viewing each of the stimuli. The data are as follows:

	Amount of Complexity		
Infant	Low	Moderate	High
A	63	112	39
B	210	73	80
C	94	314	83
D	219	232	115
E	54	396	76
F	120	352	100

Is there a significant preference among the three stimuli? Test at the .01 level of significance.

19 An industrial psychologist examines the effect of hourly wages and piecework pay on productivity. A random sample of $n = 10$ workers is studied. These workers are assembling small circuit boards for appliances and are getting paid at an hourly rate. The psychologist records the number of circuit boards assembled in 1 day for this pay schedule. The workers are later switched to a piecework rate, in which they get paid according to the number of circuit boards assembled, not the number of hours worked. Again, the number of boards assembled is recorded for 1 day. The results are as follows:

Subject	Hourly Rate	Piecework
1	74	82
2	59	70
3	70	63
4	67	91
5	79	87
6	61	75
7	80	96
8	72	68
9	69	60
10	57	67

a Perform an ANOVA to determine if a significant effect occurred. Use the .05 level of significance.

b Use a repeated-measures t test to analyze the data. Again, set alpha to .05. Compare the results of parts a and b. Remember, $F = t^2$ (Chapter 13).

***20** The following data are from an experiment comparing three different treatment conditions:

A	B	C
0	1	2
2	5	5
1	2	6
5	4	9
2	8	8

a If the experiment uses an *independent-measures design*, then can the researcher conclude that the treatments are significantly different? Test at the .05 level of significance.

b If the experiment were done with a *repeated-measures design*, should the researcher conclude that the treatments are significantly different? Set alpha at .05 again.

c Explain why the results are different in the analyses of parts a and b.

21 A researcher is examining the effect of sleep deprivation on basic mental processes. A sample of eight subjects is obtained. These subjects agree to stay awake for a total of 48 hours. Every 12 hours the researcher gives each subject a series of arithmetic problems as a test of mental alertness. The number of problems worked correctly in 10 minutes is recorded for each subject. The data are as follows:

	Hours Awake			
Subject	12	24	36	48
1	8	7	8	6
2	10	12	9	11
3	9	9	8	10
4	7	8	6	6
5	12	10	10	8
6	10	9	12	8
7	7	7	6	8
8	9	10	11	11

On the basis of these data can the researcher conclude that sleep deprivation has a significant effect on basic mental processing? Test with $\alpha = .05$.

22 The researcher in Problem 21 also wanted to examine the subjects' own perceptions of their mental functioning. Immediately before the subjects started each set of arithmetic problems, they were asked to rate their own abilities using a scale from 10 (normal) to 1 (severely impaired). The data from this part of the experiment are as follows:

	Hours Awake			
Subject	12	24	36	48
1	10	9	6	2
2	9	8	5	5
3	10	8	7	3
4	10	9	6	4
5	9	7	6	2
6	8	9	4	1
7	9	8	7	2
8	9	7	6	4

a Do these data indicate that subjects perceive a change in performance as they become more tired? Test with $\alpha = .05$.
b Write a brief description of the results of the entire experiment, combining the data from Problem 21 and Problem 22.

***23** A researcher used an analysis of variance to evaluate the results from a single-factor repeated-measures experiment. The reported *F*-ratio was $F(2, 28) = 6.35$.
a How many different treatments were compared in this experiment?
b How many subjects participated in the experiment?

24 A manufacturer of business machines would like to compare the four most popular brands of electric typewriters. A sample of eight typists is selected, and each typist spends 15 minutes testing each of the four typewriters and then rates its performance. The manufacturer would like to know if there are any significant differences among the four brands. The data from this study were examined using an analysis of variance. The results are shown in the following summary table. Fill in all missing values.

Source	SS	df	MS	
Between treatments	270	____	____	$F = 9.00$
Within treatments	____	____		
Between subjects	____	____		
Error	____	____	____	
Total	680	____		

***25** A psychology professor would like to determine whether or not the introductory course in psychology has any effect on students' opinions concerning the field of psychology. At the beginning of the semester a random sample of 12 students is selected, and each student is asked to rate psychology in terms of how interesting and relevant it is. At the end of the semester these same 12 students are asked again for their opinions. The results are as follows:

Student	Beginning	End
1	13	14
2	16	16
3	10	13
4	17	16
5	15	18
6	19	18
7	12	15
8	17	16
9	10	18
10	8	12
11	11	12
12	9	13

a Use an ANOVA to determine whether the introductory course has any effect on students' opinions. Test at the .05 level of significance.
b Use a *t* test to determine whether there is any change in opinion. Again, test at the .05 level of significance. *Note:* You should find that $F = t^2$.

CHAPTER 15

TWO-FACTOR ANALYSIS OF VARIANCE (INDEPENDENT MEASURES)

TOOLS YOU WILL NEED

The following items are considered essential background material for this chapter. If you doubt your knowledge of any of these items, you should review the appropriate chapter or section before proceeding.

- Introduction to analysis of variance (Chapter 13)
- The logic of analysis of variance
- ANOVA notation and formulas
- Distribution of *F*-ratios

PREVIEW

Imagine that you are seated at your desk, ready to take the final exam in statistics. Just before the exams are handed out, a television crew appears and sets up a camera and lights aimed directly at you. They explain that they are filming students during exams for a television special. You are told to ignore the camera and go ahead with your exam.

Would the presence of a TV camera affect your performance on an exam? For some of you, the answer to this question is "definitely yes" and for others, "probably not." In fact, both answers are right; whether or not the TV camera affects performance depends on your personality. Some of you would become terribly distressed and self-conscious, while others really could ignore the camera and go on as if everything were normal.

In an experiment that duplicates the situation we have described, Shrauger (1972) tested subjects on a concept formation task. Half the subjects worked alone (no audience), and half the subjects worked with an audience of people who claimed to be interested in observing the experiment. Shrauger also divided the subjects into two groups on the basis of personality: those high in self-esteem and those low in self-esteem. The dependent variable for this experiment was the number of errors on the concept formation task. Data similar to those obtained by Shrauger are shown in Figure 15.1. Notice that the audience had no effect on the high-self-esteem subjects. However, the low-self-esteem subjects made nearly twice as many errors with an audience as when working alone.

We have presented Shrauger's study as an introduction to experiments that have two independent variables. In this study, the independent variables are

1. Audience (present or absent)
2. Self-esteem (high or low)

The results of this study indicate that the effect of one variable (audience) depends on another variable (self-esteem).

You should realize that it is quite common to have experimental variables that interact in this way. For example, a particular drug may have a profound effect on some patients and have no effect whatsoever on others. Some children develop normally in a single-parent home, while others show serious difficulties. In general, the effects of a particular treatment often depend on other factors. To determine whether two variables are interdependent, it is necessary to examine both variables together in a single experiment. In this chapter we will introduce the experimental techniques that are used for experiments with two independent variables.

FIGURE 15.1

Results of an experiment examining the effect of an audience on the number of errors made in a concept formation task for subjects who are rated either high or low in self-esteem. Notice that the effect of the audience depends on the self-esteem of the subjects.

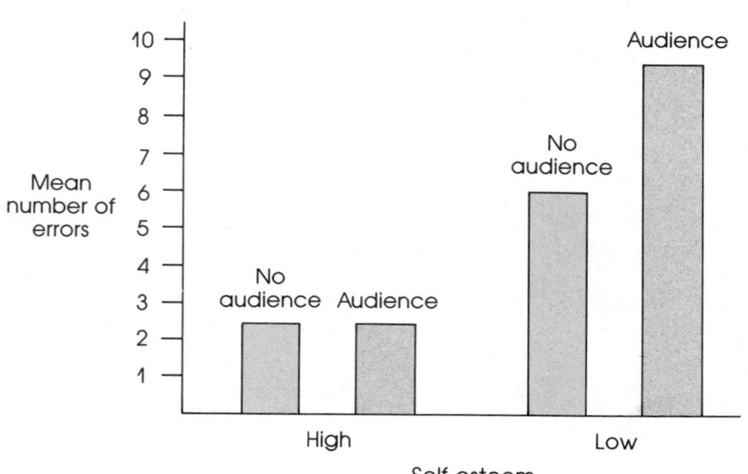

Shrauger, J. S. (1972). Self-esteem and reactions to being observed by others. *Journal of Personality and Social Psychology*, 23, 192–200. Copyright (1972) by the American Psychological Association. Adapted by permission of the author.

15.1 INTRODUCTION

An example of an experiment that combines two independent variables is presented in Figure 15.2. The independent variables in this experiment are age (one group of animals is tested at 1 month and another group at 8 months) and drug (one group receives the drug before testing, and the other does not). The dependent variable is the learning score obtained for each animal. Notice that this experiment will allow the researcher to examine several different questions:

1. What is the effect of the drug on learning?
2. How does learning performance depend on age (1 month versus 8 months)?
3. Does the effect of the drug depend on the age of the animals?

An experiment of this type is called a *two-factor* experiment. Notice that the data for a two-factor experiment always can be presented in a matrix listing the values for one factor across the top and the other factor down the first column. Each box in the matrix corresponds to exactly one value for each factor. These boxes are called *cells,* and each cell identifies a specific treatment condition. For example, the lower left-hand cell in Figure 15.2 would contain scores for those animals who received no drug and were tested at age 1 month.

Often a two-factor design is specified by the size of the matrix. For example Figure 15.2 depicts a 2 × 2 factorial design. The numbers reflect the levels of each factor.

The different values for each factor are called the *levels* of the factor. For example, the age factor has two levels, 1 month and 8 months. The drug factor also has two levels, drug and no drug.

15.2 ADVANTAGES OF A TWO-FACTOR EXPERIMENT

You may have noticed that the experiment described in Figure 15.2 could have been done as two separate experiments (see Figure 15.3). One experiment could evaluate the drug effect, and the other experiment could examine the age difference. What is the advantage of combining these two different questions into a single experiment? In fact, there are several advantages:

1. *Fewer Subjects.* The two-factor experiment pictured in Figure 15.2 uses a total of 30 subjects in the drug condition and 30 subjects in the no-drug condition. The

FIGURE 15.2

Matrix showing the experimental treatment combinations for a two-factor experiment. The factors are age and drug. There are two levels for each factor, resulting in four different treatment combinations, or cells, in the matrix.

		Factor 1 (age)	
		1 month	8 months
Factor 2 (drug)	Drug	Scores for $n = 15$ subjects given the drug and tested at age 1 month	Scores for $n = 15$ subjects given the drug and tested at age 8 months
	No drug	Scores for $n = 15$ subjects given no drug and tested at age 1 month	Scores for $n = 15$ subjects given no drug and tested at age 8 months

FIGURE 15.3

Two separate experiments that duplicate the two factors shown in Figure 15.2. Notice that it would take a total of $N = 120$ subjects to complete these two experiments, compared to a total of only $N = 60$ subjects for the two-factor experiment in Figure 15.2.

Experiment I: Evaluating the drug effect

Drug	Scores for all $n = 30$ subjects who are given the drug before testing
No drug	Scores for all $n = 30$ subjects who are given no drug before testing

Experiment II: Evaluating the effect of age

1 month	8 months
Scores for all $n = 30$ subjects who are tested at age 1 month	Scores for all $n = 30$ subjects who are tested at age 8 months

mean difference between these two groups of 30 will be used to evaluate the drug's effect. At the same time, the two-factor experiment tests a group of 30 subjects at age 1 month versus a second group of 30 subjects tested at age 8 months. Both of these tests are done with the same overall group of 60 subjects. If the two experiments were done separately (see Figure 15.3), it would require a total of 120 subjects (60 in each experiment).

2. *Experimental Control.* Often it is possible for an experimental treatment to have a positive effect on one group of subjects and no effect (or a negative effect) on others. For example, the drug we are testing could improve learning performance for the young animals but have no effect on the older animals. If we tested only the young animals, we would observe a strong effect. But if we tested a mixed group of young and old together, we would observe a mixed and inconsistent drug effect. Whenever separate groups of individuals are combined into a single sample, there is a risk that the treatment will show mixed effects. This is often called *noise* in the data because it can mask the treatment effect. The two-factor experiment allows you to control some of this noise. In the example we are considering, the two distinct groups of animals (young and old) have been separated by using age as a factor. A more-detailed example showing how a second factor can be used for experimental control is given in Example 15.2 at the end of this chapter.

By noise the experimenter is referring to variability that cannot be explained by the treatment effect.

3. *Interaction.* The greatest advantage of a two-factor experiment is the opportunity to examine the *interaction* between the two separate factors. As already noted, it is possible for a treatment to affect one group differently than it does another. Also, it is possible for the effect of a treatment to depend on the specific circumstances under which it is administered. When the effects of one treatment depend on a second treatment, you have an interaction. The two-factor experiment allows you to look at this interaction as well as each of the two treatments separately.

MAIN EFFECTS AND INTERACTIONS

It is possible to look at the data from a two-factor experiment as if they represented two separate single-factor experiments. In Figure 15.2, for example, you could ignore the age groups and look at the data as if the experiment were only comparing the drug group versus the no-drug group (the 30 subjects in the first row versus the 30 subjects in the second row). A comparison of this type is called a main effect.

· DEFINITION · The mean differences among the levels of one factor are referred to as the *main effect* of that factor. If the design of the experiment is represented as a matrix with one factor determining the rows and the second factor determining the columns, then the main effect for the first factor would evaluate the mean differences among the rows, and the main effect for the second factor would evaluate the mean differences among the columns.

For our example, we could evaluate the main effect for the drug (ignoring age), or we could evaluate the main effect for age (ignoring the drug). When discussing a general two-factor experiment, we will identify the factors as factor A and factor B. The main effect for factor A commonly is called the A-effect. Similarly, the main effect for factor B is called the B-effect. The evaluation of main effects will be one part of the two-factor data analysis procedure.

· DEFINITION · There is an *interaction* between two factors if the effect of one factor depends on the levels of the second factor. When the two factors are identified as A and B, the interaction is identified as the $A \times B$ interaction.

The examples in Figure 15.4 should make this definition a bit more concrete. Figure 15.4(a) shows results with no interaction. If you look at the main effect for

· FIGURE 15.4 ·

(a) Data showing drug effect and no interaction. (b) Data showing drug effect and an interaction. (c) Data showing no drug effect but an interaction.

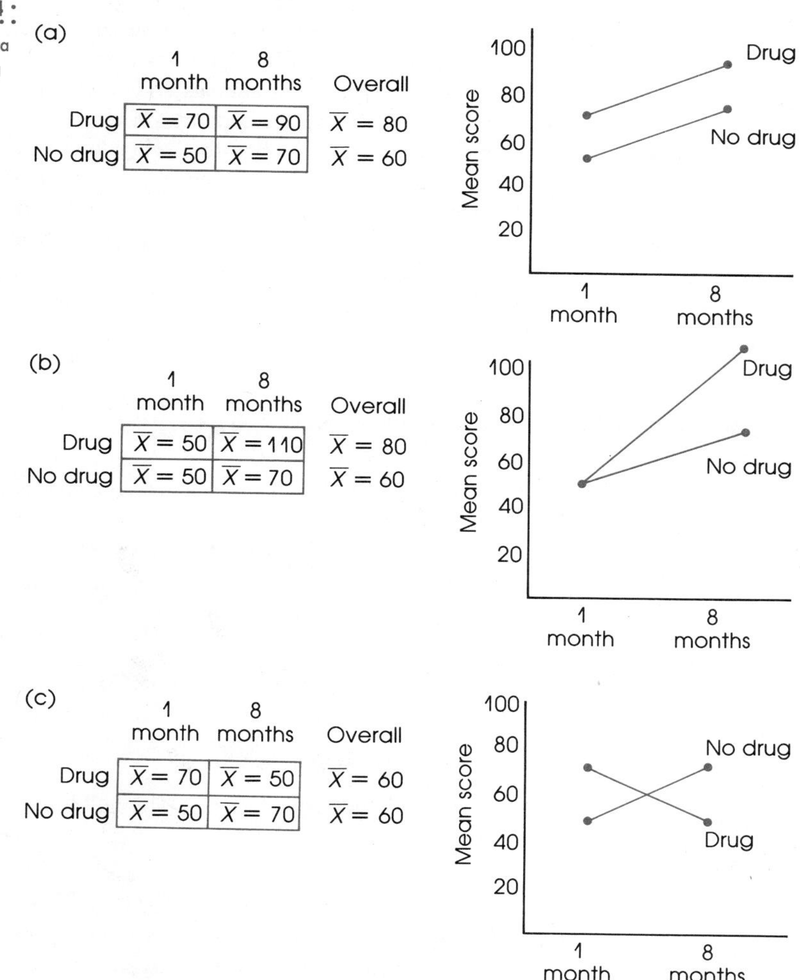
(a)

	1 month	8 months	Overall
Drug	$\overline{X} = 70$	$\overline{X} = 90$	$\overline{X} = 80$
No drug	$\overline{X} = 50$	$\overline{X} = 70$	$\overline{X} = 60$

(b)

	1 month	8 months	Overall
Drug	$\overline{X} = 50$	$\overline{X} = 110$	$\overline{X} = 80$
No drug	$\overline{X} = 50$	$\overline{X} = 70$	$\overline{X} = 60$

(c)

	1 month	8 months	Overall
Drug	$\overline{X} = 70$	$\overline{X} = 50$	$\overline{X} = 60$
No drug	$\overline{X} = 50$	$\overline{X} = 70$	$\overline{X} = 60$

the drug in these data, you should see that the overall average score for the drug group is $\overline{X} = 80$. The overall average score for the no-drug group is $\overline{X} = 60$. This means that the drug has a 20-point effect (from 60 to 80). Does this drug effect (one factor) depend on age (the levels of the second factor)? To answer, look at each age group separately. For the animals tested at 1 month, the drug effect is exactly 20 points (50 versus 70). For the animals tested at 8 months, the drug effect is still 20 points (70 versus 90). The drug effect does not depend on age. Therefore, there is no interaction. Notice that when the effect of one treatment is constant across all levels of the other factor (no interaction) there will be a constant distance between the two lines in the graph. Therefore, when there is no interaction, a graph of the data will always have parallel lines (a constant distance apart). On the other hand, an easy way to spot an interaction is to look for lines that are not parallel; that is, look for lines that converge or cross.

Now look at Figure 15.4(b). Again, the overall drug effect is 20 points ($\overline{X} = 60$ for the no-drug group versus $\overline{X} = 80$ for the drug group). But when you look at each age group separately, you find a 40-point drug effect for the animals tested at 8 months and no drug effect for the animals tested at 1 month. In this case, the effect of the drug does depend on the age of the animals. Now there is an interaction.

One final example should help solidify the concept of an interaction. Look at the data in Figure 15.4(c). For these data, the overall drug effect is zero. The drug group and the no-drug group both show an overall mean of $\overline{X} = 60$. Does this mean that the drug has no effect? The answer is *no*: The drug produces a 20-point *increase* in scores for the young animals and a 20-point *decrease* for the old animals. In this case the effect of the drug depends on which age group you are examining; that is, there is an interaction. Notice that when there is an interaction, the main effects may be misleading. In general, whenever an interaction exists, you must interpret the effects of each factor in terms of its interaction with the other factor. For this example, it would be wrong to conclude that the drug has no effect. Instead, you should interpret the drug effect for each age group separately.

15.3 LOGIC OF THE ANALYSIS

The two-factor analysis of variance actually is composed of three distinct hypothesis tests. The analysis will evaluate the following:

1. *The Main Effect of Factor A.* The null hypothesis for this test states that there are no population mean differences among the different levels of factor *A*. In symbols,

$$H_0: \mu_{A_1} = \mu_{A_2} = \mu_{A_3} \cdots$$

2. *The Main Effect of Factor B.* The null hypothesis for this test states that there are no population mean differences among the levels of factor *B*. In symbols,

$$H_0: \mu_{B_1} = \mu_{B_2} = \mu_{B_3} \cdots$$

3. *The A × B Interaction.* The null hypothesis for this test simply states that there is no interaction. That is, the effect of either factor is independent of the levels of the other factor.

In each case we are looking for treatment differences that are larger than would be expected by chance. For each of the three tests, the magnitude of the treatment effect will be evaluated by an *F*-ratio. Notice that there will be three *F*-ratios, one for each main effect and one for the interaction. Each of these *F*-ratios will have the same basic structure:

$$F = \frac{\text{variance between treatments}}{\text{variance within treatments}}$$

The between-treatments variance is assumed to be caused by three things:

1. Treatment effect (either factor A, or factor B, or $A \times B$ interaction)
2. Individual differences (there are different subjects for each treatment condition)
3. Experimental error (there always is a margin of error in measurements)

The variability within treatments will provide a measure of the variability expected by chance. Differences within treatments are assumed to be caused by

1. Individual differences
2. Experimental error

With these components of variability in mind, the three F-ratios will all have the basic form:

$$F = \frac{\text{treatment effect} + \text{individual differences} + \text{experimental error}}{\text{individual differences} + \text{experimental error}}$$

The level of significance helps us decide if the value for the F-ratio is sufficiently larger than 1.00.

As always, a value of F near 1.00 indicates that there is no treatment effect (the numerator and denominator of F are nearly the same). A value of F much greater than 1.00 indicates that the treatment effect is real.

· LEARNING CHECK ·

1 A researcher assesses verbal ability in children, both male and female, at 5 or 9 years of age. The mean test scores for the groups are as follows:

5-year-old males, $\overline{X} = 20$

5-year-old females, $\overline{X} = 22$

9-year-old males, $\overline{X} = 30$

9-year-old females, $\overline{X} = 45$

a Draw a graph of the data. (*Hint:* Put age on the X-axis and test score on the Y-axis. Use separate lines for males and females.)

b Judging from the graph, does there appear to be an interaction between age and sex? Explain your answer.

2 A two-factor ANOVA makes *three* hypothesis tests. What are they?

3 It is impossible to have an interaction unless there are also main effects present. (True or false)

ANSWERS **1 a**

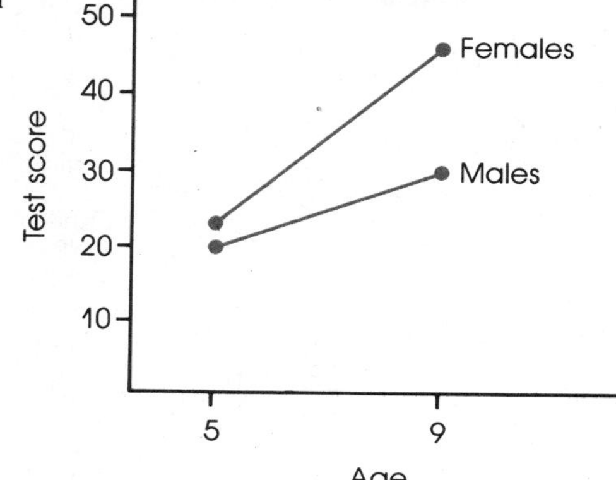

b The graph indicates an interaction because the lines are not parallel. The difference between males and females depends on age.

2 The three separate hypothesis tests in the two factor ANOVA are the main effect for the first factor, main effect for the second factor, and the interaction between the two factors.

3 False. See Figure 15.4(c).

15.4 NOTATION AND FORMULAS

The general format for any two-factor experiment is shown in Figure 15.5. Notice that we have identified the factors by using the letters A and B. By convention, the number of levels of factor A is specified by the symbol p and the number of levels of factor B is specified by q. The $A \times B$ matrix gives a picture of the total experiment, with each cell corresponding to a specific treatment condition. In the example shown in Figure 15.5, $p = 2$ and $q = 3$, so we have a total of $pq = 2 \times 3 = 6$ different treatment conditions.

It is possible to use either an independent or a repeated-measures experimental design with a two-factor experiment. In this chapter, we will only look at independent-measures designs. By definition, independent measures means that there is a separate group of subjects for each treatment condition, that is, a separate sample for each cell in the experimental design. For the experiment shown in Figure 15.5, there are six treatment conditions, so we would need six different groups of subjects.

To develop the formulas for the two-factor analysis of variance, we must be able to specify all the totals, numbers, and SS values in the data. The notation system for the two-factor design is as follows:

1. G = the grand total of all the scores in the experiment.
2. N = the total number of scores in the entire experiment.
3. p = the number of levels of factor A.
4. q = the number of levels of factor B.
5. n = the number of scores in each treatment condition (in each cell of the $A \times B$ matrix).
6. The totals for each treatment condition will be specified by using the capital letters (A and B) that represent that condition. For example, A_1B_2 would represent the total of the scores in the cell where the level of A is 1 and the level of B is 2. When we want to talk in general about the cell totals, we will refer to the AB totals (without specifying a particular cell). Notice that there are n scores in each AB total.

FIGURE 15.5

Matrix showing the general design of a two-factor experiment. The factors are identified by the letters A and B. The levels of each factor are identified by adding numerals to the factor letters; for example, the third level of factor B is identified by B_3.

		Factor B		
		Level B_1	Level B_2	Level B_3
Factor A	Level A_1	Treatment (cell) A_1B_1	Treatment (cell) A_1B_2	Treatment (cell) A_1B_3
	Level A_2	Treatment (cell) A_2B_1	Treatment (cell) A_2B_2	Treatment (cell) A_2B_3

FIGURE 15.6

Structure of the analysis for a two-factor analysis of variance.

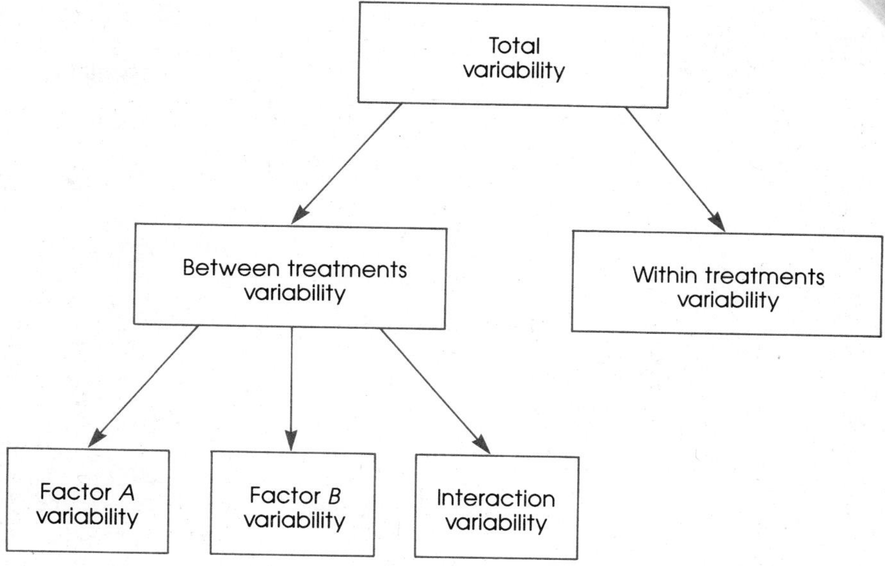

In addition, A_1 will refer to the total of all the scores for subjects in the first level of factor A (all the scores in the first row of the $A \times B$ matrix). A_2 refers to the total for the second row, and so on. When speaking in general about the row totals, we will refer to the A totals. Notice that there are qn scores in each A total. In a similar way, B_1 will refer to the total of all the scores in the first column. In general, the column totals will be called B totals. Note that you add pn scores to obtain each B total.

FORMULAS The general structure for the analysis of a two-factor experiment is shown in Figure 15.6. At the first level of the analysis, the total variability is separated into two components: between-treatments variability and within-treatments variability. You should notice that this first stage is identical to the structure used for the single-factor analysis of variance in Chapters 13 and 14 (see Figures 13.3 and 14.1). The second level of the analysis partitions the between-treatments variability into separate components. With a two-factor experiment, the differences between treatment conditions (cells) could be caused by either of the two factors (A or B) or by the interaction. These three components are examined individually in the second stage of the analysis.

The goal of this analysis is to compute the variance values needed for the three F-ratios. We will need three between-treatments variances (one for factor A, one for factor B, and one for the interaction), and we will need a within-treatments variance. Each of these variances (or means squares) will be determined by a sum of squares value (SS) and a degrees of freedom value (df):

Remember, in ANOVA a variance is called a mean square, or MS.

$$\text{mean square} = MS = \frac{SS}{df}$$

The actual formulas for the two-factor analysis of variance are almost identical to the formulas for the single-factor analysis (Chapters 13 and 14). You may find it useful to refer to these chapters for a more detailed explanation of the formulas. To help demonstrate the use of the formulas, we will use the data in Table 15.1. You should notice that the analysis consists of two parts; we must analyze the SS values as well as the df values. We will begin with the analysis of the sum of squares (SS).

TABLE 15.1

Hypothetical data for a two-factor experiment with two levels of factor *A* and three levels of factor *B*.[a]

		Factor *B*			
		B_1	B_2	B_3	
Factor *A*	A_1	1 6 1 1 1 $AB = 10$ $SS = 20$	7 7 11 4 6 $AB = 35$ $SS = 26$	3 1 1 6 4 $AB = 15$ $SS = 18$	$A_1 = 60$
	A_2	0 3 7 5 5 $AB = 20$ $SS = 28$	0 0 0 5 0 $AB = 5$ $SS = 20$	0 2 0 0 3 $AB = 5$ $SS = 8$	$A_2 = 30$
		$B_1 = 30$	$B_2 = 40$	$B_3 = 20$	$N = 30$ $G = 90$ $\Sigma X^2 = 520$

[a] The individual scores are given for each treatment cell ($n = 5$), along with the cell totals (*AB* values) and the *SS* for each cell.

ANALYSIS OF SUM OF SQUARES

Total Sum of Squares, SS_{total} SS_{total} computes the sum of squares for the total set of N scores:

$$SS_{\text{total}} = \sum X^2 - \frac{G^2}{N} \tag{15.1}$$

You should notice that this formula is identical to the *SS* formula that was used for single-factor ANOVA in Chapters 13 and 14 (see formulas 13.3 and 14.3)].

For the data in Table 15.1, this total sum of squares would be

$$SS_{\text{total}} = 520 - \frac{90^2}{30}$$
$$= 520 - 270$$
$$= 250$$

Within-Treatments Sum of Squares, SS_{within} The variability within, or "inside," the treatments is found by simply calculating *SS* for each individual cell and then adding up these *SS* values. The formula is

$$SS_{\text{within}} = \sum SS_{\text{inside each treatment cell}} \tag{15.2}$$

For the data in Table 15.1, SS_{within} is

$$SS_{\text{within}} = 20 + 26 + 18 + 28 + 20 + 8$$
$$= 120$$

Between-Treatments Sum of Squares, SS_{between} In the single-factor analysis of variance the formula for computing sum of squares between treatments focused on the treatment totals (T values) and computed *SS* for these totals:

$$SS_{\text{between}} = \sum \frac{T^2}{n} - \frac{G^2}{N}$$

In the two-factor design, each treatment corresponds to a particular cell, and the cell totals are identified by AB rather than T, so the between-treatments formula becomes

$$SS_{\text{between}} = \sum \frac{AB^2}{n} - \frac{G^2}{N} \tag{15.3}$$

This SS is also called $SS_{\text{between cells}}$. It measures between-cell variability.

Applying this formula to the data in Table 15.1 gives

$$\begin{aligned} SS_{\text{between}} &= \frac{10^2}{5} + \frac{35^2}{5} + \frac{15^2}{5} + \frac{20^2}{5} + \frac{5^2}{5} + \frac{5^2}{5} - \frac{90^2}{30} \\ &= 20 + 245 + 45 + 80 + 5 + 5 - 270 \\ &= 400 - 270 \\ &= 130 \end{aligned}$$

This completes the first level of the analysis. When you are performing the calculations for a two-factor analysis of variance, you should stop at this stage and be sure that the two components add up to the total:

$$\begin{aligned} SS_{\text{total}} &= SS_{\text{between}} + SS_{\text{within}} \\ 250 &= 120 + 130 \end{aligned}$$

We now move to the second level of the analysis. Remember, we are still measuring treatment effects or differences between treatments. But now we want to determine how much of the overall treatment effect can be attributed to factor A, how much is due to factor B, and how much is due to the interaction between these two factors. To compute the SS for each of the two separate factors, we will continue to use the same basic formula for sum of squares between treatments. The first part of this formula uses the total for each treatment condition and the number of scores in each condition (see formula 15.3). For factor A, the totals are identified by A's, and the number of scores in each level of A is given by qn. Thus, the formula for SS between the levels of factor A would be

$$SS_A = \sum \frac{A^2}{qn} - \frac{G^2}{N} \tag{15.4}$$

To get an A total, we must sum scores across the levels of factor B. Therefore, qn (or 15) scores are added to obtain an A total.

The A totals for the data in Table 15.1 are $A_1 = 60$ and $A_2 = 30$. Each of these totals is obtained by adding up a set of $3(5) = 15$ scores. Therefore, the sum of squares for factor A would be

$$\begin{aligned} SS_A &= \frac{60^2}{15} + \frac{30^2}{15} - \frac{90^2}{30} \\ &= 240 + 60 - 270 \\ &= 30 \end{aligned}$$

For factor B, the totals are identified by B's, and the number of scores in each B total is determined by pn. The formula for sum of squares for factor B is

$$SS_B = \sum \frac{B^2}{pn} - \frac{G^2}{N} \tag{15.5}$$

To get a B total, we must sum across levels of factor A. Therefore, pn (or 10) scores are added to find the B total.

For the data in Table 15.1, this SS would be

$$\begin{aligned} SS_B &= \frac{30^2}{10} + \frac{40^2}{10} + \frac{20^2}{10} - \frac{90^2}{30} \\ &= 90 + 160 + 40 - 270 \\ &= 20 \end{aligned}$$

Finally, the SS for the interaction is found by subtraction. According to Figure 15.6, the between-treatments variability is partitioned into three parts: factor A, factor B, and the interaction. Therefore, if you start with SS_{between} and subtract out SS_A and SS_B, the amount that is left will be the SS for the interaction. Thus, the "formula" for the interaction is

(15.6) $$SS_{A \times B} = SS_{\text{between}} - SS_A - SS_B$$

Using this formula on the data from Table 15.1 gives

$$SS_{A \times B} = 130 - 30 - 20$$
$$= 80$$

The complete analysis of SS for the data in Table 15.1 is presented in Figure 15.7. Notice that the separate parts at each level of the analysis add up to the total amount of variability at the level above. For example, the SS for factor A, factor B, and the $A \times B$ interaction add up to the SS_{between}.

ANALYSIS OF DEGREES OF FREEDOM

Each SS value in the analysis of variance has a corresponding degrees of freedom. Normally, SS measures the amount of variability (or differences) among a number of things. The corresponding df value is found by counting the number of things and subtracting 1. For a set of n scores, for example, $df = n - 1$. Using this general principle, we will define the df value associated with each of the SSs in the analysis.

Total Degrees of Freedom, df_{total} The df_{total} is simply the degrees of freedom associated with the SS_{total}. When we computed this SS, we used all N scores. Therefore,

(15.7) $$df_{\text{total}} = N - 1$$

For the data in Table 15.1, there are a total of $N = 30$ scores, so $df_{\text{total}} = 29$.

Degrees of Freedom Within Treatments, df_{within} To compute SS_{within}, we added up the SS values inside each of the treatment conditions. Because there are n scores

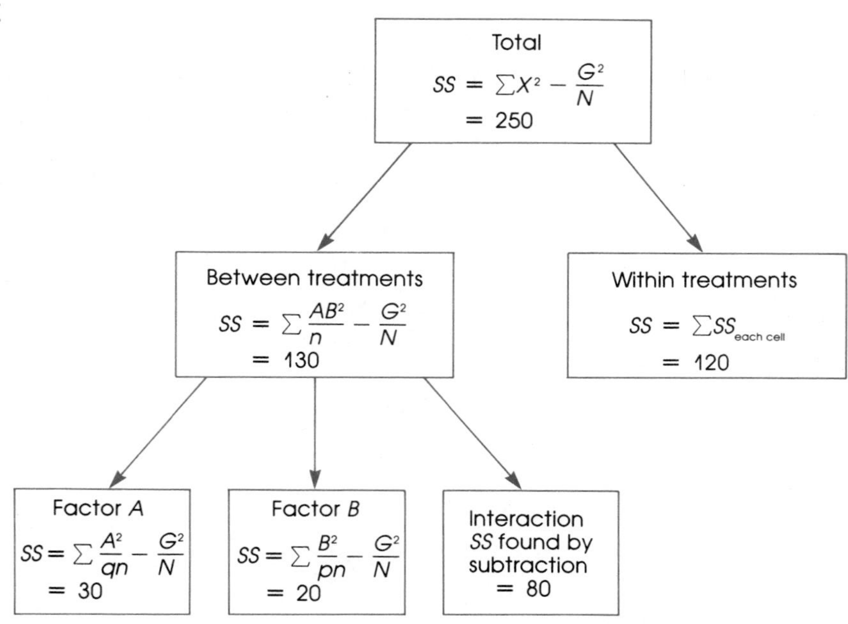

FIGURE 15.7 Analysis of the sum of squares (SS) for a two-factor experiment. The values are those obtained from the data in Table 15.1.

inside each treatment, each SS value has $df = n - 1$. When these are added up, you get

(15.8) $$df_{\text{within}} = \sum(n - 1) = N - pq$$

For the data in Table 15.1, there are $n = 5$ scores in each treatment condition. Therefore, $df = 4$ inside each treatment. Summing over the six treatments gives an overall within-treatments df of 24. This same value is obtained if we start with $N = 30$ scores and subtract $pq = 6$ treatments.

Degrees of Freedom Between Treatments, df_{between} SS_{between} was computed using the AB totals from each of the treatment cells. Because there are pq separate cells,

(15.9) $$df_{\text{between}} = pq - 1$$

The example we are considering has a total of six treatment conditions (two levels of factor A and three levels of factor B). Therefore, the between-treatments $df = 3 \times 2 - 1 = 6 - 1 = 5$.

Notice that the analysis of the df values follows the same pattern shown in Figure 15.6. Specifically, the df_{between} and the df_{within} will combine to equal the df_{total}:

$$df_{\text{total}} = df_{\text{between}} + df_{\text{within}}$$
$$29 = 5 + 24$$

Degrees of Freedom for Factor A, df_A The SS for factor A measures the variability among the A totals. Because the number of levels of factor A is identified by p,

(15.10) $$df_A = p - 1$$

Because there are two levels of factor A ($p = 2$) in Table 15.1, this factor would have $df = 1$.

Degrees of Freedom for Factor B, df_B There are q different levels for factor B, and the SS for factor B is computed by using these totals. Therefore,

(15.11) $$df_B = q - 1$$

For the data we are considering, factor B has three levels ($q = 3$), so factor B would have $df = 2$.

Degrees of Freedom for the Interaction, $df_{A \times B}$ The df for the $A \times B$ interaction can be computed two different ways. First, you can use the structure of the analysis shown in Figure 15.6 to find $df_{A \times B}$ by subtraction. If you start with df_{between} and subtract out the df values for factors A and B, the value that is left will be df for the interaction:

(15.12) $$df_{A \times B} = df_{\text{between}} - df_A - df_B$$

The data in Table 15.1 have df_{between} equal to 5, df_A equal to 1, and df_B equal to 2. Therefore, the df for the interaction would be

$$df_{A \times B} = 5 - 1 - 2 = 2$$

An easy shortcut for finding df for the interaction is to notice that

(15.13) $$df_{A \times B} = df_A df_B$$

PERSPECTIVE 15.1

ADDITIVE AND MULTIPLICATIVE RELATION BETWEEN FACTORS

One way to think about interactions is to consider the difference between factors that multiply together and factors that add together.

When there is no interaction, the effect of one factor simply adds to the effect of the other factor. This situation is shown in Figure 15.8. Notice that the effect of factor A is to add three points to each mean (the means in A_2 are each three points greater than the corresponding means in A_1). When these means are placed in a graph, the lines for A_1 and A_2 are parallel. There is no interaction. When an additive relation exists between the two factors, there is no interaction.

Alternatively, when the relation between the two factors is multiplicative, an interaction will be present. Consider the data shown in Figure 15.9. In this case, the effect of factor A is to multiply each mean by three points (each mean in A_2 is three times greater than the corresponding mean in A_1). When these means are placed in a graph, the lines for A_1 and A_2 are not parallel. This time there is an interaction.

FIGURE 15.8

Treatment means for a two-factor experiment showing an additive relation between the two factors. Notice that there is no $A \times B$ interaction.

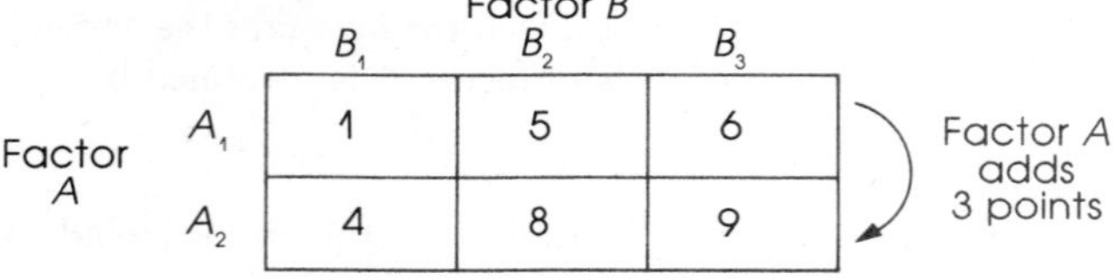

Treatment means

		Factor B		
		B_1	B_2	B_3
Factor A	A_1	1	5	6
	A_2	4	8	9

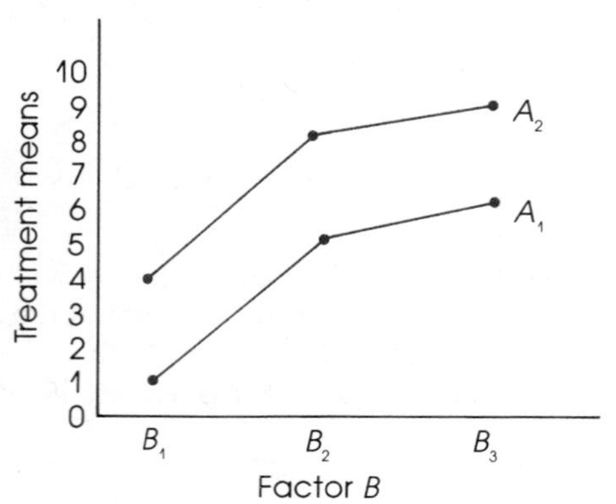

FIGURE 15.9

Treatment means for a two-factor experiment showing a multiplicative relation between the two factors. Notice that there is a large $A \times B$ interaction.

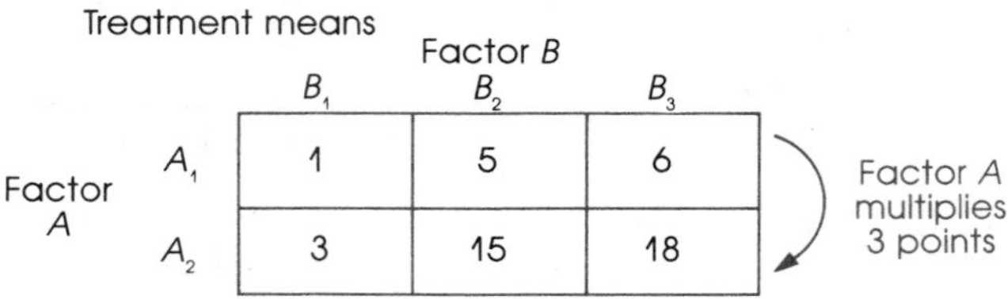

Treatment means

		Factor B		
		B_1	B_2	B_3
Factor A	A_1	1	5	6
	A_2	3	15	18

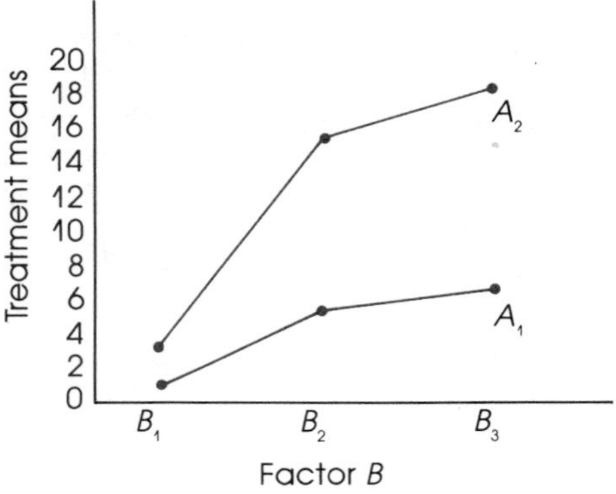

The notation used to represent an interaction is consistent with this idea of a multiplicative relation between two factors. For example, an interaction is identified as $A \times B$. Also, you can find the degrees of freedom for an interaction by multiplication:

$$df \text{ for } A \times B = df \text{ for } A \times df \text{ for } B$$

The notion that an interaction can be described as a multiplicative relation is common in areas other than statistics. For example, pharmacists often speak of "drug interactions." This term is used when the effects of one drug multiply the effects of another. You should note that in some cases the multiplication produces a much greater effect than would be expected by simply "adding" the two drugs together. In other cases, two drugs can cancel each other so that the combination is less effective than would be expected by simple addition.

Using this shortcut formula for the data in Table 15.1, the $A \times B$ interaction would have $df = 1 \times 2 = 2$. An intuitive explanation of this formula for df is presented in Perspective 15.1.

The complete analysis of df values is shown in Figure 15.10. Again, notice that the separate components always add up to the total. For example, the df_{between} (5) and the df_{within} (24) add up to the df_{total} (29).

FIGURE 15.10

Analysis of the degrees of freedom for a two-factor analysis of variance. The values are those obtained from the data in Table 15.1.

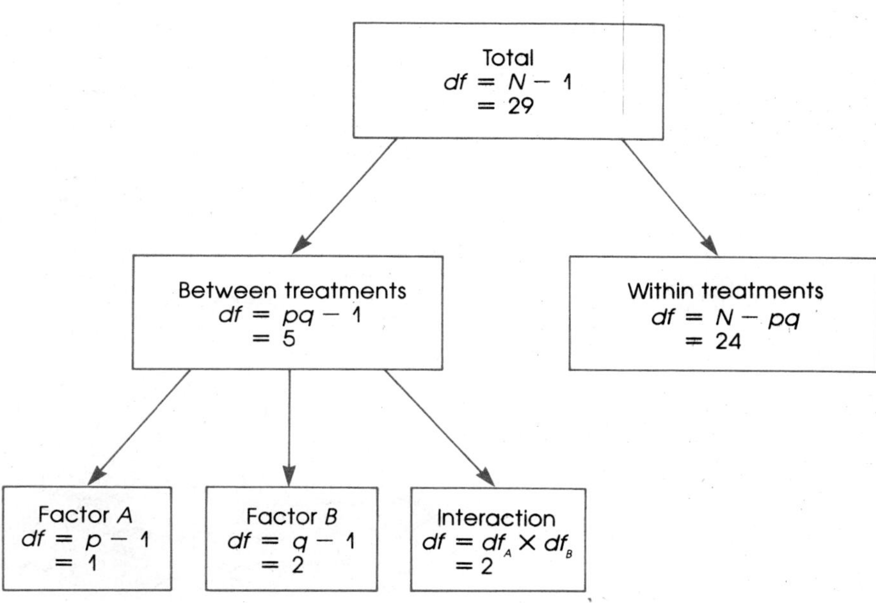

MEAN SQUARES (MSs) AND *F*-RATIOS The final step in the analysis is to compute the mean square values and the *F*-ratios. Recall that each mean square (*MS*) is actually a sample variance and is computed from the *SS* and *df* values:

$$MS = \frac{SS}{df}$$

For the example we are considering,

$$MS \text{ for } A = MS_A = \frac{SS_A}{df_A} = \frac{30}{1} = 30$$

$$MS \text{ for } B = MS_B = \frac{SS_B}{df_B} = \frac{20}{2} = 10$$

$$MS \text{ for } A \times B = MS_{A \times B} = \frac{SS_{A \times B}}{df_{A \times B}} = \frac{80}{2} = 40$$

The denominator of each *F*-ratio will have MS_{within}:

$$MS_{\text{within}} = \frac{SS_{\text{within}}}{df_{\text{within}}} = \frac{120}{24} = 5$$

For factor *A*, the *F*-ratio is

$$F = \frac{MS_A}{MS_{\text{within}}} = \frac{30}{5} = 6.00$$

This *F*-ratio has $df = 1, 24$ ($df = 1$ for the numerator of the ratio and $df = 24$ for the denominator). Commonly, this would be written as

$$F(1, 24) = 6.00$$

For factor B,

$$F(2, 24) = \frac{MS_B}{MS_{\text{within}}} = \frac{10}{5} = 2.00$$

And for the $A \times B$ interaction,

$$F(2, 24) = \frac{MS_{A \times B}}{MS_{\text{within}}} = \frac{40}{5} = 8.00$$

To determine whether or not these values fall in the critical region and thereby indicate a significant treatment effect, it is necessary to look at the distribution of F-ratios. The F distributions for $df = 1, 24$ and for $df = 2, 24$ are shown in Figure 15.11. The critical values are shown for the .05 level of significance (check the table on page 489).

Caution: Be sure to check the appropriate critical region. Factors A and B have different critical values because these factors have different values for degrees of freedom in this example.

Note that for factor A our obtained F-ratio of $F(1, 24) = 6.00$ is in the critical region. This indicates that the obtained difference between treatments (the numerator of the ratio) is significantly greater than what would be expected by chance (the denominator of the ratio). We conclude that factor A does have a significant effect.

On the other hand, the obtained F-ratio for factor B, $F(2, 24) = 2.00$, is not in the critical region. According to these data, factor B does not have a significant effect; that is, the difference we obtained is not larger than would be expected by chance.

Finally, the F-ratio for the $A \times B$ interaction, $F(2, 24) = 8.00$, is in the critical region. This indicates that there is a significant interaction. There are several equiv-

FIGURE 15.11

Distribution of F for $df = 1, 24$ for evaluating the F-ratio for factor A and the distribution with $df = 2, 24$ for evaluating factor B and the $A \times B$ interaction. In each case, the critical value for $\alpha = .05$ is shown.

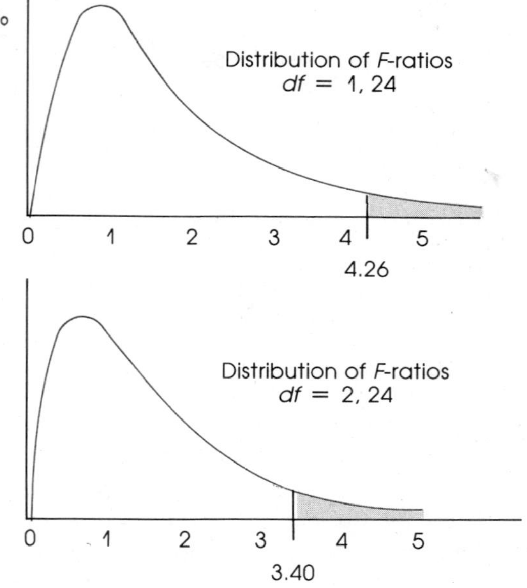

FIGURE 15.12

Graph of the data from Table 15.1, showing the means for each of the six different treatment combinations (cells) in the experiment.

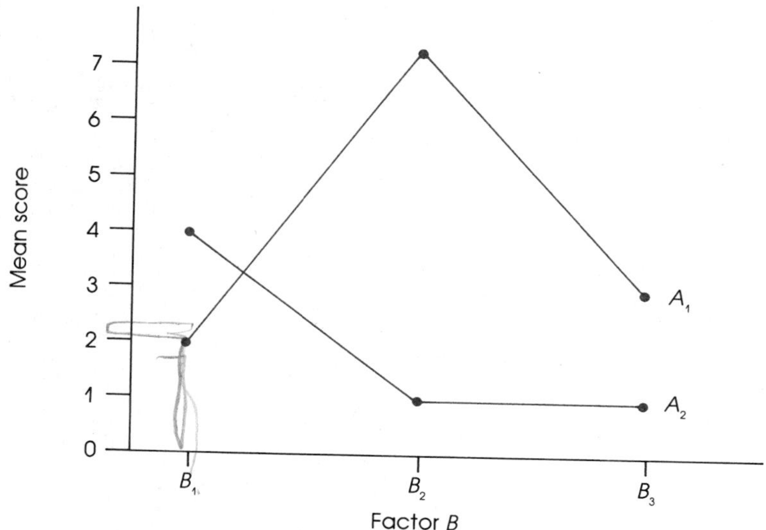

alent ways of expressing this result. You could say that the specific combinations of factors A and B produce significant differences. Or you could say that the effect of factor A depends on the different levels of factor B. Or you could say that the effect of factor B depends on the different levels of factor A.

To make these conclusions more concrete, the data from the experiment are graphed in Figure 15.12. The significant main effect for factor A is seen in the fact that the line for A_1 is generally higher than the line for A_2. The average difference between these lines is the A-effect.

To visualize the B-effect, image a point midway between the two dots above B_1 on the graph. Do the same thing for the two dots above B_2 and for the dots above B_3. Now draw a line connecting these three imaginary points. You should find that this line is nearly horizontal; as you move across the line from B_1 to B_2 to B_3, there is not much change in the mean score. This indicates that factor B does not have much effect and supports our conclusion that the main effect for B is not significant.

The interaction is easy to see because the two lines in the graph are not parallel. You can describe this interaction by focusing on the distance between the lines at each level of factor B. At B_1, for example, the A_1 line is lower. But at B_2, the A_1 line goes considerably higher than A_2, etc. This description is equivalent to saying that the A-effect (the distance between the lines) depends on the levels of B.

A concise summary of the formulas and structure for the two-factor analysis of variance is presented in Figure 15.13. This figure contains nearly all of the information you need to conduct the analysis and should help you to understand the relationships among all the parts.

A Computer Analysis of a Two-Factor ANOVA We have seen before how useful computers can be in performing statistical analyses. This is especially the case for a two-factor ANOVA, where the computations can be long and tedious. We analyzed the data in Table 15.1 using the SPSS^x software. The printout and explanation are shown in Table 15.2. The SPSS^x command that calls up the analysis is ANOVA. A second command, STATISTICS, provides means for each level of factors A and B and for each cell. The printout of cell means is especially helpful in making graphs (for example, Figure 15.12) and in interpreting an interaction if one exists. An

FIGURE 15.13

The complete analysis of variance for an independent measures two-factor design.

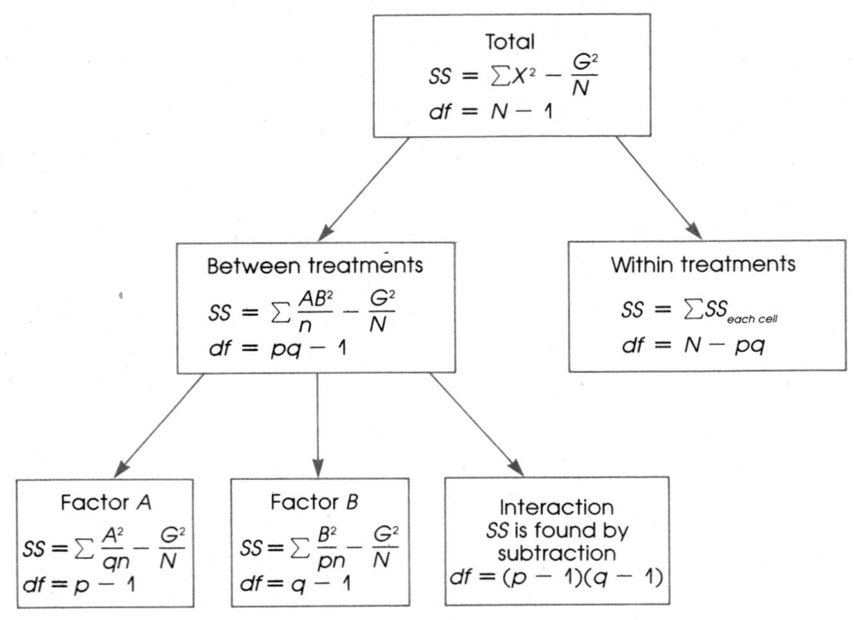

$$MS_{\text{factor}} = \frac{SS \text{ for the factor}}{df \text{ for the factor}}$$

This MS is computed for A, B, and the interaction.

$$MS_{\text{error term}} = \frac{SS \text{ within treatments}}{df \text{ within treatments}}$$

The same MS is used as the error term for all three F-ratios.

analysis of variance summary table is also provided, showing values for SS, df, MS and F-ratios.

LEARNING CHECK

1 The following data summarize the results from a two-factor, independent-measures experiment.

		Factor B		
		B_1	B_2	B_3
Factor A	A_1	$n = 10$ $AB = 0$ $\bar{X} = 0$ $SS = 30$	$n = 10$ $AB = 10$ $\bar{X} = 1$ $SS = 40$	$n = 10$ $AB = 20$ $\bar{X} = 2$ $SS = 50$
	A_2	$n = 10$ $AB = 40$ $\bar{X} = 4$ $SS = 60$	$n = 10$ $AB = 30$ $\bar{X} = 3$ $SS = 50$	$n = 10$ $AB = 20$ $\bar{X} = 2$ $SS = 40$

$\sum X^2 = 610$

a Sketch a graph similar to those in Figure 15.4 to show the results of this experiment.

b Looking at your graph, does there appear to be a main effect for factor A? Does factor B have an effect? Is there an interaction?

c Use an analysis of variance with $\alpha = .05$ to evaluate the effects of factor A, factor B, and the $A \times B$ interaction for these data.

TABLE 15.2

A printout of an SPSS[x] analysis for the data in Table 15.1.

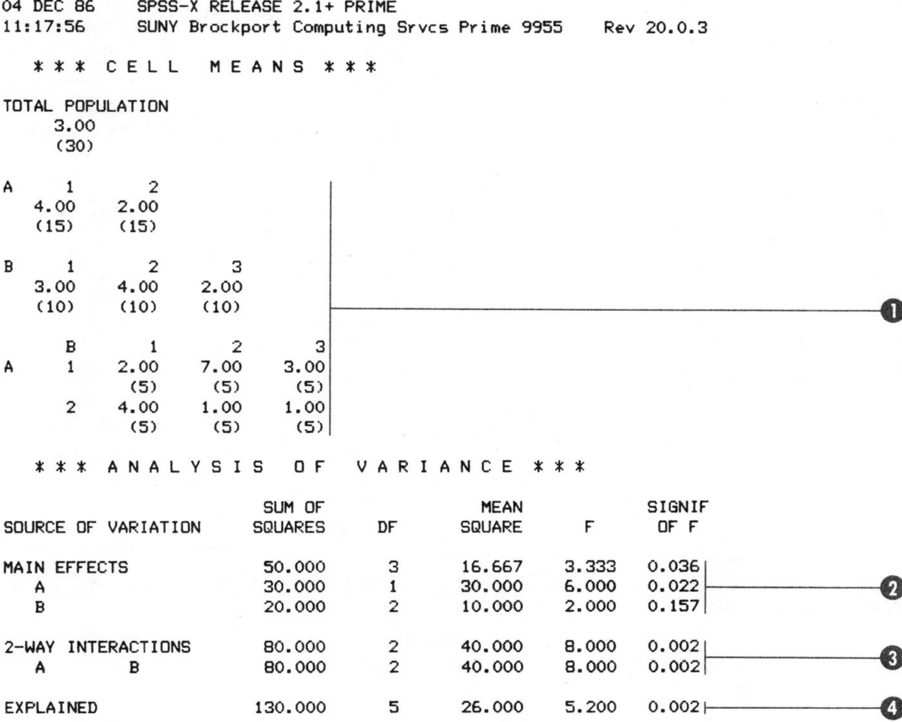

```
04 DEC 86    SPSS-X RELEASE 2.1+ PRIME
11:17:56     SUNY Brockport Computing Srvcs Prime 9955     Rev 20.0.3

   * * *  C E L L   M E A N S  * * *

TOTAL POPULATION
     3.00
     (30)

A      1        2
    4.00     2.00
    (15)     (15)

B      1        2        3
    3.00     4.00     2.00
    (10)     (10)     (10)

       B        1        2        3
A      1     2.00     7.00     3.00
              (5)      (5)      (5)
       2     4.00     1.00     1.00
              (5)      (5)      (5)

   * * *  A N A L Y S I S   O F   V A R I A N C E  * * *

                          SUM OF                MEAN              SIGNIF
SOURCE OF VARIATION      SQUARES      DF      SQUARE        F      OF F

MAIN EFFECTS              50.000       3      16.667    3.333     0.036
   A                      30.000       1      30.000    6.000     0.022
   B                      20.000       2      10.000    2.000     0.157

2-WAY INTERACTIONS        80.000       2      40.000    8.000     0.002
   A         B            80.000       2      40.000    8.000     0.002

EXPLAINED                130.000       5      26.000    5.200     0.002

RESIDUAL                 120.000      24       5.000

TOTAL                    250.000      29       8.621

     30 CASES WERE PROCESSED.
      0 CASES (   0.0 PCT) WERE MISSING.
```

EXPLANATION OF PRINTOUT:

1 The means for levels 1 and 2 of factor *A* are provided. In parentheses below each mean is the number of individuals in A_1 and A_2, respectively. Note that to get these means one must sum all A_1 cells (and the same for A_2 cells) across three levels of factor *B*. These means, therefore, give you an idea of what the main effect for *A* looks like. The next set of means are for levels of factor *B*, found by summing across two levels of factor *A*. These means reflect the main effect for factor *B*, if any exists. Finally, the matrix of means for *AB* cells is provided. This matrix is especially helpful in interpreting the interaction.

2 The summary table first presents the main effects. The values in the row labeled MAIN EFFECTS show the combined main effects for factors *A* and *B*. Below MAIN EFFECTS are the separate main effect for *A* and the main effect for *B*. For each main effect, the values for *SS, df, MS,* and the *F*-ratio are provided. The last column, SIGNIF OF F, shows the probability of a Type I error (alpha) when H_0 is rejected. For the main effect for *A*, $p = .022$. This probability value is below the generally used .05 level of significance, so H_0 should be rejected. For the main effect of *B*, $p = .157$, and thus H_0 should not be rejected.

3 The *SS, df, MS, F*-ratio, and significance values are given for the *AB* interaction. In this case, the interaction is statistically significant ($p = .002$).

4 The EXPLAINED variability is the same as between-treatments variability. That is, it is made up of the main effect for *A*, plus the main effect for *B*, plus the interaction of *A* and *B*.

5 The RESIDUAL variability is the within-treatments variability. When between-treatments variability (factor *A* variability + factor *B* variability + interaction variability) is subtracted from total variability, the *residual* is within-treatments variability.

ANSWERS

1 **a** Your graph should show two converging lines similar to Figure 15.4(b).

b In a graph, the points for level 1 of factor *A* are much lower than the means for level 2. This mean difference indicates a main effect for factor *A*. There is no main effect for factor *B*. The fact that the lines are not parallel indicates an interaction.

c The results of the ANOVA are summarized in the following table:

Source	SS	df	MS	
Between treatments	100	5		
Factor *A*	60	1	60	$F = 12.00$
Factor *B*	0	2	0	$F = 0$
$A \times B$ interaction	40	2	20	$F = 4.00$
Within treatments	270	54	5	
Total	370	59		

(*Note:* The fact that $SS_B = 0$ should be clear from looking at the data. The *B* totals are all the same; they are not variable.)

15.5 EXAMPLES OF THE TWO-FACTOR ANOVA

Example 15.1 presents the complete hypothesis testing procedure for a two-factor independent-measures experiment.

EXAMPLE 15.1 In 1968 Stanley Schachter published an article in *Science* reporting a series of experiments on obesity and eating behavior. One of these studies examined the hypothesis that obese individuals do not respond to internal, biological signals of hunger. In simple terms, this hypothesis says that obese individuals tend to eat whether or not their bodies are actually hungry.

In Schachter's experiment subjects were led to believe that they were taking part in a "taste test." All subjects were told to come to the experiment without eating for several hours beforehand. The experiment used two independent variables or factors:

1 Weight (obese versus normal subjects)

2 Full stomach versus empty stomach (half the subjects were given a full meal, as much as they wanted, after arriving at the experiment, and half were left hungry)

All subjects were then invited to taste and rate five different types of crackers. The dependent variable was the number of crackers eaten by each subject.

The prediction for this study was that the obese subjects would eat the same amount of crackers whether or not they were full. The normal subjects were expected to eat more with empty stomachs and less with full stomachs. Notice that the primary prediction of this study is that there will be an interaction between weight and fullness.

Hypothetical data similar to those obtained by Schachter are presented in Table 15.3.

For this analysis, we will identify weight as factor *A* and fullness as factor *B*.

STEP 1 *State hypotheses and select* α. For factor *A* the null hypothesis states that there is no difference in the amount eaten for normal versus obese subjects. In symbols,

$$H_0: \mu_{A_1} = \mu_{A_2}$$

$$H_1: \mu_{A_1} \neq \mu_{A_2}$$

This heading used for titles cataloged beginning January 1981, which are listed ONLY IN THE COMPUTERIZED CATALOG.

For earlier titles search the Card Catalog under:

Business Adm. 660 summer Intro to H.R. Mngmt 4 MW 8-9:30

Bus. Adm. H.R. Mngmt 701 5 MW 10-12 Intro to Org Behav.

Sociology MW 1-3 5 680 Soc. of changing Life styles 5 credits

Billups, J. O.
SW
Verifying
Imp of Ct
Odeas
Moving
SW C2960

173-80
1984

Law ~~636 Disabled + mentally~~
~~644 Law Taguing + Dev~~

Family Law 635
Aut

887 F I M
Aut

Black studies
Tues 12-3pm
1 Ue 2
Sum

TABLE 15.3

Results from an experiment examining the eating behavior of normal and obese individuals who have either a full or an empty stomach.[a]

		Factor B (Fullness) Empty Stomach	Full Stomach	
Factor A (Weight)	Normal	$n = 20$ $\overline{X} = 22$ $AB = 440$ $SS = 1540$	$n = 20$ $\overline{X} = 15$ $AB = 300$ $SS = 1270$	$A_1 = 740$
	Obese	$n = 20$ $\overline{X} = 17$ $AB = 340$ $SS = 1320$	$n = 20$ $\overline{X} = 18$ $AB = 360$ $SS = 1266$	$A_1 = 700$
		$B_1 = 780$	$B_2 = 660$	$G = 1440$ $\Sigma X^2 = 31{,}836$ $N = 80$

[a]The dependent variable is the number of crackers eaten in a taste test (hypothetical data).

For factor B the null hypothesis states that the amount eaten will be the same for full-stomach subjects as for empty-stomach subjects. In symbols,

$$H_0: \mu_{B_1} = \mu_{B_2}$$

$$H_1: \mu_{B_1} \neq \mu_{B_2}$$

For the $A \times B$ interaction the null hypothesis can be stated two different ways. First, if there is a difference in eating between the full-stomach and empty-stomach conditions, it will be the same for normal and obese subjects. Second, if there is a difference in eating between the normal and obese subjects, it will be the same for the full-stomach and empty-stomach conditions. In more general terms,

H_0: The effect of factor A does not depend on the levels of factor B (and B does not depend on A)

H_1: The effect of one factor does depend on the levels of the other factor

We will use $\alpha = .05$ for all tests.

STEP 2 *Locate the critical region.* To locate the critical values for each of the three F-ratios, we first must determine the df values. For these data (Table 15.3),

$$df_{\text{total}} = N - 1 = 79$$

$$df_{\text{between}} = pq - 1 = 3$$

$$df_{\text{within}} = N - pq = 76$$

$$df_A = p - 1 = 1$$

$$df_B = q - 1 = 1$$

$$df_{A \times B} = df_A df_B = 1$$

Notice that the F distribution table has no entry for $df = 1, 76$. A close and conservative estimate of this critical value may be obtained by using $df = 1, 70$ (critical $F = 3.98$). Whenever there is no entry for the df value of the error term, use the nearest smaller value in the table.

Thus, all three F-ratios will have $df = 1, 76$. With $\alpha = .05$, the critical F value is 3.98 for all three tests.

STEP 3 *Use the data to compute the F-ratios.* First, we will analyze the SS values:

$$SS_{\text{total}} = \sum X^2 - \frac{G^2}{N} = 31{,}836 - \frac{1440^2}{80}$$

$$= 31{,}836 - 25{,}920$$

$$= 5916$$

$$SS_{\text{between}} = \sum \frac{AB^2}{n} - \frac{G^2}{N}$$

$$= \frac{440^2}{20} + \frac{300^2}{20} + \frac{340^2}{20} + \frac{360^2}{20} - \frac{1440^2}{80}$$

$$= 26{,}440 - 25{,}920$$

$$= 520$$

$$SS_{\text{within}} = \sum SS_{\text{inside each cell}}$$

$$= 1540 + 1270 + 1320 + 1266$$

$$= 5396$$

$$SS_A = \sum \frac{A^2}{qn} - \frac{G^2}{N}$$

$$= \frac{740^2}{40} + \frac{700^2}{40} - \frac{1440^2}{80}$$

$$= 25{,}940 - 25{,}920$$

$$= 20$$

$$SS_B = \sum \frac{B^2}{pn} - \frac{G^2}{N}$$

$$= \frac{780^2}{40} + \frac{660^2}{40} - \frac{1440^2}{80}$$

$$= 26{,}100 - 25{,}920$$

$$= 180$$

$$SS_{A \times B} = SS_{\text{between}} - SS_A - SS_B$$

$$= 520 - 20 - 180$$

$$= 320$$

The MS values needed for the F-ratios are

$$MS_A = \frac{SS_A}{df_A} = \frac{20}{1} = 20$$

$$MS_B = \frac{SS_B}{df_B} = \frac{180}{1} = 180$$

$$MS_{A \times B} = \frac{SS_{A \times B}}{df_{A \times B}} = \frac{320}{1} = 320$$

$$MS_{\text{within}} = \frac{SS_{\text{within}}}{df_{\text{within}}} = \frac{5396}{76} = 71$$

Finally, the F-ratios are

$$F_A = \frac{MS_A}{MS_{\text{within}}} = \frac{20}{71} = .28$$

$$F_B = \frac{MS_B}{MS_{\text{within}}} = \frac{180}{71} = 2.54$$

$$F_{A \times B} = \frac{MS_{A \times B}}{MS_{\text{within}}} = \frac{320}{71} = 4.51$$

STEP 4 *Make decisions.* For these data, factor A (weight) has no significant effect; $F(1, 76) = .28$. Statistically, there is no difference in the number of crackers eaten by normal versus obese subjects.

Similarly, factor B (fullness) has no significant effect; $F(1, 76) = 2.54$. Statistically, the number of crackers eaten by full subjects is no different from the number eaten by hungry subjects. (*Note:* This conclusion concerns the combined group of normal and obese subjects. The interaction concerns these two groups separately.)

These data produce a significant interaction; $F(1, 76) = 4.51$, $p < .05$. This means that the effect of fullness does depend on weight. Specifically, the degree of fullness did affect the normal subjects, but it has no effect on the obese subjects.

As we saw in Chapters 13 and 14, the results from an ANOVA can be organized in a summary table, which shows all the components of the analysis (SS, df, etc.) as well as the final F-ratios. For this example, the summary table would be as follows:

Source	SS	df	MS	F
Between treatments	520	3		
Factor A (weight)	20	1	20	.28
Factor B (fullness)	180	1	180	2.54
A × B Interaction	320	1	320	4.51
Within treatments	5396	76	71	
Total	5916	79		

REDUCTION OF UNCONTROLLED VARIANCE BY A TWO-FACTOR DESIGN

We mentioned at the beginning of this chapter that one advantage of a two-factor experiment is that it allows you to "control" some of the variability within an experiment. The following example demonstrates how you can "add" a second factor to a single-factor experiment in order to reduce the error variability and thereby increase the chances of obtaining a significant treatment effect. The rationale for this technique comes from the fact that the independent-measures analysis of variance uses the variability within treatments (MS_{within}) as the denominator of the F-ratio. This variance inside the treatments provides a measure of how much variability is expected just by chance, that is, how much variability is due to individual differences and experimental error.

Often the variability within treatments is not all unexplained and uncontrolled variance. For example, a researcher may notice that a particular treatment seems to have a large effect on the young animals in the sample but not much effect on the older animals. In this case, much of the variability within the treatment condition is caused by the age of the animals. Whenever variability can be explained or predicted in this way, it is possible to measure it and remove it from the F-ratio. The following example demonstrates this process.

TABLE 15.4

Hypothetical data from a single-factor experiment comparing two treatment conditions.[a]

	Treatment 1		Treatment 2
	3		5
	3		4
	1		3
	2		5
	1	Males	3
	7	Females	7
	7		7
	5		8
	6		9
	5		9
	$T_1 = 40$		$T_2 = 60$
	$SS_1 = 48$		$SS_2 = 48$

[a]Each treatment contains a sample of $n = 10$ subjects, 5 males and 5 females.

EXAMPLE 15.2 The data in Table 15.4 represent the outcome of a single-factor experiment comparing two treatment conditions. Each treatment condition contains $n = 10$ subjects, 5 males and 5 females.

Using a single-factor ANOVA on these data, the researcher obtains

$$SS_{\text{between}} = \sum \frac{T^2}{n} - \frac{G^2}{N}$$
$$= \frac{40^2}{10} + \frac{60^2}{10} - \frac{100^2}{20}$$
$$= 520 - 500$$
$$= 20$$

The within-treatments SS for these data is

$$SS_{\text{within}} = \sum SS_{\text{inside each treatment}}$$
$$= 48 + 48$$
$$= 96$$

The MS values are

$$MS_{\text{between}} = \frac{SS}{df} = \frac{20}{1}$$
$$= 20$$

$$MS_{\text{within}} = \frac{SS}{df} = \frac{96}{18}$$
$$= 5.33$$

The resulting F-ratio is $F(1, 18) = 3.75$, which is not in the critical region. Therefore, the researcher must conclude that these data do not demonstrate a significant treatment effect.

The researcher noticed, however, that much of the variability inside the treatments appears to come from the fact that the females tend to have higher scores than the males. If this is true, then much of the within-treatments variability (the denominator of the F-ratio) can be explained. Table 15.5 reproduces the data, but this time the scores for males and females are separated by using sex as a second

TABLE 15.5

The same hypothetical data shown in Table 15.4 with a second factor (sex) added to create a two-factor experiment

		Factor A (Treatment) Treatment 1	Treatment 2	
Factor B (Sex)	Males	3 3 1 2 1 $AB = 10$ $SS = 4$	5 4 3 5 3 $AB = 20$ $SS = 4$	$B_1 = 30$
	Females	7 7 5 6 5 $AB = 30$ $SS = 4$	7 7 8 9 9 $AB = 40$ $SS = 4$	$B_2 = 70$
		$A_1 = 40$	$A_2 = 60$	

factor. If we call the original treatments factor A and use sex as factor B, the two-factor ANOVA gives the following results:

$$SS_A = \sum \frac{A^2}{qn} - \frac{G^2}{N}$$
$$= \frac{40^2}{10} + \frac{60^2}{10} - \frac{100^2}{20}$$
$$= 20$$

(Notice that the treatment effect is the same whether you use a one- or a two-factor analysis.)

$$SS_B = \sum \frac{B^2}{pn} - \frac{G^2}{N}$$
$$= \frac{30^2}{10} + \frac{70^2}{10} - \frac{100^2}{20}$$
$$= 80$$

(This is the variability due to sex differences.) The SS for the $A \times B$ interaction is zero for these data. (Check it for yourself.)

With the data arranged in a two-factor design, SS_{within} is

$$SS_{\text{within}} = SS_{\text{inside each cell}}$$
$$= 4 + 4 + 4 + 4$$
$$= 16$$

Finally, the mean square values are

$$MS_A = \frac{SS_A}{df_A} = \frac{20}{1}$$
$$= 20$$

$$MS_B = \frac{SS_B}{df_B} = \frac{80}{1}$$
$$= 80$$

$$MS_{\text{within}} = \frac{SS_{\text{within}}}{df_{\text{within}}} = \frac{16}{16}$$
$$= 1$$

The *F*-ratios are as follows:

For factor *A*: $F(1, 16) = \frac{20}{1} = 20$

For factor *B*: $F(1, 16) = \frac{80}{1} = 80$

Now the treatment effect (factor *A*) gives an *F*-ratio of 20, which is in the critical region. The researcher can conclude that there is a significant treatment effect.

The difference between the two analyses is entirely in the denominator of the *F*-ratios. In the two-factor analysis, much of the "error" variability is accounted for and removed from the denominator of the *F*-ratio. This makes it much more likely to obtain a significant result. You also should notice that the two-factor analysis provides additional information about the second factor and the interaction between the two factors.

15.6 ASSUMPTIONS FOR THE TWO-FACTOR ANOVA

The validity of the analysis of variance presented in this chapter depends on the same two assumptions we have encountered with other hypothesis tests for independent-measures experiments (the *t* test in Chapter 11 and the single-factor ANOVA in Chapter 13):

1. The population distribution should be normal.
2. The population variances should be equal (homogeneity of variance).

As before, the assumption of normality generally is not a cause for concern, especially when the sample size is relatively large. The homogeneity of variance assumption is more important, and if it appears that your data fail to satisfy this requirement, you should conduct a test for homogeneity before you attempt the ANOVA. Hartley's *F*-max test (see page 260) allows you to use the sample variances from your data to determine whether there is evidence for any differences among the population variances.

SUMMARY

1 An experiment with two independent variables is called a two-factor experiment. Such an experiment can be diagrammed as a matrix by listing the levels of one factor across the top and the levels of the other factor down the side. Each *cell* in the matrix corresponds to a specific combination of the two factors.

2 Traditionally, the two factors are identified as factor A and factor B. The purpose of the analysis of variance is to determine whether there are any significant mean differences among the treatment conditions or cells in the experimental matrix. These treatment effects are classified as follows:

a The A-effect: Differential effects produced by the different levels of factor A.

b The B-effect: Differential effects produced by the different levels of factor B.

c The $A \times B$ interaction: Differences that are produced by unique combinations of A and B. An interaction exists when the effect of one factor depends on the levels of the other factor.

3 The two-factor analysis of variance produces three F-ratios: one for factor A, one for factor B, and one for the $A \times B$ interaction. Each F-ratio has the same basic structure:

$$F = \frac{MS_{\text{treatment effect}}(\text{either factor } A \text{ or } B \text{ or the } A \times B \text{ interaction})}{MS_{\text{within}}}$$

The formulas for SS, df, and MS values for the two-factor ANOVA are presented in Figure 15.13.

KEY TERMS

two-factor experiment matrix

cells

main effect

interaction

FOCUS ON PROBLEM SOLVING

1. Before you begin a two-factor ANOVA, you should take time to organize and summarize the data. It is best if you summarize the data in a matrix with rows corresponding to the levels of one factor and columns corresponding to the levels of the other factor. In each cell of the matrix, show the number of scores (n), the total and mean for the cell, and the SS within the cell. Also, compute the row totals and column totals that will be needed to calculate main effects.

2. To draw a graph of the results from a two-factor experiment, first prepare a matrix with each cell containing the mean for that treatment condition.

		Factor B			
		B_1	B_2	B_3	B_4
Factor A	A_1				
	A_2				

Next, list the levels of factor B on the X-axis (B_1, B_2, etc.) and put the scores (dependent variable) on the Y-axis. Starting with the first row of the matrix, place a dot above each B level so that the height of the dot corresponds to the cell mean. Connect the dots with a line, and label the line A_1. In the same way, construct a separate line for each level of factor A (that is, a separate line for each row of the matrix). In general, your graph will be easier to draw and easier to understand if the factor with the larger number of levels is placed on the X-axis (factor B in this example).

3. The concept of an interaction is easier to grasp if you sketch a graph showing the means for each treatment. Remember, parallel lines indicate no interaction. Crossing or converging lines indicate that the effect of one treatment depends on the levels of the other treatment you are examining. This indicates that an interaction exists between the two treatments.

4. For a two-factor ANOVA, there are three separate F-ratios. These three F-ratios use the same error term in the denominator (MS_{within}). On the other hand, these F-ratios will have different numerators and may have different df values associated with each of these numerators.

Therefore, you must be careful when you look up the critical F values in the table. The two factors and the interaction may have different critical F values.

5. As we have mentioned in previous ANOVA chapters, it helps tremendously to organize your computations; start with SS and df values and then compute MS values and F-ratios. Once again, using an ANOVA summary table (see p. 371) can be of great assistance.

PROBLEMS

1 Sketch a graph for each of the following sets of data. (*Hint:* Place the levels of B on the X-axis and mean score on the y-axis. Use two separate graph lines for the levels of A.) State whether or not the graph indicates the presence on an interaction between factors A and B.

a

		Factor B	
		B_1	B_2
Factor A	A_1	$\bar{X} = 40$	$\bar{X} = 10$
	A_2	$\bar{X} = 60$	$\bar{X} = 30$

b

		Factor B	
		B_1	B_2
Factor A	A_1	$\bar{X} = 20$	$\bar{X} = 20$
	A_2	$\bar{X} = 10$	$\bar{X} = 50$

c

		Factor B	
		B_1	B_2
Factor A	A_1	$\bar{X} = 20$	$\bar{X} = 20$
	A_2	$\bar{X} = 10$	$\bar{X} = 10$

2 Sketch a graph showing the results of a 2 × 2 factorial experiment for each of the following descriptions:

a There is an A-effect and no B-effect and no interaction.
b There is an A-effect and a B-effect but no interaction.
c There is an interaction but no A-effect and no B-effect.

***3** A researcher studies the effects of need for achievement and task difficulty on problem solving. A two-factor design is used, in which there are two levels of amount of achievement motivation (high versus low need for achievement) and four levels of task difficulty, yielding eight treatment cells. Each cell consists of $n = 6$ subjects. The number of errors each subject made was recorded and the data were analyzed. The following table summarizes the results of the ANOVA, but it is not complete. Fill in the missing values. (Start with df values.)

Source	SS	df	MS	
Between treatments	280	____		
Main effect for achievement motivation	____	____	____	F = ____
Main effect for task difficulty	____	____	48	F = ____
Interaction	120	____	____	F = ____
Within treatments	____	____	____	
Total	600	____		

***4** The results of a two-factor experiment are examined using an ANOVA, and the researcher reports an F-ratio for factor A with $df = 1, 54$ and an F-ratio for factor B with $df = 2, 108$. Explain why this report cannot be correct.

5 The following sets of data represent three potential results from an experiment evaluating computer monitors. The two factors in the experiment are: (A) color of the monitor screen (amber versus green), and (B) the size of the monitor screen (9 inches, 12 inches, and 15 inches). The dependent variable is the ease of use for each monitor as judged by a sample of computer users. The value reported in each cell is the mean rating for the monitor.

Data set 1

	9 in.	12 in.	15 in.
Amber	5	7	9
Green	3	5	7

Data set 2

	9 in.	12 in.	15 in.
Amber	3	7	3
Green	1	5	1

Data set 3

	9 in.	12 in.	15 in.
Amber	9	5	1
Green	1	5	9

For each set of data:

a Sketch a graph showing the results of the two-factor experiment.

b In general, is one color monitor generally rated higher than the other? (Describe the *A*-effect.)

c In general, how does the size of the monitor screen affect ratings of ease of use? (Describe the *B*-effect.)

d Does there appear to be an interaction between color and size? Explain your answer.

6 The following data are from a two-factor experiment with $n = 10$ subjects in each treatment condition (each cell):

		Factor B		
		B_1	B_2	
Factor A	A_1	$AB = 40$ $SS = 70$	$AB = 10$ $SS = 80$	$\sum X^2 = 588$
	A_2	$AB = 30$ $SS = 73$	$AB = 20$ $SS = 65$	

Test for a significant *A*-effect, *B*-effect, and $A \times B$ interaction using $\alpha = .05$ for all tests.

***7** The following data are from an experiment examining the extent to which different personality types are affected by distraction. Individuals were selected to represent two different personality types: introverts and extroverts. Half the individuals in each group were tested on a monotonous task in a relatively quiet, calm room. The individuals in the other half of each group were tested in a noisy room filled with distractions. The dependent variable was the number of errors committed by each individual. The results of this experiment are as follows:

		Factor B (Personality)		
		Introvert	Extrovert	
Factor A (Distraction)	Quiet	$n = 5$ $AB = 10$ $SS = 15$	$n = 5$ $AB = 10$ $SS = 25$	$\sum X^2 = 520$
	Noisy	$n = 5$ $AB = 20$ $SS = 10$	$n = 5$ $AB = 40$ $SS = 30$	

Use an ANOVA with $\alpha = .05$ to evaluate these results. Describe how distraction and personality affect performance.

8 The following data were obtained from an independent-measures experiment using $n = 5$ subjects in each treatment condition:

		Factor B		
		B_1	B_2	
Factor A	A_1	$AB = 15$ $SS = 80$	$AB = 25$ $SS = 90$	$\sum X^2 = 1100$
	A_2	$AB = 5$ $SS = 70$	$AB = 55$ $SS = 80$	

a Compute the means for each cell and draw a graph showing the results of this experiment. Your graph should be similar to those shown in Figure 15.4.

b Just from looking at your graph, does there appear to be a main effect for factor *A*? What about factor *B*? Does there appear to be an interaction?

c Use an analysis of variance with $\alpha = .05$ to evaluate these data.

***9** Many species of animals communicate using odors. A researcher suspects that specific chemicals contained in the urine of male rats can influence the behavior of other males in the colony. The researcher predicts that male rats will become anxious and more active if they think they are in territory that has been marked by another male. Also, it is predicted that these chemicals will have no effect on female rats. To test this theory, the researcher obtains samples of 15 male and 15 female rats. One-third of each group is tested in a sterile cage. Another one-third of each group is tested in a cage that has been painted with a small amount of the chemicals. The rest of the rats are tested in a cage that has been painted with a large amount of the chemicals. The dependent variable is the activity level of each rat. The data from this experiment are as follows:

		Factor B (Amount of Chemical)			
		None	Small	Large	
Factor A (Sex)	Male	$n = 5$ $AB = 10$ $SS = 15$	$n = 5$ $AB = 20$ $SS = 19$	$n = 5$ $AB = 30$ $SS = 31$	$\sum X^2 = 460$
	Female	$n = 5$ $AB = 10$ $SS = 19$	$n = 5$ $AB = 10$ $SS = 21$	$n = 5$ $AB = 10$ $SS = 15$	

Use an ANOVA with $\alpha = .05$ to test the researcher's predictions. Explain the results.

10 It has been demonstrated in a variety of experiments that memory is best when the conditions at the time of testing are identical to the conditions at the time of learning. This phenomenon is called *encoding specificity* because the specific cues that you use to learn (or encode) new information are the best possible cues to help you recall the information at a later time. In an experimental demonstration of encoding specificity, Tulving and Osler (1968) prepared a list of words to be memorized. For each word on the list, they selected an associated word to serve as a cue. For example, if the word *queen* were on the list, the word *lady* would be a cue. Four groups of subjects participated in the experiment. One group was given the cues during learning and during the recall test. Another group received the cues only during recall. A third group received the cues only during learning, and the final group was not given any cues at all. The dependent variable was the number of words correctly recalled. Data similar to Tulving and Osler's results are as follows:

		Cues at Learning		
		Yes	No	
Cues at Recall	Yes	$n = 10$ $\bar{X} = 3$ $SS = 22$	$n = 10$ $\bar{X} = 1$ $SS = 15$	$\sum X^2 = 192$
	No	$n = 10$ $\bar{X} = 1$ $SS = 16$	$n = 10$ $\bar{X} = 1$ $SS = 19$	

Use an ANOVA with $\alpha = .05$ to evaluate these data. Describe the results.

11 The following data summarize the results of a two-factor experiment with $n = 5$ in each treatment condition (each cell):

		Factor B				
		B_1	B_2	B_3	B_4	
Factor A	A_1	$AB = 5$ $SS = 40$	$AB = 5$ $SS = 50$	$AB = 5$ $SS = 30$	$AB = 5$ $SS = 40$	$\sum X^2 = 560$
	A_2	$AB = 5$ $SS = 30$	$AB = 15$ $SS = 30$	$AB = 15$ $SS = 50$	$AB = 25$ $SS = 50$	

Use an ANOVA with $\alpha = .05$ to evaluate the results of this experiment.

***12** The following data show the results of a two-factor experiment with $n = 10$ in each treatment condition (cell):

		Factor B		
		B_1	B_2	
Factor A	A_1	$\bar{X} = 4$ $SS = 40$	$\bar{X} = 2$ $SS = 50$	$\sum X^2 = 480$
	A_2	$\bar{X} = 3$ $SS = 50$	$\bar{X} = 1$ $SS = 40$	

a Sketch a graph showing the results of this experiment. (See Figure 15.4 for examples.)

b Looking at your graph, does there appear to be an $A \times B$ interaction? Does factor A appear to have any effect? Does factor B appear to have any effect?

c Evaluate these data using an ANOVA with $\alpha = .05$.

13 Individuals who are identified as having an antisocial personality disorder also tend to have reduced physiological responses to painful or anxiety-producing stimuli. In everyday terms, these individuals show a limited physical response to fear, guilt, or anxiety. One way of measuring this response is with the galvanic skin response (GSR). Normally, when a person is aroused, there is an increase in perspiration which causes a measurable reduction in the electrical resistance on the skin. The following data represent the results of an experiment measuring GSR for normal and antisocial individuals in regular and stress-provoking situations:

		Arousal Level			
		Baseline		Stress	
Personality	Normal	27	25	15	21
		26	23	20	18
		19	24	14	21
		27	26	19	24
		21	19	13	17
	Antisocial	24	26	29	22
		28	29	27	25
		23	27	22	20
		25	22	20	29
		21	25	28	21

a Compute the cell means and sketch a graph of the results.

b Use an ANOVA with $\alpha = .05$ to evaluate these data.

c Explain the findings of this study.

***14** The following data are from an experiment examining the influence of a specific hormone on eating behavior. Three different drug doses were used, including a control condition (no drug), and the experiment measured eating behavior for males and females. The dependent variable was the amount of food consumed over a 48-hour period.

	No Drug	Small Dose	Large Dose
Males	1	7	3
	6	7	1
	1	11	1
	1	4	6
	1	6	4
Females	0	0	0
	3	0	2
	7	0	0
	5	5	0
	5	0	3

Use an ANOVA with $\alpha = .05$ to evaluate these data and describe the results (i.e., the drug effect, the sex difference, and the interaction).

15 A psychologist would like to evaluate the effectiveness of a special counseling program for students with math anxiety. Students from a freshman math class are assessed as being either high or low in math anxiety. Half of each group participates in the counseling program, while the other students continue without any special counseling. Each student's performance in the course is measured by the grade on the final exam. These data are as follows:

		Counseling		No Counseling	
Math Anxiety	High	72	61	75	64
		61	63	72	87
		85	82	85	76
		52	68	78	79
	Low	64	87	75	93
		89	94	78	71
		92	75	90	84
		61	73	84	86

a Use an analysis of variance to evaluate these data. Use the .05 level of significance for all tests.

b Based on the results of your analysis, can the psychologist conclude that the counseling program has any effect? Is the effectiveness of the program different for students high in math anxiety versus students low in math anxiety?

***16** Hyperactivity in children usually is treated by counseling, or by drugs, or by both. The following data are from an experiment designed to evaluate the effectiveness of these different treatments. The dependent variable is a measure of attention span (how long each child was able to concentrate on a specific task).

	Drug		No Drug	
Counseling	14	10	8	6
	13	15	7	4
	15	12	5	10
	10	8	9	11
No Counseling	11	13	10	13
	12	10	9	6
	14	8	12	9
	15	9	7	13

a Use an ANOVA with $\alpha = .05$ to evaluate these data.

b Do the data indicate that the drug has a significant effect? Does the counseling have an effect? Describe these results in terms of the effectiveness of the drug and counseling and their interaction.

17 A school psychologist is examining students' responses to a trial program in self-paced instruction. In this program, students are left on their own to determine how quickly (or slowly) they work through a set of required material. The psychologist suspects that self-motivated students will do well in this program but that other students may find it difficult. The psychologist identifies samples of students with "internal" personality types (self-motivated) and "external" personality types. Half of each group is placed in the self-paced program, and half remains in a normal, well-structured classroom. The final grades for these students are as follows:

	Internal		External	
Self-paced	84	64	71	86
	83	85	68	64
	91	93	75	72
	75	90	73	65
Structured Class	86	85	76	90
	83	91	81	85
	92	76	78	83
	72	84	71	72

a Use an analysis of variance to evaluate these data. Make all tests at the .05 level of significance.

b Describe the results of the ANOVA in terms of the two independent variables.

18 In addition to measuring classroom performance, the psychologist in Problem 17 also measured each student's attitude toward his or her course. Attitudes were measured on a 10-point scale with 10 being best ("I completely enjoyed the course"). These attitude scores are as follows:

	Internal		External	
Self-paced	8	8	3	4
	10	10	5	3
	10	7	3	5
	9	8	7	6
	7	9	5	5
Structured Class	8	7	8	8
	6	6	9	7
	5	7	10	6
	10	5	7	9
	7	8	9	8

a Use an ANOVA with $\alpha = .05$ to evaluate these data.

b Describe the results. (Is one type of instruction preferred over the other? Is one personality type generally more positive or negative than the other? Does preference for the type of instruction depend on personality?

***19** In the preview section of this chapter we presented an experiment that examined the effect of an audience on the performance of two different personality types. Data from this experiment are as follows. The dependent variable is the number of errors made by each subject.

		Alone			Audience		
Self-esteem	High	2	5	5	3	5	1
		3	0	4	2	4	2
		0	3	2	4	0	0
		4	1	5	1	3	3
	Low	6	8	2	11	13	9
		7	9	5	8	10	7
		3	4	3	7	8	11
		6	7	4	14	10	7

Use an ANOVA with $\alpha = .05$ to evaluate these data. Describe the effect of the audience and the effect of personality on performance.

***20** The general relation between performance and arousal level is described by the Yerkes-Dodson law. This law states that performance is best at a moderate level of arousal. When arousal is too low, people don't care about what they are doing, and performance is poor. At the other extreme, when arousal is too high, people become overly anxious, and performance suffers. In addition, the exact form of the relation between arousal and performance depends on the difficulty of the task. The following data demonstrate the Yerkes-Dodson law. The dependent variable is a measure of performance.

		Arousal Level							
		Very Low		Low		Medium		High	
Task Difficulty	Easy	10	11	16	14	20	18	15	12
		12	10	16	15	19	21	14	13
		8	12	13	12	19	16	13	14
		9	10	15	14	21	20	16	14
	Hard	5	8	12	11	9	9	5	4
		6	4	13	14	8	7	4	3
		4	6	10	13	10	11	3	4
		5	5	12	11	9	8	6	5

a Sketch a graph showing the mean level of performance for each treatment condition.
b Use a two-factor ANOVA to evaluate these data.
c Describe and explain the main effect for task difficulty.
d Describe and explain the interaction between difficulty and arousal.

21 The process of interference is assumed to be responsible for much of forgetting in human memory. New information going into memory interferes with the information that already is there. One demonstration of interference examines the process of forgetting while people are asleep versus while they are awake. Because there should be less interference during sleep, there also should be less forgetting. The following data are the results from an experiment examining four groups of subjects. All subjects were given a list of words to remember. Then half of the subjects went to sleep, and the others stayed awake. Within both the asleep and the awake groups, half of the subjects were tested after 2 hours, and the rest were tested after 8 hours. The dependent variable is the number of words correctly recalled.

	Delay of Memory Test			
	2 Hours		8 Hours	
Asleep	5	7	6	4
	6	10	8	4
	4	5	5	7
	3	8	10	8
	6	5	7	6
Awake	3	2	1	2
	4	3	0	1
	5	4	0	2
	3	2	1	0
	2	4	1	1

a Use a two-factor ANOVA to examine these data.
b Describe and explain the interaction.

22 Most adolescents experience a growth spurt when they are between 12 and 15 years old. This period of dramatic growth generally occurs earlier for girls than for boys. A psychologist studying the physical development of adolescents recorded the gain in height (in centimeters) over a 1-year period for boys and girls ranging in age from 11 to 15. Separate samples were used for each age group. The data are as follows:

	Age				
	11 Years	12 Years	13 Years	14 Years	15 Years
Males	4	4	6	8	9
	5	5	7	7	8
	6	4	5	10	6
	5	6	4	9	7
	4	4	7	10	6
	5	6	6	7	7
Females	5	8	7	4	1
	7	7	6	3	2
	6	9	6	3	2
	5	10	7	5	1
	6	9	5	3	1
	6	8	6	4	2

a Compute the mean gain in height for each of these 10 groups and draw a graph showing the results of this study.
b By just looking at your graph, how would you describe the difference between the growth spurt for boys and the growth spurt for girls?
c Use an analysis of variance to evaluate these data. Perform all tests with $\alpha = .05$.

d Do the results of the ANOVA support your description of these data?

***23** It has been demonstrated that children who watch violent television shows tend to be more aggressive than children who are not exposed to television violence. However, there is some question as to whether this effect exists only for shows with human characters or whether it also occurs for violet cartoons. A hypothetical experiment to address this question is presented here. A large sample of preschool children is obtained. One group from this sample watches a violent TV show with human characters for half an hour. A second group watches violent cartoons. Two other groups serve as control groups: One watches nonviolent human shows, and the other watches nonviolent cartoons. After watching these television shows, all four groups are placed together in a large playroom, and a psychologist records the number of aggressive actions for each child.

a Identify the two independent variables (factors) and the dependent variable for this experiment.

b Suppose that the psychologist is predicting that exposure to human violence will affect behavior but that cartoon violence will not. If the psychologist is correct, what outcomes are expected for the ANOVA? Predict both main effects and the interaction. (*Note:* It may help to sketch a graph of the predicted results.)

c Suppose that the psychologist predicts that cartoon violence and human violence will affect behavior equally. In this case, what outcomes are expected for the ANOVA? Predict both main effects and the interaction.

24 The following hypothetical data represent one possible outcome of the experiment described in Problem 23:

	Violent		Nonviolent	
Human Characters	6	2	3	5
	3	4	2	3
	2	5	1	2
	5	4	4	4
	3	6	2	3
Cartoon Characters	5	2	1	3
	4	5	3	2
	3	3	2	2
	4	3	3	3
	3	4	4	4

a Use an ANOVA to evaluate these data. Set $\alpha = .05$ for all tests.

b Describe the results of this experiment.

CHAPTER 16

CORRELATION AND REGRESSION

TOOLS YOU WILL NEED

The following items are considered essential background material for this chapter. If you doubt your knowledge of any of these items, you should review the appropriate chapter or section before proceeding.

- Sum of squares (*SS*) (Chapter 4)
    - Computational formula
    - Definitional formula
- *z*-scores (Chapter 5)
- Hypothesis testing (Chapter 8)

PREVIEW

Having been a student and taken exams for much of your life, you probably have noticed a curious phenomenon. In every class there are some students who zip through exams and turn in their papers while everyone else is still on page 1. Other students cling to their exams and are still working frantically when the instructor announces that time is up and demands that all papers be turned in. Have you wondered what grades these students receive? Are the students who finish first the best in the class, or are they completely ignorant and simply accepting their failure? Are the *A* students the last to finish because they are compulsively checking and rechecking their answers? To help answer these questions, we carefully observed a recent exam and recorded the amount of time each student spent and the grade each student received. These data are shown in Figure 16.1. Note that we have listed time along the *X*-axis and grade on the *Y*-axis. Each student is identified by a point in the graph with the point located directly above the student's time and directly across from the student's grade. Also note that we have drawn a line through the middle of the data points in Figure 16.1. The line helps make the relationship between time and grade more obvious. The graph shows that the highest grades tend to go to the students who finished their exams early. Students who held their papers to the bitter end tended to have low grades.

In statistical terms, these data show a correlation between time and grade. In this chapter we will see how correlations are used to measure and describe relations. Just as a sample mean provides a concise description of an entire sample, a correlation will provide a description of a relationship. We also will look at how correlations are used and interpreted. For example, now that you have seen the relation between time and grades, don't you think it might be a good idea to start turning in your exam papers a little sooner? Wait and see.

16.1 INTRODUCTION

Correlation is a statistical technique that is used to measure and describe a relationship between two variables. Usually, the two variables are simply observed as they exist

FIGURE 16.1

The relationship between exam grade and time needed to complete the exam. Notice the general trend in these data: Students who finish the exam early tend to have better grades.

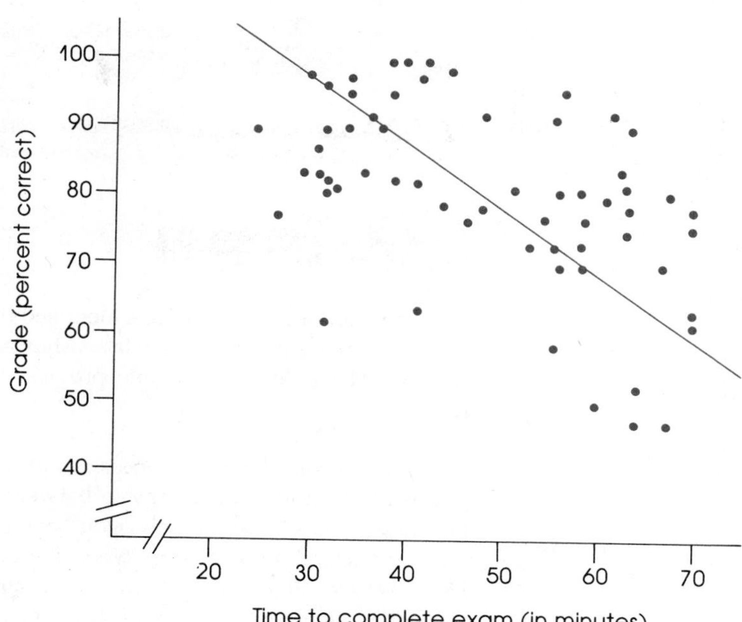

FIGURE 16.2

The same set of $n = 6$ pairs of scores (X and Y values) are shown in a table and in a scatterplot. Notice that the scatterplot allows you to see the relationship between X and Y.

Person	X	Y
1	1	1
2	1	3
3	3	2
4	4	5
5	6	4
6	7	5

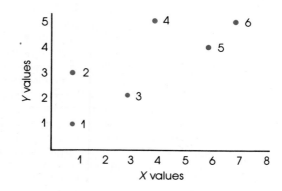

naturally in the environment—there is no attempt to control or manipulate the variables. For example, a researcher interested in the relation between nutrition and IQ could observe (and record) the dietary patterns for a group of preschool children and then measure IQ scores for the same group. Notice that the researcher is not trying to manipulate the children's diet or IQ but is simply observing what occurs naturally. You also should notice that a correlation requires two scores for each individual (one score from each of the two variables). These scores normally are identified as X and Y. The pairs of scores can be listed in a table, or they can be presented graphically in a scatterplot (see Figure 16.2). In the scatterplot, the X values are placed on the horizontal axis of a graph, and the Y values are placed on the vertical axis. Each individual is then identified by a single point on the graph so that the coordinates of the point (the X and Y values) match the individual's X score and Y score. The value of the scatterplot is that it allows you to see the nature of the relationship (see Figure 16.2).

THE CHARACTERISTICS OF A RELATIONSHIP

A correlation measures three characteristics of the relation between X and Y. These three characteristics are as follows:

1. *The Direction of the Relationship.* Correlations can be classified into two basic categories: positive and negative.

DEFINITIONS

In a *positive correlation,* the two variables tend to move in the same direction: When the X variable increases, the Y variable also increases; if the X variable decreases, the Y variable also decreases.

In a *negative correlation,* the two variables tend to go in opposite directions. As the X variable increases, the Y variable decreases.

The direction of a relationship is identified by the sign of the correlation. A positive value (+) indicates a positive relationship; a negative value (−) indicates a negative relation. The following example provides a description of positive and negative relations.

EXAMPLE 16.1

Suppose you run the drink concession at the football stadium. After several seasons you begin to notice a relationship between the temperature at game time and the beverages you sell. Specifically, you have noted that when the temperature is high, you tend to sell a lot of beer. When the temperature is low, you sell relatively little beer (see Figure 16.3). This is an example of a positive correlation. At the same time, you have noted a relation between temperature and coffee sales: On

FIGURE 16.3

Examples of positive and negative relationships. Beer sales are positively related to temperature, and coffee sales are negatively related to temperature.

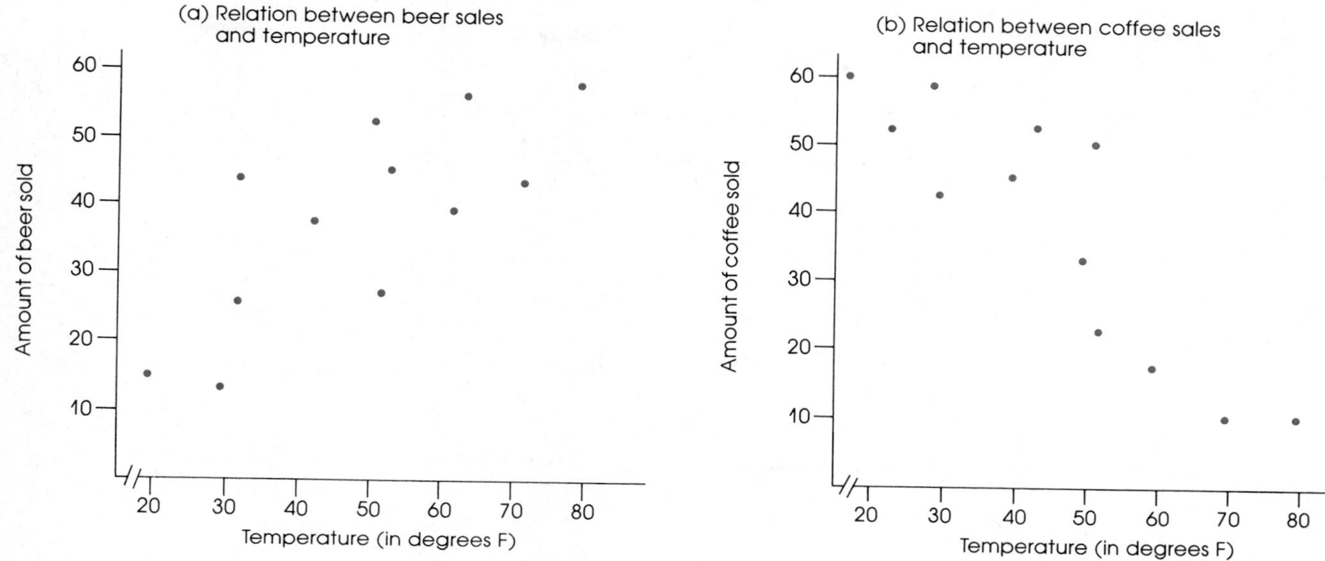

cold days you sell much more coffee than on hot days (see Figure 16.3). This is an example of a negative relation.

2. *The Form of the Relation*. In the preceding coffee and beer examples, the relationships tend to have a linear form; that is, the points in the scatterplot tend to form a straight line. The most common use of correlation is to measure straight-line relations. However, you should note that other forms of relationship do exist and that there are special correlations used to measure them. For example, Figure 16.4(a) shows the relationship between reaction time and age. In this scatterplot there is a curved relation. Reaction time improves with age until the late teens, when it reaches a peak; after that, reaction time starts to get worse. Figure 16.4(b) shows the typical relation between practice and performance. Again, this is not a straight-line relationship. In

FIGURE 16.4

Examples of relationships that are not linear. (a) Relationship between reaction time and age. (b) Relationship between performance and amount of practice.

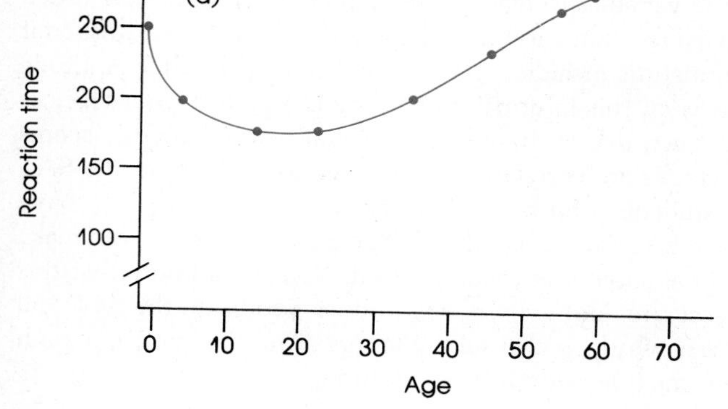

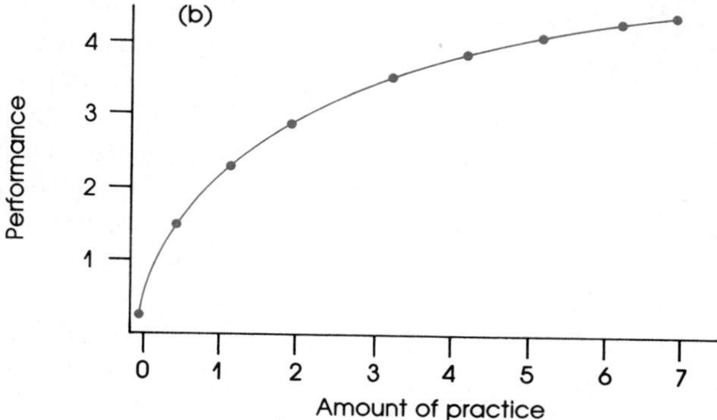

FIGURE 16.5

Examples of different values for linear correlations. (a) shows a good, positive relation, approximately +.90; (b) shows a relatively poor, negative correlation, approximately −.40; (c) shows a perfect, negative correlation, −1.00; (d) shows no linear trend, .00.

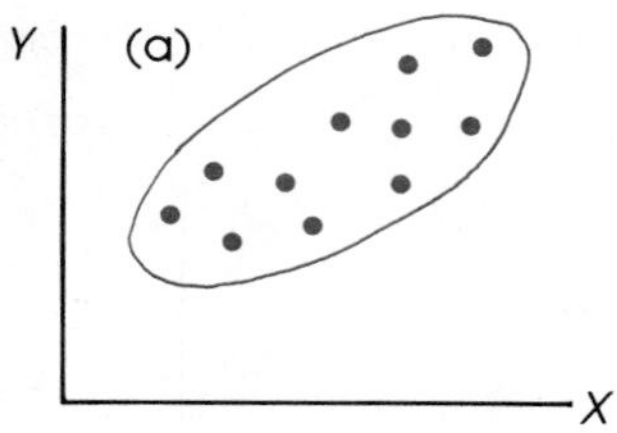

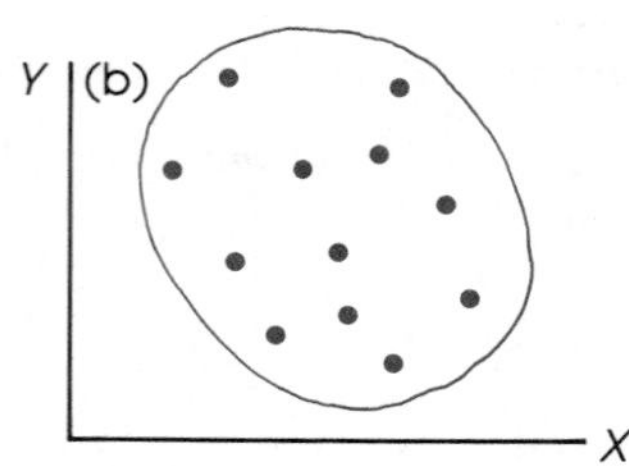

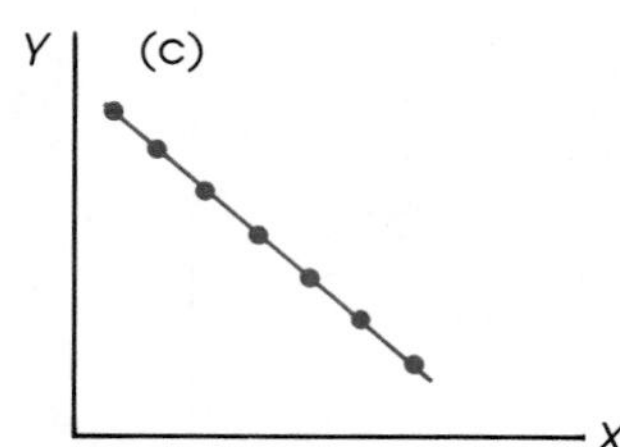

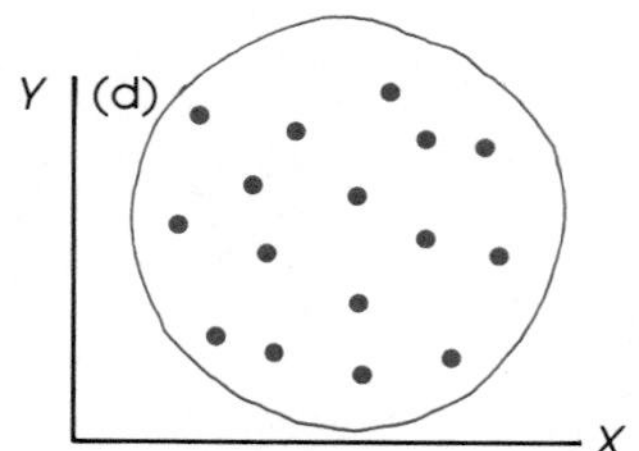

the early stages of practice, performance increases rapidly. But with a great deal of practice, the improvement in performance becomes less noticeable. (Ask anyone who has taken piano lessons for 10 years.) Many different types of correlations exist. In general, each type is designed to evaluate a specific form of relationship. In this text we will concentrate on the correlation that measures linear relations.

3. *The Degree of the Relationship.* Finally, a correlation measures how well the data fit the specific form being considered. For example, a linear correlation measures how well the data points fit on a straight line. A perfect fit always is identified by a correlation of 1.00, whereas a correlation of 0 indicates no fit at all. Intermediate values represent the degree to which the data points approximate the perfect form. Examples of different values for linear correlations are shown in Figure 16.5. Notice that in each example we have sketched a line around the data points. This line, called an *envelope* because it encloses the data, often helps you to see the overall trend in the data.

A correlation of −1.00 also indicates a perfect fit. The direction of the relation (positive or negative) should be considered separately from the degree of the relationship.

WHERE AND WHY CORRELATIONS ARE USED

Although correlations have a number of different applications, a few specific examples are presented next to give an indication of the value of this statistical measure.

1. *Prediction.* If two variables are known to be related in some systematic way, it is possible to use one of the variables to make accurate predictions about the other. For example, when you applied for admission to college, you were required to submit a great deal of personal information, including your scores on the Scholastic Aptitude Test (SAT). College officials want this information so they can predict your chances of success in college. It has been demonstrated over several years that SAT scores and college grade point averages are correlated. Students who do well on the SAT tend to do well in college; students who have difficulty with the SAT tend to have difficulty in college. Based on this relationship, the college admissions office can make a prediction about the potential success of each applicant. You should note that this prediction is not perfectly accurate. Not everyone who does poorly on the SAT will have trouble in college. That is why you also submit letters of recommendation, high school grades, and other information with your application.

2. *Validity*. Suppose a psychologist develops a new test for measuring intelligence. How could you show that this test truly is measuring what it claims; that is, how could you demonstrate the validity of the test? One common technique for demonstrating validity is to use a correlation. If the test actually is measuring intelligence, then the scores on the test should be related to other measures of intelligence, for example, standardized IQ tests, performance on learning tasks, problem-solving ability, etc. The psychologist could measure the correlation between the new test and each of these other measures of intelligence in order to demonstrate that the new test is valid.

3. *Theory Verification*. Many psychological theories make specific predictions about the relationship between two variables. For example, a theory may predict a relation between brain size and learning ability; a developmental theory may predict a relationship between the parents' IQs and the child's IQ; a social psychologist may have a theory predicting a relation between personality type and behavior in a social situation. In each case, the prediction of the theory could be tested by determining the correlation between the two variables.

LEARNING CHECK

1 If the world were fair, would you expect a positive or negative relationship between grade point average (X) and weekly studying hours (Y) for college students?

2 Data suggest that on average children from large families have lower IQs than children from small families. Do these data indicate a positive or negative relation between family size and average IQ?

3 If you are measuring linear relationship, correlations of $+.50$ and $-.50$ are equally good in terms of how well the data fit on a straight line. (True or False)

4 It is impossible to have a correlation greater than $+1.00$ or less than -1.00. (True or False)

ANSWERS

1 Positive. More hours studying should be associated with higher grade point averages.

2 Negative.

3 True. The degree of fit is measured by the magnitude of the correlation independent of sign.

4 True. Correlations are always between $+1.00$ and -1.00.

16.2 THE PEARSON CORRELATION

By far the most common correlation is the Pearson correlation (or the Pearson product-moment correlation).

DEFINITION The *Pearson correlation* measures the degree and direction of linear relation between two variables.

The Pearson correlation is identified by the letter r. Conceptually, this correlation is computed by

$$r = \frac{\text{degree to which } X \text{ and } Y \text{ vary together}}{\text{degree to which } X \text{ and } Y \text{ vary separately}} = \frac{\text{covariability of } X \text{ and } Y}{\text{variability of } X \text{ and } Y \text{ separately}}$$

When there is a perfect linear relation, every change in the X variable is accompanied by a corresponding change in the Y variable. In Figure 16.5(c), for example, every time the value of X increases, there is a perfectly predictable decrease in Y. The result is a perfect linear relation, with X and Y always varying together. In this case, the covariability (X and Y together) is identical to the variability of X and Y separately, and the formula produces a correlation of 1.00. At the other extreme, when there is no linear relation, a change in the X variable does not correspond to any predictable change in Y. In this case there is no covariability, and the resulting correlation is zero.

THE SUM OF PRODUCTS OF DEVIATIONS

To calculate the Pearson correlation, it is necessary to introduce one new concept: the sum of products of deviations. In the past we have used a similar concept, *SS* (the sum of squared deviations), to measure the amount of variability for a single variable. The sum of products, or *SP*, provides a parallel procedure for measuring the amount of covariability between two variables. The value for *SP* can be calculated with either a definitional formula or a computational formula.

The *definitional formula* for the sum of products is

$$SP = \sum(X - \bar{X})(Y - \bar{Y}) \tag{16.1}$$

This formula instructs you to first find the product of each X deviation and Y deviation and then add up these products. Notice that the terms in the formula define the value being calculated: the sum of the products of the deviations.

The *computational formula* for the sum of products is

$$SP = \sum XY - \frac{\sum X \sum Y}{n} \tag{16.2}$$

Caution: The n in this formula refers to the number of pairs of scores.

Because the computational formula uses the original scores (X and Y values), it usually results in easier calculations than those required with the definitional formula. However, both formulas will always produce the same value for *SP*.

You may have noted that the formulas for *SP* are similar to the formulas you have learned for *SS* (sum of squares). The relation between the two sets of formulas is described in Perspective 16.1. The following example demonstrates the calculation of *SP* with both formulas.

· EXAMPLE 16.2 · The same set of $n = 4$ pairs of scores will be used to calculate *SP* first using the definitional formula and then the computational formula.

For the definitional formula, you need deviation scores for each of the X values and each of the Y values. Note that the mean for the Xs is $\bar{X} = 3$ and that the mean for the Ys is $\bar{Y} = 5$. The deviations and the products of deviations are shown in the following table:

Caution: The signs (+ and −) are critical in determining the sum of products, *SP*.

Scores		Deviations		Products
X	Y	$X - \bar{X}$	$Y - \bar{Y}$	$(X - \bar{X})(Y - \bar{Y})$
1	3	−2	−2	+4
2	6	−1	+1	−1
4	4	+1	−1	−1
5	7	+2	+2	+4
				+6 = *SP*

For these scores, the sum of the products of the deviations is $SP = +6$.

PERSPECTIVE 16.1

COMPARING THE *SP* AND *SS* FORMULAS

It will help you to learn the formulas for *SP* if you note the similarity between the two *SP* formulas and the corresponding formulas for *SS* that were presented in Chapter 4. The definitional formula for *SS* is

$$SS = \sum(X - \bar{X})^2$$

In this formula, you must square each deviation, which is equivalent to multiplying it by itself. With this in mind, the formula can be rewritten as

$$SS = \sum(X - \bar{X})(X - \bar{X})$$

The similarity between the *SS* formula and the *SP* formula should be obvious—the *SS* formula uses squares and the *SP* formula uses products. This same relationship exists for the computational formulas. For *SS*, the computational formula is

$$SS = \sum X^2 - \frac{(\sum X)^2}{n}$$

As before, each squared value can be rewritten so that the formula becomes

$$SS = \sum XX - \frac{\sum X \sum X}{n}$$

Again, you should note the similarity in structure between the *SS* formula and the *SP* formula. If you remember that *SS* uses squares and *SP* uses products, the two new formulas for the sum of products should be easy to learn.

For the computational formula, you need the sum of the *X* values, the sum of the *Y* values, and the *XY* product for each pair. These values are as follows:

X	Y	XY	
1	3	3	
2	6	12	
4	4	16	
5	7	35	
12	20	66	Totals

Substituting the sums in the formula gives

$$\begin{aligned} SP &= \sum XY - \frac{\sum X \sum Y}{n} \\ &= 66 - \frac{12(20)}{4} \\ &= 66 - 60 \\ &= 6 \end{aligned}$$

Note that both formulas produce the same result, $SP = 6$.

CALCULATION OF THE PEARSON CORRELATION

By using the sum of products to measure the covariability between *X* and *Y*, the formula for the Pearson correlation becomes

$$r = \frac{SP}{\sqrt{SS_X SS_Y}} \qquad (16.3)$$

Note that you *multiply SS* for *X* and *SS* for *Y* in the denominator of the Pearson formula.

Notice that the variability for *X* is measured by the *SS* for the *X*-scores and the variability for *Y* is measured by *SS* for the *Y*-scores. The following example demonstrates the use of this formula with a simple set of scores.

EXAMPLE 16.3 The Pearson correlation is computed for the following set of $n = 5$ pairs of scores:

X	Y
0	1
10	3
4	1
8	2
8	3

Before starting any calculations, it is useful to put the data in a scatterplot and make a preliminary estimate of the correlation. These data have been graphed in Figure 16.6. Looking at the scatterplot, it appears that there is a very good (but not perfect) positive correlation. You should expect an approximate value of $r = +.8$ or $+.9$. To find the Pearson correlation, we will need SP, SS for X, and SS for Y. Each of these values is calculated using the definitional formula.

For the sum of products,

Scores		Deviations		Products
X	Y	$X - \overline{X}$	$Y - \overline{Y}$	$(X - \overline{X})(Y - \overline{Y})$
0	1	−6	−1	+6
10	3	+4	+1	+4
4	1	−2	−1	+2
8	2	+2	0	0
8	3	+2	+1	+2
				+14 = SP

For the X values,

X	$X - \overline{X}$	$(X - \overline{X})^2$
0	−6	36
10	+4	16
4	−2	4
8	+2	4
8	+2	4
		64 = SS for X

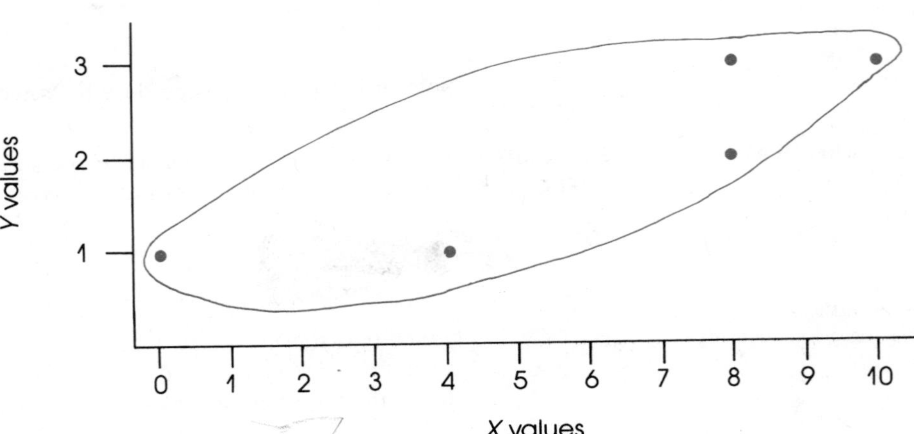

FIGURE 16.6 Scatterplot of the data from Example 16.3.

For the Y values,

Y	$Y - \bar{Y}$	$(Y - \bar{Y})^2$
1	−1	1
3	+1	1
1	−1	1
2	0	0
3	+1	1
		4 = SS for Y

By using these values, the Pearson correlation is

$$r = \frac{SP}{\sqrt{SS_X SS_Y}}$$

$$= \frac{14}{\sqrt{64(4)}}$$

$$= \frac{14}{16} = +.875$$

Note that the value we obtained is in agreement with the prediction based on the scatterplot. •

THE PEARSON CORRELATION AND z-SCORES

You should realize that the Pearson correlation measures the relation between an individual's location in the X distribution and his or her location in the Y distribution. For example, a positive correlation means that individuals who score high on X also tend to score high on Y. Similarly, a negative correlation indicates that individuals with high X scores tend to have low Y scores.

In the formula for the Pearson correlation, each individual's location in the X distribution and the Y distribution is designated by his or her deviation scores, $X - \bar{X}$ and $Y - \bar{Y}$. The product of these two deviation scores depends on the strength and the direction of the relation between X and Y. For example, with a positive relation between X and Y, individuals will tend to have the same relative location in both the X and Y distributions. A high score for X tends to be accompanied by a high score for Y, and a low X value tends to go with a low Y value. In this case, the two deviation scores for the individual will be similar (both positive or both negative), so the product of the deviations generally will be positive. The result is that the sum of products (SP) will be positive, and the correlation will be positive. On the other hand, a negative relation means that an individual with a relatively high X score (positive deviation) will tend to have a low Y score (negative deviation). Because the deviations have opposite signs, the product will be negative. In this case, the sum of the products (SP) will be negative and the resulting correlation will be negative.

You should recall from Chapter 5 that z-scores provide a precise way to identify the location of an individual score within a distribution. Because the Pearson correlation measures the relation between locations and because z-scores are used to specify locations, the formula for the Pearson correlation can be expressed entirely in terms of z-scores:

$$r = \frac{\sum z_X z_Y}{n} \tag{16.4}$$

In this formula, z_X identifies each individual's position with the X distribution, and z_Y identifies the position within the Y distribution. The product of the z-scores (like the product of the deviation scores) determines the strength and direction of the correlation.

Because z-scores are considered to be the best way to describe a location within a distribution, formula 16.4 often is considered to be the best way to define the Pearson correlation. However, you should realize that this formula requires a lot of tedious calculations (changing each score to a z-score), so it rarely is used to calculate a correlation.

· LEARNING CHECK ·

1 Describe what is measured by a Pearson correlation.

2 Can SP ever have a value less than zero?

3 Calculate the sum of products of deviations (SP) for the following set of scores. Use the definitional formula and then the computational formula. Verify that you get the same answer with both formulas.

X	Y
1	0
3	1
7	6
5	2
4	1

Remember, it is useful to sketch a scatterplot and make an estimate of the correlation before you begin calculations.

4 Compute the Pearson correlation for the following data:

X	Y
2	9
1	10
3	6
0	8
4	2

ANSWERS

1 The Pearson correlation measures the degree and direction of linear relationship between two variables.

2 Yes. SP can be positive, negative, or zero depending on the relation between X and Y.

3 $SP = 19$

4 $r = -\frac{16}{20} = -.80$

16.3 UNDERSTANDING AND INTERPRETING CORRELATIONS

Whenever you encounter correlations, there are three additional considerations that you should bear in mind:

1. Correlation simply describes a relationship between two variables. It does not explain why the two variables are related. Specifically, a correlation should not and cannot be interpreted as proof of a cause-effect relation between the two variables.
2. The value of a correlation can be affected greatly by the range of scores represented in the data.
3. When judging "how good" a relationship is, it is tempting to focus on the numerical value of the correlation. For example, a correlation of $+.5$ is halfway between 0 and 1.00 and therefore appears to represent a moderate degree of relation.

However, a correlation should not be interpreted as a proportion. Although a correlation of 1.00 does mean that there is a 100% perfectly predictable relation between X and Y, a correlation of .5 does not mean that you can make predictions with 50% accuracy. To describe how accurately one variable predicts the other, you must square the correlation. Thus, a correlation of $r = .5$ provides only $r^2 = .5^2 = .25$ or 25% accuracy.

Each of these three points will now be discussed in detail.

CORRELATION AND CAUSATION

One of the most common errors in interpreting correlations is to assume that a correlation necessarily implies a cause-and-effect relation between the two variables. We constantly are bombarded with reports of relationships: Cigarette smoking is related to heart disease; alcohol consumption is related to birth defects; carrot consumption is related to good eyesight. Do these relationships mean that cigarettes cause heart disease or carrots cause good eyesight? The answer is *no*. Although there may be a causal relation, the simple existence of a correlation does not prove it. This point should become clear in the following hypothetical example.

· EXAMPLE 16.4 · Suppose we select a variety of different cities and towns throughout the United States and measure the number of serious crimes (X variable) and the number of churches (Y variable) for each. A scatterplot showing hypothetical data for this study is presented in Figure 16.7. Notice that this scatterplot shows a strong, positive correlation between churches and crime. You also should note that these are realistic data. It is reasonable that the smaller towns would have less crime and fewer churches and that the large cities would have large values for both variables. Does this relation mean that churches cause crime? Does it mean that crime causes churches? It

· FIGURE 16.7 ·

Hypothetical data showing the logical relation between the number of churches and the number of serious crimes for a sample of U.S. cities.

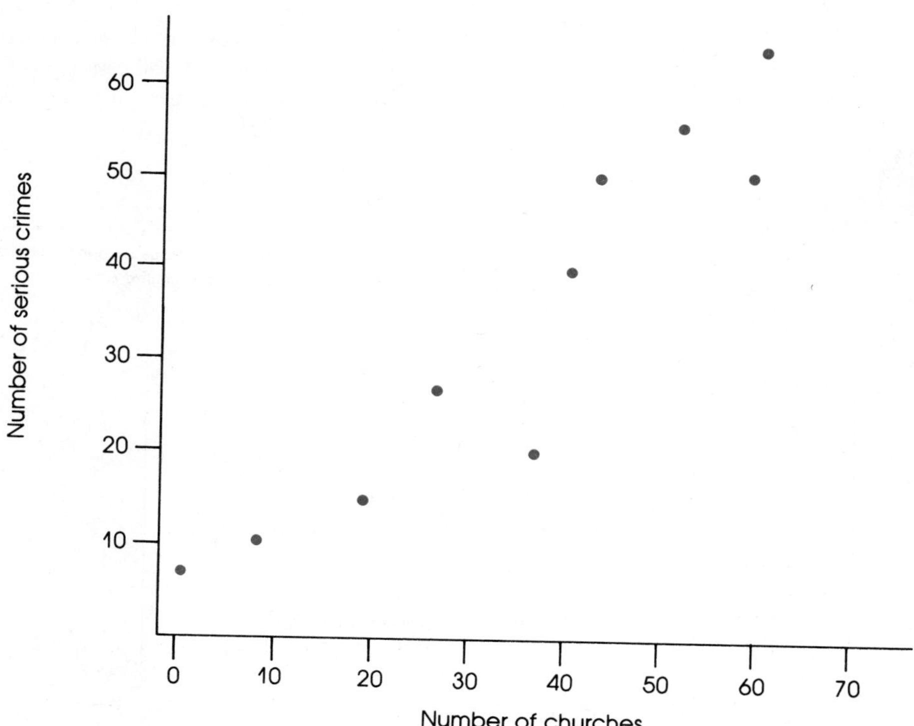

should be clear that the answer is no. Although a good correlation exists between churches and crime, the real cause of the relationship is the size of the population.

CORRELATION AND RESTRICTED RANGE

Whenever a correlation is computed from scores that do not represent the full range of possible values, you should be cautious in interpreting the correlation. Suppose, for example, you are interested in the relationship between IQ and creativity. If you select a sample of your fellow college students, your data probably would represent only a limited range of IQ scores (most likely from 110 to 130). The correlation within this restricted range could be completely different from the correlation that would be obtained from a full range of IQ scores. Two extreme examples are shown in Figure 16.8.

Figure 16.8(a) shows an example where there is a strong positive relation between *X* and *Y* when the entire range of scores is considered. However, this relation is obscured when the data are limited to a restricted range. In Figure 16.8(b) there is no consistent relation between *X* and *Y* for the full range of scores. However, when the range of *X* values is restricted, the data show a strong positive relation.

To be safe, you should not generalize any correlation beyond the range of data represented in the sample. For a correlation to provide an accurate description for the general population, there should be a wide range of *X* and *Y* values in the data.

CORRELATION AND THE STRENGTH OF THE RELATION

A correlation measures the degree of relation between two variables on a scale from 0 to 1.00. Although this number provides a measure of the degree of relationship, many researchers prefer to square the correlation and use the resulting value to measure the strength of the relationship. The reasons for squaring the correlation are discussed in Section 16.6, but a brief explanation is presented here.

One of the common uses of correlation is for prediction. If two variables are correlated, you can use the value of one variable to predict the other. For example, college admissions officers do not just guess which applicants are likely to do well; they use other variables (SAT scores, high school grades, etc.) to predict which students are most likely to be successful. These predictions are based on correlations. By using correlations, the admissions officers expect to make more-accurate predictions than would be obtained by just guessing. In general, the squared correlation (r^2) measures

FIGURE 16.8

(a) An example where the full range of *X* and *Y* values show a strong, positive correlation but the restricted range of scores produces a correlation near zero. (b) An example where the full range of *X* and *Y* values show a correlation near zero but the scores in the restricted range produce a strong, positive correlation.

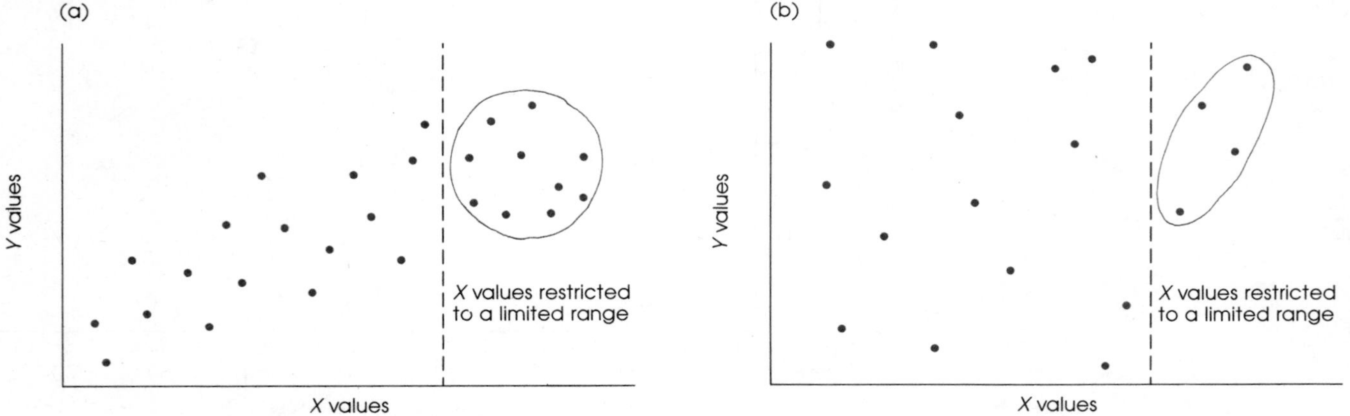

the gain in accuracy that is obtained from using the correlation for prediction instead of just guessing.

· DEFINITION · The value r^2 is called the *coefficient of determination* because it measures the proportion of variability in one variable that can be determined from the relationship with the other variable. A correlation of $r^2 = .80$ (or $-.80$), for example, means that $r^2 = .64$ (or 64%) of the variability in the Y scores can be predicted from the relation with X.

Although the coefficient of determination will be described in more detail in Section 16.6, a simple example should help make this concept more concrete. Suppose, for example, you are given the task of predicting the annual income for Mr. X. To help you with your task, we will provide three bits of information:

1. Mr. X wears a size 9 shoe.
2. Mr. X has been working in his profession for 2 months.
3. Mr. X has a monthly income of $1000.

The word *determined* means that salary is related to seniority and can be partially predicted from seniority—not that salary is caused by seniority.

It should be clear that the first bit of information (shoe size) is no help whatsoever. Because there is no correlation between shoe size and annual income, knowing shoe size will not improve your estimate of income. In this case, annual income is *not determined* by shoe size, so the coefficient of determination is zero. However, the second bit of information (length of employment) does provide some useful information. You should recognize that annual income is *partially determined* by seniority. Because Mr. X has been employed only 2 months, he probably is in an entry-level job and earning a relatively low salary. This information should improve the accuracy of your prediction. The amount of accuracy you gain depends on the strength of the correlation between salary and seniority. A correlation of .40, for example, would mean that $r^2 = .16$ or 16% of the variability in salary is determined by seniority. Finally, the third bit of information (monthly income) is extremely useful. Because there is a perfect correlation ($r = +1.00$) between monthly income and annual income, you now are able to predict annual income with perfect accuracy. In this case, annual income is *completely determined* by monthly income, so the coefficient of determination is 1.00 (100%).

16.4 HYPOTHESIS TESTS WITH THE PEARSON CORRELATION

The Pearson correlation is generally computed for sample data. Quite often, however, the sample correlation is used to provide information about the entire population. For example, a psychologist would like to know whether there is a relation between IQ and creativity. This is a general question concerning a population. To answer the question, a sample would be selected and the sample data would be used to compute the correlation value. You should recognize this process as an example of inferential statistics: using samples to draw inferences about populations. In the past, we have been concerned primarily with using sample means as the basis for answering questions about population means. In this section we will examine the procedures for using a sample correlation as the basis for testing hypotheses about the corresponding population correlation.

The basic question for this hypothesis test is whether or not a correlation exists in the population. The null hypothesis says "No, there is no correlation in the population," or "The population correlation is zero." The alternative hypothesis is "Yes, there is a real, nonzero, correlation in the population." Because the population correlation is

FIGURE 16.9

...ion of X and Y values with a ... However, a small sample of $n = 3$ ...s population shows a relatively strong, ...n. Data points in the sample are circled.

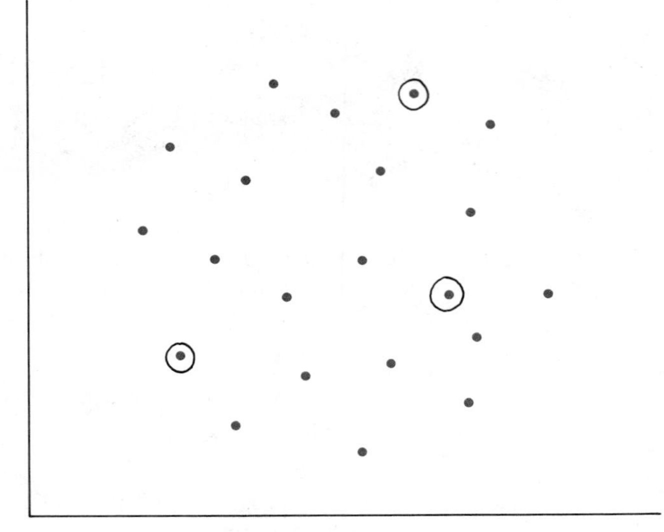

traditionally represented by ρ (the Greek letter rho), these hypotheses would be stated in symbols as

Directional hypotheses for a "one-tailed" test would specify either a positive correlation ($\rho > 0$) or a negative correlation ($\rho < 0$).

$H_0 : \rho = 0$ (no population correlation)

$H_1 : \rho \neq 0$ (there is a real correlation)

The correlation from the sample data (r) will be used to evaluate these hypotheses. As always, samples are not expected to be identical to the populations from which they come. Specifically, you should note that it is possible to obtain a nonzero sample correlation even when the population value is zero. This is particularly true when you have a small sample (see Figure 16.9). The question for this hypothesis test is whether the obtained sample correlation provides sufficient evidence to conclude that a real, nonzero correlation exists in the population. Although it is possible to conduct this hypothesis test by calculating either a t statistic or an F-ratio, the detailed computations have been completed and are summarized in Appendix B, Table B.6. To use the table, you must know the sample size (n), the magnitude of the sample correlation (independent of sign), and the alpha level. If the magnitude of the sample correlation (r) equals or exceeds the value given in the table, then we reject H_0 conclude that there is significant evidence for a correlation in the population. To demonstrate the use of the table, suppose you have a sample of $n = 30$ and want to test a nondirectional hypothesis about the population with $\alpha = .05$. In this case, the table indicates that your sample correlation must be greater than or equal to .361 to be significant.

The table lists critical values in terms of degrees of freedom: $df = n - 2$. Remember to subtract 2 when using this table.

LEARNING CHECK

1 A researcher obtains a correlation of $r = -.41$ for a sample of $n = 30$ individuals. Does this sample provide sufficient evidence to conclude that there is a significant, nonzero correlation in the population? Assume a nondirectional test with $\alpha = .05$.

2 For a sample of $n = 20$, how large a correlation is needed to conclude at the .05 level that there is a nonzero correlation in the population? Assume a nondirectional test.

3 As sample size gets larger, what happens to the magnitude of the correlation necessary for significance? Explain why this occurs.

ANSWERS

1 Yes. For $n = 30$, the critical value is $r = .361$. The sample value is in the critical region.

2 For $n = 20$ the critical value is $r = .444$.

3 As sample size gets larger, the critical value for the correlation gets smaller. The larger the sample, the more accurately the sample should represent its population. Thus, when n is very large, a sample correlation that is different from zero (even slightly), provides evidence that the population correlation also is different from zero.

16.5 INTRODUCTION TO REGRESSION

Earlier in this chapter we noted that one of the primary uses of correlation is for prediction. Whenever two variables are consistently related, it is possible to use a known value on one variable to predict the corresponding value on the other. Regression is the technical procedure by which these predictions are made. Before we introduce the detailed mathematics of regression, we will present a general example of how this procedure works and introduce the basic concepts of regression.

Figure 16.10 presents hypothetical data showing the relationship between SAT scores and college grade point average (GPA). Note that there is a good (but not perfect) positive correlation between these two variables. These data would be collected from a large group of college students. The SAT score is recorded for each individual when he or she enters college, and the GPA is recorded after 2 full years of college coursework. These data, collected from past students, define the relationship between X and Y and form the basis of prediction for new students.

Now suppose a high school senior with an SAT score of 620 applies to the college. The admissions officer first locates a score of 620 on the X-axis in the figure. The data points directly above this value correspond to the GPAs of the previous students

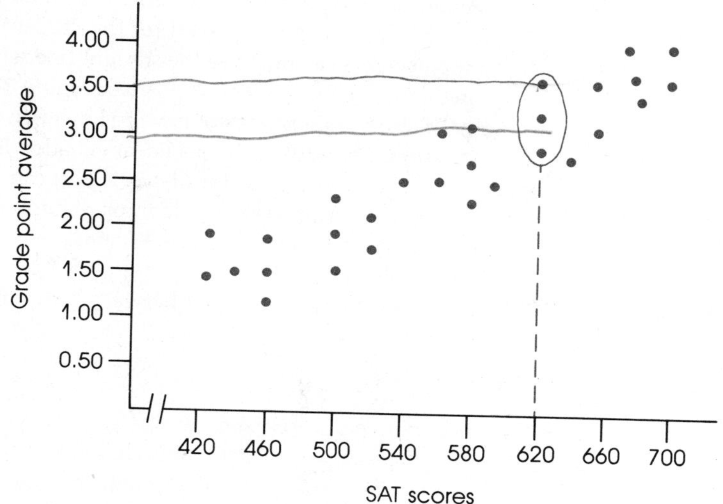

FIGURE 16.10

Scatterplot showing the relation between college grade point average and SAT scores for a set of hypothetical data. In this sample, three students had a SAT score of $X = 620$. Notice that these three students have relatively high grade point averages.

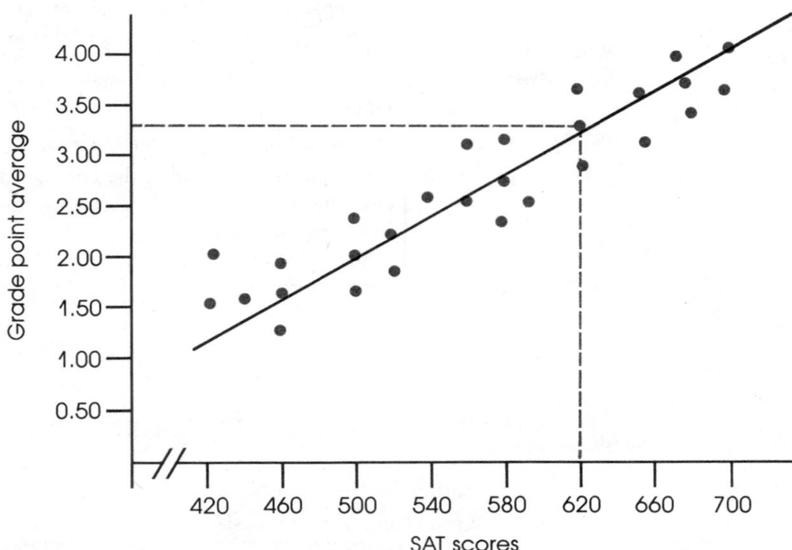

FIGURE 16.11

Hypothetical data showing the relation between SAT scores and GPA with a regression line drawn through the data points. The regression line defines a precise, one-to-one relation between each X value (SAT score) and its corresponding Y value (GPA).

who entered the college with the same SAT score. These data points provide a description of how students have performed in the past, and they can be used to predict how well the new applicant will perform.

You should note that the prediction is not perfect. The data show that three students who entered with SAT scores of 620 earned GPAs ranging from roughly 3.00 to 3.50. It should be clear that these students generally performed above the college-wide average, and the admissions officer could reasonably expect that the new applicant would also be an above average student with a relatively high GPA.

The goal of regression is to make the process of prediction simpler and more precise. Figure 16.11 again presents hypothetical data showing a relation between SAT and GPA, but this time we have drawn a line through the center of the data points. The line, which is called the *regression line,* has several purposes. First, the regression line provides a simplified description of the relation between X and Y. The line identifies the center, or *central tendency,* of the relation, just as the mean describes central tendency for a set of scores. In addition, the regression line can be used for prediction. Again, suppose a high school senior with an SAT score of 620 applies to the college. What GPA would you predict for this student? As before, we locate 620 on the X-axis. However, we can now use the straight-line relation between X and Y to make a precise prediction of the student's GPA (see Figure 16.11). As a final note, you should realize that a straight line does not have to be drawn in a graph; it can be presented in a simple equation. The advantage of a linear equation is that whenever you have a specific value for X (e.g., an SAT score of 620), you can compute a precise value for Y without sketching a graph. The problem for regression is to find the equation for the line that best describes a set of X and Y data.

LINEAR EQUATIONS

In general, a linear relation between two variables X and Y can be expressed by an equation

$$Y = bX + a \tag{16.5}$$

where b and a are fixed constants.

For example, a local tennis club charges a fee of \$5 per hour plus an annual membership fee of \$25. With this information, the total cost of playing tennis can be computed using a linear equation:

$$\text{total cost} = 5 \times (\text{number of hours}) + \$25$$

This equation describes the relation between total cost (Y) and the number of hours (X).

In the general linear equation, the value of b is called the *slope.* The slope determines how much the Y variables will change when X is increased by one point. For the tennis club example, the slope is $b = \$5$ and indicates that your total cost will increase by $5 for each hour you play. The value of a in the general equation is called the Y-intercept because it determines the value of Y when $X = 0$. (On a graph, the a value identifies the point where the line intercepts the Y-axis.) For the tennis club example, $a = \$25$; there is a $25 charge even if you never play tennis.

Figure 16.12 shows the general relation between cost and number of hours for the tennis club example. Notice that the relation results in a straight line. To obtain this graph, we picked any two values of X and then used the equation to compute the corresponding values for Y. For example,

When $X = 10$:

$$\begin{aligned} Y &= bX + a \\ &= \$5(10) + \$25 \\ &= \$50 + \$25 \\ &= \$75 \end{aligned}$$

When $X = 30$:

$$\begin{aligned} Y &= bX + a \\ &= \$5(30) + \$25 \\ &= \$150 + \$25 \\ &= \$175 \end{aligned}$$

When drawing a graph of a linear equation, it is wise to compute and plot at least three points to be certain you have not made a mistake.

Next, these two points are plotted on the graph: one point at $X = 10$ and $Y = 75$, the other point at $X = 30$ and $Y = 175$. Because two points completely determine a straight line, we simply drew the line so that it passed through these two points.

Because there is a linear relation between cost and number of hours, the Pearson correlation between these two variables is $r = +1.00$. With a perfect linear relation, you can make perfect predictions. For this example, the linear equation makes it

FIGURE 16.12

Relationship between total cost and number of hours playing tennis. The tennis club charges a $25 membership fee plus $5 per hour. The relation is described by a linear equation:

$$\text{total cost} = \$5(\text{number of hours}) + \$25$$
$$Y = bX + a$$

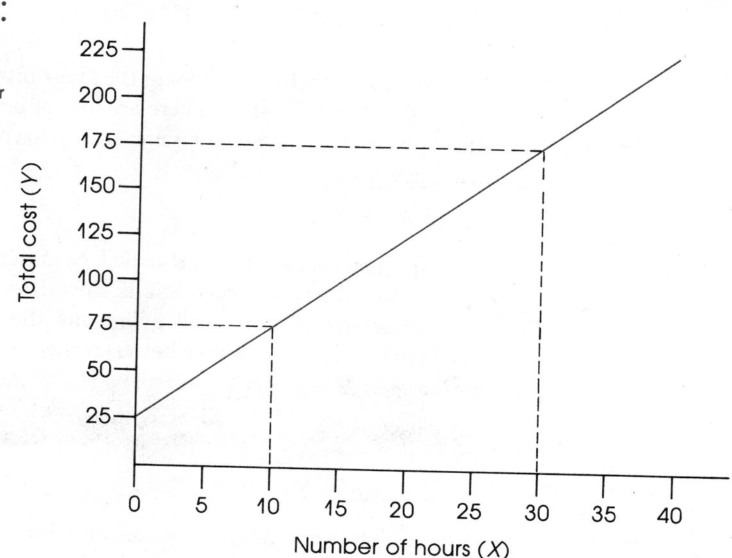

possible for you to predict one variable (total cost) for any specific value of the other variable (number of hours).

In most real-life cases, the relation between two variables will not be perfectly linear. Nonetheless, it is possible to find the equation for the best fitting straight line and then use this equation to make predictions.

· LEARNING CHECK ·

1 Identify the slope and Y-intercept for the following linear equation:

$$Y = -3X + 7$$

2 Use the linear equation $Y = 2X - 7$ to determine the value of Y for each of the following values of X.

X values: 1, 3, 5, 10

3 If the slope constant (b) in a linear equation is positive, then a graph of the equation will be a line tilted from lower left to upper right. (True or False)

ANSWERS

1 Slope $= -3$ and Y-intercept $= +7$.

2

X	Y
1	−5
3	−1
5	3
10	13

3 True. A positive slope indicates that Y increases (goes up in the graph) when X increases (goes to the right in the graph).

16.6 THE REGRESSION EQUATION: THE LEAST-SQUARES SOLUTION

The first problem in determining the "best fitting" linear equation is to define precisely what is meant by best fit. There are lots of possible straight lines that could be drawn through a set of data (see Figure 16.13). Each of the possible lines can be defined by the general linear equation

$$Y = bX + a$$

The specific values of b and a will be different for each of the different lines. The goal is to determine which line is closest to the actual data points.

To determine how well a line fits the data points, the first step is to define mathematically the distance between the line and each data point. For every X value in the data, the linear equation will determine a Y value on the line. This value is the predicted Y and is called $\hat{Y}$ ("Y hat"). The distance between this predicted value and the actual Y value in the data is determined by

$$\text{distance} = Y - \hat{Y}$$

Notice that we simply are measuring the vertical distance between the actual data

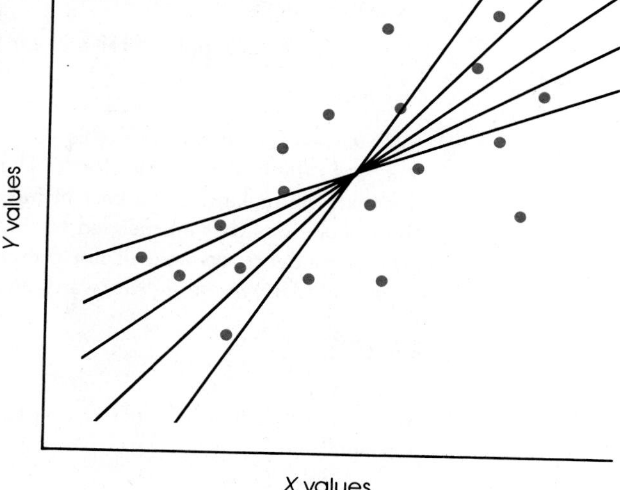

FIGURE 16.13

Scatterplot showing X and Y data points. Several lines have been drawn through the data. Note that all the lines have different slopes and different Y-intercepts; hence they have different equations. The problem for regression is to determine which is the best-fitting line for the data.

point (Y) and the predicted point on the line. This distance measures the error between the line and the actual data (see Figure 16.14).

Because some of these distances will be positive and some will be negative, the next step is to square each distance in order to obtain a uniformly positive measure of error. Finally, to determine the total error between the line and the data, we sum the squared errors for all of the data points. The result is a measure of overall squared error between the line and the data:

$$\text{total squared error} = \sum(Y - \hat{Y})^2$$

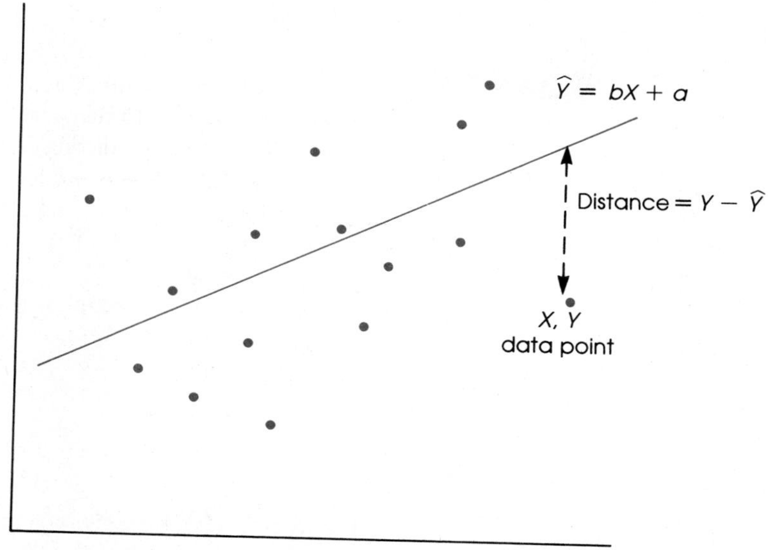

FIGURE 16.14

The distance between the actual data point (Y) and the predicted point on the line ($\hat{Y}$) is defined as $Y - \hat{Y}$. The goal of regression is to find the equation for the line that minimizes these distances.

Now we can define the *best-fitting* line as the one that has the smallest total squared error. For obvious reasons, the resulting line is commonly called the *least squared error* solution.

In symbols, we are looking for a linear equation of the form

$$\hat{Y} = bX + a$$

For each value of X in the data, this equation will determine the point on the line ($\hat{Y}$) that gives the best prediction of Y. The problem is to find the specific values for a and b that will make this the best fitting line.

The calculations that are needed to find this equation require calculus and some sophisticated algebra, so we will not present the details of the solution. The results, however, are relatively straightforward, and the solutions for b and a are as follows:

A commonly used alternative formula for the slope is

$$b = r\frac{s_Y}{s_X}$$

where s_X and s_Y are the standard deviations for X and Y, respectively.

$$b = \frac{SP}{SS_X} \tag{16.6}$$

Where SP is the sum of products (see page 388) and SS_X is the sum of squares for the X-scores.

$$a = \bar{Y} - b\bar{X} \tag{16.7}$$

Note that these two formulas determine the linear equation that provides the best prediction of Y values. This equation is called the regression equation for Y.

· DEFINITION · The *regression equation for* Y is the linear equation

$$\hat{Y} = bX + a$$

where the constants b and a are determined by formulas (16.6) and (16.7), respectively. This equation results in the least squared error between the data points and the line.

You should notice that the values of SS and SP are needed in the formulas for b and a just as they are needed to compute the Pearson correlation. Relations between the correlation and the regression equation will appear repeatedly throughout this chapter. An example demonstrating the calculation and use of this best fitting line is presented now.

· EXAMPLE 16.5 · The following table presents X and Y scores for a sample of $n = 5$ individuals. These data will be used to demonstrate the procedure for determining the linear regression equation for predicting Y values.

X	Y	$X - \bar{X}$	$Y - \bar{Y}$	$(X - \bar{X})(Y - \bar{Y})$	$(X - \bar{X})^2$
7	11	2	5	10	4
4	3	−1	−3	3	1
6	5	1	−1	−1	1
3	4	−2	−2	4	4
5	7	0	1	0	0
				$16 = SP$	$10 = SS_X$

For these data $\sum X = 25$, so $\bar{X} = 5$. Also, $\sum Y = 30$, so $\bar{Y} = 6$. These means have been used to compute the deviation scores for each X and Y value. The final two columns show the products of the deviation scores and the squared deviations for X. Based on these values,

$$SP = \sum(X - \bar{X})(Y - \bar{Y}) = 16$$

$$SS_X = \sum(X - \bar{X})^2 = 10$$

Our goal is to find the values for b and a in the linear equation so that we obtain the best fitting straight line for these data.

By using formulas 16.6 and 16.7, the solutions for b and a are

$$b = \frac{SP}{SS_X} = \frac{16}{10} = 1.6$$

$$\begin{aligned} a &= \bar{Y} - b\bar{X} \\ &= 6 - 1.6(5) \\ &= 6 - 8 \\ &= -2 \end{aligned}$$

The resulting regression equation is

$$\hat{Y} = 1.6X - 2$$

This regression equation can be used to determine a predicted Y value for any given value of X. For example, an individual with an X score of $X = 5$ would be predicted to have a Y score of

$$\begin{aligned} \hat{Y} &= 1.6X - 2 \\ &= 1.6(5) - 2 \\ &= 8 - 2 \\ &= 6 \end{aligned}$$

Regression on the Computer Just as we have seen with other statistical procedures, computer software for regression is abundant. For the data in Example 16.5, we performed regression using the SPSS^x software package. This is done with the SPSS^x command called PLOT, which provides a scatterplot, the correlation and the regression analysis. Table 16.1 shows a portion of the printout and the results of the correlation and regression. The first part of the printout, a scatterplot, was omitted because of its large size. An explanation of the printout is provided in the table caption.

TABLE 16.1

SPSS^x analysis for the data in Example 16.5.

```
07 APR 87    SPSS-X RELEASE 2.1+ PRIME
10:30:15     SUNY Brockport Computing Srvcs Prime 9955              Rev 20.0.3

5 cases plotted. Regression statistics of Y on X:
Correlation .80000  R Squared .64000  S.E. of Est 2.19089  2-tailed Sig. .1041
Intercept(S.E.)   -2.00000(  3.60000)  Slope(S.E.) 1.60000(  .69282)
```

EXPLANATION OF PRINTOUT:

1 The first line indicates that $n = 5$ pairs of scores ("cases plotted") were used in the regression.

2 The second line provides information about the correlation. From left to right the entries are the value for the Pearson correlation, the value for r^2, the standard error of estimate (see page 404), and the statistical significance of the correlation (probability of a Type I error using a two-tailed test).

3 The third line displays the Y-intercept and the slope of the best-fitting line, with the standard error for each. From the information in the printout, we can determine that the regression equation is $\hat{Y} = 1.6X - 2$.

HE STANDARD ERROR OF ESTIMATE

It is possible to determine a best-fitting regression equation for any set of data by simply using the formulas already presented. The linear equation you obtain is then used to generate predicted Y values for any known value of X. However, it should be clear that the accuracy of this prediction depends on how well the points on the line correspond to the actual data points, that is, the amount of error between the predicted values $\hat{Y}$ and the actual scores, Y values. Figure 16.15 shows two different sets of data that have exactly the same regression equation. In one case there is a perfect correlation ($r = +1$) between X and Y, so the linear equation fits the data perfectly. For the second set of data, the predicted Y values on the line only approximate the real data points.

A regression equation, by itself, allows you to make predictions, but it does not provide any information about the accuracy of the predictions. To measure the precision of the regression, it is customary to compute a standard error of estimate.

· DEFINITION · The *standard error of estimate* gives a measure of the standard distance between a regression line and the actual data points.

Conceptually, the standard error of estimate is very much like a standard deviation: Both provide a measure of standard distance. You also should note that the calculation of the standard error of estimate is very similar to the calculation of standard deviation.

To calculate the standard error of estimate, we first will find a sum of squared deviations (SS). Each deviation will measure the distance between the actual Y value (from the data) and the predicted Y value (from the regression line). This sum of squares is commonly called SS_{error} because it measures the sum of squared distances, or errors, between the actual data and the predicted values:

$$SS_{\text{error}} = \sum(Y - \hat{Y})^2 \tag{16.8}$$

The obtained SS value is then divided by its degrees of freedom to obtain a measure of variance. This procedure should be very familiar:

$$\text{variance} = \frac{SS}{df}$$

The degrees of freedom for the standard error of estimate are $df = n - 2$. The reason for having $n - 2$ degrees of freedom, rather than the customary $n - 1$, is that we

· FIGURE 16.15 ·

(a) Scatterplot showing data set 1 from Example 16.6. Notice that the data points fit perfectly on the regression equation, $\hat{Y} = 2X + 3$. (b) Scatterplot showing data set 2 from Example 16.6. In this case there is some error between the data points and the regression line.

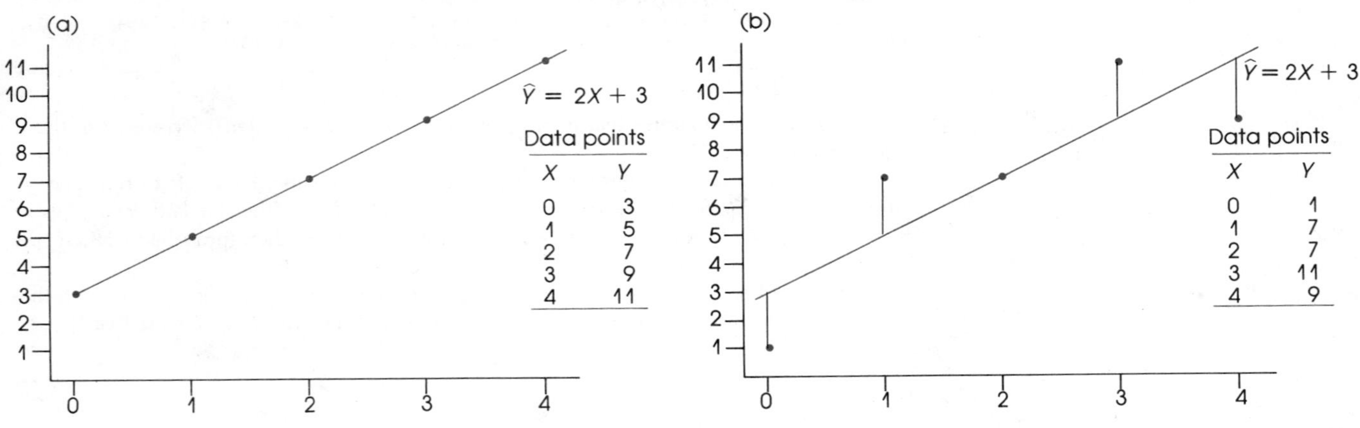

now are measuring deviations from a line rather than deviations from a mean. You should recall that it is necessary to know *SP* to find the slope of the regression line (the value of b in the equation). To calculate *SP*, you must know the means for both the *X*- and the *Y*-scores. Specifying these two means places two restrictions on the variability of the data with the result that the scores have only $n - 2$ degrees of freedom. (A more intuitive explanation for the fact that the SS_{error} has $df = n - 2$ comes from the simple observation that it takes exactly two points to determine a straight line. If there are only two data points, they must fit perfectly on a straight line so there will be no error. It is only when you have more than two points that there is some freedom in determining the best fitting line.)

The final step in the calculation of the standard error of estimate is to take the square root of the variance in order to obtain a measure of standard distance. The final equation is

(16.9) $$\text{standard error of estimate} = \sqrt{\frac{SS_{\text{error}}}{df}} = \sqrt{\frac{\sum(Y - \hat{Y})^2}{n - 2}}$$

The following example demonstrates the calculation of this standard error.

· EXAMPLE 16.6 · The two sets of data in Figure 16.15 will be used to demonstrate the calculation of the standard error of estimate. Both of these data sets have the same regression equation:

$$\hat{Y} = 2X + 3$$

However, for the first set of scores there is a perfect correlation ($r = +1$) between *X* and *Y*; that is, the points fit perfectly on a straight line. For the second data set the correlation is $r = +.845$, so there is some error between the predicted values on the line and the actual *Y* values.

For the first set of data, $SS_X = 10$, $SS_Y = 40$, and $SP = 20$. The mean for *X* is $\overline{X} = 2$, and the mean for *Y* is $\overline{Y} = 7$. By using these values, the constants in the regression equation are

$$b = \frac{SP}{SS_X} = \frac{20}{10} = 2 \qquad \hat{Y} = bX + a$$

$$a = \overline{Y} - b\overline{X} \qquad \hat{Y} = 2X + 3$$

$$= 7 - 2(2)$$

$$= 7 - 4$$

$$= 3$$

Using this regression equation, we have computed the predicted *Y* value, the error, and the squared error for each individual in the data. Notice that in every case the predicted *Y* value is identical to the actual *Y* score. All of the errors are equal to zero, so the *SS* for these errors also is zero:

Data		Predicted Y Value	Error	Squared Error
X	Y	$\hat{Y} = 2X + 3$	$Y - \hat{Y}$	$(Y - \hat{Y})^2$
0	3	3	0	0
1	5	5	0	0
2	7	7	0	0
3	9	9	0	0
4	11	11	0	0
				$0 = SS_{\text{error}}$

Because there is no error between the predicted values and the actual Y values, the standard error of estimate is zero: The regression line provides a perfect prediction:

$$\text{standard error of estimate} = \sqrt{\frac{SS_{\text{error}}}{df}} = \sqrt{\frac{0}{3}} = 0$$

For the second data set, $SS_X = 10$, $SS_Y = 56$, and $SP = 20$. The mean for the X values is $\bar{X} = 2$, and the mean for the Y values is $\bar{Y} = 7$. By using these values, the constants in the regression equation are

$$b = \frac{SP}{SS_X} = \frac{20}{10} = 2 \qquad \hat{Y} = bX + a$$

$$a = \bar{Y} - b\bar{X} \qquad \hat{Y} = 2X + 3$$

$$= 7 - 2(2)$$

$$= 3$$

Again, we have used the regression equation to compute the predicted Y, the error, and the squared error for each individual:

Data X	Data Y	Predicted Y Value $\hat{Y} = 2X + 3$	Error $Y - \hat{Y}$	Squared Error $(Y - \hat{Y})^2$
0	1	3	−2	4
1	7	5	+2	4
2	7	7	0	0
3	11	9	+2	4
4	9	11	−2	4
				$16 = SS_{\text{error}}$

This time the data points do not fit exactly on the line. The sum of squared errors for these data is $SS_{\text{error}} = 16$. With $n = 5$, these data have $df = n - 2 = 3$, so the standard error of estimate is

$$\text{standard error of estimate} = \sqrt{\frac{SS_{\text{error}}}{df}} = \sqrt{\frac{16}{3}} = 2.31$$

Remember, the standard error of estimate provides a measure of how accurately the regression equation predicts the Y values. In this case, the standard distance between the actual data points and the regression line is measured by standard error of estimate = 2.31.

RELATION BETWEEN STANDARD ERROR AND THE CORRELATION

It should be clear from Example 16.6 that the standard error of estimate is directly related to the magnitude of the correlation between X and Y. If the correlation is near 1.00 (or −1.00), the data points will be clustered close to the line, and the standard error of estimate will be small. As the correlation gets nearer to zero, the line will provide less accurate predictions, and the standard error of estimate will grow larger. Earlier (page 395) we observed that squaring the correlation provides a measure of the accuracy of prediction: r^2 is called the coefficient of determination because it determines what proportion of the variability in Y is predicted by the relationship with X. Figure 16.16 should help make this concept more concrete. In the figure we use one circle to represent the total variability in Y and a second circle to represent the

FIGURE 16.16

A graphic representation of the coefficient of determination, r^2. See text for further explanation.

(a) With $r = 0$, X and Y are independent. None of the Y variability can be predicted from X; $r^2 = 0$.

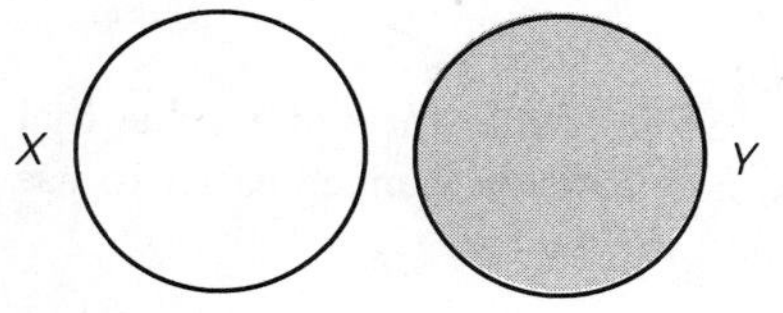

(b) With $r = 0.8$, the Y variability is partially predicted from the relation with X; $r^2 = 0.64$ or 64%.

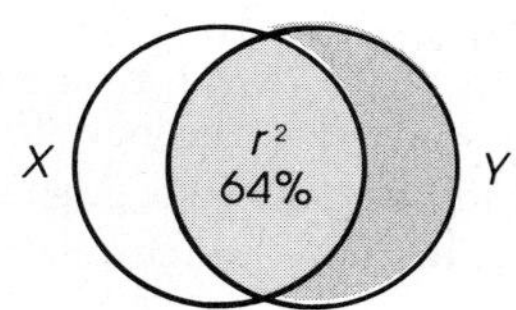

(c) With $r = 1$, all the Y variability is predicted from the relation with X; $r^2 = 1.00$ or 100%.

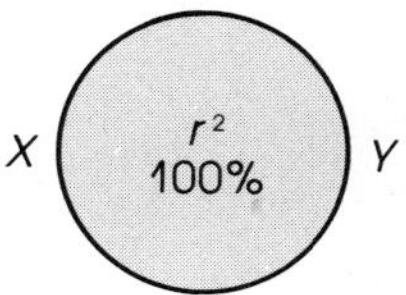

variability in X. When there is no relationship between X and Y ($r = 0$), the two circles are separated, indicating that the variability in Y is completely independent of the variability in X (see Figure 16.16(a)). However, when there is a correlation between X and Y, the two circles will overlap. Remember that a correlation means that changes in the X variable tend to be accompanied by predictable changes in the Y variable. Thus, X and Y tend to vary together, and the overlap in the two circles represents this shared variability. The coefficient of determination, r^2, measures the proportion of each circle that is contained in the overlap. With a correlation of $r = .80$, for example, $r^2 = .64$, which means that 64% of the Y circle overlaps with the X circle (see Figure 16.16(b)). In statistical terms, $r = .80$ means that 64% of the variability in Y is predicted (or determined) by the relationship with X. Finally, Figure 16.16(c) depicts the coefficient of determination when there is a perfect correlation between X and Y. With $r = 1$ (or -1), every change in X is accompanied by a perfectly predictable change in Y, which means that X and Y always vary together. Thus, 100% of the Y variability is shared with X, and the two circles completely overlap.

Because r^2 measures the predicted portion of the variability in Y, we can use $1 - r^2$ to measure the unpredicted, or *error*, portion. Looking again at Figure 16.16(b), it should be clear that when 64% (r^2) of the Y circle is predicted by X, there must be 36% ($1 - r^2$) that is unpredicted. This unpredicted variability is exactly what we have defined as error variability in the standard error of estimate. Because the total variability in Y is measured by SS_Y, the error portion can be calculated as

(16.10) $$SS_{\text{error}} = (1 - r^2)SS_Y$$

Notice that when $r = 1.00$ there is no error (perfect prediction) and that as the correlation approaches zero the error will grow larger. By using this formula for SS_{error}, the standard error of estimate can be computed as

$$\text{standard error of estimate} = \sqrt{\frac{SS_{\text{error}}}{df}} = \sqrt{\frac{(1 - r^2)SS_Y}{n - 2}}$$

The two data sets in Example 16.6 will be used to demonstrate this new formula. For the first data set there was a perfect correlation between X and Y, $r = +1.00$.

By using this value, the SS for the errors would be

$$\begin{aligned} SS_{\text{error}} &= (1 - r^2)SS_Y \\ &= (1 - 1^2)(40) \\ &= 0(40) \\ &= 0 \end{aligned}$$

For the second set of data, $SS_Y = 56$, and the correlation between X and Y is $r = .845$. By using the new formula, SS for the errors would be

$$\begin{aligned} SS_{\text{error}} &= (1 - r^2)SS_Y \\ &= (1 - .845^2)(56) \\ &= (1 - .714)(56) \\ &= .286(56) \\ &= 16.01 \end{aligned}$$

Notice that in each case the new formula for the SS produces the same value that was obtained in Example 16.6. Also note that this new formula is much easier to use because it requires only the correlation value (r) and the SS for Y.

· LEARNING CHECK ·

1 Sketch a scatterplot for the following data, that is, a graph showing the X, Y data points:

X	Y
1	4
3	9
5	8

a Find the regression equation for predicting Y from X. Draw this line on your graph. Does it look like the best fitting line?
b Use the regression equation to find the predicted Y value corresponding to each X in the data.
c Find the error $(Y - \hat{Y})$ for each data point and compute SS_{error} and the standard error of estimate.
d Compute the Pearson correlation for these data.
e Use the Pearson correlation and SS_Y to find the SS_{error} and the standard error of estimate.

2 Assuming all other factors are held constant, what happens to the standard error of estimate as the correlation between X and Y moves toward zero?

ANSWERS

1 **a** $SS_X = 8$, $SP = 8$, $b = 1$, $a = 4$.
The equation is

$$\hat{Y} = X + 4$$

b The predicted Y values are 5, 7, and 9.
c The errors are -1, 2, and -1. $SS_{\text{error}} = 6$. The standard error of estimate is $\sqrt{\frac{6}{1}} = 2.45$.
d $SS_X = 8$; $SS_Y = 14$; $SP = 8$; $r = .756$.
e $1 - r^2 = .428$; $SS_{\text{error}} = .428(14) = 5.99$; standard error of estimate $= 2.45$.

2 The standard error of estimate would get larger. As the correlation moves toward zero, the points move farther from the line.

SUMMARY

1 A correlation measures the relationship between two variables X and Y. The relationship is described by three characteristics:
a *Direction.* A relation can be either positive or negative. A positive relation means that X and Y vary in the same direction. A negative relation means that X and Y vary in opposite directions. The sign of the correlation (+ or −) specifies the direction.
b *Form.* The most common form for a relation is a straight

line. However, special correlations exist for measuring other forms. The form is specified by the type of correlation used. For example, the Pearson correlation measures linear form.

c *Degree.* The magnitude of the correlation measures the degree to which the data points fit the specified form. A correlation of 1.00 indicates a perfect fit, and a correlation of 0 indicates no degree of fit.

2 The most commonly used correlation is the Pearson correlation, which measures the degree of linear relationship. The Pearson correlation is identified by the letter r and is computed by

$$r = \frac{SP}{\sqrt{SS_X SS_Y}}$$

In this formula, SP is the sum of products of deviations and can be calculated either with a definitional formula or a computational formula:

Definitional formula: $SP = \sum(X - \bar{X})(Y - \bar{Y})$

Computational formula: $SP = \sum XY - \frac{\sum X \sum Y}{n}$

3 The Pearson correlation and z-scores are closely related because both are concerned with the location of individuals within a distribution. When X and Y scores are transformed into z-scores, the Pearson correlation can be computed by

$$r = \frac{\sum z_X z_Y}{n}$$

4 A correlation between two variables should not be interpreted as implying a causal relation. Simply because X and Y are related does not mean that X causes Y or that Y causes X.

5 When the X or Y values used to compute a correlation are limited to a relatively small portion of the potential range, you should exercise caution in generalizing the value of the correlation. Specifically, a limited range of values can either obscure a strong relation or exaggerate a poor relation.

6 To evaluate the strength of a relation, you should square the value of the correlation. The resulting value, r^2, is called the *coefficient of determination* because it measures the portion of the variability in one variable that can be predicted using the relationship with the second variable.

7 When there is a general linear relation between two variables X and Y, it is possible to construct a linear equation that allows you to predict the Y value corresponding to any known value of X:

predicted Y value $= \hat{Y} = bX + a$

The technique for determining this equation is called regression. By using a *least-squares* method to minimize the error between the predicted Y values and the actual Y values, the best fitting line is achieved when the linear equation has

$$b = \frac{SP}{SS_X} \quad \text{and} \quad a = \bar{Y} - b\bar{X}$$

8 The linear equation generated by regression (called the *regression equation*) can be used to compute a predicted Y value for any value of X. The accuracy of the prediction is measured by the standard error of estimate, which provides a measure of the average distance (or error) between the predicted Y value on the line and the actual data point. The standard error of estimate is computed by

$$\text{standard error of estimate} = \sqrt{\frac{SS_{error}}{n-2}}$$

where SS_{error} may be computed directly from the error scores,

$SS_{error} = \sum(Y - \hat{Y})^2$

or as a proportion of the original Y variability,

$SS_{error} = (1 - r^2)SS_Y$

KEY TERMS

correlation
positive correlation
negative correlation
perfect correlation
Pearson correlation
linear relationship
linear equation
slope
Y-intercept
regression equation for Y
sum of products (SP)
restricted range
coefficient of determination
standard error of estimate

FOCUS ON PROBLEM SOLVING

1. A correlation always has a value between +1.00 and −1.00. If you obtain a correlation outside this range, then you have made a computational error.

2. When interpreting a correlation, do not confuse the sign (+ or −) with its numerical value. The sign and numerical value must be considered separately. Remember, the sign indicates the direction of the relationship between X and Y. On the other hand, the numerical

value reflects the strength of the relationship, or how well the points approximate a linear (straight-line) relationship. Therefore, correlation of −.90 is just as strong as a correlation of +.90. The signs tell us that the first correlation is an inverse relationship.

3. Before you begin to calculate a correlation, you should sketch a scatterplot of the data and make an estimate of the correlation. (Is it positive or negative? Is it near 1 or near 0?). After computing the correlation, compare your final answer with your original estimate.

4. The definitional formula for the sum of products (*SP*) should be used only when you have a small set (*n*) of scores and the means for X and Y are both whole numbers. Otherwise, the computational formula will produce quicker, easier, and more-accurate results.

5. For computing a correlation, *n* is number of individuals (and, therefore, the number of *pairs* of X and Y values).

6. To draw a graph from a linear equation, choose any three values for X, put each value in the equation, and calculate the corresponding values for Y. Then plot the three (X, Y) points on the graph. Its a good idea to use X = 0 for one of the three values because this will give you the Y-intercept. You can get a quick idea of what the graph should look like if you know the Y-intercept and the slope. Remember, the Y-intercept is the point where the line crosses the Y-axis, and the slope identifies the tilt of the line. For example, suppose the Y-intercept is 5 and the slope is −3. The line would pass through the point (0, 5), and its slope indicates that the Y value goes down 3 points each time X increases by 1.

7. Rather than memorizing the formula for the Y-intercept in the regression equation, simply remember that the graphed line of the regression equation always goes through the point ($\bar{X}$, $\bar{Y}$). Therefore, if you plug the mean value for X ($\bar{X}$) into the regression equation, the result equals the mean value for Y ($\bar{Y}$).

$$\bar{Y} = b\bar{X} + a$$

If you simply solve this equation for *a*, you get the formula for the Y-intercept.

$$a = \bar{Y} - b\bar{X}$$

PROBLEMS

***1** With a very small sample, a single point can have a large influence on the magnitude of a correlation. For the following data set,

X	Y
0	1
10	3
4	1
8	2
8	3

a Sketch a graph showing the X, Y points.
b Estimate the value of the Pearson correlation.
c Compute the Pearson correlation.
d Now we will change the value of one of the points. For the first individual in the sample (X = 0 and Y = 1), change the Y value to Y = 6. What happens to the graph of the X, Y points? What happens to the Pearson correlation? Compute the new correlation.

***2** In the following data there are three scores (X, Y, and Z) for each of the $n = 5$ individuals:

X	Y	Z
3	5	5
4	3	2
2	4	6
1	1	3
0	2	4

a Sketch a graph showing the relation between X and Y. Compute the Pearson correlation between X and Y.
b Sketch a graph showing the relation between Y and Z. Compute the Pearson correlation between Y and Z.
c Given the results of parts a and b, what would you predict for the correlation between X and Z?
d Sketch a graph showing the relation between X and Z. Compute the Pearson correlation for these data.

e What general conclusion can you make concerning relations among correlations? If X is related to Y and Y is related to Z, does this necessarily mean that X is related to Z?

3 For the following set of data,

X	Y
1	2
2	4
3	1
4	3
5	3
6	9
7	10
8	7
9	8
10	9

a Sketch a graph showing the X, Y points.
b Compute the Pearson correlation for the full set of data.
c Compute the Pearson correlation using only the first five individuals in the sample (the five smallest X values).
d Compute the Pearson correlation for the final five individuals in the sample (the five largest X values).
e Explain why the results from parts c and d are so different from the overall correlation obtained in part b.

***4** A set of $n = 6$ pairs of X and Y values has a Pearson correlation of $r = +.60$ and $SS_Y = 100$. If you are using these data as the basis for a regression equation,
a On the average, how much error would you expect if the regression equation were used to predict the Y-score for a specific individual? That is, find the standard error of regression.
b How much error would you expect if the sample size were $n = 102$ instead of $n = 6$?
c How much error would you expect if the sample correlation were $r = +.80$ instead of .60?

5 a Compute the Pearson correlation for the following set of data:

X	Y
2	8
3	10
3	7
5	6
6	7
8	4
9	2
10	3

b Add 5 points to each X value and compute the Pearson correlation again.
c When you add a constant to each score, what happens to SS for X and Y? What happen to SP? What happens to the correlation between X and Y?
d Now multiply each X in the original data by 3 and calculate the Pearson correlation once again.
e When you multiply by a constant, what happens to SS for X and Y? What happens to SP? What happens to the correlation between X and Y?

6 If you obtain a random sample of $n = 2$ people and measure each person's annual salary and shoe size, what would you expect to obtain for the Pearson correlation? (Be careful. Try making up some data points to see what happens.) How would you interpret a correlation of $r = +1.00$ obtained for a sample of $n = 2$? Should you generalize this sample correlation and conclude that a strong relationship between X and Y exists in the population?

***7** For each of the following sets of scores, calculate SP using the definitional formula and then using the computational formula:

Set 1		Set 2		Set 3	
X	Y	X	Y	X	Y
1	3	0	7	1	5
2	6	4	3	2	0
4	4	0	5	3	1
5	7	4	1	2	6

8 For the following set of data,

Data	
X	Y
8	2
9	2
2	4
1	5
5	2

a Sketch a graph showing the location of the five (X, Y) points.
b Just looking at your graph, estimate the value of the Pearson correlation.
c Compute the Pearson correlation for this data set.

9 For this problem we have used the same X and Y values that appeared in Problem 8, but we have changed the X, Y pairings:

Data	
X	Y
8	4
9	5
2	2
1	2
5	2

a Sketch a graph showing these reorganized data.
b Estimate the Pearson correlation just by looking at your graph.
c Compute the Pearson correlation. (*Note:* Much of the calculation for this problem was done already in Problem 8.)

If you compare the results of Problem 8 and Problem 9, you will see that the correlation measures the relation between X and Y. These two problems use the same X and Y values, but they differ in the way X and Y are related.

10 Sketch a graph showing the linear equation $Y = 3X - 2$.

***11** Two major companies supply laboratory animals for psychologists. Company A sells laboratory rats for \$6 each and charges a \$10 fee for delivery. Company B sells rats for only \$5 each but has a \$20 delivery charge. In each case the delivery fee is a one-time charge and does not depend on the number of rats in the order.

a For each company, what is the linear equation that defines the total cost (Y) as a function of the number of rats (X)? Each equation should be of the form

$Y = bX + a$

b What would the total cost be for an order of 10 rats from company A? From company B?
c If you were buying 20 rats, which company gives you the better deal?

12 A psychology instructor asked each student to report the number of hours he or she had spent preparing for the final exam. In addition, the instructor recorded the number of incorrect answers on each student's exam. These data are as follows:

Hours	Number Wrong
4	8
0	6
1	3
2	2
4	5

What is the Pearson correlation between study hours and number wrong?

***13** **a** Calculate the Pearson correlation for the following set of data:

X	Y
7	18
12	11
1	20
18	10
3	15
9	16

b Find the mean and standard deviation for the X-scores and transform each score into a z-score. Transform each of the Ys into a z-score. Now use formula 16.4 to compute the Pearson correlation.

14 A psychologist would like to determine whether there is any consistent relationship between intelligence and creativity. A random sample of $n = 18$ people is obtained, and the psychologist administers a standardized IQ test and a creativity test to each individual. Using these data, the psychologist obtained a Pearson correlation of $r = +.20$ between IQ and creativity. Do these sample data provide sufficient evidence to conclude that a correlation exists in the population? Test at the .05 level of significance, one tail.

***15** A high school counselor would like to know if there is a relation between mathematical skill and verbal skill. A sample of $n = 25$ students is selected, and the counselor records achievement test scores in mathematics and English for each student. The Pearson correlation for this sample is $r = +.50$. Do these data provide sufficient evidence for a real relationship in the population? Test at the .05 level, two tails.

16 For the following set of data, find the linear regression equation for predicting Y from X:

X	Y
0	9
2	9
4	7
6	3

***17** **a** Find the regression equation for the following data:

X	Y
1	2
4	7
3	5
2	1
5	14
3	7

b Compute the predicted Y value for each X in the data.
c Compute the error $(Y - \hat{Y})$ for each individual and find SS_{error} for these data.

18 Find the regression equation and compute the standard error of estimate for the following data:

X	Y
3	12
0	8
4	18
2	12
1	8

*19 A college professor claims that the scores on the first exam provide an excellent indication of how students will perform throughout the term. To test this claim, first-exam scores and final scores were recorded for a sample of $n = 12$ students in an introductory psychology class. The data are as follows:

First Exam	Final Grade
62	74
73	93
88	68
82	79
85	91
77	72
94	96
65	61
91	92
74	82
85	93
98	95

a Is the professor right? Is there a significant relation between scores on the first exam and final grades? Test with $\alpha = .01$, one tail.
b How accurately do the exam scores predict final grades? Compute the standard error of estimate.

20 Sternberg (1966) reported results of a human memory experiment using regression. Sternberg presented subjects with a short list of digits to hold in memory. Then he flashed a single digit, and the subjects had to decide as quickly as possible whether or not this digit was contained in the memory list. The results showed a linear relation between the number of items in memory and the reaction time; the more items in memory, the more time needed to respond. Data similar to those obtained by Sternberg are as follows:

Number of items in Memory	Reaction Time (in Milliseconds)
1	430
2	471
3	505
4	543
5	578

Calculate the regression equation for predicting reaction time as a function of the number of items in memory. (Note that the slope of the regression equation corresponds to the amount of extra time needed for each additional item in memory. The Y-intercept is a measure of basic reaction time with zero items in memory.)

21 Data indicate that infants with low birth weight tend to lag behind in general development. The following data are infant birth weights and scholastic achievement scores at age 10 years for a sample of $n = 12$ children:

Birth Weight	Scholastic Achievement	Birth Weight	Scholastic Achievement
81 oz	58	127 oz	81
96 oz	65	108 oz	85
132 oz	78	76 oz	55
104 oz	76	86 oz	68
122 oz	81	113 oz	79
88 oz	62	110 oz	72

a Calculate the Pearson correlation for these data.
b Find the regression equation for predicting scholastic achievement from birth weight.

*22 You probably have read for years about the relation between years of education and salary potential. The following hypothetical data represent a sample of $n = 10$ men who have been employed for 5 years. For each person, we report the total number of years of higher education (high school plus college) and current annual salary.

Salary (in $1000)	Years of Higher Education
21.4	4
18.7	4
17.5	2
32.0	8
12.6	0
25.3	5
35.5	10
17.3	4
33.8	12
14.0	0

a Find the regression equation for predicting salary from education
b How would you interpret the slope constant (b) in the regression equation?
c How would you interpret the Y-intercept (a) in the equation?

*23 The marketing division of a major breakfast cereal manufacturer prepared the following table showing the monthly advertising expenditure and sales figures for the company:

Advertising Expenditure (in Thousands)	Sales Figures (in Thousands)
14	218
23	237
27	241
17	214
29	243
15	218
19	232
25	230

a Compute the Pearson correlation for these two variables.
b Do these data indicate that there is a significant relation between the amount spent on advertising and the amount of sales? Test at the .05 level of significance, two tails.
c Next month, the company plans to spend $20,000 on advertising. Find the regression equation and then use it to predict next month's sales.

24 An educational psychologist wanted to demonstrate that scores on the SAT provide a reasonably accurate indication of how a student will perform in college. A random sample of $n = 20$ students was selected. Each student's SAT score and his/her grade point average after four semesters are as shown in the accompanying table.
a Calculate the Pearson correlation for these data.
b Is there a significant relation between the SAT and grade point average? Test at the .05 level, two tails.

Student	SAT	GPA	Student	SAT	GPA
1	650	3.12	11	745	3.84
2	680	3.06	12	590	2.18
3	710	3.55	13	605	2.43
4	440	1.98	14	520	2.10
5	660	3.25	15	635	2.72
6	485	2.23	16	750	3.88
7	590	2.76	17	490	2.31
8	780	4.00	18	700	3.49
9	620	3.52	19	460	2.45
10	480	3.01	20	670	3.20

CHAPTER 17

THE CHI-SQUARE STATISTIC: TESTS FOR GOODNESS OF FIT AND INDEPENDENCE

TOOLS YOU WILL NEED

The following items are considered essential background material for this chapter. If you doubt your knowledge of any of these items, you should review the appropriate chapter or section before proceeding.

- Proportions (math review, Appendix A)
- Frequency distributions (Chapter 2)

PREVIEW

Once in a while we hear a horrifying report in which passersby observe a person in trouble and yet do not go to the victim's aid. Some people have attributed bystander apathy to the alienating and dehumanizing aspect of modern life, but Darley and Latané (1968) suggested that the number of witnesses is a key variable in determining if aid will be given. Specifically, if one person observes someone in trouble, the observer tends to feel personally responsible and is likely to assist. However, if there is a group of observers, the responsibility for the victim is spread thin among the witnesses, and it is less likely that anyone will help. This interpretation has been called *diffusion of responsibility*.

In an experimental test of this phenomenon, Darley and Latané (1968) asked subjects to participate in group discussions concerning problems adjusting to college life. To ensure anonymity, each participant sat in a separate room, and the discussion was held over an intercom. The discussion groups consisted of either 2 people, 3 people, or 6 people. Actually, there was only one real subject in each group; the rest of the people were "confederates," or research assistants posing as subjects.

At some point during the discussion, the researchers played a tape recording over the intercom, giving the appearance that one of the participants was having an epileptic seizure. Darley and Latané recorded how many subjects tried to help the "victim" and how many did not. The findings are summarized in Table 17.1. Notice that the data for this study consist of frequencies, not scores. For example, when there were only 2 people in the group (subject and victim), the data show 11 subjects helping and only 2 who did not help (85% helped). When there were 3 people in the group, the helping rate dropped to 16 out of 26 (62%). Finally, when the group size was 6, only 4 out of 13 subjects (31%) tried to help the victim. Clearly the data show a trend—the larger the group, the less likely that someone will help. However, these data represent a relatively small sample. Can we be sure that the results generalize to the entire population? This is a question of statistical inference, and what we need is a hypothesis test that works with frequency data.

In this chapter we will examine a statistic called *chi-square*, which is used to test hypotheses about the form and shape of frequency distributions. Unlike earlier hypothesis tests that used scores (X values), the data for chi-square are simply frequencies. Incidently, we will return to the bystander apathy study later in the chapter.

17.1 PARAMETRIC AND NONPARAMETRIC STATISTICAL TESTS

All the statistical tests we have examined thus far are designed to test hypotheses about specific population parameters. For example, we used t tests to assess hypotheses about μ and later about $\mu_1 - \mu_2$. In addition, these tests typically make assumptions

TABLE 17.1

The relationship between the size of group and the type of response to the victim

	Group Size 2	3	6
Assistance	11	16	4
No Assistance	2	10	9

J. M. Darley and B. Latané (1968). Bystander intervention in emergencies: Diffusion of responsibility. *Journal of Personality and Social Psychology, 8*, 377–383. Copyright (1968) by the American Psychological Association. Adapted with permission of the publisher and author.

about the shape of the population distribution and about other population parameters. Recall that for analysis of variance the population distributions are assumed to be normal and homogeneity of variance is required. Because these tests all concern parameters and require assumptions about parameters, they are called *parametric tests.*

Another general characteristic of parametric tests is that they require a numerical score for each individual in the sample. The scores then are added, squared, averaged, and otherwise manipulated using basic arithmetic. In terms of measurement scales, parametric tests require data from an interval or a ratio scale (see Chapter 1).

Often, researchers are confronted with experimental situations that do not conform to the requirements of parametric tests. In these situations you should not attempt a parametric test. Remember, when the assumptions of a test are violated, the test may lead to an erroneous interpretation of the data. Fortunately, there are several hypothesis testing techniques that provide alternatives to parametric tests. These alternatives are called *nonparametric tests.*

In this chapter and the next chapter, we introduce some of the more commonly used nonparametric tests. You should notice that these nonparametric tests usually do not state hypotheses in terms of a specific parameter, and they make few (if any) assumptions about the population distribution. For the latter reason, nonparametric tests sometimes are called *distribution-free tests.* Another distinction is that nonparametric tests are well suited for data that are measured on nominal or ordinal scales. Finally, you should be warned that nonparametric tests generally do not have as much statistical power as parametric tests; nonparametric tests are more likely to fail in detecting a real difference between two treatments. Therefore, whenever the experimental data give you a choice between a parametric and a nonparametric test, you always should choose the parametric alternative.

Remember, statistical power is the probability that a test will reject a false null hypothesis.

17.2 THE CHI-SQUARE TEST FOR GOODNESS OF FIT

Parameters such as the mean and standard deviation are the most common way to describe a population, but there are situations where a researcher has questions about the shape of a frequency distribution. For example,

> How does the number of women lawyers compare with the number of men in the profession?
>
> Of the three leading brands of soft drinks, which is preferred by most Americans? Which brands are second and third, and how big are the differences in popularity among the three?
>
> To what extent are different ethnic groups represented in the population of your city?

Notice that each of the preceding examples asks a question about *how many*—in other words, these are all questions about frequencies. The chi-square test for goodness of fit is specifically designed to answer this type of question. In general terms, this chi-square test is a hypothesis-testing procedure that uses the frequency distribution for a sample to test hypotheses about the corresponding frequency distribution for a population.

The name of the test comes from the Greek letter χ (chi, pronounced "ky") which is used to identify the test statistic.

· DEFINITION · The chi-square test for *goodness of fit* determines how well the frequency distribution for a sample fits the population distribution that is specified by the null hypothesis.

You should recall from Chapter 2 that a frequency distribution is defined as a record of the number of individuals located in each category of the scale of measurement. In a frequency distribution graph, the categories that make up the scale of measurement are listed on the X-axis. In a frequency distribution table, the categories are listed in the first column. With chi-square tests, however, it is customary to present the scale of measurement as a series of boxes with each box corresponding to a separate category on the scale. The frequency corresponding to each category is simply presented as a number written inside the box. Figure 17.1 shows how a distribution of eye colors for a set of $n = 40$ students can be presented either as a graph, a table, or a series of boxes. Notice that the scale of measurement for this example consists of four categories of eye color (brown, blue, green, other).

THE NULL HYPOTHESIS FOR THE GOODNESS-OF-FIT TEST

For the chi-square test of goodness of fit, the null hypothesis specifies the proportion (or percentage) of the population in each category. For example, a hypothesis might state that 90% of all lawyers are men and only 10% are women. The simplest way of presenting this hypothesis, is to put the hypothesized proportions in the series of boxes representing the scale of measurement:

	Men	Women
H_0:	90%	10%

Although it is conceivable that a researcher could choose any proportions for the null hypothesis, there usually is some well-defined rationale for stating a null hypothesis. Generally H_0 will fall into one of the following categories.

1. *No Preference.* The null hypothesis often states that there is no preference among the different categories. In this case, H_0 states that the population is divided equally among the categories. For example, a hypothesis stating that there is no preference among the three leading brands of soft drinks would specify a population distribution as follows:

	Brand X	Brand Y	Brand Z
H_0:	$\frac{1}{3}$	$\frac{1}{3}$	$\frac{1}{3}$

2. *No Difference from a Comparison Population.* The null hypothesis can state that the frequency distribution for one population is not different from the distribution that is known to exist for another population. For example, suppose it is known that

FIGURE 17.1

Distribution of eye colors for a sample of $n = 40$ individuals. The same frequency distribution is shown as a histogram, as a table, and with the frequencies written in a series of boxes.

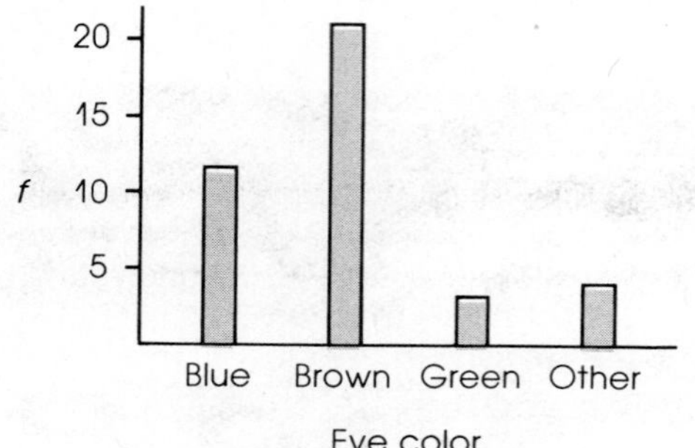

Eye color (X)	f
Blue	12
Brown	21
Green	3
Other	4

Blue	Brown	Green	Other
12	21	3	4

60% of Americans favor the president's foreign policy and 40% are in opposition. A researcher might wonder if this same pattern of attitudes exists among Europeans. The null hypothesis would state that there is no difference between the two populations and specify the Europeans would be distributed as follows:

	Favor	Oppose
H_0:	60%	40%

3. *No Change from a Past Distribution.* Suppose that in 1970 the distribution of voters in the state was 35% Democrats, 38% Republicans, and 27% Other (Liberal, Conservative, etc.). A researcher might wonder if today's distribution is any different. The null hypothesis would state that there has been no change, and today's population has the same distribution that existed in 1970:

	Democrat	Republican	Other
H_0:	35%	38%	27%

4. *No Difference from a Theoretical Distribution.* A theory may predict a particular distribution for a population. For example, a genetic theory may predict that cross-breeding two strains of mice will result in a distribution of offspring consisting of 25% that are prone to seizures and 75% that are normal. These proportions could be stated as a null hypothesis.

	Seizure-prone	Normal
H_0:	25%	75%

Of course, it is impossible to prove a hypothesis about the population (see Chapter 8), but a researcher may try to show that the theory is incorrect by rejecting this null hypothesis.

Because the null hypothesis for the goodness-of-fit test specifies an exact distribution for the population, the alternative hypothesis (H_1) simply states that the population distribution has a different shape from that specified in H_0. If the null hypothesis stated that the population is equally divided among three categories, the alternative hypothesis would say that the population is not divided equally.

THE DATA FOR THE GOODNESS-OF-FIT TEST

The data for a chi-square test are remarkably simple. There is no need to calculate a sample mean or *SS*, you just select a sample of n individuals and count how many are in each category. The resulting values are called *observed frequencies*. The symbol for observed frequency is f_o. For example, the following data represent observed frequencies for a sample of $n = 40$ subjects. Each person was given a personality questionnaire and classified into one of three personality categories: A, B, or C.

Category A	Category B	Category C	
15	19	6	$n = 40$

Notice that each individual in the sample is classified into one and only one of the categories. Thus, the frequencies in this example represent three completely separate groups of individuals: 15 who were classified as category A, 19 classified as B, and 6 classified as C. Also note that the observed frequencies add up to the total sample size: $\sum f_o = n$.

· DEFINITION · The *observed frequency* is the number of individuals from the sample who are classified in a particular category. Each individual is counted in one and only one category.

EXPECTED FREQUENCIES The general goal of the chi-square test for goodness of fit is to compare the data (the observed frequencies) with the null hypothesis. The problem is to determine how well the data fit the distribution specified in H_0—hence the name *goodness of fit*.

The first step in the chi-square test is to determine how the sample distribution should look if the null hypothesis were exactly right. Suppose the null hypothesis states that the population is distributed in three categories with the following proportions:

Category A	Category B	Category C
25%	50%	25%

If this hypothesis is correct, how would you expect a random sample of $n = 40$ individuals to be distributed among the three categories? It should be clear that your best strategy is to predict 25% of the sample would be in category A, 50% would be in category B, and 25% would be in category C. To find the exact frequency expected for each category, multiply the sample size (n) by the proportion (or percentage) from the null hypothesis. For this example you would expect

25% of 40 = .25(40) = 10 individuals in category A

50% of 40 = .50(40) = 20 individuals in category B

25% of 40 = .25(40) = 10 individuals in category C

The frequency values predicted from the null hypothesis are called *expected frequencies.* The symbol for expected frequency is f_e, and the expected frequency for each category is computed by

(17.1) $$\text{expected frequency} = f_e = pn$$

where p is the proportion stated in the null hypothesis and n is the sample size.

· DEFINITION · The *expected frequency* for each category is the frequency value that is predicted from the null hypothesis and the sample size (n).

THE CHI-SQUARE STATISTIC The general purpose of any hypothesis test is to determine whether the sample data support or refute a hypothesis about the population. In the chi-square test for goodness of fit, the sample is expressed as a set of observed frequencies (f_o values), and the null hypothesis has been used to generate a set of expected frequencies (f_e values). The chi-square statistic simply measures how well the data (f_o) fit the hypothesis (f_e). The symbol for the chi-square statistic is χ^2. The formula for the chi-square statistic is

(17.2) $$\text{chi-square} = \chi^2 = \sum \frac{(f_o - f_e)^2}{f_e}$$

As the formula indicates, the value of chi-square is computed by the following steps:

1. Find the difference between f_o (the data) and f_e (the hypothesis) for each category.
2. Square the difference. This ensures that all values are positive.
3. Next, divide the squared difference by f_e. A justification for this step is given in Perspective 17.1.
4. Finally, sum the values from all the categories.

PERSPECTIVE 17.1

THE CHI-SQUARE FORMULA

We have seen that the chi-square formula compares observed frequencies to expected frequencies in order to assess how well the sample data match the hypothesized data. This function of the chi-square statistic is easy to spot in the numerator of the equation, $(f_o - f_e)^2$. The difference between the observed and expected frequencies is found first. The greater this difference, the more discrepancy there is between what is observed and what is expected. The difference is then squared to remove the negative signs (large discrepancies may have negative signs as well as positive signs). The summation sign in front of the equation indicates that we must examine the amount of discrepancy for every category. Why, then, must we divide the squared differences by f_e for each category before we sum the category values? Basically, we would view the $f_o - f_e$ discrepancies in a different light if f_e were very small or very large.

Suppose you were going to throw a party and you *expected* 1000 people to show up. However, at the party you counted the number guests and *observed* that 1040 actually showed up. Forty more guests than expected are no major problem when all along you were planning for 1000. There will still probably be enough beer and potato chips for everyone. On the other hand, suppose you had a party and you expected 10 people to attend but instead 50 actually showed up. Forty more guests in this case spell big trouble. How "significant" the discrepancy is depends in part on what you were originally expecting. With very large expected frequencies, allowances are made for more error between f_o and f_e. This is accomplished in the chi-square formula by dividing the squared discrepancy for each category, $(f_o - f_e)^2$, by its expected frequency.

THE CHI-SQUARE DISTRIBUTION AND DEGREES OF FREEDOM

It should be clear from the chi-square formula that the value of chi-square is measuring the discrepancy between the observed frequencies (data) and the expected frequencies (H_0). When there are large differences between f_o and f_e, the value of chi-square will be large, and we will conclude that the data do not fit the hypothesis. Thus, a large value for chi-square will lead us to reject H_0. On the other hand, when the observed frequencies are very close to the expected frequencies, chi-square will be small and we will conclude that there is a very good fit between the data and the hypothesis. Thus, a small chi-square value indicates that we should fail to reject H_0. To decide whether a particular chi-square value is "large" or "small," we must refer to a chi-square distribution. This distribution is the set of chi-square values for all the possible random samples when H_0 is true. Much like other distributions we have examined (t distribution, F distribution), the chi-square distribution is a theoretical distribution with well-defined characteristics. Some of these characteristics are easy to infer from the chi-square formula.

1. The formula for chi-square guarantees that you can never obtain a negative value. Thus, all chi-square values are zero or larger.
2. When H_0 is true, you expect the data (f_o values) to be close to the hypothesis (f_e values). Thus, we expect chi-square values to be small when H_0 is true.

These two factors suggest that the typical chi-square distribution will be positively skewed (see Figure 17.2). Note that small values, near zero, are expected when H_0 is true, and large values (in the right-hand tail) are very unlikely. Thus, unusually large values of chi-square will form the critical region for the hypothesis test.

Although the typical chi-square distribution is positively skewed, there is one other factor that plays a role in the exact shape of the chi-square distribution—the number of categories. You should recall that the chi-square formula requires that you sum values from every category. The more categories you have, the more likely it is that you will obtain a large sum for the chi-square value. On the average, chi-square will be larger when you are summing over 10 categories than when you are summing over only 3 categories. As a result, there is a whole family of chi-square distributions, with the exact shape of each distribution determined by the number of categories

FIGURE 17.2

Chi-square distributions are positively skewed. The critical region is placed in the extreme tail, which reflects large chi-square values.

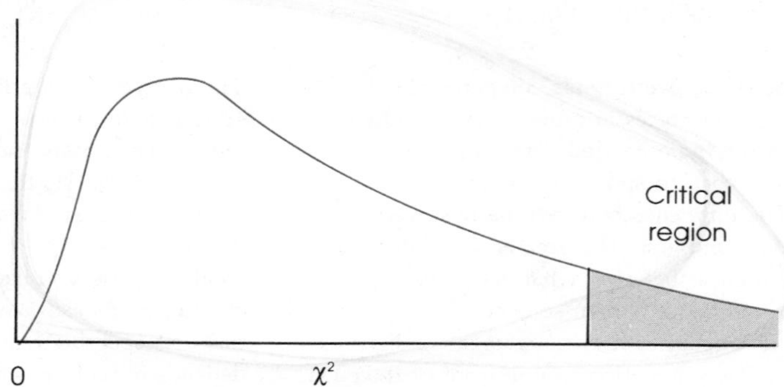

used in the study. Technically, each specific chi-square distribution is identified by degrees of freedom (*df*) rather than the number of categories. For the goodness-of-fit test, the degrees of freedom are determined by

$$df = C - 1 \tag{17.3}$$

where *C* is the number of categories. A brief discussion of this *df* formula is presented in Perspective 17.2. Figure 17.3 shows the general relation between *df* and the shape of the chi-square distribution. Note that the typical chi-square value (the mode) gets larger as the number of categories is increased.

LOCATING THE CRITICAL REGION FOR A CHI-SQUARE TEST

To evaluate the results of a chi-square test, we must determine whether the chi-square statistic is large or small. Remember, an unusually large value indicates a big discrepancy between the data and the hypothesis and suggests that we reject H_0. To determine whether or not a particular chi-square value is significantly large, you first select an alpha level, typically .05 or .01. Then, you consult the table entitled The Chi-Square Distribution (Appendix B). A portion of the chi-square distribution table is shown in Table 17.2. The first column in the table lists *df* values for chi-square. The top row of the table lists proportions of area in the extreme right-hand tail of the distribution. The numbers in the body of the table are the critical values of chi-square. The table shows, for example, in a chi-square distribution with $df = 3$, only 5% (.05) of the values are larger than 7.81, and only 1% (.01) are larger than 11.34.

FIGURE 17.3

The shape of the chi-square distribution for different values of *df*. As the number of categories increase, the peak (mode) of the distribution has a larger chi-square value.

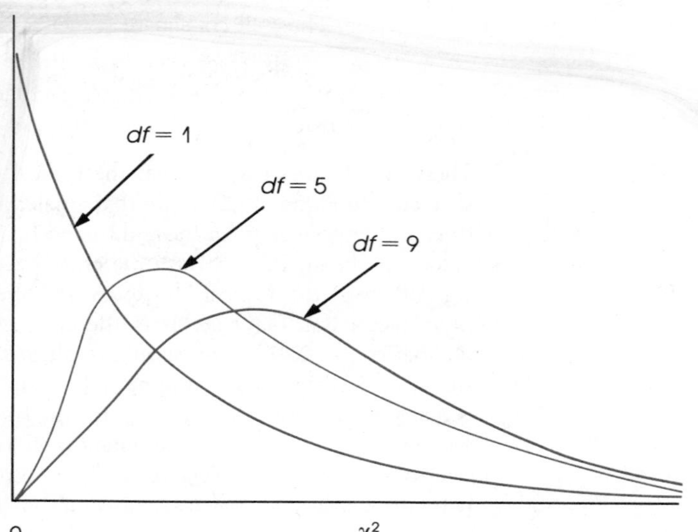

PERSPECTIVE 17.2

A CLOSER LOOK AT DEGREES OF FREEDOM

Degrees of freedom for the chi-square test literally measure the number of free choices that exist when you are determining the null hypothesis or the expected frequencies. For example, when you are classifying individuals into three categories, you have exactly two free choices in stating the null hypothesis. You may select any two proportions for the first two categories, but then the third proportion is determined. If you hypothesize 25% in the first category and 50% in the second category, then the third category must be 25% in order to account for 100% of the population. In general, you are free to select proportions for all but one of the categories, but then the final proportion is determined by the fact that the entire set must total 100%. Thus, you have $C - 1$ free choices, where C is the number of categories: degrees of freedom, *df*, equals $C - 1$.

The same restriction holds when you are determining the expected frequencies. Again suppose that you have three categories and a sample of $n = 40$ individuals. If you specify expected frequencies of $f_e = 10$ for the first category and $f_e = 20$ for the second category, then you must use $f_e = 10$ for the final category.

Category A	Category B	Category C	
10	20	?	$n = 40$

As before, you may distribute the sample freely among the first $C - 1$ categories, but then the final category is determined by the total number of individuals in the sample.

EXAMPLES OF THE CHI-SQUARE TEST FOR GOODNESS OF FIT

We will use the same step-by-step process for testing hypotheses with chi-square as we used for other hypothesis tests. In general, the steps consists of stating the hypotheses, locating the critical region, computing the test statistic, and making a decision about H_0. The following example demonstrates the complete process of hypothesis testing with the goodness-of-fit test.

EXAMPLE 17.1 A researcher is interested in the factors that are involved in course selection. A sample of 50 students is asked, "Which of the following factors is most important to you when selecting a course?" Students must choose one and only one of the following alternatives:

1. Interest in course topic
2. Ease of passing the course
3. Instructor for the course
4. Time of day course is offered

The frequency distribution of responses for this sample is summarized in Table 17.3. Do any of these factors play a greater role than others for course selection?

TABLE 17.2

A portion of the table of critical values for the chi-square distribution

	Proportion in Critical Region				
df	0.10	0.05	0.025	0.01	0.005
1	2.71	3.84	5.02	6.63	7.88
2	4.61	5.99	7.38	9.21	10.60
3	6.25	7.81	9.35	11.34	12.84
4	7.78	9.49	11.14	13.28	14.86
5	9.24	11.07	12.83	15.09	16.75
6	10.64	12.59	14.45	16.81	18.55
7	12.02	14.07	16.01	18.48	20.28
8	13.36	15.51	17.53	20.09	21.96
9	14.68	16.92	19.02	21.67	23.59

STEP 1 We must state the hypotheses and select a level of significance. The hypotheses may be stated as follows:

H_0: The population of students shows no preference in selecting any one of the four factors over the others. Thus, the four factors are named equally often, and the population distribution has the following proportions:

Interest in Topic	Ease of Passing	Course Instructor	Time of Day
$\frac{1}{4}$	$\frac{1}{4}$	$\frac{1}{4}$	$\frac{1}{4}$

H_1: In the population of students, one or more of these factors plays a greater role in course selection (the factor is named more frequently by students).

The level of significance is set at a standard value, $\alpha = .05$.

STEP 2 The value for degrees of freedom is determined, and then the critical region is located. For this example, the value for degrees of freedom is

$$df = C - 1 = 4 - 1 = 3$$

For $df = 3$ and $\alpha = .05$, the table for critical values of chi-square indicates that the critical χ^2 has a value of 7.81. The critical region is sketched in Figure 17.4.

STEP 3 The expected frequencies for all categories must be determined, and then the chi-square statistic can be calculated. If H_0 were true and the students display no response preference for the four alternatives, then the proportion of the population responding to each category would be $\frac{1}{4}$. Because the sample size (n) is 50, the null hypothesis predicts expected frequencies of 12.5 for all categories (Table 17.3):

$$f_e = pn = \tfrac{1}{4}(50) = 12.5$$

Using the observed and the expected frequencies from Table 17.3, the chi-square statistic may now be calculated:

$$\begin{aligned}
\chi^2 &= \sum \frac{(f_o - f_e)^2}{f_e} \\
&= \frac{(18 - 12.5)^2}{12.5} + \frac{(17 - 12.5)^2}{12.5} + \frac{(7 - 12.5)^2}{12.5} + \frac{(8 - 12.5)^2}{12.5} \\
&= \frac{30.25}{12.5} + \frac{20.25}{12.5} + \frac{30.25}{12.5} + \frac{20.25}{12.5} \\
&= 2.42 + 1.62 + 2.42 + 1.62 \\
&= 8.08
\end{aligned}$$

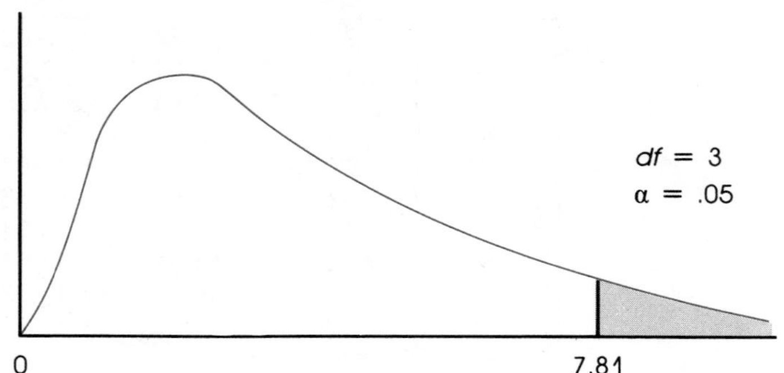

FIGURE 17.4

For Example 17.1, the critical region begins at a chi-square value of 7.81

TABLE 17.3

Part A: The Most Important Factor in Course Selection (Observed Frequencies)

	Interest in Topic	Ease of Passing	Course Instructor	Time of Day
f_o	18	17	7	8

Part B: The Expected Frequencies for Example 17.1

	Interest in Topic	Ease of Passing	Course Instructor	Time of Day
f_e	12.5	12.5	12.5	12.5

STEP 4 The obtained chi-square value is in the critical region. Therefore, H_0 is rejected, and the researcher may conclude that the subjects mentioned some of the factors more than others in response to the question about course selection. In a research report, the investigator might state:

> The students showed a significant response preference to the question concerning factors involved in course selection, $\chi^2(3, n = 50) = 8.08, p < .05$.

Note that the form of reporting the chi-square value is similar to that of other statistical tests we have encountered. Degrees of freedom and the sample size are indicated in the parentheses after the χ^2 symbol. This information is followed by the obtained chi-square value and then by the probability that a Type I error has been committed.

LEARNING CHECK

1 A researcher for an insurance company would like to know if high-performance, overpowered automobiles are more likely to be involved in accidents than other types of cars. For a sample of 50 insurance claims, the investigator classifies the automobiles as high-performance, subcompact, midsize, or full-size. The observed frequencies are as follows:

Observed Frequencies of Insurance Claims

High-Performance	Subcompact	Midsize	Full-Size	Total
20	14	7	9	50

In determining the f_e values, assume that only 10% of the cars in the population are the high-performance variety. However, subcompacts, midsize cars, and full-size cars make up 40%, 30%, and 20%, respectively. Can the researcher conclude that the observed pattern of accidents does not fit the predicted (f_e) values? Test with $\alpha = .05$.

a In a few sentences, state the hypotheses.

b Determine the value for df and locate the critical region.

c Determine f_e values and compute chi-square.

d Make a decision regarding H_0.

ANSWERS

1 **a** H_0: In the population, no particular type of car shows a disproportionate number of accidents. H_1: In the population, a disproportionate number of the accidents occur with certain types of cars.

b $df = 3$; the critical χ^2 value is 7.81.

c The f_e values for high-performance, subcompact, midsize, and full-size cars are 5, 20, 15, and 10, respectively. The obtained chi-square is 51.17.

d Reject H_0.

17.3 THE CHI-SQUARE TEST FOR INDEPENDENCE

THE NULL HYPOTHESIS AND THE CONCEPT OF INDEPENDENCE

The chi-square statistic may also be used to test whether or not there is a relationship between two variables. In this situation, each individual in the sample is measured or classified on two separate variables. For example, a group of employees at a large company could be classified in terms of salary (high, medium, low) and in terms of sex (male, female). Usually the data from this classification are presented in the form of a matrix, where the rows correspond to the categories of one variable and the columns correspond to the categories of the second variable. Table 17.4 presents some hypothetical data for a sample of $n = 130$ employees who have been classified by salary level and sex. The number in each box, or *cell*, of the matrix depicts the frequency for that particular group. In Table 17.4, for example, there were 5 men classified as having "low" salaries and 39 men classified as "medium" salaries. Notice that the data consist of frequencies, not scores, from a sample. These sample data will be used to test a hypothesis about the corresponding population frequency distribution. Once again we will be using the chi-square statistic for the test, but in this case the test is called the chi-square *test for independence*.

The null hypothesis for the chi-square test for independence states that there is no relationship between the two variables being measured; that is, the two variables are independent. For the example we have been considering, H_0 could be stated as

H_0: For the population of employees, salary is independent of sex

The alternative hypothesis, H_1, says that there is a relation between the two variables. For this example, H_1 states that salary does depend on sex. Before we begin a detailed examination of the chi-square test, we will look at some hypothetical data that demonstrate the concepts of *independent* and *dependent*.

Figure 17.5 shows two frequency distribution graphs: one displays a hypothetical distribution of salaries for men employees, and the other shows a salary distribution for women. Looking at these two distributions, does there appear to be a relation between salary and sex? When you compare the two distributions, it is clear that the

TABLE 17.4

Hypothetical data showing the frequency distribution according to salary level and sex for a sample of $n = 130$ employees.

	Salary Level		
	Low	Medium	High
Men	5	39	41
Women	19	21	5

FIGURE 17.5

Salary distributions for men and women showing a relationship between salary and sex. For these data, salary depends on sex, with men tending to have higher salaries.

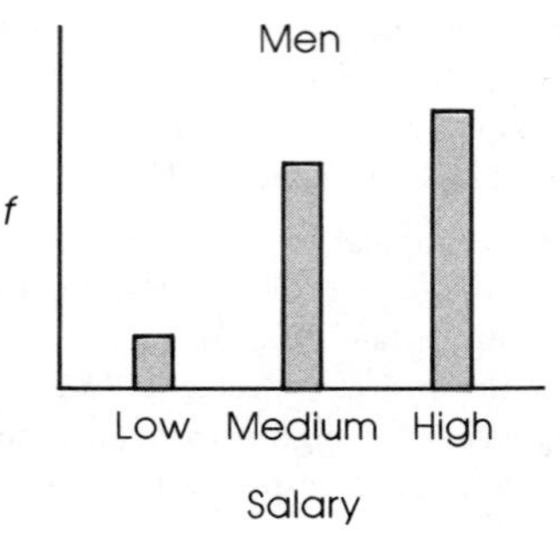

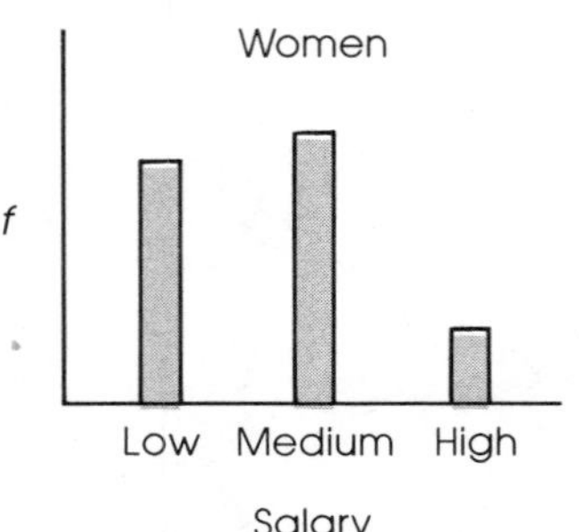

· FIGURE 17.6 ·

Salary distributions for men and women showing no relation between salary and sex. For these data, salary is independent of sex.

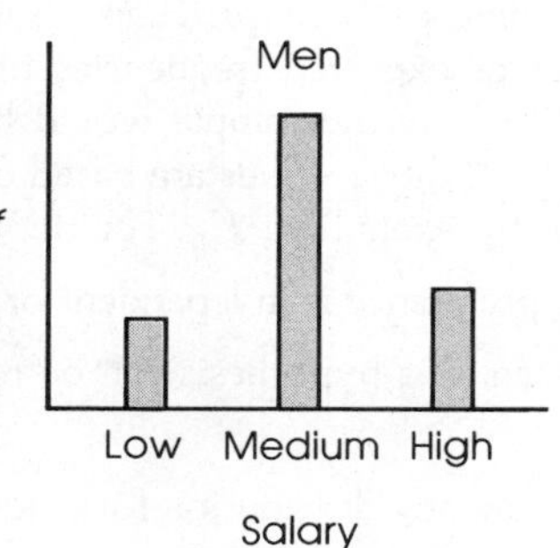

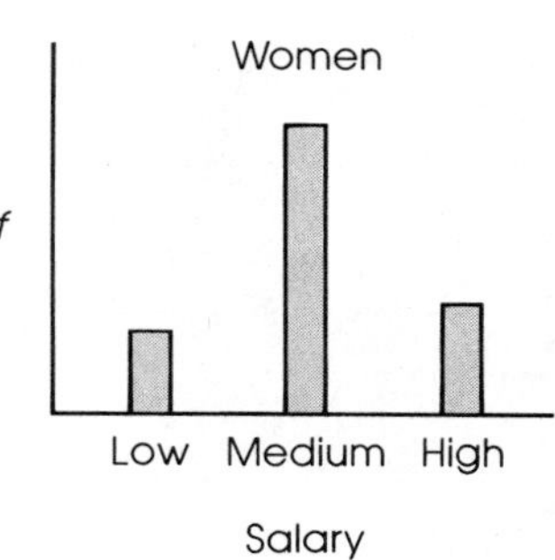

men tend to receive higher salaries, and the women tend to receive lower salaries. In this case, salary does depend on sex. In general, you can recognize when two variables are related, because the frequency distributions for one variable will have different shapes for different categories of the second variable.

Now consider Figure 17.6. It should be clear that the data in this figure show no relation between salary and sex. The two salary distributions have exactly the same shape, which indicates that salary is independent of sex. In general, when two variables are independent, the distribution for one variable will not depend on the categories of the second variable. In other words, the frequency distribution for one variable will have the same shape for all categories of the second variable.

· DEFINITION · Two variables are *independent* when the frequency distribution for one variable is not related to (or dependent on) the categories of the second variable. As a result, the frequency distribution for one variable will have the same shape for all categories of the second variable.

OBSERVED AND EXPECTED FREQUENCIES

The chi-square test for independence uses the same basic logic that was used for the goodness-of-fit test. First, a sample is selected and each individual is classified or categorized. Because the test for independence considers two variables, every individual is classified on both variables, and the resulting frequency distribution is presented as a two-dimensional matrix (see Table 17.4). As before, the frequencies in the sample distribution are called observed frequencies and are identified by the symbol f_o.

The next step is to find the frequency distribution that would be predicted from the null hypothesis. As before, the frequencies generated from H_0 are called expected frequencies and are identified by the symbol f_e. Once the expected frequencies are obtained, we will compute a chi-square statistic to determine how well the data (observed values) fit the hypothesis (expected values). Before we get to the chi-square formula, however, we must face the relatively complex task of finding expected frequencies for the chi-square test of independence. The following example will be used to help introduce the calculation of expected frequencies.

· EXAMPLE 17.2 · A researcher suspects that there is a relation between an individual's personality and his or her color preferences. A sample of $n = 400$ people is obtained. Each person is classified as either introverted or extroverted, and each person is asked to select a favorite color from among four choices: red, yellow, green, and blue. The frequency distribution for this sample is as follows:

	Red	Yellow	Green	Blue	
Introvert	20	6	30	44	100
Extrovert	180	34	50	36	300
	200	40	80	80	$n = 400$

·

The preceeding example provides a set of observed frequencies. Our problem is to find the set of expected frequencies for this example. Remember, expected frequencies specify how the sample would be distributed if the null hypothesis were correct. Therefore, the f_e values are based on the null hypothesis and the sample size. We will begin by examining H_0. For this example, the null hypothesis would state

We could state H_0 as "personality is independent of color preference."

H_0: Color preference is independent of personality

As we have seen, this hypothesis can be restated in terms of frequency distributions as follows:

H_0: The frequency distribution for color preference has the same shape for all categories of personality

Now, we are ready to look at the size of the sample.

The data in Example 17.2 represent a sample of $n = 400$ individuals. However, this total number does not completely describe the size of the sample. Specifically, this sample is already divided into a set of predetermined subgroups. For example, the sample contains 100 introverts and a separate group of 300 extroverts. Similarly, the total sample consists of 200 people who selected red as their favorite color, 40 people who picked yellow, 80 who choose green, and 80 who preferred blue. These subgroup sizes are crucial to the calculation of expected frequencies. Fortunately, the subgroup numbers are easily obtained by reading the row totals and the column totals from the data (the observed frequencies).

Part A of Table 17.5 presents an empty frequency distribution table, listing only row totals and column totals from Example 17.2. This empty table identifies the general characteristics of the sample ($n = 400$, with 100 introverts, etc.). To find the expected frequencies, we must determine how the sample should be distributed according to the null hypothesis. In other words, our problem is to fill in the empty spaces in the table.

Once again, the null hypothesis states that the distribution of color preferences should have the same shape for introverts as for extroverts. But what is the "distribution of color preferences"? The best information we have about this distribution comes from the sample data. The column totals from the sample show the following distribution (see part A of Table 17.5):

TABLE 17.5

Color preferences according to personality type

Part A. An empty frequency distribution matrix showing only the row totals and column totals. These numbers describe the basic characteristics of the sample from Example 17.2.

	Red	Yellow	Green	Blue	
Introvert					100
Extrovert					300
	200	40	80	80	

Part B. Expected frequencies for Example 17.2. This is the distribution that is predicted by the null hypothesis.

	Red	Yellow	Green	Blue	
Introvert	50	10	20	20	100
Extrovert	150	30	60	60	300
	200	40	80	80	

200 out of 400 choose red: $\frac{200}{400} = 50\%$ red

40 out of 400 choose yellow: $\frac{40}{400} = 10\%$ yellow

80 out of 400 choose green: $\frac{80}{400} = 20\%$ green

80 out of 400 choose blue: $\frac{80}{400} = 20\%$ blue

If H_0 is true, we would expect to obtain this same distribution of color preferences for both introverts and extroverts. Therefore, expected frequencies can be obtained by applying the color-preference distribution equally to the set of 100 introverts and to the set of 300 extroverts. The resulting f_e values are as follows.

For the 100 introverts, we expect

50% choose red: $f_e = .50(100) = 50$

10% choose yellow: $f_e = .10(100) = 10$

20% choose green: $f_e = .20(100) = 20$

20% choose blue: $f_e = .20(100) = 20$

For the 300 extroverts, we expect

50% choose red: $f_e = .50(300) = 150$

10% choose yellow: $f_e = .10(300) = 30$

20% choose green: $f_e = .20(300) = 60$

20% choose blue: $f_e = .20(300) = 60$

These expected frequencies are shown in part B of Table 17.5. Notice that the row totals and column totals for the expected frequencies are the same as those for the original data in Example 17.2.

A SIMPLE FORMULA FOR DETERMINING EXPECTED FREQUENCIES

Although you should understand that expected frequencies are derived directly from the null hypothesis and the sample characteristics, it is not necessary to go through extensive calculations in order to find f_e values. In fact, there is a simple formula that determines f_e for any cell in the frequency distribution table.

$$f_e = \frac{f_c f_r}{n} \tag{17.4}$$

where f_c is the frequency total for the column (column total), f_r is the frequency total for the row (row total), and n is the number of individuals in the entire sample. To demonstrate this formula, we will compute the expected frequency for introverts selecting yellow in Table 17.5(A). First note that this cell is located in the top row and second column in the table. The column total is $f_c = 40$, the row total is $f_r = 100$, and the sample size is $n = 400$. Using these values in formula 17.4, we obtain

$$f_e = \frac{f_c f_r}{n} = \frac{40(100)}{400} = 10$$

…17.6: …requencies. Once …d, all the remaining expected …ined by the row totals and the …his example has only three free choices, so

Red	Yellow	Green	Blue	
50	10	20	?	100
?	?	?	?	300
200	40	80	80	

Notice that this is identical to the expected frequency we obtained using percentages from the overall distribution.

THE CHI-SQUARE STATISTIC AND DEGREES OF FREEDOM The chi-square test of independence uses exactly the same chi-square formula as the test for goodness of fit:

$$\chi^2 = \sum \frac{(f_o - f_e)^2}{f_e}$$

As before, the formula measures the discrepancy between the data (f_o values) and the hypothesis (f_e values). A large discrepancy will produce a large value for chi-square and will indicate that H_0 should be rejected. To determine whether a particular chi-square statistic is significantly large, you must first determine degrees of freedom (*df*) for the statistic and then consult the chi-square distribution in the appendix. For the chi-square test of independence, degrees of freedom are based on the number of cells for which you can freely choose expected frequencies. You should recall that the f_e values are partially determined by the sample size (n) and by the row totals and column totals from the original data. These various totals restrict your freedom in selecting expected frequencies. This point is illustrated in Table 17.6. Once three of the f_e values have been selected, all the other f_e values in the table are also determined. In general, the row totals and column totals restrict the final choices in each row and column. Thus, we may freely choose all but one expected frequency in each row and all but one f_e in each column. The total number of f_e values that you can freely choose is $(R - 1)(C - 1)$, where R is the number of rows and C is the number of columns. The degrees of freedom for the chi-square test of independence are given by the formula

$$df = (R - 1)(C - 1) \tag{17.5}$$

AN EXAMPLE OF THE CHI-SQUARE TEST FOR INDEPENDENCE The steps for the chi-square test of independence should be familiar by now. First, the hypotheses are stated, and an alpha level is selected. Second, the value for degrees of freedom is computed, and the critical region is located. Third, expected frequencies are determined, and the chi-square statistic is computed. Finally, a decision is made regarding the null hypothesis. The following example demonstrates the complete hypothesis-testing procedure.

EXAMPLE 17.3 Darley and Latané (1968) did a study that examined the relationship between the number of observers and aid-giving behaviors (see the preview for details). The group sizes consisted of two people (subject and victim), three people, or six people. The investigators categorized the response of a subject in terms of whether or not the observer exhibited any helping behaviors when the victim (actually another laboratory worker) staged an epileptic seizure. The data are presented again in Table 17.7. Do aid-giving behaviors depend on group size?

TABLE 17.7

The relationship between the size of group and the type of response to the victim

Part A: Observed Frequencies

	Group Size 2	3	6	Totals
Assistance	11	16	4	31
No Assistance	2	10	9	21
Totals	13	26	13	

Part B: Expected Frequencies

	Group Size 2	3	6	Totals
Assistance	7.75	15.5	7.75	31
No Assistance	5.25	10.5	5.25	21
Totals	13	26	13	

J. M. Darley and B. Latané (1968). Bystander intervention in emergencies: Diffusion of responsibility. *Journal of Personality and Social Psychology, 8,* 377–383. Copyright (1968) by the American Psychological Association. Adapted with permission of the publisher and author.

STEP 1 State the hypotheses and select a level of significance. According to the null hypothesis, group size and helping behavior are independent of each other in the population. That is, the absence or presence of aid-giving behavior should not be related to the number of observers. The alternate hypothesis would state that the absence or presence of helping behavior is dependent on group size for the population. The level of significance is set at $\alpha = .05$.

STEP 2 Calculate the degrees of freedom and locate the critical region. For the chi-square test of independence,

$$df = (R - 1)(C - 1)$$

Therefore, for this study,

$$df = (2 - 1)(3 - 1) = 1(2) = 2$$

With two degrees of freedom and a level of significance of .05, the critical value for χ^2 is 5.99 (see table for critical values of chi-square).

STEP 3 Determine the expected frequencies and calculate the chi-square statistic. As noted before, it is quicker to use the computational formula to determine the f_e values, rather than the percentage method. The expected frequency for each cell is as follows:

1 Group size 2—showed aid-giving behavior:

$$f_e = \frac{f_c f_r}{n} = \frac{13(31)}{52} = 7.75$$

2 Group size 3—showed aid-giving behavior:

$$f_e = \frac{26(31)}{52} = 15.5$$

3 Group size 6—showed aid-giving behavior:

$$f_e = \frac{13(31)}{52} = 7.75$$

4 Group size 2—no aid-giving behavior:

$$f_e = \frac{13(21)}{52} = 5.25$$

5 Group size 3—no aid-giving behavior:

$$f_e = \frac{26(21)}{52} = 10.5$$

6 Group size 6—no aid-giving behavior:

$$f_e = \frac{13(21)}{52} = 5.25$$

Note that the row totals and column totals for the expected frequencies are the same as the totals for the observed frequencies.

The expected frequencies are summarized in Table 17.7. Using these expected frequencies along with the observed frequencies (part A of Table 17.7), we can now calculate the value for the chi-square statistic:

$$\chi^2 = \sum \frac{(f_0 - f_e)^2}{f_e}$$

$$= \frac{(11 - 7.75)^2}{7.75} + \frac{(16 - 15.5)^2}{15.5} + \frac{(4 - 7.75)^2}{7.75} + \frac{(2 - 5.25)^2}{5.25} + \frac{(10 - 10.5)^2}{10.5} + \frac{(9 - 5.25)^2}{5.25}$$

$$= 1.363 + 0.016 + 1.815 + 2.012 + 0.024 + 2.679$$

$$= 7.91$$

STEP 4 Make a decision regarding the null hypothesis. The obtained chi-square value exceeds the critical value (5.99). Therefore, the decision is to reject H_0 and conclude that there is a relationship between group size and the likelihood that someone will aid another person in trouble. For purposes of reporting the data, the researchers could state that there is a significant relationship between size of group and helping behavior, $\chi^2(2, n = 52) = 7.91, p < .05$. By examining the observed frequencies in part A of Table 17.7, we see that the likelihood of aid-giving behavior decreases as group size increases. •

A Chi-Square Analysis on the Computer When cell frequencies are large or when f_e values have decimals, the computation of the chi-square statistic can be quite tedious. For this reason, it has become very common for researchers to use one of several computer software packages for statistical analyses. We used the Minitab package to analyze the data of Example 17.3. The chi-square analysis is initiated by the Minitab command CHIS. The printout (Table 17.8) displays the matrix of cells for observed and expected frequencies as well as the computations for chi-square and degrees of freedom. Explanatory notes are provided in the table.

· LEARNING CHECK ·

1 A researcher suspects that color blindness is inherited by a sex-linked gene. This possibility is examined by looking for a relationship between gender and color vision. A sample of 1000 people is tested for color blindness, and then they are classified

TABLE 17.8

Minitab analysis for example 17.3

```
MINITAB RELEASE 5.1.3 *** COPYRIGHT - MINITAB, INC. 1985
U.S. FEDERAL GOVERNMENT USERS SEE HELP FGU
JUNE 10, 1987 *** S.U.N.Y. BROCKPORT - ACADEMIC COMPUTING SERVICES
STORAGE AVAILABLE 260144

 Type NEWS for information on new features in Minitab Release 5.1

MTB > READ C1 C2 C3
      2 ROWS READ

 ROW    C1    C2    C3
   1    11    16     4      ---- 1
   2     2    10     9

MTB > CHIS C1 C2 C3

Expected counts are printed below observed counts

            C1        C2        C3     Total
    1       11        16         4        31
           7.7      15.5       7.7
                                                ---- 2
    2        2        10         9        21
           5.2      10.5       5.2

Total       13        26        13        52

ChiSq =   1.36 +   0.02 +   1.81 +
          2.01 +   0.02 +   2.68 = 7.91      ---- 3
df = 2                                        ---- 4

MTB > END
MTB > STOP
*** Minitab Release 5.1.3 *** Minitab, Inc. ***
Storage available 260144  Storage used 30767
```

EXPLANATION OF PRINTOUT:

1 The original data. The three group sizes used in the experiment (see Table 17.7) appear as three columns (C1, C2, C3) of frequencies. The type of response is coded into two rows.

2 The cell frequencies. The expected frequencies are printed below the observed frequencies for all of the cells. The marginal totals are provided for the rows and columns as well.

3 Computation of chi-square. The chi-square statistic is computed, showing the values obtained for each cell.

4 Degrees of freedom. Finally, the *df* value for the test of independence is displayed.

according to their sex and color vision status (normal, red-green blind, other color blindness). Is color blindness related to gender? The data are as follows:

Observed Frequencies of Color Vision Status According to Sex

	Normal Color Vision	Red-Green Color Blindness	Other Color Blindness	Totals
Male	320	70	10	400
Female	580	10	10	600
Totals	900	80	20	

a State the hypotheses.
b Determine the value for *df* and locate the critical region.
c Compute the f_e values and then chi-square.
d Make a decision regarding H_0.

ANSWERS

1 **a** H_0: In the population, there is no relationship between gender and color vision.
H_1: In the population, gender and color vision are related.
b $df = 2$; critical $\chi^2 = 5.99$ for $\alpha = .05$.
c f_e values are as follows:

Expected Frequencies

	Normal	Red-Green	Other
Male	360	32	8
Female	540	48	12

Obtained $\chi^2 = 83.44$.
d Reject H_0.

17.4 ASSUMPTIONS AND RESTRICTIONS FOR CHI-SQUARE TESTS

To use a chi-square test for goodness of fit or a test of independence, several conditions must be satisfied. For any statistical test, violation of assumptions and restrictions will cast doubt on the results. For example, the probability of committing a Type I error may be distorted when assumptions of statistical tests are not satisfied. Some important assumptions and restrictions for using chi-square tests are the following:

1. *Random Sampling*. As we have seen with other inferential techniques, it is assumed that the sample under study is selected randomly from the population of interest.

2. *Independence of Observations*. This is *not* to be confused with the concept of independence between *variables* as seen in the test of independence (Section 17.3). By independence of observations, it is assumed that each observed frequency is generated by a different subject. A chi-square test would be inappropriate if a person could produce responses that can be classified in more than one category or contribute more than one frequency count to a single category.

3. *Size of Expected Frequencies*. A chi-square test should not be performed when the expected frequency of any cell is less than 5. The chi-square statistic can be distorted when f_e is very small. Consider the chi-square computations for a single cell. Suppose the cell has values of $f_e = 1$ and $f_o = 5$. The contribution of this cell to the total chi-square value is

$$\text{cell} = \frac{(f_o - f_e)^2}{f_e} = \frac{(5-1)^2}{1} = \frac{4^2}{1} = 16$$

Now consider another instance, where $f_e = 10$ and $f_o = 14$. The difference between the observed and expected frequency is still 4, but the contribution of this cell of the total chi-square value differs from that of the first case:

$$\text{cell} = \frac{(f_o - f_e)^2}{f_e} = \frac{(14-10)^2}{10} = \frac{4^2}{10} = 1.6$$

It should be clear that a small f_e value can have a great influence on the chi-square value. This problem becomes serious when f_e values are less than 5. When f_e is very small, what would otherwise be a minor discrepancy between f_o and f_e will now result in large chi-square values. The test is too sensitive when f_e values are extremely small. One way to avoid small expected frequencies is to use large samples.